MW01618539

Ex Libris
Todd C. Penner

The Jewish Alchemists

The Jewish Alchemists

A HISTORY AND SOURCE BOOK

Raphael Patai

PRINCETON UNIVERSITY PRESS
PRINCETON, NEW JERSEY

Published by Princeton University Press, 41 William Street,
Princeton, New Jersey 08540
In the United Kingdom: Princeton University Press,
Chichester, West Sussex

Library of Congress Cataloging-in-Publication Data

Patai, Raphael, 1910–
The Jewish alchemists : a history and source book /
Raphael Patai.
p. cm.
Includes bibliographical references and index.

ISBN 0-691-03290-4
ISBN 0-691-00642-3 (pbk.)
1. Jewish alchemists. 2. Alchemy—History. I. Title.
QD24.A2P38 1994
540′.11′2089924—dc20 93-35687

This book has been composed in Adobe Galliard

Princeton University Press books are printed
on acid-free paper and meet the guidelines
for permanence and durability of the Committee
on Production Guidelines for Book Longevity
of the Council on Library Resources

Third printing, and first paperback printing, 1995

Printed in the United States of America
by Princeton Academic Press

3 5 7 9 10 8 6 4

To the memory of
Harry Starr

Whose chance remark on Jews and alchemy,
made many years ago,
first planted the idea of this book
in my mind
and

To my brother
Saul Patai

---

the chemical encyclopedist,
from whom I learned
how much more—and less—
chemistry is than alchemy

The vocable *alchemia* (or some alternate form such as *ars chemica*) appears in the West from the twelfth century onward in reference to the medieval quest for a means of transmuting base metals into gold, for a universal cure, and for the "elixir of immortality." . . . The alchemist's quest was not scientific but spiritual.

Mircea Eliade,
"Alchemy" in *Encyclopedia of Religion*

Alchemy is the art of liberating parts of the Cosmos from temporal existence and achieving perfection which for metals is gold, and, for man, longevity, then immortality, and finally, redemption.

H. J. Sheppard,
"Chinese Alchemy" in *Encyclopedia of Religion*

At times alchemy was an organic part of a comprehensive tradition . . . which in some manner embraced all aspects of human existence. . . . The transmutation of base metals into gold is certainly not the true goal of alchemy. . . . Alchemy . . . treats the soul as a "substance" which has to be purified, dissolved, and crystallized anew.

Titus Burckhardt,
Alchemy

Alchemy is usually defined as the art of transmuting base metals into gold.

Encyclopedia Americana

CONTENTS

PART FOUR: *The Eleventh to Thirteenth Centuries*

PART FIVE: *The Fourteenth Century*

PART SIX: *The Fifteenth Century*

PART SEVEN: *The Sixteenth Century*

PART EIGHT: *The Seventeenth Century*

PART NINE: *The Eighteenth Century*

ILLUSTRATIONS

ACKNOWLEDGMENTS

IN THE PREPARATION of this volume I enjoyed the help and advice of many libraries and of esteemed colleagues and friends. My indebtedness to them can be expressed here only briefly.

To institutions in three continents for ready access to their holdings, guidance in locating items I wanted to peruse, and permission to publish my translation of manuscripts in their possession: the library of the Abadia de Montserrat, Spain, and its director, Fr. Francesc Xavier Altés; the Archivio General de la Corona de Aragon, Barcelona, and its director Sr. Rafael Conde; the Archivio Segredo Vaticano, Rome; the library of Bar Ilan University, Ramat Gan, Israel; the Bayerische Staatsbibliothek, Munich, and Hans Striedl, Munich; the library of the Ben-Zvi Institute, Jerusalem; the Biblioteca Nacional, Madrid; the Biblioteca Universitaria, Bologna; the Bibliothèque Nationale, Paris, its director, Emmanuel Le Roy Ladurie, and the head of its Service Hebraique, Madeleine Neige; the Bodleian Library, Oxford; the British Library, London; the Cambridge University Library; the Columbia University Library, New York; the Sidney M. Edelstein Collection in the History of Chemistry, Hebrew University, Jerusalem, and its curator Moshe Ron; the Engineering Library, New York; the Institute of Microfilmed Hebrew Manuscripts, Jerusalem, and its deputy director, Benjamin Richler; the John Ryland University Library, Manchester, its director, M. A. Pegg, and its Head of Special Collections, Peter McNiven; the Library of Congress, Washington, and the Head of its Hebraic Section, Myron M. Weinstein; the Library of the Jewish Theological Seminary of America, New York, its Librarian of Special Collections, Rabbi Terry Schwarzbard, and Marion Stein, in charge of its microfilm collection; the Marseille Municipal Library; the Shlomo Moussaieff Ancient Hebrew Manuscript Collection, Herzliya, Israel; the National Library of Medicine, Bethesda, Md., and its curator of rare books, Peter Krivatsy; the library of the New York Academy of Medicine; the New York Public Library, the Head of its Jewish Division, Leonard Gold, and the Head of its Oriental Division, John M. Lundquist; the Sachsische Landesbibliothek, Dresden; the Staatsbibliothek Preussischer Kulturbesitz, Berlin, and Dieter George and Hartmut-Ortwin Feistel, Heads of its Oriental Department; the Troyes, France, Municipal Library, and its Conservateur, Mme A. Plassard; the archives of the United Synagogue, London, and its archivist, Charles Tucker; and the library of the Universidad Pontificia Salamanca, Spain, and its director, Carlos Carrete Parrondo.

Also to Todd Thompson, Head of the Middle Eastern Section of the New York Public Library; to its Arabic specialists Khassam Khalil, the late Latif Khayyat, and Gamil Yousef, and its Persian specialist Massoud Pourfarrokh; Tzvi Langermann of the Jerusalem Institute of Microfilmed Hebrew Manuscripts; Moshe Sokolow of Yeshiva University, New York; the late Georges Vajda of the Sorbonne, Paris, for help with difficult Arabic and Judeo-Arabic texts. To Micheline Tison-Braun of the Graduate Center of the City University of New York, my friend Simone Boy, and Nicolas Sed of Paris for help with difficult Old French texts and French bibliographic references; to Gerald Strauss of Indiana University for help with difficult Medieval German texts; to Mrs. Joseph Adler of New York, Maria Esformes of Harvard University, Moshe Lazar of the University of Southern California, and F. Marquez of Harvard University for translating difficult Spanish and Ladino texts. To Louis H. Feldman of Yeshiva University, Edward Grant of Indiana University, James Halporn of Indiana University, Joseph Salemi of New York, Aida Slabotzky of New York, and Alex Wayman of Columbia University for translating difficult Latin texts. To Shubhra Basu of the New York Public Library for interpreting Sanskrit references. To Tuvia Preschel of the Jewish Theological Seminary for help with rabbinic literature.

For generously helping to underwrite numerous expenses attendant upon preparation of this work, to Sidney M. Edelstein, President of the Dexter Chemical Corporation of New York, the Memorial Foundation for Jewish Culture and its Executive Vice President Dr. Jerry Hochbaum, and the Lucius N. Littauer Foundation and its President William Lee Frost.

I also wish to express my thanks to the editors of the periodicals and books in which chapters included here in a revised form were originally published, to wit: *Ambix, Medical History, Hebrew Union College Annual*, and *Orient and Occident*.

ABBREVIATIONS

A.	Arabic
Berthelot, *Grecs*	Marcellin P. E. Berthelot and Charles Emile Ruelle, *Collection des anciens alchimistes grecs*, 3 vols. (Paris, 1888; reprint London, 1963)
EI^2	*Encyclopedia of Islam*, new ed. (Leiden, 1960–)
EJ(B)	*Encyclopaedia Judaica* (Berlin, 1928)
EJ(J)	*Encyclopaedia Judaica* (Jerusalem, 1972)
G.	Greek
Ger.	German
H.	Hebrew
I.	Italian
JE	*Jewish Encyclopedia* (New York, 1901–)
L.	Latin
P.	Persian
S.	Spanish
Skt.	Sanskrit

PART ONE

Prelude

Chapter One

INTRODUCTION

SCHOLARS who have written about alchemy are far from agreeing about what alchemy actually is (or was). Some go along with the popular view that alchemy is nothing but the art that tries, or claims to be able, to transmute base metals into gold. This view considers alchemy as a whole a pseudoscience, a misguided attempt at dealing with the properties of matter, which produced a few practical results before it was superseded in the late eighteenth century by Antoine Lavoisier's establishment of modern chemistry. Others, at the opposite extreme of the range of opinions, hold that alchemy is basically a spiritual endeavor whose aim is to transmute the imperfect human soul into a more perfect spiritual entity. This latter view has antecedents as far back as Maria the Jewess, the famed Hellenistic Jewish founder of alchemy.

Several Renaissance alchemists considered the stages in the alchemical work steps in the mysterious process of spiritual regeneration. Thus Heinrich Khunrath (1560–1601) interpreted transmutation itself as a mystical process occurring within the adept's soul. Highly individual is the cosmological-psychological approach of C. G. Jung (1875–1961), who held that "alchemy is pre-eminently concerned with the seed of unity which lies hidden in the chaos of Tiamat [Jung used the name of this ancient babylonian deity to designate the primordial matriarchal world] and forms the counterpart to divine unity."[1] However, the entire construct erected by Jung in his *Psychology and Alchemy* is summarily dismissed by the *Encyclopedia of Religion* with the statement that "Enticed by the resemblance between the dreams of his patients and alchemical symbols," C. G. Jung concluded that "the attribution of life to matter was the foundation of alchemical belief," which belief he "read . . . from his psychoanalytic standpoint as the projection of inner experience onto matter, and thus as the identification of matter with the Self."[2] Further examples of the great variety in the identification and interpretation of alchemy could easily be culled from the huge literature on alchemy.

During the Renaissance, alchemy broke up into competing schools among whom little sympathy was lost. The spiritual alchemists looked down with contempt at those who labored on transmuting metals, and dubbed them "sooty empirics" and "puffers." On the other hand, the claim of being in possession of spiritual truths revealed by God evoked the jealousy and wrath of many churchmen who remained indifferent to the smell of the retorts but smelled heresy in what they felt were spiritual pretensions of the alchemists, and were scandalized by such alchemical doctrines as the one that identified the philosophers' stone with Christ, since both redeemed base matter. One of the few to take a contrary view on this issue was Luther, who praised alchemy for its verification of Christian doctrine.

The contrary definitions of alchemy bring to mind the old Indian story about the group of blind men who were trying to identify an elephant. Their guide took them to the courtyard where the maharaja's elephants were kept, and let them touch one of the big beasts. One blind man happened to get hold of the elephant's trunk, and exclaimed, "The elephant is a big fat snake!" Another touched the elephant's leg and said, "No, the elephant is like the trunk of a big tree!" The third one grabbed its tail, and cried, "No, no! The elephant is like the hawser of a ship!" And so on, for the elephant's various parts.

The fact is that alchemy was everything its practitioners claimed it was, and its aims comprised everything its historians attributed to it. They included the transmutation of base metals into silver and gold, the doubling or otherwise increasing the weight of gold, the manufacturing of pearls and precious stones, the production of all kinds of tinctures and other substances, the concoction of dyes, and the making of all kinds of remedies for healing every disease of which humankind suffered, and the creation of the quintessence, the fabulous elixir, which healed, rejuvenated, and prolonged life for centuries. Because health, youth, and long life were always at least as important desiderata as riches, most alchemists were also physicians, and used their alchemical expertise for manufacturing remedies, searching for the elixir, and ministering to the sick and the old in any manner they could. All this was part of the practical aspect of alchemy.

Another of its aspects was the theoretical. Everything the alchemists did was based on theories in which they believed, and which were the guarantee that their quest would ultimately be crowned with success. The most important of the alchemical theories was that of the unity of all nature. Wherever alchemy developed—in China, India, the Ancient Near East, the Arab world, Christian Europe—it was built on the theory that all the visible forms of matter, whether mineral, vegetable, animal, or human, were manifold forms of one basic, essential substance. A rock, a piece of iron or gold, a tree, a human body—however different they appeared to be, they were but variant physical manifestations of the one and only essence contained in all of them. This is why a malfunction of a human body (i.e., an illness) could be healed with a remedy derived, or rather an essence extracted, from some mineral, vegetable, or animal substance. And this is why a base metal could be transmuted into a precious one, again by applying to it a minuscule amount of that precious essence. This was the area in which alchemy and medicine functioned not merely as sister sciences, but as identical activities: the healing of a sick person was understood to be the transmutation of a sick body into a healthy one, and the transmutation of copper into gold was understood to be the healing of a sick metal and imparting health to it. Among Jews throughout the centuries, most of the alchemists were physicians as well, and it is not easy to decide whether the outstanding role they played as physicians facilitated their entrance into the field of alchemy, or whether they became outstanding physicians because they were led from alchemy into medicine.

Connected with the theory of the unity of nature was the theory of the analogy between the growth of individual plants and animals on the one hand and the development of inanimate forms of matter in the bosom of the earth on the other. Just as a seed germinates and with time becomes a full-grown tree, and just as the human embryo grows in its mother's womb into a fully formed child, so in the earth ores and metals were believed to develop from lower into higher grades, until at the end they became gold. This theory served as the basis for the alchemist's practice of trying to transmute base metal into precious ones, by reproducing in his laboratory the developmental processes of the metals, at a very accelerated speed, always keeping in mind that transmutation was healing.

A related theory was the one that postulated an analogy between body and soul in a human being and bodies and souls in metals. Maria the Jewess said, "Just as man is composed of four elements, likewise is copper; and just as a man results [from the association of] liquids, of solids, and of the spirit, so does copper."[3] An elaboration of this theory was that some metals were bodies, others spirits, and that bodies and spirits could be transmuted into one another and back again; by doing this the adept could change one metal into another. The belief in the alchemist's ability to influence the mineral spirits led back to the human spirit, which too came to be considered subject to alchemical manipulation, and primarily to alchemical ennoblement. Thus alchemy was a comprehensive tradition embracing all aspects of human existence, which was conceived within the broader context of a universal ontology. It was this theoretical aspect of alchemy that attracted some of the greatest minds known to the Western world, including Newton and Goethe.

The main alchemical theories were supported by many subsidiary ones. One such was the identification of metals with the planets, so that when the alchemist worked with gold he felt he enjoyed the power emanating from the sun, and likewise his silver gave him a connection to the moon, quicksilver to Mercury, copper to Venus, iron to Mars, tin to Jupiter, and lead to Saturn. One of the expressions of this planetary theory was the alchemical usage of substituting the names of planets for those of metals. An alchemist spoke of "Sun," and meant gold, of "Moon," and meant silver, of "Venus," and meant copper, and so on.

Another astronomical connection of alchemy was the one between each alchemical process and a particular sign of the zodiac, with which that process was held to be mysteriously associated. Calcination was associated with Aries, congelation with Taurus, fixation with Gemini, dissolution with Cancer, digestion with Leo, distillation with Virgo, sublimation with Libra, separation with Scorpio, ceration with Sagittarius, fermentation with Capricorn, multiplication with Aquarius, and projection with Pisces—thus according to the schema developed by Dom Antoine Joseph Parnety, the eighteenth-century French alchemist.

An essential part of the alchemical theory was that the Royal Art, as it was called, went back to divine revelation accorded to the great biblical figures beginning with Adam, and hence was endowed with a certain sanctity. The success of an alchemist therefore depended not merely on his expertise in the laboratory, but also on his moral stature: it was only by the grace of God that an experiment succeeded, and God, of course, rewarded with His grace only an alchemist who deserved it. A manifestation of high moral stature was knowledge, or wisdom, whereas ignorance and folly were considered moral shortcomings. This is the basis of the frequent admonition found in alchemical writings that the teachings contained in them must be kept secret, that is, must not be divulged to the ignorant, the vulgar.

To this context belongs the relationship between alchemy and magic—a field not yet investigated. The strictly orthodox alchemist would have nothing to do with magic. He relied on his expertise and his knowledge of procedures, worked hard, and prayed to God. But there were others for whom the enticements of magic were too strong to resist. They combined alchemy and magic, much as in certain religious cults in the Caribbean and Africa Christian and pagan religious elements are joined, despite the original incompatibility of the two. As we shall see in this book, some Jewish alchemists combined alchemical work with magical proceedings.

One of the very interesting, and likewise largely unexplored, aspects of alchemy is the relationship between the three great branches of alchemy that developed more or less simultaneously in three great cultures of antiquity: those of China, India, and the Ancient Near East (especially Hellenistic Egypt). The fascination of such a study lies in the fact that, although widely separated geographically, the alchemies of these three worlds show surprising similarities in both their theoretical and their practical activities. Since, however, our interest in this book is in Jewish alchemy, which developed within the Western world (that is, the Ancient Near East, the Arab world, and Christian Europe), we shall not be able even to touch upon these issues.

THE prevailing attitude of Jewish scholars to the role Jews played in the history of alchemy is reminiscent of the scholarly position on Jewish mysticism a hundred years ago. At that time—only a generation or two removed from the *Haskalah*, the Jewish Enlightenment—Jewish scholars belittled mysticism, distanced themselves from it, and tried to show that they were true, enlightened "Europäer" by roundly condemning both the Kabbalah as a movement and the literature it produced. I remember vividly how shocked I was when, as a teenager in the 1920s in Budapest, while reading *Die Geschichte der Juden* by Heinrich Graetz—who at the time was still considered the greatest Jewish historian—I came across the sentence in which he condemned the *Zohar* and called it a "*Logbuch*" (book of lies). My shock was the greater since my father, who was the dominant influence in my young life, was a great admirer of both the Kabbalah and Hasidism, and I simply could not understand how a Jewish historian could denigrate this wonderful manifestation of lofty spiritualism in Judaism.[4] Fortunately, the *Zohar* and the Kabbalah in general have been fully rehabilitated in the last half century, due primarily to the work of Gershom Scholem and his followers. Martin Buber and his disciples have done the same for Hasidism, which is recognized today as a powerful religious movement that has played a crucial role in Jewish history since the eighteenth century. No such redemption has as yet come to alchemy.

There are, of course, basic differences between Kabbalah and Hasidism on the one hand, and alchemy on the other. First, although Kabbalah and Hasidism reflected outside influences, they were specifically Jewish phenomena.[5] Jewish alchemists, on the other hand, even though they played an important role in the origin, development, transmission, and spread of alchemy, were nevertheless only a small group of adepts in comparison to the large number of non-Jewish alchemists in the countries of the Jewish diaspora. Second, although Kabbalah and Hasidism were mass movements among the Jewish people—at times the majority of the Jews adhered to them—alchemy was always confined to a few individuals. It was an occupational specialization, comparable to medicine. The people at large may have believed in the reality of alchemy, and may even have had an inkling of the basic doctrines of the alchemical worldview, they were nevertheless as little able or inclined to engage in alchemical operations as they were to dabble in medical procedures.

Contemporary scholars, unlike their nineteenth-century counterparts, do not condemn what their research unearths, but, if they find something that is not to their liking, they try to ignore it. And this is precisely what they have done in discussing the Jewish work in alchemy. Even though the actual extent of Jewish alchemical work has been unknown, and there has existed no inventory of alchemical manuscripts written by Jews, nor even a study of references to alchemy found in printed books authored by Jews, those who have written on Jewish alchemy have taken the comfortable position that the participation of Jews in alchemy was insignificant. A few quotations will illustrate this general trend.

Moritz Steinschneider, the great master of Jewish bibliography and book lore, set the trend in the late nineteenth century. He wrote: "The Jews were much too knowledgeable about the real gold-scales to let themselves be fooled by 'the philosophers' stone.' Only later times invented [*fingierte*] a writing by Saadia and foisted another on Maimonides." He added in a footnote: "As for alchemy, I don't know a single document," and stated categorically, "The Kabbalah, as far as I know, teaches nothing of alchemy, even though it attached itself to other superstitious disciplines." He summed up his view by saying, "Hebrew literature contains remarkably little material on this subject."[6]

At the turn of the century, the well-known Jewish folklore scholar Moses Gaster wrote an article on alchemy for *The Jewish Encyclopedia*, which was published in New York in the early twentieth century. He opens with these words: "Traces of the connection of Jews with the science of Alchemy are very scanty in Hebrew literature. Not a single distinguished adept is found who has left in a Hebrew form traces of his knowledge of the subject. There is, however, scarcely a single important ancient work upon the science which is not directly related to the Jews, with their traditions and their science." And he concludes the scant four-page article (much of which is devoted to a description of a Hebrew alchemical manuscript in Gaster's possession) by saying that from the sixteenth century on, "Jews themselves apparently took no more interest in the science of Alchemy, deprived as they were, from that period on, of any further intercourse with the world of science." How unfounded these statements are will become clear from the material presented in this book.

Next in chronological order follows Judah David Eisenstein's article published in his Hebrew encyclopedia, *Oṣar Yisrael* (Berlin and London, 1924). In it he quotes more or less the same sources Gaster did a quarter of a century earlier, and then, as if to excuse the Jewish interest in alchemy, he concludes: "However, we cannot deny that alchemy was the mother of chemistry from the 17th century on and rules now in the country at the head of all sciences, and great is the number of the Jews who take part in real chemistry just as they took a great part in the study of alchemy earlier."

In the late 1920s two Jewish encyclopedias were published in German. The smaller of them, titled *Jüdisches Lexikon* (5 vols., Berlin, 1927–1930), contains a very brief and superficial entry on "Alchimie." The larger one, entitled *Encyclopaedia Judaica* (Berlin, 1928– ,) started to appear in 1928, but the advent of Nazism prevented its completion. Its first volume contains a detailed and excellent article on "Alchimie" by Bernard Suler, who utilized all or most of the material available at the time on the subject. But he was unable to rid himself of the influence of Steinschneider, and consequently we find in his article such statements as "The number of Jewish alchemists who practiced the art of alchemy is, as far as our present information goes, relatively small. But our knowledge is, in this respect, very incomplete." He goes on to state that alchemy "could not have originated among a people to whom it was forbidden to 'make gods of silver and gold.' Alchemy is not a Jewish art, and the Jews occupied themselves with it only to the extent to which they dealt also in other profane sciences."

In 1939 Joshua Trachtenberg's important study on *Jewish Magic and Superstition* was published. Although Trachtenberg did not deal with alchemy, he found it proper to state that "alchemy . . . had in general very little currency among the Jews. . . . I have not found any reference to or directions for the practice of alchemy in the literary works produced in northern Europe, although Jews were popularly believed to be adepts." One cannot quarrel with the statement of a scholar who says "I have not found. . . ." although, as we shall see in this book, references to alchemy *are* found in writings produced by Jewish scholars in northern Europe. But it is typical of the general anti-alchemical approach of modern Jewish scholars that Trachtenberg casts his statement in a negative form, whereas he could just as well have said that he had found references to alchemy in literary works produced by Jewish scholars except those of northern Europe. We may add that, as is well known, Sephardi Jews (those of the Mediterranean area), took a much greater interest in secular sciences than did Ashkenazi Jews in northern Europe, and that therefore one would have expected from them greater participation in, and more writing about, alchemy.

The most detailed survey of Jewish alchemy is contained in the 1972 *Encyclopaedia Judaica* (Jerusalem). However, the article, written by Bernard Suler, is just a reworking by the editors of the entry the same author contributed in 1928 to the German *Encyclopaedia Judaica*. Although it contains some new data, its approach remains unchanged. It asserts that "The conclusion to which De Pauw arrived 150 years ago, namely that the Jews were the creators of alchemy, is incorrect. Alchemy is neither a Jewish science nor a Jewish art. . . . While alchemic literature runs into thousands of volumes, there is no original work in this field in Hebrew literature. It seems, therefore, that Jewish adepts did not write their works in Hebrew." As we shall see, most of these statements are incorrect.

One notices a psychologically understandable correspondence between the general evaluation of alchemy and the Jewish view on the Jews' participation in it. Once alchemy came into disrepute, was considered a false science, a fraudulent art—this is how it was viewed by nineteenth-century scholarship—the position of Jewish historians and other scholars was that Jewish participation in it was minimal. However, this dethronement of alchemy was preceded by a long period, some fifteen centuries long, in which alchemy was considered the greatest of arts and sciences, sincerely believed in and assiduously practiced by some of the greatest minds, including Newton in the early eighteenth and Goethe in the early nineteenth centuries. During this long period Jewish scholars generally emphasized the seminal role Jews played in alchemy. This is a subject that requires much more research than I was able to do, but a few indications can serve as illustrations.

The earliest and most important Hellenistic alchemist, known as Maria the Jewess (Maria Hebraea), who lived in Egypt in the second or third century C.E., is quoted as having said that only "the seed of Abraham" was entitled to alchemical experimentation. Zosimus the Panopolitan (third to fourth centuries), whose writings are our main source of information on Maria the Jewess, and who was himself one of the greatest figures in Hellenistic alchemy, was considered by some medieval Arab alchemical authors a Jew.

Several medieval non-Jewish alchemists were later claimed to have been Jewish. One of the earliest of them was Khālid ibn Yazīd (ca. 668–704), a son of the Caliph Yazīd I, whom later legend made into an alchemist, and whose name became attached to important alchemical works.[7] Still later, his name was distorted into Calid ibn Yazichi or Jazikhi, and he became known also as Calid Hebraeus. Steinschneider, in an article titled "Pseudo-Juden und zweifelhafte Authoren" (Pseudo-Jews and Doubtful Authors), lists several such alchemical authors who were claimed to have been Jewish.[8]

Throughout much of the history of alchemy there was a persistent tendency to attribute a Jewish origin to alchemy as a whole. The non-Jewish alchemists were interested in providing alchemy with a respectable family tree, and since the Hellenistic, Muslim, and Christian worlds all held the Bible and individual biblical figures in great respect, the attribution of alchemical activity to biblical characters, kings, and prophets was a simple and effective way of providing alchemy with a highly prestigious, and religiously impeccable, ancestry. The next chapter will deal with the biblical figures whom later alchemists regarded as adepts, in fact, as founders of alchemy and recipients of its great secrets by divine revelation. These tendencies became especially pronounced in the later Middle Ages, when doubts about alchemy began to surface, and the alchemists felt compelled to look for arguments to marshal against the scorn of the skeptics. And in the context of their religion-directed societies, the claim of a biblical origin for their art provided the alchemists with self-legitimation.

Once biblical figures became entrenched in alchemical tradition as the original masters of the Royal Art, the next, almost inevitable, step was to attribute alchemical mastery to the people to whom those biblical figures belonged, whose Scripture contained the memory of those early adepts, and some of whose traditions were believed to preserve the secret knowledge referred to in the Bible. This is how not only Adam, Tubal-Cain, Moses, and Solomon, but the Jews as a whole became in the gentile view the first recipients of the gift of alchemy from God, or alternately, its first inventors and subsequently its developers and transmitters. This belief gave rise to the fashion, widespread among medieval and later European Christian alchemists, to seek out a Jewish master—usually in the lands of the south and the east, where ancient traditions were supposed to have survived more fully than in the west—and become his disciple in acquiring the secrets of the Royal Art. In fact, the Christian quest for alchemical expertise, which led them to Jewish masters, provides us with invaluable and reliable information concerning the work and the reputation of Jewish alchemists. Once this pattern became established among the Christian alchemists, Jews who lived among them and became interested in alchemy followed suit, and they too went to the south or the east to find a master willing to teach them. Several chapters in the present book will illustrate this search among both Christians and Jews.

Another factor in the high estimation of Jewish alchemical expertise by Christian alchemists was the attribution of alchemical-mystical efficacy to Hebrew divine, angelic, and demonic names, to Hebrew words, and even to the letters of the Hebrew alphabet. The Jew who knew Hebrew was believed, due to that very fact, to possess an advantage over the Christian when it came to acquiring mastery of the Great Art. Thus the Hebrew language had for the alchemist a greater importance than Latin has had down to the present time for the physician. Gentiles with the ambition of becoming alchemists learned Hebrew in order to be able to enter the field. Some of them became quite proficient in the language, even to the extent of trying their hand at versification in it. Many more attained only a smattering of Hebrew, barely enough to enable them to embellish their Latin, German, or French writings with a few Hebrew words or names, often written in faultily executed Hebrew characters, or in inaccurate transliteration into Latin characters. Examples of both will be presented in several chapters in this book.

Turning now to the gentile view of the Jewish role in alchemy, we must refer again to Zosimus of Panopolis, whose writings on alchemy are the oldest surviving Greek works on the subject. In them we find the earliest, most detailed, and most reliable information on Maria the Jewess, whom Zosimus quotes frequently with a respect bordering on awe, as the first of the ancient authors. Zosimus also mentions repeatedly the alchemical expertise of the Jews in general. From what he says it is clear that he considered the Jews the repositories of alchemical wisdom, even though he had no sympathy for them and accused them of having obtained the secrets of alchemy by dishonest means. In a remarkable passage he says that the sacred art of the Egyptians (that is, alchemy) and the power of gold that resulted from it were revealed only to the Jews, by fraud, and they made it known to the rest of the world.[9] In general, Zosimus held that the Jews' knowledge of alchemy was greater and more reliable than that of any other people, including even the Egyptians. Chapter 4 will present the relevant material.

Basing himself on his wide reading of ancient Greek alchemical sources Marcellin Berthelot, the author of several important collections of alchemical texts, states, "The connection between Jewish traditions and alchemy goes back very far. One recognizes it in the Leyden Papyrus [an important alchemical treatise found in Thebes, written in Demotic and Greek, and dating from about the third century C.E.], as well as in the Greek alchemical manuscripts. In both we find cited magic treatises and chemical works attributed to Moses, which date from the Alexandrian period."[10]

The widely held belief that Jews were experts in alchemy was grist for the mills of anti-Semitic authors.

Indeed, the overvaluation by gentiles of the Jewish role in the origin and development of alchemy survived the European Enlightenment and continued unabated into the eighteenth and nineteenth centuries. The earliest among the moderns to express himself on the question was Cornelius de Pauw (1739–1799), the famous historian of philosophy. In the first volume of his 1773 French book, *Philosophical Researches on the Egyptians and the Chinese*, he devotes a chapter to "Considerations on the State of Chemistry among the Egyptians and the Chinese." Being a true son of the Enlightenment, he condemns alchemy but nevertheless discusses its development in ancient Egypt, and says (in the 1773 Berlin edition): "The Jews of Egypt had to a great extent been ruined under the rule of Cleopatra, who detested that colony of monopolists and usurers who had come from Palestine under the first Lagides." In these conditions, de Pauw continues, it was the Jews whom "I suspect of having been the first to think up the foolish fable touching upon the transmutation of metals, whose secret they attributed to a Jewish woman, to a Persian magus, and to all the ancient priests of Egypt, who had never thought of it." Returning to the subject later, de Pauw adds:

> these Jewish allegorists were not unaware that the Egyptians who worked in the glassworks of the great Diospolis and of Alexandria possessed the secret procedures of forging precious stones and murrin vases that sometimes were made to cost infinitely more than the precious stones. These concealed operations of the glassworks in themselves enabled the visionaries to suspect that the priests of Egypt had to be well versed in alchemy. However, I don't doubt at all that this was not the true source of all these fables which germinated in the spirit of the Arabs when they applied themselves to the sciences, for it was they who laid the first foundations of real chemistry, or at least resuscitated this art that had been almost entirely lost.[11]

Although de Pauw's style is convoluted, what he intends to say is clear: the Jews were the first to believe in the possibility of transmuting metals, something he considers "a foolish fable," and they attributed this art to a Jewish woman—undoubtedly a reference to Maria the Jewess—and to a Persian magus, probably Ostanes, the semi-legendary alchemical ancestor figure.

Some two generations after de Pauw another historian of philosophy, August Schmölders, expressed a related idea when he said, "The astrologers and alchemists derived all their pretended science from the Hebrew writings translated from the Arabic."[12]

As late as the 1970s, the French scholar G. Monod-Herzen wrote of Hellenistic alchemy: "The oldest of the schools was Jewish. The Israelites fleeing Roman domination after the fall of Jerusalem had come in large numbers to find refuge in Egypt, by a curious return of destiny. . . . They became Hellenized to the point of translating their Holy Book into Greek. . . . This work brought them close to the mysteries of Hermes. . . . They played an important role in the first chemical researches, and their reputation remains great all through the history of alchemy." Monod-Herzen continued by quoting Sophé the Theban to the effect that the Jews, once initiated, transmitted alchemical procedures that they alone knew.[13]

These revisionist views of the Jewish role in the history of alchemy have not yet penetrated the realm of general histories of alchemy and of encyclopedias, whose articles on alchemy are supposed to be authoritative summaries of the subject. The old *Encyclopaedia of Religion and*

Ethics, published early in this century, has articles on Greek and Roman, Muhammadan, and European alchemy, but does not even mention Jewish alchemy. And in the new *Encyclopedia of Religion*, published in 1987 by Macmillan in New York, we find entries on Chinese, Indian, Hellenistic and Medieval, Islamic, and Renaissance alchemy, but none on Jewish alchemy. In fact, in the introductory "Overview" article, written by Mircea Eliade (editor-in-chief of the *Encyclopedia of Religion*), no mention at all is made of Jews, and in the article on "Hellenistic and Medieval Alchemy," although Maria the Jewess is mentioned several times, she is referred to by her later appellation as "Maria Prophetissa," or simply as "Maria," and the Jewish contribution to Hellenistic alchemy is transmuted into pious legend. Likewise conspicuous is the absence of any reference to the role of the Kabbalah and of the Hebrew language in the article on Renaissance alchemy. In sum, largely due to the Jewish scholars' negative attitude to alchemy, the Jewish contribution to the Great Art has remained hidden from the general view. I hope that the present book will make a contribution to remedying this situation.

THE overwhelming majority of Jewish alchemists wrote in Hebrew. Since the Hebrew language possessed relatively few technical terms that could be used in writing about alchemical subjects, however, we find that most Jewish alchemists interspersed their Hebrew text with foreign words. They used these foreign terms either as loan words, without bothering to explain their meaning, or else identified them as foreign words by first using a Hebrew word, and then adding, "and in Arabic . . ." or "and in Laʿaz. . . ." Laʿaz is the generic Hebrew term for "foreign language," and in the alchemical writings it refers to either Spanish or Italian. Occasionally it is not easy to determine which of these the author had in mind.

The foreign terms are always presented in the Hebrew alchemical treatises in phonetic Hebrew transliteration, and frequently there is some inconsistency when they are repeated. I have transliterated these foreign words in Latin characters the first time they appear in each document, and I have indicated in square brackets the original language of the word, added the form that the word had in that language, and followed it with its translation into English. For example: *rejalgar* [A. *rahj al-ghār*, cave dust, realgar; or, *qanalatudo* [I. *cannellatudo*, canelike]. Subsequent instances of that word within the document have usually been simply translated.

In this connection it must be pointed out that the substances designated in old alchemical texts by names that are still in use do not necessarily denote the same chemical elements or substances as do the current terms. For instance, the Hebrew *marqasita* (from the Arabic *marqashita*) designated a crystallized iron pyrite; today the same term means iron disulfide (FeS_2). Historians of alchemy have to be constantly on guard against being misled by such terminological resemblances and ambiguities.

In addition to Hebrew writings, sources on Jewish alchemy are found in other languages as well, including two of the three most widespread Jewish languages traditionally written in Hebrew characters: Judeo-Arabic and Judeo-Spaniolic (Ladino). No alchemical works have come to my attention in the third Jewish language, Yiddish. This does not necessarily mean that the Ashkenazi Jews who wrote in that language were immune to the alchemical virus. The survival of a manuscript is always a matter of chance, and the Yiddish alchemical writings may simply have been lost. It is also possible that if there were alchemists among the Ashkenazi Jews, they wrote not in Yiddish but in one of the European languages. In any case, as far as we now know, the first alchemical work undertaken by Jews from an Ashkenazi background comes from the eighteenth century (see Chapters 36 and 37). The one eighteenth-century Hebrew responsum written by an Askenazi rabbi that shows an acute interest in alchemy stems from the pen of R. Jacob Emden, whose entire intellectual orientation manifests strong Sephardi influences (see Chapter 38). As for alchemical writings in Judeo-Arabic and Ladino, the present book contains a few samples; however, this is an as yet largely unexplored field in which scholarly investigation would be a highly rewarding undertaking.

Finally, mention must be made of Jewish alchemical writings in non-Jewish languages, and of references made by non-Jewish alchemists to the work of Jewish alchemists. This type of material is found in Greek, Latin, Aramaic, Arabic, Spanish, Italian, French, and German, and some of it will be presented in this book.

The material in this book is arranged in chronological order. However, this seems easier than it actually is, because in many cases there are no fewer than three dates to which an alchemical work can be assigned. One is the lifetime of the author to whom the manuscript is attributed. But such a date would often be wrong, because the authorship is often pseudepigraphic. Thus, for example, the alchemical treatise attributed to Maimonides was evidently not written by him (see Chapter 24), and therefore to assign it to the twelfth century would be incorrect.

The second possible date is that of the actual author of the manuscript. Here the problem is that most Hebrew alchemical manuscripts are anonymous, so that it is not possible to determine their date on that basis. Only occasionally are there indications in a manuscript which allow us to estimate its date. It is on this basis that I assigned the pseudo-Maimonidean alchemical treatise to the fifteenth century.

The third possible date is that of the creation of the extant manuscript. On that basis the pseudo-Maimonidean treatise would have to be assigned to the seventeenth century. However, occasionally internal evidence in the text of an extant manuscript shows that it is a copy of an older one, in which case it would, of course, not be justified to assign the work to the date at which the surviving copy of the manuscript was prepared. (If we were to do this, we would have to assign the Book of Isaiah to the first century C.E. on the basis of its oldest extant manuscript, found among the Dead Sea Scrolls.)

All in all, each individual manuscript has to be judged separately by weighing the evidence bearing on its date. Thus I assigned the pseudo-Maimonidean treatise to the fifteenth century (when its author probably lived), and not to the seventeenth, when the extant manuscripts were probably written. On the other hand, I assigned the Jerba manuscript to the nineteenth century (see Chapter 39 and Appendix), even though it utilizes older writings, because the copyist, who seems to have lived in the nineteenth century, has added much of his own to it and considerably reshaped and recast whatever he found. Thus the assignment of dates to Hebrew alchemical manuscripts is, occasionally at least, nothing more than a matter of informed guesswork.

Despite the bulk of this volume and the considerable amount of material it presents, it should not be considered more than a prolegomenon to the history of the Jewish work in alchemy and the role of Jews in contributing to its theory and practice. For one thing, I was not able to consider all the existing Jewish alchemical writings, especially the material still in manuscript and scattered in many libraries all over the world. Although a great number of alchemical manuscripts written in Hebrew or in Judeo-Arabic and Ladino (in Hebrew characters) are accessible in the collection of the Jerusalem Institute of Microfilmed Hebrew Manuscripts, to which my indebtedness is greater than I can express, no such collection exists of alchemical manuscripts written by Jews in characters other than Hebrew. Those are still buried in hundreds of libraries all over the world, and wait to be discovered and identified. Hence the impression created by the material in this book, that the Jews wrote most of their alchemical works in Hebrew characters, is probably wrong, and will have to be corrected by locating, evaluating, and publishing Jewish alchemical writings in other languages—a truly Herculean task.

Another reason why I consider this book merely a prolegomenon is that in it I was able to refer only very occasionally to the personal relationships between Jewish and non-Jewish alchemists (such as those between the Greek Zosimus, the Arab Avicenna, and the French Flamel and their respective Jewish masters), and the literary influences between Jewish alchemical writings on the one hand, and the many times more numerous alchemical works produced in the Muslim and Christian worlds from the end of antiquity to modern times, on the other. Thorough studies comparing the alchemical theories and practices of the Jews with those of the Muslims and Christians, and investigating the contacts between them, will be needed before one can write a truly authoritative history of Jewish alchemy and its role in the development of the "Royal Art" since Hellenistic times. It is my hope that this book will stimulate younger scholars to devote their attention to this subject, and to carry on this fascinating task that time no longer permits me to undertake.

Chapter Two

BIBLICAL FIGURES AS ALCHEMISTS

THE ATTRIBUTION of alchemical mastery to biblical heroes began in Hellenistic Egypt, where alchemists were familiar with the Greek version of the Bible, and where the name of Maria the Jewess was famous as the founder of the Hermetic Art. The first Hellenistic alchemist to allude to the biblical origin of alchemy was Zosimus, who lived in Alexandria in the late third and early fourth centuries C.E. Zosimus was of the opinion that the name of Adam symbolized the four elements, which correspond to the four cardinal points of the earth. Olympiodorus, the sixth-century C.E. Alexandrian neo-Platonic author, considered Adam the first man to have been the issue of the four elements. Latin alchemists held that Adam meant red earth, the philosophical mercury, sulphur, soul, and natural fire, whereas Eve meant white earth, the earth of life, philosophical mercury, radical humidity, and spirit.[1]

In later ages Adam became not only a product of primordial divine alchemy but the first recipient from God of the secrets of the Great Art, which then was transmitted from him to Noah, Aaron, Bezalel, David, Solomon, Jeremiah, Baruch, Ezekiel, Daniel, "as well as all the other prophets."[2] Thus by the sixteenth century alchemy could boast of a complete biblical genealogy, and the alchemists were able to claim that they were the inheritors of a secret science of biblical and divine origin.

In medieval and Renaissance Europe it became fashionable to write alchemical commentaries to the first verses of Genesis, and to derive alchemy from them. This was done by Gerhard Dorn, Michael Maier, and Aegidius Guthmann, among others.[3] The great seventeenth-century compendium of alchemical writings, the *Theatrum chemicum*, contains a tract entitled *Creatio mundi ex narratione Moysis in Genesis*, followed by an *Explication duorum primorum capitum Geneseos juxta physicam*, which is a detailed alchemical commentary on the first two chapters of Genesis.[4]

By that time it had become a cherished tradition in alchemy that the processes of making gold in the *magisterium*, the Great Work, were strictly analogous to those of the creation of the world as described in Genesis 1 and 2. The philosophers' stone was therefore considered a world in miniature, a *minutus mundus*, which corresponded also to man the microcosm.[5] Consequently, Genesis 1 was looked upon by many European alchemists as a guide to the work they were to undertake, and the process of creation willed by the alchemist in his cucurbit—his distilling flask—was compared to the creation of the world by God as described in Genesis.[6] According to some historians of alchemy, the first chapter in Genesis "is the greatest page in alchemy."[7]

There follows here an overview of the alchemists' tradition about the biblical figures whom they considered the originators and early masters of their art.

Adam. In the thirteenth century, Vincent de Beauvais asserted that Adam was the first teacher of alchemy, followed by Noah and several other biblical heroes.[8] In the same century, the *Book of Sidrach* stated that God, through his angel, taught Adam the art of the smith, and that Noah took the implements made by Adam with him in the ark. The *Book of Sidrach*, written probably before 1250 in the circle of Frederick II, the Holy Roman emperor (1194–1250), contains material from Hebrew and Arabic sources, and was pseudepigraphically attributed to Sidrach, a fictitious grandson of Japheth.[9]

Paracelsus (Aureolus Phillippus Theophrastus Bombastus of Hohenheim, 1493–1541) wrote in his commentary on the alleged *Revelation of Hermes* that there is an "indestructible essence," an *una res*, which is the "perfect equation of the elements," the subject of the Art (namely, of alchemy) revealed from above to Adam. It is "the secret of all secrets," "the last and highest thing to be sought under the heavens," the life elixir, "the stone of spirit and truth," the water of life, the oil and honey of eternal healing. "It is the spirit of God which in the beginning filled the earth and brooded over the waters." It is through this spirit that the philosophers invented the seven liberal arts, and thereby gained their riches.[10]

Ben Jonson (1572–1637) was acquainted with a tradition of this kind, and says in his *The Alchemist*,

> Will you believe in antiquity? records?
> I'll shew you a book where Moses and his sister,
> And Solomon have written of the art;
> Ay, and a treatise penn'd by Adam . . .
> Of the philosopher's stone, and in High Dutch.[11]

The sister of Moses referred to is Maria, who in reality was a Hellenistic Jewish alchemist, but who was identified with Miriam, the sister of Moses.

In 1620 in Frankfurt-am-Main, an anonymous German book titled *Gloria mundi* was published and subtitled "Or the Tablet of Paradise, that is, a description of the age-old science which Adam acquired from God Himself, Noah, Abraham, and Solomon used as one of the greatest gifts of God, all wise men in every age considered above the treasures of the whole world, and left it behind only to the God-fearing, namely *de lapide philosophico, authore anonymo* [about the philosophical stone, by an anonymous author]."[12] In this book the author says that "when Adam had learned the mystery [of alchemy] out of God's own mouth, he kept it a strict secret from his sons, until at length, toward the end of his life, he obtained leave from God to make the preparation of the stone known to his son Seth." This stone, he adds, was the same one that the builders of Solomon disallowed—a statement which refers, of course, to Psalm 118:22, "The stone which the builders rejected is become the chief corner-stone." The notion that the philosophers' stone is rejected, "scorned, and trodden underfoot," appears in a medieval Arabic alchemical manuscript.[13]

The longevity of Adam and of the other antediluvian heroes of the Bible was believed to have been due to the philosophers' stone. The author of the *Gloria mundi* writes that had Adam not possessed the knowledge of this great mystery he would not have been able to prolong his life even to the age of three hundred, let alone nine hundred, years.[14]

Within a few decades of the publication of the *Gloria mundi*, Elias Ashmole (1617–1692), the famed English antiquarian whose collection became the Ashmolean Museum at Oxford University, repeated the contention that the longevity of the biblical patriarchs was due to their possession of the philosophers' stone.[15] It was from them, says Ashmole, that Hermes "obtained the knowledge of this stone," whereupon "he gave over the use of all other stones, and therein only delighted. Moses and Solomon [together with Hermes were the only three that] excelled in the knowledge thereof and who therewith wrought wonders." Among the many names Ashmole lists as being applied to the stone is *jud he voph hé*, that is, the Hebrew Tetragrammaton.[16]

Seth. Adam's third son, Seth, who was believed to have obtained the secret of the stone from his father, was identified by al-Dimashqī[17] with the Egyptian Agathodaimon, who is frequently quoted by Zosimus and others as one of the early masters of alchemy.[18]

THE next biblical personage to figure prominently in what can be called the mythical prehistory of alchemy is the antediluvian Tubal-Cain, of whom Genesis says that he was a "forger of every cutting instrument of brass and iron" (Gen. 4:22), in other words, the inventor of the smith's craft.[19] Tubal-Cain figures prominently in a book titled *Uraltes Chymisches Werck* (Age-Old Chemical Work) written by an otherwise unknown Jewish alchemist, who supposedly lived in the fourteenth century. This book is of sufficient importance to deserve detailed treatment in Chapter 17 below.

The Generation of the Deluge. The brief myth-fragment contained in Genesis 6:1–4, which tells about the sons of God who became desirous of the daughters of man and took them as wives, has been elaborated in the First Book of Enoch (written originally in Hebrew in the second or first century B.C.E.). There we read that "the angels, the children of heaven," not only took unto themselves wives from among the daughters of man, but also "instructed them in charms and enchantments, and taught them the cutting of roots and plants." One of the angels, Azazel or Azael by name, taught men knowledge of "the metals of the earth, and the art of working them, and bracelets and ornaments, and the use of precious stones, and all coloring tinctures." Other angels taught them how to resolve enchantments, how to read the signs of the stars, astrology, the knowledge of the clouds, and the signs of the earth, the sun, and the moon.[20]

Although this apocryphal source makes no reference to alchemy, what it does say about the angelic origin of technology, the arts, and the sciences was a sufficient basis for Hellenistic alchemists to impute to the instruction of those angels the origin of alchemy as well. Thus Zosimus (third or fourth century C.E.), the earliest and most important Hellenistic alchemical author, states in his lost *Book of Imouth* that when certain angels became enamored of earthly women they taught them the works of nature, that the book in which they laid down their teachings was called *Chema* (Khema), which name came to be applied to the alchemical art. This statement of Zosimus is recapitulated by the eighth-century Greek polygraph Georgius Syncellus in his *Chronographia*.[21] The treatise of Zosimus referred to by Syncellus is preserved in a Syriac version.[22]

In the same Hellenistic Egyptian alchemical circles in which this tradition originated, a connection was also made between *chymia* (alchemy) and the name Ham (Cham), son of Noah, and the notion arose that *chymia* was named after Ham, its first practitioner. After reviewing the literature on the subject, Edmund von Lippmann, the thorough German historian of alchemy, came to the conclusion that the derivation of *chymia* from Cham, the identification of Cham with Chemes (Chimes, Chimas), and the belief that this Chemes was the originator of alchemy as well as a prophet and an author, were specifically of Jewish-Hellenistic origin.[23]

The fancy that angels taught men the secrets of alchemy survived from the Middle Ages into modern times, and was restated by several later alchemical authors. Among them was the celebrated eighteenth-century French historian of alchemy, Nicolas Lenglet Du Fresnoy (1674–1755), who wrote in his three-volume history of Hermetic philosophy that, charmed by the beauty of the daughters of man, the angels seduced them, and taught them the greatest of secrets, namely that of the transmutation of metals. Noah saved this secret lore from being lost in the Great Flood, and of his sons, each of whom chose for himself a special vocation, it was Cham (Ham), or perhaps his children, who chose that of the arts and sciences. If Cham's son "Mezraim" (*Miṣrayim*) "did not practice chemistry, it is believed that it was, at any rate, practiced by his eldest son," who was none other than "Thaut or Athotis, also called Hermes or Mercurius, who became king in Thebes." Then Du Fresnoy goes on to explain that it appears likely that it was Cham, or at least his son Mezraim, who took this science into Egypt, and it was from there that alchemy spread all over the world. Even if Noah had children at the age of five hundred years (cf. Gen. 5:32), this does not mean that one has to accept it as a fact, as did the noted alchemist Vincent de Beauvais (d. 1264), that Noah practiced the most perfect chemistry and possessed the universal medicine, that is, the elixir which gave long life, and which is the most sublime part of the Hermetic philosophy. Still, Noah may have passed it on to his descendants, who cultivated it in Egypt.[24]

Thus Du Fresnoy manages to derive the Hermetic Art from Noah by the simple expedient of making Hermes (*alias* Thaut or Athotis) the son of Mezraim, the son of Cham, the son of Noah. Elsewhere he identifies the great-grandson of Noah with Hermes (or Mercurius) Trismegistus who, he says, lived in the year 1996 B.C., and whom he lists as the first in his enumeration of the "Most Celebrated Authors of the Hermetic Philosophy."[25]

Nor was the wife of Noah excluded from the genealogy of alchemy's biblical ancestry. Daniel Georg Morhof (1639–1691), the renowned author of the *Polyhistor*, informs his readers that the secret knowledge of alchemy originated from the wife of Noah, or from Sybilla, the wife of Nimrod.[26]

Abraham and Sarah. The Bible says about Abraham that he "was very rich in cattle, in silver, and in gold" (Gen. 13:2). This brief statement sufficed for some alchemists to argue that Abraham must have practiced alchemy, for how else could he have had much silver and gold? If so, from whom did he learn the Great Art? Evidently from Hermes during his sojourn in Egypt.[27]

The *Tabula Smaragdina* (Emerald Table) of Hermes, an alchemical tract dating, it seems, from the mid-thirteenth century, contains the oft-repeated legend of the original emerald slab upon which the teachings of Hermes were said to have been inscribed in Phoenician characters. It was discovered, so the legend goes, by Alexander the Great in the tomb of Hermes. Others, however, held that Sarah the wife of Abraham took the table from the hands of the dead Hermes in a cave at Hebron. This version of the legend is reproduced in the *Bibliotheca Graeca* of Johann Albert Fabricus (1668–1736) as follows:

> The tabula smaragdina, of great authority among the chemists, which, it is said, was discovered by Sarah (the wife of Abraham, as Christophorus Kriegsman does not hesitate to affirm in the aforementioned tabula smaragdina) in the valley of Hebron, in a tomb and in the hands of the cadaver of Hermes, contains in obscure words (as is the wont of chemists, to give much smoke and little light) everything, as they say, of the basis of performing the chemical magisterium of the metals, and the method of compounding a certain universal medicine, but most generally described.[28]

Jacob. Of all the biblical figures, the one in whose life a stone played a crucial role was Jacob. The story in Genesis tells about his dream of the heavenly ladder which he dreamt in Beth-el while sleeping with a stone under his head. Upon waking, Jacob anointed the stone and concluded a pact with God (Gen. 28:10–22).

Alchemical imagination latched on to this story, and considered the stone which served as Jacob's pillow as having been the philosophers' stone. The first in a series of fifteen fine copper-plate engravings, which were repeatedly reprinted in the seventeenth and eighteenth centuries, shows a young man sleeping with a stone under his head. Next to him stands a ladder reaching from heaven to earth, and on it can be seen angels ascending and descending while blowing trumpets. That the picture shows Jacob and the ladder is not open to doubt. It is also probable that the stone pillow of Jacob was accepted as a symbol of the philosophers' stone.[29] The fifteenth and last plate shows the ladder laid upon the ground, to symbolize the completion of the Work.[30]

As late as in the eighteenth century, it was still maintained by alchemists that Adam, Isaac, Jacob, Judah, and David were in possession of the philosophers' stone. This is asserted, for example, in a tract entitled *Splendor lucis* (Splendor of Light), printed in Frankfort and Leipzig in 1785 and written by AdMah Booz, actually Mich. Birkholz, who was himself a respected alchemist.[31]

Mē-Zahav. In the Book of Genesis, in the genealogy of the kings of Edom, there is a name which appeared to the medieval alchemists as a clear proof of their contention that some of the ancient leaders of Israel and the neighboring countries knew the secret of the preparation of aurum potabile, potable gold, that is, liquid gold. Genesis 36:39 (1 Chron. 1:50) records that the name of the wife of Hadar king of Edom was "Mehetabel daughter of Matred, daughter of Mē-Zahav." Although it remains unclear whether Mē-Zahav was a man or a woman, the meaning of the name is clear enough: it means, literally, "water of gold," or "gold water." The name could be an allusion to water containing gold (nuggets?), but the alchemists explained it unhesitatingly as referring to liquid gold, aurum potabile, and opined that Mē-Zahav was called by this name because he could liquify gold (see Chapter 34 below). The famed Jewish Bible commentator Abraham Ibn Ezra (1098–1164), in his comments to this verse in Genesis, states, "some say that [the name Mē-Zahav] hints at those who make gold out of copper; but these are words of wind [i.e., nonsense]."

It is possible that the name of Mē-Zahav's granddaughter Mehetabel, which in the Greek transliteration had become Metebel or Metabeel, reminded the alchemists of the Greek term *metabole*, transmutation, and this may have strengthened their belief in the alchemical interpretation of the name Mē-Zahav. They also argued that the great ages reached by the early biblical heroes—Methuselah is said in Genesis 5:27 to have lived 969 years—could have been attained only by using the "elixir of life."[32]

Job. Job had it in his grasp to become a successful alchemist, as can be seen from the words addressed to him by his friend Eliphaz the Temanite: "If thou return to the Almighty, thou shalt be built up; if thou put away unrighteousness far from thy tents, thou wilt lay thy treasure in the dust, and the gold of Ophir among the stones of the brook, and the Almighty will be thy treasure, and thou shalt have precious silver" (Job 22:23–25).[33]

Other passages in Job were also interpreted alchemically. Job named his daughters born to him after his ordeal Jemimah, Keziah, and Keren-happuch, which names were interpreted in a religious-alchemical sense. Keziah was held to mean a still, and Keren-happuch a retort which had the shape of an inverted (*hafukh*) horn (*qeren*). Yet another interpretation of Keren-happuch was the "horn," that is, the strength, of the *pukh* stone, that is, the science of alchemy.[34]

THE next biblical figures in chronological order are Moses and his sister Miriam. Moses will be discussed later in this chapter. For Miriam, with whom the Hellenistic alchemist Maria the Jewess was identified, see Chapters 5 and 6.

Korah. The biblical story of Korah tells about his rebellion against Moses and his subsequent punishment: he and his band were swallowed up by the earth (Num. 16). In the midrash, Korah and Haman are said to have been the richest men on earth. Korah's riches derived from his having discovered one of the treasures Joseph had hidden in Egypt. He perished because of his rapacity, and because his riches were not the gift of heaven. In his revolt against Moses he was encouraged by his wife.[35]

In the Koran (28:76–82), Qārūn (i.e., Korah) is said to have believed that his immense riches were given to him because of the "knowledge which is in him." This Koranic reference, based on the Bible and the midrash, was embellished by Arab authors, beginning with al-Jāḥiz (ca. 776–868/69) and Ibn al-Nadīm (d. 995 or 998). In their writings, Qārūn emerges as an adept of alchemy who had learned the art from his wife. She, in turn, had acquired it from her brother Moses. We discern in this detail of the Arab Qārūn legend an echo of the belief that Miriam, the sister of Moses, was an alchemist to whom were attributed the teachings of Maria the Jewess. Moses and Aaron, the Arab legend tells, were taught by God the art of making gold in order to cover the *tābūt al-tawrāt*, the ark of the Torah, with gold. They entrusted the work to Qārūn, who, according to one Arab source, was originally a goldsmith, and he accumulated a huge horde of gold and silver, built himself palaces with walls made of these precious metals, and at the end was punished by God for his arrogance.[36]

Gideon. The Israelite judge Gideon, of whom the Bible says that he gathered dew with a "fleece of wool" (Judges 6:36–40), is coupled with the Greek hero Jason of Golden Fleece fame by a sixteenth-century Dutch alchemist, Guilelmus Mennens (1525–1608). In his book *Aurei vellei, sive sacrae philosophiae vatum selectae unicae mysteriorumque ac Dei, naturae, et artis admirabilium libri tres*, Mennens gives an allegorical, symbolical, physical, chemical, and alchemical "history" of Gideon and Jason. The book is full of biblical quotations, and references to Hebrew kings, prophets, and so on.[37]

David. The biblical text states that King David set aside a huge amount of gold and silver for the building of the Temple: "I have prepared for the House of the Lord a hundred thousand talents of gold, and a thousand thousand talents of silver" (1 Chron. 22:14). This supplied the basis for the alchemists' speculation that David could have amassed such unheard-of quantities of the precious metals only with the help of the philosophers' stone. They found a peg on which to hang this view in the statement that King David left behind for his son Solomon, in addition to all the gold, silver, brass, iron, wood, and precious stones, also "stones of *pukh*" (1 Chron. 29:2, actual meaning uncertain). This term they interpreted as referring to the two philosophers' stones, the red one for the production of gold, and the white one for the making of silver. It was only because he inherited this stone, or these stones, from his father that Solomon was able to "make silver and gold to be in Jerusalem as stones" (2 Chron. 1:15; cf. 1 Kings 10:27).

Solomon. In their eagerness to find scriptural or semi-scriptural affirmation of the assumption that Solomon indeed possessed the philosophers' stone, the alchemists interpreted Solomon's praise of wisdom as referring to alchemical knowledge. In the apocryphal book Wisdom of Solomon, Solomon is made to say, "Neither did I liken her [i.e., Wisdom] to any precious gem, because all the gold [of the earth] in her sight is but a little sand, and silver shall be accounted as clay before her."[38] This, said the alchemists, referred to alchemical wisdom.[39]

As early as Zosimus there are references to the mystical writings of King Solomon. In his treatise *Book of the Key*, he described in detail the production and utilization of quicksilver: just as the key to everything visible and to the whole world is to be found in "The Mystery of the Nine Letters of King Solomon," so do the various kinds of mercury (the true and the metallic arsenic) contain the key to the Great Art, since everything fugacious belongs to the sulphurs; but the sulphurs, as Maria the Jewess had taught correctly, are the essential coloring agents.[40]

According to a technical treatise from the eighth century or later, one can make silver following a prescription of King Solomon that originated in the Temple of Helios (= Ptah), which calls for eastern and western quicksilver and forty days to complete the Work.[41] Moreover, according to some alchemical authors, the Song of Songs of Solomon is actually an alchemical treatise.[42]

King Solomon, who became an important figure in Arab folklore under the name Nabī Sulaymān, was according to popular belief not only the all-powerful master of demons (as in Jewish folklore), but also a master alchemist and metallurgist. The *Stone Book of Aristotle*, an Arabic treatise dating from about 850 and written by a Syrian who was well versed in Greek and Persian literature, states that Solomon made the ants dig up "red sulphur," that is, gold, from the rocks in the Valley of the Ants, and that it was from Solomon that Alexander the Great derived his knowledge of this "red sulphur."[43] According to Ibn Rusta (Abū ʿAlī Aḥmad ibn ʿUmar ibn Rusta, early tenth century), the Arabs ascribed the invention of iron ploughs, weapons, and utensils mostly to King Solomon.[44] The miraculous seal made of lead with which, according to the *Arabian Nights*, Solomon locked the evil spirits into bottles, also point to his having been an alchemist.[45]

Bonaventure de Periers, the sixteenth-century French polyhistor, makes repeated reference to King Solomon and the prophetess Maria as the greatest alchemists.[46] In 1620, the famous alchemist Michael Maier published in Frankfurt a book entitled *Septimana philosophica* or "The Philosophical week, in which the Golden secrets of all Kinds of Nature from the Most Wise Solomon King of the Israelites, and Arabia's Queen of Sheba, as well as Hiram Prince of Tyre, are Presented and Explained in Turn in the Manner of a Conversation."[47] Some fifty years later Johann Joachim Becher (1635–1682), one of the clearest heads of his time, asserted that King Solomon was in possession of the philosophers' stone.[48] According to an old English poem, preserved in Ashmole's *Theatrum chemicum Britannicum*, "the Blessed Stone Fro Heven wase sende downe to Solomon."[49]

Nor did Jewish alchemistic authors fall behind their Muslim and Christian colleagues in attributing alchemical works to Solomon. One of the foremost among them, Johanan Alemanno (1453–ca. 1504; see Chapter 23), quotes a story to the effect that the Queen of Sheba had inherited the philosophers' stone from her first husband, Sman, who was a great Nabatean sage. This was the precious stone which she presented to King Solomon (1 Kings 10:2), her purpose being to test his wisdom. But Solomon had already known the secret, and immediately recognized the stone. Although Alemanno took this story from an Arab alchemist, Abufalaḥ of Syracuse, it was originally found in the esoteric *Sefer haMaṣpun* (Book of the Treasure) ascribed to Solomon.[50] Alemanno also wrote another book, *Sefer Sha'ar haḤesheq* (Book of the Gate of Desire), which, as stated in the approbation prefacing it, was part of a larger book entitled *Ḥesheq Sh'lomo* (Solomon's Desire), and the material contained in it was attributed to King Solomon.[51] The book itself contains some references to alchemical and mystical lore, such as the *ḥokhmat haṣeruf* (science of refining gold), how to create and annihilate human beings and calves (following the example of certain talmudic sages), the letters of the alphabet as standing for the four alchemical elements, and so on.[52]

The anonymous Syriac author who reproduces and augments the text of Zosimus has much to say about the magical "talismans of Solomon," which he calls "flasks," in apparent reference to the magical flasks in which Solomon was said to have imprisoned the demons. Among other things he states that while "Solomon wrote only one work about the seven talismans [flasks], several commentaries on it were composed in different periods, to explain the things which this work contained; but in these commentaries there is fraud." However, almost all of them are in accord about the work of the talismans, which are directed against the demons. These talismans act like prayers, and like the nine letters of the name of God written by Solomon: the demons cannot resist them. Then he goes on:

> But let us return in greater detail to the subject which we are considering. The seven flasks in which Solomon imprisoned the demons were of electrum. It is fit to give credit in this respect to Jewish writings about the demons. The altered book which is in our possession and which is entitled *The Seven Heavens* contains, in brief, what follows here. The angel ordered Solomon to make these flasks. . . . Solomon made them according to the number of the seven planets, following the divine prescriptions about the work of the [philosophers'] stone, for the mixture of silver, of gold, and of Cyprian copper with the body called aurichalkos and copper of Marrah[?]. One takes one part of metal that has its shadow, and puts it face to face with all the sulphurous stones; the best of all of them will engender metal without a shadow. The necessary ingredients are in all nine in number. It is through them that everything is accomplished, as you know.
>
> The sage Solomon also knew how to conjure up demons. He gives a formula of conjuration, and he shows the electrum, that is to say, the flasks of electrum, on whose surfaces he inscribed this formula.
>
> You will find the mixture, the weight, and the treatment of each body and precious stone in the Jewish writings, and principally in those of Apilis son of Gagios. If you discover the meaning of these writings, you will discover there with sincerity that which you seek. If not, seek your refuge in the crocitidos [?], especially that which is in the manual [encheiridion?], [it being] understood that one produces the gold [*siwan*] with the iron [*sahoum*] colored red. One finds [in the manual] the complete indication of the nine necessary things.
>
> If you do not want to use this means, know that the following bodies are necessary for the preparation of the electrum: burnt gold [*siwan*], silver [*loura*] called of the ant [múrmēkos], whitened copper [*saroch*], tender and softened iron [*sahoum*], lead [?*tou*], purified silver [*lune*]. You will find their treatment everywhere.[53]

The close association between Solomon and the philosophers' stone is shown by the fact that the materia prima of the stone was sometimes represented as the two interlaced triangles of "Solomon's seal," which survives to this day as the Jewish national emblem known as the Magen David, David's Shield. For the alchemists this seal or star was the symbol of wisdom, and also the sign of the "fiery water," since it consists of a combination of two symbols: that of fire, which rises upward and hence is symbolized by the upward pointing triangle, and that of water, which descends from the sky and is represented by the downward pointing triangle.[54] The old midrashic interpretation of the Hebrew word for heaven, *shamayim*, namely, that it is a combination of the words *esh*, fire, and *mayim*, water, was known and restated by the alchemists.[55] One of them, after explaining the nature of the Upper Waters, writes, "This is why in the Hebrew language heaven is called 'Fiery Water,' from *Isch* & *Maijm*, that is, *Schamajim*."[56] The Magen David was also interpreted as a symbol of the four basic elements of Earth, Air, Fire, and Water. Sometimes it represents "universal matter."[57]

In 1687 *Arca arcani artificiosissimi* by Johann Grasshoff was published in Hamburg and Stockholm. This book, in which the author warns against hasty attempts to prepare aurum potabile, drinkable gold, was reprinted in 1753 under the new title *Philosophia Salomonis.* In his treatise *Der von Mose und denen Propheten übel urtheilende Alchymist*, published in Chemnitz in 1706, Johann Georg Schmid argued (pp. 55–59) that Solomon, wise though he was, could not have possessed an art which did not exist in rerum natura; rather, he obtained his gold and silver from mines in the usual way, without requiring the philosophers' stone or any miracle. A similar position was taken by Andreas Ottomar Goelicke (1671–1744) in his *Historia medicinae universalis* (1721, 1:61, 62). He raised the question of whether or not Solomon was a chemist, and decided in the negative.[58]

Elijah. Several of the biblical prophets were considered adepts in alchemy by the alchemists of later ages. The prophet Elijah was often referred to by Christian alchemists, several of whose works carry the name Elijah in their title. In some of these treatises Jewish influence is evident, and is manifested in statements that echo the talmudic dictum according to which, Elijah will answer all unsolved questions when he returns as a harbinger of the Messiah. Paracelsus can serve as an example. Although he claimed to have found the philosophers' stone, he wrote in his tract on minerals that "God revealed lesser things, but the most important thing [namely, the transmutation of base metals into gold] is still wrapped in darkness, and will remain so until the coming of Elias Artista."[59]

Isaiah. The prophet Isaiah ranks next to Elijah as an adept in alchemy. Leonhard Rhodius of Transylvania is quoted by the anonymous author (actually Dr. Soldner) of the treatise *Keren Happuch* to the effect that the alchemical expertise of Isaiah is shown by Isaiah 54:11, which says, "Behold, I will set thy stones in fair colors, and lay thy foundations with sapphires, and I will make thy pinnacles of rubies, and thy gates of carbuncles, and all thy borders of precious stones." The plural in "thy stones" supposedly refers to the two philosophers' stones, the red and the white; while the sapphires refer to the color of sapphire which appears at the last stage of the preparation of the stone, perhaps an allusion to the alchemical process of iosis (or oxydation). Others adduce Isaiah

60:17, which reads, "For brass I will bring gold, and for iron I will bring silver."[60]

A few biblical figures remain for us to mention. An alchemical prescription is attributed to King Hoshea, the last king of Israel.[61] A Hellenistic alchemical manuscript mentions that the solder of gold which is both an operation and a material, is designated "by the divine Daniel" as a "head of gold."[62] Valentin Weigel (1533–1588) writes in his *The Prophet Daniel Interpreted by Theophrastus* (extant in manuscript) that Daniel was a great master of alchemy.[63]

Ezra. Ezra was the last biblical figure who, in the imagination of the adepts of the Hermetic Art, became an alchemist. In the Cambridge University Library there is a Syriac collection of tracts that includes a "Book of Ezra (Esdras) the Sage Scribe." This is an alchemical treatise containing technical prescriptions analogous to those of the "Chemistry of Moses" (see below). It also contains the names of diverse plants, the planets, and metals.[64] A recipe for manufacturing ink attributed to Ezra will be found in Chapter 29 below.

Moses the Alchemist

In the alchemical literature, beginning with the earliest Hellenistic writings and down to the latest eighteenth-century alchemical treatises, and even in nineteenth-century post-alchemical writings, Moses occupies an important place as master of the Royal Art. Some alchemists even considered Moses, together with Hermes, as one of the co-founders of alchemy, which they consequently called "the Mosaico-Hermetic Art."

There seems to have lived in Hellenistic Egypt an actual alchemist by the name of Moses who appears as the author of several alchemical tracts.[65] Even in the earliest Greek alchemical sources mentioning Moses, it is difficult to separate the references to Moses the Hellenistic alchemist and Moses the Hebrew lawgiver, who was considered an initiator of the alchemical art. Thus, for example, Zosimus included in his writings copies of several detailed alchemical recipes of Moses in a manner which makes it appear that he knew that this Moses was an actual Hellenistic alchemist. But elsewhere in his treatises Zosimus speaks of Moses as if he considered him a personage of remote antiquity, that is, the Hebrew lawgiver. In one passage Zosimus says, "this is why in Jewish writings and in all writings they speak of an inexhaustible mass which Moses obtained following the precept of the Lord." Similarly, a Greek technical treatise says, "It is this about which Moses, the divine prophet, speaks in his Chemistry [the Chemistry of Moses, see below]: placing all things into a small glass ball, cook it until the product becomes the color of cinnabar and accomplishes the divine mystery."[66]

An alchemical treatise containing about five thousand words and entitled *The Domestic Chemistry of Moses* is preserved in the third-century C.E. papyrus W of Leyden. It contains sixty-two alchemical prescriptions, which are introduced with a paraphrase of Exodus 31:1–5 and 35:30–35, with the obvious intention of pseudepigraphically associating the treatise with the biblical Moses, and thereby endowing it with an aura of antiquity and authenticity: "And the Lord spoke unto Moses: I have chosen the priest called Bezalel, of the tribe of Judah, to work in gold, silver, copper, iron, in all precious stones, to work and to fashion good wood, and to be a master of all the arts." This is followed by alchemical prescriptions on the usual subjects of the treatment of mercury, copper, molybdochalkon (lead-copper), pyrite, the distillation of water, the treatment of arsenic, liquids, the purification of lead, and several instructions on how to make gold. One of the latter (no. 23) reads:

> The fabrication of gold. Taking female pyrite and that which has the color of silver, which some call the siderite stone [loadstone], treat it as you know, in a manner so as to make it liquid. If it is to copper that you add it, you will whiten it as you know how, and if it is to silver, you will yellow it by the cooking of sulphur which you know. Then project this yellow metal upon the silver, and you will tint it [i.e., obtain gold]. Nature takes pleasure in nature.[67]

The treatise both begins and ends with the blessing, "Good fabrication and success from the Creator; success in the Work, and long duration of life!"[68]

Zosimus, in his tract on "The Divine Water" (i.e., sulphur), refers to *The Domestic Chemistry of Moses*: "This is how, in the *māza* of Moses [it is said that] one burns with sulphur, with salt, with alum, and with sulphur (I mean white sulphur)."[69] The term *māza*, employed here in the sense of chemistry or a chemical textbook, otherwise means "black lead," or "magnesia"—as in the instructions of Maria the Jewess.[70] The writings attributed to Moses recommend that this *māza*, or Cyprian copper, be used as the material with which to start the alchemical work. Due to a confusion of "female magnesia" with the "male magnes" (which here means manganese dioxide [MnO_2], pyrolusite), Moses states that the "divine *māza*" has the character of *óxos* (vinegar, acridity), in that it purifies and softens everything, even glass, which it endows with a shiny white hue. The "tinting" of copper is effected by means of tin, white magnesia, white Dalmatian cadmium, Italian stimmi, quicksilver, and quicksilver of sandarac or white lead, that is, arsenic gained from red sulphide of arsenic or white arsenious acid (H_3AsO_3), which transmute and tint the copper, inasmuch as the desired "nature" or quality which is present inside is driven up to the surface.[71]

In order to obtain the effective means, the *xerion*, whose projection upon tin produces silver which, if tested, shows itself to be genuine (*dókimōs*), one uses the gold-colored auriferous pyrites from Egypt or Libya, sandyx (which here means cinnabar or native red sulphide of mercury), and "deadened" mercury (that is, either mercury in combination with another material, or mercury which is "in the depths of the nether worlds"—in other words, has trickled down to the bottom of the alchemical vessel).

Moses also prescribes the use of "horseradish oil" and "castor oil" for the treatment of the "egg white" and "egg yolk," which terms are evidently pseudonymous. On the other hand, he probably refers to the burning of real linseed oil and castor oil in describing the production of the "black, burned sulphur," presumably from smelted sulphur which, due to its carbon content and its dark color, is also called *mélan*, blackness, or soot. Preparations that require sweet water, rather than sea water, are left for a considerable time to set in dung, or are warmed in cow dung or horse manure.[72]

While there is, of course, no basis whatsoever to the attribution of these Hellenistic alchemical works to the biblical Moses, the writings themselves show strong Jewish influences and Jewish monotheistic views. At one point, for example, one of the treatises speaks of "the Creator who gives success and long life."[73] It can therefore be assumed that the author known pseudonymously as Moses was a Hellenistic Jewish alchemist. In one source he is called "Moses the thrice happy,"[74] which designation is reminiscent of the epithet given to Hermes, "Trismegistus," "thrice great."

One of the most popular of the alchemical prescriptions attributed to Moses was the so-called "Diplosis of Moses," the doubling of the weight of gold. The Greek text of it is contained in the St. Mark manuscript, which dates from the tenth or eleventh century, and in several other medieval manuscripts.[75]

It reads as follows:

> Diplosis of Moses. Copper of Calais,[76] one ounce; arsenic [orpiment], one ounce; native lead, one ounce; decomposed sandarac [a realgar], one ounce. Put it in the *acmadion* [roasting pan], and place it upon the coals, until desulphuration; then take it off, and you will find your product. Of this copper take one part and three parts of gold; melt it, carrying on the fusion strongly, and you will find all of it changed to gold, with the help of God.[77]

That the biblical Moses was well versed in, and was in fact, the founder of, the arts and sciences, was a belief current in antiquity. According to the Alexandrian Jewish philosopher Philo (c. 20 B.C.E.–50 C.E.), Moses in his youth received instruction in the wisdom of the Greeks, the Egyptians, and the neighboring nations.[78] The second-century B.C.E. Hellenistic Jewish author Artapanus, in his *Peri Ioudaiōn* identifies Moses with Musaeus of the Greek legend, and says that Moses was the master of Orpheus and the inventor or initiator of philosophy, medicine, instruments, utensils, weapons, the hieroglyphic characters, and the division of Egypt into thirty-six districts, of which he allotted one to the priests. Therefore, he says, there is nothing surprising in the divine honors paid to Moses by the Egyptians, who called him Hermes.[79] According to Pseudo-Philo, immediately prior to Moses' death great mysteries were revealed to him which, according to midrashic sources, included past and future events of the human race and of Israel, as well as cosmic secrets.[80]

In numerous magical papyri, Moses appears in a similar light.[81] Among the magical and astrological works attributed to Moses is "The Sacred Book called Monas the Eighth (or the Eighth Monad) of Moses on the Holy Name, also called the Key of Moses, the Secret Book of Moses."[82] Both the Leyden Papyrus X (from the Thebais) and the St. Mark manuscript list Moses among the twenty-six "philosophers of the divine science and art," and as early as the third century C.E., Moses appears in a Greek papyrus as a mythical author together with Homer, Orpheus, Pythagoras, and Democritus.[83] Another Hellenistic source states that Ostanes, Agathodaimon, Maria, and Moses taught that the bile of the ichneumon and the vulture, macerated for forty days with red aerugo (copper rost) are used as coloring agents.[84]

The fame of Moses as a magician (not alchemist) spread early in the Roman world. Pliny (23–79 C.E.) writes, "There is yet another branch of magic, derived from Moses . . . and the Jews."[85] The notion that Moses was a great magician is echoed in the late Midrashim, which report that in the court of Ahasuerus it was known that Moses had been "an arch-wizard, bred in the house of Pharaoh."[86]

The identification of Moses with Hermes was a remarkable feat of syncretistic ingenuity on the part of the Hellenistic and later alchemical authors. The Hermes in question was, of course, not the Greek god, but the mythical father of alchemy, who was identified also with Adam, Enoch, a fictitious son of Mizraim son of Ham, Abraham, Joseph, and so on. He was considered the personification of knowledge, of science, of the creative spirit which expresses itself in the arts, and was held to have been the keeper of all ancient hereditary wisdom.[87] As we shall see, this identification of Moses with Hermes survived well beyond the Middle Ages.

According to another, relatively late, tradition, "Hermes Trismegistus, surnamed Mercurius" was a disciple of Moses: he was instructed uncommonly [well] in the doctrine of Genesis transmitted by Moses."[88]

When viewed against the background of this legendary embroidery on the image of Moses, considered the greatest universal genius and master of all the arts and sciences, it appears as almost inevitable that the alchemists should make him a founding father of their Royal Art. This was the more easily done since the biblical story of the golden calf readily lent itself to alchemistic interpretation. When Moses came down from Mount Sinai, we read in Exodus, and found that the Children of Israel had forced Aaron to make them a golden calf and were riotously worshiping the idol, his ire was aroused, "and he took the calf which they had made, and burnt it with fire, and ground it to powder, and strewed it upon the water, and made the Children of Israel drink of it" (Exod. 32:20).

A loose reading of this verse enabled the alchemists to assert that Moses knew the secret of liquid gold, *aurum potabile*, whose production was one of the great aims of the Hermetic art. This knowledge of Moses, together with the description of the large golden vessels, weighing more than twenty-nine talents each, which Moses had Bezalel fashion for the desert sanctuary (Exod. 31:1–11; 35:30–36:1; 38:24), was taken to be proof that Moses knew the secret of the other, even greater, alchemical quest, that of making gold.

The first Arab author who refers to Moses as the founder of alchemy is Jābir ibn Ḥayyān (eighth to ninth century), one of the principal representatives of early Arab alchemy. His large opus entitled *The Book of CXII* (i.e., 112 chapters or prescriptions), a collection of essays on the practice of alchemy with many references to practitioners of the art in antiquity—such as Zosimus, Democritus, Hermes, Agathodaimon, and so on—contains a "Chapter on Moses."[89] According to Jābir, Moses was the possessor of divine science, and Qārūn (Korah) stole from him the secret of alchemy. Other Arab authors such as Ibn al-Nadīm, Pseudo-Majriti, Jahiz, and Maqdisi also refer to Moses and Korah as alchemists.[90]

Ibn al-Nadīm (d. 995 or 998) writes in his well-known *Kitāb al-fihrist* (Index Book), which he completed in 987/8,

> Others say that the revelation [of alchemy] was made by God the Most High to Moses son of Amram and to his brother Aaron—peace be upon both of them!—and that it was Qārūn who carried out the work in their name. This latter, having accumulated much gold and silver, and having

amassed treasures, was, at the request of Moses, taken away by God who perceived the arrogance, pride, and wickedness with which his riches inspired him.[91]

Korah's riches and his inordinate pride are old Jewish legendary motifs, found as early as Josephus and the Midrash but, as mentioned above, Jewish sources do not attribute the origin of Korah's fortune to his practice of alchemy, but to having found treasures hidden by Joseph.[92]

Several medieval adepts of alchemy, as well as nonadepts who had some chemical knowledge, raised the question of how Moses could burn the golden calf (Exod. 32:20), when it was a well-known fact that gold did not burn. Abraham Ibn Ezra (1089–1164), one of the foremost medieval Bible commentators, has a solution for the problem (see Chapter 11).

Five centuries later, the German alchemist and chemist Johann Kunckel (ca. 1630–1703), unaware of Ibn Ezra, restated the essence of his explanation. He argued that Moses had attained the highest degree of alchemical mastery, which comprised not only the ability to transmute base metals into gold, but also its opposite: the knowledge of how to transmute gold into base metals. He first transmuted the gold of the calf into combustible base metal, and then proceeded to burn it in fire.[93]

The *Turba philosophorum* (Assembly of Philosophers), originally written in Arabic or Hebrew (but probably based on older Greek sources), and extant only in a Latin translation, tells of a gathering of the disciples of Hermes convened by Pythagoras.[94] Among those assembled are Anaximandros, Anaxagoras, Pandolfus (Empedocles), Archelaos, Plato, Democritus, the disciple of Lucas (Leukippos), Anaximenes, Parmenides, Arsuberes (Xenophanes), Frictes (Socrates), Zimon (Zenon), Dardaris (Dardanos), Theophilus, and so on, and also Moses. When Moses' turn comes to speak, he explains the various names of quicksilver, and quotes "the Philosopher" as having said that the quicksilver which tinges gold is the quicksilver out of cinnabar (*argentum vivum cambar*), and that this is the "magnesia," while the quicksilver of the auripigmentum or orpiment (a native arsenic trisulphide, As_2S_3) is the sulphur which ascends from this mixed compound material. "You must, therefore," he says, "mix that thick thing with the 'fiery venom,' and let it putrefy, and diligently pound it until a spirit is produced which is hidden in that other spirit; then it will become a tincture for everything that you wish."[95]

Later Moses speaks of molybdochalkon:

> One must observe that the envious have named the lead of copper the "instruments of formation," in order to mislead posterity by deception. I am

> making it known to them that their "instruments of formation" are formed from our white, starlike and shining "powder" and from our "stone" which glitters like marble. But of them no "powder" is more fit for our Work and better for our composition than the powder of the "ascocia" [the gum of the acacia], out of which arise suitable "instruments of formation." Further, the philosophers have already said, "Take the instruments out of the egg," but they did not report what kind of egg, of which bird.[96] And know that the regimen of these things is more difficult than the whole Work, because if the "composition" is treated more than necessary, its light, coming from "Pelagus" [the sea] will be extinguished. Therefore the philosophers prescribed that one must observe [the heavens]. Take it, therefore, at full moon, and put it in "sand," until it becomes whitened. And know that if you have no patience for putting it in "sand," and for the repetition, you will err in the procedure, and the Work will be ruined. Therefore cook it in a gentle fire, until you have whitened it, then extinguish it with "vinegar," and you will find that one of the three has already become separated. And know that the first elixir comingles, the second gets burnt, but the third liquifies. Therefore add to the first nine ounces of "vinegar," twice: the first time while the vessel is getting warm, and the second time after it has become warm.[97]

Once the notion that the biblical Moses was a great alchemist had penetrated Christian Europe via the Latin translations of Greek and Arabic works, there was no dearth of imitative treatises composed in Latin and containing references to Moses the alchemist, amongst several other biblical figures and classical Greek and Latin authors, who were considered practitioners of the Royal Art. As a typical example of this kind of writing can be mentioned the *Margarita preciosa* (Precious Pearl) of Petrus Bonus of Ferrara (c. 1330), in which reference is made to Moses, David, Solomon, Ovid, Virgil, Aristotle, and Galen, as witnesses to the transmutability of metals.[98]

In Chapter 21 we shall discuss in some detail the fifteenth-century magico-alchemical treatise written by a certain Abraham ben Simeon of Worms. In it the author gives the biblical genealogy of the "divine science": it was revealed by God to Noah, from whom it was passed on to his descendants: Japhet, Abraham, Ishmael, Lot, Moses, Aaron, Samuel, David, Solomon, Elijah, the apostles, and St. John.

In the early sixteenth century, Paracelsus referred to the major figures in the biblical genealogy as possessors of the great secret of the philosophers' stone. He spoke of an "indestructible essence," an una res, which was first revealed to Adam.[99] Paracelsus conceived of this una res as a spiritual substance, and says that "through this spirit . . . Moses made the golden vessels in the Ark, and King Solomon achieved many beautiful works to the honor of God. Therewith Moses built the Tabernacle, Noah the Ark, Solomon the Temple. . . . By this Ezra restored the Law."[100]

The standard sixteenth- and seventeenth-century alchemical collections, such as the *Artis auriferae*, the *Theatrum chemicum* (5:57–89), and Manget's *Bibliotheca chemica* (1:467–79), contain a short tract entitled *Allegoriae sapientium supra librum Turbae XXIX distinctiones* (Twenty-nine Sections of the Allegories of the Wise about the Book *Turba*). Distinctio II begins with a dialogue between God and Moses: Moses asks God to have compassion on him and to provide a livelihood for the Children of Israel by instructing him in the production of gold.[101]

By the seventeenth century, the belief that Moses was a great alchemist was so widespread in alchemical circles and had become such a firmly established tenet that several of the more critically minded writers about the Hermetic Art found it necessary to combat it. Thus, for instance, Hermann Conring (1606–1681) wrote in 1648 and again in 1669 that it was nothing but a fable that Moses was a chemist, and asserted that in the biblical story of the golden calf which Moses pulverized nothing is said of a chemical dissolution of gold.[102]

In 1706 the same subject was discussed, and the alchemists sharply criticized, by Johann Georg Schmid, long-time pastor at Nesselbach, in a small German book entitled (in my English translation) *The Alchemist Who Passes Evil Judgment on Moses and the Prophets is Being Presented with Scriptural Proofs that Moses and Several Prophets, such as David, Solomon, Job, Ezra, and the like, Were not Adepts of the Lapis Philosophorum: Likewise that the Doctrine and the Alchemistic Pretense about the Transmutation of Base Metals into Gold is a Pure Fantasy and a Harmful Fancy*, by a Lover of Truth, Who Comforts Himself in that the Almighty is his God, Job 20:25 (? perhaps 37:22), and seeks Nothing in Gold.[103]

However, those who believed that Moses was a great alchemist were much more numerous than those who denied that he had alchemical knowledge. Among the former was Olaus Borrichius (1626–1690), who wrote in 1668 and again in 1674 that only a very good chemist could do what the Bible says Moses did, namely, reduce the golden calf by grinding it into fine powder.[104] In the same vein, Georg Wolfgang Wedel (1545–1721) wrote in his treatise *De Mose chimico* (About Moses the Chemist): "Without doubt Moses was a supreme chemist and craftsman with fire, who could destroy the golden calf so promptly." Wedel surmises that Moses may have used sulphur, acid salts, mercury, or lead for this purpose, and that he ground the calf into fine powder and, sprinkling it over water, made it not only fit for drinking but even salubrious.[105] Reference to the golden calf appears in the title of a book by

Johannes Fridericus Helvetius (Schweitzer), written originally in Latin, translated into German in 1668, and two years later also into English under the title *The Golden Calf Which the World Adores and Desires: In which is handled the most Rare and Incomparable Wonder of Nature in Transmuting Metals: Viz. How the intire Substance of Lead was in one Moment Transmuted into Gold-Obrizon, with an exceedingly small particle of the true Philosophic Stone.*[106] More on Helvetius will be found in the introduction to Part Eight.

However, it was not only religio-romantic scholars, always ready to read into the Bible indications of all the scientific and technical achievements of their own age, who maintained that Moses was indeed a master chemist. Sober scientists did the same. Thus no lesser a chemist than Georg Ernst Stahl (1660–1734), the originator of the famed phlogiston theory, developed in 1698 some ideas about the alleged dissolution of gold in water. He held that by smelting gold together with equal parts of *salis alcali* and *sulphuris citrini* it could be dissolved, and the resulting mass could then be diluted in water. And, he added, this was certainly the manner in which Moses dissolved the golden calf.[107]

In 1742 a three-volume work of Nicolas Lenglet Du Fresnoy entitled *Histoire de la philosophie hermetique* was published; it contains a brief section "Moses Knew the Hermetic Science." In it Du Fresnoy writes:

> Moses was trained in all the sciences of the Egyptians, of which the most secret, and at the same time one of the most essential, was that of the transmutation of Metals. One should, therefore, not be surprised to see him melt, calcinate, and pulverize that enormous mass of the golden calf which the people of Israel made for themselves as a divinity similar to the Apis of Egypt. This calcination could not be effected without the use of fire. What is more: Moses knew how to dissolve and dilute this calcinated gold in ordinary water, which is contrary to all experiments, since without the help of a special science the gold, in however small a quantity it be, is always precipitated to the bottom of all ordinary liquids with which one combines it. It is this science, it is this particular knowledge, which changes the nature of metals, to which we have for a long time given the name of philosophy, or of Hermetic chemistry, and very likely [it was called] by the Egyptians the Sacred Art, the Divine Science.[108]

Du Fresnoy's opus contains an extensive listing in chronological order of "the most celebrated authors of the Hermetic philosophy." He puts Hermes (or Mercurius Trismegistus) at the head, stating that he lived in 1996 B.C. In the second place comes Moses, to whom the date 1595 B.C. is assigned, with the accompanying statement that "there is in his name a supposed book on the Hermetic science."[109]

Although Du Fresnoy thus places four full centuries between Hermes and Moses, the identification of the two nevertheless survived to the very end of the eighteenth century. Fabricius in his *Bibliotheca* quotes Artapanus to the effect that the Egyptians intimated (*innuunt*) that Moses and Mercurius (= Hermes) were one and the same person.[110] To this Gottlieb Harles, the editor of Fabricius' magnum opus, adds in a footnote that Basnage in his history of the Jews "denies that Mercurius and Moses were one and the same man, since before Moses and before Joseph the art of writing was known, and written books did exist."[111]

The question of the identity of Hermes and Moses still agitated the minds of not only alchemists but also historians well into the second half of the nineteenth century. W. Herapath, upon studying silverlike hieroglyphics on the linen wrappings of Egyptian mummies, found that the linen was eaten away next to the writings, and suspected that the writing was done in silver dissolved in nitric acid. Hence he concluded that nitrous ether was known to the ancient Egyptians, and went on to conjecture:

> A very probable speculation might be raised upon this to account for the solution of the Golden Calf by Moses, who had all the mundane knowledge from the Egyptian priests. It had been supposed that he was acquainted with and used the sulphuret of potassium for that purpose; how the inference arose, I know not; but if the Egyptians obtained nitric acid, it could only have been by the means of sulphuric acid, through the agency of which, and by the same kind of process, they could have separated hydrochloric acid from common salt: it is therefore more probable that the priests had taught Moses the use of the mixed nitric and hydrochloric acids with which he could dissolve the statue, rather than a sulphuret, which we have no evidence of their being acquainted with.[112]

Within a year of the publication of the above article, another chemist, J. Denham Smith, raised objections to Herapath's theory, and argued that the biblical text says nothing about Moses having *dissolved* the gold of the calf, but merely states that he "reduced it to an impalpable powder, and thus rendered it potable when mixed with water . . . 'he burnt it with fire,' that is, he fused and alloyed it with a substance capable of rendering gold brittle."[113]

In conclusion, some reflections seem to be called for on the motivation underlying the persistent claim that Moses was a master alchemist. The great quest of alchemy—to fathom the secrets of nature, including those of metals, on the one hand, and of the human being, on the other—was seriously hampered by the disrepute incurred by frauds perpetrated by charlatans who claimed to be able to make gold. In this predicament it became of paramount importance for alchemists to be able to show that their science had a respectable genealogy. And no other ancient great figure could serve the purpose as perfectly as Moses, the man of God, the great lawgiver, whose sacred Five Books were held in the greatest awe by the whole Christian world, and in no less reverence by the Muslims as well. Hence, if Moses was an alchemist, alchemy itself had to be not merely reputable but a praiseworthy endeavor, approved and indeed originally taught by angels or even by God Himself.

Moses had one great advantage over other biblical figures from the alchemical point of view: although the others may have made golden vessels and utensils or had them made, only about Moses does Scripture say that he burned and pulverized gold. Here then was a religious leader of the greatest distinction, a man of God of unmatched sanctity, whose biblical image was, so to speak, tailor-made to serve as the alchemical equivalent of a patron saint.

Chapter Three

ALCHEMY IN BIBLE AND TALMUD?

As we have seen in the preceding chapter, despite the claims of alchemists, the fact is that the Bible contains nothing that would indicate familiarity with either alchemical theory or alchemical practice. The attribution of alchemical expertise to biblical figures was clearly the figment of later generations' imagination.

This observation does not mean that the Hebrews in biblical times were ignorant of metals, their mining, smelting, and use. Quite to the contrary: although the Bible does not have a generic term for "metal," it mentions seven metals several times: gold, silver, copper, iron, tin, lead, and antimony. Excavations conducted in various parts of Ereṣ Israel have unearthed remnants of those metals in both raw and processed forms. A closer look at biblical metallurgy seems warranted, since metallurgy is an indispensable prerequisite of practical alchemy.

It is a well-known anthropological-linguistic observation that there is a direct correlation between the importance of an item in the life of a people and the number of words in its language to designate that item and its varieties. There are the proverbial hundred words in Arabic for the camel, and in Eskimo languages many words designating the varieties of snow. Likewise, one may conclude that the many words found in biblical Hebrew for gold must indicate that gold was of great importance in the life of ancient Israel, whereas other metals, covered by fewer terms, had lesser significance.

In the Bible the following seven nouns have the meaning "gold": *zahav, paz, ketem, ḥaruṣ, s'gor, ophir, baṣer.* Whether they referred to various kinds of gold, can no longer be established. In addition, there are in the Bible five adjectives regularly associated with gold: *zahav shaḥuṭ* (beaten or polished gold); *zahav ṭov* (good gold); *zahav ṭahor* (pure gold); *zahav m'zuqqaq* (refined gold); and *zahav sagur* (closed [?] gold). Moreover, kinds of gold were differentiated according to their places of origin: there was Ophir gold, Sheba gold, Uphaz gold, Parvayim gold, gold from the north, and gold from the land of Havila. Ophir, Sheba, and Havila seem to have been located in East Africa; the location of Parvayim and Uphaz is unknown. Four of these determinants were used also together with *ketem*: there were *ketem ṭahor, ketem ṭov, ketem ophir*, and *ketem uphaz*. Finally, the noun *paz* appears in combination with three other nouns denoting gold: *zahav uphaz, ḥaruṣ uphaz, ketem paz*. There was also a *ḥaruṣ nivḥar* (choice *ḥaruṣ*), and a *y'raqraq ḥaruṣ*, in which the first word originally was yet another synonym for gold. This rich nomenclature makes it clear that the ancient Hebrews carefully differentiated among various kinds of gold according to place of origin, quality, purity, color, and so on.

From other biblical passages it is possible to conclude what processes went into the production of gold objects. The raw gold was melted in a special crucible (Prov. 17:3; 27:21), given the shape of ingots or large "tongues" or "wedges" weighing up to fifty shekels (Joshua 7:21). In the course of smelting, the gold was separated from the impurities (Mal. 3:3; Job 28:1; 1 Chron. 28:18), and thereafter was also assayed (Zech. 13:9; Job 23:10). If the gold was to be used for coating other objects or for making jewelry, it was first beaten into thin plates or cut into threads (Ex. 39:3).

As for metals other than gold, from passages in Jeremiah (6:29–30) and Ezechiel (22:18, 20) it appears that the metallurgists worked with bellows (*mapuaḥ*) to increase the temperature of the fire under the crucible (*kur*), and to separate (or "consume") the lead from the silver, and to remove the dross (*sig*) of silver which consisted of such base metals as copper (*n'ḥoshet*), tin (*b'dil*), iron (*barzel*), and lead (*ʿoferet*).

That metallurgical processes of purifying gold and silver were known in ancient Israel becomes clear from a passage in Malachi (3:1–3): "Behold, I send My messenger, and he shall clear the way before Me. . . . But who may abide the day of his coming? And who shall stand when he appeareth? For he is like a refiner's fire, and like fullers' soap; and he shall sit as a refiner and purifier of silver, and he shall purify the sons of Levi, and purge them as gold and silver." The key words in Hebrew are *esh m'ṣaref* (refiner's fire), *m'ṣaref um'ṭaher kesef* (a refiner and purifier of silver), *v'ṭiher . . . v'ziqqeq otam kazahav v'khakesef* (and he will purify . . . and purge them as gold and silver).

This verse is explained in the medieval commentary *M'ṣudat David*: "That messenger will be like the fire which refines the silver and burns away the dross, and like the soapwort of the washers which removes the spots from the clothes, that is how he will destroy and remove all the sinners and the rebellious." It is evident from the use of such a simile in a prophetic admonition that the work of the refiner and purifier of precious metals was well known to the audience addressed by the prophet; the effect of his words hinged upon striking a familiar chord in the consciousness of the people.

There is a passage in Job that gives a poetic description of the mining of various metals in biblical times. Job is speaking:

For there is a mine for silver, and a place for gold to refine:
Iron is taken from dust, and stone is molten to copper—
An end he puts to darkness, and searches what is remote,
Midst lightless rocks, in the shadow of death,
Breaks open a shaft where no man dwells,
Where no foot treads, where no soul moves,
In earth from which no bread will sprout,
And in whose depth the fires churn.
Among its crags is found sapphire,
And it is rich in dusts of gold.
No bird of prey can know that path,
Nor was it seen by falcon's eye,
No wildebeest has pawed that way,
Nor has the lion strutted there—
Man's hand alone has touched the stone,
Torn up the mountains' mighty root,
Broken channels in the midst of rocks,
His eyes espied the precious bits,
He led the flow of streams across
And brought to light the hidden things.

(Job 28:1–11; my free translation)

To counterbalance this poetic description of a mine in the wilderness, let us mention that archaeological work in the southern parts of Israel, carried out by Nelson Glueck and others, has located several copper mines that were exploited in the days of King Solomon. Likewise, both biblical references and archaeological finds testify to the general use of bronze, and later iron, implements and other objects in biblical Israel. Hence it is clear that in the biblical period the metallurgical preconditions were present for the subsequent development of Jewish interest in alchemy.[1]

When we proceed to the talmudic period (c. 100 B.C.E.-500 C.E.) we find more abundant sources, though it is surprising that there are so few references to knowledge of alchemy.[2] Much of the talmudic period overlapped with the Hellenistic age, during which there was a sizable Jewish community in Egypt, where alchemy was beginning to flourish, and there was considerable contact between the rabbis of the Talmud and the Jews of Hellenistic Egypt. In Alexandria the trades of the gold and silversmiths, gold and silver workers, and coppersmiths were among the most important occupations—this can be concluded from the statement in the Talmud that practitioners of these five crafts, plus that of the weavers, were the only ones seated in separate groups in the huge synagogue of the city.[3]

Although Jewish goldsmiths supplied important pieces of furnishing and ritual objects to the Jerusalem Temple, no overt traces of, or references to, Hellenistic alchemy are found in the entire talmudic literature, except for one passage of doubtful authenticity which we shall discuss below in Chapter 30. Given the interest in alchemy that characterized Hellenistic Egypt, however, it is more than likely that among the many Jewish metal workers there were some who tried their hand at alchemy. It almost appears as if the sages of the Talmud purposely shut their eyes to this important aspect of Greek and Jewish culture in Hellenistic Egypt. In any case, the talmudic references that lend themselves to an alchemistic interpretation are few and vague.

The locus classicus is the discussion of the seven kinds of gold, which is a passage found, with some variations, in several talmudic and midrashic sources.[4] It is a homily on the seven terms for gold which the sages found scattered in the various books of the Bible, and which they believed designated seven different kinds of gold. The explanations given to the biblical terms are purely midrashic, based mostly on popular etymology of words whose actual meaning was unknown to the sages. I give here the literal translation of the shortest and oldest, and of the longest and most recent of these four versions, with the biblical source references added in parentheses.

The shortest and oldest version is found in the Babylonian Talmud:

> R. Ḥisda said: There are seven kinds of gold: gold, good gold, Ophir gold, *Muphaz* gold, *shaḥuṭ* [beaten] gold, closed gold, and *Parvayim* gold. Gold and good gold, as it is written, "and the gold of the land is good" (Gen. 2:12). Ophir gold, which comes from Ophir (1 Kings 10:11). *Muphaz* gold (1 Kings 10:18) which is like *paz* [shining gold; Rashi explains: "it shines like a pearl"]. *Shaḥuṭ* gold (1 Kings 10:16), which can be stretched like a *ḥuṭ* [thread. Rashi: "Because it is soft"]. Closed gold (1 Kings 10:21)—when its sale opens, all the stores are closed down [Rashi: "because no other kinds of gold are then being bought"]. *Parvayim* gold (2 Chron. 3:6)—thus called because it is like the blood of *parim* [bulls]. . . . We have, in fact, learned thus (in Mishna Yoma 4:4), "Every other day its gold was yellow, on this day [on Yom Kippur] it was red"—this is the *Parvayim* gold which is like the blood of bulls.[5]

The etymologically impossible explanations of the three difficult terms *Muphaz, shaḥuṭ*, and *Parvayim* shows that this is pure aggadah or legend, and that R. Ḥisda was not in possession of any concrete tradition or information concerning actual differences in the quality of gold designated by the seven biblical terms.

Some traces of an alchemical grasp of the characteristics of gold may be contained in the expanded version found in two Midrashim with almost identical wording. In my translation I have combined the two texts:

> There are seven kinds of gold: good gold, pure gold, *shaḥuṭ* [beaten] gold, closed gold, *Muphaz* gold, purified gold, and *Parvayim* gold. Good gold—as its simple meaning. . . . Pure gold—if it is put into the melting pot it does not diminish at all. R. Judah in the name of R. Ami said: Solomon put a thousand talents of gold into the melting pot a thousand times, until only one talent remained. But has not R. Yose ben R. Yehuda taught: It so happened that the Menorah of the Temple was heavier than that of the desert [Sanctuary] by the weight of one Gordian denar, whereupon they put it into the melting pot eighty times until it was reduced? [No contradiction, because] at the beginning it was reduced much, and thereafter it was reduced only little by little. *Shaḥuṭ* gold—it could be spun like a thread (*ḥuṭ*) and stretched like wax. Hadrian had an egg's weight [of this gold], Diocletian had a Gordian denar's weight, this nation has none of it. Closed gold—it caused all the works in gold to close shop. . . . *Muphaz* gold—R. Paṭroqi, the brother of R. Drosa, said in the name of R. Abba bar R. Buna: It looked like sulphur set on fire. R. Abin said: It is called after the name of its country, *me Uphaz* [from Uphaz]. Purified gold—those of the school of R. Yannai said: They cut it up like olives and feed it to ostriches, and it comes out purified. Those of the school of R. Yudan said in the name of R. Shimᶜon that they hide it in dung for seven years, and it comes out purified. *Parvayim* gold—R. Shimᶜon ben Laqish said: It is red like the blood of the bull [*par*]. And some say that it brings forth fruit [*perot*], for when Solomon built the Temple, he fashioned in it all kinds of trees, and in the very hour when the trees of the field brought forth fruit, the trees in the Temple also brought forth fruit, and they let their fruit drop, and [the priests] gathered them and put them aside for the repairs of the Temple. But when Manasseh set up an idol in the Temple, all those trees dried up.[6]

Most of the passage is again pure aggadah, but it also touches on a few matters of alchemical concern. It evinces interest in the question of whether or not gold loses some of its weight when melted down. It assumes that there is a kind of gold which is so soft that it can be spun like a thread and stretched like wax, and another which is like burning sulphur in appearance. The belief that the ostriches can ingest and digest gold recurs in several medieval Jewish alchemical tracts. The notion that if gold is put into dung for seven years it comes out purified reappears in a modified form in medieval alchemical writings: certain substances, if buried in dung for periods of varying length become transformed into other substances which in turn can be used for producing gold.

The other great quest of the alchemists—to be able to produce a miraculous substance or essence that could give health and youth, and banish death—was also known to the rabbis of the Talmud. They called it in Hebrew *sam ḥayyim*, and in Aramaic *samma diḥayya*, that is, "elixir of life," and believed in its actual or possible existence. The references to it in rabbinic literature are few and indirect, but clear enough to render the presence of such a belief indubitable. The following midrash is a good example:

> There was a spice seller who used to make the rounds of the villages near Sepphoris [in the Galilee], and he used to announce and say, "Who wants to buy the elixir of life?" The people crowded around him. R. Yannai, who was sitting and studying in his parlor, heard him announce "Who wants the elixir of life?" and called out to him, "Come over here and sell it to me!" The spice seller said to him, "Neither you nor those like you need it." But R. Yannai persisted, whereupon the spice seller went to him, took out a copy of the Book of Psalms, and pointed out to him the verse, "Who is the man who desireth life?" [and said,] What is written after it? "Keep thy tongue from evil . . . depart from evil and do good."[7]

According to a parallel source it was the daughter of R. Yannai who heard the spice seller hawking his ware and told her father, who asked the man to approach him; when he heard the answer, he rewarded him with six *selaᶜ*s.[8]

Although the intent of the story as it stands is pietistic and moralistic, since it teaches that the true elixir of life is righteousness (or, according to one parallel source, the study of the Torah), it presupposes not only a familiarity with the concept of "elixir of life," but also a strong desire among both the simple people and the learned rabbis to acquire it. Hence we may conclude that the search for the elixir constituted part of Jewish life in Palestine in the third century, in which R. Yannai lived. In other talmudic passages, too, the Torah is likened to the elixir of life.[9] However, none of this proves that any talmudic sages who lived in Palestine and Babylonia were actually familiar with alchemy, let alone engaged in its practice.

PART TWO

The Hellenistic Age

Introduction to Part Two

ALTHOUGH there is no agreement on the question of whether alchemy emerged first in China or in Hellenistic Egypt, there is no doubt that in the Western world alchemical tradition goes back to the latter place and era, and that the first language in which alchemical writings were produced was Greek. Thus it is remarkable that Hellenistic alchemy was from its very inception informed by the belief that it owed its origin to a Jewish, or Hebrew, secret and sacred alchemical science. One form taken by this tradition, which is not supported by any historical evidence, was the creation of a mythical biblical prehistory for alchemy; another the frequently voiced but historically unprovable assertion that the Jews alone were in possession of true alchemical knowledge.

There is historical evidence, on the other hand, that among the Hellenistic alchemists there were several Jewish adepts, one of whom, Maria the Jewess, was considered by them the founder of their art. She is constantly referred to by Zosimus and others as the ultimate authority in both the theory and the practice of alchemy, and her teachings, in many cases in the form of pithy aphorisms, are quoted as if they had been prophetic pronouncements.

This part presents what I was able to learn about Maria and the other Jewish alchemists in the Hellenistic world from extant Greek texts.

Chapter Four

JEWS IN HELLENISTIC ALCHEMY

INFORMATION on Jewish alchemists in the Hellenistic world is contained primarily in the writings of (Pseudo-)Democritus and Zosimus the Panopolitan, and in the so-called Papyrus W of Leiden; these groups of treatises constitute the bulk of all Hellenistic alchemical writings.

(PSEUDO-)DEMOCRITUS

The treatises that go under this name date, as best one can determine, from between 100 B.C.E. and 100 C.E. They deal with a large number of alchemical subjects, and contain occasional direct or indirect references that afford an insight into the role Jews played in the alchemical activities of the Hellenistic world. In his treatise entitled *Planetary List of the Metals*[1] (Pseudo-)Democritus transcribes the names of certain precious stones, such as *smaragdos* (sapphire), sardonyx, jasper, chrysolite, *margarites* (pearl), minerals such as *lithos magnites* (lodestone), *lithargyros* (litharge), and alloys such as *claudianos*, *asem*, *diargyros*,[2] and so on, in Hebrew characters. It appears, says Berthelot, that the author "wanted to deny their knowledge to uninitiated people; this is an indication of an old mystical tradition."[3]

This interpretation is supported by a statement of Maria the Jewess, and by another pronouncement of (Pseudo-)Democritus. As we shall see in the next chapter, Maria the Jewess intended to limit the knowledge of the philosophers' stone to "the race of Abraham" that is, to Jews. In the light of this saying it is more than likely that the following passage in (Pseudo-)Democritus's treatise entitled *On the Assembly of the Philosophers* also refers to Jews:

> The philosopher [(Pseudo-)Democritus], answering clearly about the things known to them, expressed himself thus: "It is not befitting to those of our race, originating in one single species, that we should be reproached for our books, and that imprecations should be hurled at our heads. Concerning the tincture of gold which one wants to obtain, this is what has been indicated to me by the people of the craft: if somebody comes to expose the instructions relating to the multiplicity of the species, it is an error, for the goal to be pursued is another one. The furnace is unique, unique is the road to be followed, unique also the Work.[4]

In interpreting this admittedly obscure passage we can go along with Berthelot, who remarks that "It seems that there is here an allusion to the role of the Jews among the alchemists; analogous phrases, but more precise, are attributed to Maria." We may add that if the expression "those of our race" actually refers to the Jews, as seems to be the case, then there is an indication here that this (Pseudo-)Democritan treatise was written by a Jewish alchemist.

Another passage from (Pseudo-)Democritus speaks explicitly about the role of Jews in the alchemy of Hellenistic Egypt: "It was the law of the Egyptians that nobody must divulge these things in writing. . . . The Jews alone have attained a knowledge of its practice, and also have described and exposed these things in a secret language. This is how we find that Theophilus son of Theogenes has spoken of all the topographic descriptions of the gold mines; the same is the case with the description of the furnaces by Maria and with the writings of the other Jews."[5]

Theophilus son of Theogenes was evidently an otherwise unknown Egyptian Hellenistic Jewish alchemist. He is referred to again, many centuries later, in the Treatise of Stephanus, a philosopher, physician, astrologist, and courtier of the Emperor Heraclius (c. 620), as having said, "There exists an excellent stone in the Land of Egypt."

Zosimus

Zosimus of Panopolis lived in the late third to early fourth century C.E., professed himself a disciple of Maria the Jewess, and was the earliest authentic, non-pseudepigraphic, and reliable author on the state of alchemy in Hellenistic Egypt. What he says on the subject, together with his frequent references to Maria, conveys a good idea of the seminal role Jews played in developing both the theory and the practice of alchemy in Hellenistic Egypt.

Part of the Zosimean corpus is a treatise entitled *On Virtue*, in which Zosimus asks a series of questions, which are in effect enigmatic sayings very similar to those he quotes in the name of Maria the Jewess:

> What do these words signify: "Nature triumphant over natures"? And this: "The moment it is achieved, it [nature] is seized by vertigo"? And again: "Restrained in research, it [nature] takes on the common visage of the work of All, and it absorbs the proper material of the species"? and this: "When, speaking a barbaric tongue, it [nature] imitates the one who speaks the Hebrew language; then, defending itself, the wretched one makes itself lighter by mixing together its own members"? And this: "The liquid totality is driven to maturity by the fire"?[6]

I am unable to interpret these questions, each of which states more than it asks, but it seems clear that the one referring to the Hebrew language is based on the premise that Hebrew was superior to the other, "barbaric" languages.

In his treatise entitled *On the Evaporation of the Divine Water*, addressed to his sister Theosebeia, Zosimus states clearly that on the highly important subject named in the title he could find information only in the books of the Jews.[7] He writes:

> Finding myself once in your residence, O woman, in order to hear you, I admired the whole operation of that which is called by you the "structure." I became greatly amazed at the sight of these effects, and I started to venerate the *poxamos* [an instrument] as something divine. . . . What surprised me was the cooking of the bird,[8] subjected to filtration; it was to see how it undergoes cooking by means of the sublimated vapor, of the heat and of an appropriate liquid, when it partakes of the tincture. Surprised, my spirit returned to our object of study: it examined whether it is as a result of the emission of the vapor of the divine water that our mixture can be cooked and tinted. Then I searched whether any of the ancients had mentioned this instrument, and nothing presented itself to my mind. Discouraged, I examined the books, and found in those of the Jews, next to the traditional instrument named *tribikos*, the description of your own instrument.[9] This is how the matter is presented:
>
> "Taking the [sulphurated] arsenic,[10] whiten it in the following manner. Make a fatty paste, of the size of a small very thin mirror, pierce it with small holes, in the manner of a sieve, and place above it a small receptacle, well adjusted, containing some sulphur. Put into the sieve some arsenic, as much as you wish. After having covered it with another receptacle, and having sealed the points of junction, after two days and two nights you will find ceruse.[11] Take of it a fourth of a *mine*[12] and let it breathe for a day, adding to it a little bitumen, etc. Thus is the construction of the apparatus."[13]

Another of the treatises of Zosimus is entitled *The True Book of Sophé the Egyptian and of the Divine Lord of the Hebrews [and] of the Powers of Sabaoth.* "The Divine Lord of the Hebrews" refers to the God of the Jews, and "Sabaoth" is, of course, the Greek transliteration of the Hebrew divine name *ṣ'va'ot*, which in the Bible usually appears in the combination *Yahweh Ṣ'va'ot*, that is, "Lord of Hosts." The treatise begins as follows:

> There are two sciences and two wisdoms: that of the Egyptians and that of the Hebrews, which latter is rendered more sound by divine justice. The science and the wisdom of the best dominate both: they come from ancient centuries. Their [present] generation is devoid of a king, is autonomous, insubstantial; it does not search for material and corruptible bodies; it op-

> erates without submitting to [foreign] action, sustained now by prayers and [divine] grace. The symbol of chemistry is drawn from Creation [in the eyes of its adepts], who save and purify the divine soul enchained in the elements, and who, above all, separate the divine spirit commingled with the flesh. Just as there exists one sun, the flower of the fire, a celestial sun, the right eye of the world, so the copper, if it becomes a flower [that is, if it takes the color of gold] by purification, becomes a terrestrial sun, which is the king on earth just as the sun is king in heaven.

Zosimus goes on to tell of alchemical procedures for the transmutation of copper into gold, and other alchemical works.

In his treatise *On Furnaces and Apparatus*, Zosimus goes in for some comparative mythology. He writes:

> The Chaldeans, the Parthians, the Medes, and the Hebrews call him [the first man] Adam; which signifies virgin earth, bloody earth, igneous earth, and carnal earth. These things are found in the library of the Ptolemies, deposited in each sanctuary, notably in the Serapeum. [They were put there] when Asenan, one of the high priests of Jerusalem, sent Hermes who interpreted the whole Hebrew Bible in Greek and in Egyptian.
>
> It is thus that the first man is called Toth by us, and by them Adam, a name given by the voice of the angels. One calls him symbolically by means of the four elements, which correspond to the cardinal points of the sphere, and by saying that his body was composed [of them]. In fact, the letter A of his name designates the Orient (*Anatolē*) and the Air (*Aer*). The letter D designates the setting sun (*Dúsis*), which goes down by reason of its weight. The letter M points to the South (*Mesēmbria*), that is to say the fire of the burning which produces the maturation of the bodies, the fourth zone and the middle zones.[14]
>
> Thus carnal Adam, in his apparent form, is called Toth. But the spiritual man contained in him [has a name] proper and appellative. But we to this day don't know what is this proper name; for only Nicotheus, that personage whom one cannot find, knows these things. As for the appellative name, it is that of *fōs* [light, fire]: this is why men are called *fōtes* [mortals].
>
> When he was in Paradise, in the form of light [*fōs*], subject to the inspiration of destiny, they persuaded him, profiting from his innocence and his incapacity to act, to reclothe [the personage of] Adam, the one which [was subject to] destiny, the one which [corresponded] to the four elements. He, owing to his innocence, did not refuse; and they prided themselves on having captured [in him] the exterior man.
>
> It is in this sense that Hesiod[15] has spoken of the chains with which Jupiter tied Prometheus. Thereafter, after those chains, he sent him another one [that is to say] Pandora, whom the Hebrews call Eve. Now Prometheus and Epimetheus are one and the same man in allegorical language—

the soul and the body. Prometheus is sometimes the image of the soul; sometimes [that of] the spirit. This is also the image of the flesh, owing to the disobedience of Epimetheus, committed with respect to Prometheus, his brother.

Our intelligence says: The son of God, who can do everything and who can become everything if he wants to, manifests himself to everybody as he wants to. Jesus Christ joined Adam and brought him back to Paradise where the mortals had previously lived.

He appeared to people deprived of all power, having [himself] become man, subject to suffering and to blows. [Meanwhile,] having secretly cast off his proper mortal character, he [in reality] did not experience any suffering; he seemed to trample death underfoot, and repell it, for the present and until the end of the world: all this in secret. Thus relieved of appearances, he advised his people to exchange likewise their spirit secretly with that of Adam which they had in themselves, to beat it and to put it to death, this blind man being led to rivaling the spiritual and luminous man: it is thus that they kill their proper Adam.

In the sequel Zosimus continues to present, in a similar combination of Hebrew, Gnostic, Manichean, and Persian ideas, the struggle between God and Antimimos, the "counter-actor," for the soul of Adam.[16]

In his treatise entitled *The First Book of the Final Reckoning*, Zosimus discusses the Jews' knowledge of the important alchemical field of tinctures:

As for the proper tinctures, nobody either among the Jews or among the Greeks has ever revealed them. In fact, they put them in images formed with their own colors and destined to be preserved. The operations performed on the minerals differ greatly with regard to the suitable tinctures. They [the Jews and the Greeks] were very jealous of divulging the art itself; and they did not let a manipulator remain without punishment. He who made a search without authorization could be thrown down [and put to death] by the overseers of the town markets charged with the collection of the royal taxes. Likewise, it was not allowed to operate the furnaces secretly, or to fabricate in secret proper tinctures. Also you will not find anybody among the ancients who reveals that which is hidden, and who exposes anything clearly in this regard. I have found among the ancients only Democritus who gave a clear understanding of something in this respect in the enumerations of their catalogs.[17]

What is interesting in this passage is that it affords a glimpse into the social position of the Jewish and Greek alchemists in Hellenistic Egypt. It would appear that they had the power to prevent unauthorized individuals from engaging in alchemical work and research, and that their control over the trade (or Art) was backed up by the forces of the royal government.

In the sequal Zosimus quotes some statements by (Pseudo-)Democritus on mercury, magnesia, and other substances used by the alchemists as tinctures. He then explains that Democritus and the Egyptian alchemists recorded their procedures in such a manner that even if "somebody dared to face the darkness of the sanctuary in order to obtain the knowledge in an illicit fashion, he would not succeed in understanding the characters, despite his daring and his efforts." As against them, he continues,

> the Jews, having been initiated, have transmitted these procedures which had been confided to them. Behold what they counsel in their treatises: "If you discover our treasures, abandon the gold for those who want to destroy themselves. After having found the characters which describe these things, you will assemble all these riches in a short [time]. But if you restrict yourself to taking these riches, you will destroy yourself, in consequence of the envy of the kings who reign, and that of all men."[18]

After this warning, which was to be repeated frequently by medieval authors who wrote about the life of alchemists, Zosimus expatiates about the jealousy among alchemists, and advises Theosebeia to follow in her alchemical endeavors the example of King Solomon:

> Let your body rest, calm your passions, resist desire, pleasure, anger, sorrow, and the dozen fatalities of death. In thus conducting yourself you will call to you the divine being, and the divine being will come to you, he who is everywhere and nowhere. Without being asked, offer up sacrifices: not only those advantageous to these men and destined to nourish them and to please them; but also those which remove them and destroy them, sacrifices such as those that were recommended by Membres when he addressed himself to Solomon, king of Jerusalem, and principally those which Solomon himself described according to his own wisdom. Operating in this manner you will obtain the proper, authentic, and natural tinctures. Make these things until you become perfect in your soul. But, when you recognize that you have arrived at perfection, then beware of [the intervention of] the natural elements of the material: descending toward the Shepherd, and plunging into meditation, you will thus re-ascend to your origin.[19]

Next Zosimus returns to quoting Jewish alchemists in his treatise on *The Coloring of Precious Stones*, in which, as we shall see, he frequently quotes Maria the Jewess. He writes:

> The biles of animals, when losing their aqueous material, are desiccated in the shade. In that condition one incorporates them into the rust of our

> copper, just as into the *comaris*; one cooks all of it together according to the rules of the Art. Colored by the [divine] water, they assume a stable tint. This water being removed, the stones are heated, and while still hot mixed in the tincture, according to the precepts of the Hebrews.[20]

From the material presented above it becomes evident that Zosimus had a close familiarity with the work of Hellenistic Jewish alchemists, went along with the view that the Hebrew language was superior to all other tongues, and held that the alchemical knowledge of the Hebrews was "rendered more sound by divine justice" than that of the Egyptians. In addition, in one of his writings, addressed to Eusebeia, he refers to the Jewish legend based on Genesis 6:1–4 and embellished by the Midrash, according to which the angels were seized with passion for the earthly women and were expelled from heaven.[21] He enriches this legend by adding an alchemical interpretation of the angels' sins:

> The ancient and divine books say that certain angels were taken by passion for women. They descended to earth and taught them all operations of nature. It is about them that our book says that those angels who became proud were driven from heaven because they had taught men all the evil things which do not serve the soul. They were the ones who composed [chemical] works, and from them derives the first tradition concerning these arts. Their book is called *Chema* [Khema], and it is from it that chemistry [*kumia*] received its name. The book is composed of twenty-four sections. . . . One of them is called *Imos*, another *Imouth*. . . .[22]

The reference in this passage to the Bible as "our book" was interpreted by Julius Ruska as possibly indicating that Zosimus was a Jew. Long before Ruska, the thirteenth-century Arab alchemist Abu ʿl-Qāṣim al-ʿĪrāqī in his *Book of Knowledge Acquired Concerning the Cultivation of Gold* introduced a long quotation from Zosimus's opuscule "Distinctions of Religions" by identifying the author as "Zosimus the Jew" (A. *Zismus al-ʿIbrī*), which of course is an indication of the existence of an Arab alchemical tradition according to which Zosimus was a Jew.[23] Whether or not this tradition is based on fact cannot be decided on the basis of presently available information.[24]

The Leiden Papyrus W

Papyrus W of Leiden, published in the original Greek, translated into French, and commented upon by Berthelot, is a treatise of alchemy and magic, and contains references to the relationship between magic and Jewish Gnosticism.[25] The Jewishness of its author is shown by references to the Temple of Jerusalem and the Cherubim, and by the names of

Abraham, Isaac, Jacob, and Michael that appear in it. It also contains an invocation that points to the author's affinity with Jewish Gnostic views, colored by an alchemical perception of the deity. He addresses himself to God in this language:

> All is subject to You, but none of the gods can see Your shape, because You transform Yourself into all. . . . I invoke You by the names which You have in the language of the birds, in that of the hieroglyphics, in that of the Jews, in that of the Egyptians, in that of the Cynocephals . . . in that of the sparrow hawks, in the hieratic language.[26]

These references to the alchemical knowledge and practices of the Jews are in themselves meager. But when they are read together with the frequent references Zosimus makes to Maria the Jewess, they create the impression that Zosimus considered the Jews in general, and Maria in particular, the most important sources of learning about age-old alchemical theories and practices that were kept jealously hidden by the Egyptians and the Greeks.

The Power of Hebrew

Among the treasures of the Paris Bibliothèque Nationale there is a large folio volume of 342 leaves containing several dozens of alchemical treatises, all written in Greek and claiming to be works of Pythagoras, Ptolomaeus, Hermes Trismegistus, Zoroaster, Hippocrates, Aristotle, King Solomon, and other authors famous in the gallery of alleged ancestor figures of Hellenistic alchemical tradition, as well as anonymous works, magical formulas, and so on. The hefty volume, identified as MS Grec 2419, is beautifully bound, and is supplied with a Latin table of contents, evidently of later provenance than the Greek manuscripts themselves. One of the treatises included in the volume is described in this table of contents as follows: "Albumazar qui et Jafar et Aboazar, astrologus, vixit circa annum Christi 540," that is, "Albumazar, who like Japhar and Aboazar, astrologer, lived about the year 540 of Christ." It is the treatise of this Albumazar, contained on folios 37a–69b, which constitutes an eloquent example of the attribution of power to the Hebrew letters by the Hellenistic alchemists, and their heirs in the worlds of both Christianity and Islam.[27] The author referred to in the manuscript as Albumazar was Jaʿfar ibn Muḥammad ibn ʿUmar Abū Maʿshar al-Balkhī. He is well known in the history of Arabic literature, but he lived not about A.D. 540 but in the first half of the ninth century.[28] He was born in Balkh in eastern Khurāsān, studied in Baghdad, and became celebrated as an astrologer, even though he was known to be guilty of plagiarism. Several of his works dealing with astrology were translated into Latin in the twelfth century by Johannes Hispalensis, and printed in the late fifteenth and early sixteenth centuries. They were influential in Christian Europe, and introduced a theory of the tides and the law of the ebb and flow of the sea.

That treatise contains, among other matters, a list of the correlations between the planets and metals, and thus is undoubtedly alchemical. However, with its attribution to Abū Maᶜshar there is a problem. The usual direction of the flow of literary transmission was from Greek into Arabic, and not vice versa. Hence it would be quite unusual for a treatise written in the ninth century in Arabic to be translated into Greek. This consideration makes me inclined to assume that we have here an anonymous treatise, written originally in Greek, and then mistakenly attributed to Abū Maᶜshar.

Marcellin Berthelot, who printed, translated, and described the Albumazar treatise, noticed that several pages of the manuscript contain Greek words written in Hebrew characters, which he explained by saying that it was done because those words had a "mysterious meaning."[29] In his translation of the text he noted that the Greek words (I transliterate them into Latin characters) *lithárgyros, gagátes kai klaudianos, diárgyros, theĩon, líthos magnítes, sámfyros, margarítes*, and *sardónyx* are transliterated in Hebrew characters. He observed that Albumazar's list merits special attention because "it corresponds to a more complete and older astrological tradition, probably going back to the Chaldeans, and because it is included in a list of plants and animals also consecrated to the planets. A certain number of the names of precious stones (sapphire, sardonyx, jasper, chrysolith, pearl), minerals (lodestone, litharge), and alloys (claudianos, asem, diargyros) are transcribed in Hebrew characters, as if to interdict their knowledge to noninitiated persons: this is a sign of an old mystical tradition."[30]

Berthelot confined his remarks to a few pages of Albumazar's Greek text, and either did not notice, or found it unnecessary to comment upon, the fact that on several other pages such Hebrew transliterations of Greek words appear with the Greek letters written above them.[31] Since the Greek superscriptions seem to be later additions, what probably happened was this: At first the Greek author of the treatise wrote the "words of power" in Hebrew characters in accordance with the prevalent view that the Hebrew letters themselves lend additional "power" to the word. At that time it was assumed that the adepts who were likely to peruse the manuscript were able to read not only Greek but Hebrew as well. Subsequently, as familiarity with the Hebrew alphabet declined among the late Hellenistic alchemists, a reader of the Greek manuscript who knew Hebrew thought it would be helpful for other readers to have the Hebrew words transliterated in Greek, so that those ignorant of the

Hebrew alphabet should at least be able to pronounce the "power words" (which themselves were Greek!). It should also be pointed out that the Hebrew words themselves in the Albumazar treatise were evidently written by a copyist who did not know Hebrew and who copied the words rather clumsily, leaving considerable spaces between the letters, and reproducing them so inaccurately that some of them cannot be deciphered at all.

Despite this decline of the knowledge of Hebrew, the belief in the power and efficacy of Hebrew survived in alchemical circles into the Middle Ages and beyond. One can easily convince oneself that this indeed is the case by glancing at practically any alchemical work written, down to modern times, in Latin or any European language: they all contain a few, and occasionally more than a few, key Hebrew "power words" that were supposed to lend them authenticity, originality, and reliability.

Chapter Five

MARIA THE JEWESS

THE FIRST nonfictitious alchemists of the Western world lived, as far as can be ascertained, in Hellenistic Egypt. And the earliest among them was Maria Hebraea, Maria the Hebrew, or Maria the Jewess, for whom our chief source is Zosimus the Panopolitan. Zosimus is the first Greek alchemical author whose actual writings have survived. He lived in Hellenistic Egypt, about 300 C.E., and wrote an impressive number of works; twenty-two treatises of his were published in the Greek original and in French translation by Marcellin Berthelot.[1] He also wrote, together with his sister Eusebeia, a chemical encyclopedia in twenty-eight books, of which only fragments survived, also published by Berthelot. Nothing is known of Zosimus's life, but it is generally assumed that he was originally from Panopolis in Thebais, and lived in Alexandria.

For the most part, Zosimus's writings consist of extensive quotations from older alchemical authorities. The ones whom he quotes most frequently are (Pseudo-)Democritus, to whom he refers as "the philosopher," and Maria the Jewess, whom he calls in most cases simply Maria, although occasionally he styles her "the divine Maria."[2]

Despite the frequent references Zosimus makes to Maria, his writings contain practically no clue as to when and where she lived. In his tract on "The Divine Water," however, Zosimus says: "The operation of burning [is] one which all the ancients extolled. Maria, the first, says, 'The copper burnt with sulphur.'"[3] Elsewhere Zosimus refers to a treatise, *On Furnaces and Apparatuses (Peri kaminon kai organon)*, which seems to have been written by Maria, as a writing of "the ancients." He does this while refusing to comply with the request of his sister Theosebeia, who asked him for information on the subject: he concedes that he is unable to treat it more authoritatively than was done in that ancient treatise.[4] From these references to Maria as the first of the ancient authors one can conclude that she must have lived at least two generations before Zosimus himself. We can thus tentatively assign her to the early third century C.E. at the latest.[5]

MARIA'S INSTRUMENTS

There are several alchemical apparatuses which Maria either invented or whose description she provided; from the way Zosimus quotes her it is impossible to say which of these is the case.

Maria constructed and described various ovens and apparatuses for cooking and distilling made of metal, clay, and glass. She connected, tightened, and caulked the various parts of these instruments by means of fat, wax, starch-paste (size), fatty clay, and the "clay of the philosophers." She considered glass vessels especially useful, because "they see without touching," and permit the safe manipulation of dangerous materials such as mercury, which she describes as "the deadly poison, since it dissolves gold, and the most injurious of metals," as well as "sulphurous" (by which she often means arsenical) substances, serving the preparation of "divine water."[6]

The most famous alchemical apparatus either invented or used and described by Maria is the *balneum Mariae*, or water-bath, which consists of a double vessel, the outer one of which is filled with water while the inner one contains the substance(s) which must be heated to a moderate degree. Whether Maria actually invented this apparatus or whether, as Lippmann tried to show, it had been in use for centuries before her, described by Hippocrates and Theophrastus, and attributed to Maria as a result of a chain of fortuitous circumstances, the fact remains that the fame and prestige of Maria led to the association with her of the water-bath, which to this day is known in both chemistry and cooking as *bain Marie* in French, and *Marienbad* in German (see Figures 5.1–3).[7]

The oldest description of a still is again given by Maria. The typical still consisted, and still consists, of three parts: a vessel in which the material to be distilled is heated, a cool part to condense the vapor, and a receiver (see Figure 5.4).[8] The Greek name of the still, *kerotakis*, was derived from the name of the palette on which the ancient Greek painters mixed their four basic pigments—white, black, yellow, and red—with wax (*keros*). The triangular or rectangular metal plate which served as the kerotakis had to be kept warm in order to prevent the wax from hardening.[9] The alchemists used the kerotakis in a similar manner for softening the metals and mixing them with their coloring agents, which was one of their chief procedures in attempting to transmute base metal into gold or silver. Subsequently the kerotakis became a three-part apparatus, which in its simplest form consisted of a vessel under a plate into which were placed vaporizable substances capable of attacking metals, while over it was an inverted cup in which the vapors were condensed to liquid. On the plate itself were placed the metals to be treated.[10]

A more complex alchemical still is described by Maria under the name *tribikos*:

> I shall describe to you the tribikos. For so is named the apparatus constructed from copper and described by Maria, the transmitter of the Art. For she says as follows: "Make three tubes of ductile copper, a little thicker than that of a pastry cook's copper frying pan. Their length should be

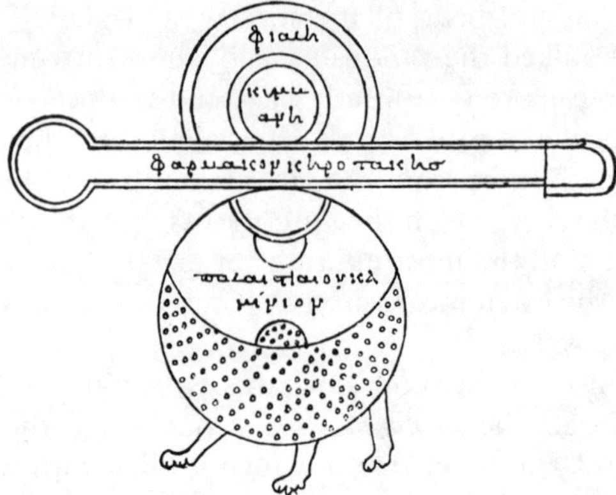

Figure 5.1. Drawing of the *bain Marie.*

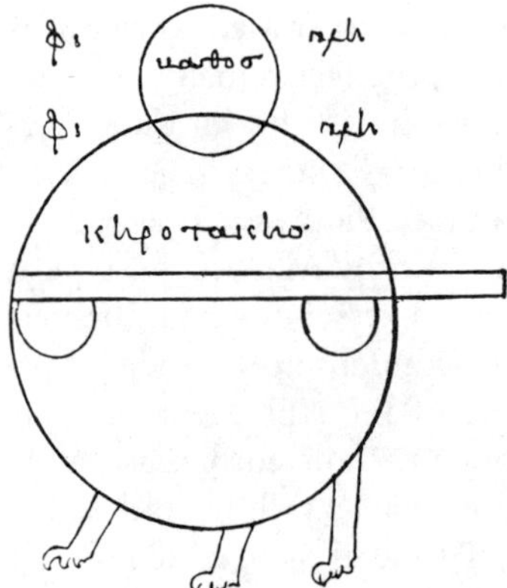

Figure 5.2. Another drawing of the *bain Marie.*

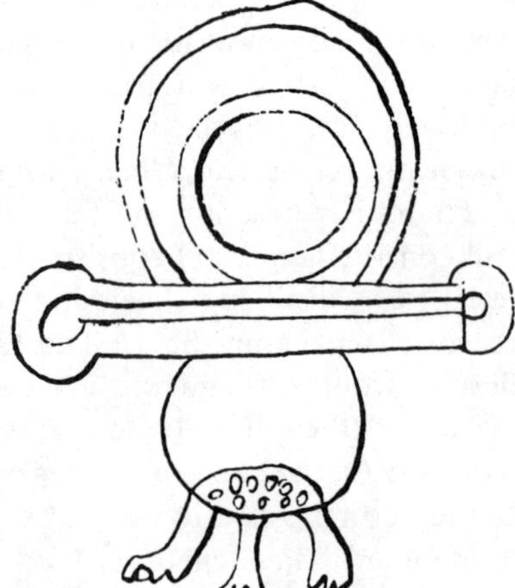

Figure 5.3. Sketch of the *bain Marie.*

about a cubit and a half. Make three such tubes, and also make a wide tube of a handbreadth width and an opening proportioned to that of the still-head. The three tubes should have their openings adapted like a nail to the neck of a light receiver so that they have the thumb-tube and the two finger-tubes joined laterally on either hand. Toward the bottom of the still-head are three holes adjusted to the tubes, and when these are fitted they are soldered in place, the one above receiving the vapor in a different fashion. Then, setting the still-head upon an earthenware pan containing the sulphur, and luting the joints with flour paste, place at the ends of the tubes glass flasks, large and strong, so that they may not break with the heat coming from the water in the middle. Here is the figure" [see Figure 5.5].[11]

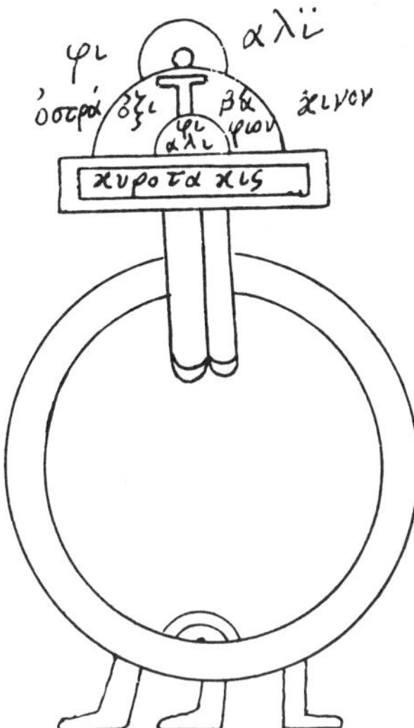

Figure 5.4. Drawing of the *kerotakis*.

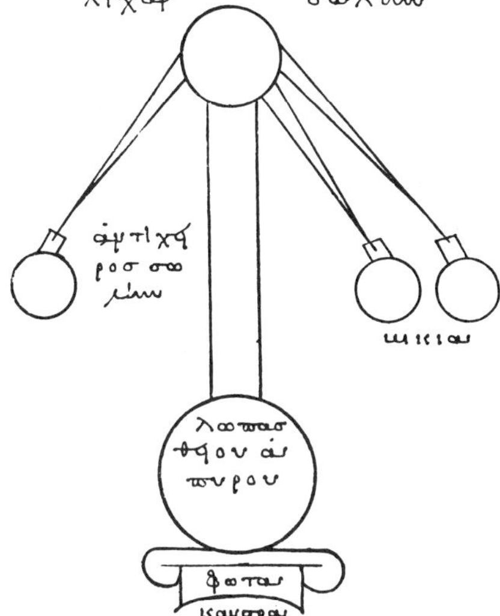

Figure 5.5. Drawing of the *tribikos*.

In his treatise *On Furnaces and Apparatuses*, from which the above quotation is taken, Zosimus apparently does little more than quote or paraphrase the text written by Maria. More on Maria's instructions will be found in the next chapter.

Maria's Procedures

We begin with Maria's prescription for the preparation of the philosophers' stone. According to the early seventh-century anonymous alchemistic author usually referred to as Christianos, she discoursed as follows:

> Invert nature and you will find that which you seek. There exist two combinations: one pertains to the action of whitening, the other to that of yellowing; one is done by trituration [reduction to powder by grinding], the other by calcination [reduction to a friable state]. One pulverizes in a saintly fashion, with simplicity, only in the holy house; there takes place the dissolution and the deposition. Combine together, says Maria, the male and the female, and you will find that which you seek. Do not be anxious to know whether the work is on fire. The two combinations have many names, such as brine water, incorruptible divine water, vinegar water, water of the acid of sea salt, of castor oil, of horse radish, and of balsam. One also calls it water of the milk of a woman who gave birth to a male child, water of the milk of a black cow, water of the urine of a young cow or of a ewe, or of a male ass, water of quicklime, of marble, of tartar, of sandarac

> [realgar, arsenic sulphide], of schistose alum, of niter, of the milk of a she-ass, of a goat, of the ashes of lime, water of ashes, of honey and oxymel [a mixture of vinegar and honey], of the flowers of the arctium, of sapphire, etc. The vessels or the instruments destined for these combinations must be made of glass. One must beware of stirring the mixture with the hands, for the mercury is deadly, just as the gold which is found there is corrupted.[12]

Although much remains unclear in this remarkable passage, Maria appears in it not only as an expert practitioner of alchemy, but also as a person of great erudition in its traditions and lore.

As for the alchemical procedures used, described, and recommended by Maria, in addition to the older methods of performing the Great Work, such as placing base metals into cow dung or horse manure or into a bath of ashes (*thermospodion*), and the like,[13] she employed various new procedures which, according to later authors, she herself had invented.

She taught that the Great Work can be performed only in one particular season, in the Egyptian month Pharmuthi (which corresponds to March-April). The materials must be wrapped tightly in linen, then subjected to salting (*taricheia*), and finally cooked in the "water of Pontus."[14] In the course of the transformation, Maria says, one-quarter, or even one-third, of the materials becomes lost, but whatever is left over can be multiplied by means of the *diplosis* (doubling) of Maria.[15] This can be carried out with mercury, and, in particular, with an alloy of four metals which she calls "our lead."[16]

These four metals—copper, iron, lead, and zinc—constitute the *tetrasomia*. They are "four in one" said Maria according to Olympiodorus, and hence are also called the "egg of the philosophers," because the egg, too, is one thing that comprises four components: the shell, the skin, the egg white, and the yolk.[17] This mixture can be prepared by means of "our lead," which term designates either "black lead" (*molybdos melas*) or antimony (*molybdos hemeteros*), whose melted state is also called "black brew" or "black juice."[18] The four metals are, according to Maria, also called "our copper," or "their copper," and it resembles in its quadruple composition the human body.[19]

In order to make gold, the tetrasomia must be heated and "burned" with certain substances: with sulphur, which becomes vaporized in heat by itself and thereby colors everything—two features it shares with "all sulphurous materials"; with mercury; with "round alum," that is, morsels of arsenious acid derived from the arsenic sulphides;[20] with the "divine water," which can always mean a solution or a molten alloy, prepared from the smoke or soot (*aithale*) of substances containing a sulphur or arsenic, with the addition of vitriol (*chalkanthos*), or two substances termed gallnut and *kiki* (the Egyptian word for the castor-oil plant). Maria's instructions relating to the "divine water" will be found in the next chapter.

But to return to the materials with which, according to Maria, "our lead" and "our copper" must be treated, they include alabaster (probably a white oxide of antimony), and sulphurlike stimmi (sulphide of antimony).[21] If the "copper" is properly nourished with solids and liquids, it undergoes four phases of color transformation: it becomes, in turn, black, white, yellow, and red. These metamorphoses must be considered the "effects of the stone," that is, of the compound powder prepared by the philosopher, which he sprinkles upon the "copper," thus effecting the transformation whose essence consists of a marriage, that is, the "union of the female and the male," for "nature charms, dominates, and conquers nature."[22] Another procedure either invented by Maria or learned by her from earlier alchemists and described in her writings used by Zosimus was the method of making precious stones shine in the dark. Berthelot assumes that this was probably done by producing a temporary phosphorescence, because Maria advises that mixtures of certain organic substances, such as the gall of fish and tortoises, the juice of jellyfish, oils of plants, resins, and so on—all of which are readily oxidized in the air—should be added in "the proper proportion" to the "tints and varnishes." Lippmann prefers to explain it as the luminosity, often very intensive, which persists, often for several hours, after certain precious stones, as well as other minerals and alloys, are exposed to high heat.[23]

Maria's Doctrines

Probably the most interesting part of Maria's teachings was her doctrine about the nature of nature, which underlies all her alchemical work, and which she herself proffered in numerous enigmatic axioms as the bases of the procedures she describes and recommends.

From what Zosimus says on the subject, one gathers that Maria held that all substances or bodies found in nature were basically one. This, of course, was the alchemical doctrine prevalent in Alexandrian circles. Maria, taking this for granted, states that "All" can be produced by means of the kerotakis.[24] As for the precise nature of All, there is considerable uncertainty in the statements listed by Zosimus. He quotes "the philosopher," that is, (Pseudo-)Democritus, as having called the body of magnesia "the All."[25] Chymes seems to have held that this All comprised all the metallic bodies; he is cited by Zosimus as "having declared with truth: One is the All, and it is through it that the All is born. One is the All, and if the All does not contain all, the All will not be born."[26]

Christianos gives this statement a more succinct form and says that Maria uttered it in an ecstatic shriek (*kraugazein*): "Therefore the Hebrew prophetess shrieked, 'One becomes two, two becomes three, and by means of the third and fourth achieves unity; thus two are but one.'"[27] Medieval alchemists continued to quote this axiom with some variations. Thus, for example, in the *Turba philosophorum*, which probably dates from the twelfth century, we read: "Out of two one must make three, out of four make one, out of two make one."[28]

C. G. Jung calls this utterance of Maria "one of the central axioms of alchemy," which, he says, "runs like a *leitmotiv* throughout almost the whole of the lifetime of alchemy, extending over more than seventeen centuries." He reads a deep psychological meaning into the transformation of one into two, and two into three, and the emergence of the one as the fourth out of the third. The even numbers, he asserts, "which signify the feminine principle, earth, the regions under the earth, and evil itself, are interpolated between the uneven numbers of the Christian dogma."[29] While this interpretation may or may not hold good for Christian alchemy, it cannot be applied to Muslim alchemical schools, which were ignorant of, or unconcerned about, Christian dogma. Nor can one assume that Maria who, as we shall see, was a devoted and fervent Jewess, had Christian doctrine in mind when coining her famous axiom. It seems much more likely that we have here an encapsulated and purposely enigmatic reference to a complex alchemical procedure, consisting of several consecutive stages which, Maria taught, must be performed in order to bring about a unity (or union) of various materials and hence a production of gold. In simplest terms, what she says is that the transmutation must be accomplished by a successive combination of three or four metallic bodies which to begin with are distinct, and then at the end of the operation become identical.[30]

In a manner reminiscent of the midrashic concept of parallelism between the composition of the material world and the human body, which concept was in her days at least a century old, Maria draws an analogy between the kind of nourishment required by man and that which must be supplied to the copper in order to transmute it into gold.[31] Elsewhere too Maria is reported to have made a statement that parallelled a midrashic (and Jewish-Hellenistic) concept: that the human body is composed of four elements. She says: "Just as man is composed of four elements, likewise is copper; and just as man results [from the association of] liquids, of solids, and of the spirit, so does copper."[32]

From the analogy between man and metals it follows that the latter, too, are of two sexes. This notion underlies the enigmatic saying of Maria, "Join the male and the female, and you will find what is sought."[33]

Another feature shared by man and metal is death. In one of her prescriptions concerning the transmutation of base metals into gold, Maria speaks of the "death" of copper and silver: "We do not want to extract their quality, for their body, by its death, becomes useless. Plants, too, are useless, for they are consumed by fire."[34] This rather enigmatic saying seems to mean that in the transmutation of copper and silver neither their quality nor their proper color is preserved; nor is their body, which becomes changed into that of another metal. As for plants, if one understands the term as referring to vegetable dyes, they are, in effect, destroyed by fire. In a figurative sense, the metallic flowers and certain corresponding colorations are likewise evaporated or destroyed by fire.[35] In any case it is clear that Maria saw in the destruction of a metal by fire the death of that metal. At the same time she held that by oxidation the alchemist could "make the nature concealed in the interior [of bodies] come to the fore," and thus, "in effect, you can transform their very nature, and you will find that which you seek [i.e., you can make gold]."[36]

The analogy between man and metal, according to Maria, goes even further. Just as man is composed of body and soul and spirit so, says she, are the metals: "The vapor [produced by volatilizing the sulphurous substances in the metals] is the spirit of the body. The soul differs from the spirit."][37]

A related doctrine is that the metallic bodies can be rendered incorporeal, and incorporeal substances can be made corporeal. Maria says: "If the bodies are not rendered incorporeal, and the incorporeal corporeal, nothing of that which one expects will take place: that is, if the fire-resistant materials are not mixed with those which evaporate in fire, one will obtain nothing of that which one expects."[38] A later, fifth-century alchemist, Olympiodorus, quotes the same passage in a somewhat expanded form: "'How is it ["our lead"] produced?' said Maria. 'If you do not render the corporeal substances incorporeal, and the incorporeal substances corporeal, and if you do not make the two bodies one, nothing of the expected will be produced.' "[39]

The crux of the procedure prescribed by Maria is the assumption that there are two categories of bodies: volatile and fixed, or incorporeal and corporeal. Metals such as copper, lead, and zinc, are corporeal and fixed. One must take away their bodies by subjecting them to sublimation, that is, by rendering them volatile and incorporeal, in the state of oxides (by the action of the air), or in the state of sulphides (by the action of sulphur or of sulphides), or in the state of chlorides (by the action of sea salt), and so on. Then one must restore or regenerate these oxides, sulphides, or chlorides to a metallic state with new properties and colors, either through their purification or through the formation of alloys.[40]

> She [Maria] said: "The philosopher (Pseudo-)Democritus said: 'Why should you take many things when nature is One?' " He said: "True, and I shall teach you that the body is one. If you treat this body until you make it become water [i.e., until it melts], then solidify it, you have achieved nothing, and you will not satisfy your soul. Do you not see how the philosopher said, 'Transform nature, and make the spirit which is hidden inside this body come out?' " She said: "And how is it transformed?" He said: "Destroy the body, and make it become water, and extract that which is in it."[41]

The Arab alchemical author al-Ḥabīb (dates unknown) says that Maria was a disciple of (Pseudo-)Democritus, and the teacher of "King Aros (Horus)."[42] Since al-Ḥabīb took almost everything he wrote from Hellenistic sources, his information about the dialogue between Maria and Aros must have come from some lost Greek manuscript. Aros, as the disciple, puts many questions to Maria which she answers in detail. Occasionally there is reference to the theoretical basis of her procedures. Thus she says on one occasion that "the precious nature [of the metal] which it contains internally" can be extracted by means of "a delicate operation."[43]

Al-Ḥabīb, probably again relying on Hellenistic sources, states that Maria opposed some views held by alchemists in general. One example is the question of the total volatility of the sulphur which, in contrast to other alchemists, Maria denied:

> I [Maria] say that it [the sulphur water] does not escape [i.e., is not volatile], but remains fixed [and] thereupon it tints. For Maria has said that wherever it penetrates it tints. And if one must admit with the philosophers [alchemists] that it does escape, I say that [the part] of it which escapes is but that [part] which is entirely on top, while the finest of its spirit, the tincture, remains with [the material] with which it is mixed, and therefore she [Maria] called it "deep heat," the finest tincture, because it remains permanently and does not escape, and she then also called it "rust."[44]

Elsewhere al-Ḥabīb quotes Maria on the souls of the metals: "In effect, as Maria reported it, the souls [of the metals] can be seen only in restoring these seasons [of summer and winter] to unity."[45]

More about Maria's alchemical doctrines is provided by the tenth-century Arab author Abū ʿAbdullah Muḥammad ibn Umail al-Tamīmī, whose treatise, *The Silvery Water and the Starry Earth*, is based on fragments in circulation since Hellenistic times:

> Mariya also said: "The 'water' which I have mentioned is an angel, and descends from the sky, and the earth accepts it on account of its [the earth's] moistness. The water of the sky is held by the water of the earth, and the water of the earth acts as its servant, and its Sand [serves] for the

> purpose of honoring it. The *kiyān* [vital principle] holds the *kiyān*, and the *kiyān* is whitened by the *kiyān*." She meant [by this] the coction of the "soul" with the "spirit" until both mix and are thoroughly cooked together and become a single thing like marble.

Maria's statement about the "angel" is explained by Ibn Umail:

> She meant by this the divine water which is the soul. She named it "angel" because it is spiritual, and because that water has risen from the earth to the sky of the *birbā* [i.e., from the bottom to the top of the alembic]. And as for her statement "[The water] descends from the sky," she meant by this the child which they say will be born for them in the air, while conception had taken place in the lower [region]; this being [through] the higher celestial strength which the water has gained by its absorption of the air. Regarding this Hurmus [Hermes] said: "The strength of the highest and the lowest will be found in it."

Furthermore, says Ibn Umail, "Mariya the Sage in several places in her books named it [this water] 'the rennet,' because it coagulates their water in their second earth, which is their second body. It is the crown of victory. . . . Consequently Mariya said, 'The water is not coagulated save by rennet, this being the ash.'" Remarkably, Ibn Umail reverses the usual chronological sequence assumed by the Hellenistic alchemists, and makes Maria not a disciple but a teacher of Ostanes: "Astanas [Ostanes] states: 'Mariya has said: The water possesses a retentive power.'"[46]

Returning to the philosophers' stone, and translating molybdochalkos by the Arabic *abār nuḥās* (lead-copper), Ibn Umail writes: "Mariya has called the honored stone *abār nuḥās*, and this is the completely perfect and super-perfect *abār nuḥās* that imparts color. Consequently it gives birth to the perfect gold, which is inferior to it, because the gold is only perfect, whereas the *abār nuḥās* is super-perfect. Surely and undoubtedly this *abār nuḥās* is [completely] perfect."[47]

Several of the concepts, doctrines, and terms (angel, *kiyān*, the expected child, the rennet, the two waters, and so on) which Ibn Umail quotes from Maria are found neither in the Greek nor in the other Arab authors who frequently and copiously quote her. This seems to indicate that Ibn Umail was in possession of "books" by Maria that were unknown to other alchemical authors.

Maria's Jewishness

The Jewishness of Maria is attested by internal evidence, in addition to the epithet "Hebraea" attached to her name. In sayings quoted in her name she spoke of the Jews as the chosen people, and held that only they, not the gentiles, should know the deepest alchemical secrets. In several Greek manuscripts she is reported to have said: "Do not touch the philosophers' stone with your hands; you are not of our race, you are not of the race of Abraham."[48] According to a later version, found in Olympiodorus's commentary on Zosimus, she said: "If you are not of our race, you cannot touch it, for the Art is special, not common."[49]

Indirectly, the Jewishness of Maria is manifested in the numerous references she makes to God. She does this occasionally in quite unexpected contexts, such as when she claims that God had instructed her in certain alchemical procedures, and revealed them to her directly. This claim is reminiscent of the utterances of the biblical Hebrew prophets, who typically opened their prophecies by stating that God addressed them and told them what to do and say.

Also, in speaking of God Maria always uses the singular form ("God"), and not the plural. Even though references to "God," or even to the "only God," occur also in the writings of other Hellenistic Greek authors,[50] still, the consistent use of the singular "God," or "the Lord," and especially in such statements as "the wisdom of the Lord hidden from the gentiles" (see below), definitely suggests Jewish religio-national pride.

Maria's claim that alchemical secrets were revealed to her by God became a part of the medieval alchemical traditions about her. One of those who refer to it is the Byzantine monk Maryanus, also known as Morienus Romanus, of whom nothing concrete is known, although alchemical tradition made him the teacher of the likewise legendary Arab alchemist Khālid ibn Yazīd, who in real life was an Omayyad prince (c. 668–704; see Chapter 9 below). One of the several alchemical treatises attributed to Maryanus is the *De compositione alchemiae*, which was translated into Latin by Robertus Castrensis. In it Maryanus writes that the philosophers (i.e., alchemists), having assembled in the presence of Maria, said to her: "Happy are you, O Maria, for the divine hidden and always splendid secret is revealed to you."[51]

The Arab alchemical author al-Ḥabīb, whom we have already encountered, reports that after Maria explained that the philosophers called a certain tincture "incombustible sulphur" because "the fire has burned it and transformed it into ashes in such a way that no humidity remained" in it, and that "that which comes out of these ashes is the power of our Work and its agents," she exclaimed, "Thanks to the will of God, Who should be glorified!"[52]

A person to whom God speaks and reveals His word and will or His secrets is, of course, a prophet. Accordingly, Maria was endowed with the title "Prophetissa" and, from the early sixteenth century at the latest, she was so styled. By that time her reputation as a true prophetess in possession of divine secrets was so well established that Bonaventure Des Périers (1500?-1546?), in his spirited satire in which he accuses the alchemists of fraud and cheating, charges that they promise the believers the secrets of King Solomon and the Prophetess Maria, but then put them off with empty talk.[53]

An important selection of Maria's teachings is contained in a small treatise entitled *Dialogue of Maria and Aros*, a Latin translation of which, possibly based on an Arabic version (which in turn may have been a translation or reworking of a Greek original), was included in the late sixteenth-century anthology *Artis auriferae quam chemiam vocant.*[54] In it the philosopher Aros, a fictitious figure, comes to Maria to learn the ultimate secrets of the Great Work. He greets her respectfully, and asks her many questions, most of which she answers willingly, often at considerable length, and always with a rich admixture of pithy statements. In the course of the conversation Maria refers several times to God, in a style and manner that can best be characterized as those of Jewish piety. The treatise, although certainly apocryphal, is of interest because it shows the extent to which Maria was considered one of the greatest authorities on matters alchemical. In the following I give my translation of the whole treatise, based on the version contained in the *Artis auriferae.* As we shall see, Maria is identified with Miriam (= Maria) the sister of Moses—just as Maria the mother of Jesus was identified in the Koran with the sister of Moses (Koran 3:35ff.). To the historically unschooled, identity of names signified identity of persons.

> Here begins the practice of Maria the Prophetess in the alchemical art. Aros the philosopher met with Maria the sister of Moses, and approaching her paid homage to her and said to her:
>
> "O Prophetess, I have heard so much of you—that you can whiten the stone in one day."
>
> And Maria said: "So it is, Aros; indeed, even in part of a day."
>
> Aros said: "O Lady, how will be that work which you claim? How shall we whiten, and then add the black?"
>
> Maria said: "O Aros, is it not that the nations are [come] from that part? Or, O Aros, do you not know what is the water or the thing which whitens the Hendrax?"
>
> Then Aros replied and said to her: "It is as you say, O Lady, [but it takes] a long time."
>
> Maria answered: "Hermes said in all his books that the philosophers whiten the stone in one hour of the day."
>
> Aros said to her: "O how excellent that is!"
>
> Maria said: "This is the most excellent thing for him who does not know."
>
> Aros said: "O Prophetess, if there are in men all the four elements which he [Hermes] said they can contain, then they should be encompassed and their fumes coagulated and retained within one day, until they become complete."

Maria said: "O Aros, by god, if your reasoning was not firm, you would not hear from me these words until the Lord filled my heart, by grace of the divine will. Nevertheless: Take alum from Spain, white gum and red gum which is the *kibric* [A. *kibrīt*, sulphur] of the philosophers, and their sun [gold], and the major tincture, and join the gum with the gum in true matrimony. Did you understand, Aros?"

"Yes, my Lady."

Maria said: "Make it like unto running water, and vitrify this water, when a day has elapsed, by means of the two *zubechs* [from A. *zībaq*, mercury] over the fixed body, and liquify it by the secret of the natures in the vessel of philosophy. Did you understand us?"

"[Yes,] O Lady."

Surely Maria said: "Preserve the fume and take care lest any of it escape. And the measure of the small fire [must be] like the measure of the heat of the sun in the month of June or July. And remain near the vessel, and pay attention to how it becomes black and red and white in less than three hours of the day. And the fume will penetrate the body, and the spirit will be condensed, and they will become like milk, wax-like, liquifying, and penetrating. And it is a secret."

Aros said: "I do not say [i.e., I do not believe] that this will always be like this."

Maria said to him: "Aros, there is a more admirable thing which did not exist among the ancients, nor did it reach them through mediation. And it is: Take the white, clear, precious herb which grows upon the small mountains, and pound it freshly as it is in its hour, and it is the body which truly does not become fugacious in fire."

And Aros said: "Is that not the Stone of Truth?"

And Maria said: "It is. Truly, however, the people do not know this regimen because of their haste."

Aros said: "And what then?"

Maria said: "Vitrify over it sulphur and *zubech* (that is, *zibeic*) [mercury], and they are the two fumes which envelop the two luminaries, and throw out over it the complement of tinctures and of the spirits and the weight [or: a pound] of truth, and grind all of it, and put in on the fire, and you will see of them marvels. The entire regimen consists of tempering the fire. O how wonderful is the way it moves from color to color in less than one hour of the day, until it reaches the point of redness and whiteness. Then extinguish the fire, and let it cool, and open it, and you will find a body, pearl-like, clear, of the color of the poppy of the woods mixed with white, and it is waxing, liquifying, and penetrating, and its golden color falls over a thousand and two hundred. It is a hidden secret."

Then Aros fell on his face. But Maria said to him: "Lift up your head, Aros, for I shall tell you the matter briefly. Take that clear body which grows on the small mountains, which is not subject to either putrefaction or movement, and pound it with the gum elsaron and with the two fumes, for the gum elsaron is a seizing body, and grind it all. Approach it, therefore, since it becomes totally liquified. If you project it upon its wife, it will become like distilled water, and when the air penetrates it, it will become congealed and become one body. And project it [upon base metals] and you will see wonders. O Aros, this is the hidden secret of the *scholia* [science]. And know that the two aforementioned fumes are the roots of this art, and they are the white sulphur and the humid lime. But the fixed body is the heart of Saturn which comprises the tincture and the fields of wisdom or of the science. And the philosophers called it by many and all names. And the clear and white body is taken from the small mountains. And those are the medicines of this art, some [of which] are prepared, and some found on the small mountains. And know Aros, that . . . in these sciences there is nothing except wonderful things. For into it enter even those four stones. And its regimen is true, as I have said. And it is this: at first "scoyare Ade & Zethet"[55] and about it Hermes spoke allegorically in his study books. And the philosophers have always made its regimen long, and pretended that the work consisted of various things which [in fact] it was not at all necessary to perform for that Work, and spent a whole year in performing the magisterium. But they did this only in order to hide it from the ignorant folk, until it became established in people's hearts and their senses that the Art could not be accomplished except with gold, because it is a great secret of God. And those who hear of our secrets do not test its truth because of their ignorance. Did you understand, Aros?"

Aros said: "I did. But tell me of that vessel without which the Work cannot be accomplished."

Maria said: "It is the vessel of Hermes which the Stoics have hidden, and it is not the vessel of the necromancers, but it is the measure of your fire."

Aros said to her: "O Lady, did you listen to the students' society [*scoyari*]? O Prophetess, did you find the secrets of the philosophers who in their books set it down that one can perform the Art by means of one body?"

And Maria said: "Yes. Hermes did not teach that because the root of the *scholia* is the unbreakable, irretrievable body, and it is a poison which kills all bodies and pulverizes them, and it congeals the mercury with its odor."

And she said: "I swear to you by the Eternal God that when that poison is dissolved until it becomes subtle water—and I do not care what the solution is—it congeals the mercury into *luna* [silver] with the power of truth, and it occurs in the dominion of Jupiter, and it transmutes them into *luna*. And there is a science of all bodies, but the Stoics have hidden it because of the shortness of their lives and the length of the Work. And they found these coloring elements, and they themselves increased them, and all the philosophers teach those things rather than the vessel of Hermes, because the latter is divine, and, by the wisdom of the Lord, hidden from the gentiles. And those who do not know it are ignorant of the regimen of truth because of their ignorance of the vessel of Hermes."

On "the white herb on the mountain," which figures prominantly in this treatise, we shall have more to say below. The "vessel of Hermes" referred to in Maria's peroration seems to be more than a simple alchemical apparatus. It seems to serve as a symbol of the secrets of alchemy in general. As for "the wisdom of the Lord hidden from the gentiles," these words could have been said only by a Jew, and their attribution to Maria, added to her admonition to gentiles not to touch the philosophers' stone, proves that in medieval alchemical tradition she was believed to have been a Jewish woman.

Maria's Legend

It has still not been established precisely when the identification of the Alexandrian Jewish alchemist Maria with Miriam the sister of Moses took place. Lippmann says that this was done by Zosimus himself, but gives no sources for this assertion, nor do there appear to be any in Zosimus's treatises as published by Berthelot.[56]

Within a few decades after Zosimus, however, Maria had become a sufficiently famous figure for at least one church father to claim that she had a vision of Christ. This was done by Epiphanius (c. 315–402), who was born in Palestine, studied in Egypt, and became the bishop of Salamis. In his *Against Eighty Heresies*[57] Epiphanius refers to two works of Maria (whom he does not further identify), entitled *Great Questions* and *Small Questions*, in which, he reports with indignation, Maria describes a vision she had:

> In the *Questions* of Maria which are called "Great" (for there are also others which have been fabricated [called] "Small"), they suppose that he [Jesus Christ] revealed himself to her—after he had taken her to a mountain, and after he had prayed, and after he had produced a woman from his side, and after he began to have intercourse with her, and after he had thus transferred his flow [of semen]—that he showed that it was necessary to do thus in order that we may live. And they say that Maria was perturbed and fell to the ground, and that he, raising her again, said to her: "Why have you doubted, O one of little faith?" And they say that this is the very thing which has been said in the Gospel, that "If I have told you earthly things and you did not trust me, how will you believe the heavenly things?" and "When you see the son of man going up where he was formerly," that is, the flow [of semen] being taken back whence it had gone out.[58]

If this Maria is identical with Maria the Jewess (as Jung unquestioningly assumes),[59] and if the two books of *Questions* (otherwise unknown) were written by the alchemist Maria, and if the passage quoted was actually contained in one of them, then we have here perhaps the first historic reference to a Jew or Jewess believing in Jesus—the dream-vision described must be based on a familiarity with the Christian belief in Jesus, and probably on a (subconscious?) sharing of that belief. However, it is more likely that the entire scene as described by Epiphanius belongs to the realm of early Christian legend, from which we can only learn what beliefs had developed about Maria within a century or so after her lifetime. For fifteen centuries after Epiphanius, during which Maria figured prominently in alchemical literature, no student of alchemy read any Christological meaning into her traditionally transmitted words. The only one who has finally followed in the footsteps of the bishop of Salamis was Jung, who gives a Christological interpretation to Maria's most famous axiom, as quoted above.

The legendary transformations of Maria pushed her lifetime further and further back into antiquity. In an Arabic manuscript of unknown origin in the Leyden library she is styled "the matron Maria Sicula."[60] In the *Kitāb al-Fihrist* (c. 987) and in other Arabic sources she is called "Mariya al-Qibtiyya" (Maria the Copt), and is described as having carried the infant Jesus on her shoulder, and holding a spindle in her hand. But she is also supposed to have been a student or fellow instructor in alchemy of Ostanes, to whom she was supposed to have said, "The Work is derived from me and from you," alluding thereby to its accomplishment through the female and the male substances.[61] The authors who make her the contemporary of both Jesus and Ostanes are blissfully unaware of the double anachronism they are committing. Ostanes, who gained the reputation of having been the greatest Persian magus, was a historical figure, a Persian satrap and brother-in-law of Xerxes (519?–465 B.C.E.), who participated in the latter's Greek campaign. Later he was considered one of the fathers of alchemy, medicine, mineralogy, and botany, the *magorum omnium magister* (the master of all magi),[62] and to have taught at Memphis in Egypt, where Maria was his disciple or fellow instructor.[63]

Georgius Syncellus (ninth century C.E.) mentions in his *Chronographia* that Ostanes the Mede was sent by the Persian kings to Egypt, and there he instructed the priests and the philosophers, among them Maria Hebraea, in all the disciplines of an occult nature. He wrote about gold, silver, and precious stones, but did it all by careful circumlocution. Maria and Democritus, who used the same methods of presentation and spoke about the Art enigmatically, were praised for their restraint; Pammenes, who wrote amply and openly about it, was condemned.[64]

In a medieval Arabic manuscript, Maria is called "Mariya the Sage, daughter of the king of Saba," and is quoted as having said, "This [the philosophers' stone] is a great mystery. It is scorned, and trodden underfoot. But this scorn is a grace from Allah, may He be exalted, so that the fools should not know it, and it be forgotten."[65] Arnaldus de Villanova (1235–1315) calls Maria "the daughter of Pluto."[66] In medieval and later Latin writings, finally, she is referred to as the sister of Moses, or the sister of Aaron, or, to make the identification crystal clear, "Maria Prophetissa soror Moysis et Aaronis."[67] Therewith the lifetime of Maria was pushed back a full sixteen centuries.

The White Herb on the Mountain

The mountain which, according to Epiphanius, figured in Maria's vision of Jesus, reappears in her description of the procedure of making gold. The recipe is, perhaps, the best known and most frequently referred to of all her teachings and prescriptions. In the dialogue between Maria and Aros, as we saw, Maria refers repeatedly to the "white, clear, precious herb which grows on the small mountains," and when she mentions it a third time she explains that "the two fumes are the roots of this Art" and that "the clear and white body is taken from small mountains."

The enumeration of these basic ingredients of the Great Art—the two fumes and the clear, white, precious herb growing on the small mountains—recurs again and again in alchemical literature. Michael Maier, a leading figure in early seventeenth-century alchemy, has in his *Symbola aureae mensae duodecim nationum* a section entitled *Mariae Hebraeae symbolum*, in whose introductory remarks he characterizes Maria as having been the nearest to Hermes. These remarks, which are interesting because they show the importance Maria had for post-medieval alchemy, are given here in a literal translation with all the convolutions of Maier's style:

> When Hermes the Egyptian had imposed a limit upon his deliberations, as was the law, Pyrgopolynices, now unmindful of his own more gigantic virtue, which had so often been displayed, stood, as if suffused with blushing, bringing an offering to Harpocrates, since he had nothing to present. And so the succession passed to Maria the Hebrew, who was closest to Hermes, and who, being a maiden, was of the weaker sex and seemed unfit for fighting with a very keen enemy, so that consequently she would have been able to enjoy, not undeservedly, the privilege of frailty and bashfulness. Yet, since she had to contend on behalf of Maiden Chemistry, she herself, endowed with a clearly virile spirit and with that of an Amazon, as it were, declared that she by no means dreaded her adversary who, in order to re-

> gain his strength, earnestly meditating, ceased from the fight. Meanwhile we shall survey the life and writings of this courageous female warrior, as well as other things that pertain to her race and to those connected with her.[68]

Following this introduction Maier explains that there is a great controversy about whether Maria was a fictitious person, or the sister of Moses, or another woman of the Jewish race. Basing himself on the consensus of the chemists of all ages and of other most learned men, he excludes the first possibility. Discussing the remaining two, he says that it would appear that the book attributed to Maria, that is, the *Dialogue of Maria and Aros*, although extant only in a Latin translation, was originally written in Hebrew. No copies of the Hebrew original have survived, because the knowledge of Hebrew among gentiles is very rare, found only among theologians who deal with theological matters to the total neglect of profane literature. As for the Jews, their low status and the perpetual servitude to which they are condemned make them unfit for such studies.

Maier found it difficult to make up his mind as to whether Maria was identical with the sister of Moses. It is quite possible, he says, that the sister of Moses had prophetic powers, but there is no evidence to show that she was an expert in chemistry. On the other hand, it is entirely possible that she learned the Art from her brother Moses, who was a most skillful chemist—such was the generally held view among alchemists in all ages. At the end Maier inclines to the conclusion that Maria the alchemist was not the sister of Moses but another Jewish woman who had perfect knowledge of chemistry. He approves Maria's method of presenting chemical teachings. Maria, he says, did not clothe her teachings in a garb of allegories, fables, and poetic figments, but presented them in a veiled language, enigmatically. She

> speaks of two gums, white and red, and of their matrimony; also of two fumes, of the white and clear herb which grows on the small mountains. But the whole secret, she says, is in the knowledge of the Vessel of Hermes, because it is divine, and is, by the wisdom of the Lord, hidden from the *gentes* [gentiles]. Those who do not know it are ignorant of the regimen of truth, because of their ignorance of the Vessel of Hermes. These words of hers, even if they are very obscure for the ignorant, still appear clearer to those educated by long experience, and to those who are well versed in the seven mountains of the world, day and night. That vessel is that of the Brahman philosophers of India who use it in order to moderate the dryness of the summer, or is not unlike it, and was received by Hermes for the first time. But that vessel, says Maria, which the Stoics have hidden, is not the vessel of the necromancers, but is the measure of your fire. Therefore, in

> the bowl of fire, whose flame is of the color of lead, it was moderated by an element contrary to itself, nor did it ever exceed the rim of the bowl. He who understands this properly grasps the truest mind of Maria, and she will open up to him those secrets of chemistry which, as a rule, all have wrapped in dark silence.

In the sequel Maier says that Maria was one of four women who knew how to produce the philosophers' stone—the other three having been Cleopatra, Taphnutia, and Medera—and that her book is circulated everywhere.[69]

On the page following Maier's introductory remarks there is an engraving showing Maria the Jewess, superscribed as follows: "Fume is completed by fume, and the white herb growing upon the small mountains captures both." The engraving itself shows Maria as a stately woman dressed in an ample robe with a hoodlike cap over her head, pointing with her left hand to a small mountain on which grows a white herb, exhibiting five branches, each topped with a flower. At the foot of the mountain stands an urn from which rise two columns of smoke, which separate so as to circle the white herb like a wreath, and unite with two other fumes that descend from an inverted urn which is the mirror image of the one below, and which seems to be suspended from heaven (see Figure 5.6). This picture was reprinted many times through the ages, from the *Viridarium chymicum* by Daniel Stolcius (Frankfurt-am-Main, 1624), to C. G. Jung's *Psychology and Alchemy* (Zurich, 1944), and John Read's *Prelude to Chemistry* (New York, 1937). Stolcius (or Stolcz) was a disciple of Michael Maier, and his *Viridarium* consists of 107 copper engravings, each with a Latin epigram. Among them are reproductions of the "Twelve Chosen Heroes" (from Michael Maier's *Symbola*). The only woman among the twelve is Maria Hebraea (fig. xvii, the figure reproduced here), and the accompanying epigram reads:

MARIA HEBRAEA

Gente Palaestina Moysis soror, ecce Maria
  In Chymico pariter gaudet ovatq; choro.
Abdita cognovit lapidis mysteria magni
  Erudijt dictis nos quoque docta suis.
Fumus amat fumum, rursusqu; adamatur ab illo:
  Alba sed herba alti montis utrumque capit.

[Of Palestinian race, Moses' sister, behold Maria,
  Equally rejoices and triumphs in the Chymic choir.
She knew the hidden mysteries of the great stone.
  Sage that she is she taught us with her words,
Smoke loves smoke, and is loved by it in return:
  But the white herb of the high mountain captures both.]

Figure 5.6. Maria the Jewess.

The "white herb" may be the lunary (*Botrychium lunaria*), which possesses a peculiar significance in alchemy because of its imagined "impregnation with a celestial vitality," and which was believed to be derived from the moon, whence its name, moonwort. All kinds of healing and magical qualities were attributed to it, and it represented the white stage in the Great Work, that is, the first color transformation from the basic black, followed by yellow and red. The white and red fumes (or smokes) signified the mercury and sulphur of the philosophers.[70]

THE quintessence of Maria's alchemical works and teachings was aptly summed up by Arnaldus de Villanova (1245–1313), the learned friend of Pope Clemens V, in these lines:

Maria mira sonat breviter, quod talia tonat
Gummis cum binis fugitivum figit in imis
Horis in crinis tria vinceat fortia finis
Maria lux roris ligam ligat in tribus horis
Filia Plutonis consortia iungit amoris
Gaudet in assata sata per tria sociata.[71]

[Maria utters wonders briefly, for she thunders such things
She fixes the fugacious matter with the double gum in the last hour
She binds three powerful substances into the ends of the tubes
Maria, the light of the dew, binds a band in three hours.
Daughter of Pluto, she unites love's affinities
Delights in things roasted, sown, assembled in threes.]

Practically each phrase in this poem requires elucidation.

Line 1. "Maria utters wonders briefly" refers to her preference for expressing her teachings in brief, enigmatic sayings. "She thunders" refers to the tradition that she, on one occasion at least, "shrieked" enthusiastically when expressing the essence of her insight into a fundamental alchemical procedure.

Line 2. "She fixes the fugacious matter with the double gum" refers to the volatile material which, Maria taught, must be fixed, and which she did fix with the use of the white gum and the red gum.

Line 3. The "tubes" into which Maria ties "three powerful substances" are the three tubes of the tribikos invented or described by her.

Line 4. "Binds a band in three hours" refers to the alchemical tradition according to which Maria performed the Great Work in three hours, binding together, or uniting, various substances.

Line 5. "Daughter of Pluto" is an allusion to Maria's ability to make gold, thereby becoming, as it were, the daughter of Pluto (Hades), to whom Greek myth attributes fabulous riches. "Unites love's affinities" refers to Maria's teaching according to which the transmutation consists of a marriage, or union, of male and female substances.

Line 6. "Delights in things roasted" refers to the burning of the tetrasomia, the copper, or the sulphur prescribed and described by Maria. Things "sown" refers to the mysterious white herb on the mountains. "Assembled in threes" may refer to the tribikos, or to the three kinds of "divine water" (the whitened, yellowed, and blackened), or to Maria's doctrine according to which two must become three.

Chapter Six

ZOSIMUS ON MARIA THE JEWESS

ZOSIMUS refers frequently and in detail to Maria the Jewess, and his references to her are of such importance due to their unique authenticity that it seems appropriate to present here the remaining material about her that has not already been quoted.[1] Zosimus's treatise entitled *On the Sacred and Divine Art of the Fabrication of Gold and Silver* begins:

> Taking the soul of copper which is under the water of mercury, make a volatile body; for the soul of copper retained in the material in fusion rises up; the liquid part remains below in the apparatus of the kerotakis,[2] and must be fixed by means of the gum:[3] this is the flower of gold, the liquor of gold, etc. Others mean by it the coloring, the cooking, the work of the mystical doctrine. In the beginning, the projected copper, after treatment in the apparatus of [its] fabrication, charms the eyes. When it loses its glitter, one combines it with the gilded gum, the liquor of gold, etc. [Behold this is what] he [Zosimus] has written on the subject of the manufacture of gold, of which also the fixation is proclaimed.
>
> Maria says: "Take the water of sulphur[4] and a little gum, put it in the bath of ashes; they say that it is in this fashion that the water is fixed." Maria also says: "For the preparation of the flower of gold, place the water of sulphur and a little gum in foil of the kerotakis, so that it becomes fixed. Make it digest in the heat of manure for some time." After the words "for some time" Maria [added]: "Take a part of our copper, a part of gold; soften the foil formed by these two metals united by fusion, put [it] on the sulphur, and leave [all of it] for three times twenty-four hours, until this product becomes cooked" (3:148).

In his treatise entitled *On the Substances Which Serve to Support and On the Four Metallic Bodies According to Democritus*, Zosimus writes:

> The four [metallic] bodies serve as the support [of tincture], and none of them volatilizes. . . . Maria says: "Remove the sulphurous [nature] from the lead; wherever the sulphur enters, it will tint." She wanted to show by this that we have no reason to burn the sulphur. She used strange names for the Arts in the description of their operations. It is not thus that those who operate act when they speak of our copper or any other metallic body (3:150–51).

In the section of this treatise dealing with "The Weights of the Raw and the Cooked [Substances]," Zosimus returns to quote Maria.

> According to what the writings say in this regard, assuredly the sulphur must be expelled by insufflation. This is what Maria wanted to make us understand when she said: "You will find five parts less the fourth, that is to say less the sulphur driven away by the insufflation. Likewise at the end of her statement she says that the copper, when it is refined by melting, diminishes by one-third of its weight. She says that the changes are also accomplished when one whitens and when one makes yellow; for these sulphurous [substances] tint but volatilize themselves. We get rid of the sulphurous substances by volatilization. It is the same with the plants when they are totally dissolved; thus it happens when one cooks them with the water of sulphur, rejecting the ligneous part (3:151–52).

In discussing "the vapor which is the spirit, the spirit which penetrates the bodies," Zosimus states that "in no passage of the [alchemical] writings is there mention of any other support [for the tincture] except copper alone. Thus Maria says that copper is treated and later burnt. It is in this sense that it plays the role of support. This is [the role of] copper or of silver, in our operation."[5]

> Agathodemon says: "The magnesia, the antimony, and the litharge become volatilized, after having lost their purity."[6] Maria [said]: "Blow away the vapors until the sulphurous products become volatilized with the shadow (which obscures the metal), and until the copper gains all its glitter." Thus our copper receives from them the sublimated vapor. Now the vapor is the spirit of the body. The soul differs from the spirit (3:153).

In his treatise discussing the importance of timing, Zosimus again quotes Maria:

> Maria occupied herself with it in describing the treatment of the small object: "The divine water will be lost for those who don't understand what has been written, to know that the [useful] product is sent upward by the long-necked vessel and the tube. But it is customary to designate by this water the vapor of the sulphur and of the sulphurated arsenics. Because of this you have jeered at me, because in one and the same discourse I have revealed to you such a great mystery.
>
> This divine water, whitened by the whitening materials, whitens. If it is yellowed by the yellowing materials, it makes yellow. If it is blackened by means of vitriol and gallnut, it blackens, and carries out the blackening of silver and that of our molybdochalkon.[7] I have spoken to you previously of this molybdochalkon, [when talking] of our traditional silver. Thus the water blackens, attaching itself to our molybdochalkon, and gives it a permanent black tint; and even though this tincture is nothing, all the initiates desire very much to know it. Now the water capable of taking on such a color produces a fixed tincture, the oil and the honey having been eliminated (3:157).

Somewhat later in the same treatise Zosimus again quotes Maria's instructions on the proper method of applying fire for the purpose of absorbing the water of sulphur, and he does this in a manner which clearly shows that he lifted out the essential phrases from her more detailed discourse on the subject. "Maria said: 'the flames progressively'; and then, 'the fire gradually'; in order to make it understood that it has to be operated according to a suitable progression, beginning with the [instant of the] flame" (3:158).

The extent to which Zosimus is dependent on the instructions of Maria is well illustrated in his treatise entitled *On the Detailed Account of the Work: A Discourse to Philaretes.* This treatise, as indicated in its first sentence, contains what (Pseudo-)Democritus was supposed to have written to Philaretes. Nevertheless Zosimus attributes to (Pseudo-) Democritus a reference to Maria, disregarding the fact, or perhaps unaware, that she lived some hundred years after (Pseudo-)Democritus. He writes:

> Let us speak of the four bodies[8] which resist fire, the [bodies] which serve as support [to the tincture], that is to say, to the ultimate composition. After having composed it, we take a part of it, and adding the divine water[9] until the color is produced and the tone of the corresponding body [the gold or the silver], according to Maria. When one has obtained the ultimate composition, one not only projects on the four bodies which serve as support the composition of the ferment of gold, but also the composition of the water of sulphur (3:160).

Another Zosimean treatise is a one-page discussion entitled *On That Which the Art has Said about All the Bodies in Treating a Unique Tincture.* It reads as follows:

> 1. According to the catalogue one knows that Hermes and Democritus have spoken summarily of a unique tincture, and others have alluded to it. This is also what Africanus says: "That which one uses for tincture are the metals, the liquids, the earths, and the plants." Chymes has said about it truthfully: "One is the All, and it is through it that the All becomes born. One is the All, and if the All did not contain everything, the All would not have become born.[10] Hence it is necessary that you project the All in order to produce the All." Plebichius: "By means of the four bodies." Maria: "By means of the foil of the kerotakis." Agathodaimon: "After the refining of the copper, [its] attenuation, and [its] blackening, and thereafter its whitening, there will take place a solid yellowing." All the other [materials] are explained similarly by them.
>
> 2. When Maria speaks of this question, she says: "There exists a great number of metallic bodies, from lead to copper." When she speaks of diplosis, she says: "There are, in effect, two kinds of materials employed,

whether for alloying copper and silver, or alloying gold and silver; molybdochalkon and all the others are comprised in it." As for the purification of silver, or its blackening, I have spoken of it previously. How one single tincture is applied to all [the materials] is stated by Maria alone and proclaimed in these terms: "When I speak of copper, or of lead, or of iron, I mean by it [their] *ios* (3:168–69)."[11]

Zosimus's short treatise entitled *The Four Bodies Are the Aliment of the Tinctures* is in its entirety a summary of Maria's teachings. It reads as follows:

1. Here is how: Maria says that the copper is tinted at first, and that then it tints. Their copper: that is the four bodies. Behold the tinctures: [they comprise] the solid and liquid species of the catalogue, and also the plants . . .

2. Thus, just as we [humans] are nourished by means of solid and liquid materials, and as we are colored only by their proper quality, so copper behaves in the same way; and just as we are not nourished by means of solids or liquids alone, in the same way neither is copper. In fact, if we receive [as food] only solid material, we become inflamed, burnt, poisoned; the same is the case with their copper. Contrarywise, if we take nothing but liquids, we become inebriated, we have a heavy head, we have cheeks of high color, and we vomit; [the same] is the case with copper. When it has taken the color of gold by the action of the divine water, it becomes heavy and rejects, and immediately thereafter [its color] becomes fugacious. But if we have taken good nourishment in the right proportion composed of the two orders of material, solid and liquid, we are reasonably nourished; our cheeks are colored reasonably, and the nutritive faculty distributes the nourishment in the stomach, by reason of its ability to retain it. Likewise copper, receiving the solids on the one hand by virtue of nourishment, on the other hand nourishes itself by the divine water united with the gum by virtue of the wine; it becomes colored by reason of the faculty to retain that which resides in it. It is thus that she said in the [aforementioned] work: "The sulphurous [things] are dominated and retained by the sulphurous." Hence this truth: "Nature charms, conquers, and dominates nature."

3. "The same way," she says, "as man is composed of four elements, so also is copper. And just as man results from [the association of] liquids, solids, and the spirit, so does copper. Now Apollo, in his oracles, says that the vapor is the spirit: "And a spirit more black, humid, pure."

4. Maria has spoken appropriately of the vapor, [saying]: "Copper does not tint, but is tinted; and when it has been tinted, then it tints; when it has been nourished, it nourishes; when it has been completed, it completes." Good health!

In his treatise entitled *Round Alum Must be Employed*, which deals with the whitening of metals by mercury, the preparation of mercury, and the use of arsenical sulphur (which is meant by "round alum")[13] for tinting copper and the alloys derived from it, Zosimus again quotes Maria, this time together with Chymes:

> All the writings, and [notably] Chymes and Maria, speak of a lead mortar and of a lead pestle [for pounding the cinnabar[14] and reducing the mercury]. One dissolves the lime and the cinnabar with vinegar, in the sun, until mercury develops. One produces the same effect with tin. The heated, or calcinated, or fixed, or tinted [species] are susceptible to furnishing mercury, if the operation is performed according to the precepts of the Art. Whichever material one works with, if it is potentially cinnabar, it furnishes vapor and this escapes, the mixture being delayed with all kinds of bodies. . . .
>
> According to a certain author one must use round alum instead of the vapor [of mercury].[15] Maria expresses herself in conformity with this opinion when she says: "The infusion of the tinctures takes place in green flasks, submitted to a gradually growing fire. The furnace in the shape of a kiln has nipples at its upper part. If you don't succeed, use the double of the round alum, of the color of cinnabar;[16] that is worth more for achieving the same result. One can succeed also with other pastes. In effect the sublimated vapor fixes itself only on the four bodies. Some say that it is absorbed by the other bodies, together with the chrysocolla. I on my part know well that chrysocolla alone does not retain it; [but] all the dead and diluted metallic bodies conserve the vapor." . . . These things have been reported by me, who wanted to show that round alum acts similarly, as was stated above all by the divine Maria (3:170–73).

In his treatise *On the Sulphurs*, entitled in one manuscript *On the Divine Waters*, Zosimus says:

> Some, and Maria [among others], have mentioned the figure below. "It is thus that they have prepared mercury," says she, "as well as sulphur and *ios*, by diluting the ensemble in the sun until everything becomes *ios*. They say that [prepared this way] it is more active. Some have accomplished this iosis[17] in the sun alone, without adding anything, and they assert that they have obtained the object of their search. Others have diluted with divine water, asserting that it is their sulphur—it is also their mercury. I admit the opinion of these, more than that of the others. Others have projected the mercury, sometimes raw, sometimes in the state of yellow coagulation. Some, after the operation of the *iosis*, have effected nothing beyond it" (3:174–75).

In his treatise *On the Measure of Yellowing*, Zosimus quotes not only Maria but also Moses:

> Maria [places] in first line molybdochalkon and the [processes of] fabrication. The operation of burning [is] that which all the ancients recommended. Maria, the first, says: "Copper burnt with sulphur, treated with the oil of natron,[18] and recovered after having undergone the same treatment several times, becomes excellent gold, and without shadow. Behold, this is what God says: 'Know all, that according to experience, by burning the copper [first], the sulphur produces no effect. But if you burn [first] the sulphur, then it not only renders the copper without blemish, but also makes it approximate gold.' " In the description situated under the figure, Maria speaks a second time and says: "This was graciously revealed to me by God, to know that the copper is first burnt with the sulphur, then with the body of magnesia; and one blows it until the sulphurous parts escape with the shadow: [then] the copper becomes without shadow."
>
> This is how everything burns. This is how in the *maza* [chemistry][19] of Moses one burns with sulphur, with salt, with alum, and with sulphur (I mean white sulphur). This is how also Chymes burns in many places, above all when he operates with celandine. Thus in Plebichius the operation of burning in laurel wood[20] is expressed enigmatically by paraphrase; the leaves of laurel signify white sulphur. This is the explanation concerning the measures.
>
> Behold, this is what Maria has said, here and there, in a thousand places: "Burn our copper with sulphur and after having recovered it will be without shadow." Not only does she know the burning with white sulphur, but also the whitening and the rendering shadowless. It is also with [sulphur] that Democritus burns, whitens, and renders shadowless. And again, "not only do they burn yellow sulphur, but they render the metal shadowless and make it yellow." Behold what Democritus says: "Saffron has the same action as the vapor; the same as cassia with respect to canella." In the *Chemistry of Moses*, toward the end, there is this text: "Sprinkle with water of the native sulphur, it will become yellow and without shadow." That is evidently to say burnt (3:180–81).

In speaking On the Preparation of Ocher[21] Zosimus says: "What rank has to be assigned [to ocher] outside the coloring materials is explained at this point in all the writings. If, consequently, you want to assign it a rank, it is there that you will find the result sought; above all if you follow Maria and the philosopher [Democritus]" (3:184).

In his treatise *On the Body of the Magnesia and on Its Treatment*, Zosimus again quotes Maria at length and repeatedly:

> Behold, this is what Maria explains liberally and clearly about the subject that she calls the breads of magnesia. The first stage in the truth of the mystery finds its explanation in these [passages]. Thus, therefore, Maria wants the body of the magnesia to be there: she proclaims this not only in this passage, but in many others. In another place she says: "Without the

concourse of black lead one cannot produce the body of the magnesia, concerning which we have specified and accomplished the preparation. These are," she says, "the doctrines." And without growing tired, teaching [them] for the second and third time, she calls the body of magnesia the black lead and the molybdochalkon. On this subject she speaks of cinnabar, or lead, and of etesian stone. It is this body which produces potentially the simultaneous fusion of all the materials cooked and gilded. It cooks the raw materials, and it brings about their diplosis. It produces, says she, potentially all the materials gilded by cooking; for this no longer exists in actuality. On this [point] I shall write another discourse, but for the moment let us occupy ourselves with our subject.

It was therefore explained by Maria that the body of magnesia is black molybdochalkon; for it was no longer tinted. "It is molybdochalkon which you must tint, by projecting on it the *motaria* of yellow sandarac,[22] so that the cooked gold should no longer exist [only] potentially, but actually." This is how Maria [expresses herself] after having named the body the breads of the magnesia.

We must, above all, show that the philosopher [Democritus] is of the same sentiment in that which [concerns] the body of the magnesia, which they call THE ALL. This molybdochalkon was black lead. When they said that mercury is fixed with the body of magnesia, they wanted to say by the complete body, that which has been explained in my first memoir, and that which Maria said above about the body of magnesia. She [also] says: "You will find the black lead: use it after having mixed it with mercury" (3:188–89).

. . . This is why Maria says: "The body of magnesia is the secret thing which comes from lead, from etesian stone, and from copper" (3:190). Maria on the subject of chrysocolla: "After having weighed [it, operate] with molybdochalkon, for one day" . . . Or again: "Taking chrysocolla and cinnabar, dilute them with white litharge and make [the nature of the metal] disappear. If copper is modified and brought to the state of a [metallic] body, project on it the color of gold, and you will have gold." Thus chrysocolla receives this qualification of the body when it has been well mixed, and although it is fugacious by itself, because you make it into a body by transmutation (3:191). In the chapter of the sulphurous it is discussed which [substance] acts without the help of fire. Maria [calls it] the [substitute for] igneous preparation. She also says that if the bodies are not rendered incorporeal, and the incorporeals corporeal, nothing of that which one expects will take place: that is to say, if the materials resistant to fire are not mixed with those which evaporate in the fire, one does not obtain anything of what one expects.

Which, then, are the bodies and the incorporeals in our Art? The incorporeals are pyrites[23] and its likes, magnesia and its likes, mercury and its likes, chrysocolla and its likes, all incorporeal [materials]. The bodies are copper, iron, tin, and lead: these [materials] do not evaporate in the fire; these are the bodies. When some [of these materials] are mixed with others, the bodies become incorporeal, and the incorporeals become bodies. Mix in this manner mercury, the one which is designated in the classes, and you will produce that which is expected, about which Maria has said: "If two do not become one"; that is to say if the volatile [materials] do not combine themselves with the fixed materials, nothing will take place of that which is expected. If one does not whiten it, and if two do not become three,[24] with the white sulphur which whitens [nothing will take place of that which is expected]. But when one renders yellow, three become four; because one renders yellow with the yellow sulphur. Finally, when one performs *iosis* [tints violet], all the [materials together] attain unity (3:192).

Zosimus's notes called *On the Philosophers' Stone*, a title given them in the Middle Ages, open with quotations from Maria:

Maria says: "If our lead is black, that is what it has become; for common lead is black from the outset. Now, how is it formed? If you do not deprive the metallic bodies of their state, and if you do not bring back the bodies deprived of their state to the state of [metallic] bodies; if you do not make of two things one single one, nothing of that which one expects will take place. If the All is not attenuated in the fire, if the sublimated vapor reduced to spirit does not rise, nothing will be brought to a conclusion." And again: "I am not speaking of ordinary lead, but of our black lead. Behold, how one prepares black lead: it is by cooking that one reaches [the reproduction of] common lead. For common lead is black from the outset, while our lead becomes black, not having been black to begin with" (3:194).

Further on, Maria is quoted several more times:

Maria says: "If all the metallic bodies are not attenuated by the action of fire, and if the sublimated vapor reduced to spirit does not rise up, nothing will be brought to conclusion." Molybdochalkon is the etesian stone. In the whole operation the preparation is black from the beginning. When you see that all turns into ashes, understand that you have operated well. Pulverize this *scoria*, drain it of its soluble part, and wash it six or seven times in sweetened water after each melting. One operates by fusion and according to the richness of the minerals. In effect, following this course and the washing, says Maria, "the composition is sweetened and provided with its elements." After the end of the *iosis*, a projection having taken place, the stable yellowing of the liquids is produced. In doing this, you induce nature which is hidden in the interior to come out. In effect, "transform," said she, "their very nature, and you will find that which you seek."

Maria says: "Join the male and the female, and you will find that which is sought." And elsewhere Maria says: "Don't come to touch it with your hands, for this is an igneous preparation" (3:196).

The Zosimean corpus contains two treatises called *The True Book of Sophé the Egyptian and of the Divine Lord of the Hebrews [and] of the Powers of Sabaoth.* The first one consists almost entirely of a quote from Maria. This is its complete text:

1. Behold the measure of the mercury.

Agathodaimon says: "Cook it, extract the gold." One projects the copper. One obtains the foil of Maria, formed of two metals; one cooks it on fire, in view of the tincture by means of the oil and of the honey, and one recaptures through the mercury: this is the [regular] work, so that the copper, brought anew to the state of *ios*, should dissolve with the gold, according to the measure of the mercury.

Maria says: "When the composition is formed by itself, or else by means of vinegary brine,[25] and when one has cooked it, dilute it with sulphur, that is to say with sublimated sulphur, be it in a flagon, [or] on a kerotakis, then pour or dilute, and see whether you have accomplished the work. If you have not accomplished [it] with a certain yellow, use our *ios* with the material which precedes the coloring: there is that which is necessary for making the gold perfect; otherwise the gold will not become yellow. Project it anew with the material which precedes the coloring, or else dilute with the transformed silver: [take] of the sparkling black one part of *ios*, of the raw *misy*,[26] and also of the material which precedes the coloring, in order to dissolve one portion of the copper.

2. It is cooked; for even if it does not contain mercury, it must be cooked, considering that before the action of the fire it has no tincture. One must make it undergo the purifying action by [appropriate] materials, in order to ascertain that it is pure. Try, or else make it melt. If you know the two steps, those of the Jews and of . . .[27], do not be afraid to try, [executing] in detail all the things which I have revealed to you.

This exposition allows no room for any equivocation; rather its purpose is to induce you to try whether fortune is favorable to you, and whether you have been wholly successful. And, relying on this [knowledge] you will not fail; but by this method you will conquer poverty, especially if you have talent and the ability to surmount the obstacles. In thousands of works it is taught how copper is whitened and yellowed properly; but it will not become alloyed properly by diplosis unless it is changed into *ios*. It can be treated methodically by a thousand [means]; but it is made into a proper alloy only in one single way, by becoming our true copper: this is the whole formula. Such is the efficacious coloring, the one which they have taught them, the coloring sought for centuries, which cannot be discovered otherwise, except in this fashion. What the appropriate principle is for these effects I have shown you in writing about vitriol. There it is told how copper tints, and there lead is spoken of and all that which is susceptible to receiving the tincture (3:205–6).

The second *True Book of Sophé the Egyptian* has been referred to above in Chapter 4. Another of the treatises of Zosimus entitled *On Furnaces and Apparatuses*, has also been mentioned. From the second paragraph of this treatise it appears that Maria was the only source, or, in any case, the most reliable source, for the construction of furnaces. He writes:

> A great number of constructions of apparatus have been described by Maria; not only those which concern the divine waters, but also many more species of kerotakis and of furnaces. The apparatus for sulphur are those which one must explain in the first place. Among them, one must speak above all of the glass receiver with the earthen tube, the glass vase *udcoé* [?] with a narrow neck, into which penetrates the tube placed in right proportion with the opening of the receiver (3:216).

In his treatise *On the Tribikos and the Tube*[28], Zosimus again invokes the authority of Maria, then, discussing other furnaces, he reproduces in detail the instructions of Maria:

> On Other Furnaces. Since the continuation of our discourse has for its subject furnaces and the tincture, I do not want to repeat to you what is found in the writings of others. In effect, the description of furnaces presented here does not figure in [the writings of] Maria. The philosopher [Democritus] does not mention [them], but only prisms and other [apparatuses], of which I have spoken in passing, in [his] commentary on the rules of fire. But so that nothing should be lacking in your writings, speak there of the furnace of Maria, the one which Agathodaimon mentions in these terms: "Here is the description of the class of kerotakis destined for sulphur put in suspension. Taking a cup, make divisions, that is to say with a stone make a central and circular groove in the bottom of the cup, so as to catch there at the lower part a saucer of corresponding dimension. Take a slender earthenware vase, fitted and suspended on the cup, retained by it in its superior part, and projecting toward the kerotakis of fire. Arrange the [metallic] foil as you wish, conforming to the writing, on top of the vase and under the kerotakis, at the same time as the cup, so that you should be able to see its interior. After having luted the joints, cook it as many hours as our writing says. This is for sulphur in suspension. For arsenic in suspension one operates similarly. Make a little needle-hole in the center of the vase.
>
> Another glass cup placed beneath. The earthenware vase should be of such a dimension that it should fit the rounded parts and conform with those parts.
>
> This is the furnace in the shape of a kiln, says Maria, having at the upper part three holes, intended to retain [the big pieces] and to let through the

melted parts. Heat it progressively, so as to burn the Greek reeds for two or three days and nights, according to what the coloring requires, and let it be completely roasted in the furnace. Then let the asphalt descend for a whole day, while adding that which you know, plus white or yellow copper. [This] can also be done thus: the apparatus in the form of a sieve whitens, yellows, produces the *ios.* Cook gently, as is done for the production of paint, the tincture of the mixtures and all that you can imagine. This is the fabrication (3:230–31).

In his treatise *On the Final Reckoning*, Zosimus returns to quoting what Maria said about coloring: "There are two steps of appropriate tinctures, according to whether one operates with raw or with cooked species. The process of cooking does not involve great effort; [but] it requires great adroitness and it is shorter, as the divine Maria says. For this process of cooking there are many varieties of liquids and of fire" (3:236).

Maria's methods are referred to again by a commentator on Zosimus in a treatise called *The Species Is Composed and Not Simple*: "If any one of these special parts fails to appear, the composition will be incomplete; whether it underwent [only] dilution, or cooking, or calcination, or decomposition effected in the water-bath [*bain-Marie*] heated with the fire of sawdust; or in a bird-beaked vase; or [when it is deposited] in the kerotakis; or in an alembic heated with naked fire; and this, if it is a case of diplosis carried out by means of mercury, according to the procedure of Maria, or any other kind of treatment" (3:261–62).

In conclusion, Zosimus, who was by far the greatest authority among the Hellenistic alchemists, considered Maria the greatest authority among all the alchemists who preceded him and whose teachings and practices he presents in his numerous treatises.

PART THREE

The Early Arab World

Introduction to Part Three

WITHIN a few centuries after the decline of Hellenistic culture—of which alchemy was an integral part—the new and vigorous Arab civilization became its heir, and began to build its own intellectual world on the foundations laid down by the Greeks. Among the constituent elements of the great medieval Arab culture were the sciences of religion (an Arabic term: *ʿulūm al-dīn*), philosophy, all the natural sciences, medicine, geometry, and astronomy, as well as alchemy.

As in the Hellenistic world, so in the Muslim Arab orbit, alchemy was regarded a science, or art, received through the grace of divine revelation by Adam. From him alchemy was transmitted to a chain of adepts, the earlier ones of whom were biblical figures, followed by Greek masters (some of them mythical), and finally by Muḥammad and early caliphs and princes. The latter included Khālid ibn Yazīd (660–704), Jaʿfar al-Sādiq (died 765), and Jābir ibn Ḥayyān (died c. 812).

It was not until the ninth century that these unsubstantiated traditions began to be supplemented by alchemical writings that can be definitely dated, even though their authorship remains doubtful. The two most important Arabic alchemical corpora, the one attributed to Jābir ibn Ḥayyān and the other consisting of the writings of Muḥammad Zakariyyā al-Rāzī, came into being about the turn of the ninth to tenth centuries.

By that time alchemy among the Jews could look back to a history of some seven centuries, although so far no solid evidence has come to light bearing on it between the demise of the Hellenistic age and the rise of Arab alchemy. There are indications which permit us to suspect that, notwithstanding the absence of data, Jewish activity in alchemy did not cease in the intervening period. The fact that Avicenna mentions two Jewish alchemists, and highly praises one of them as his teacher and master in the Great Art, can be considered a proof that in his day alchemy was a specialization in which Jews had achieved expertise and renown, something that could have been developed only in the course of centuries. The legend-studded alchemical writings of Abufalaḥ of Syracuse (eleventh century), preserved in Hebrew manuscripts, also point in the same direction, as does the extant Hebrew version of the *Book of Alums and Salts*, traditionally attributed to al-Rāzī.

There is also the tradition which turned the seventh-century Muslim prince Khālid ibn Yazīd, a legendary founder-figure in Arab alchemy, into the Jew Calid son of Iazich, because—at least in the medieval Christian world—Jewish alchemists had a reputation that outshone that of their Muslim colleagues. The alternative explanation, which I embrace below in Chapter 9, is that a Hebrew alchemical manuscript was attributed by its author or copyist to Khālid ibn Yazīd because the Jews who lived in the Muslim world shared with the Arabs the belief that Khālid was the most honored of alchemists. In either case, the existence of such a pseudepigraphic treatise in Hebrew indicates that Jewish alchemists were known to be at work in the period in question, and that old Hebrew alchemical treatises circulated among them.

Questions such as these apart, the material presented in the following chapters also indicate that alchemy was yet another of those fields of Arab scholarly, artistic, or intellectual activity in which both Jews and Muslims participated, and in which Jewish achievement was appreciated by the Muslims. Especially noteworthy in this connection are the words of Avicenna about the "law of the philosopher" which requires learning from "the instructed man to whatever religion he belongs." Since Avicenna quotes this maxim in the name of his master Jacob the Jew, it appears that it expresses the position taken by the Jews in the Arab world which made possible, and justified in their eyes, their active participation in all the fields which made medieval Arab culture the greatest of the age.

Avicenna's Jewish Master

Avicenna, as the Latin world knew the Arab encyclopedic philosopher and scientist Ibn Sīnā (980–1037), was one of the shining lights of the medieval Muslim world. Born near Bukhara, at the time the capital of the Samanid dynasty, he learned Arabic in his childhood (his mother-tongue was Persian), and while still in his teens he became known as an outstanding physician. By the age of eighteen he had mastered all the sciences then known. He led an unsettled life, serving various courts in eastern Persia, while laboring tirelessly on producing in Persian and Arabic an astounding number of books on philosophy, metaphysics, medicine, natural history, mathematics, phonetics, and all the sciences of the age. His Arabic books, and especially his most important *Healing of the Soul* and *Canon of Medicine*, were translated into Persian, Hebrew, Latin, and the modern European languages, and were republished again and again. For example, the *Healing of the Soul* was reissued repeatedly in Latin in 1485, 1508, 1546, and as recently as in 1968 a critical edition of its medieval Latin translation was published.[1]

Berthelot in his *La chimie au moyen age* makes a brief presentation of Avicenna's statements on alchemy on the basis of the *Liber abuali abincine de anima, in arte alchimiae*, of which a manuscript is found in the

Paris Bibliothèque Nationale.[2] This work contains a list of mystical and real alchemists, beginning with Adam, Noah, Idris (cf. Koran 19:56/56–58/57; 21:85–86), and Moses. Among the latter-day alchemists is mentioned "Isaac the Jew." Avicenna has more to say about a certain "Jacob the Jew" whom he acknowledges as his master in alchemy:

> Jacob the Jew, a man of penetrating mind, also taught me many things, and I shall repeat to you what he taught me: if you want to be a philosopher of nature, to whichever religion you belong, listen to the instructed man of whatever religion, because the law of the philosopher says: thou shalt not kill, thou shalt not steal, thou shalt not commit adultery, do unto others as you do to yourself, and don't utter blasphemies.[3]

This brief statement is remarkable for several reasons. First, Avicenna professes himself to be the disciple of a Jewish alchemist. Second, of "the many things" he learned from Jacob he quotes him as having taught him not the art of alchemy as such, but the manner in which knowledge should be acquired: by learning from wise men of whatever religion. In the Muslim environment in which Avicenna lived and worked, it was an extraordinary thing to advocate that believers should seek knowledge from unbelievers. That Avicenna himself did learn from Jacob the Jew is eloquently demonstrated by the "law of the philosopher" which Jacob taught him: the basic Jewish ethical commandments which constitute the sixth, seventh, and eighth of the Ten Commandments (Exod. 20:13), quoted literally, followed by a rephrasing of Leviticus 19:18, "thou shalt love thy neighbor as thyself," probably in the light of Hillel's famous reformulation: "What is hateful to you do not unto your neighbor—this is the entire Torah."[4] The prohibition of uttering blasphemies is a reference to the Third Commandment, which in post-biblical Jewish religion developed into the concept of *ḥillul haShem*, "desecration of the name of the Lord."[5]

It is a pity that we know nothing of this Jacob the Jew who made such an impression on one of the greatest minds of the age.

Chapter Seven

ABUFALAḤ'S ALCHEMY

IN THE BRITISH Library is preserved a short but important Hebrew alchemical manuscript numbered Or. 3659 which begins: "Said Abufalaḥ the Saraqusti: Thanks to God who ordered the things and taught the sons of men their knowledge."[1] The author, who seems to have lived in Syracuse, Sicily, in the eleventh century, is known for another work as well, also preserved only in Hebrew, entitled *Sefer haTamar* (Book of the Palm-Tree).[2] MS. Or. 3659 is identified on folio 1v as *The Book of Em haMelekh*, that is, "Mother of the King." Its numerous Arabisms show that it is a translation from the Arabic. Also the references to King Solomon as *hamelekh Sh'lomo al-Yahūd*, that is, "King Solomon the Jew," and *Salmōn al-Yahūd* (8v), show that it was written by a Muslim Arab. Definitely of non-Hebrew origin is also the vacillation in the spelling of the name of the king: it is spelled not only *Salmōn*, but also *Salāmōn* (1v, 2v), and *Sulaymōn* (8r). Moreover, occasionally the Hebrew translator was at a loss to find the Hebrew equivalent of an Arabic term, in which case he used a circumlocution; after writing "the properties of the *sagra*," for example, he adds, "and in our language the properties of the soul of the living" (2r).

Even though the treatise is the work of a Muslim Arab alchemist, the very fact that it was translated into Hebrew testifies to the interest Jews, or at least certain circles of Jews, had in alchemy in the Middle Ages. Moreover, essential parts of the treatise (including the detailed discussion of the metals, 2v–4r), were incorporated verbatim by Gershon ben Shlomo into his *Shaʿar haShamayim* (Gate of Heaven), which shows that the treatise was influential among medieval Jewish alchemists, and was utilized some two centuries after its composition.

Gershon ben Shlomo of Arles was a Provençal scholar of the late thirteenth century, of whose literary output only one book, the *Gate of Heaven*, has survived. It was published first in Venice in 1547, and thereafter several more times. The *Gate of Heaven* is a popular compilation, summing up the sciences as of the thirteenth century, including astronomy, meteorology, mineralogy, alchemy, zoology, botany, anatomy, physiology, and medicine, as well as psychology, heredity, and theology. Gershon lists a great number of Greek, Latin, Arabic, and Jewish authors, but even though he lifted out major parts from Abufalaḥ's *Em haMelekh* and incorporated them word for word into his *Gate of Heaven*, he did this without giving credit to his source. None of the scholars who have so far discussed the *Gate of Heaven* noticed or commented upon Gershon's borrowing from Abufalaḥ.[3] The fact is that the Second Gate of the Second Article (pp. 9b–10b in the Venice 1547 edition) of the *Gate of Heaven* is in its totality copied from the First Part of Abufalaḥ's manuscript presented below, most of it verbatim, here and there with slight changes, and occasionally with a transposition of paragraphs or inadvertently omitted passages. Only on a very few occasions did Gershon add anything to Abufalaḥ's text. In Chapter 24 we shall see that a long section of this treatise was incorporated into a pseudo-Maimonidean tract as well.

After the opening sentence quoted above, the treatise starts with the customary address to a friend or a disciple:

> You, O successful son, at your request, as the disciple beloved by us, Ibn Masʿūd the Ashbelite, may God let you attain your good desire, and may He in His mercy protect you from evil. Your messenger has reached me here in Asro [?], with your letter of apology, and with your request [presented in] pleasantly flowery language, which arouses desire and yearning. You yearn and desire to comprehend the truth of the wisdoms. . . .

After some more general pleasantries Abufalaḥ gets down to his subject proper:

> (1r) . . . It is my wish to reveal to you everything you asked me, so that you apprehend the truth and wisdom of the intellectual work that is called among the sages *alkīmīyah.* With it you will achieve success in accumulating money and gathering a fortune, for the secret of one single operation of it should suffice for [to satisfy] your need of bread [for yourself] and of bread for your house.
>
> The many troubles I had with the practice of medicine and service of the king have caused me harm, and I reached the decision not to reveal anything of this science in a book, but only to a single person, and face to face. . . . I know also that you are perfect in all kinds of natural sciences, and [I know of] your endeavor to pursue honesty and the religious laws. You were elected judge in that kingdom, and this science will be with you so that none of the usual harm should befall you. . . .
>
> (1v) I am sending you the *Book of Vexation*[4] together with this book, for you are very greatly in need of it in this Work. . . . In order to lighten the burden of my troubles I chose brevity, and I called this book *Mother of the King*, because in it I mention the operation of the precious and wonderful stone that the Queen of Sheba brought to King Shlomo *al-yahūd* [the Jew] as a present . . . as King Salmōn testified in a book which he wrote about this science, called *HaMaṣpen* (The Compass).

BEFORE presenting the alchemical teachings of Abufalaḥ, which begin at this point in his manuscript, it will be of interest to discuss the story about the provenance of the mysterious *Book of the Compass.* Information about it is given by Johanan Alemanno, the sixteenth-century Italian Jewish alchemist, in his *Sefer haLiqqutim* (Book of Collectanea), in the name of Abufalaḥ himself, and in the form of a colorful folktale. It was published in Hebrew by Yiṣḥaq Sh'muel Reggio in 1836,[5] and the following is my translation:

> We found in the *Collectanea* of the sage R. Yoḥanan Alemanno of blessed memory, who wrote in the name of Abufalaḥ haSaqruti. . . . It is the story of the reason why the Queen of Sheba decided to travel from her country to a faraway land and come to Jerusalem: to hear the wisdom of Solomon of the seed of Jesse the Bethlehemite. . . . And these things which were told by the aforementioned sage were written in the book of Yathra the Ishmaelite, who wrote an explanation to the work of figures and alchemy, copying it from the *Sefer haMaṣpun* [Book of the Occult], a book attributed to King Solomon, which he left behind in another language, and perhaps it is the *Sefer haR'fu'ot* [Book of Remedies], which was hidden by Hezekiah king of Judah, and which is still in existence in the Kingdom of Armenia and the Kingdom of Sheba. . . . And this is the language of the aforementioned sage:
>
> Our ancestors have told us about the sages of this Work, and especially about Suleyman the ancient king in his book entitled *Sefer haMaṣpun*. . . . And there in that book, in the chapter about bringing the spirituality of the planet Mars, he said that there was a great sage among the sages of the Copts or Nabateans, by the name of Seman, who was engaged in philosophical speculation about the wisdom of spirituality, and he had . . . a venerable image which foretold the future before it came to pass. Seman in his great wisdom married into the family of the King of Sheba after the death of the king, and took his daughter to wife, and she is the Queen of Sheba mentioned in Scripture. Her father the king, at the time of his death, had commanded his princes and councilors concerning her, that when his only daughter grew up to be married, she should be given to a wise man who would rise in his wisdom high above all the other sages in the land, for the king did not want bride-price and property, but only wisdom, which is more precious than pearls, and nothing can equal it.
>
> And it came to pass after the death of the king that the time arrived in which the maiden reached her full beauty, her breasts developed and her hair grew. And the princes said: "The time has come to give her in marriage and to raise up seed for the kingdom to reign in the land, for, behold, now is the time of love, and it is proper to find rest for her, as the king, our lord, her father, had commanded."

And they issued a decree, and chose wise and old men, noted in all the kingdoms of Sheba and of Dedan and of the children of Aden, and they made them judges according to the decree which the princes prepared. And they sent heralds to all the lands saying: "Who is the man who wishes to come and stand before the wise men, to make his wisdom known before them, who can answer all their questions, each word in its fashion, and can stand in the breach, in all their discussions, for ten days, and can defeat them in his wisdom? He will marry the princess, and will be the successor of the king on the royal throne. But if he cannot prevail, and spoils her happiness, then, because he was so insolent as to come before the princes and the judges, he will be put to death, and his head will be removed from him, lest a stranger who is unworthy come and aggrandize himself, saying 'I shall reign,' and mock the sages and the elders, and become for them a burden with false words in which there is no understanding."

And the sages gathered together in the appointed place, and the days grew many, but no man came forth, for who is he who has daring in his heart to come to the house of assembly of great wise men and men of note such as these, and can leave in peace, without harm, and without forfeiting his head to the kingdom? Only one man, Seman, came forward and approached them, even though they warned him and cited to him all the conditions of the decree which the princes of the land had issued. Despite all this he did not withdraw, for his heart was sure that he would stand up and come out a victor. And he came before the wise men and judges, and held forth before them, and he gave correct answers to all their words, even though they asked him very deep questions and tested him with riddles. No secret was unknown to him, and he stood and spoke throughout the ten days.

And it came to pass that when the judges and princes saw the greatness of his wisdom, and that he had answered everything they asked him, and that there was no way they could withhold the princess from him, they dug deeper in council among themselves to ask him one more great and difficult question, which was in the realm of impossible things. It was whether he could make in his wisdom a thing small in quantity and size but great on account of its wondrous qualities and importance, a thing worth more than the whole kingdom? This [they said] he should bring in his hands as a gift to the princess to be a pledge in her hand of the kingship which would come to him through her. And thereupon they all would agree to make him king and to cry *abrekh*[6] (majesty) before him.

Seman did not hesitate to accomplish that [demand] in his great wisdom, for he wanted the princess. He asked for time, and with the spirituality which was known to him he made the precious stone of the philosophers, which all the things in the world cannot equal, and he brought it in his hand to the princess, before all the princes and councilors. When the sages saw the stone in his hand they laughed at him for they did not know what was its nature, and they threw that sage [Seman] in jail and prepared to cut off his head, for they did not believe him. But the sage commanded that they bring before him all the vessels in the house of the queen, made of copper, tin, iron, and lead, and all kinds of metals which were in the house, and he cast them into a fire, and then he scraped off a little from that stone over the metals, and out came pure gold from the fire, purified sevenfold. Then all the people were amazed at the wisdom of the man, and they all cried, "Long live the king!" And they put the royal crown on his head, and gave him the princess to wife. She took the stone and put it in her treasury to be her greatest treasure and the most precious thing in all her kingdom.

And it came to pass that she lived with him seven years, but she received no male seed from him. And at the end of seven years he fell ill with the illness in which he died,[7] and the queen remained a widow in the house of her father, and she had no child. And all day the princes and the councilors pressed her to remarry in order to raise up royal seed. But she sighed and sat back, for she wanted to wait until she would find as wise and understanding a consort as Seman, her first husband. And in the course of days she heard the fame of Solomon, whose name traveled far, and of his great wisdom and virtue. And she decided to visit him, so as to test him with riddles. Perhaps [she thought] the king will become desirous of her beauty and of the greatness of her kingdom, and will take her to be his wife.

And she came to him with great pomp, with much gold and silver and spices and precious stones to present as gifts to the king, as Scripture testifies.[8] And also it is found written in the Book of Chronicles of the Kings of Sheba that she brought with her that precious stone of the philosophers which Seman had made, to test with it Solomon, whether he would know its hidden secret, and whether he too could make one like it, with the condition that if the king told her the secret of her stone and its working, then she, and the stone, and her kingdom would become his. And if not, she would return home and not marry him.

And the king answered all her questions, and told her the secret of the stone and its nature and its working, and other secrets which do not have to be related. And the stone remained in the hands of the king. And in order to appease her after he had gone in unto her and she became pregnant by him with male seed fit for kingship, he let her return to her kingdom on condition that the son whom she would bear should reign after her and should be called by his father's name. And so it was, for the son who was born to her was called thereafter by the name of his father Sulayman son of David, of the seed of Jesse the Bethlehemite. And this has continued to this day: all the kings are called Sulayman the first, the second. And this was done by the princes and the noblemen, the chiefs of the kingdom, so that the royal seed not be lost. . . .

And because she brought the precious stone to King Solomon, this was the reason why the king wrote in the *Sefer haMaṣpun* about its working and the manner of the work of its wisdom, and thus Abufalaḥ the Saqruti testifies, as we have written.

Reggio concludes the above story by stating that "the science of alchemy is a divine science and a work about which many ancient sages have written, and it is of the secrets of nature and creation, to know the intrinsic meaning of the natures of the minerals, and to make them work one upon the other. For it is by means of natural wisdom that the philosophers' stone can be made, which is the precious stone that Seman made and about which Solomon wrote to the Queen of Sheba in the *Sefer haMaṣpun*, by bringing spirituality down upon the bodies through the preparation of mixtures and the receipt of exalted forms . . . as attested by Abufalaḥ the Ishmaelite, who gathered his words from the books of Solomon which are found in the Kingdom of Sheba."

We now return to the text of Abufalaḥ himself as preserved in the Hebrew translation.

(1v) I find it proper to begin with the section which I shall call "Theory [or The Part of Scrutiny]" (*Ḥeleq haʿIyyun*). . . . I shall follow it with a second section . . . which I shall call "The Part of Practice" (*Ḥeleq haMaʿaseh*), for in it I shall explain the order of the operations and the Work that I consider necessary to mention in these operations concerning matters of whitening, coloring, melting, coagulation, distillation, and sublimation—all these are necessary for this sought-after work, and I do this in three sections. In THE FIRST I shall enumerate what I took from the books of wisdom concerning the essence of the kinds of things that receive power from natural action on the part of the supernal bodies, and their origin and composition, such as the kinds of metals and mineral stones that are being born, and the resemblance of their appearance and their nature according to the stars that affect them. In THE SECOND I shall describe the forms of the operations with a mention of the drugs that should be placed in this Work, and those that absorb the power of that action. In THE THIRD I shall mention the operation of the precious stone and the accounts of its inventor with which this operation is completed; it is a selection of all the properties (2r) and operations, and it is at it that this book aims; it is a great secret from among the secrets of the ancient Salāmōn, which is worthy of a place in the treasuries of kings. And I also thought it desirable to write in this book a section about the coagulation of *zībaq* [A., quicksilver], since they are important operations that we have received from the oldest sages and the elders of this Work. Also our tests are directed at those operations to make sure there is in them no failure nor harm, and I ask of God the help and the support.

The First Part: Which is the Part of Theory

The sage Abufalaḥ said: Know, O longed-for son, that the ways of scrutiny to which I have already called your attention are five, and behold, I have alluded to them and explained them in the *Book of Vexation* and the *Book of Competition*; I do not consider it necessary to mention them here except very briefly, and I shall not present their explanation here, for there is no place for them in this book: A. The way in which one can achieve something remote from that which is intended. B. The way in which one can achieve the thing itself without an intermediary. C. The way in which one can achieve the near matter which adheres to the matter itself. D. The way leading to that which is outside of what is proper. E. The way of taking the essence of things out of their husks. . . .

(2v) And he said: Know, O longed-for son, that all things of the plants and the minerals in this world are controlled by the wheel [zodiac], and its power influences them through the intermediacy of the elements. And what comes into being first is two kinds of vapors: the moist and the dry. When the moist rises from the earth there comes rain, and from the dry thunder and winds. And when they come into being inside the earth, out of the dry and smoky vapor are born two kinds: one is mineral stones that come out of the earth, which are not pure, like red arsenic and *siqra* [rock-lichen, fucus], and of these there are two kinds: one is a kind of colored ash, and the other like marcasite and its like. From the moist vapor are also born two kinds: one melts like copper, gold, silver, and their like, and the other breaks like iron. . . . And the appearance of metals is in accordance with the determining powers that work on them and bestow power upon them by means of the elements, for the appearance of gold is due to the sun and its sparks, and the whiteness of silver is due to the moon, and similarly the appearance of each kind is due to one of the moving stars, for blackness is due to Saturn, and red to Mars, and green to Jupiter, and blue to Venus, and that which is compounded of various appearances to the star Sun. And behold, the dusty parts are more abundant in gold and silver, the parts are attached and mixed well, which is not the case with lead and iron. The reason that some metals such as gold and silver take longer to melt, whereas others like lead and tin melt quickly is that the watery and airy parts are attached well and fused better with the dusty parts in gold, silver, and iron, which is not the case with lead and tin. And the greater heaviness of one kind as against the other has two aspects: one is because the attachment of the parts to one another is much greater in gold, and this is the reason why gold does not deteriorate and does not rust a long time, and its melting is very retarded in the fire. And the other is because of the abundance of the parts of dust (3r) in the lead. And behold gold: no dross comes out of it when it is melted, as it does from the other metals, because of the purity of its nature and its cleanness. And it is in its nature that it fuses with silver and copper when they are melted with it, but if the marcasite stone is put on it, it will separate from them. And gold does not melt quickly in fire but it melts in the body of ostriches, *otrosi* in Laʿaz, for it is their food, and even though the heat of ostriches is weaker than the heat of the fire, [it melts] because there is a special quality in them.

And the reason why the appearance of gold is red and the appearance of silver is white is the vapor that goes into them: for if that vapor is very warm because the smoky vapor is intermixed with it, without which it cannot be, it [the gold] becomes red. And silver is white because the heat does not prevail in that vapor, and this tends toward the appearance of water.

Quicksilver: Its origin and nature are of two aspects. One: it has an origin and source like the other silver, and the reason that it does not coagulate is that there is much humidity in it, which the cold of the earth cannot coagulate and turn into a dusty [i.e., solid] body and make it thick and hard, but turns it humid like water as it results from the vapor; because of its great humidity upon the water it does not coagulate in the cold so as to become a dusty body, but becomes water. And the other reason is that the minimum of cold does not prevail upon it, so [cold] cannot turn it into a hard body and it remains moist, close to the nature of its material.

And it is the view of the sage Ben Rushd[9] that heat has thickened it from the beginning, but only a little, and then cold coagulated it, and because the action of the heat has not prevailed upon it, its nature became cold and moist. And in the opinion of some sages the substances that are closest to all kinds of metals is quicksilver and sulphur, for the moist vapors that develop in the space of the earth are affected by the heat [at the time] of origin, and it ripens them and purifies them during the long time of their stay there, and they add thickness and weight and purity of appearance. . . .

And if the quicksilver is very pure and the sulphur clean, and the two get mixed in equal measure as is proper, and the sulphur draws off the moisture of the quicksilver and dries it, and the heat of origin is average during its ripening, and if nothing cold happens to them, nor dryness prior to their ripening, then good gold will come into being out of them. And if cold happens to them prior to their ripening, white silver will come into being out of them. If dryness happens to them due to the great heat [at the time] of origin and the abundance of the dusty particles, (3v) then red copper develops from them. And if cold happens to them before the parts of sulphur and quicksilver mix, prior to ripening, then iron[10] develops out of them. And if cold happens to them prior to ripening, and the dusty particles prevail over the moist ones, then black iron develops out of them. And if the quicksilver prevails over the sulphur, and the heat is very weak in them, then lead comes out of them. In this manner do metallic substances change for reasons that happen to them: more sulphur and less quicksilver, or less sulphur and more quicksilver, or because the heat becomes strong prior to their ripening, or because of the cold, as we have explained.

Next follows a list of metals, each briefly defined or described.

(3v) TIN is . . . near in its nature to silver, and differs from it in three respects: in smell, in softness, and in tone. And these features became attached to it at [the time of] origin. Indeed, its softness is due to the abundance of its quicksilver, or due to the small measure of the cold which dried it or desiccated it; and the cause of the tone of its sound is the thickness of the sulphur that is in it; and its bad smell is due to the insufficiency of its ripening. Behold, through a known procedure it will become quicksilver, for it is close to its nature, as I shall reveal to you in the Gate that follows this, and due to a slight cause it will be saved from its traits, as we have said about silver, which is close to the nature of gold, and with thoughtful work we can transmute it into gold, as I shall reveal unto you likewise after this. And if one of those who deny this argues against us, saying that it is impossible that one kind should be transmuted into another—except for a kind of wheat which changes into a kind of *go"l* [variant: *yo"l*] [?], and a kind of hazel tree which also changes into another kind—we shall answer them that this is not a transmutation of one kind into another, because silver, if it ripens for a long time in the warmth of the earth will turn into gold, and the master of this work brings about the ripening in a short time. AND LEAD is also close to the nature of silver, and its ripening has not been completed, as with tin, and I shall tell you of its operation in the next Gate. AND LATUN [*laiton*, brass, an alloy of copper and zinc] is a kind of copper, but mixed in it are some known drugs, and it becomes hard through them, and I shall tell you also about this later. AND METAYL [metal] is a thing mixed of two metals which are tin and copper, or tin and lead, and a kind of iron; also from all the other metals you can transmute them with the devices of this Work into either silver or gold, as I shall reveal unto you the secrets of this Work in the next Gate.

And know that out of lead they make the white [substance] which is called *blanqet difoila* [ceruse, white lead?] with vinegar. And *mina* [minium] is a red color which is made out of lead and sulphur; and the vermilion out of quicksilver and sulphur; and *verdet* [aerugo, verdigris] of copper and vinegar. These are five good kinds.

And know that quicksilver if they put it on fire, will all go up in the smoke of the fire because of the abundance of its moistness, and if it is mixed with [other] kinds of metals it will soften them (4r) and weaken them, and this is why the refiners put [some] of it into silver and gold so that it should melt like water, and they gild vessels with it, and then they put the vessel on a fire, which destroys all the quicksilver in smoke, and the vessel will remain gilded, retaining the hardness and nature [of gold]. And with the devices of this Work we can coagulate it [the quicksilver] and transmute it into the nature of good silver in every respect, and that is among the important works which I shall reveal unto you in the third Gate. AND KNOW that if you mix three parts of it [quicksilver] with two parts of good gold and melt all of it, and then weigh the mixture, you will find that it gained in its weight one-sixth of what you put into it, and suffice it for him who understands.

AND BEHOLD there are artificial substances of other kinds, and they are divided into [several] kinds, such as the kinds of salts, and the kinds of alum, and the *salnitri* [saltpeter, potassium nitrate or sodium nitrate, or the like], and the *naft* [naphtha, bitumen], and all of them enter into these works. And among the salts there are those that are sweet, such as the salt which is mined from a certain mountain called Basqar [variant: Qardoya, Qardona], and there is bitter salt with which the refiners clean silver vessels. And these traits develop with moisture and the waters which mix in the space of the earth, and the heat of the sun burns them away, and because of much burning bitterness develops in them. All this I saw in this first Gate.

We now reach a passage which is significant because in it Abufalaḥ disclaims any originality for his alchemy, and admits that it is a mere compilation from older sources. He writes:

(4r) And you, O successful son, understand concerning this Gate that I extracted it from the books of nature, and this should suffice for you to study. And to give preference to natural over artificial knowledge is the great secret of this Work. If you will deal with it wisely, with the artifices and operations which are known in it, you will transmute the unimportant kind to one more important than it, and will succeed with it in accumulating a fortune in a short time, while you will also preserve the Third Composition which I indicated to you in the First Book, with the five ways which I mentioned there as well. And behold I shall present to you hereafter the Second Gate, which will discuss the manner of the artificial operations and the order of the Works and the artifices which are used by the sages of this Work who describe the whitenings and the colorings and the meltings and the coagulations and the distillations and the sublimations and other operations to transform the unimportant to the more important than it is, with a mention of the drugs that are needed to be put into these Works, as we have written.

The Second Gate

The wise said: Know, O my brother, that just as I have presented to you in the preceding Gate a discussion of the natural operations which take place due to the power of the supernal bodies by means of the elements, and I presented to you their origin from the two kinds of vapors, the moist and the dry, which are born with in the space of the earth, and their resemblance and their mixture—so it is meet that I present to you in this Gate a description of the kinds of accidental and artificial operations.

Next follows a summary interpretation of Plato's doctrines concerning the universal and particular souls: the universal soul is found in metals, in vegetation, and in the earth in general, and likewise the powers of the particular soul are found in each of the bodies, including the metals. Love between two individuals is due to the essential similarity of the power of the particular souls in the two persons. This is how Abufalaḥ puts this idea: "The power of one particular soul which is in a person, if it is similar in true quality to the power of the soul of another person, the one will desire the other, and there will be a powerful love between them, even if they should differ in years and in temperament" (4v.).

Following his excursion into Platonism Abufalaḥ turns to concrete alchemical details, and writes:

> There are things which produce their effect by whitening and coloring, for they color and whiten the metal, or by the quality of the cleansing power that is in them, such as vinegar and salt and their like. Or through addition or subtraction they unite with them and endow them with whitening and coloring in their appearance, as *zingar* [verdigris], *verdet* in Laᶜaz, and *ruga* [?] and *ruma* [?]. Or they have a relation to that metal, such as *zarnīkh* [arsenic], and the red [?], and their like. Or they relate to the weight, as ashes of the basilisk in water of the cock [see below]. And there are those that exert their effect by weight and adherence, for they adhere to all parts of that kind or those kinds and make them heavy, thus to transmute them to the kind which is sought, whether due to its quality such as the smoke of quicksilver and the smell of silver and their like, or due to its combination and beauty, as the beautification of metals and iron and natron water and their like, or by its relationship, as *marqasiṭa* [marcasite] and the stone that attracts iron, which is called *iymant* [S. *iman*, magnet] and their like. And there are those that exert their effect by way of penetration, for they infuse the power and nature of one kind into the power of the other kind, and they are like a wing for the other things that enter into these kinds of Work; or by means of their quality such as the smell of musk and its like. Or through a combination such as the rind of citron and the moistness of resins and their like. Or through their relations such as hair and naphtha and their like. And I shall begin, with the help of God, with those Works which exert their effect by means of whitening and coloring, with the power of the things that enter into them by means of their quality, relations, and qualitative combination.

DESCRIPTION: To add beauty and color to sun [gold]. [Take] verdigris and *nushādir* [sal ammoniac] and alum in equal weight, grind it and mix it with strong vinegar, and smear it [the gold] with it, and put it into fire, and it will come out a commensurate quality operation. . . .

DESCRIPTION. Of the operation of copper into sun [gold]. Heat copper plates many times, and quench them in the water of alum and *garya* [?] and salt and *ruga* until they become well softened and the blackness is removed, and take *tūtiah* [vitriol] and *atinqar* [alkali, salt], *borias* [borax] in Laᶜaz, and pure white glass (5v) and grind it well and sift it in a sieve, and knead it with black seedless raisins and with the juice of figs, and grind it with salt, and drench it with strong vinegar, alum water, and the water of *azig* [?], *vitrionol* in Laᶜz, and sal ammoniac, and thereafter dry it and grind it, and put it into the well-known *tasᶜīd* [sublimation] vessel, that is the *alanbīq* [alembic], and sublimate it from four to seven times in weak fire as long as four hours, and then sublimate it for four hours in strong fire; there is nothing like them. It is a great secret like the mixture of moon or sun; keep it because it is good.

DESCRIPTION: Coloring. Take the bark of a willow and soak it for nine days until it turns red, and you can color anything with it.

DESCRIPTION: Whitening. Take the globules which you find at the foot of the river willows and press them and squeeze out their water, and put the metal into it while it is warm, and it will become white.

DESCRIPTION: Copper into moon [silver]. Used to be practiced by Barakhia the sage. Take of good green arsenic one weight, and grind it well with strong and good vinegar many times, and sublimate it until all of it becomes white, and let its vapor rise into the well-known sublimation vessel, then make of it a compound with *mask* [musk] and pure fine flour, and sublimate all of it with the arsenic that was worked upon with the vinegar and was sublimated, until it rises like white [i.e., silver] and nothing remains in the bottom of the sublimation vessel, and then grind all this compound well and mix it with the well-known oil of those eggs. . . . One weight of this on seven weights of copper and one weight of silver—and it will come out good.

DESCRIPTION: Another whitening of copper into quality moon [silver]. Take sal ammoniac in the well-known manner and put it on melted copper, and it will become white inside and out.

DESCRIPTION: A wonderful and exalted operation to whiten all operations which are performed with copper into moon [silver] so that they should come out white from the fire each time, even a hundred times, and this is the number of [illegible word] in the experiments. Take *shabī* [A. *shibh*, copper] which is *m'ruqqeh* [H., made thin], alum, and *albish* [A. *bish*, poison plant, Napellus moysis] and *garia* and *ruga* and salt, and grind all of it well, and put half of it into cold and pure water, and the other half into boiling water in a copper vessel in which there is no tin, and heat the essence of that operation in an iron bowl, and when it is well heated throw it into the aforementioned cold water and then into the boiling water, and do this many times, heat it and put it into cold water and then into boiling water, and then rub it and dry it with a linen cloth, and then rub it between your hands and dry it and put it into fire as many times as you wish, and each time it will come out white [or: moon, silver] from the fire, but by way of melting it will not come out white [or: moon, silver]. And preserve it.

DESCRIPTION: The operation of coloring copper into gold. Take copper and make it into thin layers, and put them into another melting pot; (6r) sprinkle on them some tutty powder, and melt it and throw it into pure olive oil, and do this three or four times, and it will come out good sun [gold] in its appearance and nature. And if you heat it and extinguish it in the gall of an ox and *zaᶜfrān* [saffron] and *ruga* and sal ammoniac it will be more beautiful, and if some good sun [gold] is mixed into it it will be good for any Work.

DESCRIPTION: An operation to make sun [gold]. Six weights of sun and one weight of moon, and melt it, and it will come out good sun; give it beauty by washing, and it will be better; it is good for using in a mold, and the mold is made with linen oil and egg white.

DESCRIPTION: A distinguished combinatory operation, tested by Rusis [Rases, Rāzī] the ancient, copper into sun [gold]. Take the rind of dry *ethrog* [H., citron] which had ripened thoroughly on the tree, and *qost* [A. *qusṭ*, costus, a marine medicinal plant] and *ḥarida*,[11] explanation: burnt copper, and *zarnīkh* [arsenic] which has been prepared and sublimated until it has become most white, in equal amounts one part from each; ground *qoral* [coral] and vitriol in equal amounts, one-eighth part of each; and all of it should be ground and sifted and kneaded with the milk of figs and *ṣāg [ṣamgh] ᶜaravi, gumma arabica* in Laᶜaz, and sublimate all of it. Then take it and put one part of it, of good gold, well grated, into thirty parts of it, and knead it in water of copper, and water of the soul, of whose operation I shall tell later in the next Gate, well mixed to the limit of their kneading; return to sublimate it once more, and then take everything out and take of the copper which was melted three or four times and was extinguished in olive oil, ten weights, and of this compound one weight with a little of the copper stone about whose operation I shall tell in the following Gate, and put it into a melting pot whose description is this: take white raisins, cleansed of dirt, and let them be ground well with a little musk[12],and let him make of it a melting pot and put it into another melting pot made of clay, and let him seal it on top with dough of the raisin pot, and melt it in strong fire, and throw it into the aforementioned waters, and out will come for you good gold, and put one part of it on ten parts of red copper, and it will be very good gold.

DESCRIPTION: Another from copper into sun [gold]. Let him take copper and melt it on a fire and put on it the burnt and extinguished and ground *tutia* and human blood burnt in a vessel, and *gariya* [?], and yellowed and dried cock's excrement, one part of each, filings of good gold one-tenth of a part and musk a tenth of a part, and let him make a dough and sublimate it once in the vessel of sublimation, and let him take the sublimated [matter], and grind and mix it a second time with the aforementioned water of copper on the fire, and a little sal ammoniac which has been prepared, and let it be removed from the fire, and let him throw it while hot into the water of the hair whose operation I shall describe in the following Gate, and when it cools down it will dry, and it should be ground, and let him take twenty *sheqels* of good gold and half a *sheqel* of that stone, and let him melt it in fire, and out will come gold good in color and shape none like it (7v) and let him take if off and throw it on the copper water, and out will come for you important [i.e., fine] moon [silver]; in all the Works there is none more honored and important than this, as long as you preserve in it the traces of the third composition, and this has been tried by us.

DESCRIPTION: Another to increase and add to the weight of the sun [gold]. Take *nitro* [niter] and put it in an eggshell, and hide it in a pit which you should make in the earth in a very moist place, and there it will melt by itself, and will be like water. Then heat the sun and immerse it into that water, and you will find that it increased and added to its weight over and above what was in it, and this suffices to one who understands and succeeds like you.

AND HERE is a description for you of making *lutun* [brass]. Make a dough out of black raisins cleaned of their seeds, and ground glass, and black human hair cut with scissors very fine, and *tuṣiah* [i.e., tutiah, tutty] of its two kinds, and smear with it pieces of copper which you should make into thin sheets, and put it into the melting pot and on top of it another melting pot luted with philosophers' clay [see below], and melt it, and instantly take it off the fire and throw upon it a little sal ammoniac, then dip the melting pot gradually into cold water, and then everything will be made quickly in the water.

THIS IS FOR YOU another description of increasing the weight of sun [gold]; it is from among the operations of our friend the refiner, and it has been tried by us. Take the human sweat which accumulates in the pits of the walls in the bathhouse, and the vapor of sublimated quicksilver, with one part of lead whose operation I shall tell you hereafter, ground; knead all of it in the water of human excrement which is found in the distilling vessel in the known manner, and put all of it into an eggshell under the earth in a moist place, and it will melt and become like water; and then heat that which is cleansed, or the double of the sun, and throw it into the water, and let it stand there about an hour, and then take it out, and it will dry by itself, and you will find that it added much to its weight. Preserve it, for it is a secret of secrets and marvelous.

AND BEHOLD I shall tell you now about the sublimations as I promised.

DESCRIPTION: The sublimation of killed [extinguished] quicksilver with lead. Take lead and melt it in a fire, and when it is melted throw upon it the quicksilver, and when it is mixed together grind it with a little *zag* which is called vitriol, until it becomes dust, and then put it into the melting pot and light under it a gentle fire all day and all night, and then leave it for about five hours so that it cools down well, then take it out and grind it a second time as you did the first time, and return it to the fire a day and a night, and do this as many as ten times, and each time grind it and burn it, and at the tenth time leave it until it cools down, and collect it and operate with it.

DESCRIPTION: The sublimation of killed quicksilver with the arsenic. This is how you should kill it: put it in an iron mortar and put on it half of the arsenic by weight, and grind it until it becomes dust, and then put it into a melting pot well covered with philosophers' clay, and put it into the furnace of fire, and light a fire in it a full day and night, (8r) and then take it out, and when it has cooled down well take it out and grind it a second time and return it into the fire a second time. Do this a full seven times, and then take the vapor which rises from it, and you will see that it is similar to frost. Collect it and operate with it.

DESCRIPTION: The sublimation of quicksilver with shavings of iron. Take one part of the quicksilver, and two parts of the iron shavings and grind all of it well, and mix it and put it into two melting pots well luted with philosophers' clay; light under it strong fire. Make sure to make a small hole in the lid, and when it begins to make steam like cinders, then you should have with you a little philosophers' clay; close that hole well, and then take it off, and when it has cooled down take it and operate with it.

DESCRIPTION: The operation [superscribed: sublimation of sal ammoniac]. Take sal ammoniac and kitchen salt, two parts. It should be well ground and mixed and put into two melting pots covered with philosophers' clay, and do it in the manner of the quicksilver which was killed with the shavings of iron.

DESCRIPTION: Philosophers' clay. Take *gimoliah* [?] and fine sand, and excrement of an ox, and cattle hair cut small with scissors, mix it all and make a kind of mud.

DESCRIPTION: The preparation of the salt which enters into these Works. Put it into the oven in an empty pan until it becomes burnt and is transformed into coal, and then grind it and dissolve it in water until all the salt is finished, and then let it drip and transfer all that water into two vessels;

in one vessel the water should stand in the heat of the sun, and in the other vessel let the thin [liquid] drip in this manner: take a strip of thin cloth of linen or a piece of felt cloth, and put it as mentioned above[13] and put on the fire the water that dripped down in a pot and let it boil until it thickens into pure and white and clear salt.

DESCRIPTION: The preparation of arsenic. Pound it with salt and mix it with vinegar and dry it, and again pound it and mix it and dry it, and do this four times, and put it into the oven for one night after the bread has been taken out, and then use it for any Work.

AND SUFFICE for you what I have mentioned until now of these operations in this Gate. And I shall tell you in the Third Gate many wonderful and honored things in which we have found overt and well-known usefulness. I have examined them with our friend Abū Artūs[h], the teacher with whom we joined together to try out these operations, through a faithful and wise refiner who lived in our generation and instructed us in the true way of attaining the desired success. And in my hands was a secret book written by the philosopher Aristo for King Alexander his pupil, which explains all that is hidden in these Works from that which the philosopher took out of the book of Sulaymon the ancient about the secret of the precious stone called by the sages *Mother of the King*, after the name of its first inventor, and she [the Queen of Sheba] brought it to King Sulaymon the ancient as a present, and she introduced it with a full and wonderful performance of this Work. And she was familiar with the operation and the quality of the work, and was instructed in spiritual wisdom, and the deity was revealed to her, and that book was intended for her, for no one is worthy to use this rare and honored operation except kings and sultans. However, when I saw the honesty (8v) of your nature and the pleasantness of your traits I was enticed by your desire, and decided not to hide this secret from you. But I warn you a second time not to pass on the [word illegible] of this secret to another, as the sage said, "Guard well your secret, he who reveals it kills it." . . .

And now I shall begin in the Third Gate to tell about the precious stone and the stories of its inventor and its effect and its occurrence and its wonderful utility, together with a description of the coagulation of quicksilver and other weighty operations which I have not mentioned in the Second Gate. I shall mention them now in this Third Gate because of the great importance and verity of their experiment; I have tried them. I received them from the ancient ones and the sages, and we established their truth, and from God will be my help.

THE THIRD GATE

Behold, our predecessors told us: The sages of this Work, and especially Salmon al-Yahūd [Solomon the Jew] the ancient king, in his book called *Sefer haMaṣpen* [Book of the Compass] tells about the secret of the quality of the spreading of spiritual powers in flesh and blood. There he tells the story about the image called "image of the pictures," which [served] to bring the image of spirituality out of the vapors, according to a great sage from among the sages of the contemplatives [*hebeṭiyyim*; possibly *Nabaṭiyyim*, Nabateans, or *Qabaṭiyyim*, Copts], whose name was Kamhan the philosopher in spiritual science. He was in possession of the aforementioned image of the picture, a very honored and wonderful image, which foretold the future before it came to pass. And he married into the house of the King of Sheba. Because of his great wisdom and good fortune they gave him the daughter of the king for wife after the death of the king, for that is what the king commanded: to search for a great sage in all lands of his kingdom and to give him his daughter. It was the law of the kingdom in those days to enthrone none other but a wise man and philosopher, and she was the only one, no son was left to the king nor another daughter. And they searched and found this one, exalted and philosophizing above all the sages of India, and he accepted the condition between them: if he should not tell in his wisdom everything they would ask him, [he would lose the throne,] and this story is very long, but I do not want to be long-winded.

MY BROTHER, take for yourself the stone of copper powder, which is an artificial stone the description of whose Work I shall tell hereafter, and the magnet stone, and the marcasite stone of all three kinds, one weight of each, and the pregnant stone, and *al-zundar* [probably *zingar*, verdigris] stone, and the stone of the bull's gall, and the stone called wolf stone which is known among the physicians . . . (9r) as a stone born in the sand from the urine of the wolves at the summer solstice from the heat of the sun—of each half a weight—and cinnabar stone and *garia* [?] and glass and *ḥadīda* [A., iron] and vitriol of both its kinds, and red and pure arsenic and *zaigma* [?], one-third of a weight. Pulverize all of it well, and add to it pure and good gold well pulverized in purity, and put in one-third of the good and important musk, and knead all of it in the water of the quicksilver and sal ammoniac, the description of whose Work I shall also tell you hereafter, and make all of it one body. Thereafter put it into two melting pots well sealed and closed with philosophers' clay, and sublimate it in the furnace of fire, light in it a strong fire for a full day and night. Then take it out, and when it cools down grind all of it a second time to fine powder, and add to it *nushādir* and *durmig* [perhaps A. *darmaq*, flour] and copper and saffron and *nitra* [niter] and frankincense, and this is the gum arabic, ground and sifted, of each an equal weight, all of them together should be half of the weight of the one powder which you took out of the melting pot. And thereafter add to it of the good and pulverized gold, one-third of the weight of the two powders, and two-thirds of the musk, and knead all of it a second time in oil of *k'lil harim* [perhaps *klil ḥoresh*, Judas tree, redbud, cercis, siliquastrum], the description of whose work I shall also give you hereafter. Make of all of it one body and sublimate it a second time as you did at first, and take it out and grind it to fine powder, and add to it one-third of its total weight of the powder of the soul, the description of whose preparation I shall give you, and of the good gold dust one-third of a weight, and of the good musk two-thirds of it. Knead all of it in the soul-water the description of whose preparation I shall also give you hereafter, and make all of it one body also, and sublimate it a third time as you did at first. Take it out and grind it and add to it the powder of viper which is separated from the eggs of the cock [*sic*], whose operation I shall also tell you hereafter, one-third of the weight of all this, and of the good gold dust one-third of one weight, and of the good musk two-thirds, and knead all of it for about an hour, whose Work I shall also tell you hereafter, and make of it one body. And then put it into the furnace a fourth time and sublimate it as you did at first, and then take out all the sublimate and grind it to fine powder, and then knead it in the water of the gold whose operation I shall tell you hereafter. When it has dried thoroughly grind it and then put everything into a glass vessel closed and sealed with philosophers' clay [and put it] into warm dung and let it stand there thirty consecutive days, and every five days put it into warmer dung, and when the time has passed take it out and you will find it water. Then put that water in a round, thick glass vessel which should have only one hole well sealed and closed with philosophers' clay, and put that vessel into another big vessel made like the shape of the glass vessel in which they show the urine of the sick, and fill the big vessel with pure olive oil and then seal (9v) well that vessel also with philosophers' clay and put it into a *farid* or a kettle full of pure and sweet water. That kettle should be placed in the opening of the furnace and should be coated all around with philosophers' clay; light the fire under it day and night, let it not go out. Seven full months should pass in this operation, the power of seven which is upon it will endow and infuse it with its strength.

And this too is one of the hints that I gave you in the Third Composition. And when the water diminishes due to the power of the boiling be careful to add to it little by little every hour, do not wait until the water diminishes to a great extent, because then you will have spoiled the operation and toiled in vain. And the ancients said of each toil that yields no benefit—death is better. And after the mentioned time break the vessel, and you will find those waters have coagulated and become tied together, and become a stone of beautiful shape, precious and wonderful. And if you take it and scrape off a little of it with a knife, and you have in front of you any of the metals that can be melted in fire, it will transmute them to the nature of the sun [gold] in its appearance and nature by power of the virtue that is in it; even if they be a thousand talents they will endure many meltings and will come out of the fire with the nature and appearance of the sun. And there are some metals which will receive the power of that stone even without melting, through mere heating with fire. However, beware of giving any of this artificial sun to any person to eat or to drink, and do not mix any of it into medications, lest a misfortune overtake him [who uses it], and guard this secret.

AND THIS IS the description of the copper stone which is mentioned in this operation. Take red and good copper—for there are two kinds of it—and white glass, one part of each, and put it into fire, it will melt like water, then sprinkle upon it half a part good *burag* [A. *būraq*, borax, saltpeter], and when everything is well melted throw it while warm into water, and out will come a stone of the appearance of good gold. That stone has several virtues, but they have no place in this book. And operate with it.

AND THIS IS for you the operation of the water of quicksilver and sal ammoniac. Take eight parts quicksilver and nine parts sal ammoniac, and sublimate them in the known vessel; its operation is like the operation of quicksilver with iron filings of which I told in the preceding Gate. And then put them upon a marble stone and grind them and mix them well and put them in a glass vessel, well sealed with philosophers' clay, and put it under warm dung, and every five days put it into warmer dung, and mix it; it should stand twenty-five days, and it will flow [like] water. They have other operations apart from this, but this is not their place. And operate with it.

AND THIS IS for you the *k'lil harim* [Judas tree?] which is called *romani* [?] or [word illegible]. Collect many flowers, at their known time, and gather of them as much as you can, put them into a new soup pot, and make a hole in its bottom; under the pot put another plastered glass or another glass vessel in which they show the urine of the sick, and put it under the earth and let it stand there a full year so that the power of the constellations should pass over it (10r). Then you will find those flowers dissolved and their water fallen into the lower vessel, and then take them and put them into a glass flagon, well sealed, and let them stand there for another year in the ground, and there it will become purified, all the sediments will go down into the bottom of the vessel and their pure part will go up, and that is the good oil suitable for this work. This oil has several other virtues, but they have no place here. Also the sediment is good for several things, and it is the great *tiryāq* (A., theriac, panacea) among expert physicians. And operate with it.

AND THIS IS the description of the hair water which is very efficacious and wonderful in this Work and also in other Works which have no place here. Take hair from a red youth, and none other, as much as you can, and put it in a soup pot well covered with philosophers' clay, and hide it in warm dung for ten days. Then take it out and you will find in it black creatures similar to worms, and their appearance is frightening to him who sees them, and each has a head and two tails. And take tongs of iron and collect them in a vessel, for to touch them is dangerous, and cover the vessel well, and let it stand there until they eat one another. And after nine days open the pot and you will find a big snake or several snakes, and take them with the tongs and put them into the distilling vessel known for the operation of rose water, on a mild fire, and take out its *m"m* [?] water with supreme caution, and put it into a glass vessel, and operate with it.

AND THIS IS for you the description of the soul water and the soul dust which were mentioned, and it is an efficacious and very wonderful operation in this Work and also for other operations which have no place in this book. Take blood by bleeding a man's ears and fill with it a glass vessel well sealed with philosophers' clay, and let it stand forty days in the warm sun in the summer days. And then you will see that a creature has come into being in it, and take it and put it into flour, and let it be there as [long as] you wish. Then take the creature and put it into the known distilling vessel which was mentioned, and out will come its water which is called the soul water, that is to say, the water of the blood, and what is left in the bottom of the vessel is the soul dust, and operate with it with great caution.

AND THIS IS for you the description of the basilisk ashes which you can make out of cock's eggs, and this operation was the most exalted and wonderful of all the kinds of mentioned Works, and this Work has a great virtue and also other virtues which have no place to be mentioned in this book. Take of cock's eggs, that is to say the long and pointed eggs out of which male cocks hatch, and of the short and round eggs from which come the females, take thirty to forty of them, and break them and put them into another pot and hide it in the warm dung under the earth, and the pot should be closed and sealed well with strong clay, and in the lid make another hole (10v) and insert there a somewhat crooked hollow reed, either of metal or of real reed if you can find it, so that its vapor should rise over the earth, and let forty days pass so that those eggs become moldy and a kind of basilisk will be formed, which will cause decay and death to everything else that his [the basilisk's] glance falls upon, also every plant, tree, or grass will wither. Therefore when these [days] are up you should have with you a frying pan; melt in it what you want, and when it is hot throw upon it [the basilisk] with the hollow reed, and kill the basilisk with it. And behold I instructed you that the reed should be crooked so that the basilisk's glance should not fall upon any thing lest the air decay and danger increase. And then dig it up and take it out and burn it any time of the day, for thereafter you will no longer be in danger. And those ashes are the basilisk ashes whose operation is known among the sages of this Work. However, this operation has in truth no value. Yet, don't miss its operation, for as long as you observe, while carrying it out, the signs of the Third Composition, which I have explained to you in the First Book, to perform it in these operations at the time when the *maggid* [H., herald, narrator?] gives its special power, and keep away from its opponents at the time of the dissolutions and the distillations and the sublimations and the congelations and the burnings[14] for then you will be saved from the errors and the mistake of the *maggid* in giving his power. And do not think that when I present the intention of the book I shall give you the particulars of the indications in detail, for what I have included of this work should suffice you, and together with what you will extract from the books of the laws of the stars [astronomy] it will establish this composition properly. And also look up the preceding Gates, and there you will find how some *maggid* is found to be related, such as the sun to gold, and the moon to silver, and likewise the others, and understand this. And behold, what is necessary to be observed in the burning of the basilisk is that it should be done on a day when the sun is shining and in its hour, and when there is the constellation of the Lion and the sun, and the moon should be on the increase and in the first rise of *Tleh* [Aries], and let the evils be far from them. And if you observe all this and put your heart in every one of the operations to observe in them the aforementioned composition, and to select its impressions which are suitable for this Work, then you will reach the desired success and will be saved from errors and mistakes. And observe this.

AND THIS IS for you the description of the operation of the water of gold which was mentioned, and it is very wonderful in this Work. Take pure and good gold and grind it and add to it sal ammoniac, half of its weight, saffron and musk one-quarter of its weight, and mix and grind it until nothing is left of the gold, and put it into a glass vessel of rose water, and put it on a hot fire, and keep it there until the steam that rises from it ceases, and receive the dripping in a glass vessel, and then take out what is found, and grind it again as at first, and grind it and return it to the rose water and add to it of the sal ammoniac, half of its weight, and of the saffron and the musk one-quarter of its weight, and return it to the fire as at first, and do it in this manner up to ten times, and each time add of the sal ammoniac half a weight, and of the saffron . . .

Here ends the last extant leaf of MS 3659.

Chapter Eight

A HEBREW VERSION OF THE *BOOK OF ALUMS AND SALTS*

THE *Book of Alums and Salts* (hereafter *BAS*) is one of the famous treatises of medieval Arab alchemy. Only fragments of its original Arabic text survive; its Latin translations have been published repeatedly. In 1937 Julius Ruska published the extant Arabic fragments, the complete Latin version originally published by John Garland in 1560, a German translation, and an extensive analysis.[1] The *BAS* was traditionally attributed to Muḥammad ibn Zakariyyā' al-Rāzī (864–925), the celebrated Persian physician, philosopher, and alchemist, whose writings were for centuries required reading in both Muslim and European medical schools. Modern historians of alchemy agreed with this attribution, but Ruska's own conclusion was that the book was not written by al-Rāzī but by an anonymous Arab alchemist who lived in Spain in the eleventh century.[2] Nevertheless, Ruska considered the *BAS* one of the most important medieval alchemical treatises. He made no reference to a Hebrew version of the book, and seems to have been unaware of its existence.

The Hebrew version of the *BAS*, as noted by Steinschneider,[3] is contained in MS Orient. Oct. 514 of the Berlin Staatsbibliothek, which we shall discuss in its entirety in Chapter 33. It contains numerous insertions, most of them in the text itself, with a few added on the margin. These additions always begin with the abbreviation *n'l*, the initials of the Hebrew words *nir'eh li*, that is, "it seems to me," followed by corrections or explanatory comments.[4]

The first nineteen folios contain alchemical recipes, among them several quoted in the names of authorities (for example, f. 1a: "And I have heard from Menase . . ."; f. 13a: "Miriam [i.e., Maria the Jewess] said . . . ," etc.). The translation of *BAS* begins at the bottom of f. 19b under the heading "I shall begin the Book of *Alume* [Alums] and Salts," followed by the explanatory comment, "The treatise of the *alums* and salts needed for this work. And this is the nature of the *atramento* [L. *atramentum*, vitriol]."[5]

A comparison of the Hebrew text with the Latin and Arabic versions published by Ruska reveals, first of all, a basic difference in the order of sections in the Hebrew, which makes it clear that the Hebrew is based on neither of the others, but on another prototype whose order of sections it followed. In the Hebrew version the order of sections is more logical than that of the Arabic or the Latin. It begins with a discussion of alums and salts and *nishdera* (sal ammoniac), then goes on to the souls and spirits of the minerals, arsenic, sulphur, mercury, the bodies, gold, silver, iron, tin, lead, glass, and talc. The Latin and the Arabic (assuming that two missing sections of the latter were in the same order as those of the Latin), on the other hand, begin with a discussion of the souls and the spirits, and only after treating the metals do they turn to general statements on alums and salt. Given the title of the book, one would expect it to start with this subject, and this expectation is reinforced by the opening statement, which in Ruska's Latin version stands not in the beginning of the book but after seventy-one paragraphs: "[Here] Begins the Book of Rasis on the Alums and Salts which are Necessary in This Art" (p. 79).

A comparison of the Hebrew text with the text of the two others also shows that it conforms at times to the Arabic and at times to the Latin and at other times differs from both. Hence one is led to the tentative conclusion on the basis of this comparison that the Hebrew translator used neither the Arabic nor the Latin text published by Ruska, but had before him a different, older Arabic text, as we can see from the following excerpt.

Hebrew Version Berlin MS 514, f. 32b

Another thing, fine and good. Take *limatura* [I., filings] of copper, one *litra* [pound], and the like of it of quicksilver (it seems to me: tin. Another view: four times like it), and grind it well *peri antribalo* [in like manner?] until it becomes like dough. Then wash well with salt and vinegar until it becomes well purified. And then wash it with pure water, then dry it. And take *atramento* [L. *atramentum*] one pound and dissolve it in double of old urine of boys, and filter it. And put on it one pound of *nishdera* [sal ammoniac]. (It seems to me: water it and roast it.) And *incera* [I. *incerare*, to wax, i.e., soften] with this water little by little until it drinks all of it. And it will be colored in a color between yellow and red which is called in the Arabic language *aṣfar* [yellow]. (It seems to me: anoint with it purified silver filings or silver or tin, and heat it little by little until it penetrates it, and do it until it becomes gold. Then melt it and put it on them.) We have already combined the quicksilver with the copper, now work it with it, and rejoice. (It seems to me: or roast it, coagulate it in a glass ball fully covered with clay, and drench it until it coagulates and does not smoke. Then dissolve it and coagulate it until you achieve it, or distill it. Or coagulate it in a melting pot covered with another melting pot and sealed with clay according to the method of *Yabar* [Jābir] in the coloring of the white [i.e., silver] into red [i.e., gold]. Or fill an *anpula* [I., ampolla] and coagulate it in the fire of brass or in hot ashes. Or coagulate it and melt it.) And if you wish to whiten [i.e., to make silver], put instead of the *zāj* [A., vitriol] *alume yamīnī* [Yemenite alum], and do with it as we said, that you should put it on the copper and it will be transmuted to silver, with the help of God. (Nazar tried this method, and roasted it in a moderately hot bread-oven, and at the sixth time it melted.)

This Hebrew version can be compared with the Arabic and Latin texts:

ARABIC VERSION, RUSKA P. 47, AG§54, P§64

Another. Take copper filings and place of them a portion, and of quicksilver a portion, and grind them until they are mixed together, and work it with water and salt until purified, then work it with sweet water and dry it, and take of the vitriol like the copper and dissolve it in the like of it of old urine of boys, and put it aside or filter it, and put on it a weight of eagle [i.e., sal ammoniac], and soften it with this water little by little, drench it, and it will become like marble. Already some of it has been combined, and work it. You will rejoice in it, if Allah wills. And if you want whitening, make in place of the vitriol Yemenite *shabb* [A., alum or atrament-stone], and work it as before, and throw of it upon the copper. It will come out silver if Allah wills.

LATIN VERSION, RUSKA P. 73, G§54 P§64

A Medicine which converts copper into silver. Take *limatura* [I., filings] of copper, any part, and just as much quicksilver, and grind it well until they become dough. Then work well with salt and vinegar until they are well purified, and then with pure water, and then dry it. And take *atramentum* [L., vitriol] in the amount of the copper, and dissolve it in double that much of puerile urine, and filter it. And put on top of it as much sal ammoniac, and soften it with this water gradually until it drinks all of it. And it will be colored in the color of pale red glass, which color is called in Arabic *firfir*. We have already combined the quicksilver with the copper; therefore work it and rejoice. And if you wish whitening, put in place of the atramentum alum of Aleman, and do with it as it has already been said. Which you should put over copper, and it will be converted into silver, if God wills.

A comparison of the Hebrew with the two other versions shows that the Hebrew is closer to the Latin than to the Arabic, but there are indications that the Hebrew is based on a different Arabic text than the Latin. For example, the Latin refers to the Arabic term *firfīr* (marble), which, incidentally, it misinterprets as the word for a color, whereas the Hebrew quotes the Arabic term *asfar* in its correct sense, yellow. The

Hebrew also renders correctly the Arabic *shabb yamānī* as *alume yamīnī* (Yemenite alum), where the Latin has the corrupt *alumen de Aleman*.

Most interesting in this excerpt are the numerous and lengthy *n'l* (*nir'eh lī*—it seems to me) additions, the like of which appear in many places throughout the Berlin MS 514. The character of these added comments makes it clear that the person who wrote them—whether he was the Hebrew translator or the copyist of the translation—must have been himself an expert alchemist with broad knowledge of the procedures described in the text, who occasionally disagreed with them and suggested what he considered better alternatives. In one of his additions he refers to a method of Jābir ibn Ḥayyān, the famous Arab alchemist. At the end of the section he refers to "Nazar," that is, the alchemist Giovanni Battista Nazari, who lived in the sixteenth century, and whose book *Della Tramutazione Metallica* was first published in Brescia in 1564. Nazari is mentioned also in an addition appended to the Hebrew version at the end of the section titled *Raṣio bᶜoferet usrub*, that is "Discourse on the lead *usrub* [A., lead]."[6] This addition (exceptionally not introduced with "it seems to me") reads, "Nazari told me that he tried and distilled tin filings, and out came of it white *viline* water. And of copper filings red water came out, which tended to blackness." This brief addition indicates that the Hebrew translator/copyist had personal contact with Nazari, and therefore must have lived in Italy in the sixteenth century.

Apart from the "it seems to me" additions, the Hebrew version also contains a few passages that seem to have been contained in the original Arabic from which the translator worked, and which are missing in both the Arabic and the Latin of Ruska. Thus before the discussion of talc the Hebrew has these added introductory sentences: "And let us begin with the Ninth [i.e., talc, or mica] *deqondimenṭo* [I. *di condimento*, of the preparation] of stones, and the light compounds of it, that which is much needed by students and peoples. And the peoples compound great works. The method of *qondimenṭo* [preparation] with the Ninth." Then follows, as in the Latin, "Take of the white Ninth . . . " (Ruska, 77: *Accipe de altalc foliato albo* . . .). The term "ninth" for talc is not known to me from other sources. In fact, Steinschneider, in discussing the Berlin MS 514, stated that the meaning of *t'shīᶜī* (ninth) was unknown to him.[7] However, the designation of metals by ordinal numbers was not unusual in medieval Arab alchemy. Mercury was called "the second," copper "the third," iron "the fifth," tin "the sixth," lead "the seventh,"[8] and now we learn that talc was termed "the ninth." The use of "the fourth" is also attested in the Hebrew version of the *BAS*, in an "it seems to me" addition to folio 35b, but its meaning is not stated. I have not come across the use of "the first" and "the eighth." However, on the basis of the traditional order of the planets and their associated metals, we get the following sequence:

The First – Moon – silver
The Second – Mercury – quicksilver
The Third – Venus – copper
The Fourth – Sun – gold
The Fifth – Mars – iron
The Sixth – Jupiter – tin
The Seventh – Saturn – lead
The Eighth – ? – ?
The Ninth – ? – talc

It should be noted that the term "the ninth" was also used to designate a compound poison described by Ibn al-Waḥshīya (ninth century) in his treatise *Kitāb al-Sumūm*.[9]

The names of authorities quoted in the Latin and Arabic versions published by Ruska, except for Jābir ibn Ḥayyān and Pythagoras, appear in different forms in the Hebrew version. Where Ruska's texts have *filius Gilgil Cordubensis* and *filius Inthuelis Cordubensis*, the Hebrew (f. 20a) has Ben Julio of Cordova. For Ruska's *Lialich filius Iasich* the Hebrew (f. 23b) has Lial. For Ruska's Anfridius the Hebrew has Asidro (34a, perhaps to be read Isidoro?). Marginal additions by the translator/copyist refer to Florentino (possibly Antonius de Florentia who is mentioned in Nazari, or Florentinus de Valentia)[10] as a comtemporary ("Florentino told me . . ." f. 29b). Another marginal addition on folio 31b refers to Tastoiani.

The style of Berlin MS 514 is frequently clumsy and grammatically sloppy, occasionally to the point of being unintelligible without recourse to the Arabic or Latin versions. The translator/copyist may have been a good alchemist, but Hebrew was certainly not his best language. He frequently took the easy way out by using Italian (and on a few occasions Arabic) terms in Hebrew transliteration instead of troubling with finding their Hebrew equivalents, and did this occasionally even where perfectly good biblical or talmudic-midrashic Hebrew words were readily available. Thus he uses repeatedly the Italian *vegetabile* in inconsistent Hebrew transliterations (*vyytyble*, *vyytbyle*, *vyytible*), even though the Hebrew *ṣemaḥ* would have served just as well (f. 21a). He writes *preparare* instead of the Hebrew *l'hakhin* (f. 22a); *qurento* (that is I. *currento*) instead of *nozlim* for "running (water)" (f. 22b); *liberare* instead of *l'shaḥrer* for "to liberate" (f. 22b), and so on.

Occasionally, instead of actually translating, he simply transliterates entire phrases: "and others said that the vinegar *meliora esso dimeliorazione inqorutibile*" (f. 23b), that is, "improves it with an incorruptible improvement." On folio 28b he writes about gold that it is of *uguale sustansia adurante amitente*, that is, "equal substance, durable, permanent." And occasionally, as if being unsure of the clarity of the Hebrew word he uses, he adds to it the Italian equivalent in transliteration. Thus he writes *b'taḥtit infondo hasir*, that is, "in the bottom *infondo* of the pot" (f. 23a). The linguistic confusion is compounded due to the fact that the copyist of the extant Hebrew manuscript seems to have had only a rudimentary knowledge of Italian and therefore occasionally distorted the words which in the original Hebrew version were given in Hebrew transliteration. Thus the original *suo stridore* (its crackling) became *hasantridore shelo* (f. 24a), by adding the Hebrew article *ha-* (the) and the Hebrew possessive pronoun *shelo* (its) to the Italian two words which he misread as *santridore.*

Despite these linguistic shortcomings, the Hebrew version of the *BAS* (like the entire Berlin MS 514) is a rich storehouse of medieval Hebrew alchemical terminology. It contains hundreds of Hebrew alchemical terms, and its very existence is an eloquent testimony to medieval Jewish interest in alchemy. Moreover, this particular manuscript happened to have preserved more completely, or at least more faithfully, the original text of the *BAS* than the Arabic and Latin versions published by Ruska.

Chapter Nine

PSEUDO-KHĀLID IBN YAZĪD

AMONG the most problematical personages in the history of Arab alchemy is that of the anonymous master (or masters) whose works have been attributed to Khālid ibn Yazīd. The historical Khālid ibn Yazīd ibn Muᶜāwiya (c. 668–c. 704), one of the sons of the caliph Yazīd I, spent his life in relative obscurity governing his emirate of Ḥims. It was only later that legend made Khālid into an alchemist and that alchemical works were attributed to him, including the *Firdaws al-ḥikma*, a large collection of alchemical poems, and treatises such as the Marianus legend.[1] Perhaps the most important alchemical work attributed to Khālid is the *Liber secretorum artis* (Book of the Secrets of the Art) or *Liber secretorum alchimiae* (Book of the Secrets of Alchemy), with whose authorship there are additional serious problems.

The *Liber secretorum alchimiae* has in due course taken its place in the standard medieval and Renaissance collections of alchemical classics. It is included in the important alchemical compendium published in 1541 in Norimberg (Nürnberg) under a long title which reads in part *In hoc volumine de alchemia continentur haec gebri Arabic philosophi solertissimi rerumque naturalium . . . item liber secretum alchemiae Calidis filii Iazichi Iudaei.* The treatise itself is found on pp. 338–62, and carries the title *Liber secretorum alchemiae compositae per Calid filium Iazichi translatus ex Hebreo in Arabicum & ex Arabico in Latinum, incerto interprete*, that is, "The Book of the Secrets of Alchemy by Calid son of Iazich, translated from Hebrew into Arabic and from Arabic into Latin by an uncertain translator." "Iazich" is evidently a corrupt form of Yazid.

The treatise was subsequently included in Manget's *Bibliotheca chemica curiosa*, one of the richest and most complete collections of ancient alchemical works. Here too it is stated that the treatise was translated from Hebrew into Arabic and from Arabic into Latin, and the name of the author is given as *Calid filius Iaichi*, that is, the name Iazich has been further corrupted into Iaich.[2]

The problems represented by the attribution of an originally Hebrew alchemical treatise to an Arab prince can best be tackled by asking whether there is any indication in the text of the treatise itself relative to its authorship. In fact, the treatise starts with a "Preface on the Difficulty of the Art" in which the author first "gives thanks to God the creator of everything who led and directed us, and taught and gave us understanding and knowledge." Then he goes on to say, "Know, O brother, that this magisterium of ours about the secret stone and the honored observance is the secret of secrets of God which He kept hidden for His people, and did not want to reveal to anyone, except to those who faithfully, like sons, deserved it, and who knew His goodness and greatness."

The expression "His people" (in Hebrew *'amo*), that is, God's people, is used so often in the Bible that it has subsequently become a stereotypical designation of the Jews in the writings of Jewish authors. Moreover, the statement that God kept secret the philosophers' stone and revealed it only to the Jews is but a variant of an old idea of Jewish alchemists, first expressed in the third century C.E. by Maria the Jewess, who insisted that the great secret should be known only to "the seed of Abraham." From the Middle Ages on, pronouncements to this effect have become commonplace in the writings of Jewish alchemists. In the recurrence of this statement in the treatise attributed to Khālid (as we shall refer to the unknown author of the book), there is a clear indication that he was a Jew and that he shared the early Jewish alchemists' desire to confine the knowledge of the Great Art to the adepts of their own people. It thus seems reasonable to accept at face value the statements contained in the two title pages, that the treatise was written originally by a Jew and in Hebrew. How, then, did it come about that the author was termed "the Jew Calid son of Iazich"?

The answer, probably, lies in the prevalent medieval tendency to attribute writings pseudepigraphically to famous authors. Whether this attribution was made by the author or by a later copyist or translator, its aim was to secure acclaim for the treatise by claiming that it was written by a famous alchemical author (that Khālid ibn Yazīd was not only famous but also legendary was not known at the time). On the other hand, the author (copyist, translator) was unwilling to forego the prestige Jewish expertise enjoyed in the alchemical world, and thus we get the peculiar hybrid author: a Hebrew-writing Jewish author whose name is Calid son of Iazich, that is, Khālid ibn Yazīd!

In the sequel, Khālid tells about the efforts his most outstanding disciple Mūsa made to understand the writings of the "noble philosophers," studying more than a hundred of their books. When Khālid saw that Musa struggled in vain, he decided to help him out of his quandary by writing for him the present book, in which he described clearly and explicitly what the earlier philosophers concealed behind obscure sayings. He has, he writes, mentioned in this book

> whatever is necessary for the investigator of this science or magisterium, in a language suitable for its understanding and for the perception of the researcher. And I named in this book the four highest and best magisteriums

which the wise men have performed. Among them are the elixirs, one mineral and the other animal. In fact there are two remaining minerals, which we call bodies, and they are not one, and their artifice is in washing them. Yet another [magisterium] is to make gold out of live *azoth*[3] whose formation is [by] generation, according to the generation or the series of generations in the minerals, which exist in the heart and in the interiors of the earth. And these four magisteriums and artifices were explained by the wise men in their books about the composition of that magisterium. But there were not many of them and they did not want to put anything in their books about its operation, or if there is found [anything about it] it cannot be understood and nothing more serious is found in them than that. Therefore I shall speak in this book of mine about it and its making. Therefore he who would read this book of mine should read some geometry, and should learn in addition measuring, so that he should properly accomplish the construction of furnaces, nor exceed their dimensions by increasing or diminishing it [the furnace] or the quantity of the fire.

Chapter I
On the Four Magisteriums of the Art, that is, Dissolution, Congelation, Albification, and Rubification

I shall begin to speak of the major artifice, which is called alchemy, and I shall certify my saying, and shall hide nothing, nor shall I keep silent but speak of it here, except of that of which it is not proper to speak or which should not be named. Let us therefore say that the major artifice is the four magisteriums about which the wise men have spoken, namely, to dissolve, to congeal, to whiten, and to redden. . . .

But this dissolution and congelation, which I mentioned, is the dissolution of the body and the congelation of the spirit, and they are two but have one single operation, because the spirit cannot be congealed except with the dissolution of the body, and similarly the body cannot be dissolved except with the congelation of the spirit. And the body and the soul, when they are joined at the same time, each acts on its partner, making it similar to itself. An example of this is water and earth: for when water is joined with earth, it attempts to dissolve it with its moisture and its virtue and quality, which are in it, and makes the earth more subtle than it was before, and makes the earth similar to itself, for water is more subtle than earth. And the soul acts similarly in the body. And in the same manner water is thickened by earth and becomes similar to earth in density, because earth is thicker than water. . . .

For the composition in this artifice or magisterium is the conjunction or matrimony of the congealed spirit with the dissolved body, and their conjunction, and their *passio* [occurrence] is over fire. For the heat is their nutriment, and the soul does not release the body, nor is joined to it in all kinds of conjunction, unless by the change of both from their [original] virtue and quality, and after the conversion of their nature. And this is the dissolution and congelation of which previously the philosophers spoke. And know that the sages concealed this dissolution and congelation, and spoke of them in a subtle fashion and in obscure and covered sayings, so that the perception of the searcher should be kept away from their understanding.

And here is an example of the covered and obscure sayings of the philosophers about it: "Smear the leaf with the poison (*toxicum*), and the beginning of your function or its magisterium will be verified." Or: "You operate the strong bodies with dissolved broth until both of them are converted into its subtilty." Similarly a saying of the sage about it is this: "Unless you convert the bodies into subtilty so that they be subtle and impalpable to the touch, you will not be led to what you seek. And if they [the bodies] will not be ground, return to the operation until they are ground and become subtle; for if you will do this you will be led to what you desire." And in this manner they uttered many such sayings. But nobody can achieve in any respect a testing of this fact thus concealed, until a good and manifest unfolding of its proof becomes visible. . . .

Although Khālid does not identify "the sage" whose words he quotes, the quotation itself is but a rephrasing of the sayings of Maria the Jewess we quoted above: "If the volatile [materials] do not combine with the fixed materials, nothing will take place of that which is expected," and "If you do not make out of two things one single thing, nothing of that which you expect will take place." Evidently Khālid had in mind an alchemical doctrine that went back to Hellenistic times and in particular to the school of Maria the Jewess.

Chapter II
On the Things and Instruments Necessary and Suitable for this Work

You need to know the utensils in this magisterium, that is, the *aludela* [aludels], which the sages called cemeteries or sieves, for in them are the parts divided and purified, and in them is performed, completed, and purified the matter of the magisterium. And each of these should have a baking vessel (*clibanus*) suitable for it, and both of them should have a similarity and a shape suitable for the Work. And Mezleme and several philosophers in their books have already named all of them and taught their size and form. And know that the sages agreed in this in their sayings, and hid [them] by signs, and then wrote several books, and made instruments which are necessary in those aforementioned four. And they are two. One is the cucurbit with its alembic, and the other is the aludel, which is well made. And likewise those which are required for them are four. They are the bodies and souls and spirits and waters. And on these four are based the magisterium and the mineral act (*factum*). And they are explained in the books of the wise, and I took from them for my book, and I mentioned in it that which the philosophers had not mentioned. He who has any intelligence will know which those things are. I did not write this book for the ignorant and unknowing, but composed it for the prudent and for those who have sense and wisdom and for the knowledgeable.

The mention of Mezleme in this chapter is important for the establishment of the date of Khālid's book. Mezleme is none other than Abu'l-Qāsim Maslama al-Majrīṭī, the Arab mathematician and astronomer who lived in Spain in the second half of the tenth century, and to whom several alchemical works were attributed, including the *Sirr al-Kīmīya* (Secret of Alchemy).[4] The mention of Maslama in Khālid's book proves that it could not have been written prior to the end of the tenth century, that is, three centuries after the historical Khālid. Moreover, the reference to a Spanish Arab alchemist makes it appear likely that the anonymous Jewish author of the book lived in Spain, where an Arabic alchemical treatise of Spanish provenance would be more easily accessible than in other Arab countries.

Chapter III
On Things of Nature Pertaining to this Magisterium

Know that the philosophers called it [the philosophers' stone] by many names. Some of them called it minerals, and some animals, while some called it herbs, and some by the name of the natures, that is, naturals. Others again called it by whatever names they pleased, according to what seemed right to them. Also know that their medicaments are near nature, as the philosophers said in their books that nature approaches nature, nature is similar to nature, nature is united with nature, nature is submerged in nature, nature whitens nature, and nature reddens nature; and one generation is retained by the other, and one generation vanquishes the other.

This chapter calls for one brief comment only. The pronouncements about nature are but an elaboration of the saying quoted by al-Tamīmī, a contemporary of Maslama, in the name of Maria the Jewess: "The *kiyān* [vital principle] holds the *kiyān*, and the *kiyān* is whitened by the *kiyān*."

Chapter IV
On Decoction and its Effect

Know that the philosophers spoke in their books of decoction. They said that one should make decoction with things. For that is what generates them [the things] and changes them from their substances and colors into

> other substances and colors. Do not transgress that which I tell you in this book, but proceed properly. Consider, O brother, the seed, which is in the life of man, how the heat of the sun works on it until the seed comes out of it, and men and other animals eat it. Afterward nature with its heat works in it, in man, and impacts flesh and blood. And such is the operation of our magisterium. Hence our seed which, from the sages, is such that its perfection and process is fire, which is the cause of life and death, which does not impart life to it except with an intermediary and with its spirituality, which do not mix except with fire. I have already stated for you the truth which I saw and did.
>
> CHAPTER V
>
> ON REFINING, DISSOLVING, CONGEALING, AND COMMINGLING THE STONE, AND THEIR CAUSE AND LIMIT
>
> Know that unless you refine the body until it becomes all water, it will not become moldy, nor will it putrefy, and cannot congeal the fugaceous souls when fire touches them. For it is the fire that congeals them with its own help in relation to them. And similarly the philosophers taught [us] to dissolve the bodies, and we dissolve [them] so that the heat should cleave to their depths. Then we return to dissolve the same bodies, and after their dissolution to congeal them with a thing which is close to them, until we join all of it together in a good and suitable commingling, which is of a moderate quantity. Then we join together fire and water and earth and air, and when the thick and the thin (*subtilis*) are mixed, and the thin with the thick, the different remains with the different, and their natures become converted into equals, while earlier they were simple, because the part is generative, it adds and contributes its virtue to the thin which is air. . . .

The rest of Chapter V deals with the four properties of heat, cold, dryness, and moisture.

Chapter VI is entitled "On the Fixing of the Spirit."

Chapter VII is "On the Decoction, Grinding, and Washing of the Stone."

Chapter VIII is "On the Quantity of Fire and Its Advantage and Disadvantage." In this chapter Plato is quoted, as well as Hermes, who says to his father: "Father, I fear the enemy in my dwelling," whereupon his father gives him detailed instructions about the ingredients to be used in producing fire of controlled heat.

Chapter IX is "On the Separation of the Elements of the Stone." In it God is invoked and an alchemist named Garib is referred to.

Chapter X is "On the Nature of the Stone and Its Origin." It reads:

> Take it [the stone] therefore and operate with it, as the philosopher has said in his book when he spoke of it thus: Take a stone which is not a stone, that is neither a stone nor of the nature of a stone. It is the stone whose

> mineral is generated on the summit of mountains, and the philosopher wanted to say mountains for animals. He said: My son, go to the mountains of India, and to its caves, and take from them the honored stones which become liquified in water when they are mixed with it. And that water is, evidently, the one which is taken from other mountains and their caves. And they are, my son, stones and not stones, but we call them [stones] because of the similarity which they have to them. And know that the roots of the minerals themselves are in the air, and their head in the earth, and when they are plucked out of their places, a great shout (*rumor*) arises and can be heard, and hasten, my son, with them, because they quickly lose their effect (*evanescunt*).

In this description of "the stone that is not a stone" it is unmistakable that what Khālid had in mind was not so much a stone as a plant. The words "the roots of the minerals are in the air and their head in the earth" can refer only to plants, such as carrots or potatos, whose "heads," that is, tuberous roots, are in the earth, while their "roots," that is, their leafy branches, are "in the air," that is above ground. The added detail that when these plants are plucked out "a great shout arises," that is, they cry aloud, shows that the specific tuberous plant Khālid had in mind was none other than the mandrake (*mandragora officinarum*). The mandrake, whose roots often bear some resemblance to a human body, has attracted a great amount of folklore among various peoples, some of whom believed that when it is torn out of the earth it emits a horrifying shriek.[5] Josephus Flavius (first century C.E.), who describes such a mandrakelike plant, alludes to this feature when he says that "it is not easily taken by such as would do it, but recedes from their hands, nor will it yield itself to be taken quietly." Shakespeare refers to this belief repeatedly. In *Romeo and Juliet* he says, "Shrieks like mandrakes torn out of the earth, That living mortals, hearing them, run mad," and again in the second part of *Henry VI*, "Would curses kill as doeth the mandrake's groan?"[6]

The reason for trying to obtain the mandrake despite the dangers attendant to its uprooting was anchored in the belief in its quasi-miraculous beneficial properties: it could endow those who ate of it with the power of arousing sexual passion, and could make barren women fertile. This belief underlies the biblical story of Rachel and the mandrakes, and was shared by the ancient Greeks.[7] From these sources the folklore of the mandrake spread to many other peoples, including the Arabs. The Arab botanist and pharmacologist Ibn al-Bayṭār (twelfth to thirteenth centuries), a native of Spain who spent the second half of his life in the East, gave in his *Dictionary of Simple Medicaments and Nutriments* a description of the virtues of the mandrake: it is a remedy for all maladies caused by jinn, demons, and Satan; it cures lameness, cramp, epilepsy, elephantiasis, insanity, and loss of memory, and affords protection against mishaps of all sorts, including theft and murder.[8] This belief in the mandrake as the universal medicine may well have influenced Khālid in attributing mandrakelike features to the mysterious philosophers' stone to be sought in the mountains. The additional detail that the plant-stone is found not simply on a mountain, but in a cave in it, can also be traced back to ancient Jewish sources. Josephus Flavius, in the passage quoted above, says that the root is found in "a certain place called Baaras, which produces a root of the same name." The name Baaras is puzzling, but it has been explained by Louis Ginzberg as an abridgement of *yavruḥa di-m'ara*, that is, "mandragora of the cave," Baaras being the Greek form of Hebrew *m'ara*, cave.[9]

We have seen above that in medieval sources also, Maria the Jewess was said to have identified the philosophers' stone with a mysterious "white herb of the mountain."

Chapter XI is "On the Commingling of Separate Elements."

Chapter XII is "On the Dissolution of the Composite Stone."

Chapter XIII is "On the Coagulation of the Dissolved Stone." It describes the properties and uses of the philosophers' stone, quotes Jābir ibn Ḥayyān, and reads as follows:

> Some of the sages said: congeal it [the stone] in a bath very thoroughly, as I told you, and it is the sulphur luminous in darkness, and it is the red hyacinth, and the fiery and lethal poison, and it is the elixir, above which nothing remains, and the victorious maleficent lion, and the cutting sword, and the healing *tyriaca* [*theriaca*, theriac, antidote] which heals all infirmities. And spoke Geber son of Hayen [Jābir ibn Ḥayyān]: All the operations of this magisterium are contained under six things, which are: *fugare* [to make fugacious], to melt, and to incerate, and to whiten as is marble, and to dissolve, and to congeal. "To make fugacious" means to make the blackness fugacious and to remove it from the spirit and the soul. "To incerate" is to liquefy the body and make it subtle. "To whiten" is to melt the body quickly and properly. "To congeal" is to congeal the body with the prepared soul. Contrarywise, "to make fugacious" pertains to the spirit and the soul, and to melt and to whiten and to incerate and to dissolve pertain to the body, and to congeal pertains to the souls; and understand!

There are several points of interest in this chapter. It identifies the philosophers' stone with the elixir and the theriac, the universal healing substance, but also with luminous sulphur and the "red hyacinth." Moreover, the stone is also a lethal poison, and a cutting sword. The identification of the stone with the "victorious maleficent lion" is an unusual image: as a rule the lion (frequently the "green lion") is an alternative of the unicorn, a metaphor for gold, and more often for mercury.

The attribution of both good and evil qualities to the stone is a remarkable example of the coincidentia oppositorum in alchemy. (It is a pity that this text was unknown to Jung, or, in any case, not considered by him—he surely would have been able to make much of it in connection with his manifold interpretations of the philosophers' stone.)[10]

In Chapter XIV, entitled "That There Is Only One Stone, and of Its Nature," the author presents additional details about the wonderful philosophers' stone:

> Said Bauzan, the Greek philosopher,[11] when they questioned him: Is it true that anything sprouting can become a stone? He said thus: Certainly there are two prime stones, the alkali stone and our stone, which is the life of him who knows it and its making. And he who does not know and does not make it and is not aware of how it is born, either considers the stone or, because he does not comprehend above all what I said of the mode of this stone, already appears to have died and to have lost his money. Because, unless he found this honored stone, no other will emerge in its place, and the natures will not be victorious over it. Its nature is much warmth in due proportion. Therefore he who knows it has already taught it, and he who does not know it has not taught it.
>
> Truly, it has many qualities and virtues. For it cleanses the bodies of contracted accidental illnesses, and conserves the healthful substances, so that they do not appear, nor are seen, in their disorders of opposites, nor escaping their chains. This therefore is the soap [cleanser] of the bodies and their spirit and their soul: when it is mixed with them, it dissolves them without detriment. This is the life of the dead and the resurrection, the medicine which preserves the body and purges it of superfluities. And he who knows it knows, and he who does not know, knows not. For its performance does not augment its price, nor is it acquired by sale or purchase. Understand its virtue, value, and honor, and how to operate. And said a certain sage: This magisterium is not given to you by God solely because of your boldness, fortitude, and eagerness, without much work. But men work, and God bestows fortune upon men. Worship, therefore, God the creator, who was willing to grant you so much favor of his blessed works.

In Chapter XV, entitled "The Manner of Operating with the Stone for Whitening," the author describes how the stone can and should be used for transmuting base metals into silver, but does it in a manner that leaves much essential information purposely unstated:

> If therefore you want to make this honored magisterium, take the honored stone, and put it in a cucurbit, and cover with an alembic, and seal it well with philosophers' clay, and let it dry. When you do this, whenever you seal it with philosophers' clay, thereafter leave it in the hottest dung; then distill

it, and put it under the receptor in which the water is distilled, and leave it thus until all the water is distilled, and the humidity dried up, and it drinks the dryness above it. Then take it out dry, and preserve the water which has been distilled out of it, as long as you deem it necessary. Then take the dry body which has remained in the bottom of the cucurbit, and grind it, and put it in a *chalcosolario* [brass] vessel, whose quantity should be according to the quantity of the medicine, and bury it in moist horse manure, extremely hot, as much as possible, and seal that vessel well with pestels and philosophers' clay, and thus leave it there. And if you notice that the dung is about to become cold, prepare other very hot dung, and put the said vessel into it. Do thus with it for forty days, renewing the warm dung often, as is necessary, and let the medicine dissolve in it, and let it become thick white water.

And when you see it thus, know its weight, and add to it half of the weight of the water which you have previously preserved, and then seal that vessel with philosophers' clay, and again put it into warm horse manure: because in it is the humidity and the heat. And do not omit (as we have said before) to renew the manure when it begins to cool, until the forty days are completed. Because then the medicine is congealed in the same number of days in which it finished being dissolved at first. Thereafter take it, and you will know its weight correctly, and take the same quantity of the water which at first you fashioned, and grind the body and the fine matter, and put the water over it. And again put it in warm horse manure for one week and a half, or for ten days, and then take it out and you will find that the body has already drunk the water. Then grind it, and put on it that water in the stated amount. And bury it in the manure, and leave it there for another ten days. And then extract it, and you will find that body which has already drunk the water. Then grind it as at first, and put upon it and the said water together the aforesaid quantity, and again bury it in the abovementioned manure, and leave it there for ten days, and then take it out. And do thus four times, then, after the fourth has been completed, take it out and grind it, and sublimate it in the manure, until it dissolves. Then take it out, and repeat this once more, because then its origin will be perfect, and already its preparation will be complete. Then, in truth, when it has become thus, and you have brought, O brother, the matter to this honored state, take 250 drachmas of lead or tin, and melt it. Then, when it has become liquified, throw upon it one drachma of cinnabar, that is, of this medicine which you have brought to this honored state and to this high order, and let that tin or lead be retained lest it fly away from the fire, and it will whiten it, and will extract its detriment from it, and its blackness, and convert it into a perpetual permanent tincture. Then take one drachma of those 250, and throw it upon 250 [drachmas] of tin, or brass, or copper, and it will convert it into silver better than the mineral one, and this is the best you can do, and the ultimate, if God wills.

Chapter XVI, the last chapter, is entitled "The Conversion of the Aforesaid Stone in Red." It reads:

> If you want to convert this magisterium into gold, take of this medicine, which (as I have said) you have brought to this honored status and to this high order, one drachma in weight, and [do] this according to the manner of the example which I told you above. And put it in a brass vessel, and bury it in horse manure for forty days so that it should dissolve. Then give it to drink the water of the dissolved body, first a quantity which is half of its weight, then, when it has congealed, bury it in very hot manure as said before. Then in turn do in this chapter of gold as you did above in the chapter of silver. And it will be gold, and can be worked as gold, if God wills. Preserve, O Son, this most secret book, and put not the secret of secrets of God in the hands of the ignorant. Thus you will achieve what you want. Amen.

On this pious note ends the *Book of the Secrets of the Art*, which, quite apart from the question of its authorship, is one of the important alchemical treatises of the Middle Ages. It presents the gist of alchemical theory and practice in a clearer and more understandable language than most other treatises of the age, which undoubtedly contributed to its popularity once it was translated into Latin.

PART FOUR

The Eleventh to Thirteenth Centuries

Introduction to Part Four

THE ELEVENTH to thirteenth centuries were the golden age of Arab culture in general and of Arab alchemy in particular. Ibn Sīnā and al-Rāzī, both of whom we met in the preceding part, were but two of a galaxy of great and creative minds who enriched the Arab world, and through it the intellectual history of man. Since it would lead us beyond the limits of our subject to speak even of the most outstanding of them, I want to mention only a single development which makes tangible the importance of alchemy in the intellectual climate of the age. By the eleventh century the popularity of alchemy created a counter-movement of opinion denying its value and even its reality: Ibn Sīnā himself was willing to recognize only that the alchemists were able to produce something that had external resemblance to the precious metals. In the person of Ḥusayn ʿAlī al-Ṭughrā'ī (d. 1121?) alchemy found a spirited and able defender. In his *Kitāb Ḥaqā'iq al-Istishhād fi al-Kīmiyā* (Book of the Truths of Evidence in Alchemy), written in 1112, Al-Ṭughrā'ī argues that alchemy does not create an absolutely new *faṣl* (*differentia specifica*), but merely prepares matter to take in the *faṣl* granted to it by the Creator. This argument took the wind out of the sails of the orthodox theologians, but by no means put an end to the Muslim polemic about alchemy, which continued into the fourteenth century and in which Ibn Khaldūn joined the anti-alchemist side.

Almost nothing of these storms reverberates in the few passages referring to alchemy contained in the writings of the leading Jewish thinkers of the period. Baḥya ibn Paquda seems to have believed unquestioningly that alchemists can produce gold. Judah Halevi denied the validity of alchemical experiments. Abraham Ibn Ezra believed that the production of drinkable gold was possible, and that there existed a substance which causes gold to be burnt and become black. Judah ben Solomon believed that gold matures gradually in the bosom of the earth out of base metals, but denied the ability of alchemists to duplicate that process in their laboratories. Each of these views is an individual opinion with nothing in common among them, and it is difficult to gauge whether they represent reactions to the strongly held and defended competing views of the Muslim alchemists of the period.

As for the Jewish kabbalistic thinkers of the thirteenth and subsequent centuries, among whom Moses de Leon has the pride of place, they were much more interested in the confirmation they thought they could find in alchemy for the kabbalistic mysteries they discovered in the universe, and in the seemingly limitless possibilities of *gematria* calculations, than in scrutinizing the feasibility of alchemical operations. When, during the Renaissance, the Kabbalah reached the Christian world, it was in these aspects of the strange Jewish mysticism that the Christians found immediate interest, while their own alchemy was slower to penetrate the Jewish kabbalistic spiritual strongholds.

In the introduction to Part Three it was mentioned that the master from whom Ibn Sīnā acquired his alchemical expertise was a Jewish alchemist by the name of Jacob the Jew. Two centuries later we hear of the first Jewish alchemist who taught the Great Art to a Christian scholar. He was Jacobus Aranicus, of whom practically nothing is known, except that he lived in France and was the teacher of Vincent de Beauvais (d. 1264), one of the most celebrated scholars and alchemists of medieval Christian Europe.[1] As we shall see in Chapter 15, by the fourteenth century Jewish alchemists were recognized in the Christian world as masters and authorities whom the Christians sought out when they wished to be initiated into the secrets of the Great Art. Although the available data are too scanty to serve as a basis for any generalization, still there is in them some indication that Jewish alchemists were the teachers of both Muslim and Christian alchemists in the Middle Ages, just as they had been of Hellenistic alchemists in antiquity.

The thirteenth century is notable in the history of Jewish alchemy for one more reason. It is the last century in which all the Jewish alchemists lived in a Muslim environment, although they by no means ceased to write in Arabic, occasionally at least, for several centuries thereafter. In the thirteenth century Jewish alchemists make their first appearance in the Christian world, and thereafter the center of gravity of Jewish alchemy gradually shifted to the West.

Chapter Ten

ARTEPHIUS

ARTEPHIUS, who lived in the twelfth century, was one of the most famous and most respected medieval alchemists. His works are included in the standard alchemical collections, such as the *Theatrum chemicum* and Manget's *Bibliotheca chemica curiosa*, and have been translated into French and German beginning with the early seventeenth century. In 1832 Karl Christoph Schmieder, one of the earliest historians of alchemy, listed them and summarized their contents in his *Geschichte der Alchemie.*[1]

One factor that materially contributed to Artephius's fame was his claim, put forward in his book *Tractatus de vita proroganda* (Tractate about the Prolongation of Life), that with the help of his secret tincture, which he used as a medicament, he had reached the age of 1025 years by the time he embarked on writing this book. Schmieder, after mentioning this detail, adds: "A great word!! No other champion of the panacea had gone this far. This audacity should deprive the adept and inventor of all credit. However, the party of the moderates considers this treatise a counterfeit and falsely attributed to him. This could be the reason why it was never printed and is found only in manuscripts."[2]

Bernard Suler's learned article "Alchemy" in the *Encyclopaedia Judaica*, published in Jerusalem in 1972, states that

> Artephius, the great alchemist of the twelfth century, "before whom there lived no other expert equal to him," was, according to the author of *Keren ha-Pukh* [*Keren Happuch*], a baptized Jew. He is said to have brought the creation of the philosopher's stone to perfection. He wrote three books on alchemy "whose importance is invaluable." . . . Some scholars believe that Artephius was an Arab. However, the fact that he did not write anything in Arabic (all his works were written in Latin), seems to belie this contention.

Suler's source, not easy to trace, was a small pamphlet of forty-two pages, with a preface dated Arnheim, 1700,[3] and an introductory part in which the author recapitulates the well-known biblical pseudo-prehistory of alchemy, with due mention of Adam, Moses, David, Solomon. Then comes the body of the treatise, which consists of a numbered sequence of brief paragraphs, each offering the author's opinion on an alchemist of past ages: Isis "regina Aegypti," Ostanes, Zosimus, Democritus, Virgilius, Papias, Morienus, and so on. No. 19 reads: "Artephius is supposed to have been a converted Jew. In his still extant treatise he is so explicit and clear that he would properly be liked and valued by everybody. What is stated about his great age is rightly doubted, yet his writings remain incomparable."[4]

An expression such as "is supposed to have been a converted Jew" shows nothing more than that there was a rumor to that effect, and cannot be taken as proof positive. Similar uncertainty appears in other sources. In the great four-volume *Bibliotheca Hebraea* published in Hamburg in 1715–1733, the Christian Hebraist and bibliographer Johann Christoph Wolf (1683–1739) presents a list of all the Hebrew books which he either saw himself or found mentioned in other bibliographies. In it the following item appears: "Artephius, pro ex Judaeo venditatur in libro vernaculo. *Fegfeuer der Chymisten* p. 12 ibique scriptio ejus Chymica, satis nota, a perspicuitate laudatur & incomparabilis appellatur, vita vero ejus longior in dubium vocatur (Artephius is praised as an ex-Jew in the vernacular book Purgatory of the Alchemists, p. 12, and in the same place his alchemical writing, sufficiently known, is praised for its clarity and called incomparable; his life, however, has long been called in question."[5]

A still earlier source is the great *Theatrum chemicum*, in which the following prefatori remark introduces Artefius's (spelled thus) *Liber qui clavis majoris sapientiae dicitur* (The Book Called the Key of Major Wisdom): "It is not sufficiently agreed, however, who this Artefius was. Somebody thinks that he was a Jew; about him there are certain things in Roger Bacon and Cardan: of how much erudition, morever, this book will be able to demonstrate, in which there are some things beyond credibility; I should like to persuade you that they are enigmas; those things which, indeed, are clearly physical have been woven together with marvelous skill."[6] Although these statements do not prove that Artephius was Jewish, or a converted Jew, they at least indicate that in the early seventeenth century (or perhaps even earlier) he was rumored to have been one.

On the other hand, Artephius is frequently identified as an Arab. The title of his earliest printed book reads: *Artefii Arabis liber secretus artis occultae* (The Secret Book of the Occult Art of Artefius the Arab). In the late eighteenth century, Gmelin wrote that the disciples of Artephius considered him a descendant of Arabs.[7] In 1870, M. Chevreul inclined to the view that Artephius was of Arab origin.[8] In 1876, a German scholar, Gildemeister, identified Artephius with the Arab poet and alchemist al-Ṭughrā'ī, who was put to death about 1119–1120 or 1121–1122.[9]

On the other hand, Schmieder argued in 1832 that Artephius "was not an Arab, as some want to suppose; nor is it proven that he descended from Arab parents. He wrote only in Latin. . . . He quotes Adfar often, and is himself quoted by Roger Bacon; for which reason one can place him between the two, that is, in the year 1150."[10] Several other historians of alchemy speak of Artephius without mentioning any theory or assumption as to his descent.

It is interesting that Artephius was not at all consistent in the interpretation of alchemical terminology. He explains, for example, the frequently used term *laton* as gold (par. 1), and as "the body compounded of sol [gold] and luna [silver] by our first water" (par. 15). He gives his own interpretation to the *balneum Mariae* (*bain Marie*) as "our fiery and sulphureous water" (par. 31). In another passage (par. 6) he gives a variant interpretation of *balneum Mariae*. *Azoth* for him is "our water, which can take from the perfect bodies of sol and luna their natural color, making the red body white[11] (par. 32). Following the restrictions enunciated by Maria the Jewess, who wished to reserve alchemical knowledge to the Jews, Artephius states that he is willing to reveal everything one needs to know in order to perfect the philosophers' stone "excepting one certain thing which is not lawful for me to discover to any, because it is either revealed or made known by God himself" (par. 30). As against the mystifying references to the "great arcanum, viz. a water of saturnine antimony, mercurial and white" (par. 2), he states explicitly that this water "brings back bodies to their first original of sulphur and mercury, [so] that of them we may afterwards in a little time, in less than an hour's time, do that above ground which nature was a thousand years doing underground, in the mines of the earth, which is a work almost miraculous" (par. 10). However, the "ultimate or highest secret is, by this water, to make bodies volatile, spiritual, and a tincture, or tinging water which may have ingress or entrance into bodies, for it makes bodies to be merely spirit[11] (par. 11). Nor was sexual imagery foreign to Artephius, as can be seen from this statement of his: "Between the body and the [philosophers'] water there is a desire and friendship, like as between the male and the female, because of the propinquity and likeness of their natures" (par. 14).

Chapter Eleven

THE GREAT JEWISH PHILOSOPHERS

THE ELEVENTH, twelfth, and thirteenth centuries were the great age of medieval Jewish philosophy. After a deep sleep of several centuries following Philo of Alexandria, Jewish philosophy awakened to new life under the impact of Arab philosophy, which in turn, was the child of Greek philosophy made available in Arabic translations.[1] The writings of several of the great medieval Jewish philosophers show that they were familiar with alchemy, that they were willing to go along with its theories, and that they accepted the alchemists' claims of being able to transmute base metals into precious ones. In addition, statements made by some Jewish philosophers about alchemy and alchemists give us an insight into the social position occupied by alchemists, their way of life, and the benefits and dangers of their work.

In this chapter we shall discuss briefly what four outstanding medieval Jewish philosophers had to say about alchemy and what we can learn from their statements about the place of alchemy in their society. As we shall see, nowhere do the authors state that the alchemists they speak about were Jews. But given the close participation of the Jews of Muslim and Christian Spain and of other Mediterranean countries in the social and intellectual life of their non-Jewish environment, and data culled from other sources, we can take it for granted that when our authors wrote about alchemists their observations applied to both non-Jewish and Jewish adepts.

Baḥya Ibn Paquda

Baḥya ibn Paquda was a Jewish religious philosopher who lived in the second half of the eleventh century in Muslim Spain, probably in Saragossa. He wrote his major work, *Kitāb al-Hidāya ilā Farā'id al-Qulūb* (Book of Guidance to the Duties of the Hearts) in Arabic, about 1080.[2] It was translated into Hebrew in 1161 by Judah ibn Tibbon under the title *Ḥovot haL'vavot* (Duties of the Hearts), became popular, and had a profound influence on all subsequent Jewish moralistic-ethical literature. Although the book evinces strong Muslim-Arab, Neoplatonic, and possibly also Hermetic influences, it remains an essentially Jewish book. Its purpose is to lead the reader to a spiritual perfection in strict accordance with the teachings of Jewish religion. In modern times it has been translated into the major European languages as well as into Yiddish. Although a fine English translation is available (it was done by M. Hyamson and published in 1962), I have given the excerpt below in my own translation (based on Ibn Tibbon's Hebrew version to which the book owes its popularity), to make sure that all the nuances of its typical medieval style are reproduced exactly.

In its chapter 4, titled "On Trusting in God, Blessed be He," Baḥya compares the advantages accruing to him who puts his trust in God with those acquired by a master alchemist who can make gold. He concludes, as could be expected, that trust in God is a much more valuable attainment than alchemical mastery, and in the course of comparing the two achievements paints a rather dismal picture of the worries and dangers to which the alchemist is constantly exposed.

However, what is more interesting for us in the present context is that of all the possible careers open to talented individuals (including Jews) in eleventh-century Muslim Spain, which included such positions as that of statesman, army commander, physician, poet, philosopher, astronomer, geometrist, cartographer, architect, and the like, Baḥya should have selected that of the alchemist to compare with the values inherent in the trust in God. It is possible that among the Jewish intellectual elite of Muslim Spain, the work and the social position of the alchemist were considered the most appealing and rewarding, so that when Baḥya searched for a foil against which to offset the supreme good man could derive from trusting God, he selected the career of the alchemist. By so doing, he was saying in effect, "You believe that the supreme good one can attain in this world is to be a master alchemist; lo, I shall show you that even that is a paltry thing compared to the benefits one can derive from trusting God." He marshals ten arguments, each of them interspersed with many biblical quotations which are not included in the following. Baḥya begins by saying that he who puts his trust in God

> will in the quietness of his soul and the breadth of his heart and the smallness of his worries about his affairs be like the master of alchemy, that is, a man who can transmute silver into gold, and copper and tin into silver, through wisdom and deed. However, he who trusts in God will have the advantage over him [the alchemist] in ten things:
>
> The first of them is that the master of alchemy needs special things for this work and cannot complete anything without them, and cannot find them every time and in every place. . . .
>
> Second, the master of alchemy needs acts and works without which he cannot obtain that which he desires, and it can happen that the smell and smoke will kill him due to the constant work and length of the effort he devotes to them night and day. . . .

Third, the master of alchemy does not entrust his secret to anybody else for he fears for his life. . . .

Fourth, the master of alchemy cannot escape from ordering much gold and silver to have ready in time of need; or he will order nothing of them but only as much as is sufficient for a short time. And if he orders much of it, he will live in fear for his life all his days lest some of it get lost, and his heart will never be tranquil and his soul will not rest, because of his fear of the king and the people; and if he orders of them only as much as is required to fill his need for a short time it can happen that he will be unable to accomplish the work at the time when his need will be great, because one of the factors will be withheld from him. . . .

Fifth, the master of alchemy always trembles because of his work for fear of the king [and] down to the smallest of the people. . . .

Sixth, the master of alchemy is never safe from illnesses and pains which are mixed in with his joy and richness, and these never let him enjoy what he has, nor to take pleasure in what his hands have achieved. . . .

Seventh, the master of alchemy risks not to be able to obtain his food with all the gold and silver he possesses, because food may not be available in his city in certain times. . . .

Eighth, the master of alchemy does not tarry in any place for fear lest his secret be discovered. . . .

Ninth, the master of alchemy is not accompanied by his alchemy at the end of his life, and he achieves through it nothing but security from poverty and human need. . . .

Tenth, the master of alchemy, if he knows his work, it will be the cause of his death, because that which he endeavors to achieve is the opposite of the way of the world, and the leadership [i.e., the king and the government] will send somebody to kill him when he can no longer hide his secret.

A number of interesting things emerge from this portrait of the alchemist. First of all it becomes clear that Baḥya believed in the ability of the alchemists to transmute base metals into precious ones. Second, he knew that alchemical experimentation can be dangerous, and that the smoke and smell produced by it can cause serious illnesses and pain to the alchemist, and can even kill him. From the third, fourth, and fifth points we can conclude that Baḥya's alchemist acquaintances were secretive and feared for their life. The fourth point also informs us that the alchemists known to Baḥya used gold and silver in their work, probably for operations to "multiply" these precious metals by increasing their bulk or weight with the addition of base metals. From point eight we can conclude that the alchemists frequently moved from place to place. And, finally, point ten seems to indicate that the life of alchemists was frequently in danger from the powerful of the society in which they worked. Although Baḥya undoubtedly exaggerates each of the features he describes—he does so in order to give more weight to his argument that piety was a better way of life than the practice of alchemy—there must have been at least some truth to each of his points.

Juda Halevi

Information on the position of medieval Jewish thinkers on alchemy can be gleaned from Judah Halevi's *Book of the Kuzari*. Judah Halevi (before 1075–1141) was born in Tudela, or possibly in Toledo, lived most of his life in Spain, practiced medicine, apparently in the service of the king and his nobles in Toledo, and in 1140 set out for Palestine, but after reaching Egypt he remained there for several months until he died. Considered the greatest medieval Hebrew poet, Halevi wrote love poems, poems of eulogy and lament, *piyyuṭim* (liturgical poems), and songs of Zion which express his longing for Ereṣ Israel. He wrote one philosophical work, the *Kuzari*, on which he worked for some twenty years and which he completed shortly before he set out on his voyage for Palestine.

The frame-story of the *Kuzari* is this: The king of the Khazars (the Kuzari) is induced by a dream to discover what proper conduct is, and invites first an Aristotelian philosopher and then representatives of Islam, Christianity, and Judaism to learn of their respective beliefs. In the course of the discussion the king has with the Jewish scholar, the latter has an opportunity to present a detailed picture of Jewish religion, history, beliefs, and worldview, and to offer a Jewish polemic against Aristotle, Christianity, and Islam. The rabbi also argues that all science originated with the Jews, and that other nations can approach God only through the intermediacy of Israel, since the prophetic faculty is hereditary and unique to the people of Israel. At the end the Kuzari is convinced, and converts to Judaism.

The rabbi is, of course, a mask of Judah Halevi himself, and from his words we learn what Halevi considered the beliefs and tenets of Judaism. In addition, they reveal what he knew and believed about various issues that were of importance in the intellectual environment in which he lived. One of these was alchemy, and it is of interest in our present context to examine what this exponent of Jewish philosophical thinking of his times has to say on the subject.

Two passages in the *Kuzari* deal with alchemy. In the first the rabbi explains to the king that the species of plants and animals are developed

> according to the proportion of heat and cold, moisture and dryness. . . . We are unable to determine these proportions, and could we do it, we

> might produce blood or milk, etc., from liquids mixed according to our calculations. We might eventually create living beings endowed with the spirit of life. Or we might produce a substitute for bread from ingredients that have no nourishing powers, simply by mixing the right proportions of heat and cold, moisture and dryness, and particularly if we knew the spherical constellations and their influences which, in the opinion of astrologers, assist in bringing forth anything that is desired in this world. We have seen, however, that all alchemists and necromancers who have tried those things have been put to shame. Do not raise the objection that these people are able to produce animals and living beings, as bees from flesh, and gnats from wine. These are not the consequence of their calculations and agency, but of experiments.

In the second passage the rabbi explains that "the alchemists and necromancers" are in error.

> The former thought, indeed, that they could weigh the elementary fire on their scales, and produce what they wished, and thus alter the nature of materials as is done in living beings by natural heat which transforms food into blood, flesh, bone, and organs. They toil to discover a fire of the same kind, but are misled by accidental results of their experiments, not based on calculation, just in the same manner as the discovery was made that from the planting of seed within the womb man arises.[3]

The first thing we learn from these passages is that Judah Halevi believed, together with his contemporary scholars and philosophers, that a precise knowledge of the four Aristotelian qualities of heat and cold, moisture and dryness, would enable the experimenter to produce any substance and even life forms. Second, we learn that he also believed that an essential ingredient in the proper proportion of substances and living beings was the influence of "the spherical constellations." Third, he believed that the alchemists and necromancers did not succeed in their efforts in this field, because their calculations were inadequate, but they did succeed in producing some living beings by experiments that by chance led to results.

From the second passage we learn that Judah Halevi believed that it was "natural heat" that transformed food into the bodies of living beings. The alchemists thought, he reports, that by weighing the elementary fire on their scales—by which he probably refers to an accurate method of controlling the heat of fire—they could likewise alter the nature of materials. However, he states, the alchemists are in error, and whatever they do achieve by their experiments is due not to calculation but to mere accident.

Thus Judah Halevi went along with the general views of his time and place on the nature and composition of substances and of the bodies of living beings, and believed that by lucky chance experimenters can produce results that duplicate that which the influence of the constellations and of elementary fire creates in this world. However, he denied the value of these chance outcomes of experiments—a position similar to that of modern science, which insists that experiments must be capable of being duplicated and repeated. Most interesting, however, from the point of view of the history of alchemy is that from his references it appears that alchemists in his time were not concerned with the possibility of transmuting base metals into gold and finding the mysterious philosophers' stone—he makes no mention of these things—but concentrated on using the power of fire to create living beings.

Abraham ibn Ezra

A younger contemporary of Baḥya ibn Paquda was Abraham ibn Ezra (1089–1164), one of the greatest figures of Spanish Jewry. Born in Toledo, Ibn Ezra spent the first fifty years of his life in Spain, although he may have paid extended visits to various North African Jewish centers during those years. The last twenty-five years of his life he spent wandering in Italy and France. Despite his unsettled life, Ibn Ezra's literary output was nothing short of phenomenal. He was a great Hebrew poet, wrote several philosophical works, was an important Hebrew grammarian, the author of numerous books on astrology, astronomy, and mathematics, and, last but not least, an outstanding biblical commentator. Ibn Ezra's commentary on the Bible retained its value through the ages. In the *Miqraot G'dolot*, a valuable and popular edition of the Bible with thirty-two commentaries published in Warsaw in 1860, it is given a place of honor: the sacred text is flanked by Rashi's commentary on one side, and by Ibn Ezra's on the other.

Two brief comments in Ibn Ezra's biblical commentary touch upon alchemical matters. The first is his explanation of the personal name Mē-Zahav (Gen. 36:39), the name of the grandfather (or grandmother) of Mehetabel, the wife of Hadar, king of Edom. The literal translation of Mē-Zahav is "water of gold," and Ibn Ezra comments, "This is his name, and the Gaon said, refiner of gold, and others said, a hint at those who make gold out of copper, but these are *divrē ruaḥ* [words of wind, that is, empty words]."[4]

This comment of Ibn Ezra can be interpreted as meaning that he did not believe in the possibility of transmuting copper into gold, but it can also mean that he considered baseless the explanation of the name Mē-Zahav as meaning "refiner of gold," or as hinting at those who made gold out of copper.

The second comment relating to gold shows that he was both acquainted with, and believed in, the alchemical manipulation of gold. It is appended to Exodus 32:20, which states that after Moses came down from Mount Sinai and saw the Children of Israel worshiping the golden calf, "he took the calf which they had made, and burned it in fire, and ground it until it became fine, and scattered it upon the face of the water, and made the Children of Israel drink it." Ibn Ezra explains: "Some say that Moses burned it means that he melted it down in fire. But this [explanation] is unnecessary, for there is a substance which, if put into the fire with the gold, the gold is instantly burned and becomes black, and will never again become gold. And this is proven and true." This biblical passage has become the locus classicus for medieval alchemists who wanted to prove that their quest for aurum potabile, drinkable gold, which they considered a form of the elixir, was within the realm of the possible, for behold, Moses did produce a liquid gold or a gold liquid which he gave the Children of Israel to drink.

Judah ben Solomon

An early thirteenth-century Jewish philosopher who showed interest in alchemy, was Judah ben Solomon haKohen ibn Matka. Born in Toledo, Judah became a disciple of Meir Abulafia, and in 1245 wrote in Arabic an encyclopedic work on logic, physics, metaphysics, psychology, geometry, astronomy, and other topics, based primarily on Greek authors. He also wrote several other books, some of which he himself translated into Hebrew. He was a highly respected scholar, was recognized as such by the gentiles as well, and corresponded with Frederick II (1194–1250), the Holy Roman Emperor, who was a man with considerable scientific interest.

Judah believed, together with all the alchemists of the Middle Ages, that gold developed in nature, slowly, out of base metals. But this is how far he went in accepting the claims of alchemists. After a discussion with a non-Jew, he remarked:

> Research is not the main thing, but the act. Of what use is their wisdom to the wise? Does one not find among them more bad mores and deception than among all the fools? For they use their wisdom only for images [*ṣ'lamim*], or for sensual gratification [*ḥesheq*], or for the pretense or fabrication of gold which they call "the Great Art," but in which they will never succeed, because it is impossible. It is about such vain words that Solomon said (Prov. 29:3), "He that keepeth company with harlots wasteth his substance."[5]

This brief passage shows that some medieval Jewish scholars who were acquainted with alchemical theory and went along with it drew the line when it came to the alchemists' claim that they were able to transmute base metals into gold. As for Judah's pronouncement that the alchemists would never succeed in fabricating gold, it gives the impression that it must have been preceded by some actual observation of alchemists at work or by a discussion of the issue with knowledgeable people.

Chapter Twelve

KABBALAH AND ALCHEMY: A RECONSIDERATION

IN THE FOURTEENTH century, when the Kabbalah emerged as a powerful factor in Jewish religious life, alchemy had been entrenched in the Muslim world for centuries, and could look back upon a history of several generations in Christian Europe. The Jews, who up to that time were actively involved with secular culture primarily in the Muslim countries, participated, as could be expected, in the alchemical work practiced there, and translated into Hebrew several alchemical treatises which were either written originally in Arabic or were Arabic reworkings of Greek originals. In some cases such treatises survived only in their Hebrew versions, so that, occasionally at least, the Jewish alchemists saved originally non-Jewish alchemical writings for posterity.

We have no way of knowing how many of the Jewish authors who became followers of the Kabbalah had a previous familiarity with alchemy. Inasmuch as Sephardi authors and scholars in general were acquainted with the arts and sciences of their Muslim, and later Christian, environment, it is likely that all of them knew of the theories and practices of alchemy, and most of them accepted if not the feasibility of transmuting base metals into gold at least the alchemical theory of their gradual ripening into gold in the earth. This theory was easily reconcilable with biblical teachings and, in fact, was shown to harmonize with biblical passages.

Given these antecedents, it was practically inevitable that those Jewish scholars who fell under the sway of kabbalism should utilize alchemical theories that readily lent themselves to a mystical interpretation (or reinterpretation), and thus were felt to be grist to the mill of kabbalistic thinking. Where the alchemists spoke of the gradual transformation of the metals in the bosom of the earth, until, in the course of time, they matured and reached the ripe stage of the perfect metal, gold, the Kabbalists understood this to be a "great mystery," a hidden process taking place under the influence of mysterious supernal powers. When the alchemists spoke of gold as "sun," and of silver as "moon," the Kabbalists sensed in this a reference to the mysterious influences emanating from the supernal realm and exerting an effect on the likewise mysterious spiritual essence contained in earthly substances. In the kabbalistic references to alchemical ideas there is a surfeit of "mysteries" or "secrets" (the Hebrew *sod* and Aramaic *raza* mean both), and by inserting this term frequently into their comments touching upon alchemical matters they gave the latter a theosophical coloration, and fitted them into the complex kabbalistic imagery of a mystical-spiritual universe. At the end of this chapter, in discussing the writings of Moses de Leon, we shall present examples to support this generalization.

There was, moreover, a certain a priori affinity between the world view of alchemy and that of the Kabbalah. The alchemist considered all existing things, whether mineral, vegetable, animal, or human, as containing a basically identical essence—this is emphasized in every study discussing alchemy—and an almost identical doctrine underlay kabbalistic thought. One kabbalistic manifestation of this idea was the belief in metempsychosis, the transmigration of souls, which assumed that one and the same soul (i.e., spiritual essence) could inhabit in turn a human being, an animal, or a plant, and move from one such body into another. For people habituated to believe in this doctrine there was nothing strange in the idea that lead, copper, silver, gold, and so on were essentially the same, and were but disparate forms containing the same metallic "soul."

The alchemists, building on concepts of ancient Greek philosophers such as Empedocles and Aristotle, postulated four "elements"—fire, water, air, and earth—indwelling all the existing substances, each in a specific proportion of its own. In this again there was nothing extraordinary for the Kabbalists, who readily adopted and spiritualized the idea by the simple expedient of pronouncing it "a supernal mystery."[1] By the same mental process, the Kabbalah spiritualized the other basic alchemical idea, that there were four qualities—heat, cold, dryness, and moisture—which too had their share in the formation of every existing thing. Of course, they pronounced this too a great mystery.

An original contribution of the Kabbalah to this alchemical world view was the mystical theory that there was a dichotomy, or duplication, between the two worlds of the Above and the Below, that there were mutual influences emanating from each of the two, and that not only did powers from the Above, such as the power of the (spiritualized) sun, bring about a ripening into gold of the metals down here Below (as alchemy taught), but also human acts down here could produce major changes in the Above—as, for example, when King David brought about the "perfection" of the moon.[2] Thus for kabbalistic alchemy there was not only a "mystery of the seven metals," but also a "mystery of the supernal and the lower silver and gold"[3] and a rich array of other such discoveries of mysteries in the physical realm.

Although the influence of alchemy on the Kabbalah was confined to such theoretical considerations, and to a contribution of certain concepts that the Kabbalists were able to add to their storehouse of "mysteries," the flow of influence in the reverse direction was stronger. From the fifteenth and sixteenth centuries on, the Kabbalah attracted the attention of Christian scholars of the ilk of Johannes Reuchlin (1455–1522), Pietro Galatinus (1460–1540), and Pico della Mirandola (1463–1494), whose writings made the doctrines and methods of the Kabbalah accessible to Christian alchemists. Foremost among them was the Cardinal Egidio da Viterbo (ca. 1465–1532), who translated, or sponsored the translation of, extracts from the Zohar and various esoteric tracts (such as the *Ginnat Egoz, Raziel*, etc.), and composed a treatise on the ten sefirot, the ten stages of emanations that form the realm of God's manifestation in His various attributes.[4] As Hermann Sprengel observed, "Theosophical ideas received a significant impetus from the spread of the Kabbalah, or the Oriental system of emanations, presented by scholarly Jews with even more cunning [!], and interlaced with related fancies of the Neo-Platonics."[5] The Christian alchemists pounced upon certain doctrines that they found in the kabbalistic literature, and that they felt had important alchemical implications. One of those doctrines was that of the kabbalistic sefirot, which they forthwith proceeded to interpret alchemically; the other the so-called *gematria*, the kabbalistic method of interpreting biblical (and other) words by calculating the numerical value of the letters (consonants) contained in them, which the Christian alchemists adopted for use in their work.

By the beginning of the sixteenth century, the connection between the kabbalistic doctrines in general and the kabbalistic sefirot in particular was established. Cornelius Agrippa (1486–1535) in his *De incertitudine* mentions that "the learned Jews attribute the number thirty-two to Wisdom, for so many are the ways of Wisdom described by Abraham."[6] In his *De occulta philosophia* (published 1533; III, ch. 10) Agrippa discusses the Kabbalah along with alchemy and astrology, refers Saturn to the sefira of Binah (Intelligence), Jupiter to Ḥesed (Mercy), Mars to Gevurah (Power), the Sun to Tif'eret (Beauty), Venus to Neṣaḥ (Lasting Endurance), Mercury to Hod (Majesty), and the Moon to Yesod (Foundation). In another part of his book (I, chs. 23–29), Agrippa fully develops the correspondence between the planets and the metals. This book was written prior to 1510, since it is prefaced by a letter written by the Abbot Trithemius dated 1510. Soon after its publication the relationship between the metals and the kabbalistic sefirot came to be presented in the *Esh M'ṣaref* (The Refiner's Fire), written in Hebrew or Aramaic by a Jewish author who codified in it the correspondence between the ten kabbalistic sefirot and the seven metals. Chapter

26 will present the full text of the *Esh M'ṣaref* together with a discussion of its alchemical ideas.

Gematria (pl. *gematriyot*; from the Greek *grammateion*) was introduced into talmudic hermeneutics from ancient Near Eastern Gnostic and Hellenistic cultures to serve as a basis for midrashic interpretations of biblical words and passages, and to attribute to or derive from them totally extraneous meanings. Its use became widespread in the post-talmudic age, in midrashim and rabbinic literature. The gematriyot are based on the fact that each of the twenty-two letters of the Hebrew alphabet has, in addition to its phonemic value, also a numerical value (alef = 1, bet = 2, . . . yod = 10, kaf = 20, . . . qof = 100, resh = 200, shin = 300, and tav = 400). In traditional Hebrew literature, down to the twentieth century, no other numerical notation was used. Numbers of chapters and of pages, measurements, amounts, years, and days of the month, and so on, were always written in letters of the Hebrew alphabet. Thus, for instance, the famous 613 commandments the rabbis counted in the Torah were always referred to as the *TaRYaG miṣvot* (tav = 400, resh = 200, yod = 10, and gimel = 3; the vowels do not count).

This method opened up almost unlimited possibilities of biblical interpretation. For instance, Rashi (1040–1105), the greatest of biblical commentators, explains that when Jacob said "I have sojourned with Laban" (Gen. 32:5), what he intended to convey was that "even though I sojourned with evil Laban, I observed the 613 commandments," which Rashi derives from the gematria of the letters of the word GaRTY (*garti*, "I sojourned"): G = 3 + R = 200 + T = 400 + Y = 10 = 613.

It was in kabbalistic literature that the most extensive use was made of gematriot, and several (according to Moses Cordovero no fewer than nine) gematria systems were developed. The systems became so comprehensive and flexible that practically any idea could be supported by a gematria. In Chapter 26 there are several examples of the use of Gematriot by a Jewish alchemist.

The opening up of the hidden mysteries of the Kabbalah to the Christian scholarly world also made the secret methods of the *gematria* calculations available to it. This in turn led rapidly to their adoption by Christian alchemists and their utilization in the theoretical underpinning of the Great Work. It was thus that "kabbalistic alchemy" developed—not, as one would have imagined, among Jewish alchemists, but among their Christian colleagues. This led the latter to a revival of the Hellenistic alchemical attitude: the attribution of mysterious potency to Hebrew words in general. Even when Christian scholars did not explicitly make use of gematria calculations, the very fact that Hebrew words concealed in themselves the possibilities of an unforeseeable variety of meanings, connections, and hints was sufficient to make Hebrew words, and even single letters of the Hebrew alphabet, of awesome esoteric value in the eyes of the Christian adepts. In fact, from about the fifteenth century on, there was scarcely an alchemical book or treatise written by Christian alchemists that did not display conspicuously some Hebrew power-words on the title page or inside the text. A striking example is one of the most influential alchemical compendiums, Heinrich Khunrath's *Amphitheatrum sapientiae*,[7] which has a very impressive large, circular illustration. Unless one has a close look and notices that in its middle there is depicted a small naked human figure with horizontally outstretched arms, and around it the Latin words *Vere filius* DEI ERAT IPSE (Truly, he was the Son of God), one has the impression of seeing a complex Jewish emblem written in Hebrew (Fig. 12.1). On top of the big circle there is a small triangle inscribed with the Hebrew letters Y, YH, YHW, YHWH, the last line of which gives the sacred Tetragrammaton. Under the triangle is the Latin word OMNIA. All around are eight concentric circles, five of them in Hebrew letters, which are a veritable brief anthology of important quotations and names of Jewish religious significance. The outermost circle contains the Hebrew text of the Ten Commandments. The second circle, the Hebrew angelic names Tarshishim, Ḥayyot haQodesh, Ofanim, Er'elim, Ḥashmalim, S'rafim, Mal'akhim, Elohim (not an angelic but a divine name), Bne Elohim (sons of God), K'ruvim (cherubim), Ishim (men). The third circle has in Latin translation the beginning of the Shemaʿ prayer (Deut. 6:5), with the added words "and with all thy mind": *Diliges Dominum Deum tuum ex toto corde tuo et ex tota anima tua, et ex omnibus viribus tuis et ex tota mente tua*, followed by the Latin translation of the famous basic Jewish religious commandment, *et proximum tuum sicut teipsum*, that is "and [love] thy neighbor as thyself" (Lev. 19:18).

The fourth circle consists of the twenty-two letters of the Hebrew alphabet. The fifth lists, in Hebrew, the ten sefirot: Keter, Ḥokhmah, and so on, and inserted into them is at the top the Hebrew word *En Sof*, infinite, and at the bottom *Emet*, truth, and in between are drawings of clouds. The sixth circle is double: it consists of the Hebrew letters Y H sh W H, which looks like an attempt to transliterate the name Jesus into Hebrew, and of the divine names Ehyeh, Yhwh, El, Elohim, Gibbor, Adonay, Melekh, Shaddai, Elohim Ṣ'vaot, Yhwh Ṣ'vaot, Eloah. Inside this is the seventh circle containing the words IN HOC SIGNO VINCES (In this sign you will conquer). Then follows the smallest, innermost circle already mentioned, with the small figure of Jesus in the center, and under it the picture of the burning Phoenix. Outside the outermost circle, in very small letters, is the identification of the author and the illustrator: "Henricus Khunrath Lips. Theosophiae amator et Medicinae utrius Doctor. Dei gratia in vintor Paulius vander Doorf Antwerp scalpsit."

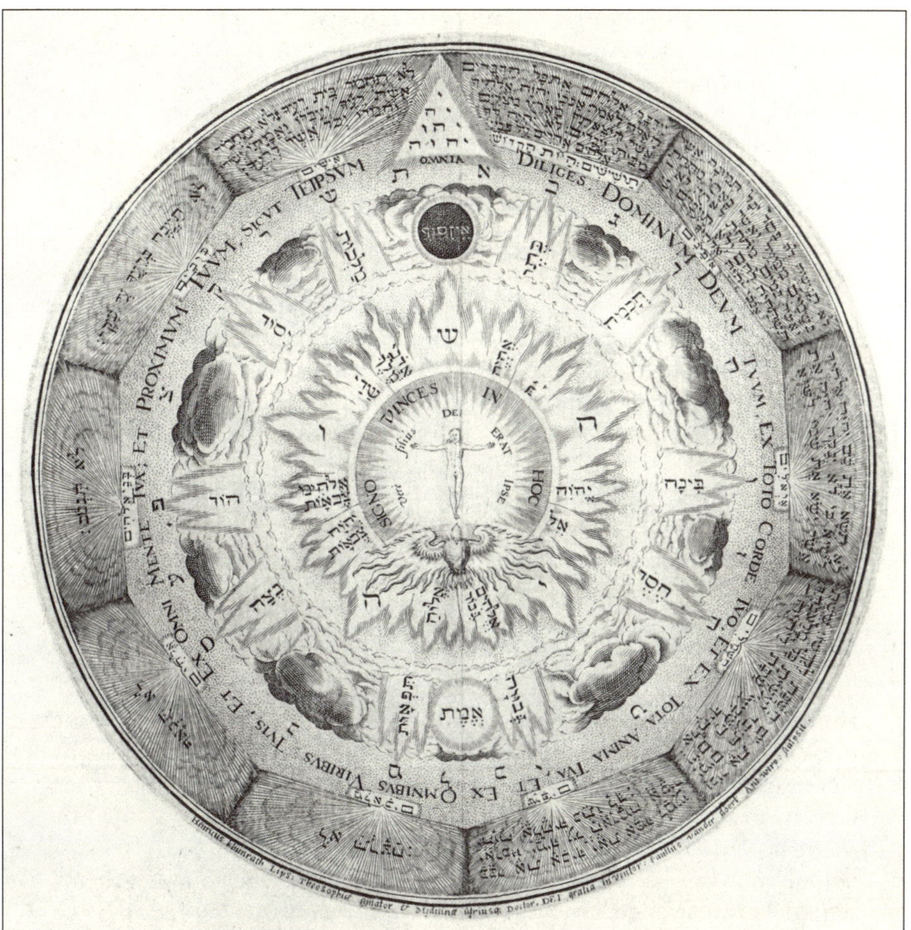

Figure 12.1. The World of the Spheres.

Khunrath says in this book that the philosophers' stone is said to be identical with the *Ruaḥ Elohim*, the Spirit of God, which brooded over the waters during the first period of Creation.[8] This is perhaps the most striking example of the daring reinterpretation of the biblical text by Christian alchemists in their efforts to anchor alchemical concepts in the Holy Scripture.

An important contribution to the study of the relationship between Kabbalah and alchemy is the treatise of (Pseudo-)Simeon ben Cantara, entitled *Cabala mineralis* (Mineral Kabbalah), which was published in 1986 in a scholarly edition, with detailed analyses of its context and background.[9] *Cabala mineralis* has survived in two manuscripts, both probably dating from the seventeenth century, one preserved in the British Library (MS Add. 5245), the other in a private collection. The latter is reproduced in the book in its entirety, and its relationship to other kabbalistic-alchemical treatises of the period is discussed.

The treatise is a review of alchemical interpretations of the biblical creation story of Genesis, as well as of the opposition to them. It follows in the footsteps of Giovanni Agostino Pantheus, the Venetian priest, who in his *Voarchadumia* (published in Venice in 1518) pioneered in establishing a relationship between alchemy and rabbinical science, and maintained that the very word "alchemy" was derived from the Hebrew. After it, many of the speculative alchemical treatises had the word "Kabbalah" in their title. Among them was Franz Kieser's *Cabala chymica* (Frankfurt, 1606), Stephen Michelspacher's *Cabala sive speculum artis et naturae in alchymia* (Augsburg, 1615–1616), the *Cabala chymica ab anonymo quodam compilata* (Hamburg, 1680), and Johann Grasshof's *Cabala chymica* (published in the *Philosophia Salomonis*, Augsburg, 1753). This reliance on the Kabbalah being the general trend of sixteenth- to eighteenth-century alchemy, it was inevitable that Hebrew words should be found frequently in the texts, notably in those of Bang, Muller, Maulius, Sallwigt, and Wienner.

Hand in hand with this "Hebraization" of alchemy went the doctrine that even the legendary ancestor figure of alchemy, the "thrice-great" Hermes Trismegistus, obtained his knowledge of the Royal Art from the Book of Genesis of Moses. This was stated several times, for example, by Gerhard Dorn: "All agree that Hermes Trismegistus was taught by the Genesis of the Hebrews, even though he was an Egyptian, as stated by Augustine [in his] book *De civitate Dei*, Suidas, etc."[10]

One more aspect of the relationship between Kabbalah and alchemy should be mentioned briefly. The Jewish alchemists who came to the Royal Art from a kabbalistic background brought with them a mindset predisposed to having a profound sympathy for and a deep understanding of the central tenet of alchemy, which taught that the many substances of the physical world were but multiform manifestations of the same basic ultimate essence that informed them all. This was the doctrine that underlay the major preoccupation of alchemists, which was to track down and isolate that essence, and thus to be able to change any one of the many forms of matter into any other. The Kabbalists were suffused with the idea of the identity of the most varied manifestations in the spiritual realm. For instance, they were taught in their most revered books, and therefore unquestioningly believed, that the Shekhina, the mystical spouse of God the King, was at one and the same time also the divine Matronit (matron), the Sefira (emanation) of Malkhut (kingship), and the oral Torah, the Community of Israel, Mother Zion, and so on, and was, in addition, identified with dozens of other mystical entities, such as the Queen, the Holy Spirit, the Moon, the River, the Lower Mother, Rachel, and so on.

This kabbalistic tendency of multiple identifications is found as early as the writings of Philo of Alexandria, so that it preceeds the Spanish Kabbalah by more than a millennium.[11] In the Middle Ages one of its expressions was the use of gematria, which presupposed a basic identity of the most disparate concepts, hidden but discernible in the identity of the numerical value of the letters of which the words denoting them were composed. One particular expression of this kabbalistic tendency to identify multiformities was the tradition called Ḥokhmat haṢeruf, which has a suggestive double meaning: it means "Wisdom of Combination," that is, of the gematria, and also "Wisdom of Refining," that is, of refining the heart by concentrating on divine matters, which recalls the work of alchemical *ṣeruf*, of refining and thus ennobling the quality of metals. The common feature between these kabbalistic ideas and those of alchemy is the tacitly accepted axiom that beneath all diversities lies a hidden essential identity or an identical essence.

To this context belongs also the remarkable correspondence, on the one hand between the sacred marriage of God the King and his spouse the Matronit, which is a central theme in kabbalistic mysticism, and, on the other, between the *conjunctio*, the alchemical marriage, or "chymical wedding," of sun and moon (and we must not forget that sun and moon in alchemy stood for gold and silver), of king and queen, of spirit and body. Nor did the Jewish alchemist find it too strange that in alchemical imagery the two partners in the *conjunctio* were often spoken of as brother and sister; after all, from his readings in kabbalistic literature he was well acquainted with the idea that the King and his Matronit, whose unification was the major purpose of mystical practice, were brother and sister.

What all this amounts to is that there were a priori facets of sympathy between Kabbalah and alchemy: the Kabbalists were prepared and predisposed by their teachings to take up alchemy, in which they found application to the physical world of doctrines that they believed were valid in the worlds of the divine, of the spirit, and of the soul; whereas the alchemists found much in the Kabbalah which not only served their purposes but added a new dimension to their alchemical philosophy. The alchemical view of the nature of substances and the transmutability of one of them into another penetrated the mystical world of the Kabbalah, and contributed additional, previously unsuspected, mysteries to its worldview, and to its interpretation of the mutual interdependence of the Above and the Below. The Kabbalah, in turn, enriched alchemy with its numerological-mystical gematria, in which alchemists found a legitimation of their belief in the interrelationships among substances, and of their search for the common essence which had to underlie the baffling multiplicity of tangible forms. More important, the Kabbalah supplied the alchemists with a quasi sanctification of their views by opening up to them its doctrine of the cosmological structure of the sefirot, which taught them that not only the hidden essence of materia but even the divine unity itself was expressed in multiple mystical manifestations.

Moses de Leon

Of the great variety of types of literature produced by the Jews in the course of the three millennia of their history there is none as difficult to understand, translate, or merely describe as that of the Kabbalah. The typical kabbalistic mode of thinking is replete with symbolism, often vague and obscure, with interchangeable concepts, with ideational jumps from one subject to another, with the equation of disparate matters on the basis of purely formal characteristics of the words designating them which have nothing to do with the meaning of those words, and the like. To what extent these features characterize kabbalistic literature, and in particular the *Zohar*, to which we now turn, will be amply demonstrated by the excerpts which we present from that magnum opus of the Kabbalah.

The *Zohar* is a huge book, published in three volumes in the standard edition and comprising a total of some 850,000 words. It is written almost entirely in Aramaic, and the claim is made in it that it was written by R. Shimʿon ben Yoḥai, a leading *tanna* (mishnaic master), who lived in the second century C.E. in Palestine, and had the reputation of a miracle worker. Formally it is a commentary on the Bible, but in fact it is a rambling mystical discourse on God, the world, man, moral issues, and many other esoteric subjects that were of interest to its author. It was not until the twentieth century that critical scholarship, headed by Gershom Scholem, established that the *Zohar* was in fact written by Moses de Leon (ca. 1240–1305), a Spanish Kabbalist who has to his credit several other books as well, dealing with both traditional Jewish and mystical-kabbalistic subjects.

Since De Leon wrote the *Zohar* in the persona of a second-century *tanna*, we cannot expect to find in it any direct reference to alchemy, since the very term is missing in the entire talmudic literature. However, De Leon lived in a time and a place in which alchemy was an integral part of the cultural atmosphere, and thus it is not surprising that references to alchemical ideas and subjects are found in various contexts in the *Zohar*. In fact, what is surprising is that, given the live interest in alchemy that characterized the Jewish society in which De Leon lived, he allowed so few references to matters of alchemical interest to appear in his great work. Since the extant references do not follow any logical order, but derive from De Leon's haphazard association of ideas, I present them here in the order in which they are found in the *Zohar*, and do so with the most painstaking fidelity to the Aramaic original, even if thereby the clarity of the English translation occasionally had to suffer.

To begin with, here is a passage which reflects a familiarity with the alchemical concept of relationship between the moon and silver and the sun and gold:

> [King David] sought all his days to bring the moon to perfection, and to sing songs of melody and praise [here] below. And when David passed away from the world, he left the moon in a state of perfection. And Solomon received the moon in all its riches and perfection. For this moon had left behind poverty and entered into riches. And with those riches Solomon ruled over all the kings of the earth. And therefore [it is written], "Silver counted for nothing in the days of Solomon"(1 Kings 10:21), but everything was of gold, for gold became superabundant. And of that time [it is written], "And he had dust of gold" (Job 28:6), for that dust which was on the surface—the sun looked at it and with its glance and its power it made the dust turn into gold and increased it.
>
> Come, see: From the mountains where there is the light of the power of the sun, the dust of the earth among the mountains became all gold. And had it not been for the wild beasts that crouched there, the sons of men would not have been poor, for the power of the sun increased the gold [and they could have taken of it at all]. It is for this reason that in the days of Solomon silver counted for nothing, for the power of the sun looked at the dust and turned it into gold. Moreover, that dust was [of] the side of judgment: when the sun looked at it, it took power and the gold increased. When Solomon looked at it, he uttered a[n exclamation of] praise and said, "All are from the dust" (Eccl. 3:20) (*Zohar* 1:249b–250a).

What De Leon expresses here in his own style is the well-known alchemical idea that telluric elements ripen under the influence of the sun and ultimately become gold. And he repeats no fewer than six times the simple idea that the power of the sun turned dust into gold and thus the amount of gold increased.

The alchemists, as is well known, were keenly interested in colors and coloring. De Leon gave a mystical coloration to the phenomenon of colors:

> One day R. Shimʿon sat, and his son R. Elʿazar and R. Abba with him. Said R. Elʿazar: This verse, which says, "I appeared unto Abraham, unto Isaac, and unto Jacob, etc." (Exod. 6:2). Why "I appeared"? It should have said,

"I spoke." He [R. Shimᶜson] said to him: My son, it is a supernal mystery. Come, see: There are colors that are visible, and there are colors that are invisible. Both are part of the supernal mystery of faith, but the sons of men do not know it and do not consider it. Those colors which are visible, no man has merited to perceive them, until the Fathers [Abraham, Isaac, and Jacob] came and perceived them. This is why it is written, "I appeared." For they saw those colors which are visible. And which are those colors? They are those of *El Shaddai* [God Almighty], which are the appearance of the supernal colors, and they became visible. And the supernal colors are hidden, and cannot be seen. No man has grasped them, save Moses. (*Zohar* 2:23a).

Close on the heels of this passage follows another, much longer one, which discusses another classical alchemical theme, that of the four elements, their four qualities, and their influence on the birth of metals, all of it wrapped, of course, in the mantle of "supernal mystery."

R. Shimᶜon said: Come, see! The four primordials (*qadma'ē*) are a mystery of faith: they are the fathers of all the worlds, and are the mystery of the Supernal Holy Chariot. They are the four elements (*y'sodin*): fire, wind, water, and dust. They are a supernal mystery, and from them come gold and silver and copper and iron, and beneath them other metals that are similar to them.

Come, see: Fire, wind, and water and dust—these are primordial, and the roots of the Above and the Below, and the things below and above are based upon them. And these four [spread out] to the four winds of the world, and they exist in these four: north and south and east and west. These are the four winds of the world, and they exist in these four: fire on the north side, wind on the east side, water on the south side, dust on the west side. And these four are tied to those four, and they all are one, and they produce the four metals which are gold and silver and copper and iron. Thus they make twelve, and [yet] they are one.

Come, see: Fire is on the left, on the north side, for fire has the power of warmth, and its dryness is strong. And north is its reverse, and the one commingles with the other, and they become one. Water is on the right, on the south side. And the holy One, blessed be He, in order to mix them together made the mixture of one like the mixture of the other. The north which is cold and moist [was mixed with] fire [which] is hot and dry, and He turned them around on the south side: the south, which is hot and dry, [was mixed with] water [which] is cold and moist, and the Holy One, blessed be He, mixed them together, for water comes forth from the south and goes to the north, and from the north the water spreads. Fire comes from the north and comes into the power of the south, and from the south comes forth the power of heat over the world. For the Holy One, blessed be He, causes them to borrow from one another, and each of them lent to the other from its own, as it was fit. In a similar fashion wind and east, so that each one of them should lend to the other, and one becomes encompassed in the other, and they unite and become one.

Come, see: Fire from this side, water from that side, and they are in conflict. [But then] the wind comes between them, gets hold of the two sides. This is what is written, "And the *ruaḥ* [wind or spirit] of God hovered over the face of the water" (Gen., 1:2). For fire stands on high on this side, and water stands upon the face of the earth [below]. The wind came between them, got hold of the two sides, and settled the conflict. As for the dust [i.e., the earth], the water and the wind and the fire stand upon it, and it receives from all of them the strength of these three which stand upon it.

Come, see: Wind and the east. The east is hot and moist. The wind is hot and moist, and because of this it gets hold of the two sides, for the fire is hot and dry, and the water cold and moist, and the wind is hot and moist. The side which is hot gets hold of the fire, and the side which is moist gets hold of the water. And thus it harmonizes them and ends the conflict of fire and water.

The dust is cold and dry, and therefore it receives upon it all of them, and all of them accomplish their task upon it. And it receives from all of them, so as to produce, with their strength, nourishment for the world. For the dust gets hold of the west, which is cold and dry, and that side which is cold gets hold of the north which is cold and moist, for the cold unites with the cold. Thus the north gets hold of the west in this side. The south which is hot and dry gets hold with its dryness of the dryness of the west, on the other side, so that the west is got hold of by two sides. Likewise, the south unites with the east, for the heat of the south unites with the heat of the east. And the east unites with the north, for its moisture unites with the moisture of the north. Now, then, we find southern-eastern, eastern-northern, northern-western, western-southern, all contained in one another, commingled one with the other.

In this manner the north produces gold, for from the side of the power of fire gold is produced. And this is what is written, "From the north cometh gold" (Job 27:22). For the fire gets hold of the dust and gold is produced, and this is what is written, "And it hath dust of gold" (Job 28:6). And this is the mystery of the two cherubim of gold.

Water gets hold of the dust, and the cold with the moisture produces silver. Now this dust gets hold of two sides, of gold and of silver, and is placed in between them. The wind gets hold of water and gets hold of the fire, and joins the two into one, which is "the color of burnished copper" (Ezek. 1:7).

As for the dust which we have mentioned, when it is by itself, with its dryness and coldness, it brings forth iron, and your sign is "If the iron be blunt" (Eccl. 10:10). And this dust gets hold of all of them, and all of them produce in it something similar to themselves.

Come, see: Without dust there is no gold, nor silver, nor copper, for each of them lends the other something of its own, to combine one with the other, and the dust takes hold of all of them. For two sides are united in it, namely, fire and water. And the wind is joined to it, because of those two, and exercises its influence on it. Thus we find that the dust, when joined together with them, produces and gives birth to other dusts, similar to them. Dust brings forth something like unto gold, namely green *suspita*, which closely resembles gold. Like unto silver it brings forth lead. Like unto superior copper it brings forth tin, which is a minor copper. Like unto iron it brings forth iron, as you can learn from "Iron with iron together" (Prov. 27:17).

Come, see: Fire, wind, water, and dust—all of them are cleaving to one another, are joined with one another, and there is no separation between them. But when this dust brought forth [its products], thereafter they were no longer joined one to the other, [nor] to those supernal [elements], as it is said, "From thence it was parted and became four heads" (Gen. 2:10). In these there was separation. For when this dust brought forth, by strength of the three supernal [elements], it produced four streams in which are found precious stones, and they are in one [particular] place, as it is written, "There is bdellium and the onyx stone" (Gen. 2:12). And those precious stones are twelve in number, and they are toward the four sides of the world as against the twelve tribes, as it is written, "And the stones shall be according to the names of the Children of Israel, twelve, according to their names" (Exod. 28:21). And they are the twelve oxen which were under the sea [i.e., the basin, in the Temple, cf. 1 Kings 7:25].

Come, see: Although the four supernal sides [of the world] of which we have spoken are tied one to the other, and are the sustenance of the Above and of the Below, there is more to the existence of the world: the wind (spirit), for if the wind (spirit) were to be removed even for one moment, the soul could not exist. This mystery is referred to in the verse, "Also without knowledge the soul is not good" (Prov. 19:2). The soul without spirit is not good, and cannot exist.

Come, see: Those twelve which we have mentioned, those twelve stones, are the twelve oxen under the sea [basin]. This is why the twelve princes [of Israel] took "each one an ox and presented them before the Tabernacle" (Num. 7:12). All this is a supernal mystery, and he who comprehends these things comprehends the mystery of supernal wisdom in which is the root of all things (*Zohar* 2:23b–24b).

Most of the concepts propounded in this passage were commonplace ideas in medieval alchemy. The four elements of fire, wind (air), water, and dust (earth); the four qualities of heat, cold, dryness, and moisture; their intermixture in varying proportions; their influence in producing the four basic metals of gold, silver, copper and iron—all this is elementary alchemy. New in De Leon's presentation are the ideas centering upon the conflicts, influences, harmonizings, and causalities among the primeval elements, and their close association with the four sides of the earth. Also new, and nonalchemical, but emphatically Jewish religious-mystical-kabbalistic, is the ascription to God of such quasi-physical acts as mixing together the various elements, causing them "to borrow from one another," and the like. And typical of De Leon's thinking and style is the repetitious assertion that what he is saying is a great mystery.

Apart from these general observations, the foregoing passage requires only a few specific elucidations. The Supernal Holy Chariot mentioned at its very beginning is a well-known Jewish mystical concept developed in talmudic literature, in which the term *maʿase merkava* (matters of the chariot) refers to dangerous esoteric speculations. The term itself is based on Ezekiel's vision of God's throne-chariot (Ezek. 1), and in the Kabbalah it became the designation of speculations about the nature and the suppositional visible manifestations of God.

As for the equation of wind and spirit, this is made inevitable by the Hebrew word *ruaḥ*, which means both. It is under the influence of this powerful word that De Leon substitutes it for the talmudic word *avir* (air) when speaking of the four primeval elements. In using *ʿafar* (dust) instead of the likewise biblical word *adamah* (earth) in the same context, De Leon was influenced by the frequent biblical usage of "dust" when referring to the substance of which the earth or the ground consists.

The green *suspita* mentioned in connection with gold has given rise to various interpretations. The *Zohar* commentary *Niṣoṣē Orot* explains: "It is called in Arabic *zarnīkh* [arsenic], and in Laʿaz *orpimento*, and it causes men's hair to fall out." Later commentators explained it as "green copper which is called *allatun*." Robert Eisler, in a 1925 article on the terminology of Jewish alchemy, emended the reading of the word to *susepta*, and suggested that it stood for the Greek *sussептē*, meaning decayed or putrefied gold, in accordance with the alchemical process known as *putrefactio*.[12] This is a possible explanation, although it is hard to see why De Leon should use an uncommon Greek word for an alchemical process which in the western world was called everywhere either by the Latin *putrefactio*, or by its derivative in one of the medieval Romance languages.

In view of the thought processes typical of Moses de Leon we should not be surprised to find that he applied the idea of the seven kinds of gold to physical features of King David, to whom he refers as "the first Messiah":

> I saw in the Book of the First Adam that it said thus: the appearance of the First Messiah [David] was like that of the moon. His color was greenish gold in the face; his color was Ophir gold in his beard; his color was Sheba gold in his eyebrows; his color was Parvayim gold in the lashes over his eyes; his color was *sagur* (closed) gold in the hair of his head; his color was Muphaz gold on his chest on the tablet upon his heart; his color was Tarshish gold on his two arms. All these seven colors were incised in all those places of his hair (*Zohar* 2:73a–b).

Although it is somewhat difficult to imagine how all the seven colors of gold could be visible on various parts of the First Messiah's body and also be incised into his hair, which at the same time was characterized by the color of one single kind of gold, such a question should perhaps not be raised in connection with a book allegedly written by Adam. But this type of presentation is typical of the style of the *Zohar*, and is part of the enchantment with which it held in thrall many generations of Jewish mystics.

It is interesting that in this passage the appearance of the First Messiah is stated to be like that of the moon, whereas in view of the unvarying alchemical association of the moon with silver and the sun with gold one would expect of a mystical human, or superhuman, figure sparkling in the colors of seven kinds of gold to have the general appearance of the sun. But, again, our logic must not be applied to the pronouncements of the *Zohar*.

The *Zohar* discusses the "mystery of gold" elsewhere, too, but its teachings have in general no alchemical significance. However, one passage states that "copper comes from gold, and it changed to a diminished thing" (*Zohar* 2:148a), which idea has a definite alchemical coloration.

Alchemical concepts figure also in another, smaller, and much less known book by Moses de Leon, titled *Sefer Sheqel haQodesh* (Book of the Holy Sheqel). It was written in 1292, but remained unpublished until 1911. In it we find the following passages dealing with alchemical matters:

> Gold is most precious of the metals, and about the mystery of this matter they said: There are seven kinds of gold in the world, and they are different, and one is more precious than the other: Ophir gold, Parvayim gold, Muphaz gold, beaten gold, greenish [or: yellowish] gold, Sheba gold, closed gold. These are the seven kinds of gold. Verily, they said that the most precious of all is the closed gold, because it is gold which is closed from the eye and closed from everything. And this is the mystery of the name of God, which is common in seven places more than in other places. The living God is the mystery of the supernal world, and as against this is

> the closed gold. Therefore it is more closed than the other degrees. God is the Fear of Isaac, and as against it is Sheba gold. And this is the mystery of what is said, "And he lived and gave him of the gold of Sheba" (Ps. 72:15). For the King Messiah is of that side which receives the left side. God—this is the Eternity of Israel, and as against it is the Parvayim gold, the matter of the thighs [?]. God [is] the totality of the Community of Israel, as against it is the greenish gold. And of this mystery they [i.e., our sages] of blessed memory said, "Esther was greenish" [B. Meg. 13a], and this is the mystery of the *ethrog* [citron]. God is the mystery of the loftiness of the earthly court of law, the seventy [members] of the Sanhedrin, who surround the throne of Glory. And as against it is the beaten gold. God is the mystery of the judges of below in this world. And as against it is Ophir gold. Verily, in these seven places [there is] the continuation of the participation of the name of God, as against the seven kinds of gold which are in the world. And in any case, the continuation of the quality of [stern] justice is continued to several armies, to several powers which have no number, as they said, "Who can utter the powers of the Lord" [Ps. 106:2].[13]

One must truly be steeped in kabbalistic-mystical thinking in order to fathom the meaning of this passage.

The second passage in the *Sheqel haQodesh* which has an alchemical reference consists of only a few words: "Dust. We have already explained this. And, truly, this dust is gold dust. And this is the proper matter, for its cause is the gold of above, and from there she receives, for always the cause of the point is the left. And this is why the dust begets and gives off seed to grow."[14] Again, I must admit that I have difficulty in understanding this passage.

The last passage I wish to quote from the *Sheqel haQodesh* is similar to the one quoted above from the *Zohar*, but is exceptional in that it refers to the opinion of the natural scientists:

> The masters of natural science [say that] fire produces the nature of gold. Truly, they said as a mystery, "From the north cometh the gold" (Job 37:22). For the mystery of the four metals, which are gold and silver and copper and iron, [is that they] do not come into being except out of these elements. And were it not for these three elements, the dust could not produce the realization of any thing. For gold comes into being and is attached to the mystery of the fire, and on the north side, for in any case, when the natural warmth approaches a cold thing it produces its thing, for it is green [or: yellow], and that is the mystery of the gold through the nature of the craft on that side, and in the matter of that element.
>
> Silver adheres to the mystery of the water and to the south side, for when the wind and the sun approach each other, it produces a white nature, and that is the mystery of silver. Copper is red, and this produces the nature of

both [gold and silver], because those who know the Work in the manner of their nature [know that] copper produces, and they make of it the nature of gold and silver, and it is [done] with the art of the sun in the wind. And in any case, the matter of the production of gold and silver and copper, their cause is in a great true matter, and it is a deep mystery.

And when the elements are transformed and are comprised one in the other, you will find in this that occasionally water produces gold and fire silver. Verily, the cause of iron in the dust is in the mystery of the west, for its cause produces by being helped by the sun, and by its light being reduced the dust produces iron whose nature is drier than all the others, because it is of the west side out of the products of the dust. For the dust, when it combines with the three supernal elements, when that element stays with it longer, then it produces something like each one of them.

For you will find that when the power of the fundamental fire, the natural heat, which is on the north side, approaches the dust which is below, the dust begets the gold when it approaches it together, and when all the three come together, which is one thing, then the gold produces dust. For when the dust approaches the heat of the fire on the north side, then the product of the dust is gold. And from this you can understand the mystery of the two golden cherubim.

And likewise the dust: when it approaches the water it gets tied up in it on the south side, due to the power of the south and of the water. For water is cold and moist and the south is warm and dry. Hence you can recognize that the dust, which is the receiver, when it approaches any one of the other elements, produces in every case [substances] like itself [and] like each one of them. And we have already been alerted to this mystery in the Book *Shoshan ʿEdut.*

And even though these four elements are the fathers of the fathers of all the offspring, there are nevertheless also other elements below, which stand beneath them, and they are the lower elements whose continued existence is in this low world. And verily they are like those productive elements, verily, for the dust is the one which produces offspring in their likeness according to their families and houses.

And verily the four metals which we have mentioned, and they are the supernals which originate in the mystery of the four elements, produce them with the power of those four, for each one produces in its likeness. And each one of these four lower metals emerges from the power of the supernal metals which are the four elements which we have mentioned. For there is a metal which emerges in the likeness of gold and it is the one called the gilded copper, a *metal* [*sic*] of dust. And in any case it is in the likeness of gold but is not gold. And it emerges due to that power and is like it. And the silver produces the lead which is white and it emerges in the likeness of silver. And understand. And verily, just as the gold is on the north side, as

> we have said, and that metal emerges to that side, so the silver which produces the lead is on the south side and produces it to that side. And the copper likewise is of the power of dust and by reason of fire there emerges the strong lower copper which is connected to the iron, and it is to the east side. And everything is due to the power of the supernal elements which we have mentioned, which produce in their likeness below.
>
> And the mystery is as we have said, and this is "and a river went out of Eden to water the garden, and from thence it was parted and became four heads" (Gen. 2:10), and they are the four metals of below which are the lower ones. And the precious stones are connected with the metals which we have mentioned. And the precious stones are twelve, which are mentioned in the Torah, and they are connected in the *ephod* [the high priest's breastplate] and the stones according to the names of the Children of Israel emerge with the power of the primeval elements, "like the engravings of a signet, every one according to his name" (Exod. 28:21), and everything is from the continuation of those supernal elements, for with their power and due to them each man moves out to his camp and each with his flag. And understand, for it is a great principle above.[15]

Although these passages quoted from the writings of Moses de Leon show that he was familiar with certain alchemical concepts and perhaps even procedures, they also show that his interest in them was merely tangential, and that he referred to the elements, the metals, and so on, only to express, or illustrate, his mystical religious ideas. Nevertheless, we have here evidence that an extraordinary thinker such as Moses de Leon, who created an entire world of ideas of his own, and constructed an intricate edifice of original concepts, also utilized building blocks which he found lying about in the alchemical byways of his age. While De Leon was not an alchemist, he was certainly aware of the alchemical ideas of his society, and believed in the alchemical doctrines and tenets as firmly as he believed in the teachings of the Bible and the Talmud upon which he built his Kabbalah.

Two more brief comments. The book *Shoshan ʿEdut* (Lily of Testimony), referred to by De Leon as his first book, was written in 1286. The word *metal* appearing in this pericope is one of the very few foreign words De Leon used in this book. He evidently considered it a technical term, and that is why he used it instead of the Hebrew *matekhet*, which he used on all other occasions.

PART FIVE

The Fourteenth Century

Introduction to Part Five

WHEN SURVEYING medieval European alchemical literature, one becomes aware of the marked increase in sources in the fourteenth century. The greater number of both original manuscripts and books printed later but based on older manuscripts must be evidence that in the fourteenth century more alchemists were engaged in what they called the Great Art than in the thirteenth or earlier centuries. What can explain this? The most probable answer lies in the assumption that increased production is an indication of increased demand. In other words, if alchemical work increased, this must mean that in the fourteenth century there was a greater need of precious metals, whose production out of base metals was claimed by alchemists to be their great achievement. It was of course this claim, to which general credence was given in the Middle Ages, which made kings, seigneurs, and princes of the Church employ alchemists, and induced many others who could afford it to seek out their services.

Why should there have been a greater demand for alchemical gold and silver in the fourteenth century? The answer lies in the economic conditions in Central and Western Europe in that century, characterized by a shortage of available gold and silver coinage, which in that period reached almost catastrophic proportions. This has been pointed out recently by the French historian Emmanuel Le Roy Ladurie:

> A huge crisis of liquidity, a great monetary famine, peaked between 1395 and 1415. Its causes were not far to seek: the commercial balance between Europe and the Orient had shown a deficit ever since the year 1000 due to the purchase of spices, silks, and pearls, and also because of the pilgrimages, the Crusades, and the payments of ransoms. This unfavorable balance was worsened about 1400 by internal disasters in the West, and it was not helped by the still growing purchases of spices, and by the drying up of Sudanese gold. In France, not much different in this respect from England, Spain, Italy, Flanders, and Bourgogne, the worst decade, the one most lacking in money, was that of the years 1392–1402. The district of Briaude, deep in the heart of the *massif central* and isolated, was reduced about 1423–1425 to minting coins of lead! In Western Europe as a whole the stock of precious metals was diminished from approximately the equivalent of 2,000 metric tons of silver in ca. 1340, to 1000 tons ca. 1465.

To indicate how abysmally small was this coin supply, Le Roy Ladurie adds that by 1809 the coin supply of Europe had grown to the equivalent of 50,000 tons of silver, that is, to no less than fifty times that of 1465.[1]

The relevance of this situation for the work of Jews in alchemy is obvious. Since, on the one hand, the Christians were prevented by Church law from engaging in moneylending at interest, and, on the other, the Jews were barred by state and municipal statutes from trying to make a living in many occupations in which they would have competed with the Christians, moneylending had become in the Middle Ages a trade in which the Jews were represented far above their proportions in the general population. The drying up of coinage was thus a much greater hardship for Jews than for Christians. This meant that when circumstances brought about a growth in the demand for alchemical gold and silver, a larger number of Jews, who were specialists of long standing in the money business, branched out, or switched to, what was after all in its basic practical aspect an occupation related to the one they had been engaged in for generations.

Since firm data concerning the numbers of Christian and Jewish alchemists do not exist, the above argument is nothing more than a conjecture. But the increase of the number of Jewish alchemical texts is a fact.

Chapter Thirteen

RAYMUND DE TARREGA: MARRANO, HERETIC, ALCHEMIST

IN THE SIXTEENTH century one of the most popular alchemical-medical works was the *De secretis naturae sive quinta essentia* (On the Secrets of Nature or the Fifth Essence). It was first printed in 1514, was reprinted some ten times before the end of the century in Venice and in several German cities, and was translated into Italian and partially into English.[1] In the seventeenth century, the book (hereafter referred to as *De secr.*) continued to be reissued, and it was again translated into Italian in an abridged form as late as 1924.[2] In all these editions the name of Raymund Lull appears as that of the author.

Raymund (or Ramón) Lull (ca. 1234–1315) was a native of Majorca, the son of noble Catalan parents. After a rather profligate youth he saw a vision of Christ in the shape of a crucifix, and heard the Lord addressing him: "Raymund, follow me!" The vision moved Lull to give up his worldly life and devote himself to God.[3] He lived to the age of eighty, and became the foremost Catalan philosopher, logician, theologian, metaphysician, mystic, preacher, and missionary to the Jews and the Muslims. At the age of seventy-eight he pleaded at the ecclesiastical council of Vienne (1312) that, in order to be able to hold its own against Islam, the Church ought to foster the study of Arabic, Syriac, Hebrew, and Greek. He succeeded in convincing the council and having it resolve to establish chairs for these languages at Paris, Oxford, Bologna, and Salamanca. Lull visited Africa several times, and during his last visit, when he was eighty, he was attacked and stoned by the Moors. He died of injuries aboard the ship which was taking him back to his native Majorca, thus achieving his lifelong desire to become a martyr of his faith.[4]

Lull's literary output was monumental and staggering in its variety. He wrote 321, or according to another count 488,[5] works in fields as diverse as general art, grammar, rhetoric, logic, metaphysics, politics, medicine, military science, cavalry, astronomy, astrology, geometry, arithmetic, spiritual and contemplative studies, preaching, disputations, theology, and so on. Historians of Spanish literature agree that he was one of the most original and most wide-ranging thinkers of his age.[6] His admirers and followers bestowed upon him the title *doctor illuminatus*, (the enlightened doctor). The study of his thought and work spread in the sixteenth century to France, where a chair of Lullism was established at the Sorbonne. The preoccupation with Lull continued down to the 1940s, when a Lullian Archeological Society functioned in Majorca and issued papers on him.[7]

His great reputation prompted several other authors who lived shortly after Lull to attribute their own works pseudepigraphically to him. Nicolas Antonio Hispalensis (1617–1684), in his comprehensive *Bibliotheca hispana vetus*, lists no fewer than eighty-one works which, as he says, "were circulated under the name of Lull," but not actually written by him.[8] Among them were several alchemical works, whose spuriousness was recognized by church historians in the sixteenth century at the latest. However, the conclusion that these alchemical treatises could not have been written by Lull seems never to have reached alchemical circles, whose admiration for Lull the alchemist continued to secure him an honored place in alchemical literature.

Thus Lull figures prominently in the large compendiums of alchemical treatises that were published in the seventeenth century. The 1625 *Musaeum Hermeticum* contains a work entitled *Hydrolythus Sophicus seu aquarius sapientum, hoc est opusculum chemicum* (The Sophic Water-Stone or the Water Carrier of the Wise, which is a Small Chemical Work), with an inner title page framed by imaginary portraits of the six most famous alchemists of all times: Hermes, Geber, Morienus, Raymund Lull, Roger Bacon, and Paracelsus.[9] Likewise, the *Gloria mundi* (Glory of the World), another alchemical work reprinted in the same volume, has a title page framed by pictures of the twelve most famous alchemists, including Maria Hebraea and Lull.[10] The very first treatise contained in the same *Musaeum Hermeticum* is the *Tractatus aureus de lapide philosophico* (The Golden Treatise on the Philosophical Stone), which quotes (on p. 15) Lull as having said in his *Codicillus* (Short Note) that "Our Mercury has the property that it can undergo coagulation from its own sulphur," and as having stated in his *Testamentum* that "Quicksilver floats on top and flows with humidity that prevents combustion."[11]

The conclusion that the alchemical books published under the name of Lull cannot be authentic is based on two considerations. One is that Lull himself had an adamantly and consistently negative view of alchemy. In several passages of his unquestionably authentic writings he went on record condemning alchemy in general, and denying that alchemists were able to produce gold, in particular.[12] The second consideration is chronological. The dates mentioned in several manuscripts of alchemical works attributed to Lull as the dates of their completion render

Lullian authorship impossible. This was pointed out meticulously as early as in the seventeenth century by Lucas Wadding (1568–1657) in his *Annales minorum*. Thus the pseudo-Lullian book *De 24 experimentis* (On 24 Experiments) contains a statement at its end to the effect that it was completed in 1330—fifteen years after the death of Lull. The *Testamentum novissimum* (The Newest Testament), also attributed to Lull, contains the statement:

> We made our testament by the virtue of God, in the island of England, in the Church of Sancta Catharina, facing part of the Tower before the chamber (*versus partem castelli ante cameram*) in the reign of Edward by the grace of God, in whose hands we placed in custody, by the will of God, the present testament, in the year 1332 after the incarnation.[13]

A third pseudo-Lullian book, *De mercuriis* (On Mercuries), states at the end of chapter forty that it was completed in 1333. In the *De 24 experimentis*, says Wadding,

> the author who calls himself Raymund tells in the introduction how King Edward of England while young put aside a great treasure in order to declare war against the Saracens, but then he diverted it for attacking the king of France. However, he says, led by repentance, the same Edward, when already old, asked forgiveness for having wrongfully diverted the money. This Edward, however, to whom he [Raymund] delivered his testament, was the third of this name. He began to reign in 1327 at the age of fourteen, and died in 1377, in the fifty-first year of his reign and the sixty-fifth of his life.[14]

In the sequel Wadding adduces more data to show that the alchemical books circulated under the name of Lull could not have been written by him, and mentions in particular the book *De secr.*, three copies of which he consulted in the Vatican Library, as being falsely attributed to Lull.[15] The earliest extant manuscript of this book is dated Paris, 1319.[16]

In addition to the aforementioned books there are several other alchemical works attributed to Lull which are identified by colophons in the manuscripts themselves as having been written between 1330 and 1357, that is, decades after the death of Lull. These colophons are important evidence for the pseudo Lull's identity. The colophon of *Lucidarium totius testamenti* (Lighting up the Whole Testament) reads: *Finitus est iste liber in praeclaro studio Montis Pessulani, anno 1330* (This book was finished in the celebrated place of study of Mons Pessulanus [Montpellier], in the year 1330).[17] The colophon of *Liber naturae et lumen nostri lapidis* (The Book of Nature and the Light of Our Stone) reads: *Fecimus in Sancta Catharina Londini, 1337* (We wrote it in St. Catharine in London, 1337). The colophon of *Liber de conservatione vitae humanae et de quinta essentia* (The Book on the Preservation of Human Life and on the Fifth Essence) reads: *Factus est his liber anno 1349* (This book was completed in 1349). The *Liber ad serenissimam Reginam Eleanorem uxorem serenissimi regis Anglorum Eduardi* (The Book [addressed] to the Most Serene Queen Eleanor Wife of the Most Serene King of the English Edward) concludes with the words: *Factus Londini in Sancta Catharina, 1355* (Completed in London, in St. Catharine, 1355). And the *Quatuor libri angelorum testamenti experimentorum* (The Four Books of Angels of the Testament of Experiments) states: *Fecimus in Sancta Ecclesia Divae Catharinae Londini, anno salutis 1357* (We wrote it in the holy church of the Divine Catherine in London in the year 1357 of salvation). There is yet another pseudo-Lullian alchemical treatise, the *Opus Abbreviatum super solem et lunam* (The Abbreviated Work on the Sun and the Moon), whose colophon states that it was written in the same church of St. Catharine in London, but it gives no date.[18]

It may be added that Daniel Georg Morhof (1639–1691), who lived some two generations after Wadding, lists in his *Polyhistor* (The Learned Man), among the pseudonymous and anonymous books, a treatise titled *Manipulus quercuum sive ars comprehendi transcendentia* (A Bundle of Oaks, or the Art of Understanding Transcendence), as written by a Raymund the Second.[19]

Colophons giving the place and date of writing of a manuscript are usually considered reliable, and these give testimony as to the lifetime of the alchemist Raymond who actually wrote the books attributed to Lull. They indicate that this alchemist was in Paris in 1319 (or 1330/33), in Montpellier in 1330, in London in 1332 and in 1337, in an unnamed place in 1349, and again in London in 1355 and 1357. The dates in these colophons were accepted as authentic by Lynn Thorndike, who argued that since there could be no logical reason for a forger to give a treatise attributed to Lull a date after his death, the manuscripts in question "are perhaps the work of another Raymond."[20]

Before addressing ourselves to the problem of the identity of this second Raymund, we must have a closer look at the royal personages named in the books mentioned. King Edward poses no problem. As Wadding asserted, he was Edward III, who reigned from 1327 to 1377, that is, throughout the period during which, according to the testimony of the colophons, the alchemist Raymund lived in London. There is, however, a problem with the wife of Edward III to whom Raymund dedicated his 1355 book: she was not Eleanor, but Philippa of Hainault (Hainaut), whom Edward married in 1328, and who died in 1369. The only King Edward whose wife was called Eleanor was Edward I (r. 1274–1307); she was a half-sister of Alfonso X of Castile. How the alchemist Raymund could have dedicated a book in 1355 to Queen Eleanor wife of King Edward is a puzzle. The only possible explanation is that Raymund made a mistake, and that instead of "Queen Philippa" he wrote "Queen Eleanor" which name, being that of several Spanish queens and princesses, as well as that of the wife of an earlier King Edward and of several other English queens, was more familiar to him. Once we assume this, several other parts of the puzzle fall in place. In another pseudo-Lullian work, the *Animae transmutationis* (The Soul of Transmutation), the author claims to have come to England at the invitation of King Edward, who, of course, must be Edward III. Moreover, in the likewise pseudo-Lullian treatise entitled *Experimenta Raymundi Lullii Majoricani philosophi docissimi* (Experiments of Raymund Lull, the Most Learned Majorcan Philosopher, already mentioned above under the abridged title *De 24 experimentis*), the author states that "we performed this operation for the English king, who pretended that he would fight against the Turk, but who subsequently fought against the king of France, and incarcerated me, though [ultimately] I escaped."[21] The operation referred to was the transmutation of base metals into gold according to the method of Arnold of Villanova.

Independent confirmation of the sojourn in England of an alchemist called Raymund is available in *The Testament of Cremer*, a tract included in the *Tripus aureus* (The Golden Tripod) compiled by Michael Maier (1568?–1622) and published in Frankfurt in 1618. The full title of the third of the three treatises contained in this book is "The Testament of the Englishman Cremer, formerly abbot of Westminster, not published until now, now in the esteem of diverse nations, edited and embellished with figures skilfully cut in copper with care and zeal." According to the internal title page (p. 181), Cremer was a member of the Benedictine order. The introductory part of Cremer's *Testament* reads as follows:

> Even though I was a zealous follower of this art and skill [i.e., alchemy], I was in a peculiar manner impeded by the thing, to me obscure, explained in the many and diverse books which I read, and with which I kept busy for thirty years, at great cost to me and to the detriment of my Work. The more I read, the more I lost my way, until I betook myself by divine providence to Italy where, by the grace of the most good and most great God, it was shown to me in the company of a man endowed with as great a dignity as with all kinds of knowledge, by the name of Raymund . . . in whose company I remained for a long time. Indeed, I found such favor in the eyes of this good man that he revealed to me a certain part of this entire mystery; therefore I impressed on him with many entreaties that he should come with me to this island, and he remained with me for two years. In the course of that time I attained completely the entire Work. Thereafter I

> brought this eminent man into the presence of the most glorious King Edward, by whom he was received with the honor he deserved, and was treated with all kindness. And there, persuaded by the king with many promises, pacts, and propositions, he undertook to make the king rich with the promise of his divine art. This with the condition that the king, in his own person, would wage war against the Turks, the enemies of God, and would spend it on the House of the Lord, and under no condition in haughtiness or in waging war against Christians. But (O pain!) this promise was broken and violated by the king, whereupon that pious man, afflicted in spirit and in his innermost heart, fled from here overseas in a lamentable and miserable condition, which pains my heart exceedingly, and I daily request earnestly that I should be with him in body, for the aspect and integrity of his daily life can easily induce even obstinate sinners to penitence.
>
> I, O most blessed Raymund, pour out my prayers for you to the most good and most great God, and my brothers do likewise. All wisdom belongs to God.[22]

The foregoing account of Raymund's experiences in England is not without its difficulties. As Waite has pointed out, there was no Cremer among the abbots of Westminster, and the statement that Cremer took Raymund to England and two years later introduced him to King Edward contradicts the assertion, contained in Raymund's own tract, the *Animae transmutationis*, that he went to England at the request of King Edward. Despite these discrepancies, Waite is satisfied that Cremer was not a fictitious person, and that his Testament was "a valuable testimony borne in England to the truth of the story told concerning himself" by the author of the aforementioned alchemical books dated in England.[23] By and large, Cremer's account bears out what Raymund says in his *De 24 experimentis* about his relationship with King Edward. It also contains three features familiar from the lives of other contemporary alchemists.

The first is Cremer's trip to the south in quest of alchemical knowledge, his encounter there with a great adept of the Royal Art, and his return to his home country accompanied by that alchemist. All this is duplicated in the story told by Nicolas Flamel, the fourteenth-century French alchemist.[24] The second common feature is that in both encounters the master alchemists involved were converted Jews—we shall see below that this was indeed the case with Raymund. The third feature in Cremer's story recurring in other alchemical accounts is the agreement made between a king and a Jewish (or Marrano) alchemist. Such agreements were not extraordinary at the time, as shown by the one concluded, also in the fourteenth century, between King Pedro IV (r. 1343–1387) of Majorca, who was greatly interested in alchemy, and a local Jewish physician, astrologer, and alchemist named Magister Menahem.[25]

BUT, to return to the story of Raymund, whose pact with King Edward III is made more than likely by the above parallels, the brief and rather vague contemporary references to the relationship between him and the king leave several questions unanswered. How was Raymund able to produce the gold which King Edward used to finance his war or wars against France? Did Raymund actually dare to reproach the king for not having kept his promise? Or was there some other reason for Raymund's incarceration? And, how did Raymund manage to escape from prison? A partial answer, possibly fictitious, is supplied by a note Elias Ashmole (1617–1692) appended to an alchemical poem titled "Hermes Bird," included in his *Theatrum chemicum Britannicum.* The poem, Ashmole says, was originally written in French by Raymond Lully(!) and translated into English by his disciple Cremer. Then Ashmole adds that after Edward III led his first military expedition against France in 1337,

> finding that Lully (after he had seen him violate his faith in destroying Christians instead of Mahumetans) refused to further his Ambition with new supply of gold, He clapt him up in the Tower where he lay a long time, and seeing no possibility of release, begun to study his Freedom, and to that end made himself a Leaper (i.e., leper), by which means he gained more Liberty, and at length an advantage of escaping into France, where in all probability he penned this Peace.[26]

Let us add a single comment: for the author of *De secr.* it was a simple thing to simulate leprosy or even to produce symptoms taken as those of the dreaded disease by his jailers, who thereupon undoubtedly kept their distance from him, which facilitated his escape.

A variant tradition about the imprisonment and escape of Raymund found its way into the French *Bibliothèque des philosophes alchimiques:*

> Raymond Lull [still the same confusion of Raymund the alchemist with Raymund Lull], disciple of Arnaldus de Villanova, having been presented to Edward III, king of England, by an abbot of Westminster, who had brought him up from Milan to London, performed considerable transmutation for that prince, who had persuaded him that he was preparing himself for waging war against the Turks. After some time had passed, Raymund saw that Edward turned his arms against the king of France. He complained of the use which the king made of the gold which he had supplied with the sole object of fighting the infidels. For fear that Raymund would seek out the protection of his enemy, Edward commanded that he be seized. But later Raymund regained his liberty, trusting the vigilance of his physician, for the promise which Lull made to cast a golden bell which would be heard all over the world. While he was transmuting the imperfect metals for this work, he seduced the physician, promising him the secret of transmutation. The latter then made arrangements with the owner of a ship

who took them to France, when the materials were near the point of being poured into the mold of the promised bell. Informed of the escape of Raymund, Edward gave orders to pursue him, but it was of no use. In order to record the memory of this event for posterity, Edward commanded that a coin be minted which is called *rosa nobilis* (noble rose), which the curious keep to this day as a precious medal, and on which can be seen a rose above a ship propelled by oars.[27]

It is, of course, a historical fact that Edward III declared war on France in 1337, began actual hostilities in 1339, and fought against France on and off for decades. After suffering reverses, he concluded a peace treaty with France in 1360, promising to renounce his claims to the throne of that country and to territories other than those ceded by France in the treaty itself. It is also a historical fact that Edward did not honor his pledge, which makes it likely that he had no scruples breaking his word given to a lowly alchemist. On the other hand, if Raymund was indeed a Marrano, it seems at first glance puzzling that he should have tried to induce Edward III to fight the Turks instead of the French. Why should a crypto-Jew, whose secret loyalties lay with Judaism, be interested in a war between England and the Turks, and try to prevent fighting between England and France? The Ottomans were at that time struggling to consolidate their hold on Anatolia, and were for several years allied to the Byzantine emperor John VI Cantacuzene (c. 1295–1383), who gave his daughter Theodora in marriage to the Ottoman ruler Orhan (Orkhan, r. 1326–1362). By about 1360 the Ottomans held a firm bridgehead in Europe along the Marmara coast, but the expansion of Turkish power into the Balkans lay far in the future, as did the Ottoman conquest of Palestine (1527), which was to motivate the Jewish adventurer and messianic pretender David Reubeni (d. 1538?) to seek European Christian intervention in the Holy Land. It is, of course, possible that the term "Turk" in the account of Raymund's falling out with Edward was used loosely and inaccurately in the sources quoted, and that their intention was to refer not to the Ottoman Turks, but to the Muslim Mamluks who ruled Egypt from 1250 to 1517, and under whose first, Bahri, dynasty the Jews (as well as the Christians) of Egypt, Palestine, and Syria were actively persecuted. If so, this would explain the interest Raymund, as a Marrano whose loyalties were with his old Jewish, rather than his new Christian, coreligionists, had in seeing an armed confrontation between a Christian and a Muslim power.

The memory of Raymund's sojourn in England and of his successful accomplishment of the Great Art survived for several centuries after him. In 1555 Robertus Constantinus affirmed that he had been shown a coin of very pure gold, under the name of "Raymund noble," which was said to have been struck from the precious metal manufactured by Raymund in the Tower of London. Also John Stow's *A Survey of London* (1598) mentions a work on alchemy written by Raymund in St. Catharine's Hospital.[28] And, as we have just seen, Elias Ashmole in the seventeenth century, and the *Bibliothèque des philosophes alchimiques* in the eighteenth, still knew of remarkable, albeit disparate, details about his imprisonment and escape.

We mentioned above that the earliest manuscript of the *De secr.* states that it was written in Paris in 1319. This date fits with the statement contained in text of the book itself (p. 9 of the 1542 edition), according to which the author was asked by King Robert for certain alchemical information. On page 33 of the same edition the author states that he sent a "compendium" to King Robert that contained alchemical instructions. Several other pseudo-Lullian alchemical manuscripts also state that they were written for King Robert or Rupert.[29] The king referred to must have been Robert I the Bruce, who was king of Scotland from 1306 to 1329, defeated King Edward II of England at the battle of Bannockburn in 1314, and obtained the pope's recognition of his title as king of Scotland in 1323. If King Edward III was interested in our alchemist because of his promise of gold, King Robert turned to him in the hope of obtaining relief through alchemical medicine for the leprosy which afflicted him and of which he ultimately died in 1329. In his *De secr.* (p. 9), Raymund hints at having the fabled "elixir" in his possession, and his quinta essentia is repeatedly described by him as a magical panacea which could cure practically any disease if added to the more commonly used medicaments.

One more royal personage is mentioned in yet another pseudo-Lullian work: an earlier version or copy of the *Testamentum novissimum* is dedicated to "King Charles" by its pseudonymous author, "Raymond Lully the Majorcan." In it the author addresses the king as "my dear Charles," and says that "I choose you as the most beloved son, as the enlarger of the Catholic faith."[30] The king in question was probably Charles IV ("le Bel"), king of France (r. 1322–1328), who also reigned as Charles I in Navarre. If so, Raymund probably stayed on in Paris, or at least in France, for several years after completing his *De secr.* in 1319.

In 1330 we find him in Mount Possulanus (Montpellier) in the south of France, from where he must have returned to London and then gone on to Italy. From Italy he went with Cremer again to London, where he wrote his three treatises dated 1337, 1355, and 1357. Whether Raymund stayed throughout these years in England is uncertain. If we can give credit to the story of his escape from the Tower, he went to France some time after 1337 (the year Edward III declared war on France), and then, prior to 1355, returned to London. It is very unlikely that in the course of these years he returned to his native Spain, for had he done so the Inquisition would undoubtedly have got hold of him.

The "fifth essence" was a favorite subject of Raymund the alchemist, which occupied him on and off for more than thirty years. The full title of his first treatise on the subject, which he wrote in Paris in 1319, was *Tertia distinctio quintae essentiae quae est de cura corporum* (The Third Distinction of the Fifth Essence which is about the Healing of Bodies). According to a statement contained in the opening passage of Raymund's *Compendium animae transmutationis artis metallorum* (The Compendium of the Art of Transmutation of the Soul of Metals), which he sent to King Rupert, he wrote "the third book of the fifth essence" in the Abbey of St. Benedict in Paris.[31] And in 1349 he returned to the subject and wrote the *Liber de conservatione vitae humanae et de quinta essentia* (The Book of the Conservation of Human Life and of the Fifth Essence).

Who, then, was the author of *De secr.* and of the other alchemical books which subsequently were attributed to the famous Raymund Lull? The direct light of history is thrown on this unknown alchemist only in the last three years of his life, after the Inquisition began its proceedings against him. If the data given in the colophons of the books referred to above are correct, however, this second Raymund had to be born about 1295 in order to be able to complete his first book, the *De secr.*, in 1319. The name by which he became known, Raymund (or Ramón) de Tarrega, indicates that he was born in the town of Tarrega, in the bishopric of Vich (later Solsone), and since all the references to him, including those contained in the inquisitorial proceedings that ultimately cost him his life, are unanimous in identifying him as a converted Jew, we can accept it as a fact that he was born to Jewish parents. This means that he must have received a Jewish education and adhered to the Jewish religion until his conversion to Christianity.

The town of Tarrega was the home of an important Jewish community that dated from the early thirteenth century. At first it was under the jurisdiction of the community of Lérida, but in 1325 King Jaime of Aragon granted it independence. In 1345 King Pedro IV of Aragon (r. 1336–1387) gave the Jews of Tarrega permission to rebuild their synagogue, and recommended to the vicar-general of Vich that he should authorize its reconstruction, which the latter did in August 1346. In 1350 the populace of Tarrega attacked the Jews and killed three hundred men and women among them. But all this happened long after Raymund de Tarrega had left the town.[32]

According to the minutes of the inquisitorial tribunal that interrogated Raymund about 1370, he stated that he had converted to Christianity in his twelfth year. However, this statement about his pre-adolescent conversion is contradicted by the fact that in secret he remained faithful to Judaism to the end of his life. It is hard to imagine that such Marranism should be based on impressions or knowledge a young child had absorbed from his parents. It is much more likely that his conversion took place years later, after he had saturated himself with the doctrines and practices of Judaism. In fact, according to later annalists, Raymund de Tarrega grew up a Jew, became "a rabbi of the Hebrews," and only thereafter did he undergo an insincere conversion to Christianity.[33] Also the two papal letters that deal with Raymund de Tarrega's heresies (see below) and were written, the first before his death, and the second soon thereafter, state that he "lately," or "once," "returned from the error of Judaic blindness to the light of Christian faith," which is unlikely to refer to a child who was converted in his twelfth year. Finally, the appellation "neophyte," by which he was known, seems to refer to a person who converted to Christianity in adulthood rather than in childhood. As Francisco Peña explains, "This Raymund de Tarraga is called Neophytus, as it were a new sprout or twig. For those are called neophytes who were not born of original Christians but converted to the Catholic faith."[34]

Apart from his Jewish origin and the incident in London, all we know of the alchemist Raymund de Tarrega's life prior to his incarceration by the Inquisition is what can be derived from the colophons of his books. We do not know when and how he became interested in alchemy, nor when and how he developed the theological ideas that the Church considered heretical and that brought down the wrath of the Inquisition upon his head. We can only conjecture that the reason he left his native Spain at an early age and spent most of his life in France, Italy, and England might have been his desire to live in a religiously less oppressive environment, in which he would not have to fear inquisitorial censure and punishment for the doctrines he expressed in his writings. In any case, he did live and work in those countries for close to four decades. By 1319, when he wrote the first version of his *De secr.*, he must have been known as an adept of the Great Art, whose services were sought by royalty. From the testimony of Cremer it appears that he never pretended to be anybody but himself, Master Raymund, an alchemist. It was only after his death that his works came to be attributed to Raymond Lull.

If very little is known of most of Raymund de Tarrega's life, this is not true of his last years, when the Inquisition caught up with him. During Raymund's long sojourn abroad, a Dominican friar and master of theology, Nicolas Eymeric (1320–1399) by name, became inquisitor general of Aragon, Valencia, and Majorca. One of Raymund's books, titled *De invocatione demonum* (On the Invocation of Demons), came to Eymeric's notice. He found it full of heretical errors, and during the reign of Pope Innocent VI (1352–1362) he had it burned in Barcelona. What happened was recorded by Eymeric himself in his book *Directorium inquisitorum* (The Inquisitors' Directory), which he wrote (in third person) in Avignon, c. 1365.

> Also in the time of the same Pope Innocent VI, the same Fray Nicolas Eymeric, inquisitor, and Arnaldus de Buchetis, publicly condemned in Barcelona, and caused to be burned, a certain large and bulky book, *Demonum invocatione*, in seven separate parts, which is titled *The Book of Solomon*, in which were described sacrifices, discourses, offerings, and very many nefarious things with which the demons can be consulted.[35]

The *De invocatione demonum* is no longer extant, but some idea of its contents can be had from the listing by Eymeric of the heretical doctrines it proposed. In question 27 of his *Directorium*, Eymeric states that Pope Gregory XI (r. 1370–1378) condemned this book written by Raymund de Tarrega, and in his question 10 he enumerates twenty-two heresies the book contained.[36] Eymeric's listing is redundant, and hence I present here a somewhat shorter formulation given to the Tarregan heresies by Natalis Alexander (1639–1724), which is practically identical with Eymeric's list. Raymund, then, was accused of having taught that

1. The distorted dogmas of Almaricus, Arius, Sabellius, and many heretics were not heretical in themselves, but only in respect of those who by their own intention choose to be stubborn.
2. It was permitted to adore creatures and to participate in the cult of their worship, inasmuch as they represent the Creator.
3. It was permissible, for the same reason, to worship demons.
4. He who sacrificed to demons should be excused equally as, and more than, the Christian who worshiped the images of Christ and the saints; to them [the demons] adoration and sacrifice were due by the law of nature.
5. Those who, as victims of torture, denied God with their mouth, but worshiped him in their heart, not only did not sin, but indeed deserved a reward.
6. A layman should not be held to believe explicitly any article of faith: and therefore, if he held or believed the opposite of any article out of ignorance or through the temptation of the devil, he did not sin.
7. All those who did not obey the precepts of God or of the Church must be considered heretics.
8. Every sinner, even while he sinned, conformed his will to the divine will, for good and evil pleased God equally; the recklessness (*desperatio*) of Judas as much as the contrition of Petrus.

9. It was not possible to observe in this life any precept, nor could charity be had from any person.

10. Man, [even] without charity imparted (*infusa*) to him, could love God above everything, and merit eternal life.

11. Without charity nobody could be faithful.

12. The sect of Mohammed[37] was equally catholic as the faith of Jesus Christ.

13. It was more perfect to be a schismatic than a catholic; Christ, the apostles, the angels, [and] all the inhabitants of heaven were schismatics.

14. Only God the Father was the best, God the Son was good in the first degree, the Holy Spirit in the second degree, all the creatures in the third degree.[38]

It is, of course, questionable whether this list of heresies actually and faithfully represents the doctrines expounded by Raymund de Tarrega in his *De invocatione demonum*, or whether they were intentionally slanted by Eymeric who, for reasons of his own, was interested in having his superiors condemn the book and its author. This being the case, it is difficult to say whether Raymund's teachings in that book were indicative of any belief that would be held by a Marrano Jew rather than by a Christian thinker with an original and independent bent of mind. The worship of demons was certainly as sharply condemned by Judaism as by Christianity. However, in paragraph 5 one could see an attempt to justify and excuse the Marranos who denied their old religion "with their mouth" but continued to worship "in their heart" according to the faith of their fathers. Remarkable is Raymund's positive attitude toward Islam, although this would not be a specifically Jewish position. His assertion that Christ and the apostles were schismatics becomes understandable if they are considered from a Jewish point of view. Also his point in placing God alone in the highest position while assigning to Jesus and the Holy Spirit lower statuses can perhaps be interpreted as a Jewish attempt to justify strict monotheism as against Christian trinitarianism. Whether Eymeric was sufficiently familiar with Jewish theology to recognize Judaizing tendencies in Raymund's heresies is unknown. But he knew that Raymund was a former Jew and hence suspect of Judaizing, which suffices to explain his animus against Raymund.

Later historians took it for granted that Raymund de Tarrega was a Marrano, a crypto-Jew. Thus Francisco Peña, in his commentary on Eymeric's *Directorium inquisitorum*, writes: "This Raymund . . . called Raymund de Tarrega, who, after first having been a Jew (*Hebraeus*) converted to the faith of Christ, became a monk of the Order of the Preachers. Otherwise, as the matter itself demonstrated, he did not change his mores, even though he changed his religion."[39] Henricus Spondanus

(Henri de Sponde, 1568–1643), speaking of the annalist Bzovius (Abraham Bzowski, 1567–1637) says that Bzovius erred in attributing to Raymund Lull "the errors which were those of Raymund Neophitus . . . who had converted from Judaism to the faith of Christ, but nevertheless retained his old errors."[40] Jaime Custurer (1657–1715) says that "Raimundo Neophito, or Raimundo de Tarraga . . . was a Jew, and although he made himself a monk, he did not abandon his customs."[41] Similarly, Theophilus Raynaudus (1583–1663) writes that "Raimundo Lullio de Tarrega, whom others call Raimundo Neofito, because he converted from Judaism to the faith of Christ, and thereafter became a monk . . . but he did not relinquish the errors of which he had been accused before. Finally, by command of Gregory XI, he was examined in the year of Christ 1372, and convicted of grave errors, was condemned, and all his books were burned."[42]

Giulio Bartolocci (1613–1687) presents the following information about Raymund de Tarrega in his *Bibliotheca magna rabbinica* (written in Hebrew):

> Raymund the latter (*aḥaroni*), a false neophyte of the Order of the Preachers, wrote several evil books against our holy community, which were burned in fire by order of Pope Gregory XI. . . . About the year 1372 of our Lord our Messiah Jesus. Note: And know that Raymund de Tarraga the second is not Raymundo the first from the island of Majorca, who visited Africa and died there at the hand of the Ishmaelites for the holy faith of our Messiah, and so say many of our religion: and he was of the sect of the monastic order as stated by the author of the book of names who wrote books of chronicles of that minor order.[43]

Bartolocci is misquoted by Johann Christoph Wolf (1683–1739) to the effect that Raymund de Tarrega underwent a feigned conversion to Christianity and joined the Dominican order with the express purpose of deceiving and misleading "the simpler minds" among the Christians:

> Raimundus, whom Bartolocci, vol. 4, p. 363, calls *aḥaroni*, or the latter, in order to be distinguished from Raymund Lull. Of him he thus: "Raymundus the latter, called de Tarraga, neophyte, having in external appearance abandoned the superstition of the Jews, simulated adherence to Lord Christ, not from his soul but deceptively, and, in order to be able to deceive the simpler minds with the appearance of holiness and of a more confined life, he assumed the habit of the sacred Dominican Order, and about the year 1370 wrote certain minor works in which were contained several heretical and erroneous things. Of them the first was *On the Invocation of Demons*, and another whose beginning is "Whether an unbeliever is required to obey both the divine and the apostolic canons," and several oth-

ers, which, by order of Pope Gregory XI, about the year 1372, were condemned and given over to the flames.[44]

The assertion that Raymund de Tarrega, despite his feigned conversion, "continued to Judaize," is repeated by Johann Jacob Hofmann (1635–1706) in his *Lexicon universale*, published in 1698.[45]

Basing himself on the aforementioned sources, Johann Albert Fabricius (1668–1736) becomes guilty of some inaccuracy in stating that Raymund de Tarrega "ex-Jew, joined the Dominican order in 1370, but entirely as a pretense in order to deceive the Christians."[46] The fact, of course, is that by 1370 Raymund de Tarrega had been in the carcer of the Dominican monastery for more than two years. It is most likely that he joined the order in his youth, prior to 1319, by which time he was in Paris. Fabricius takes it for granted that Raymund de Tarrega is the author of the *De secr.* and of another alchemical book entitled *De alchymia*.[74]

The above reconstruction of Raymund de Tarrega's literary activity and sojourns in France, Italy and England, based on the evidence of the colophons in manuscripts and on Cremer's account contained in his *Testament*, is at variance with the data published by José M. Coll in the January-December, 1948, issue of ILERDA under the title "¿Ramón de Tárrega fué formalmente hereje?" (Was R. d. T. Formally a Heretic?). Coll was either unaware of, or disregarded, the colophons and Cremer's account, and based his life of Ramon only on references to him found in the archives of provincial church institutions. From them he pieced together the following story:

Ramon was born in Tarrega, of Jewish parents, about 1335. At the age of eleven and a half, that is to say, in 1346 or 1347, he embraced the Catholic religion, and some two years later he entered the Order of the *Predicadores* (Dominicans), not in his own town of Tarrega, as some have supposed, or in Barcelona, as others have thought, but in Cervera, in which monastery, founded in 1318, he received the habit of a *Predicador* friar, most probably in 1350. All this is conjectural in Coll's reconstruction of Tarrega's life.

The first official document to mention frater Raymundus de Tarrega dates from September 1351, when the Acts of the Capitulo Provincial de Balaguer state that he was sent for one year to the monastery of Santa Catalina of Barcelona to complete his grammatical studies. In 1352 he was assigned to the same monastery to study first-year logic. One of his colleagues there was Nicolas Eymeric, who years later became Raymund's chief inquisitorial prosecutor. In 1353 Ramon de Tarrega's name appears among the second-year students of logic in the monastery of Barcelona. In 1354 Ramon was sent to the monastery of Lerida to study logic. Coll remarks that Raymund completed his studies in logic in three years, while other students needed five years for the same studies. Next, in the records of the Capitulo de Pamplona for 1355, Raymund is stated to have been assigned to the monastery of Majorca to study philosophy. In 1357, after two years of study, the young scholar was appointed lecturer of logic at the monastery of Lérida, where he had several students who were to become well-known theological authors.

Raymund's independence of mind and unwillingness to submit to superior authority surfaced for the first time in 1358, when he was but twenty-three years old. In that year he was assigned to teach logic at the monastery of Urgel, where he soon found himself in disagreement with its sub-prior, Fr. Antonio Laver. Details of the conflict are not known, but its result was that Raymund, together with a colleague, Fr. Gabriel Ribes, was found guilty of acts of insubordination, for which both young scholars were duly punished. The extant document which specifies the punishment meted out to them reads as follows:

> Because Fr. Raymund de Tarrega and Fr. Gabriel Ribes, together with several other clerics, carried out deceitfully and maliciously an investigation against Fr. Antonius Laver, at present the Ilerdan sub-prior, therefore they are deprived for three years of all voice and study and other favors. As punishment we confine the said Fr. Raymund de Tarrega to the Sangones monastery, and Fr. Gabriel Ribes to the Stellensian monastery, imposing severely upon them that while they will be in the said monasteries they should fast twenty days on bread and water.

The term of banishment of the two young scholars was completed in September 1361. From that date until 1365 Raymund is not referred to in the few surviving records, and thus Coll is unable to say anything about his life in those four years, except that those were precisely the four years in which Raymund *was supposed* to study theology. In any case, in 1365 Raymund was appointed lecturer in theology at the monastery of Cervera, where he stayed for two years. Coll suspects that it was in the course of his lectures that Raymund began to put forward certain theories or propositions which sounded theologically wrong. The prior of the monastery felt obliged to alert his superiors to the problem. From the local superior the matter was passed on to the provincial, who in turn handed it up to the general of the order. On January 6, 1368, the general, Fr. Elias Raymund, wrote a "very paternal and affectionate letter" to Tarrega, exhorting him to give up his false and erroneous view in matters of the faith.

Tarrega, however, resisted his superiors' persuasion, whereupon, a short time thereafter, legal proceedings against him began. Ramon was sent to Barcelona and detained there in the monastery that was the principal provincial seat of the order. In the sequel Coll recapitulates an account given by Torres Amat of the inquisitorial proceedings against Tarrega, which we shall present below.

Coll's conclusion is that the image of Ramon de Tarrega "the alchemist, the adept of occult sciences, the Judaizer, the necromancer, etc." is "pure legend and fantasy." The historical Raymund de Tarrega was, he says, what he appeared to be in the lawsuits, a Dominican theologian, whose doctrinal errors were greatly exaggerated by the authors who wrote about him. Coll even suggests that it is most likely that the sea of confusions around the person of Raymund de Tarrega arose from confounding him with the Jew Estruch de Piera, who, according to Eymerich, was not only an invoker of demons but also actually offered them sacrifices.

Obviously, one person could not have studied and taught at the monastery of Santa Catalina in Barcelona, and at the same time been engaged in writing alchemical books in the church of Sancta Catharina in London—to mention only one of the discrepancies between the two life histories, made the more intriguing by the coincidence between the names of the two ecclesiastical institutions. One must therefore ask whether it is possible that there were two men by the name of Raymund de Tarrega, the younger one of whom (born c. 1335) never left his native Spain and never wrote any alchemical books. If so, who was the other Raymond, some forty years his senior, who lived from 1319 to 1357 in Paris, Montpellier, and London, and wrote during those years at least nine alchemical books which are extant and are considered by most historians the work of Raymond de Tarrega? This is one of the many puzzles in the annals of alchemy whose solution awaits the work of future historians.

BUT to return once again to the closing years of Raymund de Tarrega, from the brief statement by Eymeric quoted above it appears that the burning of his *De invocatione demonum* was carried out by Eymeric and Arnaldus de Buchetis in Barcelona between 1352 and 1362, without papal authorization. There the matter rested for a number of years, probably because de Tarrega, living abroad, could not be reached by the arm of the Inquisition. It is likely that in the course of the ensuing years, however, Eymeric managed to obtain copies of the other books written by Raymund and, having studied them, decided that he would have to deal again with their author. Then, some time after 1357, perhaps even several years later, Raymund committed the fatal error of returning to Spain, therewith making himself available to the inquisitorial jurisdiction of Eymeric. Why he returned, even though he must have been aware of the danger in doing so, is a puzzle. Perhaps, having reached the seventh decade of his life, he felt that he wanted to spend his last years in his homeland, for which, as we know from historical sources, the Spanish Jews had an extraordinarily strong love. In any case, return he did, and Eymeric went after him.

How long a time passed between Raymund's return and the beginning of the inquisitorial proceedings against him we do not know. Since he must have joined the Dominican order prior to his leaving Spain for his long sojourn abroad, it is probable that a Dominican monastery became his home upon his return, so that Eymeric, who was also a Dominican, had no difficulty in tracking him down. As the first step, it seems, Eymeric merely admonished Raymund to retract his errors. When Raymund refused, Eymeric summoned him, and, as Torres Amat puts it, "exhorted him charitably" to retract his false propositions, or else he would have to experience the full weight of inquisitorial justice. Raymund, however, "resisted with various cavilings," whereupon, in 1368, Eymeric had Raymund incarcerated in the Dominican monastery of Barcelona, and commissioned a number of theologians to examine his doctrines.[48]

During Raymund's imprisonment the inquisitorial tribunal obtained depositions from witnesses and also a declaration from Raymund himself, who, as Torres Amat puts it, tried to protect himself "with the subtlety of his genius [*ingenio*], neither retracting his propositions nor manifesting enmity to the Church." The general of the Dominican order, troubled by the unfortunate situation of "Maestro P. Tarrega," sent him a letter (dated January 6, 1368) in which he tried to persuade Raymund to repent of his heresies. He reminded him of the honor of his order, which he had disgraced, and its holiness, which he had desecrated with his deviations, and informed him that he, the general, had caused Raymund's doctrines to be examined many times by the most celebrated theologians of the order, who were unable to reconcile them with the doctrines of the Church. In fact, they found in them twenty-two erroneous propositions which were viciously heretical. The general sincerely counseled him to respect his own honor and that of his order, and to subject himself to the judgment of Fr. Nicholas Eymeric, the inquisitor of the faith, "who had treated him with greater benevolence than he himself could hope for." And he warned him that, should he remain uncontrite, he would be surrendered as a heretic to the secular arm, which would impose upon him a just punishment.

But Maestro Raymund, Torres Amat goes on to relate, disobeyed "these salutary advises," and "resorting to various turns and evasions tried to elude" the inquisitorial sentence. He even had the temerity to complain to the Roman Curia "that they oppressed him and used force against him." Consequently, by order of the pope given on February 15,

1371, Cardinal Guido, bishop of Perusa, wrote to Eymeric instructing him that the proceedings against Raymund, who by that time had been incarcerated for more than three years, should be brought to a conclusion without further delay. When nothing happened for several more months, the pope himself sent on September 10, 1371, to the archbishop of Tarragona and to Eymeric a papal decree of which the relevant parts are as follows:

> Quite recently, not without great displeasure, it has come to our attention from a trustworthy source that Raymund de Tarrega, a member of the order of preaching friars, who lately returned from the error of Judaic blindness to the light of Christian faith, at the damnable instigation of the sower of evil works, publicly holds, asserts, and preaches some errors in his sacrilegious and perverse doctrine. You, son Nicholas, the apostolically authorized inquisitor into heretical wickedness in those parts, inquired into those errors against this same Raymund, as befits your office. Since the aforesaid things, if they are based on truth, ought not to remain unpunished . . . by apostolic writ we do commit and charge you that with due proceedings you should punish the abovementioned Raymund according to canonical sanctions, with no appeal, if he should hold, set forth, or defend some heretical errors, unless he should freely abjure them, do penance, and show adequate satisfaction. But if on account of the power, malice, or dread of someone or some persons you should be unable to carry out the above, do not delay to send us as soon as possible the said Raymund with all the proceedings against him . . . with all the documents . . . sealed with our seals, with a trusty guard. . . . Let the aid of the secular arms be invoked if necessary. . . . Given . . . on the tenth day of the calends of September, in the first year [of our pontificate].[49]

What Eymeric did upon receipt of this papal decree he recorded in his *Directorium inquisitorum* in a brief paragraph:

> The 27th question is: Which are the heretical and erroneous books which were condemned by special order of the Lord Pope Gregory XI, outside the Curia, by apostolic authority?
>
> To this we reply that in the time of the Lord Pope Gregory XI, the Lord Petrus, archbishop of Tarragona, and the friar Nicolaus Eymericus of the order of the preachers, inquisitor of Aragon, sententiously condemned a certain booklet *De daemonum invocatione*, which begins Misericordia et veritas (Compassion and truth) and a certain other book which begins Utrum quilibet infidelis tam divinis quam Apostolis canonibus teneatur obedisse (Whether any unbeliever is obliged to obey both the divine and the apostolic canons), and certain other minor works, as wholly heretical and erroneous, written by a certain Raymund Neophyte, because of the

heresies and errors contained in them, which were enumerated above, question 10.[50]

It is not clear which "other minor works" were, according to Eymeric, condemned by the pope. They may have been one or more versions of Raymund's *De secr.*, and the other alchemical work he wrote, *De alchimia et metallorum metamorphosi* (On Alchemy and the Metamorphosis of Metals),[51] or, as seems more likely, other theological books of which no trace has survived.

The papal rescript was followed three days later (September 13, 1371) by a letter the confessor of the pope wrote to the archbishop of Tarragona informing him that the pope had formed a commission of thirty theologians entrusting them with the examination anew of Raymund's doctrines. Once they reached their conclusions, there should be no more delay, and sentence should be passed expeditiously.

This letter seems to have been the death knell for Raymund. On the 20th of September, that is, barely a day or two after the papal confessor's letter could have reached Tarragona, Raymund "was found dead, thrown on his bed" in his cell. After the archbishop of Tarragona learned of Raymund's death, he wrote (on October 21) to Francisco Botella, prior of Sta. Ana de Barcelona, instructing him to investigate and ascertain, jointly with Eymeric, whether Raymund died a natural or a violent death. The very fact that a month after the death of Raymund the archbishop found it necessary to order an investigation into its circumstances shows that there must have been good reason to suspect that Raymund was murdered. The results of the investigation, if indeed it took place, are not known. Torres Amat concludes his brief biography of Raymund by saying, "Thus the case against Raymund remained without a verdict."[52]

The death of Raymund de Tarrega did not put an end to the preoccupation of the Church with his heresies. In January 1372 Pope Gregory XI again wrote to the archbishop of Tarragona and to Eymeric, ordering them to burn all the books of Raymund that contained heretical errors:

> To our venerable brother the Archbishop of Tarraco, and our beloved son Nicholas Emmerich, member of the order of preaching friars, master of theology, our chaplain and inquisitor into heretical wickedness in all the lands subject to the authority of our dear son in Christ the illustrious Pedro King of Aragon, greeting and esteem. Recently it came to our attention . . . that Raymund de Terraga, a member of the order of preaching friars, who once returned from the error of Judaic blindness to the light of Christian faith, at the damnable instigation of the sower of evil works, at one time publicly held and asserted some errors in his sacrilegious and perverse doctrine. You, son Nicholas . . . had inquired into those errors against this

> same Raymund, as befits your office. We charged in our commission to you that . . . with due proceedings you should punish the abovementioned Raymund according to canonical sanctions, with no appeal. . . . But since, as we have heard, the said Raymund (who while he lived is said to have produced several different books and writings that contain heretical errors) has gone the way of all flesh . . . we do commit and charge you that by apostolic authority you should cause each and every book and writing of this man to be shown to you, and all his books and writings which contain heretical errors . . . you should burn or cause to be burned. . . . Given at Avignon . . . of January, in the second year [of our pontificate].[53]

Having thus disposed of Raymund de Tarrega, Eymeric turned his inquisitorial attention to Raymund Lull and found him, too, wanting. He informed Pope Gregory XI of his findings, whereupon the pope, in a letter dated June 5, 1372, and addressed to the archbishop of Tarragona, authorized him to burn the books in question. However, Eymeric was not able to lay his hands on all the extant copies of Lull's works, nor did the pope consider the matter closed, for on October 1, 1374, he wrote yet another letter to the bishop of Barcelona instructing him to send to Avignon the copy of the heretical book which Eymeric had deposited with the bishop. Another two years later, in a letter dated February 1, 1376, and addressed to the archbishop of Tarragona, Pope Gregory XI instructed the archbishop to have the twenty books written by Raymund Lull that were examined by a commission of theologians sent to Avignon, as well as other books by the same author which contained similar errors.[54]

It seems fitting to conclude the story of Eymeric's destruction of Raymund de Tarrega and his accusation of Raymund Lull with countless heresies, with a brief reference to what happened thereafter to Eymeric himself. In 1386 Lullism was declared sane and wholesome by the inquisitor Emangaudius of Barcelona. Eymeric was demoted, and subsequently sent by King John of Arragon into exile where he died in 1399, at the age of seventy-nine.[55]

What remains now is to present a brief summation of the book *De secr.*[56] *De secr.* begins on page 6, with a preface entitled, "The Preface to the First Book of the Secrets of Nature or the Fifth Essence by Raimund Lull, the most acute philosopher, and most celebrated Physician." It takes up the whole page and reads as follows:[57]

> This is the book of the secrets of nature, or the Fifth Essence, which teaches its extraction and application to human bodies, for the accomplishment of wonderful and nearly divine works. When it is hidden, true medicine is hidden, and also the transmutation of metals is prevented; when it is unlocked, anything having to do with them is unlocked also. Indeed, this book is the

epitome of all books treating of these subjects, a thing which glorious God has shown to us in order that it might preserve our body from corruption insofar as it is naturally possible, right up to its end fixed for us by God; and also so that imperfect metals may be perfected and transmuted into one another. It is my desire that the artists of this art, contemplating God, should prefer to know, worship, and love God through good works by aiding paupers, widows, and indigent orphans, without a large fee, and by doing divine works of this sort. Let them not be like unto him who hid the Lord's talent, and did not show it forth for the purpose for which it had been entrusted to him, as Matthew writes in his 26th chapter.[58] But by trusting Him who says through Moses, "I will be in thy mouth, and teach thee what thou shalt speak,"[59] we have decided that this most hidden secret of hidden secrets ought to be declared to you. With divine virtue inspiring me and the infinite goodness of the same helping me, I will make brief mention of its principles and rules, and of the process of its nature.

The first book itself begins (p. 7) with the description of the three basic "principles" which underlie all alchemical work: *materia* (matter), *medium* (means), and the *quinta essentia* (fifth essence). On page 9 occurs the first reference to King Robert: "Besides, we are of the intention to treat briefly the testimony and the codicil as we have been requested by the illustrious Lord King Robert." Then our author goes on to explain that the elixir, which is the Fifth Essence, is applicable to three purposes: in human medicine, in the transmutation of metals, and in connection with precious stones (p. 13).

After some theological digressions, touching upon Christ, Paul, Adam's expulsion from the Garden of Eden, and the divinely ordered limit of human life (pp. 16–17), our author describes the immeasurable value of the fifth essence:

> It preserves the body from corruption, strengthens the basic constitution (*elementativa*), pristine youth is restored by it, it unifies the spirit, dissolves the crudities, solidifies that which is loose, loosens the solid, fattens the lean, weakens the fat, cools the inflamed, heats up the cold, dries the humid, humidifies the dry; in what way soever, one and the same thing can perform contrary operations, the sole act of one thing is diversified according to the nature of the recipient, just as the heat of the sun has contrary effects, for it dries the mud and liquifies the wax (p. 18).

References to Hippocrates, Galenus, and John Damascene (pp. 20–21) show that our author was acquainted with the medical literature available in the Middle Ages. He concludes this first part with the pious admonition: "This is only revealed to you by us so that you comprehend, love, and contemplate God, and be aware of your end, everything to be devoted to the honor and praise of God" (p. 21).

The second part explains "how to extract the fifth essence from plants, and primarily from wine":

> Therefore, in the name of our Lord Jesus Christ, take red or white wine, and it should be the best that can be obtained, or take reserved wine, which is not vinegary in any way, neither too little nor too much, and distill burning water (*aqua ardens*), as it is customary, through the tubes of the arms of copper, and then rectify it four times until the major rectification. But I tell you that it is sufficient to rectify it three times, and to seal it well so that the burning spirit should not escape. And you have an infallible sign when you see that sugar soaked in it and placed into fire burns like water. After you have thus prepared the water, you have the material from which the fifth essence can be extracted in performance (*ad actum*) which is one foremost thing which we intend [to treat] in this book. Take it, therefore, and place it in a vessel which is called [vessel] of circulation or in a pelican which is called a Hermetic vessel, whose form appears below, and seal its opening most tightly with *clibano* [dough or clay] or soft mastic or live lime mixed with egg white, and put it in dung which is very hot by its nature or in *vinacia* [wine flasks] to which no heat should be applied by accident, as you can do if you place a great quantity of any of those things in the corner of the house, which quantity should be thirty portable loads (*onera gerularia*).
>
> It is necessary that the vesel should not lack heat, for if heat is lacking the circulation of the water will be spoiled, and what we seek will not come to pass unless constant heat is administered to it through continuous circulation. Our fifth essence will be separated in the color of the sky, which you can see by the diametrical line which divides the upper part, that is, the fifth essence, from the lower, that is, from the impurities which are of a muddy color. Its nature is almost incorruptible and immutable because from it, it reaches to total glorification. For it has this in respect of the whole body of the world, to the extent that it is possible to change nature by an artifice (pp. 25–26).

Our only comment on these instructions of how to produce the fifth essence is that the author, evidently on purpose, hides more than he divulges, and that for actual experimentation his instructions are all but useless.

The second canon describes how the finished product of the fifth essence can be recognized, once the vessel of circulation is opened, by its "more than miraculous odor with which no fragrance in the world can compare" (p. 26).

The third canon tells "how our fifth essence or vegetable mercury can be obtained without great expenses by him who, due to the greatest poverty, is prevented." For God "created the fifth essence not only in burning water, but also in all plants, stones, and metals . . . and even in animals, snakes, etc." (p. 26).

The fourth canon (p. 28) teaches how to extract the fifth essence from fruits, roots, meats, eggs, and blood. The fifth (pp. 31–32) explains how "to extract the four elements from all things, namely, plants, animals, and metals." The sixth (pp. 33–34) refers to "a compendium which I sent to King Robert, and in which I revealed the composition of pearls." Then our author addresses directly the person for whom he wrote the present book, and says, "but to you we revealed in this chapter the calcinations. . . ." The seventh (pp. 34–35) "contains the science of extracting the fifth essence from all things so as to apply it to human bodies according to what is needed."

Canons 8 to 44 contain lists of plants and other natural substances used as medicaments, arranged in the following categories:

Canons 8–11. Hot plants of the first to fourth grades.

Canons 12–15. Humid plants of the first to fourth grades.

Canons 16–18. Cold plants and substances of the first to fourth grades.

Canons 19–22. Dry plants and substances of the first to fourth grades.

Canon 23. The doctrine of the application of the aforementioned substances for medical purposes, and a lengthy discussion of the qualities characterizing them. The last four pages of this long canon (pp. 59–62) are written in the form of questions and answers.

Canon 24. Missing in the printed text.

Canon 25. The "attractive things, so that it should be possible to remove from our body every injurious object, such as iron, wood, abscesses, etc." Among the items listed are magnet, sulphur, petroleum, asafoetida, parsley, etc. (pp. 62–63).

Canon 26. Purgatives.

Canon 27. "Substances constricting the belly and the blood, so that you attach them to our heaven [i.e., the fifth essence], and thus make it constrictive." The long list of these substances includes dragon's blood, *terra sigillata* [a kind of clay], gum arabic, *mummia*,[60] alum, etc. (pp. 65–66).

Canons 28–43. Lists of hardening, mollifying, maturing, corrosive, binding, opening, cleansing, attenuating and dissolving, opening and dividing, sweat-producing, repellent, soporific, stinging, strengthening, and poison-repelling substances (pp. 66–80).

Canons 43–44. Explanations as to the administration of the aforementioned drugs.

As an example of Raymund de Tarrega's pharmacopia I am listing here in his original Latin (with the translation in parentheses) the substances he enumerates in his eighteenth canon as those of the fourth (the highest) grade of frigidity (pp. 46–47):

Opium
Mandragora (mandrake)
Camphora (camphors)
Semen papaveris (poppy seed)
Iusquiamus (hyoscyamus, henbane, or Aster atticus
Semen eius (its seed)
Semperviva (aizoon, evergreen, houseleek)
Salamandra (salamander)
Aqua eius (its water)
Mucilago psilii (musty juice of psyllion, fleabane, fleawort)
Cicuta (Cicuta virosa L., or Conium maculatum L., hemlock)
Semen eius (its seed)
Ebenus (Diospyris ebenum L., Hebenus, ebony)
Verbascus (mullein, a plant of the figwort family)

Following this list the author adds: "Apply these things to our heaven, and you will have it the coldest." It should be noted that his instruction throughout the lists of his medicaments is to add them to "our heaven," that is, the fifth essence, whereby the original medicinal property and effectiveness of the substances in question will be maximized.

With page 83 begins the second book of *De secr.*, which carries the following superscription: "Here begins the second book of this volume which is called On the Ultimate General Remedies for the Preservation of the Good Condition of our Body."

The Introduction gives the purpose of this second book as follows:

> In this present book we intend to deal with the application of the fifth essence to the human body for the purpose of curing it of all the infirmities which are incurable according to the judgment of the most recent physicians. . . . Because in this book the doctrine of healing all diseases from head to foot is specified, we composed it despite our intention of which we have said earlier that it was to be brief. Because of which we shall give one general rule, with which everything can be cured, from head to foot, with our fifth essence. Thereafter truly we shall get down to some specific cases of comparisons [*collationes*], so that according to the doctrine which we shall present concerning it, any investigator should know how to practice it and what is the appropriate method of application in each case.

This introduction is followed by seventeen canons:

Canon 1. How to avoid insomnia.

Canon 2. "Teaches the magisterium of resuscitating the dead, which is one of the greatest secrets in this book."

Canon 3. "Contains the science of healing the leprous so that they should revert to pristine health and be cleansed."

Canon 4. The science of curing paralysis.

Canon 5. Remedies for consumptives.

Canon 6. "Which teaches us the perfect cure of demoniacs, melancholics, and all epileptic diseases (*morborum caducorum*)." We shall have more to say on this canon below.

Canon 7. "Teaches the curing of those who have fear, and of inconstancy."

Canon 8. Cure of those infected by poison in a drink or in other ways.

Canon 9. Cure of infectious humors of our body, and of hotness (*calefactiones*), itches, and of lice.

Canon 10. How to cure quaternary fever.

Canon 11. The perfect cure for tertiary fever.

Canon 12. The cure for daily fevers (*quotidianis febribus*).

Canon 13. The science of curing all continuous fevers.

Canon 14. The science of pestilential fevers.

Canon 15. The science of the true cure of spasms.

Canon 16. The science of how to administer laxatives, and how it is possible to cure sciatica, podagra, and kinds of *guttae*.

Canon 17. "Which teaches you how to conduct yourself in all cures of chirurgy, according to which it will be possible to repair wounds through nature."

Each of the above prescriptions and medical instructions contains references to the use of the fifth essence. For example, the very last item (p. 107) reads: "Likewise a fistula, a cancer, an infection (*plaga*) can be cured, first with the corrosive fifth essence, then with the cleansing [fifth essence], then with that which makes flesh grow; and this should be the general rule in chirurgical cure."

Since Raymund de Tarrega was the author of the book *On the Invocation of Demons*, which caused his downfall when in his old age he returned to Barcelona, and which evidently evinced what could be characterized as a soft or friendly attitude toward demons, it is of special interest to see whether *De secr.* reflects in any way this unusual position.

Canon 6 of Book Two of *De secr.* (pp. 90–93), as mentioned above, deals with the curing of demoniacs, as persons believed to be possessed by demons were called. In it Tarrega states:

> Truly, experience teaches us that all melancholics are occupied with horrible cogitations. The malicious humor has its origin in the spleen, and its fumes ascend through channels in the body until they reach the brain, and they move the fantasy and the imagination, and fabricate horrible fantasms with the perturbation of the intellect while asleep, and while awake they think horrible things. At times that humor is excessively malicious and generates epilepsy or apoplexy. In fact the demons frequently mingle with these infirmities to such an extent that the infirmity mixed with the demons

tortures the patient. At other times, however, they are crazed (*stulti*) and talk to themselves, and oftentimes seem as if they were discussing with other people and not only with themselves, and also reach such a state of desperation that they kill themselves.

The cure for them lies in the use of our fifth essence or in its addition to those medicines, that is to say to the fumigations (*fumusterrae*), the *centaurea maior*,[61] *epithimus*,[62] thyme, lapis lazuli, black hellebore.[63] And let it stand in our fifth essence for three hours, and then give it to him in a potion twice a day and once at night, and from the leftover anoint the whole body and the region of the spleen. This medicine surely cleanses the brain and purges the melancholy, and restores cheer to the patient, and [makes him] perfectly healthy in ten days, if he continues taking it.

Question. How can it be that the demons can be expelled from the bodies, when they have no bodies in which they could receive the impressions of medicines, all whose potency has an effect [only] in respect of an object?

Answer. Many reasons can be adduced in answering this question, both from the texts of the Holy Scripture and from the necessary reason that the demons are driven away by virtue of the perceivable medicines. I shall begin by stating the reason from the Holy Scripture. The Holy Scripture shows in the Book of Thobias that the demons are driven out through the virtue of sensate things in a creditable and sacred manner, that is, with fumigation, sacrifice, etc. For it is said in that book, in chapter 6, that Thobias placed part of a liver over coals and the demon fled from the whole house. Also in the same chapter, Thobias placed part of a heart over coals and its smoke drove away the entire race of demons. Here is the clear answer to the question from the Holy Scripture which, however, is by belief. But if you want to understand how the solution can be found by natural reason, take these principles: cause, effect, justice. Whence I conclude that once all causes are removed, their effect is removed. For justice is that which is reasonably given to every man.

From the first maxim we set forth this reason: The demons are attached to human bodies because of bad disposition and corrupt humor, or because of melancholic infection which generates evil, black, and horrible images in fantasy, and disturbs the intellect, for the demons habitually take on such forms, and generally dwell in obscure and solitary places. When by virtue of the fifth essence and of other things this humor, which is the reason they enter such a body, is expelled from it, then at the same time also the demons vanish at once together with the humor.

Another reason is this. Just as the power of God is and was able to make the qualities of the elements become fixed in the Acheron [the Lower World] after the Day of Judgment without proper co-essential substances for the vindication of His divine justice, so He is able to make the demons themselves subject to the action of sensate things, so that the truth of His power, which is directed with that justice, should have a subject in which He can perform His act according to the quantity of the sin; otherwise the inequality of the truth would be destroyed because of the failure of the free will over whose exercise (*ratio*) God has no power of disposition, according to the disposition of the merit in creatures, which is impossible. It is therefore true that God has free will, as it is used according to the disposition of their merit in created principles, and metes out punishments according to the quantity of the sin, and merit and glory according to their measure. It can therefore not be doubted that God, for the vindication of His divine justice, subjects the demons to the effect of sensate things.

The answer to the foregoing question is also made clear by Solomon's acts of necromancy, with which the demons were forced to perform good works; or with the evil virtue of words, stones, and plants. It is therefore clear how the demons are subject to the action of sensate things.

The same can be clearly understood from the action of Avernian [infernal] fire, with which the souls of the damned are tortured, and even the demons themselves, in order to multiply their punishment, even though their substance is not composed of the four elements; but so that their punishment should be greatly multiplied they feel the punishment by order of divine justice.

For he who sins against the infinite substance is guilty of infinite sin. Hence the sinner, in whatever fashion, can suffer greater punishment, but beyond the divine vision nothing can give them a greater one than that to which they are submitted by the action of sensate things.

And because of this there exists a revelation of how the sensate medicines have the effect of expelling demons from any body. Use, therefore that aforementioned medicine, and you will cure any demoniac, apoplectic, and melancholic, and, most importantly, if you add to the said medicines the herb called ypericon,[64] which otherwise is called *fuga demonum* (flight of demons) or *perforata*. For a fumigation of its seed drives away all demons from the vicinity of the body or the house.

Perhaps I am reading too much into this passage in which Raymund presents his views of demons, but my impression is that he did not consider the demons with any deep loathing, but rather saw in them instruments of God's punishment of the wicked. It is also remarkable that in this context he should make reference to the "good works" which King Solomon forced the demons to perform. This shows the demons in a somewhat favorable light, precisely as one would expect it from the author of *De invocatione demonum*. That book, as stated by Eymeric, also carried the title *The Book of Solomon*, and hence one can assume that the relationship of Solomon with the demons was discussed in it.

Incidentally, from his reference to Solomon's control over the demons one can perhaps conclude that Raymund was familiar with talmudic and midrashic literature. The story that Solomon forced the demons to perform "good works" (for example, to help in the building of the Temple of Jerusalem) is not found in the Bible, whose narratives were known to the learned Christians, but in the Talmud and the Midrash, sources generally unknown to non-Jews.[65] Of course, it is always possible that Raymund knew of the dominion of Solomon over the demons from the apocryphal *Testament of Solomon* or from Josephus (*Antiquities of the Jews*, 8:45ff.)—if, that is, he read Greek. I hold it much more likely that Raymund's familiarity with these legends went back to the early period in his life when he studied the Talmud and the Midrashim.

Another point of similarity between the *De secr.* and the *De invocatione demonum* is the author's preoccupation with grading. In the *De secr.* he groups all substances and diseases into four grades, and speaks for nine solid pages (pp. 54–63) of "the doctrine of degrees." In the *De invocatione demonum*, as we have seen, Tarrega applied his penchant for grading to the doctrine of the Trinity, expressed the view that "only God the Father was the best, God the Son was good in the first degree, the Holy Spirit in the second degree, and all the creatures in the third degree." That is, he arranged taxonomically the totality of the spiritual and the human realm into a scheme of four (God the Father, God the Son, the Holy Spirit, and the creatures), which corresponds to his grading of all medicinal substances into four grades.

In this connection it is of interest to note that in the latter fourfold grouping he repeatedly uses the simile of a royal household: the dominant quality in a substance is for him "the king," the next strongest quality "the queen," the third "the soldier," and the fourth "the slave woman." In speaking of the medicinal qualities of pepper he says, for example, "In the pepper the heat is the king, and since dryness agrees more with fire than the others, therefore dryness in the fire, or in pepper, is the queen. And since after dryness humidity agrees with heat, therefore humidity in pepper is the soldier. And since coldness is opposed to heat, water or coldness in pepper is the slave woman" (pp. 52–53).

All in all, the foregoing summation shows that the *De secr.* is a medical rather than an alchemical treatise. More precisely, one can characterize it as a handbook of medicaments concentrating on the application of an alchemically derived elixir, the mysterious *quinta essentia*, also referred to as "our heaven," whose preparation is given only in rather obscure and vague terms.

Chapter Fourteen

THE QUINTA ESSENTIA IN HEBREW

AS WE HAVE SEEN in the preceding chapter, among the many Latin writings published under the name of Ramon Lull there are several that deal with the fabulous quinta essentia, the purest of essences, which was supposed to have the power to rejuvenate the old and to cure all kinds of diseases, including mental aberrations. The popularity of Lull is attested, among other things, by the fact that *De secr.* was reprinted at least eight times between 1514 and 1557.[1] Another Lullian work on the quinta essentia, *Libellus Raimundi Lullii Maioricani de medicinis secretissimis* (The Majorcan Raimund Lull's Book on the Most Secret Medicines, hereafter *De med.*), is contained in a collection of Lullian writings entitled *Raimundi Lullii Maioricani philosophi suit temporis doctisssimi libelli aliquot chemici* (Some Chemical Writings of the Majorcan Raimund Lull, the Most Learned Philosopher of His Time).[2] Lullian treatises on the quinta essentia continued to appear even in the seventeenth century.[3]

De secr. was certainly available to Johannes de Rupescissa in the latter half of the fourteenth century, for his book *De consideratione quintae essentiae rerum omnium* (On the Consideration of the Fifth Essence of All Things) relied heavily on it.[4] Rupescissa wrote most of his works while imprisoned in Avignon by Pope Innocent VI (r. 1352–1362). He seems to have been burned at the stake in 1362. (The Lullian alchemical treatises, as we have seen, were burned in 1372 at the order of Pope Gregory XI.)

Lullian authorship is also claimed for a brief Hebrew manuscript in the Bibliothèque Nationale, Paris.[5] The manuscript also contains chapters 3 to 7 of the Canon of Avicenna, written in Arabic in Hebrew characters. Steinschneider devoted two pages to its discussion in his book on medieval Hebrew translations.[6] Apart from copying the name Ramon incorrectly as Romon, however, Steinschneider said nothing about the Hebrew manuscript itself, and instead described in some detail the *De secr.*, which, he suspected, was its source. But even a cursory comparison of the Hebrew manuscript with *De secr.* shows that the former is neither a translation of the latter, nor a summary of its contents, nor a reworking of it. Nor does it have any relationship to *De med.* In fact, not a single paragraph or sentence contained in either Lullian treatise reappears in our manuscript. Although all three works deal in the main with the quinta essentia, the contents of each are different.

The Hebrew manuscript begins with the words, "And now I shall copy for you a great secret of the fifth essence. . . . It was written by a great sage whose name is Raimon, and he placed introductions in front of it, and they are these. . . ."[7] The anonymous author of this manuscript seems to have claimed Lullian authorship for the same reason that Ramon de Tarrega—if indeed he was the author of *De secr.*—attributed his book to Lull: the desire to endow it with the prestige and respect commanded by Lull in the fourteenth century among the philosophers, theologians, and physicians of Spain.

The spuriousness of this Lullian claim becomes evident immediately after the two prefatory sentences. Contrary to the Hebrew author's statement that "Raimon" wrote introductions to his work on the quinta essentia, which he purports to "copy," that is, translate, neither the *De secr.* nor the *De med.* contains any introduction. The seven brief introductions with which the Hebrew manuscript opens are definitely original with the Hebrew author, who summarizes in them his views on the origin of diseases, the harmful effect of fear, and the nature of the quinta essentia. Echoing a statement by Rupescissa to the effect that "This fifth essence is the human heaven which the Most High created for the conservation of the four qualities of the human body, just as [he created] the heaven for the conservation of the whole universe,"[8] our author amplifies it and presents in some detail the similarity between heaven and the quinta essentia, "the human heaven."[9]

The conclusion that our author did not intend to summarize, let alone translate, the *De secr.*, the *De med.*, or Rupescissa's book on the quinta essentia is further borne out by his text. Where the two Lullian works give long lists of the materials from which the quinta essentia can be produced, arranging them in groups of minerals, animals, herbs, roots, fungi, and so on, and proceed to describe "the mode of the preparation of the quinta essentia from gold," and its composition, of all this there is no trace in the Hebrew manuscript, whose author evidently was not interested in such details. Instead, he states briefly in his Sixth Introduction that the fifth essence can be distilled "from the edibles, such as meat or fruit or herbs."[10]

The next part of the Hebrew manuscript, which deals with the diseases that can be cured by an admixture of the fifth essence into specific medicines or drugs, shows a certain resemblance to the Lullian works. This was inevitable, since they were all intended to serve as medical guides, and therefore had to specify such diseases as were recognized and diagnosed in their time, and their cures. Yet here, too, the differences are greater than the similarities. Where Lull groups the diseases into sixty-one "canons" (of which forty-four are contained in the first, and seventeen in the second, book of *De secr.*), the Hebrew author treats them under nineteen "benefits." The actual treatments prescribed are not identical, or even similar. For instance, in discussing the cure for poisons, both *De secr.* and *De med.* enumerate the venomous animals, whereas the Hebrew manuscript does not. In addition, whereas the two Lullian works rely primarily on the effect of "the fifth essence of things" in curing poisonings, the Hebrew manuscript recommends the fifth essence mainly as a solvent for "antidotes of poisons" whose identity it does not specify, probably because it assumes that they were well known to its readers. Another important difference is that the Hebrew author recommends the use of an emetic, whereas the Lullian treatises prefer purgatives, and external applications. It may be of interest to mention here that Maimonides (1135–1204), in his book on poisons and their antidotes (which our author may have known), recommended all the three types of therapy: emetics, purgatives and external treatments.[11]

As for the identity of the author, all that can be said is that he was a Jewish physician-alchemist who lived in Spain in the fourteenth or fifteenth century, and knew, in addition to Hebrew, also Latin, Spanish, Arabic, Persian, Turkish, and Sanskrit.

Was our author a practicing alchemist? He undoubtedly was influenced by the alchemical teachings of his time, in which the quinta essentia occupied a prominent place. He repeats again and again that the admixture of the quinta essentia will increase the effectiveness of drugs. Like the Lullian treatises, he considers that the quinta essentia can cure almost anything, from melancholy to pestilential fever, and from poisoning to demoniac possession; it can remove any foreign object, such as an arrow or thorn, which has penetrated the body; it can even renew the spirit of life, rejuvenate old men, and endow women with beauty. Yet, despite these clearly alchemical features, one gains the impression that the author relies more on the curative power of the drugs themselves than on that of the quinta essentia added to them. Nowhere does he recommend the use of the quinta essentia by itself; he always suggests it as an agent intensifying or augmenting the curative power of drugs. Hence, one is led to the conclusion that he was primarily a physician, and only in the second place an alchemist.

In the translation that follows, the notes contain translations or explanations of the Hebrew, Spanish, Latin, Greek, Arabic, Persian, Turkish and Sanskrit terms used by our author, and references to other Hebrew medical texts, to corresponding terms in the Lullian works, and to the use in folk-medicine of the materia medica mentioned in the text.

Translation

(155v) And now I shall begin, with the help of God, to copy for you a great secret of the fifth essence, which is called in their language[12] *qinta esensia*. It was written by a great sage whose name is Raimon, and he placed introductions in front of it, and they are these:

The first introduction. The diseases come because of a lack of natural strength, and the medicine which is capable of restoring health must be one which is not subject to putrefaction,[13] and is capable of renewing the spirit of life which has been lost, and of adding the radical humidity and strengthening the natural heat which has become weak.

The second introduction. Everything which is affected by fear is sick and weak, and if the afflicted [person] is given a thing which is affected by fear he will become more affected. And since physicians act against all the things, they will harm, and afflict, and kill. And it also happens to those who cannot comprehend this secret which the physicists[14] have comprehended. Therefore it is proper to search and to seek a thing in which are found the four qualities which are in us, and the four *materiae* of which our bodies are composed, and this will not be subject to corruption[15] in the arrangement of the four elements. And this is why the physicists called heaven by the name "fifth essence," because heaven is not subject to corruption, for it is not hot as fire [and] is not a thing foreign or alien to the four elements. And this thing of which we speak is called "human heaven," or "fifth essence," for it is in them, in the arrangement of the four *materiae*. And it is not subject to corruption, for it is not hot as fire, nor cold as water, nor dry as dust. And just as heaven bestows humidity when it is needed, and heat when it is needed, and likewise coldness and dryness, so the fifth essence bestows upon us what is called "spirit of life," which is composed of the four elements and can be separated from them through human artifice.[16]

The third introduction. It is proper that you know that our fifth essence is not cold, for it warms the coldness; and not hot, for it cools the heat; and not humid, for it dries the humidity; and not dry, for it humidifies the dryness. And it nourishes the body and protects it from all corruption and putrefaction, and thus it seems like a true marvel, for if [it is] put in a vessel and then if one puts into it a slaughtered fowl or a piece of meat, it will not putrefy as long as it is there, and then it will dry, since it has this effect [also] on a live body.

The fourth introduction. Just as the highest heaven does not on its own influence the existence of the world, but [does this] through the intermediacy of the luminaries and the stars, and through them produces enormous and awesome effects, so for our Human Heaven it is proper that it should be aided by the things which are influenced by it, such as the medicines, or the herbs which have virtues for the limb that we intend to cure. For instance, if we intend to cure the head, it is proper that we should put into our heaven those things which help the head, and thus for the other limbs.

The fifth introduction. It is proper that you should take the water which rises from the wine in a very clear distilling vessel. And let it rise at least four times in the distilling vessel in which there should be many rising and descending tubes, for the more it rises the more it will become purified and the farther it will be from putrefaction.

And let me tell you what I heard from a man whose words are trustworthy, who saw it in the court of the king of Spain where they did it in this manner. After they made it rise in the distilling vessel four times, they hid it in horse manure in a glass vessel tightly sealed. And after four months they took it out gently and transferred it into another vessel, so that the sediment should not be mixed up, and they buried it for another four months. And so they did for yet another four months, until a full year. And then they took it out, and there was not found in the bottom of the vessel even the thinnest dust, so thoroughly it was purified. And its scent rose as if it had issued from the Garden of Eden. And this is the proper way for you to proceed in order to achieve your desire.

The sixth introduction. Likewise it is proper to distil all things which you want to purify and to make of them the fifth essence: from the edibles such as meat or fruit or herbs, and mix them with the aforementioned heaven to cure with them any malady you wish.

The seventh introduction. Likewise it is proper for you, if you want to prepare a potion for a disease, to place those drugs which are appropriate for that potion into our fifth essence, and it will become like the potion, and it will be more effective, one part of it to a hundred. And likewise the things which constipate, or the fragrant drugs, and thus all things of this kind, and thus all the cordial drugs[17] must be pounded to utter thinness, until one can feel it by palpation, and then they must be put into the aforementioned water. And prepare in like manner the laxative medicines, for this water will add power of effectiveness a hundredfold, without doubt. Also, if a man is given a deadly poison, put of the water which received the poison into the aforementioned water, and he will instantly vomit up the poison which he swallowed or imbibed. Also, in order to remove an iron arrow or any object or thorn from any place, put into the aforementioned water the things which attract. Also, in order to clean any wound, put into it the cleansing drugs. And likewise, to make flesh grow, put [into this water] the drugs which cause the flesh to grow, and likewise those drugs which constipate, and which contract, and all of them in this manner.

Now I shall begin to explain the virtues of the aforementioned water in their general benefit, although we have already mentioned some of them above when we spoke of their importance. However, I shall tell here a little of the secrets which no man has comprehended, except him to whom their virtues have been revealed by word of mouth of those present. And they are powerful things for curing, with the help of the True Beneficer, all serious diseases which the physicians have despaired from curing, except those which are come by divine will, decreed upon him from his allotted lifetime.

The first benefit is to restore the strength of old men which has become very much debilitated, and it will restore it, with the help of God in whose hand is the strength and the power. Take the aforementioned precious water after it has been purified most thoroughly, and add to it of the essence of the gold and the crystal. Thus for the debilitated, each time half an egg full. And if the True Physician so decrees, he will be almost cured, and his strength will return to him like one of the young men, thirty years of age. And after he returns to the days of his youth he should no longer take of it.

The second benefit is to cure with it those who have been debilitated by disease to the point of a depression of the soul, except for those whom God wants to take, whose days have reached their end, or as a punishment, or, as in the case of the anointed of God, King David, peace be upon him, [who said] of Saul, "If his day comes, or if God smites him," etc.[18] And this on condition that the sick person is able to drink it. And also give of the aforementioned water to the old and debilitated, and as soon as the medicine goes down into the stomach it will endow the heart with a new spirit of life, and augment the natural heat which had diminished, and his strength will return to him as it was in the beginning. And if you want him to arise in his time and become healthy, give him the aforementioned water of the fifth essence which arises from the herb *salidonia*,[19] about [as much as] a grain of wheat, and you will see a mighty miracle, as if he had never been sick, and he will walk on his staff, if the True Powerful so decrees. And this secret is [one] of the most important secrets of nature which can be found; no physician has comprehended it in these our times.

The third benefit is that it heals leprosy, except if it is an ensnaring one, for [to heal] that is [one] of the impossible things. And it is proper that you should know that this water, with the help of the True Helper, will cure him of leprosy, because this medicine devours all corrupt and putrefied material, of whatever humidity it be. And I can attest to you that this (156v) water, with the water of gold and crystal, and with even more power if one puts into it the fruit which is called in their language *frasas*, and in Laᶜaz *fraulas*, and in Turkish *jilek*,[20] which is a small round fruit like the grapes of the thorn bush which is called *mora sarsa*,[21] and its leaves are like its leaves, except that they grow near the ground and they have no thorns, and their taste is sweet, leaning a little to sourness, and they have a good smell. And the aforementioned water with the aforementioned fruit strengthens nature very much, and drives away all poison and corruption and putrefaction from the human body, and brings their menses to women, and helps to pregnancy, and is beneficial to cure the cataract in the eye. And I saw a woman in whose face the traces of leprosy were visible, and she washed in this water, and the leprosy was instantly cured.

The fourth benefit is to cure all growths or scrufs or discharges of whatever kind. Let there be put into the aforementioned fifth essence some *tartaro* which is called *rasuras*,[22] after having burned it to lime, and let him anoint with it the spot, and it will be cured.

The fifth benefit is to cure *perlesia*.[23] If you put into this water some of those things which destroy the white [humor],[24] such as *farfiyun turbid*,[25] [and] the husk of *shawqu* root,[26] for these have the virtue of strengthening the vessels of feeling and motion, and also put on the paralyzed places a plaster of cooked and ground *bazr qatuna*,[27] and take of it five parts, and olive oil three parts, and wax two parts, and let the patient drink of their decoction thirty consecutive days.

The sixth benefit is for the sufferer of blight which is called *tisica*,[28] and for all kinds of shrivellings. An infant or child, or a youth, or a mature man, or an old man, whether man or woman, let there be given to them of the aforementioned water with that which comes up from the aforementioned *salidonia*, and they will, within a short time, return to their strength and fatness, as if they had never been sick at all.

The seventh benefit is for insanity or madness or *melakhonia*,[29] rage or spleen. Give them of the aforementioned water, with the fifth essence of gold and crystal, with a little of the drugs which purge the sharpened black humor,[30] and the seed of *fuagia*,[31] and its root.

The eighth benefit is for weakness of the heart or fainting, or beating or fluttering, and the like. Give him the aforementioned essence of gold and crystal and the herb *peonia*,[32] and the *toronjil*,[33] which is called *badrang buya*,[34] and saffron, and he will be cured entirely with the help of God.

The ninth benefit is to cure the bewitched and those who were injured by demons or an evil spirit. [Give] the patient of the aforementioned water with the water of gold and crystal, and put into them the seed of *perforata*,[35] that is, *qorasonsilio*,[36] and he will be saved with the help of God.

The tenth benefit is against lice and the kind which is called *adadores*,[37] which come into being in the flesh between the skin and the flesh, and which cause plague spots and great friction in the body. These things are born from the heat, in addition to being [born] from the putrefaction of wetness. And if the patient washes his body the . . .[38] of the fifth essence he will be saved from the aforementioned affliction, and especially if you mix into it quicksilver and *mozaj*.[39]

The eleventh benefit is to save from all poisons and deadly drugs. Take of the aforementioned essence, and put into it of the remedies which are the antidotes[40] of poisons, and give them to the patient, and with the help of God he will instantly vomit out the poison which he has eaten or drunk or which has come from the outside, from (157r) the bite of a poisonous animal. And if a person takes of the aforementioned things, and [thereafter] some kind of poison is given to him, it will not harm him, with the help of God.

The twelfth benefit is to cure the quartan fever[41] and all the diseases which come from the black [humor].[42] There are some physicians who say that there is no use in removing it quickly, but [only] in prolonging the time of its cure. And if you want to cure it quickly and easily, give the patient of the aforementioned water. And if you want to add to it some of the things which are antidotes of the black [humor], it will be more effective, on condition that he give it to the patient slowly, so that he does not weaken the nature.

The thirteenth benefit is for all those who were damaged by a laxative or emetic drug, which did not work or which worked in excess. For the laxative drugs must be viewed from three points of view. First, the laxative must not weaken the vital force. Second, it must not be [one] of the sharp and deadly drugs. Third, one must try to remove from, or diminish in, that drug any sharpness or poisonousness as far as possible. And [since] the physicians cannot do this as far as possible, at times they cause damage, and at times [the medicine] does not help and does not save, for the constitutions[43] and the years and the time are not the same for all people and diseases. Let him put the medicines into the aforementioned water, [and] they will act gently and without weakening the strength. Therefore it is proper that the physician should give the patient only one grain of our Essence, and he will see wonders. And if he needs to give more let him give the second time two grains, and thus gradually, according to the nature of the patient and the nature of the disease, and open your eyes and see!

The fourteenth benefit. All physicians agree that the permanent fever[44] is caused by a mixture of all putrefied materials, and its cure is to empty the blood and clean it of all rust and of the mixture of bad humors which are mixed into it. This is done completely by our fifth essence, which removes and separates from the blood all putrefied material, because it differs from the four qualities, for it is neither hot nor cold, neither humid nor dry. Therefore you can give it constantly without any fear, and especially if you mix into it the essence of gold and crystal and blood which were mentioned above. And if you anoint with it the temples and the neck and the veins and pulses, and the palms of the hands and the soles of the feet, and if you add to it the herb called *marqurial*,[45] you will add a wonderful thing to its effectiveness.

The fifteenth benefit is for curing tertiary fever. Tertiary fever is born of red and putrefied things.[46] It you want to cure it, put immediately into the [ingredients] mentioned some of the things which draw out the red [humor] and part of the cured liquid,[47] and give it to the patient to drink in the evening and in the morning, and he will be cured with the help of God.

The sixteenth benefit is to cure the day and night fever, which is generated by the putrefied white [humor].[48] And since the white [humor] is cold and humid, take our water with a little *farfiyun*,[49] and a little *shawqu*,[50] with other drugs which are antidotes of the white [humor], and let him drink it in the evening and the morning, and it will help with the help of God.

The seventeenth benefit is to cure epileptics of all kinds, and the acute fevers, and the *sirsam*.[51] Know that the acute fever is seated in the head. And since this fever is produced by the red, acute, and burned [humor], and also by burned blood, and at times by the burning of the three substances except the black one, therefore the physicians became confused in their cure. However, all these are cured by our medicine. Therefore one must take of our (157v) essence with the essence of gold and crystal and blood, and put into them rose water and *violas, boraja, lijunas*,[52] and therewith the patient will be cured with the help of God.[53]

For the healing of ringworm; pitch, one rotl; olive oil, one ounce; sesame oil, half an ounce; clarified butter, half an ounce; colophony, half an ounce; and the *daruru*,[54] peel it, roll it, burned [?]; and dog dirt; and every four [days?] cover its incision. And for him whose head trembles, let him take sesame oil, half an ounce; olive, half; clarified butter, half; mastic, half; pitch, half. Make an ointment and anoint the head, and every three days a hot bath, and between each plaster and plaster bathe.

And if you want to cure the *sirsam*, take of the *popilion*-ointment,[55] and choice vinegar, and ground garden rue,[56] mix all of them together with the essence of blood,[57] and dip into this medicine pieces of linen cloth, and put them on the brain of the patient and on his nostrils, and thereby he will be cured with the help of God. And know that this thing helps to cure epileptics and all kinds of insanity.

The eighteenth benefit is to heal pestilential fevers, that is to say, epidemic. If one is in the habit of using it at such times, with the help of God he will be saved from the pestilence, and patients will be cured with the help of God by the essence of blood, half of this and half of that with the roots of ox tongue[58] and the vinegar herb which is called *agritas y si se paliare el ribas o el jarope de el es munju mejor*,[59] and a little of *suqutri* aloe[60] and a little *firfion*[61] and *gira pigra*[62] and essential *lilio*[63] root, all this mixed also with the Essence of gold and crystal with a little *papili Veneris*[64] and hyssop, and he should do this regularly three times a day so that they should purge him of the empty substances, and he should use all the medicines which are antidotes to the poisonousness of the pestilence, and especially calf's stomach,[65] and these mixed with the aforementioned essence so that its effectiveness should be stronger and more apparent, with the help of God.

The nineteenth benefit is to cure the disease of spasms.[66] The physicians are in agreement that fever is a good sign in this disease, and the experimenters[67] said that if all the joints of the limbs are anointed with the juice of the herb called *flamula*[68]—which is a herb that grows in the ashes and its leaves are similar to the leaves of the celery, and its flower is green—if they smear him many times with its juice, the spasm will be cured, and therefore there is nothing as good for this as our essence, for this will make him completely healthy, with the will of the Creator, and God is the True Physician.

And I shall now reveal to you other hidden secrets which remained hidden from the eyes of the physicians who preceded us.

Take of the herb called *agrimonia*,[69] rue, fox-testicles[70] with their roots, *selidonia*, sugar,[71] and let them be pounded and put into the vessel of the alembic, on a gentle fire. And the water which ascends from it has powerful properties, for there is no pain in the eye, even the strongest, which does not become cured by it. And it helps, if imbibed, to save from all kinds of deadly poisons, and it cleans the stomach and strengthens it, and it helps against all kinds of dropsy,[72] which come from the cold, and it cures the Persian fire[73] in three days if they dip into it chaff of hemp and put it on the afflicted spot. It also is utterly effective against the illness of cancer if it is imbibed with *sabar*[74] and it should be put on the afflicted spot as mentioned above, and changed three times a day.

Take *pinpinela*[75] seed and mustard seed, and *perisil*[76] seed, and celery seed, and clove, and *mastaqi*,[77] an equal part of each, and they should be pounded well, and kneaded with the blood of a he-goat and mixed with strong vinegar, and put into the *resentor*[78] for three days, and then it should be distilled. This water is effective in breaking up kidney and bladder stones, if it is drunk on an empty stomach, and it cures scabies[79] if the head is washed with it, and it helps all kinds of boils if they are washed with it, and if they drink it twice it helps the *parilisia*,[80] and it helps epilepsy if it is drunk evening and morning.

Take chicks of *golondrinos*,[81] and burn them and pulverize them and mix them with *qastorio*,[82] that is to say *qashni*,[83] and put them into strong vinegar, and put it into a distilling vessel, and this water has many virtues. One is that if they drink it on an empty stomach it cures epilepsy completely if the patient drinks it for forty consecutive days, and it strengthens the brains, and clears the mind, and clears the stomach and the chest, and softens the nerves and removes the . . .[84] from them, and strengthens the nature (158r) and helps those who have a cold. And if hyssop is cooked in this water it will help the rheum which comes from the cold, and it will cure all kinds of fevers. But beware lest you give it to a pregnant woman, for she would instantly miscarry. And it helps cold headache, and [those who take it] will sleep comfortably. And it strengthens digestion and softens the belly, and it makes the urine flow, and it causes the hair to fall out and it will not grow again. Take hyssop and *avhal*[85] and *akheronto*[86] in equal parts in the distilling vessel, and the water which will come out will cure all kinds of headaches that come from the cold, and all old fevers, and will cause the menses to flow. But the woman should not be pregnant, for at times it [the menstruation] is kept back because of pregnancy, and the woman will be weak. It also helps all kinds of diarrhea, and it kills the worms which are born in the body if it is drunk on an empty stomach, and it cleans the stomach of all decayed substances, and if it is mixed with *qastorio* it will cure all kinds of *falij*.[87]

Take a bat and burn it and pound it with sulphur and mix it with the juice of *selidonia*,[88] and put it in a vessel up to six days, and then distil it, and this water has many uses. One: If any black hair is washed in it, it will turn white. Two: If you mix it with *sabar*[89] *and wax, and smear with it the pain of gout,*[90] *it will cure it, and it will cure the kind of cancer which grows on the face, which is called noli me tangere*,[91] that is to say, touch me not, if it is smeared over it, and it will cure scabies[92] by smearing.

Take *pirosil*[93] and pound it and distil it and it will help to expel all kinds of winds and bloatings from the body, and will strengthen the digestion, and if they drink it with *canela*[94] it will cure coughing and clean the chest. And if you distil also the *artemisa*[95] and the *polio*,[96] and mix them together with the water of the *perisil*,[97] it will help more for all the abovementioned things.

Take white *papaver*[98] seed and pound it fine and mix it with the abovementioned water, and it will help the chest and the cough very much, and if *qastorio*[99] is mixed into it it will help the *falij*.[100]

Take *salvia*[101] and *polio*[102] and pound them and distil them, and the water which comes up will warm bodies which have caught cold, and will strengthen the head and the limbs, and improve the tonic,[103] and will cure all kinds of boils, and produce good blood. And if one drinks of this water three times a day, up to forty days, it will cure all kinds of old diseases. And I call your attention to a great secret: if one takes of the abovementioned water and puts it into the distilling vessel a second time and mixes with it the water of *al butm*,[104] that is to say the fruit which is called *ḥub al khadhra*,[105] distilled in the distilling vessel and with *qastorio*,[106] it will cure all kinds of diseases which are born in the body, whether in its interior or on its exterior. This medicine was invented by a great sage, and many old diseases came upon him, and he saw this in his dream, and made it, and was cured, and he put it in writing so as to help many people. And it helps internal [diseases] by drinking, and external [diseases] by way of a plaster with chaff of *qanavos* (hemp).[107] And we have tried this medicine many times, and all those who take of the abovementioned mixture will be saved from leprosy and from *perselia*,[108] and from bad diseases which have no [other] cure.

And now I shall tell you the manner of preparing the abovementioned water of *al butm*. Take one pound of *tarmantina*,[109] half a pound of honey of which the frost has been removed, one pound of *aqua vita*,[110] very fine Indian *ʿand*,[111] *ṣandal*,[112] in equal parts. Arab *samg*,[113] *juz bawwa*,[114] *kholanjan* root,[115] *kababa*,[116] reed, *mastaqi*,[117] *qaranfal*,[118] *sanbal*,[119] of each three drachms. They must be pounded well and put into a distilling vessel made of glass, and it must be well covered, and put on a gentle fire. And the first water which will come up will be pure, and receive it in a vessel while it comes up pure; and then it will come up with the appearance of fire, red and bright, receive it in another vessel. And increase the fire a little, and when you see that the head of the distilling vessel is black and the water is coming out thick like honey, remove the second vessel and put on another vessel, and increase the fire more, and do this until nothing more comes out. And know that these three are hot, to wit, the second is hotter than the first, and the third is hotter than the second. And know that the first is called "the mother of medicine," and the second "the substance of medicine," and the third "the complete medicine." The first, if it is taken lukewarm with wine will strengthen the stomach and expel from it the white [humor] which is closed in, and it arouses the desire to eat, and preserves the heart so that no evil vapor should go into it. And I tried this often. And if a thin piece of linen is dipped into it and put into the nostrils with the little finger when going to sleep, it will be very helpful against all kinds of drips. And it will improve the odor of the mouth and of the nostrils if drunk in the evening and in the morning. And it whitens the teeth if one gargles with it, and removes all aches from them. And if a piece of linen is soaked in it and then put on the face, it cures the redness of the face which is called *barosnat.*[120] And it cures heaviness of the tongue by drinking [it] and gargling. And if a piece of linen is soaked in it and then put on hemorrhoids, it will cure them, and it will also cure deafness if cotton-wool is soaked in it and put into the ear.

Now I shall reveal to you the secret of the other two drops. They are good for cancer of the face which is called *nujmi Tangier,*[121] which was mentioned above,[122] and for pain of the hips and the kidneys and the neck and the throat, if a cloth soaked in them is placed on the sore spots. And they are good for him who has fallen down from a high place, or was smitten by . . .[123] or broken a bone, if he is bandaged with them, and they drive off all kinds of poisonous creeping [158v] things. This is the rule: they are good for all diseases and all wounds, and all afflictions. And the third drop even more so.

Take the herb *marqurial,*[124] and *qandero*-sugar,[125] in equal parts, and pound them together and put them in the distilling vessel, and let them stand there ten days, then distil them as [you did with] the drops of water which were mentioned before, and if the third is put into a clean vessel it will shine at night like a candle. The third water is like oil. If a man or woman anoints his face with it, it will cleanse it and beautify it, and if he drinks of this water every morning, even if he be a hundred years old, his youth will return to him as if he were twenty, and likewise all his limbs will shine brightly like [those of] a youth, and neither in his face nor in his body will any wrinkles be left at all. And if the epileptic drinks of it for forty days, he will be saved from his disease, and if *qastorio*[126] is mixed into it, it will cure crushed nerves and all the pains of the limbs of the body. And if it is put into eyes which are afflicted by any disease whatsoever, it will cure them. And if pulverized gold and fine crystal and *raubaibaro*[127] are mixed into it and pounded well and mixed, and the leper drinks of it, he will be cured completely, on condition that he drink of it until the freshness of his face becomes beautiful.

Take *rubia* roots[128] and pound them and cook them with olive oil and with *perisil,*[129] in the amount of the roots, and it will cure the disease which is born in the bladder. And if you cook the *rubia* with *parro,*[130] and give it to drink to him who has a diarrhea of blood, it will cure him. And if you cook it with bran, and the gouty[131] part is bandaged with it, it will cure it.

Take *pinpinela*[132] seed and put it into good red wine for ten days, and then dry it and make oil of it, and it will be good for stones in the bladder. And also the juice of the *pinpinela*, if he drinks it, will dissolve the stone and the patient will get it out in his urine in the form of sand.

Wondrous water which makes youth persist, and health remain, and this is its description: Take good white wine, three pounds, uncooked honey of the beehive, one pound, and pulverized gold, and distil them, and let him drink of this morning and evening. This good medicine was sent by the king of Egypt to the king of Garnata [Granada], who was smitten with blindness which is called *cataras*,[133] and he was cured by it. And this is its description: Take flowers of *romero*,[134] with their leaves removed, and spread them on a rug so that the wind should blow on them, for two days, and then put them into a flagon, but do not fill it completely, and cover it with a lead tablet, and paste the bottom of the flagon with clay of the philosophers,[135] and put it in the garden into a hole full of very fine sand, and let it stand there ninety days of the days of the summer. And when the days are up, open the flagon, and you will find the flowers softened like honey, and distil it in a glass vessel, and keep the distillation for both drinking and putting into the eyes, and it will help wonderfully, with the help of God.

Pills came from India, written in their language, and called in the language of Hind "pills of father and mother," for their benefit for a person is like the benefit of his father and mother, and this is their description: *Tirpola tirqota tangargayad ras u-bis gindek arhertal.* And this is their explanation: *tirpola*,[136] three kinds of pepper, that is, black, and red, and *zanjabil*,[137] and because of its sharpness he calls it pepper. *Tirqota*[138]—three kinds of *mirabulanos*,[139] Babylonian, yellow, and *amlaj*.[140] *Tangargayad*[141]—*atinkar*.[142] *Ras*[143] is quicksilver.[144] *Bis* is *bish*.[145] *Gindek*[146] is sulphur. *Arhertal*[147] is *zarnik*.[148] Equal parts should be pounded well and kneaded in the urine of goats and a decoction of *apsantin*.[149] And let it dry in the shade, and then be pounded a second time, up to seven times. And make [of them] pills like peppercorns. Seven to be taken.

To release the menses strongly take *dar*[150] of pepper, one drachm, *darsini*,[151] one drachm, *juz bawwa*[152] one drachm, *zangabil*[153] one drachm, *zaᶜfran*[154] one drachm, pure incense one drachm, sulphur one drachm, *misk*[155] a grain. They should be pulverized and kneaded in a little glue which is called *jaris*,[156] and *hukaro*[157] water, and let them make *farazjat*,[158] and let the woman suffer[159] one of them, and it will help with the help of God.

For pregnancy. The tooth of an elephant should be ground and mixed with *theriak faruq*,[160] and let the woman eat one-third at the time of her menses, and one-third when she becomes purified, and one-third after her immersion, and she will conceive with the help of God.

Chapter Fifteen

FLAMEL'S JEWISH MASTERS

FEW ALCHEMISTS have ever received as much attention and been studied so thoroughly and repeatedly as Nicholas Flamel (c. 1330–1418), the Parisian scribe and clerk, famous for his *Book of Hieroglyphic Figures.* In a 1983 paper, the Belgian scholar Robert Halleux listed some of the studies on Flamel which, he found, fell into two categories. One of them consists of those works which tell about Flamel's long, and ultimately successful, quest for "the Great Work," his gold making, his acquisition of great riches, and founding of huge charitable establishments. Studies of this type began to be written in the early seventeenth century and are still being produced in the late twentieth. The second type of studies describes Flamel as having married a rich widow, working in his métier as a scribe, and also dealing in real estate. He acquired a modest fortune, and set up numerous but rather insignificant charities. These studies began to see the light of day in the eighteenth century, and continue to appear down to the present day.[1]

Our present context does not allow us to discuss the arguments on which these two views of Flamel are based, nor even to go into the question of whether the autobiographical sketch circulated in the name of Flamel is authentic, as many scholars believe, or is a later pseudepigraphous work, as others maintain. Our interest is in the role Jewish alchemists played in medieval France, and it is with that view in mind that we will look at the Flamel story.

That story was first published in 1612, when the Paris firm of the widow M. Guillemot and S. Thiboust printed a book by the otherwise unknown Pierre Arnauld de la Chevallerie, with the long title (in my translation): *Three Treatises on Natural Philosophy, hitherto unprinted, the secret book of the very old philosopher Artephius treating of the occult art and metallic transmutations, Latin French, plus the hieroglyphic figures of Nicholas Flamel, as he put them on the fourth arch which he had constructed in the cemetery of the innocents in Paris, entering through the great gate from St. Denys Street, & taking the right hand, with their explication by the same Flamel, together with the true book of the learned Synesius, taken from the library of the Emperor on the same subject, all translated by P. Arnauld sieur de la Chevallerie of Poitou.*[2] The following is my translation of the book's introductory part:[3]

> I, Nicolas Flamel scribe and inhabitant of Paris, in this year 1399, and living in my house in the Rue des Écrivains [Street of Scribes], near the chapel of Saint-Jacques-de-la-Boucherie, although, I say, I learned but a little Latin because of the small means of my parents . . . there fell into my hand, for the amount of two florins, a very old and very large gilded book. It was not on paper or parchment as are other books, but was made (so it seemed to me) only of thin barks of tender leaves. Its cover was of well-beaten copper, all engraved with strange letters of figures, and as for me, I thought that they could be Greek characters or of another similar ancient tongue. Thus it happened that I was unable to read them, and that I knew well that they could not be Latin or Gaulois [old French] notes or letters, since we know a little of those languages. As for its inside, its leaves of bark were engraved, and written with a very great industry, with an iron point, in beautiful and very neat colored Latin letters. It contained three times seven leaves, for they were thus numbered on top of each leaf, every seventh being always without writing, in place of which it had a painted rod and serpents swallowing themselves;[4] on the second seventh a cross on which a serpent was crucified; and on the last seventh were painted deserts in whose midst flowed several beautiful sources from which emerged several serpents that ran hither and tither. On the first leaf was written with large, gilded capital letters ABRAHAM THE JEW, PRINCE, PRIEST, LEVITE, ASTROLOGER AND PHILOSOPHER TO THE NATION OF THE JEWS SCATTERED BY THE WRATH OF GOD IN THE GAULES [FRANCE], SALVATION D. I. After that it was filled with great execrations and maledictions (with this word MARANATHA that was frequently repeated there) against every person who cast his eyes into it, unless he was a sacrificer or a scribe.

The word "maranatha," which Flamel saw frequently repeated in the book and which he believed to be a malediction, comes from 1 Corinthians 16:22: "If any man loveth not the Lord, let him be anathema. Maranatha." It consists of the two Aramaic words māran āthā, or *māranā thā*, meaning "the Lord has come," or "O Lord, come!" The context shows that it was an expletive, an exclamation akin to "Halleluyah!" that is, "Praise the Lord!" Nevertheless, it was frequently taken to have the same meaning as anathema, an execration. On the first page of Abraham the Jew's book, as we shall see below, the word is explained as meaning "malediction," not in Aramaic, but "in Greek and in Arabic," which, of course, is erroneous. We may add that the use of this expression taken from the New Testament is the first indication pointing to a non-Jewish authorship or revision of Abraham the Jew's book. But let us return to Flamel's own story.

> He who sold me that book did not know what it was worth, and as little did I know when I purchased it. I believe that it was taken by force from the

> miserable Jews, or found in some hidden spot in the old place of their lodging. In this book, on the second leaf, he comforted his nation, counseling it to flee vices, and above all idolatry, to wait with sweet patience for the coming of the Messiah who would vanquish all the kings of the earth, and would rule with his people in eternal glory. Without doubt, he was a man of great wisdom. On the third and all subsequent written leaves, in order to help his captive nation to pay tribute to the Roman emperors, and in order to achieve other things about which I shall not speak, he taught them the metallic transmutation in plain words, depicting the vessels on the side and showing the colors and all the rest, except for the first agent, about which he said not a word. However (as he said on the entire fourth and fifth leaves), he depicted and represented it with very great artistry. For again, even though it was represented and depicted very intelligibly, nevertheless nobody could understand it without being advanced in their traditional Kabbalah, and without having studied the books.

In this paragraph Flamel quotes Abraham the Jew as saying that he taught his people the art of making gold in order to help them pay the tribute imposed upon them by "the Roman emperors," that is, evidently, the rulers of the Holy Roman Empire. Flamel also states here that Abraham presented his alchemy in such a manner as to make a thorough knowledge of the Jewish Kabbalah a prerequisite of being able to understand it. And—he introduces these statements by citing Abraham's admonitions to his "captive" brethren, warning them to repent and to wait patiently for the coming of the Messiah. There can be no doubt that these thoughts reflect an authentic Jewish spirit that must have characterized Abraham's book. Then Flamel continues:

> Therefore, the fourth and fifth leaves are without writing, all full of beautiful illuminated figures or the like, for this work was very exquisite. At first, he painted a young man with wings on the heels, holding in his hand a caducean rod surrounded by two serpents, with which he struck a helmet that covered his head. In my modest opinion he seemed to be the god Mercury of the pagans; toward him came running and flying with open wings a very old man who had an hour-glass attached to his head, and in his hands a scythe like [that of] death, with which, terrible and furious, he wanted to cut off the feet of Mercury.
>
> On the reverse of the fourth leaf he depicted a beautiful flower on the summit of a very high mountain shaken roughly by the north wind. It had a blue stem, the flowers were white and red, the leaves shining like fine gold, and around it the dragons and boreal griffins made their nests and dwellings. On the fifth leaf there was a beautiful flowering rosebush in the midst of a garden, leaning against a hollow oak at whose feet a spring of very white water bubbled up and fell headlong into the abyss, passing how-

> ever at first between the hands of a great many people who were digging in the earth in search of it; but since they were blind, none of them recognized it, except one who paid attention to its weight.
>
> On the reverse of the fifth leaf there was a king with a big cutlass who ordered his soldiers to kill in his very presence a great multitude of small children whose mothers were crying at the feet of the pitiless gendarmes. The blood of the little children was thereafter collected by other soldiers and put in a big vessel in which the Sun and the Moon came to bathe. And since this history represented most of the story of the innocents killed by Herod, and since it was from this book that I learned most of the Art, this was one of the reasons why I put these hieroglyphic symbols of this secret science into their cemetery.
>
> This, then, was in those first five leaves. Now I shall not tell that which was written in beautiful and very intelligible Latin on all the other leaves, for God would punish me, since I would commit a greater evil than he who (as is said) wished that all men in the world should have but one head so that he could cut it off with one blow.

For information about the alchemical symbolism contained in the pictures Flamel describes the reader can be referred to any of the numerous books dealing with the Flamel story. The monster who wished he could cut off the heads of all men with one blow was the Roman emperor Nero (A.D. 37–68), or at least it was he to whom the wish was attributed.

Having completed the description of the book, Flamel now turns to telling of his persistent efforts to understand it.

> Once I had this beautiful book in my possession, I did nothing but study it night and day, learning very well all the operations it described, but not knowing with what material it should be started. This caused me great sorrow, kept me in solitude, and made me sigh incessantly. My wife Perrenelle, whom I loved like myself, and whom I had married only recently, was greatly astonished at this, comforting and asking me with all her courage whether she could not deliver me from the distress. I have never been able to keep from her anything, so I showed her this beautiful book, with which, the moment she saw it, she fell as much in love as I, taking extreme pleasure in contemplating the beautiful covers, engravings, images, and portraits, of which figures she understood as little as I did. Nevertheless, it was for me a great consolation to talk about it with her, and to consider what could be done in order to find out their meaning.
>
> In the end I had these figures and portraits of the fourth and fifth leaves copied as faithfully as I was able to, in my lodgings, and showed them in Paris to several great clerics, who, however, did not understand them better than I. I even informed them that they were found in a book that taught the philosophers' stone, but most of them mocked me and the blessed

> stone, except one, named Master Anselm, who was a licentiate in medicine and had thoroughly studied that science. He became very anxious to see my book, and was ready to do anything to see it. But I always asserted that I did not have it, even though I gave him a full account of its method. He told me that the first picture represented time which devours everything, and that it required the space of six years, according to the six inscribed leaves, to perfect the stone, maintaining that thereafter one should have to turn the time-glass and cook no more. And when I told him that it was depicted only to show and teach the first agent (as it was said in the book), he answered that this coction of six years was like a second agent, that surely the first agent painted here, which was the white and heavy water, was undoubtedly the quicksilver which one could not fix [solidify], nor could its feet be cut off, that is to say, its volatility be removed, that by this long decoction in the very pure blood of young children, which is [shown] here, this quicksilver, uniting with gold and silver, becomes transmuted with them at first into a herb similar to that which was depicted, and thereafter, through corruption, into serpents which, being subsequently totally dried and cooked by the fire, will become reduced to gold powder, which is the stone.

Flamel refrains from expressing any criticism of Master Anselm's alchemical expertise, and instead goes on with his story:

> This was the reason that for the long space of twenty-one years I made a thousand errors, although never with blood, which is evil and villainous. Moreover, I found in my book that the philosophers call blood the mineral spirit that is in the metals, principally in the Sun [gold], the Moon [silver], and Mercury, whose assemblage I had always attended to. Also, these interpretations were, for the most part, more subtle than veritable. Therefore, never perceiving in my operations any of the signs at the times described in the book, I always had to start anew. Finally, having given up the hope of ever understanding these figures, at last I made a vow to God and to Monsieur Saint-Jacques de Galice that I would seek their interpretation from some Jewish priest in some synagogue of Spain.

It took Flamel no fewer than twenty-one years to hit on the idea that his best hope of finding the meaning of the book by Abraham the Jew lay in seeking out the help of contemporary Jewish alchemists. In his day, the Jews of France were going through a very difficult period. They suffered repeated massacres, confiscations, fines, imprisonments, expulsions, and other persecutions, and were, on the whole, an oppressed and dispirited community. These circumstances were certainly not favorable to delving into the secrets of alchemy, which required capital, time, and peace of mind. Hence when Flamel conceived the idea of seeking out Jewish alchemists, he had to turn to places outside France. The natural choice was Spain, the home of an old, well-established, prosperous, and highly educated Jewish community. One cannot know whether Flamel was familiar with the situation of the Jews in Spain, but in the fourteenth century there were several Spanish Jewish alchemists who served kings and princes both in Spain and elsewhere, so that if he was not, his decision to go to Spain to find for himself a Jewish master in alchemy was surely a serendipitous one. In any case, his reference to "some Jewish priest in some synagogue of Spain" shows that Spanish rabbis, or at least some of them, had the reputation in France of being adepts of the Royal Art.

> Therefore, with the consent of Perrenelle, carrying with me an extract of them [the hieroglyphic figures], I took the habit and the staff, in the same manner in which one can see me [depicted] outside of the arch on which I placed these hieroglyphic figures, in the cemetery, where I also put against the wall on both sides a procession in which are represented in order all the colors of the stone, as they arise and end, with this French inscription:
>
> | | |
> |---|---|
> | *Moult plaît à Dieu procession* | Much pleases God the procession |
> | *S'elle est faite en dévotion.* | If it is done in devotion. |
>
> (this, which is, so to speak, the beginning of the book of Hercules [Heraclius] treating of the colors of the stone called Iris, in these terms: *Operis procession multum Naturae placet*, etc. [The procession of the work much pleases Nature, etc.], which I put there intentionally for the great clerics who will understand the allusion).
>
> Then, in this manner, I betook myself on the road, and so it happened that I arrived at Montjoye, and then at Saint-Jacques, where, with great devotion, I fulfilled my vow. That done, in Leon, on the way back, I met a merchant from Boulogne who made me acquainted with a physician, Jewish by nation, but now a Christian, living in said Leon, who was very knowledgeable in the sublime sciences, called Master Canches. When I showed him the figures of my extract, he asked me forthwith, enraptured with great astonishment and joy, whether I knew about the book from which they were taken. I answered him in Latin, in which language he had interrogated me, that I hoped to have good news if somebody would decipher these enigmas for me. Carried away by great ardor and joy, he instantly began to decipher the beginning for me. To cut a long story short, he was very content to get the information on the whereabouts of the book, and to hear me talk about it. (And surely he had heard discussions about it for a long time, but only as about a thing one believed completely lost, as he said.)
>
> We resumed our voyage, from Leon we proceeded to Oviedo, and from there to Sanson, where we set sail for France. Our voyage was pleasant enough, and by the time we reached this kingdom he very veritably had

interpreted most of my figures in which, even down to the dots, he found great mysteries (this I found very marvelous). When we arrived at Orleans, this learned man became very ill, afflicted by severe vomitings that had remained with him of that which he had suffered at sea; he was so afraid that I would leave him that he could not imagine anything like it. And however faithfully I remained by his side, he called me incessantly. In the end he died on the seventh day of his illness, which caused me great grief. The best I could do for him was to have him interred in the Church of the Sacred Cross at Orleans, where he still rests. May God keep his soul! For he died a good Christian. And certainly, if I am not prevented by death, I shall give that church an allowance to have some masses said for his soul every day.

Having thus learned from the Jewish alchemist within a few weeks what had eluded him for twenty-one years despite sustained efforts and the help of some Parisian Christian adepts, Flamel returned home in a happy mood and proceeded forthwith to put in practice the teachings of Master Canches:

He who wishes to see the manner of my arrival, and Perrenelle's joy, can see the two of us in this city of Paris, on the gate of the Chapel of Saint-Jacques-de-la-Boucherie, next to my house, where we are depicted, I giving thanks at the feet of Monsieur Saint-Jacques de Galice, and Perrenelle at those of Monsieur Saint Jean to whom she had so often prayed. For it was by the grace of God and the intercession of the blessed and holy Virgin and of the blessed Saints Jacques and Jean that I attained that which I had desired, that is to say, the first principles, not always their first preparation which is the most difficult of all things in the world. But I achieved that too in the end, after long errors of three years or thereabout, during which time I did nothing but study and work, as one can see me doing outside this arch where I placed the sequence [of figures] against the columns that are there, at the feet of Saint Jacques and Saint Jean, praying to God, with rosary in hand, reading very attentively in a book, and pondering the words of the philosophers, and attempting thereafter the diverse operations that I imagined only according to their words. Finally, I found that which I desired, that which I instantly recognized by its strong scent. Once I had that, I easily accomplished the mastery; also, knowing the preparation of the first agents, following my book to the letter, I could not fail even if I had wanted to.

Thus, the first time that I made a projection it was upon Mercury of which I transmuted about half a pound into pure silver, better than that of the mines, as I assayed it and had it assayed several times. This was on January 17th, a Monday, about noontime, in my house, in the presence of only Perrenelle, in the year 1382 of the restoration of human lineage. And thereafter, always following my book word by word, I did it with the red stone upon a similar (quality) [quantity] of Mercury, in the presence of only Perrenelle, in the same house, on the 25th of April that followed in the same year, at the hour of five in the evening, that I veritably transmuted into about as much pure gold, very certainly better than the common gold, softer and more pliable.

I can say with truth: I achieved it three times with the help of Perrenelle, who understood as well as I to help me in the operations, and undoubtedly had she wanted to undertake its performance alone she could have reached the same point. I had quite enough by accomplishing it one single time, but I had very great pleasure in seeing and contemplating the admirable works of Nature in the vessels. To indicate to you how I accomplished it three times, you can see on this arch, if you are acquainted with it, three furnaces similar to those which served our operations.

The foregoing part, as stated at the very beginning of the book, was written in 1399, and tells of events that took place up to the year 1382. In the next part we are suddenly in a much later year, a point in time from which Flamel looks back upon the year 1413. No explanation is given in his text as to this time lapse.

When I wrote this commentary, in the year 1413, at the end of the year, after the passing of my faithful companion whom I shall mourn all the days of my life, she and I had already founded and endowed fourteen hospitals in this city of Paris, had built three completely new chapels, decorated seven churches with great donations and goodly endowments, with several repairs in their cemeteries—apart from that which we did in Boulogne, which is not less than what we had done here. I shall say nothing of the good that we together did to individual poor people, principally to widows and poor orphans; should I mention their names and how I did those things, apart from being rewarded in this world, I would cause displeasure to those good people (whom God should bless), which I would not want to do for anything in the world.

Having built therefore these churches, cemeteries, and hospitals in this city, I resolved to have depicted on the fourth arch of the Cemetery of the Innocents, entering through the great gate from Saint-Denis Street, and taking the right hand, the most true and essential signs of the Art, but only under the hieroglyphic veils and covers, in imitation of those of the gilded book of the Jew Abraham. They can represent two things, according to the capacity and knowledge of those who contemplate them: first, the mysteries of our future and indubitable resurrection on the Day of Judgment and the coming of the good Jesus (may it please him to have mercy on us), a story well suited to a cemetery, and then again they can signify for those who are knowledgeable in the natural philosophy all the principal and necessary operations of mastery. These hieroglyphic figures will serve as the

> two paths leading to celestial life, the first, more open sense, teaching the sacred mysteries of our salvation (as I shall show hereafter), the other teaching every man, however little he understands of the stone, the straight path of the Work which, if perfected by anyone, changes him from evil to good, removes from him the root of all sin (which is avarice), making him liberal, soft, pious, religious, and God-fearing, however evil he was earlier, because thenceforth he will remain always entranced by the great grace and compassion which he has received from God, and by the profundity of His divine and admirable works.

Flamel concludes his story with the warning that neither in the hieroglyphic Figures nor in his commentary will be found any teaching or indication concerning the First Principles and First Agents that could in any way be used by those who are not adepts.

Let us now have a look at the two Jewish masters from whom Flamel claims to have acquired his knowledge of alchemy. Flamel is very laconic in speaking of Master Canches, but we do learn something about him. He was a Jewish physician who lived in Leon, Spain, was a master alchemist, and by the time Flamel met him had converted to Christianity. As we shall see in subsequent chapters, among the Jews of Spain there were others too who combined medicine with alchemy. Canches had heard about the book in Flamel's possession even before Flamel told him about it. He had no problem in understanding the pages Flamel had copied and shown him, and on that basis, and probably also drawing on his own alchemical expertise, he instructed Flamel in the art of making gold and silver. We would like to know what induced him to accompany Flamel to France, but are told nothing on this point. He died of an illness before reaching Paris, and was buried in the Church of the Sacred Cross in Orleans. He left behind nothing in writing. His instructions enabled Flamel within three years to transmute quicksilver into silver and gold.

As for the Jew Abraham, two alchemical authors by the name Abraham are known. They seem to have lived in the fourteenth and fifteenth century, respectively. I shall discuss them and their work in Chapters 17 and 21. The book purchased and described by Flamel seems to be identical with an illustrated manuscript work of which several copies are available in various French libraries.[5] I consulted them and found that the one in the Paris Bibliothèque Nationale (MS Français 14765) is the best and most complete (see Figure 15.1). The following description is based on it.

The manuscript has a printed title page with a richly decorated frame, identified in the lower right corner as having been designed and engraved by F. N. Martinet, and dated 1760. It reads (in French):

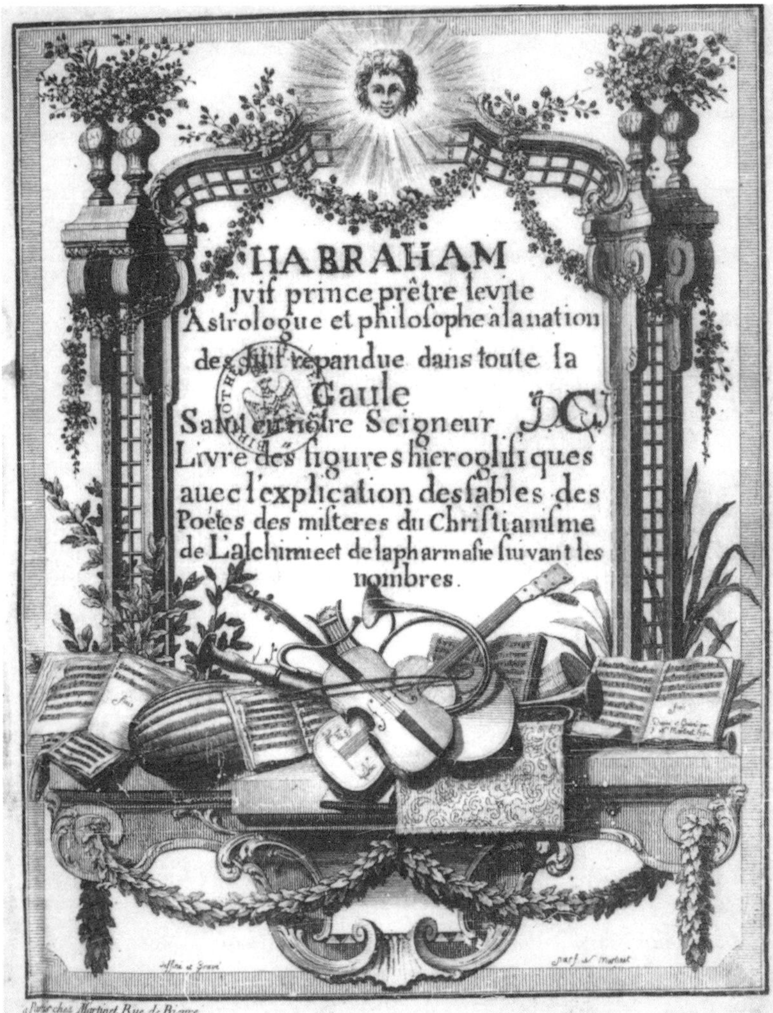

HABRAHAM
Jvif prince prêtre levite
Astrologue et philosophe a la nation
des Juifs repandue dans toute la
Gaule
Salut en nostre Seigneur D.C.J.
Livre des figures hieroglifiques
auec l'explication des fables des
Poetes des misteres du Christianisme
de L'alchimie et de la pharmasie suivant les
nombres.

Figure 15.1. Title page of the *Book of Hieroglyphic Figures* by Abraham the Jew.

"HABRAHAM Jew Prince Priest Levite Astrologer and Philosopher to the Nation of the Jews Scattered in all Gaul. Salvation in Our Lord. Book of the hieroglyphic Figures with applications of the Fables of the Poets of the Mysteries of Christianity, of Alchemy, Pharmacy according to Numbers." That is to say, although the book, or part of it, is claimed to have been written by "Habraham Jew," it is presented in Christian garb and with the addition of extranous material.

This title page is the only printed part of the book. It is followed by 395 manuscript pages in eighteenth-century French hand, with inserted hand-painted illustrations in color, corresponding to the descriptions of the figures given by Flamel. The text begins as follows:

> Our respectable Jewish priest has issued no more forceful and more frequent warnings and commandments than to preserve at the bottom of the heart the most hidden secrets of the kabbalistic art, and he uttered a thousand maledictions against those who, with an ignorant sacrilege and a shameless temerity, reveal them to unworthy people in order to be profanated. He inveighs against those who would explicate them with less restraint and respect than fits the curses which it is horrible to hear and which the most penetrating spirit has pain to understand. Maranatha (which in Greek and Arabic signifies ✠ malediction) in the city and in the country ✠ maranatha ✠ malediction upon the children, upon the animals, upon the flocks, maranatha ✠ malediction upon the barns and upon the crops as well as upon the houses if the secrets are not treated with all the piety required. Maranatha if one does not observe with regard to them the silence of *Pythagoras* and of *Harpocrates.* He adds to all this the pestilence, the fever, the heat and the cold and the seasons infested with a malignant air, and finally all that which can ravage and destroy the world (and that to infinity) against those who will mock it, who will consider it as stories of the old people.

We discussed maranatha above; the curses listed, although not a quotation, are closely reminiscent of those enumerated in Deuteronomy 28:16ff.

On page 4 we find a genealogy of the prophetic blessing: it was passed on from Isaac to Jacob, from Jacob to Judah, and so down to Jesus (p. 6). From page 9 on, the text is surrounded by marginal notes, seemingly from the same hand, including drawings of alchemical vessels. Opposite page 9 is the first hand-painted colored plate, followed by six more, opposite pages 14, 21, 37, 43, 51, and 59. Each picture is followed by several pages of explanatory text.

A Christological tendency is evident in a comment on page 37: "All the Hebrew doctors make mention of the cross, and wished that one give it great veneration, since it contains all the secrets of physics, of magic, and of religion."

Page 71 reads: "First book of the sacred numbers with the miraculous prayers appropriate according to the Kabbalah," and then follows a prayer to Jesus Christ.

Page 72 reads: "The manner of making the mirror of Solomon with the prayers for rendering this operation effective," and goes on to describe how to prepare such a mirror with the four names Adonai, Jehovah, Eloin (Elohim), and Mitatron (i.e., Metatron, the chief angel). The prayer to be said asks God to allow the supplicant to see in the mirror "your angel Anäel." Then follows an incantation: "Come, O Anäel, in the name of the terrible Jehovah." On the left margin of the page there is a sketch of the "Mirror of Solomon" (see Figure 15.2).

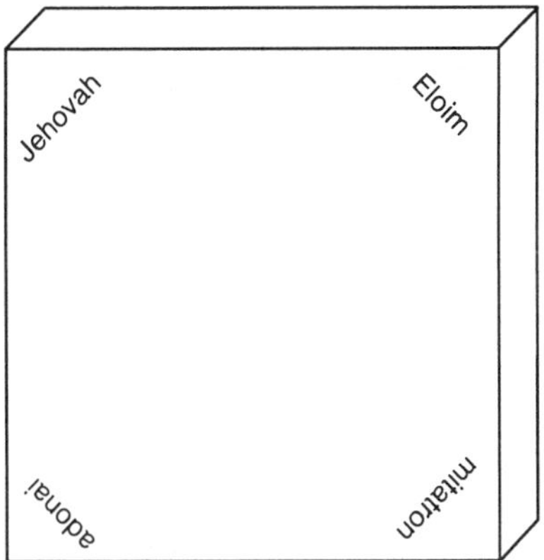

Figure 15.2. Sketch of the Mirror of Solomon.

Page 99 contains a "conjuration of the angel Raphael." Page 124 speaks of the mystery of the incarnation. On page 134 an alchemical operation is stated to be "capable of being taken for a symbol of the proof of the death of Jesus Christ." Page 141 says that "several theologians of the Kabbalah of the Hebrews believe and even assert that Jesus Christ assumed a human body independently of Adam's sin." On page 157 we read that "the resurrection of King Sulphur represents allegorically the resurrection of Jesus Christ himself," and that "all the doctors and masters of the Hebrews have asserted that the seeds of Immortality and of glorification were scattered in all, the things, from which they inferred the resurrection of Jesus Christ and of the bodies." All in all the book is replete with Christological interpretations of alchemical processes. At the same time, Hebrew-Jewish theological terms are frequently used. Thus page 296 mentions "the great Adonay," and pages 300ff. tell of seven temples dedicated to "the great Yahweh" (the word is written in neat Hebrew characters) of which the seventh was that of Solomon. The first was that of Adam, the second of Cain, the third of Enoch, the fourth of Noah, the fifth of Abraham, the sixth of Moses. In connection with the temple of Abraham the text refers to the months of Nissan and Tishri (p. 302). All this shows that even if the book was originally of Jewish authorship, it was subsequently thoroughly reworked by one or more Christian authors. Of Jewish relevance is the repeated appearance of the Tetragrammaton in Hebrew script and of the David's star (on pp. 206, 315, 325). This being the case, it seems justified to interpret Flamel's emphasis on the Jewish authorship, provenance, and decipherment of the book as a reflection of the prestige Jews had in his eyes—and must have had in the eyes of the Christian circles to which he belonged—as masters of alchemy.

A REMARKABLE sequel to the story of Flamel and his Jewish masters in alchemy took place in the early eighteenth century, four hundred years after Flamel's death. In that period Paul Lucas (1664–1737), a French traveler and antiquarian, made repeated trips to the Orient and described them in several books.[6] In the first volume of his 1712 travelogue there is a chapter entitled "Conversations with the Dervishes. History of Flamel: Is He Still Alive?" In it Lucas describes how one day, taking a walk in the streets of Bursa, Turkey, he met a dervish who told him that he had come from the land of the Uzbeks (in Central Asia).

> He seemed to me to be more learned than the others. I think he knew all the languages of the world.[7] Since he did not know that I was French, after having spoken Turkish for some time, he asked me whether I knew Latin, Spanish, or Italian. [Then] he spoke to me in French like a man who was brought up in Paris. . . . Finally I mentioned to him the illustrious Flamel. I told him that despite the philosophers' stone, he was dead in all respects. Hearing that name he started to laugh at my simplicity. Since I had almost begun to believe him in the other things, I was extremely astonished to see him doubt that which I stated. Having noticed my surprise, he again asked in the same tone whether I was good enough to believe that Flamel was dead. "No, no," said he, "you are mistaken. Flamel is alive, neither he nor his wife have as yet known what is death. It is not yet three years hence that I have left both of them in India, and he is one of my most trusted friends." He even went on to state for me the time when he made Flamel's acquaintance, but then he restrained himself and told me that he wanted me to learn his history, which undoubtedly is unknown in my country.
>
> "Our sages," he continued, "although rare in the world, are found equally among all sects, and in this respect no sect is superior to the other. In the days of Flamel there was one [among us] of the Jewish religion. In the early times of his life he became desirous of not losing sight of the descendants of his brothers; and knowing that for the most part they had gone to live in France, the desire to see them prompted him to leave us and to undertake the voyage. We did all we could to dissuade him, and several times he changed his plan at our advice. In the end, his extreme desire to go there made him depart, with the promise, however, to rejoin us as soon as would be possible for him. He arrived in Paris, which was at that time,

as it is at present, the capital of the kingdom. He found that the descendants of his father were held in great esteem among the Jews. He saw, among others, a rabbi of his race who appeared to want to become a *savant*, that is to say, who sought the true Philosophy, and labored on the Great Work. Our friend did not disdain to make the acquaintance of his small nephews. He established with him [the rabbi] ties of close friendship, and gave him many explanations. But since the first material takes long to make, he was content with putting in writing the whole science of the Work, and in order to prove to him that he did not write falsehoods for him, he made in his presence a projection of 30 *ocques*[8] of metal which he transmuted into the purest of gold. The rabbi, full of admiration for our brother, made every effort to induce him to stay with him. But this was in vain, he was determined to keep the word he gave us. Finally the Jew [i.e., the rabbi], not being able to obtain anything from him, changed his friendship into mortal hatred, and the avarice that suffocated him made him resort to the black scheme of extinguishing one of the lights of the Universe. But, wishing to dissimulate, he asked the sage to give him the honor of staying with him a few more days, and during that time, with incredible treachery, he killed him and took from him all his medicine. The horrible deed could not for long remain unpunished. The Jew was discovered, put in prison, and, for several other crimes of which he was also convicted, was burned alive. The persecution of the Jews of Paris began shortly thereafter, and you know that all of them were expelled. Flamel, more reasonable than most of the other Parisians, had no difficulty in establishing relations with some Jews; he was considered even by them a person of honesty and of well-known probity. This was the reason why a Jewish merchant conceived of the plan to entrust to him his registers and all his papers, persuaded that he would not use them for evil, and that he would want to save them from the general conflagration. Among these papers were found those of the rabbi who was burned, including the books of our sage. The merchant, undoubtedly busy with his commerce, had not paid much attention to them. But Flamel, who later examined them, noticing the figures of furnaces, alembics, and other similar vessels, and judging with good reason that this could be the secret of the Great Work, felt that he must not stop there. Since these books were in Hebrew, he arranged for the translation of the first page. This little having confirmed him in his thought, in order to use prudence and not to be discovered, this is the manner to which he resorted: he betook himself to Spain, and since there were Jews there almost everywhere, in every place he asked someone to translate for him one page of his book. Having in this manner translated all of it, he took the road back to Paris. On the way there he found for himself a faithful friend whom he took with him to labor on the work, and to whom he planned to divulge subsequently his secret. But an illness carried him off prematurely.

"Thus Flamel, upon reaching home, decided to work with his wife: they achieved their goal, and having acquired immense riches they caused the construction of several large public buildings, and enriched several people. Fame is sometimes a very annoying thing, but a sage knows, with his prudence, how to extricate himself from all difficulty. Flamel saw clearly that he would be arrested if he should be believed to possess the philosophers' stone, and it would be unlikely that much time could pass without that science being attributed to him, in consequence of the glitter which his largess brought him. Thus, like a true philosopher who does not care about living in view of the human race, he found the means to escape by publicizing his death and the death of his wife. At his advice, she feigned illness, which took its course, and when she was pronounced dead, she was near her *suisse* [?] where she was instructed to wait for him. They buried in her place a piece of wood and clothes, and in order not to lack a ritual this was done in a church which she had caused to be built. Subsequently he had recourse to the same stratagem for himself: since one does everything for money, he had no trouble in winning over the physician and the people of the Church. He left a testament in which he recommended explicitly that they should bury him with his wife, and erect a pyramid over their tombs. A second piece of wood was buried in his stead, while the sage himself was on his way to join his wife. After that time the two of them led a philosophical life with one another, sometimes in one country sometimes in another. Behold, this is the true story of Flamel, and not that which you believe, nor that which people foolishly think in Paris, where few have the knowledge of the true wisdom."

This account seemed to me, and in fact was, very strange. It was the more surprising for me since it was told to me by a Turk who, I believe, had never set foot in France. In fact, I report it only as a historian, and I pass over several other things, even less credible, which he nevertheless told me in affirmative tones. I content myself with remarking that one has in general too low an idea about the science of the Turks, and that the one about whom I speak is a man of a superior type.[9]

We cannot undertake here an investigation of the truth of this remarkable story, but sightings of a famous alchemist after his death by individuals who believe that he did not die—could not die since he possessed the philosophers' stone which is the elixir of life—have remained quite common down to the twentieth century, so that this part of the story need not surprise us. What is interesting in the present context is that although Paul Lucas's story (or the dervish's story) knows nothing of the book of the Jew Abraham, it attributes Flamel's alchemical expertise to another Jewish source: this time it is an anonymous Jewish sage, a member of an interreligious brotherhood of Oriental sages, who goes from an unnamed eastern country to Paris, is murdered there by a fellow

Jew, and leaves behind secret Hebrew alchemical notes or books. Subsequently, when the Jews are persecuted in Paris, these books fall into the hands of Flamel. This version too knows of Flamel's voyage to Spain, where several Jewish sages are able and willing to translate for him the Hebrew text page by page. However, in this version Master Canches has paled into an anonymous "faithful friend," whom Flamel meets in Spain, who is not among his masters but a would-be disciple whom Flamel is ready to instruct in alchemy, but who, like Canches, dies prematurely. All these details, even though changed and distorted, bear a definite resemblance to the original Flamel story. What is new in this version is the faking of death by Flamel and his wife, their false burials, and continued life thereafter in many countries down to the present (eighteenth century), and as far east as India.

The Flamel story demonstrates that in both the fourteenth and the eighteenth centuries the Jews are presented as adepts of the Royal Art, as its past masters, whose writings and oral instructions are the only truly reliable sources from which its Christian students can obtain real mastery. Whether or not Jewish alchemists actually possessed superior knowledge in alchemy, there can be no doubt that the gentile alchemical circles were suffused with the perception that they did. This view was probably nourished by the fact that the Jewish alchemists knew Hebrew, a language difficult for the gentiles to acquire, and that Hebrew, with its close association with Kabbalah and gematria, was considered by gentiles the key that opened a door to the mysterious realms of the Great Art.

It is not my intention to draw too close an analogy between medieval Jewish medicine and Jewish alchemy—although many Jewish physicians were alchemists as well—but just as Jewish doctors had the reputation in royal and princely courts of being the best, so did Jewish alchemists; and just as kings and princes preferred to employ Jewish doctors as their personal physicians, so they preferred to employ Jewish alchemists, as shown by examples discussed in the present book. It seems that in both medicine and alchemy Jewish practitioners constituted a disproportionately high percentage, and if so, they must have made a considerable contribution to both arts. In view of this it is remarkable—and unfortunate—that from the entire span of the Christian Middle Ages the works of no great Jewish alchemist identified by the author's name have survived to take their place next to those of Albertus Magnus, Ruysbroek, Flamel, Trevisanus, Valentinus, Zachaire, and others.

Chapter Sixteen

TWO SPANISH-JEWISH COURT ALCHEMISTS

THE STORY of Flamel's meeting with Master Canches contains an indication of the reputation Spanish Jewish alchemists enjoyed far beyond the borders of the Iberian Peninsula. Flamel's account creates the impression that the Jewish alchemists in Spain plied their trade openly, that the people at large were well aware of the presence of an alchemist in their midst. Otherwise, it would be hard to imagine how a visiting gentile merchant from France could locate, apparently without any difficulty, a Jewish alchemist.

Contemporary historical sources preserved in Spanish archives confirm this impression. They contain documentation pertaining to the life and work of two Jewish alchemists, one in the middle of the fourteenth century, and the other toward its end. The earlier one was Magister Menahem, who was a physician and alchemist like Master Canches, whereas the later, Caracosa Samuel, was one of the heads of the Jewish community of Perpignan and an alchemist with a royal license.

MAGISTER MENAHEM

The name of Magister Menahem appears the first time in a document dated June 1345, which tells about a lawsuit brought by a certain José Maria Quadrado in Palma de Mallorca, accusing Jacobus Rubeus and "Magister Menaym [Menahem] Judeus" of defrauding people with counterfeit silver and gold. Points III through VII of the indictment read (in Dr. Joseph Salemi's translation):

> III. That the said Jacobus and certain others, through dishonest substitution and by means of wicked and counterfeiting art, caused false and counterfeit gold and silver to be made in his house, and he exchanged them and sold them and deceived some persons. And this is public knowledge.
>
> IV. That the said counterfeiting of metals was accomplished through the work of Magister Menaym the Jew, and this is public knowledge.
>
> V. That the said Menaym is a great experimenter and necromancer, and he is known in the street or among the Jews.
>
> VI. That for many months he dwelt almost continuously, day and night, in the house of Jacobus Rubeus, eating, drinking, and sleeping there—so

much so that he sometimes remained there for a full week, right up until Sabbath evening.

VII. That the said Jacobus gave clothing and a great quantity of florins to Magister Menaym as wages for his work.

Furthermore, the indictment alleged that:

> since Magister Menaym the Jew and Senata the silversmith, who are accomplices in the counterfeiting of gold and silver, are persons suspected of wanting to flee, and likewise Marcus de Santa Cruz, who has been accused of stirring up the populace with his words—that is, if they should become aware of the aforesaid [indictments]—it is requested that they be apprehended without delay and thrown into one of the royal fortresses, since they cannot be detained safely in a common prison for the reason expressed to you.[1]

No information is available as to the outcome of the lawsuit, but if Magister Menahem was actually imprisoned in one of the royal fortresses, that seems to have been the opening for him of a fabulous career, somewhat reminiscent of that of the biblical Joseph. Within a year, King Pedro IV (r. 1336–1387), who only shortly before had gained control over the Kingdom of Majorca, appointed him his personal physician, and one month later, on July 7, 1346, he concluded an agreement with him concerning certain experiments and *opera*, whose nature is not stated in the surviving letter patent, but which could not have been anything but alchemical in character.[2] Thus the man who in the summer of 1345 stood before the law court of Palma accused of manufacturing false gold and silver, and defrauding with them his fellow citizens, became a year later an influential high official of the royal court, and entrusted officially with precisely the type of work that he had been accused of having engaged in fraudulently.

Magister Menahem retained his position for several years, and became a confidant of the king, who considered him his master in both alchemy and astrology. This is recorded by Geronymo Çurita (Zurita), the sixteenth-century chronicler of Aragonese history, who devotes a few lines to sketching the intellectual and literary interests of Pedro IV, and in that connection speaks of Menahem: "[King Pedro IV] was much devoted to all kinds of letters, especially to astrology, and was fond of alchemy, in which he found as master a Jewish physician of his, whose name was Menahem."[3]

Caracosa Samuel

Perpignan, located in the eastern Pyrenees, was from 1276 to 1344 the capital of the Kingdom of Majorca, and in the fifteenth to seventeenth centuries changed hands several times between Spain and France. The name of Caracosa Samuel appears the first time in 1367 as one of the *ne'emanim* (trustees) who headed the *aljama*, the Jewish community of Perpignan.[4] Six years later he appears again in an order issued by King Pedro IV and addressed to several Jewish notables, Samuel among them, instructing them to appear within six days in Barcelona to render their expert opinion in a question that had to be decided according to Jewish law.[5]

In the decades that had passed since he first employed Magister Menahem, King Pedro's interest in alchemy did not abate, and on April 1, 1384, he issued a decree that permitted three Christian alchemists to practice their art in *ville Montisalbi* (Montblanch), and empowered them to work "together with those Christians, Jews, or Saracens who might want to take part in the said labor, as often and wherever it will seem expedient to them."[6] This document, incidentally, testifies to cooperation in Spain among alchemists of the three faiths.

The successor of Pedro IV on the throne of Aragon, John I (r. 1387–1396), was, like his predecessor, a patron of the arts and an aficionado of alchemy. Under him, Caracosa Samuel came to play an important role as an alchemist authorized by royal decree to practice his art. The decree in question has survived, and the following is its translation:

> We John, etc., noting that it shall be illicit for no one to direct his attention to the workings of philosophy, whether they be natural or artificial, and for that reason agreeing to the request of some members of our domestic household who have interceded before us on your behalf, Caracosa Samuel, Jew of the city of Perpignan, we concede to you that you have the right to, and can experiment with, the art of alchemy anywhere in our territories, without incurring anyone's penalty; you may freely use, and try through experimentation to the fullest degree, whatever you think fit in this art; you may do and fabricate each and every thing which is consonant with, necessary to, and convenient in whatever manner to, the said art and to its practice and exercise. We command by this same document in specific terms and expressly our governor-general and appointees everywhere and their lieutenants, that under pain of incurring our wrath and indignation they should honor and observe, and neither contravene nor permit anyone else to contravene, our concession and license to you, and all contained in it, for any reason. In testimony of this thing we have ordered the present document to be made and ratified with our seal. Given at Perpignan, on the fifth day of April in the year 1396 from the nativity of our Lord.[7]

Two conclusions can be reached from these sparse historical references. One is that to be an alchemist was an honored profession among the Jews of Perpignan in the fourteenth century, since otherwise they would not have elected an alchemist to be one of the trustees of the community. Moreover, since there is no reason to suspect that the situation in Perpignan was exceptional in this respect, and since there is additional evidence supplied by other data, one can generalize and assume that this was the case in the medieval Jewish communities in the Western world in general.

The second conclusion, likewise confirmed by collateral evidence, is that kings and princes put special reliance on Jewish alchemists, endowed them with the right of practicing their secret art all over the royal domains, and appointed them as court alchemists whose official functions included teaching alchemy to the royal aficionados, and producing gold for the treasury. To put it differently: the historical data, even though scarce, do indicate that alchemy was an important field in Jewish cultural and economic life, and that Jewish alchemists played an important role in the practice of the "Great Art" in the gentile world.

Royal sponsorship of alchemy in general, and of Jewish alchemists in particular, inevitably raises a serious question: since the scientific information at our disposal today makes us certain beyond the slightest doubt that no alchemist was ever able to transmute base metal into gold, how then were the alchemists employed by royal heads to make gold for them able to escape the ultimate unmasking of their failure, and the ultimate penalty that would inevitably have followed? I cannot answer this question satisfactorily, even though quite a number of technical, legal, circumstantial, and psychological factors could be cited to show the great difficulty to be encountered in any attempt to prove fraud by an alchemist working under royal license. In any case, it is a fact that in all the historical sources relating to Jewish alchemists I have studied, I found not a single case in which such a practitioner was in any way penalized for failing to produce gold. Hence it seems legitimate to conclude that the alchemists in question were astute enough to protect themselves one way or another, so that, even if a lawsuit was initiated against them (as it happened in the early life of Menahem of Majorca), the authorities did not muster enough evidence to lead to their conviction.

Chapter Seventeen

ABRAHAM ELEAZAR

ALCHEMICAL treatises, as a rule, deal with practical, realistic or quasi-realistic subjects, such as the transmutation of metals, or the production of the great elixir, and, on the theoretical side, with the nature of nature, the origin and development of metals, and the like. These matters are of equal concern to members of all religious and ethnic groups, and one would not expect to find in alchemical treatises references to particular religio-ethnic concerns. In fact, at the most one finds in them a few brief general phrases, such as "thank God," "with the help of God," and so on, which are nothing more than commonplace expressions of the prevalent religious sentiments. The most remarkable exception to this rule I have encountered is Abraham Eleazar's *Uraltes Chymisches Werck*, which is unquestionably the most Jewish alchemical book in existence.

Nothing is known of Abraham Eleazar except what can be deduced from his book, which was printed in Erfurt in 1735 and which carries the following long descriptive title (in German):

> R. Abraham Eleazar's *Age-Old Chymical Work* [*Uraltes Chymisches Werck*] which was ere now written by the Author partly in Latin and Arabic, partly also in the Chaldaean and Syriac Language, subsequently translated into our German Mother-Tongue by an Anonymous. Now, however, delivered to public Print with appertinent Coppers, Figures, Vessels, Ovens, a brief Preface, the requisite Indices, as well as added Keys of the foreign Words occurring in it, with the usual Approbation for the Benefit and Use of all Lovers of the noble Hermetic Philosophy, in Two Parts, by Julius Gervasius of Schwarzburg, P. M. & J. P. E.

As the title page states, the book contains two parts, each with an inner title page of its own. The first follows Gervasius's Preface, and reads:

Covenant[1]
God without Beginning and End
Abraham Eleazar the Jew, A Prince, Priest, and Levite
Astrologer and Philosopher, born of the Stock of Abraham
Isaac, Jacob, and Judah

Figure 17.1. Frontispiece of Abraham Eleazar, *Uraltes Chymisches Werck*. The Hebrew words on top read *ha'orah sefer*, but they are faultily vocalized and reversed. They should read *sefer ha'orah*, i.e., Book of Light. The Hebrew word under the feet of the figure reads "torah."

The title page of the second part reads:

> *Donum Dei* [Gift of God] of Samuel Baruch, the Rabbi, Astrologer and Philosopher, born of the Stock of Abraham, Isaac, Jacob, and Judah, which teaches the great Secret of the great Master Tubal-Cain, from his Tablet, found by the Jew Abraham Eleazar, I. N. J. CXI.[2]

These three title pages in themselves purport to give quite a lot of information about the provenance, authorship, and contents of the two parts of the book, but the problem is that of the four individuals mentioned only one, the mythical biblical figure Tubal-Cain, is known, and the three others—Abraham Eleazar, Samuel Baruch, and Julius Gervasius—are totally unknown. As often happens with books of such problematic authorship, the provenance of this one has given rise to scholarly controversy.

The *Uraltes Chymisches Werck* (hereafter *Werck*) was first examined by Johann Friedrich Gmelin, a late eighteenth-century historian of chemistry, who states that there are in it "instructions for the preparation of mineral acids," and considers it valuable in connection with "the Great Work of Transmutation." He attributes the book to the beginning of the fourteenth century, a period preceding that of Flamel, but does so without any supporting argument.[3]

After Gmelin, Hermann Kopp, the outstanding nineteenth-century historian of alchemy, subjected the book to critical scrutiny, and found that on page 6 of part 2 of the 1760 edition there was a Latin passage taken from the *Tabula Smaragdina*,[4] which could not be earlier than the twelfth century. He also examined the political references in the book, and found that they reflected the conditions in the seventeenth century. Moreover, he asked his colleague, the Orientalist Gustav Weil (author of the classic *Biblische Legenden der Musulmänner* [1845] and many other important books) to check over the text of the *Werck*. Weil's opinion was that the book contained several incorrect quotations from the Old Testament, a prayer that did not confirm to the Jewish faith, a Chaldaean quote that was partly unintelligible (in part 2, p. 11), and so on. On this basis Kopp concluded that the author, Abraham Eleazar, was supposititious, that the book was spurious, that it could not have been written earlier than the seventeenth century, and that its real author was Julius Gervasius.[5]

This view was unquestioningly accepted by Moritz Steinschneider, who in 1894 pronounced categorically that the book was a forgery.[6]

Another twelve years later, John Ferguson, the conscientious cataloger of alchemical literature, recapitulated Kopp's views and stated that he could not entirely agree with them. His own conclusion was that "Gervasius may . . . have based his adaptation on some old manuscripts, if he did not actually reprint one, as he professes to have done."[7]

Ferguson's view was either unknown to, or disregarded by, C. G. Jung, who in 1963 opined that the *Werck* was a late forgery from the beginning of the eighteenth century, that the author, Abraham Eleazar, purported to be a Jew but was clumsy enough not only to perpetrate anachronisms, but to reveal "his own unquestionably Christian psychology."[8] I am not sure what "anachronisms" Jung refers to, and as to the "psychology" of the author, we shall return to it anon. First, however, let us tackle the question of whether the book could have been written by Gervasius, as Kopp concluded.

Gervasius (whose name, I repeat, is known only from this book), brought the book to press, as stated on the main title page, and contributed to it the preface that he signed. Even a cursory reading of this preface shows that, as far as his opinion of Abraham Eleazar's Judaism was concerned, Gervasius was a typical son of his age: he speaks of the author's "Jewish blindness" in matters of faith, and criticizes him for mixing in his text, "in accordance with his Jewish rudeness, not only many impertinent phrases, strange fables, empty consolations, adventurous prophecies, and idolatrous formulas of prayer, but also occasionally very great mistakes here and there, which one would either have liked to change, or else to omit entirely, had one not been apprehensive that thereby the position of the whole book could possibly be nullified." And he adds, "One could, if time and space permitted, easily and at length refute the drivel scattered in the book by this Jew, with which he tries to defile Christendom," but feels that since this was done effectively by the anti-Jewish authors Wagenseil, Eisenmenger, Gerson, Hosemann, and Müller, it is unnecessary to do so.

Of the Jews in general Gervasius had a similarly dim view. He writes: "the curse that the ancestors of this miserable people wished upon their own necks in the days of our most beloved Savior Christus Jesus, Matth. 27:22,[9] is still lying upon their souls" (f. 7b). Utterances such as these make it evident that Gervasius was a typical eighteenth-century anti-Semite who, in publishing a book by a Jewish alchemical author, felt obliged to make sure that his own negative views of Jews and Judaism were clearly stated in the preface. It is difficult to imagine that all this was a devious ploy and a ruse, and that he himself wrote the "drivel scattered in the book" only to censure them in the preface.

However, if Gervasius did not write the book, but merely edited a manuscript that was written by a Jewish author—and we shall show that such was the case—the question arises: why did he bother with publishing it at all? The answer, I believe, lies in the great respect that Christian alchemists had for Jewish adepts, despite their unfriendly attitude toward Jews in general. Some of the most renowned Christian (and Muslim) alchemists had learned their art from Jewish masters and Gervasius was evidently one of them. Even though his view of Jews was negative, he nevertheless recognized the Jewish author's alchemical mastery, and considered his book important enough to publish, and thereby enhance his own reputation as an alchemist, while at the same time taking care to emphasize his objections to Jewish views that had nothing to do with alchemy. With this understanding, let us now have a look at Gervasius's preface and see what we can learn from it about Abraham Eleazar.

Gervasius states that he published the book on the basis of "a very rare and precious manuscript." He takes it for granted that this manuscript was identical with (or a copy of) the one that fell into the hands of Flamel, which Flamel spent twenty-one years seeking to understand. Gervasius refers to a German edition of Flamel's "Chymical works," printed in Hamburg in 1681, and, in order to point out the importance of Abraham's manuscript he quotes Flamel to the effect that "he would never have found the true vessel of the philosophers had not the Jew Abraham depicted it with its proportionate fire, in which consists a great part of the secret."

Gervasius also quotes another, anonymous, alchemical author, who in his book, entitled *Curieuse Untersuchung* (Curious Investigation), "praises singularly this Jew for giving indications about how, where, and when to find the prima materia of the philosophers' stone."

As for the person of Abraham Eleazar, Gervasius says that "One cannot precisely determine when this rabbi lived, but words contained in Part One, pages 7 and 8, indicate that he flourished quite some time after the destruction of Jerusalem." He explains that the many Chaldaic, Syriac, Arabic, and Greek words contained in the *Werck* are attributable to the fact that after the Jews returned from the Babylonian Captivity, they forgot Hebrew, and within seventy years acquired not only Chaldaic but also the languages of the nations with whom they mingled. Then he goes on to recapitulate the story of the biblical origin of alchemy as it was current in the sixteenth to eighteenth centuries, including, of course, the names of (the original) Abraham, Tubal-Cain, and Moses. He asserts that what Abraham Eleazar did in his book was to explain clearly the transmitted *formas hieroglyphicas*, that is, the pictorial representations, originally made by Tubal-Cain. In this connection he refers to Josephus Flavius, *Antiquities of the Jews*, 1:3:7, who, he says, states that Tubal-Cain invented the art of metal-working.[10] All this is merely a rehashing of what was commonplace in alchemical circles in the eighteenth century.

As for the period in which Abraham Eleazar lived, we can learn nothing definite from Gervasius's preface. However, he either believed or pretended to believe that Abraham Eleazar lived prior to the time of Flamel, that is, before the fourteenth century. Nor can we learn more from the text of the book itself, except for one thing: the author evidently lived in the midst of a Jewish community that was suffering oppression, persecution, rapine, and rapings, and had great difficulty in defraying the taxes imposed upon it by the "Roman Emperor," which designation could apply to the head of the Holy Roman Empire, which is generally considered to have been founded by Charlemagne in 800, and lasted for a thousand years.

What is unusual in Abraham Eleazar's book is that in it he gives repeated expression to his deep concern for the misery of the Jews, emphasizes that he reveals the alchemical secrets for the explicit purpose of alleviating their sufferings, and constantly mingles the mysterious alchemical recipes he presents with expressions of commiseration and of consolation. The tendency to be the comforter of his people is evinced right after the inner title-page of the first book. The lower part of that page reads:

> I wish my brothers, who by the wrath of the great God lie scattered and captive in slavery here and there in the world, much luck and salvation in the name of the soon-to-come Messiah and the great prophet Isaiah who already calls out to all his brothers: *Deni Adonai Bocitto Ochysche*, 60 F.[11] Therefore wait patiently until the Hero comes, but Maranatha[12] [curse] upon all and every one of those who are not of the stock of Judah, who get this book into their hands, so that they should become darkened, and perish like the band of *Korah, Datan, Abiram*, and perish in אֵשׁ *esh* [fire], or disappear.
>
> I.N.U.C.XI.[13]
>
> AZOTH HYLE SHAMAYIM[14]

In the first few pages of his book Abraham Eleazar reminds his brothers of the sins of their fathers whose consequences they were still suffering, and calls on them to repent their own sins. These pages set the tone of the whole book, throughout which Abraham Eleazar shows himself to be full of aching concern for the fate of his people.

After a lengthy quotation from 4 Ezra 14:39–47 (which may have been added by Gervasius), Abraham Eleazar holds out the promise to his brothers that the Messiah (the word is written in Hebrew characters) would soon come and redeem them. Addressing God, he describes in heartbreaking detail the suffering of his people: "O Lord, they make our virgins subservient to them, and violate them in front of our eyes; our elders and princes are mercilessly murdered by them; our youths are put to death under the burden . . ." (p. 4). Then he switches to a description of the messianic age which is soon to come, and asserts that he is revealing in this book "the secrets of our fathers so that you should be able to pay the tribute to the Roman Emperor, and . . . to redeem the poor captives. . . . Therefore I want to teach you the preparation of the metals in Asophol [gold melted through antimony][15] and Diana [silver], and to depict it with invariable words and figures, so that you should be able to grasp it with your hands, and [know] how to prepare the △[16] [fire] of the Lord, which was lost, when the time comes to intimidate with it your enemies, so that you should have it in your hands for your protection" (pp. 6–7).

The passage that follows is interesting because it contains a reference, unusual in alchemistic literature, to Jewish alchemical secrets hidden in the ruins of Jerusalem:

> Furthermore I want to show you the place where our Fathers walled in and buried the secrets, when Jerusalem was destroyed by the emperor Titus Vespasianus, so that you should be able to tell and show it to your children, for no heathen will find the spot, only our brothers. For the signs stand to this very hour, so that even a blind man among you will find it, which however will happen when the great prophet Elijah will be present, for prior to that time, even if you have all the signs, you will still not obtain it. For already out of curiosity some went there, and searched for the place, and even found it, but when they opened it △ [fire] came out so that they partly perished. Therefore beware lest this book get into the hands of your enemies, lest the wrath of the great God be kindled against you even more. For then your enemies would have even more reason to afflict and torture you. Therefore let Maranatha come upon all those who get this book into their hands and to whom it does not belong. Maranatha must darken and destroy them (p. 7).

The subject of the secret hidden in (or under) the ruins of the Jerusalem Temple preoccupied Abraham Eleazar to such an extent that on the next page he returned to it:

> The great יְהֹוָה Jehova will not maintain his wrath forever, but will shortly gather us, to occupy again our inheritance, so that you, when the time comes, should be advised where our priests hid the most noble secrets at the time when Titus Vespasianus wickedly burned and destroyed the holy city and the Sanctuary. The same will be found at the entrance to the Holy of Holies toward morning [the east], where there is a vault 500 spans deep, through a narrow passage, and it is paved with broad hewn flat stones, with ▽ [earth] two cubits deep upon them, then again flat stones. This is hidden until the present hour, and will be found at the time when Elijah comes with the Maschiach [Messiah]. Therefore, dear brothers, moan and groan with yearning for it; for at that time you will everywhere destroy your enemies. There have been a few brothers who received word about this secret from their fathers. They dared, went there to help their brothers, this was a good intention; but because they were not of the stock of Judah, and also did not understand the signs, because they started to work without instruction, they did not find it. Had they, however, understood the *Signa* [signs], they would have found that which was hidden, had not the God of Abraham and Isaac held his hand over it. But so that you should be sure of the figures and the indications which you will find in your search, I want to paint for you and reveal those which I received from my fathers. 1) When

> you come to the place where the Holy of Holies stood and when you have found the spot and the entrance to it toward morning [the east] on the right side, clear it away, and then you will find a stone which lies two cubits deep: it is marked thus: אֵשׁ [*esh*, fire]; lift it up, it lies 200 spans deep. If the passage is ruined, you must continue to clear it until you come to the place where you will find all the secrets which our fathers possessed, and will know how you should make use of them. For at that time your enemies will begin to torment you. But be of good cheer, for you will get the sword into your hands which will devour your enemies. But so that you should have a consolation until the time comes, and you can come to the aid of your poor captive brothers to redeem them of their servitude, pay attention to what these appointed figures indicate. For you should know that God the Highest will promise and give you His blessing so that you should enjoy the breadth of the land and drink the dew of heaven (pp. 8–10).

At this point Abraham Eleazar breaks off his prophetic pronouncements, divests himself of his Jewish religio-nationalistic considerations, and assumes the mantle of the alchemical adept, by continuing in a totally different vein: "For our father Hermes says: *Pater eius est Sol, Mater Luna, Ventus portavit in ventre suo*, that is, "His father is the sun, his mother the moon, the wind carried it in its belly." "Our father Hermes" refers, of course, not to the Greek god whom the Roman called Mercurius, but to the mythical Egyptian alchemist Hermes Trismegistus, whom Hellenistic and later alchemists considered the father of their Art. This is followed by alchemical-mystical pronouncements which are difficult to understand:

> *Sal ⦶ ri nostrum in mari mundi versans. Ω acris, invisibilem, congelatum coelum nostrum, ▽ m manus non madefacientem* [(Take) our *salnitri* (sodium nitrate) turning into the sea of the world. The spirit of the air, our invisible congealed heaven. Water which does not moisten the hand]. For the spirit of the Lord is unfathomable. It hovers in the air, it signifies the winged serpent, and permeates men and all creatures that are created in the earth, for the winged serpent signifies the Ω *mundi universalem* [universal spirit of the world], permeates all things under the heaven, this is our *Materia* which we prepare out of the coagulated air. This is the Ω [spirit] which is extracted out of the dew, and with which we prepare our ⊖ [salt]. The lowest serpent, however, signifies our *Materia* which is found everywhere, and is earthly as well as heavenly, for it is the true ▽ *Virginea & Adamica* [virginal and Adamic earth].

Abraham Eleazar continues in this vein for several more pages, then switches to alchemical recipes, usually bracketed in expressions of concern for the Jewish people's fate. A good example of this is found in the second chapter (Book 1, pp. 26–44) which consists of one long and involved mystico-alchemical recipe, and begins as follows:

> I Abraham Eleazar continue, dear brothers, to teach you. Dear brothers, since our fathers with their idolatry sinned against the Lord in the deserts, Moses made for them a brazen serpent, fastened it to a cross, so that it should be seen by the whole people, and so that they should recover from the plague which they deserved and suffered. Therefore know that if you can fasten the serpent Phython to this cross with a golden nail, you will lack nothing in wisdom. Therefore, dear brothers, nature which the great Creator created is unfathomable and this is the whole secret of the Art: that we extract the ♎ [spirit] of Phython.

Phython, or, as he also spells it, Python, is an old alchemical concept that made its first appearance in the writings of Greek alchemists who speak of the "oil of Python" and the "serpent Python."[17] For Abraham Eleazar the Python has special importance:

> Nothing in the world has such power to destroy metals as the Phython alone; but, dear brothers, it is not the common Phython, but our ♎ Phythonis [spirit of Python], since with the common Python our ♎ *Phythonis in infinitum* [spirit of Python to infinity] is multiplied, for our ♎ Phythonis transmutes the common Phython into its own nature, just as he transmutes the ☉ [gold] and all metals into its own nature. For it is the *primum ens metallorum* [the first essence of the metals], that is, the well of the ancients, the flower which is covered and guarded by the griffins and the poisonous dragons . . . (pp. 27–28).

As we can see, this is more mysticism than alchemy, or perhaps it can best be characterized as mysticism clothed in an alchemical garb. A few pages later Abraham Eleazar interrupts his presentation, and again addresses his brothers:

> With this you can subdue the whole world. Therefore, dear brothers, pay attention to my teaching, for I want to reveal to you here a still greater secret, and teach you two ways to achieve the great quintessence. Take our *materiam magnesiam* [magnesia material], *plumbum nigrum* [black lead] also called bismuth or *puch* [H. *pukh*, antimony], as it comes out of those mountains, ten or twelve pounds, make that Old One [i.e., the *plumbum nigrum*] into an incomprehensible powder, after you have purified it of all rock; put this powder into a distinct broad *alabazus* [sand-cupel]; place it so that the moon should be able to shine on it and the dew to fall on it, but no sun must shine on it, also no rain come to it; leave it stand thus four weeks; but you must stir the powder every day; when the time is over, take

Figure 17.2. Figure illustrating the unification of the air, symbolized by the winged dragon, with the earth, symbolized by the serpent. The two German words on top read *Vereinige sie*, that is, "unite them," followed by the misspelled Hebrew word *awir* (air). At the bottom is the Hebrew word *eres* (earth). From Abraham Eleazar, *Uraltes Chymisches Werck.*

this powder, as our Old One, and put it in an *acures* [round glass vessel] with a crooked neck [see Figure 17.3], place it into an *alabazus* filled with sand, so that the sand should cover the *acures*, upon an oven, and give it *algir* [the fourth and strongest grade of fire], *termon* [another grade of fire], *heruo* [the first grade of fire], *humor* [the third grade of fire] . . . (pp. 29–30).

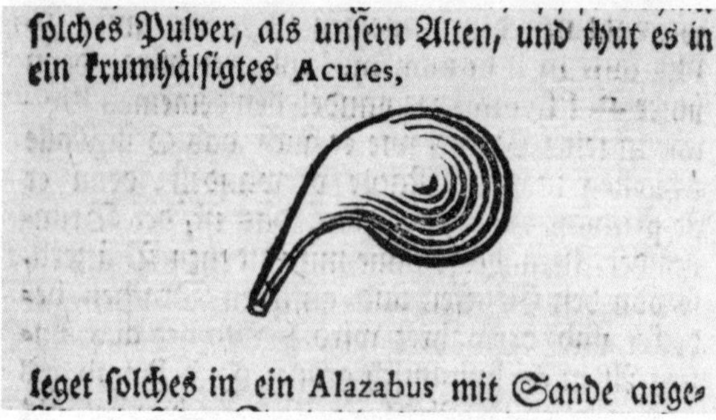
solches Pulver, als unsern Alten, und thut es in ein krumhälsigtes Acures,

leget solches in ein Alazabus mit Sande ange-

Figure 17.3. Alchemical vessel: "*acures* with crooked neck." From Abraham Eleazar, *Uraltes Chymisches Werck.*

After continuing to specify the recipe in this vein for several more pages, Abraham Eleazar again returns to his concern for his brothers:

> Thus I have shown to you again, dear brothers, a way so that you should be able to help yourselves and your poor, and also help those of your brothers who lie captured by the enemy, and who are otherwise in need and in misery. Do not forsake the widows and the orphans, so that you should be able to pay the tribute to the emperor. Be taciturn, lest you be overtaken by misfortune. Cry and moan for your redemption, until the hero comes, the Messiah, to redeem you from your tormentors, and lead you out. Then your days will change, and your mourning will turn into joy. Dear brothers, at that time our brothers will again gather from Assyria, Egypt, and the other countries, they will cross with dry feet the Euphrates and the Nile River. Yes, from all four corners of the world, morning, evening, midday and midnight, the angels which rule the four winds will bring you together, and collect all Israel in the holy places . . . (pp. 42–43).

A distinct element in the teachings of Abraham Eleazar is his reliance on pictorial representation of the ideas he wishes to put across. His chapter 4 begins as follows:

> Dear brothers, Oh if only you would understand me, what I depict for you now! For I speak to you as to children, and not in dark words. Learn, and begin the work, so that your poor brothers should be redeemed of fear. Think of how your souls are distressed under the pressure, that they can not even raise their heads, this is why my heart breaks to show you a way, to help you and them. If you cannot work, entreat the Lord that He give you wisdom, Daniel 11.12, 22. It is easy and a small matter if only you will abandon all the high things in the world. Therefore, dear brothers, I have

Figure 17.4. The Python, from Abraham Eleazar. *Uraltes Chymisches Werck*. German inscription: "With this cut off the Pithon's feet or burn them off with the △ [fire] prepared out of the green dragon."

here again painted for you a figure where you have again two ways before your eyes. Firstly you see how the old *albaon* [black lead] with his blade wants to cut off the wild, winged feet of the Python, and that the Python has a stick in his hands, which means that when this happened he then had two natures, for this is what the two serpents indicate [see Figure 17.4]. This old father-begetter (*Zeuge-Vater*) is being drawn once out of the *primordial chaos*, this is what the △ [fire]-spewing dragon signifies. That the Old One floats in the air signifies the *universal* ♎ [spirit] or Python, the beginning of all things, as I taught you, dear brothers, at the very beginning; and these figures are obvious. That the Old One has a scythe or a

> sickle, and wants to cut off the feet of the Python is an indication that this can be prepared also from another *materia* than the *albaon*, which is a black-grey and heavy *materia*, and one can get it in abundance; and that the Old One floats in the △ [air] has the meaning that one should, as I previously taught you, prepare out of this Old One the *columbam Dianae* [dove of Diana, or of the moon, or of silver], and mix it with the Python, and let it rise again, and thus you get the double Python, or the right *gluten* [glue], the △y [fiery] dragon, in a humid way; but out of the green lion a creeping dragon is being prepared, you have it before your eyes, and you can compare the Old One to the humid way, but in the work they result in the same thing, only that in the dry way there is in the pre-Work a different *modus* than in the humid . . . (pp. 62–64).

I must leave it to students of the general history of alchemy to tackle the question of whether the alchemical concepts and symbols—other than the Python, on which we commented above—appearing in the above text were known in the fourteenth century. The answer to this question could supply additional testimony as to the date of the original manuscript of the *Werck*.

At a later point Abraham Eleazar is again drawn away from his mystical alchemy into an exhortation to his brothers, on which occasion he describes the upheavals he expected would shake the gentile world in the messianic times:

> Then the Messiah of the tribe of Judah will come. Oh! Daughter of Zion, if your king comes, hurry to receive him with a humble heart. Then you will no longer be the forsaken one, but your light will shine again. When the sound of the trumpets comes, the whole ▽ [earth] will be shaken, and all your enemies will tremble in fear and fright, yes, in fright, and know not where to go. Have this for a certain and true emblem. All the nations round about you, and also those among whom you dwell, will rise up one against the other, France against the West, as well as Spain, and the Roman Emperor against France; also the Northerners against one another, the Poles against the Turks, the Turks against the Persians, the Muscovites against the Tartars. One kingdom will destroy the other, which will be followed by pestilence and famine, and then your enemies will be humbled, and their power will become nothing. Therefore, dear brothers, let them always take up the sword, and have nothing to do with them. Keep to humility, and wait with patience. For your king will rise at the same time, and lead you out with a strong arm . . . (pp. 93–95).

This seems to be the passage on which Kopp based his conclusion that the *Werck* must have been written in the seventeenth century. However, the "prophetic" statements contained in it are much too vague to be interpreted as reflecting conditions of a definite period; they seem simply to enumerate all the major powers known to the author, and predict wars between them in the style and tradition of the biblical prophets.

The most problematic passage in the book of Abraham Eleazar, as far as its Jewish authorship is concerned, is the one in which he refers to an epidemic caused by the poisoning of wells. As is well known, when the great plague raged in Europe (1348–1350), killing between one-quarter and one-half of the total population, the Jews were accused of having caused it by poisoning the wells. Under torture, several Jews confessed that they, or other Jews they knew, had indeed committed this terrible crime. This was widely believed by the Christians despite the fact that the Jewish communities suffered as much from the plague as did the Christian population. This seems to be the background of the following passage in Abraham Eleazar's *Werck*:

> Do not dare, without Elijah and our King [the Messiah] to gather against the heathen in order to destroy them, as some of our brothers did, by which they only made the exigency worse, so that often 1,000 of them fell in one day, as with Barchocheta [?]. He taught, because he understood the science, how to prepare the *Mysterium*, to prepare for the people a horrible, poisonous ▽ [water] . . . and they made out of it by *Cohobation* [?] such a horrible smoke of poison that they themselves had partly to perish through it. They poured this into the wells, and when the sky was thick, dark, and gloomy, they poured it into a vessel. This they placed in abundance in addition upon the △ [fire], so that it started to smoke, and thus they poisoned the 🜁 [air] so that men and beasts perished. A terrible sickness and plague spread among the people, they got a horrible burning pox which began to putrefy and to stink; some became black like pitch, and fell down suddenly, and if it entered a house the poison raged so strongly that there was no rescue. Those who were attacked by this poison sought to save themselves and fled into the country, whereby the whole land was ruined. Therefore beware of such things, so that you don't make the burden even heavier upon you. But if you will walk in the commandments of your God, He will preserve you and you will see an early redemption. Be vigorous and watchful, for the yoke will soon be lifted from your necks.

This passage reads as if its author had believed in the libel of poisoning of the wells and the responsibility of the Jews for the Black Death. Could a Jew, who lived during that epidemic or some time thereafter, believe such a thing? Alas, the answer must be yes: the "confessions" were sent to various cities, the accusation spread like wildfire, and the belief in their truth was general in the Christian population.[18] In this atmosphere it is little wonder that a Jewish alchemist like Abraham Eleazar came sufficiently under the influence of the general conviction to believe that one of his colleagues (to whom he referred by a possibly invented name) took unauthorized and reprehensible action to destroy the "heathen" by poison, and that he felt it necessary to warn his brethren not to follow his example. If any historical conclusion can be based on this passage, it is that it seems to have been written soon after the Black Death, that is, probably in the second half of the fourteenth century.

THE second part of the work, attributed to the otherwise unknown Samuel Baruch, is basically an alchemical-mystical commentary on Genesis. Its opening statement, purportedly written by Abraham Eleazar, tells how he found its text:

> My brothers! In the first part I have left behind for you faithfully that which the great God and Creator had revealed in the book of the secrets of Tubal-Cain, for your pressing need, so that you should be able to comfort yourselves and your children, and find help in need. However, so that it should lack nothing, I want to explain to you the secret book, word by word, as far as I have illumination from the God of Abraham, Isaac, and Jacob. Dear brothers, you should know how I obtained it. I found this secret written on copper tablets by Samuel Baruch of our race, in figures, in Chaldaic, Syriac, and Arabic language. Although at first it was difficult for me to understand it, to comprehend the proper meaning of the △ [fire] for sacrifice; however, the great Jehova soon opened it up for me, by His power, so that I could grasp and understand these secrets. Therefore I want to depict for you everything, as much as I understand of this secret, for the elucidation of my first little book, confidentially, as well as the figures engraved on these barks and described. . . .

There can be no mistaking the effort at mystification in this opening statement. Abraham Eleazar says that he found the secret writings of Samuel Baruch engraved on copper tablets, and that he copied their text onto tree bark—a claim reminiscent of what Flamel says about the Book of Abraham the Jew: "it was made of thin barks (as it seemed to me) of tender shrubby trees. Its cover was of very thin copper."[19] While this correspondence cannot be used for attributing Abraham Eleazar's book to the fourteenth century (the time of Flamel), it indicates that the idea of associating copper plates and bark leaves with books goes back to that century at least. Abraham Eleazar's introductory statement is followed by Samuel Baruch's own preface which begins as follows:

> My sons, I have sketched in figures the secrets of the great world, and also its meaning according to its inner secret understanding, as Moyses our brother had learned it from Tubal-Cain, and left it behind, to your great joy, to find the Mighty One in Israel, in figures, as well as His servants and

angels, together with the powers of the innermost receptacle in *centro* of the natures; the food of the hidden angels and spirits, the life, the movement of the stars of heaven, and the power of the soil; the light in △ [fire], the movement and rotation of the earth and ▽ [water]; the effluence of יְהוָֹה Jehova; the clarity of the picture of the great Creator; the splendor of the Holy One and Most merciful; mine and your power, the blessing of Jacob; the power of Isaac, the preserving fruit of Joseph's chastity; the refreshing power of Daniel; the effluence of all spirits. So, take care, and beware, lest the enemies of the highest Creator find it and get it. Keep hidden these marvels which Adam brought out of Paradise for a consolation of his descendants, his brothers who are his equals. Therefore, search in darkness, without being seen, in quiet. When you have found it, do not forsake your brothers who lie caught in need, for you must be a consolation for them. Fear the Creator in the great אֲדוֹנָי Adonai, keep yourself pure, and your souls chaste, then you will be equal to the substance (*Wesen*) of these inner, holy, wonderful things, and of life, of the great world, to perform miracles, to tread the rivers with your feet, to go through mountains, and to command the light of the great world. Yes, so that the earth will tremble before you, and the rocks shake and fall; for the Lord is with you. Up! And be wise and love the תּוֹרָה [Torah], and be [among those] *qui ingrediuntur sine macula & operantur iustitiam* [who enter upon and serve justice without blemish].[20]

Following this introduction, chapter 1 discusses and explains the alchemical mysteries of Creation which, at the same time, are taken to contain secret instructions for alchemical operations:

The *primum ens* [first entity or essence] has appeared, and, after the movement, was lying in itself, out of steam and smoke, and out of the highest became that which is down here, *inferiora haec cum superior[i]bus illis* [these lower things with those higher things], which, according to the Arabic, is *quod est inferius centrum, est sicut est quod superius circumferentia* [that which is the lower kernel is as that which is higher in circumference]. Therefore the high one is heaven, and the lowest is the elementary earth, and all flowed out of the *primo enti* [first essence] (Book 2, pp. 1–4).

Soon thereafter Samuel Baruch introduces the mystical concept of

the supernal serpent [which] is the *spiritus mundi* [the spirit of the world], the most lovely and also the most terrible, who makes everything live, and who also kills everything, and takes on all shapes of nature. In sum: he is everything, and also nothing.

Therefore, *the earth from the separated fire, the subtle and thin from that which is thick and dense, in this it ascends from the earth into heaven, again descends from the earth and from the sky into the earth, and receives the power* and efficacy of the higher and the lower, in this way you will acquire the glory of the entire world; therefore, you will ward off all darkness and blindness. Thus you have one out of two, which contain in them the third and the fourth. It is the most volatile and also the most fixed, it is a [fire], which burns everything, and also opens and closes everything. *For this strength [more than] any other, carrying off the palm for strength and power, for it is able to penetrate and overcome all subtle and dense and hard things.*[21] Then you will have the power of the Creator in your hands, with which you can pursue Wisdom and work wonders. Cook this fire with fire until it remains standing, so you have the most fixed, which penetrates all things, and this figure emerges. [see Figure 17.5]

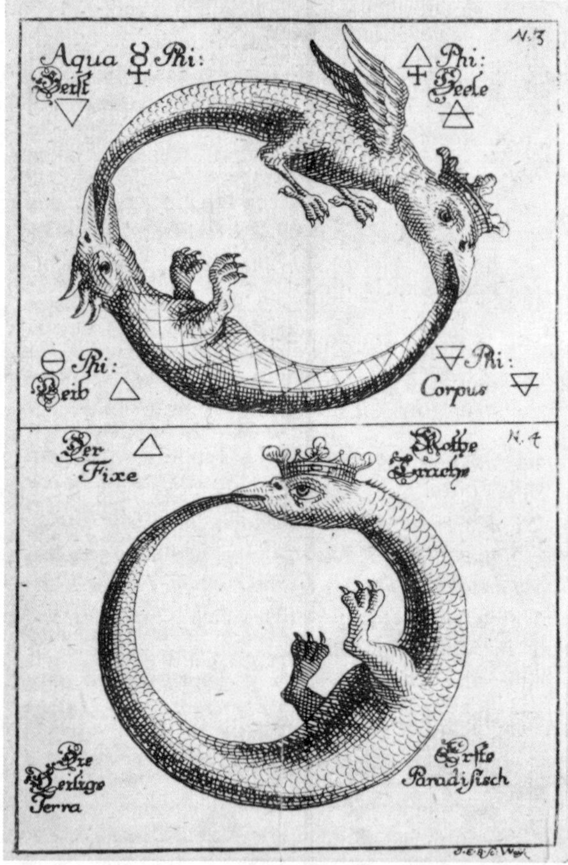

Figure 17.5. Top: the unification of the spirit, the soul, and the body. Bottom: the red dragon of fire. From Abraham Eleazar, *Uraltes Chymisches Werck.*

Here you have made these two into one. Now you can make this worm volatile again: this happens again with the spirit of the world: rub it and make this fixed *carfunkel* [carbuncle, a mineral] or △ y [fiery] worm, red dragon, to ♁, put it again into an *acures* [round glass], give it to drink of its spirit and of its blood until this worm swells up in its *abrasatim* [a spirit, the sharp ☿ ♎, mercury balance], and becomes fruitful in this brood, and bears many thousands of the same. That is, this much one will say: one should put this red △ y [fiery] stone again into a glass, and water it with the double *abrasatim* (or double spirit) of the world (it is also called a penetrating poison, a double △ [fire], is also the life of nature), until the noble one swells up, i.e., becomes pregnant, and then let it stand in a soft warmth until the parturition, until your paradisiac fruit or earth again becomes dry and coagulates. Then do the same again, and as often until the great secret appears: the △ y [fiery] coagulated ▽ [water], the great mystery of the world, the life and food of the holy souls and angels, out of whose dew the heaven [comes] and the fatness of the earth (p. 9).

In the sequel the author explains that the bowl for which Esau sold his birthright to Jacob was a secret medicine, and in it was hidden "the sun of riches" which he desired greatly. Jacob, on the other hand, wrestled for the blessing of God and obtained the heavenly coagulated water. He instructs his brothers to mix this heavenly water with a coagulated fire, thus to obtain the quinta essentia. That quintessence is

> a holy balsam and also a poison, שאסיא כולה (נלא) [בלא] סיעתא דאלהיא לא יהני וגרים (מהית) [מיתה][22] This is all medicine, [and] without the help of God it is without fruit, it kills and destroys. . . . This is the great secret of the fathers, this is what God gave them as a consolation, which they used when they were in plight and trouble; otherwise they did not use it, because they were satisfied with the Highest, and with little. This was the masterpiece of the wise masters with which they prepared everything necessary that belonged to the Temple (p. 11).

The second book ends (on p. 87) with this comment, evidently written by Abraham Eleazar:

> There were many other important things described in the book of Baruch, and in figures on tables. But they are incomprehensible. I have therefore described and depicted for you only the necessary things of which the Ancient Fathers made use with many effects, so that the supernal Creator should thereby be praised, extolled, and glorified.

There is a star of David printed at the end of the book.

When I started this chapter by saying that the *Werck* was "the most Jewish" alchemical treatise known to me, what I had in mind was the fervently religio-nationalistic spirit that pervades it and makes it as much a "Zionist" work as an alchemical-mystical one. The above excerpts and analysis show clearly that Abraham Eleazar's purpose in divulging the secrets of alchemy to his brothers was to help them in their misery and oppression, and to enable them to use alchemical mastery for the alleviation of their sufferings. At the same time, he again and again resorted to fatherly exhortation, and warned them with unrelenting religious insistence to repent their sins, and return to the Lord, who in His great mercy would then send the Messiah to lead them back to the land of their fathers. It is in connection with this hoped-for messianic redemption and restoration that Abraham Eleazar depicted the Armageddon-like events he expected to overtake the gentile world in the not-too-distant future. In sum, we have here the work of a Jewish mystical alchemist whose aim was to use his expertise to help his brothers.

As for the period in which the author lived, there are two factors in the book which allow a tentative conclusion. One is the reference to the Black Death. The other factor, also pointing to a fourteenth-century origin of the *Werck*, is the similarity between it and Flamel's famous *Livre des figures hieroglyphiques*, which we have discussed in some detail. The resemblance begins with the title pages of the two books, which describe their respective authors in a series of epithets much too similar to be coincidental. They read:

Flamel	*Abraham Eleazar*
Abraham the Jew, prince, priest, Levite, astrologer and philosopher of the nation of the Jews . . .	Abraham Eleazar the Jew, a prince, priest and Levite, astrologer and philosopher born of the stock of Abraham, Isaac, Jacob, and Judah . . .

When Flamel describes the contents of the mysterious book of the *Hieroglyphic Figures*, he does it in terms that read like a summation of the detailed and repetitious statements contained in Abraham Eleazar's *Werck*.[23] Apart from the close correspondence between this summation and the detailed presentation in the *Werck*, and the appearance in both books of such mystical-alchemical terms as *azoth*, the serpent Python, and the like, there are two non-alchemical details appearing in both books that are noteworthy. One is the use of the word "Maranatha." Abraham Eleazar uses it repeatedly in a self-evident and matter-of-fact manner, indicating that the term was well known to him. Flamel, on the other hand, finds it necessary to explain its meaning. This can be taken to indicate that Flamel was not familiar with the word until he found it in the text of the *Hieroglyphic Figures* which he summarized, and in the original version of which that word appeared without comment, as it does in Abraham Eleazar's text.

The other detail is the statement made in both books that the master alchemist whose work is described in them taught alchemical procedures to his people in order to enable them to pay the tribute to the Roman Emperor, and to obtain other benefits as well. This idea is much too specific to appear independently in two different sources, and can be taken as pointing to a definite connection between the two books.

The question then arises of which book has influenced the other. Can one explain the similarity between Flamel and Abraham Eleazar by assuming that the latter was familiar with Flamel's book, took it as the basis for his own treatise, and expatiated on the brief statements contained in it? This seems to be most unlikely, for a number of reasons. First, Abraham Eleazar provides many details to which there is no reference at all in Flamel. These details are so many and so varied that they preclude the possibility that the book is but an amplification of the brief statements contained in Flamel. Second, it is rather unlikely that the brief references in Flamel should have been sufficient to stimulate another author to write a book, so to speak, around them. Third, Flamel explicitly states that he merely summarizes the contents of pages two to five of the book of Abraham the Jew, that is, he had in his hands a much longer text from which he worked. Fourth, the deeply Jewish religio-national sentiment and quasi-prophetic fervor that characterize Abraham Eleazar could hardly have been produced or evoked by working on an enlargement of Flamel's brief, matter-of-fact statements.

This leaves only one plausible explanation of the similarities: Flamel obtained from the unnamed Jewish vendor a manuscript book, and summarized it in his *Livre des figures hieroglyphiques.* Such a book could have existed in several manuscript copies (and even in several languages) representing, in all probability, differing versions. Another copy, or version, was obtained in Germany by the anonymous translator, who then proceeded to produce a German version of it, which in turn was printed by Gervasius. It is likely, all in all, that Abraham Eleazar's *Uraltes Chymisches Werck* goes back to a fourteenth-century original, written by a Jewish alchemist.

Chapter Eighteen

THEMO JUDAEI

THEMO JUDAEI was a French astronomer and alchemist of German Jewish descent whose major work has survived in toto, and whose life is relatively well documented, but of whose Jewishness (or Jewish origin) nothing is known except for the fact that he called himself, and was called by others, Themo Judaei, that is, Themo of the Jew, probably meaning Themo son of the Jew. A variant of his name, in the form of Themo Judaeus, i.e., Themo the Jew, appears in the *Historia universitatis Parisiensis* (History of Paris University, Paris 1665–1673) of César Egasse du Boulay (d. 1678), who also calls Themo *clericus* (clergyman, priest), which designation was subsequently translated by some authors as "rabbi."[1] On the basis of the evidence, Pierre Duhem concluded that "if Thémon's father was Jewish, he himself was Christian." The particulars known about Themo's life also indicate that he was accepted as a Christian, and it was as such that he played an important role in the life of the University of Paris and of a monastery in Erfurt. On the other hand, the witness of the name cannot be denied, and it is an irrefutable testimony to Themo's Jewish parentage and birth.

The date of Themo's birth is unknown, but it can be assumed that he was born about 1325, for in 1349 he and his brother Nicolas, both identified as hailing from Munster, Westphalia, and surnamed "[sons] of the Jew," passed the *déterminance*, or *baccalauréat* examination given by Maitre Henri de Herne of Unna.[2]

The specific conditions that prevailed at the University of Paris in the fourteenth century are responsible for the survival of details about Themo's early life at that institution. At the time the teachers and students of the university who came from foreign countries formed four "nations": German, Scottish (or English), Dacian, and Swedish, each of which was headed by a Procureur, elected for a month, from among the young masters. In 1353 the "English Nation" elected Themo to the office of Procureur and then reelected him in 1355, and again in 1356.

It appears that young Themo was either well supplied with funds by his Jewish father or else he himself managed to acquire money while associated with Paris University, for the records show that he repeatedly financed drinking bouts of his colleagues, and helped them out otherwise, as well. In 1357, and repeatedly until 1361, he was elected Receveur, a position of financial responsibility at the university, and in

1359 he was entrusted by the assembly of the "English Nation" with an important mission to Pope Innocent VI.[3]

After his departure from Paris, the historical notes about Themo Judaei become more meager, but some years later he is referred to in the records of the monastery of St. Augustin in Erfurt (together with two other clerics) as a witness, and is styled *magister Thymo de monasterio rector scolarium scole monasterii nostri* (Master Themo of the monastery, rector of the students of the school of our monastery). This indicates that, probably soon after his association with the Faculty of Arts at the University of Paris, he went to Erfurt to head the school of the Scottish Benedictine monastery in that city. At a later date he seems to have returned to Paris, where he taught at the Sorbonne until 1371.[4]

Themo's life and work are discussed in several studies. As early as in the beginning of the eighteenth century, Johann Christoph Wolf in his great *Bibliotheca Hebraica* stated briefly: "Rabbi Timon wrote questions in Aristotle's Meteorological books, and in books about Generation and Conception."[5] In the early years of our century Pierre Duhem showed that Leonardo da Vinci knew, used, and was influenced by Themo's work, which served him as a guide in his meditation.[6] Recently, Henri Huggonard-Roche discussed in considerable detail Themo's life and work, and subjected his astronomy to a thorough scientific analysis.[7]

Manuscripts of Themo's writings have survived in the libraries of Paris, Erfurt, Vienna, the Vatican, and elsewhere. His astronomical book, titled *Questiones in quatuor libros meteororum [or meteorum] Aristotelis* (Questions in the Four Meteorological Books of Aristotle) is included in the *Questiones et decisiones physicales insignium virorum* (Physical Questions and Decisions of Distinguished Men), an anthology edited by the Scotsman Master George Lockert, and published in Venice in two editions, in 1516 and 1518, and then again in 1522.[8] The incipit of Themo's treatise describes him as *doctissimus philosopiae professor Thimo* (the most learned professor of philosophy Thimo), and is the only source known to me which omits the epithet *Judaei* after Themo's name.

Although Themo was first and foremost an astronomer, he was a man with a wide range of interests, and devoted a chapter in his treatise to problems of alchemy. He quoted Ibn Sīnā's *De mineralibus*, and the *Liber perfectionis* attributed to Jābir ibn Ḥayyān. He believed in the possibility of metallic transmutation. His approach to the problems of the natural world was expressed in the epigram, *omne possibile est cognoscibile vel intellegibile* (every possible thing is knowable or intelligible). What follows is a translation of that passage of the concluding part of his chapter on alchemy in which this sentence occurs, and which contains Themo's philosophical views on the nature of alchemy:

WITH THESE THINGS ASSUMED, WE CAN TURN TO THE QUESTION. And let this be the first conclusion: that with the aid of the existing or possible art [of alchemy] metals can be made, just as a rainbow or a halo [can be made artificially]. This can be proved [as follows]: if someone should know how to apply both passive and active [principles] by means of the art [of alchemy], just as they are applied under the earth in nature, then they would make and cause similar effects, just as there [in nature]. The consequence is obvious and the antecedent is also obvious, for this reason: because such things require nothing other than that they should be approximate, so that they act unimpeded here [on the earth] just as they do below the earth. [This is so] because we see the same thing with respect to other things, so that fire burns here [on earth] just as it does in its own sphere.

The second conclusion is this: that it is possible that such an art [alchemy] can be known and understood. This is proved because such an operation or mixture of primary qualities does exist; therefore it can be known. The consequence is obvious, because every possible thing is knowable or intelligible. But the antecedent is obvious because every day these things are generated and born under the earth. Therefore such a mixture exists.

The third conclusion [is] that although it is possible, it is nevertheless very difficult, and for many reasons it is dangerous to insist on the study of this art. This is proved because sometimes counterfeit specimens are made of gold and silver by which a whole region can be deceived, and the one making it will be a counterfeiter if he uses it as good currency, or, if not he himself, nevertheless he could do so through others, until someone is deceived.

Again, many often make great expenditures which they lose, and the laborers and those who delve [into these matters] suffer similar tribulations. And sometimes, if they do achieve perfection, they are destroyed because of envy, [and] not because their work is less good than that of others, because, according to Aristotle in the *Politics*, the potter hates the potter. And perhaps men take pride in doing such things, but they commit evil deeds. Therefore the lesser evil is to abandon [it], and to exert oneself [lit., "to sweat"] in other good arts.[9]

PART SIX

The Fifteenth Century

Introduction to Part Six

THE NUMBER of Jewish alchemists whose writings survived, or on whose work information is contained in treatises written by others, is somewhat greater in the fifteenth than in the fourteenth century. An interesting indication of the important place alchemy occupied in Jewish thinking in the fifteenth century is contained in a Spanish document which shows that some Jews believed that the expected Messiah would be a kind of alchemist. This document tells of a posthumous lawsuit that took place in 1491 against a certain Fernando de Madrid, a *converso* (converted Jew) of Torrelaguna in the archdiocese of Madrid. A Christian witness testified that fifteen years earlier (i.e., 1476), when Fernando de Madrid was evidently still an adherent of the Jewish faith, he made a prediction about the Messiah, whom the document terms *el ante cristo*, that is, the Antichrist. He predicted "that the Antichrist would come to the city of Palos, and they say that he would bring a philosopher's stone, and that if he should touch with it an iron rod it will turn into silver, and if one of steel it will turn into gold, and the sea will reveal its treasures to him." The outcome of the appearance of this "Antichrist" would be that the Christians would cease believing in Jesus Christ, and instead follow him. The lawsuit ended with the condemnation of the accused, who had long been dead by that time.[1]

Chapter Nineteen

SIMEON BEN ṢEMAḤ DURAN

ONE MEDIEVAL Jewish scholar whose position on alchemy was ambivalent was R. Simeon ben Ṣemaḥ Duran (1361–1444). He was born in Majorca, studied there in Palma in the yeshivah of Ephraim Vidal at a time when the city was a center of Jewish alchemical activity. His curriculum comprised mathematics, astronomy, science, logic, and medicine. After going on to study in Aragon, he returned to Palma, and worked as physician and surgeon. In the massacre of 1391, in which his master Ephraim Vidal was martyred, Duran lost all his fortune, but managed to leave Majorca together with his family; he settled in Algiers, and took a post as rabbi. In 1408 he was appointed chief rabbi of Algiers. He greatly admired Maimonides, but went against his views in believing in astrology, and considered himself primarily a disciple of the Kabbalists, whom he terms "masters of the truth," and often quotes in his works.

Duran was a many-sided author. His writings fall into the fields of religious philosophy, Hebrew religious poetry, responses dealing with religious and legal problems, as well as Hebrew grammar and philology, biblical exegesis, Kabbalah, and the scientific subjects of mathematics and astronomy. He was also a polemicist, attacked the doctrines of the Karaites, engaged in polemics with the Christians, and expressed himself critically about the Koran. His philosophy forms a major part of what is perhaps his most important book, the *Magen Avot* (Shield of the Fathers), an encyclopedic work treating astronomy, natural sciences, animal and human physiology and pathology, and psychology. It is in this book that Duran manifests his thorough knowledge of alchemical theory and his unquestioning acceptance of them, while at the same time expressing himself critically on the alchemists' claim of being able to transmute base metals into precious ones. This is what he says on the subject:

> AND ALREADY in a special book of Aristotle are found the characteristics of more than 400 stones, for some of them serve the sustenance of men, such as silver and gold; some are for the improvement of his food, that is salt; some in which fire is hidden, and they are of many kinds; some, if another mineral falls on them their body becomes strengthened, and they are quicksilver; some, if water falls upon them their body becomes strengthened, such as lead and its like; and hence comes the error of the people in

the work of alchemy [who think they can] improve lead and quicksilver with the remedy of other admixtures, and they think that thus they can use remedies to turn other metals into silver and gold. And many were ruined by this, and their days were cut short, for the nature of the desire to hoard causes men to be seduced by this, and there has never been anybody who succeeded in it.

And there are among the metals those which, if they fall into fire, are ruined and melted, like quicksilver; and those which, if they fall into fire, become strengthened and acquire more glitter and luster and good scent, [like] the precious stone which is called *yaqut* [A., sapphire]. And there are those that are water in the womb of the earth, and when they come out into the air they turn to stone. And there is such that will change by fire from one shape into another, such as the lead out of which they make *zarqon* [A., cinnabar], and such also is iron, for iron is taken from dust, and such is *zanzar* [A. *zinjār*, verdigris] that is made of copper, and *ofidas* that is made out of lead, and also *zanzafur* [A. *zunjufr*, minium, cinnabar] out of quicksilver that comes out by fire in a glass vessel. And some say that *marqasiṭa*, when it is melted, makes quicksilver freeze [i.e., coagulate], and likewise *alsalaq* [A. *al-silaq*, liquid] stone, and this is an error of the alchemists. And from lead [comes] *al-martaq* [A., litharge, oxide of lead]. And there are among the stones such as attract iron, and they are called *magtinas* [magnitas], some of which attract iron, and some flesh, and some hair, and some gold, and some silver, and some straw, and some the water that is in the belly, *hidroqen* [dropsy], and some attract the poison that kills by drinking, and they are the topaz that is called *zmurda* [A. *zumrud* or *zumurrud*, emerald] (and in Laʿaz *marqadi*), and some are good for opening the [bladder] pebbles that are in a person, and some grow like coral, and some in which fire is hidden and if water touches them the fire will come out and conflagration [will be] all around it like the *magtinas* [magnitas] and lime stone, and there is a stone in which there is another stone and it rattles like a bell, and there is a stone that contracts and glues the flesh in abscesses, and there is a stone that puts to sleep, and there is a stone that begets wakefulness, and there is such that if fire touches it [there is] a conflagration around it, such as the sulphur, and there is such that plucks out hair such as lime, and also *zarnīkh* [A., arsenic], and there are such that are found in animals such as the water-lobster [or crayfish], and also in the gall of the ox and of man, and there is such that if it is burned in fire it freezes [i.e., coagulates] and becomes a stone like *tabashir* [A., chalk], and there are those that come out of the water like crystal, and who can know the number of the stones and all their characteristics but God, blessed be He, who created them, in addition to those that are in the various plants and in the various animals whose kinds are very numerous, as I shall explain with the help of God when we shall speak about the soul. However: how did these elements get mixed together until these substances came to exist? For is it not that the place of each one of the elements is fixed, one above the other, and that it does not have the nature of moving out of its place and nature? However, their moving out of their places came about through compulsion, and the compulsive [factor] in this is the movement of the spheres, due to which a part of the elements of fire moves out of its place and enters into the belly of the earth and brings in with it a part of the air and of the water, and there they mixed and mingled in a wonderful mixture with the help of mixtures of the sparks of the stars which have traces in the moistening, and likewise the other sparks of the stars which have such traces.

And in general the light and the darkness are the causes of all beings, for in the light is warmth and in the darkness is cold, and through their commingling come into being all the emerging substances (*mithawim*), and behold the darkness is a substantial feature of the earth while the light is an accidental feature of the earth and it acts in the darkness. And in the recognition of the movements the elements move out of their place, and due to the mystery of the compulsive [factor] they want to return to their natural place, and when they come out of the earth the substances according to their kinds come into being.

And the matter of their commingling is that the water and the dust mix together like mud, and a part of the air enters into them, for were it not so, all the substances would be heavy like water and dust, and were it not for the element of fire which ripens[1] them, all the substances would remain like the potter's clay, but by reason of the element of fire they divest themselves of that form and assume [other] forms according to the measure of the mixture. And the forms that it [they] assume is the lower world.

Out of the commingling of the elements come four [forms]. The first form is the form that becomes inanimate: the parts which are inanimate [bodies] and the minerals which are dead bodies; they have no movement except the movement from above downward when they have come out of their place due to a compulsion, and by the mystery of the compulsive [force] they return to their natural place, and this is their nature, as I have written above. And in the totality of this form are all the metals according to their kinds, and all the stones according to their kinds, and they all agree in this form, and differ [only] in their quality according to the mixture of their elements. And all of these were created on the third day, when the earth became revealed.

The second form is the form of vegetation, for in it was added to the first form the form of sprouting and growth, and of producing seed that remains in it. This is the life-force to preserve the species, and this is the form which is called soul, for there are in it movements that change, downward and upward, for the roots move downward and branches upward, and the roots sense the sweetness of water and move toward it, and move away from he bitter water.

In the sequal Duran speaks in a similar style about "the third form," which is that of the animals, and then of "the fourth form," which is that of the "speaking living form," that is, man.

It is evident that the printed version of the quoted passage from which I translated[2] is occasionally corrupt (some statements are duplicated, some of the Arabic words are faultily transliterated, etc.), but those are minor blemishes that do not detract from the value of the passage as a whole as a testimony to Duran's extraordinary knowledge of the chemistry-alchemy, mineralogy, and medicine of his age. It also shows the extent to which in Duran's day medicine and mineralogy were intertwined, and shows the uncritical acceptance of imaginary properties of minerals next to actual ones (types of magnets which attract iron, flesh, hair, gold, silver, straw, water, poison, etc.).

Duran mentions a "stone in which there is another stone and it rattles like a bell." This undoubtedly refers to the stone called *aban e-re-e* or *aban a-la-di* in ancient Assyria, *aetites* in ancient Rome, and *even t'quma* in the Talmud, which was known also to the medieval Arab naturalists al-Baytar and al-Qazwini (both thirteenth century), and in European folklore under the names "eaglestone," "Adlerstein," "Klapperstein," and so on. It was everywhere believed that if a woman wears such a stone around her neck while she is pregnant it will protect her from miscarriage.[3]

The "special book of Aristotle" Duran mentions in the first line of the quoted passage is the well-known *Stone-book* or *Book of Stones*, attributed to Aristotle, which was popular in medieval Arab scientific circles. It was published in 1912 by Julius Ruska, who discussed the extant Arabic, Hebrew, and Latin versions of the book, which contain practically all the terms and ideas appearing in the foregoing passage of Duran.[4]

Chapter Twenty

SOLOMON TRISMOSIN AND HIS JEWISH MASTER

ONE of the several Christian medieval alchemists who reported that they had traveled to the south or the east and there acquired the "Great Art" from one or more Jewish alchemists was Solomon Trismosin (variant spellings Trissmosin, Trismorin). Trismosin lived in the fifteenth century, was German by birth, and his book, entitled *Aureum vellus*, or "Golden Fleece," became almost as popular as Flamel's book of the hieroglyphic figures.

Trismosin's title goes back to the Greek legend of the Argonauts' search for the Golden Fleece, to which by the seventh or eighth century was added the fantastic feature that the inestimable value of the Golden Fleece lay in the fact that it was a skin inscribed with a prescription for making gold. Trismosin's *Aureum vellus* was first published in 1598–1599 in Rorschach am Bodensee. Its German title page reads as follows: *Aureum vellus or Golden Treasure and Art Chamber. In it [are] Workings and Books of the Most Noble, Most Excellent, Choicest, Most Wonderful and Most Valued Authors, from Age-Old Treasure of the Surviving Hidden Reserved Relics and Monuments of the Kings and Sages of the Egyptians, Arabs, Chaldeans and Assyrians. By the Noble, Highly Inspired, Excellent and Trustworthy Philosopher Solomon Trismosin (Who Was Preceptor of the Great Philosopher and Physician Theophrastus Paracelsus), Arranged in Specific Separate Little Tractates, and Brought into German. . . .*

Within a few years after its original publication, the *Aureum vellus* was translated into French, and printed in Paris is 1613. The French version takes liberties with the title page, and adds that the book, called *La toyson d'or*, "treats succinctly and methodically of the philosophers' stone," that it is "enriched with figures and proper colors," and that it was gathered from "the most weighty monuments of antiquity, such as Chaldean, Hebrew, Egyptian, Arab, Greek, and Latin."[1]

On the very first page of the *Aureum vellus*, Trismosin tells something of his early life and years of wandering. He relates that, desirous of finding the secrets of alchemy,

> from the year 1473 I betook myself to the road, and wandered here and there. Wherever I heard of an artist, I was diligent in going to him, and I

spent one year and a half in these wanderings, and I came to know all kinds of arts of alchemy which I do not want to specify, but I saw the truth in several *particularibus* [details], and spent 200 florins, and still did not think of giving up.

I thought, and had the diligence, to raise expenses among my friends, and set out on a journey with a foreigner to Labach, and from there to Milano, and I came to a monastery where I served as an amanuensis, and attended lectures for a whole year. Thereafter I wandered all about in Italy, and came to an Italian merchant and a Jew who knew German. They knew how to make English tin look like the best fine silver, they sold much of it. I offered myself to serve them if it pleased them: the Jew persuaded the merchant that he should take me on as a servant. I had to guard the fire when they made their art with the tin. I was diligent, and they liked it well, and therefore they kept nothing hidden from me. Thus I learned also the art which was carried out with poisonous things, and I was with them fourteen weeks.

Thereafter I traveled with the Jew to Venice [where] he sold forty pounds of the silver to a Turkish merchant. While he negotiated with the merchant I took six lots of the silver and went to a goldsmith, who had two journeymen. He knew Latin, and I asked him to assay the silver. He referred me to St. Mark's Place, to an assayer who was very portly and rich. He had three German assistant assayers. They quickly carried out the assay, with very sharp things, and thereafter they subjected it to the test, but it did not stand any of the tests, everything flew away in the fire. And they asked me harshly from where I had taken the silver. I indicated that I had had it assayed in order to see whether it would stand up as good silver. When I saw the fraud, I did not return to the Jew, and no longer paid attention to this art, and thought I would be caught in a misfortune with the Jew and the false silver. And I went after that to a school in Venice, and requested that they give me food twice a day. The rector referred me to a hospital in which there were several Germans, and they gave me ample food; it was founded for all kinds of nations and foreigners.

Had Trismosin ended his story here, we would have been left with the impression that his Jewish companion or teacher of alchemy was a common charlatan who tried to pass off cheap metal as silver. But the sequel of the story shows that—whatever the quality of the batch of silver he gave to be assayed—subsequently Trismosin came to believe that he had indeed acquired from the Jewish alchemist the art of transmuting base metal into gold. He reports that the same assistant assayer who had found the first sample to be false silver, offered him a job in a laboratory the next day, when the two met again. Trismosin does not report whether he took up that offer, but he informs his readers that he was employed in a large alchemical establishment outside Venice, went to work, and within two days succeeded in producing "three lots of fine gold." Evidently, he had learned well the "Great Art" from the Jew.

Subsequently, Trismosin reports that he went on to master more and more of the secrets of alchemy. He writes, "From Venice I went to a better place where kabbalistic and magical books in the Egyptian language were entrusted to me; these I had to translate into the Greek language, and from it into Latin."[2] Trismosin claims that from these magical books he learned the secret of the preparation of the philosophers' stone, of which he gives the following description:

> One sublimates mercury with alum, saltpeter, and cooking salt, and in the meantime eats bread thickly spread with butter so that the vapors should not harm one. The sublimate is distilled repeatedly with *spiritus*, and the distillate always poured back, until the sublimate becomes over-distilled. This distillate is the mercury of the philosophers. To it one adds pulverized gold which dissolves in it like fat. One half of the dissolved gold is putrefied with alcohol for fifteen days, so that it turns red and becomes lion's blood. One replaces this with the other half of the dissolved gold, and digests it in a well-sealed still, so that the mixture will turn black, grey, white, yellow, red, one after the other. The substance which one thus obtains, if one puts it on a thousand times as much molten gold or heated mercury, transmutes these into the true stone of the philosophers, with which one can ennoble tin, lead, copper, and iron into good gold.[3]

Little more is known of the life of Trismosin. He seems to have traveled from the West to the East, for Paracelsus records that he met Trismosin in 1520 in Constantinople, and was instructed by him there.[4] Trismosin claims in one of his writings that he was able not only to produce the philosophers' stone, but to use it for rejuvenation. He writes that when he was extremely old and suffered senile decay, he rejuvenated himself with half a grain of the coveted stone: his wrinkled, yellow skin became again smooth and white, his cheeks red, his grey hair black, his bent back straight, and youthful stirrings awakened in him. He also claims to have rejuvenated others: women aged seventy to ninety became so young again that they gave birth to several children. It would, he asserted, be possible for him to live as long as he wanted, and "were it not against the eternal wisdom of God, one could sustain oneself with this *arcano* [secret] until the day of the Last Judgment."[5]

Chapter Twenty-one

ABRAHAM BEN SIMEON'S *CABALA MYSTICA*

THE COMBINATION of mysticism and alchemy in the minds of medieval Jewish thinkers is, as we have seen, strikingly illustrated by the writings of Moses de Leon. No such illustrious testimony can be cited to demonstrate the existence of a similar mental conflation between practical magic and alchemy in the thinking of some medieval and later Jewish authors. In fact, the writer who left behind the most voluminous book treating magic and alchemy in combination is otherwise unknown. Before we discuss that book and its author, however, a few comments are in order about the relationship between magic and alchemy in medieval thought in general.

In the second half of the nineteenth century, Paul Lacroix (1806–1884), the famous French historian, offered a scathing opinion of the alchemical literature of the fourteenth to sixteenth centuries. In his classic *Science and Literature in the Middle Ages*, he termed that literature "a chaotic collection of absurdities," in which "everything grand or mysterious was attributed by the alchemists to the demons which people the air, fire, and water, to the stars which are superior to humans, and to divine will, to mysterious sympathies existing between the Creator and his creatures, and to the hybrid combinations of mineral and vegetable substances."[1] Although Lacroix does not mention the word magic, what he has in mind in the first part of this statement is clearly to condemn the combination of alchemical procedures with magical practices resorted to for conjuring up and controlling demons. His condemnation is the more justified since in their unadulterated forms there is an unbridgeable abyss between magic and alchemy.

The magician (by which term we designate in the present context the practitioner of magic who lives in a Jewish, Christian, or Muslim religious environment, and believes that his magic has a legitimate place within the framework of his religion) believes that by reciting certain secret formulas (incantations), and/or performing certain likewise secret acts or rites, he can force, or at least persuade, supernatural (angelic or demonic) powers or beings to do his bidding. This belief, which was as widespread in medieval Europe as in the Muslim world, had existed among the Jews ever since biblical times, and traces of it could be found, especially among the Middle Eastern Jewish communities, down to present times.

The alchemist, by contrast, believes that there are in nature certain hidden processes, properties, forces, and powers which the adept can duplicate in his laboratory, and thus achieve within a few weeks, days, or even hours that which nature requires years or eons to produce. If he succeeds in learning the correct procedure, and follows the instructions meticulously, he can transmute base metals into precious ones, produce precious stones and pearls, and concoct the even more precious elixir, the quinta essentia, or the philosophers' stone, which gives strength, health, eternal youth, and can delay death almost indefinitely; this is the alchemist's credo.

In the belief system and work order of the true alchemist there is no place for magic. Although he pays lip-service to God, whose help he feels bound to invoke, he performs his art on a purely empirical basis, relying solely on experience gathered and transmitted by his predecessors, often illustrious and greatly venerated, and on his own patient and painstaking experimentation. He does not invoke demons and spirits, because supernatural spiritual forces have no place in the scheme of his work. He believes only in the possibility of modifying the physical properties he *knows* characterize the metals, the minerals, and the elements; and of changing the materials contained in the bodies of plants, animals, and men, all of which can be subjected to physical, technological manipulation by bringing the influence of heat and cold, of dryness and moisture, to bear on them. Characteristic in this connection is the fact that even the terms "soul" and "spirit" are used by the alchemist to designate certain elements or material substances, and do not have for him the common connotation with which we are familiar from the usual contrasting of body and soul, of flesh and spirit.

But in addition to the uncompromisingly puristic (or shall we call them orthodox?) devotees of magic on the one hand and of alchemy on the other, there existed, in many places and many ages, many others of a less rigorous bent who could not resist the promise held out by either magic or alchemy of breaking through the bounds of a confining and often painful physical existence, and resorted to the techniques of both indiscriminately, alternatingly, or in combination. It is a man of this ilk who speaks to us from the pages of the *Cabala mystica*, also entitled the *Book of Sacred Magic*.

Abraham ben Simeon's book has survived in several versions in Hebrew, German, and French. The Hebrew manuscript in the Bodleian Library (Oxford MS Opp. 594) is fragmentary. The most complete is the German manuscript preserved in the Sachsische Landesbibliothek in Dresden (MS Dresden N. 161, Nr. 56), and the French manuscript found in the Paris Bibliothèque de l'Arsenal (MS 2351). Both manuscripts were probably written in the eighteenth century, but both are evidently copies of older originals. These two manuscripts serve as the main basis for our discussion.

The title page of the German manuscript reads: "The Mystical Kabbalah of the Egyptians and the Patriarchs, which is the Book of the True Old Divine Magic, Written by Abraham Son of Simon for His Younger Son Lamech."

The French manuscript is divided into three books, each with a separate title page, the first of which reads: "FIRST BOOK of the Sacred Magic which God gave to Moses Aaron David Solomon & to other Saints Patriarchs & Prophets, which teaches the true Divine wisdom, left by Abraham to Lamech His Son translated from the Hebrew 1458."

The wording of the French title raises the question of whether the book was written by a Jewish or a Christian author. The listing of "saints" together with patriarchs and prophets could indicate a Christian author, although the French "saints" could mean not saints canonized by the Church but holy men in a general sense; this would be in harmony with the Hermetic traditions which claim that the secret knowledge of alchemy had been passed on to the holy and wise men of all nations.[2] On the other hand, the name of the author and the claim that the book was translated from the Hebrew clearly point to a Jewish author. Who then was the author? Furthermore, does the date 1458 mean that the book was written in that year or that 1458 is the year of its translation into French?

Abraham ben Simeon is mentioned in no historical document other than this book, but that source contains a number of clues. His full name was Abraham ben Simeon ben Judah ben Simeon. He grew up in his father's house in Worms, Germany, and received from his father, a Jewish scholar, a Kabbalist, a good Jewish education that included an introduction to the Kabbalah. The book is written in the first person, and is addressed to Lamech, who is the younger son of the author. His older son is called Joseph, and Abraham also had two daughters.

The German manuscript states that on the sixth of Tebeth 1379 (the Hebrew manuscript also has this date but the year is missing), when Abraham was twenty, his father Simeon died. This gives 1359 as Abraham's birth date. Four years later he set out on an extended study trip in search of mastery of "the true magic" and the "divine wisdom." He went first to Mayence, where for four years he studied under a certain Rabbi Moses. While there he became friendly with a young man from Bohemia, Samuel by name, and the two of them decided to go to Constantinople. They set out in the month of Kislev 1387 (according to the French manuscript on February 13, 1397), and passed through Germany, Bohemia, Austria, Hungary, and Greece. In Constantinople the two young scholars stayed two years, probably studying under local masters. At that point Samuel fell ill and died, and Abraham continued the journey alone. He spent four years wandering in the Near East, and then, as he writes, "I went to the old promised fatherland, where I found nothing but woe and misery." Nevertheless, he spent a year in Palestine, and then, in the company of a Christian youth named Christoph, he went on to Arabia. His book contains not a word about what he did during all that time.

Having been away from home for five years, Abraham felt it was time to return. He reports in a single sentence that he parted from Christoph and returned to Worms. In the next sentence we learn that he set out again for the East in pursuit of his quest. He spent another year in Arabia, and then went on through Palestine to Egypt. There he spent yet another year—he does not say where—and then settled in a small town called Arki (in the Hebrew manuscript Arāqī, in the French Arachi) near the Nino (in the Hebrew manuscript "river Nilus"). After having stayed for six months in the house of an old Jew Aaron, he complained to his host of his inability to find what his heart desired, whereupon Aaron advised him to seek out an old and very wise man named Abrahamelim, who lived in the desert not far from Arki. Aaron provided Abraham with a guide, and one and a half days after they set out from Arki they came to a hill covered with bushes and trees. The guide told Abraham that on that hill lived the sage Abrahamelim, but he himself did not want to go further. So the guide returned to Arki, and Abraham, left alone, called upon God for help, and climbed the hill.

And there he encountered an old man, who greeted him in "the Chaldaic [in the Hebrew manuscript 'Aramaic'] language," and bid him welcome. It was Abrahamelim. Abraham is again silent about what happened next, except for stating in general terms that in Abrahamelim he finally found the master for whom he had searched all his life. He remained with Abrahamelim for a whole year, during which the master taught him all the great, secret, divine mysteries. He instructed him orally, and then gave him two little books to copy, which Abraham did. Those two books were of inestimable value, and Abraham, in turn, left them to his younger son Lamech.[3]

In contrast to his silence concerning the year he spent as the disciple of Abrahamelim—the crucial year during which he learned everything that shaped his life thereafter—Abraham describes in detail the scene that took place on the day he took leave of Abrahamelim to return to Germany, quoting the very words of his esteemed master. I translate from the French manuscript, which is the most detailed at this point.

I presented myself to Abramelim [*sic*], who . . . led me into his own apartment, where I took the two little manuscripts that I had copied, and he asked me whether I desired the divine magic really and without any feint. I answered him that it was the only aim and the sole motivation which had obliged me to undertake such a long and arduous voyage in the hope of receiving from the Lord His grace. "And I," Abramelin said to me, "I am confident of the mercy of the Lord, I give you and accord you this sacred science which you will have to acquire in the manner prescribed in these little books, without omitting the least thing imaginable from their contents, and without expanding on what could be and what could not be. Because the Artist who created the Work is the same God who out of nothing created everything. You will not make use of this sacred science for offending the great God, and for harming your neighbor. You will not communicate it to anybody alive whom you don't know very well from long contact and conversation with him, examining thoroughly whether such a person has the intention of using it for good or for bad. When wishing to give it to him you will observe well and precisely the style which I have used toward you. If you act otherwise, the one who would receive it would obtain no fruit from it. Guard yourself as you would from a snake from trading this science, and from making it a merchandise, because the graces of the Lord are given to us free and gratis, and one does not sell them."

Upon receiving the two small books I wanted to throw myself on my knees, but he scolded me saying that one must not flex the knees except before God. I acknowledge that the two books were written exactly so as you, Lamech my son, will be able to see them after my death, and you will recognize the regard I have for you. It is true that prior to my departure I read them thoroughly and studied them, and where I found difficult obscurities I had recourse to Abramelin who, with charity and patience, explained them to me. Being well instructed, I took leave of him and, having received his paternal blessing, which is in use not only among the Christians but also among our predecessors, I left and took the road to Constantinople, where, having arrived, I fell ill, and my illness lasted two months [according to the German version: six months]. But the Lord, in His mercy, delivered me from it, so that a short while after I had regained my strength, having found a vessel about to sail for Venice, I boarded it, and arrived there. Having rested a few days, I left for Trieste, where, having disembarked, I took the land route of Dalmatia. Finally I arrived in my paternal home, where I lived among my relatives and brothers.[4]

The German manuscript supplies the date: Abraham arrived home in "Wormbs" (Worms) on the twelfth of Elul. Thereafter, to the end of his life, Abraham felt indebted to the Egyptian Jewish sage for everything he knew and was able to accomplish with his magic, and in his book he again and again mentions Abrahamelim with gratitude and awe bordering on adulation.

After returning home, Abraham embarked upon a career of what today we would call professional magician and spiritual adviser, and in this capacity—so he informs us—helped princes, kings, and popes, as well as a large number of simple people. He reached a ripe old age: according to the German version of his book he was seventy-nine years old when he wrote it; according to the French, ninety-six. In the book he appears as a man of great piety, who always adhered to the highest principles of morality, and who succeeded in his work as a magus because he was deeply religious and always relied on the help of God.

BEFORE presenting the alchemical aspect of Abraham's book we must take a closer look at the question of the author's identity, and the other question, closely connected with it, of whether the book was originally written in Hebrew. These questions have been discussed by several scholars since the early eighteenth century. Their opinions are widely separated. Neither Johann Christoph Wolf nor A. Neubauer expressed any doubt about the original having been written in Hebrew.[5] For this they were reproached by Moritz Steinschneider, who found that the book was "evidently" written by a Christian "swindler" (*Betrüger*) who pretended to have traveled all over the world, and that it was full of "unabashed lies." His final judgment was that "not a word was true in this book."[6]

In 1927, Gershom Scholem had a critical look at Abraham ben Simeon's book and came to the conclusion that the *Book of Sacred Magic* was "one of the most important, internationally known texts" whose "Jewish origin does not seem to be a mere fabrication." Scholem found that the Christian interpolations were few, and assumed that the book originated in the fifteenth century. He argued that the author could not have been a "Christian swindler," because if he were, he would have had to possess "a surprisingly good knowledge of Hebrew."[7] However, forty-five years later, when Scholem briefly returned to the book, he asserted that "the book was no doubt written originally in German, although the author claims it to be a translation from Hebrew," and retreated somewhat from his earlier position by stating that "the question of its authorship, whether Jewish or Christian, is a matter of dispute. The general style of the book shows the author's knowledge [no longer 'surprisingly good knowledge'] of Hebrew. The work may well have been written by a Jew, with the passages of clearly Christian content added later. It may also have been written by a Christian kabbalist who had read the writings of Pico della Mirandola and Johann Reuchlin." He added that "the book had great influence among those interested in the occult in England and France since the end of the nineteenth century," and concluded by stating that "the magic material in the book is essentially of Jewish origin and constitutes one of the main channels of Jewish influence on late Christian magic."[8]

Another two years later Scholem changed his mind concerning the author of the book. Whereas in 1972 he considered it "a matter of dispute" whether he was Jewish or Christian, in 1974 he wrote that the book "was not in fact written by a Jew." At the same time he returned to his 1927 opinion on the author's mastery of Hebrew, and again considered it not merely "knowledge," but "uncommon command."[9] Such vacillation by a scholar who is generally considered the foremost modern authority on Jewish mysticism only serves to increase our curiosity about the author of the *Cabala mystica* and the original language in which he wrote it.

To tackle the second question first, we must compare the available Hebrew, German, and French manuscripts.[10] In doing so, one notices that the fragmentary Hebrew manuscript is briefer and more terse than the manuscripts in either German or French. Moreover, the Hebrew manuscript abounds in Hebraisms, that is, in turns of phrase typical of rabbinic writing, and is replete with biblical and talmudic references, as one would expect of a medieval Jewish author thoroughly at home in traditional Jewish literature. It seems most unlikely that this style should be found in a book translated from a European language into Hebrew.

Second, the Hebrew manuscript is much more modest in the types and numbers of miraculous acts that it claims Abraham performed than either the German or the French manuscript. We shall return to a discussion of the significance of this feature.

Third, a scrutiny of the magic squares that form the concluding part of the manuscript in both the German and French versions reveals, I believe, important information concerning the original language of the book. In general, Hebrew magical texts abound in non-Hebrew magical names and words used in conjurations, as can be seen, for instance, from the *Sepher Mafteaḥ Sh'lomo* (Book of the Key of Solomon) published in facsimile by Hermann Gollancz.[11] In Abraham's book, too, there are many non-Hebrew magical words inscribed in the squares, but by far the largest number of such words is in Hebrew, transliterated in Latin capital letters.

These magic squares usually consist of a basic word appearing in the first horizontal line of the square, then the same word written on the left side perpendicularly from the first letter; at the bottom of the square the same word appears written backward, and on the right side the same word is written from the bottom up. Finally, the spaces left inside these four words are filled in with words also written back and forth and down and up. The significant feature for our consideration is that the basic words in the great majority of the squares (there are several hundreds in the book) are, in both the German and French versions, Hebrew words transliterated in Latin capital letters, mostly correctly. These Hebrew words have in every case a direct relationship to the purpose subserved by the magic square as stated in the manuscript. Here are a few examples of the basic words, given precisely as they appear in the German manuscript (in the French they are in most cases identical), followed in parentheses by the correct transliteration and the translation, and by the purpose of the magic square as stated in the manuscript:

ALMANAH (*almanah*, widow): to gain the friendship of a widow
BASAR (*basar*, meat): to make the spirits bring meat
CALLAH (*kallah*, bride): to gain the friendship of a bride
CATAN (*ḥatan*, bridegroom); to gain the friendship of a bridegroom
DOBERAH (*dov'rah*, raft): to make a bridge appear
EBENIEKARAH (*even y'qarah*, precious stone): to make the spirits bring precious stones
GARAGAR (*gargeret*, throat): to make a person sick in his neck
GEBLINAS (*g'vinah*, cheese, with the Spanish *s* added for the plural): to make the spirits bring cheese
IEDIDAH (*y'didah*, woman-friend): to gain the friendship of a woman
MATBA (*maṭbeʿa*, coin): to obtain small coins
MELACAS (*m'lakhah*, work, with the Spanish *s* added for the plural): to know secret works
MILCHAMAH (*milḥamah*, war): to get to know secret wars
PEGER (*peger*, corpse): to make dead bodies come alive
SEARAS (*sʿarah*, storm, with the Spanish *s* for the plural): to bring a storm
SITUK (*shittuq*, paralysis): to heal a paralytic

The sum total of the rich Hebrew vocabulary appearing in the magic squares attests not merely to a thorough knowledge of both biblical and post-biblical Hebrew but also to a familiarity with the nuances of living Hebrew as used by the learned elements in the Jewish communities in books, treatises, letters, and other forms of written expression.

An additional important point emerges from a consideration of these transliterated Hebrew words: in both the German and French manuscripts the words are transliterated in accordance with the Sephardic pronunciation of Hebrew. Had the author written in German, he would have transliterated the Hebrew words following the Ashkenazic pronunciation that had become prevalent in Central and Eastern Europe from the thirteenth century on. In that case the German manuscript would have had *zoraas* instead of *tsaraat; scholaum, scholem*, or *schulaym* instead of *salom; choson* instead of *catan* (*ḥatan*), and so on.

The occasional addition of the Spanish plural *s* allows us to conclude that the person who translated the book from the Hebrew manuscript into German was a Sephardi Jew who transliterated the Hebrew words as he pronounced them, and where he felt that the plural was more appropriate than the singular added the Spanish plural ending. After the Spanish expulsion the presence of Sephardi Jews in German lands was not unusual.

Yet another feature that speaks for a Hebrew original is the style. The style of both the German and the French is characterized by long run-on sentences, and by a frequent use of two synonyms in expressing one idea. Both of these features are so typical of Hebrew style throughout the ages that it is superfluous to illustrate them with examples. But let me give one example to show how these features appear in the Hebrew text of Abraham. I translate part of one sentence verbatim from the Hebrew manuscript (book 1, chapter 2), with the duplications in italics:

> He [R. Abraham Elim] *led me on the straight road and brought me to the right path*, as I shall tell below, and the aforementioned Abraham Elim was among my helpers to find *favor and mercy* in the eyes of God, who is *the great and awesome God*, who *graced me with his mercy and increased my understanding from day to day and opened my eyes to see light and to achieve divine wisdom, and I became understanding and knowledgeable in the great holy and awesome secrets* with additional knowledge every morning, until I learned to recognize *the sacred and pure angels, and to be a friend to them and to speak with them mouth to mouth*, and it was they who revealed to me in the end the science of magic to its very essence and how to subdue the evil spirits.

I should add that in the original Hebrew this is a perfectly acceptable style, as it is not, of course, in a European language. The above quoted sentence is translated (or, rather, paraphrased) in French as follows (I again put the duplications in italics):

> Abramelim, who put me on the true road, as I shall tell later, and he gave me the best *instruction and doctrine* of all the others. But this particular grace was granted me by the Almighty Father of all mercy, that is to say, the almighty God, who *enlightened my understanding little by little, and opened my eyes to see and admire, contemplate and learn*, his divine wisdom, so that it was possible for me *to understand and comprehend more and more* of the sacred mystery through which I became knowledgeable of the holy angels, enjoying *their sight and their sacred conversation* whereby I received thereafter the foundations of the veritable magic, and how I could *dominate and command* the evil spirits.

The German version of this passage is very similar.

The French and German versions of the Hebrew original take considerable liberties, and the French manuscript contains occasional evidences of tampering with the text in the form of Christological additions (which, of course, may have been made not by the original translator but by a later copyist). In the beginning of Book Two, where the biblical genealogy of "the divine magic" is given, founder-figures of other religions are included: God gave the divine science "to Noah and his children Japhet, Abraham and Ishmael; this was the science which delivered Lot from the conflagration of Sodom, Moses learned the same science in the desert from the burning bush and taught it to his brother Aaron, Joseph, Samuel, David, Solomon, Elijah, and the apostles, and Saint John in particular (from whom there is an excellent book of prophecies)."

As for the magic and demonic names invoked in the conjurations (whose original Hebrew text, as mentioned, is not extant), quite a number of them are not of Jewish or Hebrew origin, including Magot, Aviton, Lucifer, Oriens, and Paimon. This, however, should not be surprising, since such names appear frequently in Hebrew magical texts and incantations. A glance at the Hebrew *Sefer Maphteaḥ Sh'lomo*, referred to above, will show that the old Hebrew conjurations contained in it are full of non-Hebrew magical names, all written in Hebrew characters, such as Lucifer, Mahel, Aglaut, and the Tetragrammaton.

It is time now to look at the indications in the book that its author, although undoubtedly a practitioner of magic conjurations (he even calls himself a magus), was also an expert alchemist. The first such indication is found in chapter eight of the First Book (French manuscript), where Abraham reports that while he was in Herbipolis (Würzburg), he performed "the operation of the eighth chapter of the Third Book," and "was assigned (?) a very old treasure of gold" and thereafter "struck and converted that gold "into the same weight of gold florins with [the help of] the spirits," and achieved this within a few hours. Since, however, chapter eight of the Third Book deals with magical means for arousing tempests and bringing down hail, snow, rain, and thunder, it is evident that the author, or his translator or copyist, made a mistake, and his intention was to refer to chapter seven of that book, which deals with alchemical operations. This is how that chapter reads in the German manuscript (in my literal translation):

Chapter seven

To make the spirit perform all kinds of alchemical works. 1. That the spirits should perform all kinds of alchemical work. 2. That the spirits should produce all kinds of metals and alchemical arts. 3. To learn all kinds of alchemical art from the spirits.

1	2	3
T A B B A T	M E T A H O	I N I H I N O
A R U U C A	E Z A T E H	N A M A M A N
B U I R U B	T A R A T A	I M A C O R I
B U R I U B	A T A R A T	H E L A L E H
A C U U R A	H E Z A T E	I R O C A M I
T A B B A T	O H A T E M	N A M A M A N
		O N I H I N I

In this version not a single word contained in these three magic squares has a recognizable meaning. In the French version, however, the basic first word in square 2 (which in the French is square 1) reads METALO, the common noun "metal" in general use in medieval Hebrew alchemical writings. Also, in the French version of square 3 the central word is not HELALEH but MELACAH, which is the transliteration of the Hebrew *m'lakhah*, meaning "work," and was the term applied also to alchemical operations.

The three sentences defining the purposes of the three magic squares show clearly that Abraham was not only a magus, but also an alchemist. Had he been only a magician, he would have been satisfied with demanding of the spirits that they produce precious metals and perform alchemical operations for him. But being also an alchemist, who believed in his ability to bend the spirits to his will, he wanted them to teach him the methods of "all kinds of alchemical art."

Additional testimony that Abraham was an alchemist is contained in the second book of his *Cabala mystica*. That book is a kind of medical-magical handbook that provides methods of healing all kinds of diseases, of overcoming enemies, of obtaining friendship, love, fertility, of making parturition easy, of quieting storms on the sea, of finding favor in the eyes of potentates, and so on. In this book, in the course of instructions he gives to his son Lamech, he speaks repeatedly of the elements and metals, and in doing so uses the common alchemical signs, for water, air, gold, silver, copper, iron, lead, and so on. At the same time he also reveals considerable interest in and knowledge of astronomy and astrology, and employs the alchemical signs designating metals in referring to the planets corresponding to them.

ALCHEMY apart, one of the most interesting parts in Abraham's book is chapter eight of his First Book, in which he briefly enumerates cases of miraculous help he was able to render to emperors, counts, and popes with his magic art. This chapter is the only one in which historical figures are mentioned, all of them rulers who lived in the late fourteenth and early fifteenth centuries.

Since this passage contains a number of concrete numerical details, it can also serve as a basis for tackling the question of the time sequence of the various versions in which it has been preserved. The general tendency of medieval and later translators and copyists (who were often paraphrasers) was to embellish the original text, to substitute greater and more remarkable deeds for those told in the original, and to multiply or at least increase the numbers appearing in the first version. Hence one can assume that the more modest variant is older than the more extravagant one. Keeping this in mind we start with the Hebrew version.

> So that you should know how a man should behave, with the help of God, and do them [his deeds] for the honor of God and for good to settle the earth, and also so that you should know to thank God for His goodness and for the plenty of His mercy and charity to you which He gave you to teach you such a wonderful wisdom through me without your having any trouble and effort, I shall now let you know briefly some of the operations which I have performed with patent faith for all peoples, with proper knowledge, as a servant of God, and I understood how to augment the honor of God and how to do good to settle the earth so that the honor of God should be told and his wisdom praised. And the rest of the things which I did and tried with this wisdom you will find after my death when you will have access to my book(s) which I wrote and engraved with a human stylus to serve as a memorial from the day I started to operate in this science until the present day. Behold, there are some four or five persons whom I liberated from the enchantment that was imposed on them, apart from many Jewish and Christian men and women who fell ill due to sorcery done to them, and I healed them, and apart from other sicknesses and illnesses of which I shall not speak in this book.
>
> 1. Our lord the Emperor Zigmundus [Sigismund], may his splendor be exalted, apart from having given him as his share one of the spirits which are subordinated to me to be his servant, I also helped him to wed his wife the queen.
>
> 2. The lord Count Friederich and a thousand horsemen which were with him I liberated from the pit of captivity, as I instructed you to do in the Fourth Part. And had I not done it he would have remained in captivity and in countries inhabited by foreigners.
>
> 3. The bishop of Wormiza [Worms]: I revealed to his ear saying that his servants, and especially the Duke of *Qerin* Burg, would betray his secret, and at the end of half a year it was found that what I said was true and correct, apart from many other things and operations which I performed for him.
>
> 4. Who is he who liberated your uncle Yitzḥaq from the prison in which he sat in Speyer, if not I with the help of God and his wisdom?

> 5. And did I not help the lord the Duke with the Pope so that they should not be captured?
>
> 6. Pope John XXIII and Pope Martin V asked me several times in secret that I let them know the future and tell them what would happen, and what I wrote to them came to pass, and they did not find falsehood and lies in any of my words.
>
> 7. This has already been known to you: when I traveled to the Duke of Bayern [Bavaria], while I was on my way, burglers broke into my house, into the small room which was mine, and took silver and gold and things worth money, in the amount of three thousand gold [ducats]. And when I returned to my house the thieves were forced to return the stolen things without the loss of a penny.
>
> 8. Believe me that about half a year before the fall of the Emperor of Greece in the city of Constantina I wrote to him a letter saying that perhaps he could be spared of all the evils which I worried would come upon him within a short time.
>
> Many more the like, which I do not want to write about, did I accomplish with this science, I myself and alone, and the faithful God did always help me, so that I was never put to shame, and no thing was ever turned back, because [I obeyed] all His commandments and the advice of His angels, according to what R. Abraham Elim had taught me. I walked and observed and performed them as much as possible without turning left or right to the science of the gentiles and their idols, for the ways of the Lord are straight, the pious walk in them and tread in his wisdom.

A German version of this chapter was printed in Johann Christoph Wolf's great *Bibliotheca Hebraea*, from which I translate:

> Briefly now, *inquit* [he says], to relate to you several of the previously mentioned operations, which, after my departure from this world, will be found described in a book, where it is recorded how, from the time when I began to practice this art, which happened in the year 1409, until the day when by the mercy of God I reached the seventy-ninth year of my age, I healed and made healthy some forty-five persons who had various illnesses and infirmities, were bewitched and crippled, among whom there were men as well as women, without [mentioning] innumerable others, who, praise God! were by my efforts restored to health.
>
> With the invincible emperor, our most gracious lord, Sigismund, I not only discoursed concerning my *spiritibus familiaribus* [familiar spirits], but also brought it about by means of my art that he was able to possess the empress, his wife.
>
> Count Friederich I equipped by means of my art with 1,000 horsemen through the power of the contents of chapter XXIX of the last Part of this book, to liberate him from the hands of Leopold, the Duke of Saxony, for

otherwise he would have been captured by him and removed from his office.

To the bishop of this city, our temporal lord, I have half a year earlier revealed and made known the treachery planned by his governor at Krauenburg, not to mention many other particular things which I showed him and with which I was of service to him.

In addition, I set free your cousin Isaac from the prison in Speyer.

I was with him who helped the duke and the pope to flee from the Council of Constance, otherwise both of them would have been captured by the Emperor, their enemy.

I sent for both popes, John XXIII, and Martin V, to come to me in my secret council, and there I told them and showed them what would happen in the future, and they never found any fraud or error in my responses.

You know that when I went the last time to Regenspurg to the Hertzog [duke] of Bavaria, my house was burglarized, and up to 3,000 florins in money, gold, and jewels were stolen. But as soon as I reached home again, he [the burglar] was forced to restore everything to me.

If the Greek emperor had given credence to my letter which I wrote to him six months ago, then perhaps his affairs would not take such an evil turn, as he has to expect within a few years.

All this and much more which is not seemly to describe, have I, my dear son, accomplished solely through the art described in the two last parts of this book and God helped me at all times, so that I was never, in any of my expectation, exposed to shame and derision.

The German manuscript is, by and large, identical with the above version except for the following instances: in the first paragraph it mentions not forty-five but four hundred fifty persons whom Abraham claims to have restored to health, and it adds that they were both Jews and Christians; Count Frederick is stated to have been provided by Abraham not with one thousand horsemen, but with an indeterminate number of *vorgekünstelten* (that is, produced by artifice) horsemen; the amount stolen from Abraham in Regensburg is stated to have been not three thousand but three hundred florins.

There exists yet another German version not mentioned so far. It was published by Johann Richard Beecken, who does not state on what manuscript he based his edition.[12] It differs in several respects from the two discussed above. The most significant deviation is that the person whom Abraham claims to have freed from the prison in Speyer was "a nobleman, whom I redeemed from the prison in Speyer without anybody having noticed it."

In the French manuscript Abraham's exploits are considerably augmented in number and dimension. As one would expect of a later reworking, all the numbers are changed to higher ones. In the German versions Abraham writes his book in his seventy-ninth year, in the French in his ninety-sixth. The one thousand horsemen become "two thousand artificial horses." The three hundred or three thousand florins stolen from him become "eighty-three thousand *Hongres*" (Hungarian gold pieces). And it is not his son's "*Vetter* [cousin] Isaac" whom he liberates from prison in Speyer, nor an unnamed nobleman, but "the Count of Varvick [Warwick?] from the prison in England." And as to the common people whose lives Abraham claims to have saved, their number is not a modest fourty-five or four hundred fifty as in the German versions, but 8,413, and they were not simply sick, but bewitched: "I have until the present healed people of all sorts who were bewitched to death, 8,413 of all kinds of religions without any exception" (p. 65).

Since the Hebrew version is brief, simpler, and more modest in its claims to magic achievements than either the German or the French version, it stands to reason that it is the earliest, upon which were based the German and French versions as embellished and augmented translations or paraphrases. This, of course, does not mean that the extant Bodleian Hebrew manuscript is the original version of the book. On the contrary: it is fragmentary, and the cursive Ashkenazi hand in which it is written shows that it is a late (seventeenth- or eighteenth-century) copy.

As for the historical personages, all from the late fourteenth to early fifteenth century, can easily be identified. The ruler to whom Abraham refers as "Our lord the Emperor Zigmundus, may his splendor be exalted" (in the Hebrew version), is the Emperor Sigismund of the Holy Roman Empire (1368–1437), the protector of the Council of Constance (1414–1418), who was chiefly responsible for the deposition of Pope John XXIII (r. 1410–1415) and the elevation of Martin V (r. 1417–1431) to the papal throne. John had to flee from Constance in March 1415, and was offered protection by Duke Frederick of Austria (1382–1439). Both the duke and the pope took refuge in Switzerland, at the time a Hapsburg appanage. It is this flight to which Abraham refers.

Abraham mentions also another Frederick, whom he calls "Count Frederick." This could be Frederick I (1369–1428), called *der Streitbare* (the warlike, bellicose), who became the duke and elector of Saxony. However, there was no Leopold Duke of Saxony, and, of course, there was no clash between Frederick and the non-existing Leopold. Abraham's "Count Frederick" could therefore refer to another Frederick, the Burggraf of Nuremberg, who became the first margrave of Brandenburg in about 1415, but in that case the Leopold mentioned is erroneously identified by Abraham as Duke of Saxony; he was Leopold (Ludwig *im*

Bart) of Bavaria-Ingolstadt, with whom Frederick did, in fact, have a long and renowned feud.

The mention of Abraham's sojourn in Regensburg with the Duke of Bavaria, on which occasion his rooms were burglerized, could refer to one of several meetings held in that city at which matters of highest moment were discussed. An especially important one took place in 1422, and had something to do with the Council of Constance.[13]

The Greek emperor to whom Abraham claims to have addressed a warning letter "half a year before" the fall of Constantinople must have been Constantine XI Dragases (r. 1449–1453), the last Byzantine emperor, whose capital Constantinople fell to Sultan Mehmed II on May 29, 1453. The style of this reference in Abraham's book clearly intends to demonstrate two things: that he possessed prescience, and that he wrote his book (or at least this passage of it) prior to the fall of Constantinople. If, as indicated in an early part of his manuscript, Abraham was indeed born in 1359, and he was still alive in 1453, then he must have been at that time ninety-four years old, an age which in itself would have been considered a mark of magic powers.

Do the historical references contained in the book prove, or at least indicate, that it was actually written in, or soon after, 1453? The medievalist Gerald Strauss, whom I consulted in this matter, felt that they do not. He found the clues contained in chapter eight "ambiguous as indicators of contemporary familiarity. The references to Emperor Sigismund and the Council of Constance certainly aren't compelling. Sigismund and the Council were the focal points of the reform agitation that swept the entire fifteenth and much of the sixteenth centuries; everyone knew about them (the *Reformatio Sigismundi* was the most widely circulating reform tract in the entire Reformation period). The problems of the eastern empire were certainly widely known; references to the siege and fall of Constantinople were commonplace in the political and moral literature of the time. . . . The writer seems to get the popes confused. . . . This suggests lack of direct acquaintance with events. A contemporary would probably not have made such an error. I would guess that the writer lifted all these references from some chronicle, most likely that of Ulrich von Richental, whose chronicle of the Council of Constance (printed in 1483 and 1536 in Augsburg, and in 1575 in Frankfurt) was the period's standard source of information." Also the inconsistencies about Frederick and Leopold "suggest later date and indirect source of information for the material in this chapter." As for the Hebrew words in the magic squares, Professor Strauss points out that by the sixteenth century Christian magicians had "easy access to Hebrew grammars and dictionaries, for example those published by Sebastian Munster in Basel. From these it would have been easy to cull words and phrases." Hence the Hebrew words in the magic squares do not necessarily mean that the squares, and the book as a whole, are a translation from an original Hebrew. "All in all," he concludes, "I would guess that the treatise is later than the fifteenth century. I would guess the sixteenth, but that's only because I find the excerpt so similar to other such texts I have seen."

The points Professor Strauss raises are concrete and weighty (much more so than, for example, Gershom Scholem's unsupported views mentioned in the early part of this chapter), but, I feel, they can be countered. To begin with the Hebrew words in the magic squares: they are so many, and show such a familiarity with both biblical and postbiblical Hebrew, including nuances of meaning, that it seems most unlikely that they could be the work of a Christian Hebraist magician. As for assigning the manuscript to a later date, the question arises, why should an author writing in the sixteenth century select precisely the period of 1359 to 1453 as the time-frame for his story, assign dates within those decades to a series of events he records from the life of his fictitious hero, and then go to the trouble of reading up chronicles of that time in order to insert references to historical figures who acted, and events that took place, strictly during his hero's adulthood and at no other time, so as to connect him with them and illustrate thereby his extraordinary magical powers? This would indicate a concern with scholarly accuracy one would not expect from a sixteenth-century magical author who concocts a pseudepigraphic story set in a past age.

On the other hand, if we assume that the author actually was a Jewish magus-alchemist who tells his own story in the book, and that he did indeed live at the time he says he lived, then it is easy to understand that in trying to furnish proof of his powers he should quote events that took place during his own lifetime, refer to troubles the leading historical figures of his time were known to have had, and then put forward the fictitious claim that it was he who in secret, with his magic, helped those great men and saved their lives. Claims of this type of achievement could count on being believed, since, as Professor Strauss himself points out in his letter, "Jews had the reputation of being the most effective conjurers and spell-binders . . . [and] there are many instances of Jews traveling about Europe to offer their knowledge of the secret arts to those who could pay for it."

Nor can, I believe, the historical errors and confusions that have crept into Abraham's accounts of the magic work he performed for popes and secular rulers be considered as proof of the later provenance of those stories. A Jewish magus who lived in fourteenth- to fifteenth-century Germany, a country comprising many principalities competing and at war with each other, could not be expected to have had accurate knowledge of contemporary events, especially if they took place in remote parts of the vast German lands. Rumors of armed conflicts and the names of the warlords who clashed in them spread across frontiers, but the precise identification of the many emperors, kings, princes, and counts who were involved was difficult, especially since there were several Sigismunds, Fredericks, and Leopolds.

In sum, I think that there are sufficient indications in Abraham's *Cabala mystica* to attribute its authorship to a Jewish magus-alchemist who lived in Worms around 1400, wrote in Hebrew, and pretended (or believed himself) to be favored by God.

Chapter Twenty-two

ISAAC HOLLANDUS AND HIS SON JOHN ISAAC

THE SAME critical list of true and false alchemists which identifies Artephius as a converted Jew also devotes one sentence to the "Hollandi," of whom it says: "The *Hollandi* lived not long before Paracelsus, and are known through their writings, but they are very obscure, and cover things under sophistries."[1] Although this source does not say so, the two Hollanduses belong to that group of alchemists rumored to have been Jews. This was explicitly stated by Karl Christoph Schmieder ("the two Hollands, whom some consider to have been Jews"),[2] who adduces them as examples of the Jewish predilection for anonymity or, as he puts it, *Verschwiegenheit* (reticence, secretiveness). He is correct, since despite the great number of their surviving works practically nothing is known of these two men. Even their family name is unknown, Hollandus being merely the designation of their home country. Nevertheless, Edmund O. von Lippmann, the thorough historian of alchemy, unhesitatingly pronounces them Jewish.[3] Following him, Bernard Suler, in his article "Alchemy" in the 1972 *Encyclopaedia Judaica*, states that in the fifteenth century—according to Lippmann, the seventeenth century—

> two Dutch Jews became famous as alchemists: Isaac and his son John Isaac, both called "Hollandus," since their family name was unknown. The father was a diamond cutter and his son a physician. They led solitary lives, and became famous only posthumously, through the works which they left behind; some authors consider them equal to Basilius Valentinus. They knew how to prepare "royal water" out of nitrate and sea-salt, as well as the "spirit of urine" (ammonia), and produced artificial gems.

Schmieder discusses the work of the two Hollanduses in some detail and presents his arguments for placing them in the first quarter of the fifteenth century. Isaac the father quotes Arnaldus de Villanova, the famous author of the *Rosarium philosophorum*, who is known to have lived from 1245 to 1313, and both Isaac and John Isaac are quoted by sixteenth-century authors, and especially by Paracelsus (c. 1493–1541), who copied passages of their works without, however, mentioning the source. Schmieder argues that one must assume, on the one hand, that reclusive scholars could not be expected to become acquainted with the newest literature within a short time, and, on the other, that the works of such isolated scholars took a long time before it came to the notice of other alchemical authors. For these two reasons, Schmieder says, students of the history of alchemy "concluded that they [the Hollanduses] should be placed in the middle between Arnaldus and Paracelsus, that is, about the year 1425." And he adds that in this respect Torbern Bergmann is wrong by placing them in the early seventeenth century, on the basis that their writings were only printed at that time.[4]

Schmieder goes on to adduce the opinions of leading chemists among his own contemporaries, who lauded the Hollanduses and one of whom, Robert Boyle (1627–1691), even subjected their procedures to repeated experiments. Another, Kastner, spoke highly of Isaac Hollandus and surmised that his operations involved the decomposing of base metals into substances of unequal calorific capacity by subjecting them to a disoxidizing treatment with carbohydrate.[5]

Both the father and the son describe transmutations with a certainty that gives the impression of being based on actual experience. John Isaac states in his *Opus Saturni*[6] that his tincture was so powerful that if one part of it was thrown upon a thousand parts of molten lead or silver, it oversaturated the metals. And only thereafter, when one of these thousand parts was put on ten parts of metal, was the latter transmuted into gold, the best gold that could be found on earth. That is, the Hollanduses not only saw this, but claim that they actually did it several times, with varying experiments, measured with scales and weights.

It appears that the Hollanduses wanted to speak to posterity, but without any ambition. About the preparation of the philosophers' stone both of them speak only with great restraint, although they make it apparent that it must be composed of substances from all three realms. In his book *De triplici ordine elixiris et lapidis theoria* (On the Threefold Order of the Elixir, and the Theory of the Stone)[7], Isaac mentions by name four stones, one mineral, one vegetable, one animal, and one composite, the last one clearly a product of the first three.

Schmieder suspects that John Isaac was a practicing physician, for no other alchemist before him wrote in such detail about the utilization of the tincture as a panacea. He wrote in the *Opus Saturni*:

> This stone makes all leprous people healthy, it heals the pestilence and all contagious diseases. Take of it as much as a grain of wheat, put it into good wine, and give it to the patient to drink. Very soon it will be drawn to the heart, will course through all the blood vessels, and will pursue all humors. The patient will perspire from all pores of his body, but will not become fatigued, but feel more cheerful, stronger, and lighter. For the perspiration will last only until all the bad humors are driven out, whereupon it stops.

> Next day let the patient take again as much as a grain of wheat in warmed-up wine, and go to the closet. This will not diminish as long as he still has something obnoxious in the body, but make him feel the better. If on the third day he takes again the same amount in wine, his heart will be strengthened. One feels elevated over human nature, so light and nimble will be the members.

The same tincture can also be used as a prophylaxis: "One should take as a preservative as much as a grain of wheat in wine once a week, thus one will always remain healthy until the very last hour of one's term of life as destined by God."

In most of the writings left behind by the Hollanduses they are explicitly named as the authors. One can conclude from the style, the manner of writing, and the views expressed in some other treatises, published anonymously, that they were written by these two. However, since father and son had very similar styles and views, it is impossible to attribute such writings to one or the other of them with certainty. Schmieder says that their books are considered to have been written originally in Dutch, but that the extant Dutch manuscripts leave one in doubt on this point, and that it is possible that the originals were in Latin. Most of the writings are contained in the Latin collection titled *Isaaci et J. I. Hollandi Opera universalia et vegetabilia, sive de lapide philosophorum* (The Universal and Vegetable Works of Isaac and J. I. Hollandus, or on The Philosophers' Stone) printed in Arnheim in 1617.[8]

As an example of John Isaac's alchemy, I present here the concluding part of his brief treatise on the urine, which contains instructions of how to prepare the much sought-after quinta essentia. The first part of the treatise tells how to subject "old and pure" urine to a series of alchemical procedures until an "ineffably subtle" substance is obtained. Then he instructs the alchemist to take of that substance

> six parts, of distilled vinegar four parts, and of aqua vita three parts, half a *libra* [pound] of salt, half a pound of common quicklime, mix all of it together, finally dissolving it in clear water of which the sediments have been removed. And you will have an admirable material which reduces into mercury all the limes of the bodies. With this water can be extracted the blessed fifth essence [quintessence] out of antimony and out of all things which are white or red. . . .
>
> *The Way of Extracting All Tinctures with the Precedent Water*
>
> Take sulphur or auripigment or ochre or the like from whatever the extracting of tincture is desired, make of it the finest powder, and mix it with vinegar until it becomes like a *smegma* [paste]. Then put it in a big receptacle and place it on ashes in an oven or on sand, and sprinkle over it from

that aforementioned pure urine or water so that your receptacle should be half filled. Seal it with a cork, and shake it with your hands so that it should be well absorbed. Having done that, replace it on the ashes or the sand, giving it at first gentle fire, until it gets extremely hot, and note that the paste or lid must frequently be removed so that the air should pass under it, otherwise the glass will burst apart, and [note] that the material must always be kept shaken with the hands so that it should be mixed, and the vinegar should be able to operate well. When you see that the vinegar is saturated with color, then, while it is hot and clear, pour it out, but be careful lest the sediments also go at the same time. Preserve what you poured out, well sealed. . . . This done, you have extracted all the tincture, then throw away the sediment, or you can apply it to any use you wish.

Now put your tincture in any receptor vessel, and evaporate the humidity until a thin skin appears. Then, without letting it cool, put the material upon the skin that shows itself in the jug, well sealed with its alembic, and draw out all humidity in ashes or in sand, and there will remain a white or red tincture at the bottom, conditioned by the material you placed there, which will be the quinta essentia: if you have put on it a white material your V. ESS. [quintessence] will be white like snow, if however a red material, it will be red like sparkling gold. In the same manner can the quinta essentia of mercury be extracted from red or white. Likewise from the *limatura* [filings] of Mars [i.e., iron], or from verdigris, cinnabar, or burnt copper, and also from the lime of gold and silver, or from copper; in brief, from all things of the world.

Note. So that the urine should be stronger, if you wish, instead of *salarmoniac* [sal ammoniac] and common salt add one drachma of *ana* [?], and then extract the nobler tincture.

Note. Out of these extracted tinctures it is possible to make cements with which you can cement, which is a certain secret art. Likewise, a certain aqua fortis, red and sparkling like a Rubinus [ruby?]. With that water one can bring to pass miraculous things, which, however, it is not permitted to reveal.

Praise to God.

Chapter Twenty-three

JOHANAN ALEMANNO AND JOSEPH ALBO

WE HAVE already met Johanan Alemanno (1435–c. 1504) in connection with our discussion of Abufalaḥ's alchemy. Alemanno was a fifteenth-century Italian Jewish Kabbalist, philosopher, and scholar with a wide-ranging interest in the occult. It was he who introduced Pico della Mirandola (1463–1494) to the Kabbalah, and thus had a role in the rise of the Christian Kabbalah. Of Alemanno's literary output two books have been printed. One is a kabbalistic miscellany titled *Sefer haLiqqutim* (Book of Collectanea) which quotes Abufalaḥ; the other, titled the *Sefer Shaʿar haḤesheq* (Book of the Gate of Desire) was printed in Livorno in 1790. He also left behind in manuscript a commentary on the Torah titled *ʿĒnē haʿĒdah* (The Eyes of the Community), and an untitled work on the Kabbalah.[1]

Alemanno's *Shaʿar haḤesheq* is characterized by a deeply religious spirit. He explains that all the sciences (among which he counts *geomanṣia, astrologia*, and music) have the one basic purpose of enabling man to serve God better. A point he emphasizes is that the knowledge of other nations, such as the Egyptians, was based on experimentation, whereas King Solomon had knowledge "by the spirit of wisdom and by the holy spirit that rested upon him" (f. 6b). All in all, the *Shaʿar haḤesheq* is a valiant attempt by a deeply religious man of science to organize all the sciences into one organic whole under the aegis of religion and of the divine wisdom which God granted to King Solomon.

At the same time, Alemanno's writings show that he was seriously interested in alchemy. Had that not been the case he would certainly not have included in his *Collectanea* Abufalaḥ's tale about the Ethiopian connection of King Solomon's mastery of the philosophers' stone. His *Shaʿar haḤesheq* contains two sections that betray considerable familiarity with contemporary alchemical theory. One speaks of the relationships between the planets and the metals:

> We saw in the books of the ancients fearsome things which they did in their days because of the greatness of their desire to make an image of the supernal world and its miracles down here on earth. They said that Japheth the son of Noah built a palace in the land of Zin which is on the edge of the east, a very wonderful one, and what is written among us is that in it were

seven windows. In each window there stood an image, according to the shape of one of the seven planets, and each image was of a stone attributed to that planet. And its appearance was like the appearance of gold for the sun, and whiteness for the moon, and blackness for Saturn and redness for Mars, and greenness for Jupiter, and azure for Venus, and a combination of colors for Mercury. And he drew in that palace many figures from which any wise man could undertand the nature of the supernal figures, and the way in which the supernal is represented in the physical form of that which is below, and everything that emerges anew from them as a result of their movements and influences and sparks, and other such indications. And with our own ears we heard a Greek who had gone from one end of the world to the other, and who had neither read nor studied, and he related to us something similar about the building in Zin where he had been. And we questioned him and investigated him as is proper in order to verify in our heart the words of the sages and their dark sayings which appear in the light of the intellect as vanity of vanities, but they are wise sages and wonderful words.[2]

What Alemanno does in this passage is to take the well-known alchemical doctrine about the connection of the seven planets and the seven metals, and attribute its invention to a biblical figure, Japheth the son of Noah. When he says that each "stone" was attributed to a planet, he simply uses the alchemical terminology that was customary in his age, when metals were frequently referred to as "stones." It is, however, noteworthy that he mentions by name only one metal, gold, and replaces the names of the other six metals by names of colors. As for "the land of Zin" in which Alemanno locates his mystical astrological-alchemical palace, its name is, of course, taken from "the wilderness of Zin" located, according to Numbers 34:1–4, at the southern borders of the Land of Canaan.

The other passage shows clearly that Alemanno was a firm believer in the "miraculous things" that could be performed by those who knew the secrets of alchemy. He writes:

And you, if you would know the relations of the metals which affect each other, you could transmute the whole world into silver and gold and precious stones and pearls. And likewise with the relations of the living things and the plants you could perform miraculous things never imagined by the ancients. And if, in addition, you would know the science of the relations of the stars and their representations on earth and all that which they pour out [i.e., emanate] day after day, nothing would be too miraculous for you in judging the future and the past and the present, and all that the Lord has wrought, to find its solution in the [things] inanimate, vegetative, speechless living, and the living which has the power of speech. As for the inanimate, behold, gold is dear in value, [and] is endowed with seven properties. One, that if [somebody] eats [of it] as a charm, it makes him cunning like unto running water, or if it is cooked with food, behold, it will be in its power to restore to life the soul of the sick who is close to death. The second, that if he is used to his wine in which it [the gold] is extinguished many times, then, behold, it purifies the intellect to sharpen [the mind of] the man who uses it. The third, that its sight gladdens souls with the special quality that is in it, and even more so in eating and drinking, if one drinks from a golden vessel. The fourth, that it greatly purifies and improves the digestion when it is found in the stomach, just as it makes it hard if it is swallowed whole in the shape of a skull. Behold, it improves the vision darkened by bad digestion, and not only the vision, but it also lights up the face darkened by leprosy or by ugly moisture. The fifth, that even if it is left for thousands of years in caves or in wet places underground, it will not be affected, nor will it be damaged, for it preserves its truth [i.e., original character] forever, for it is not possible to forge it or to exchange it for another thing, even though the masters of alchemy do forge it and make beaten gold which resembles it to such an extent that one can as little distinguish between the two as between a dust-mouse [i.e., born out of dust] and that which is born of its own kind. But as for verification, so that it should not be falsified, there is a feature preserved in it which cannot be forged by means of a charm, for the gold that is made by [alchemical] work raises blisters in burning, whereas the real gold does not raise blisters. This is a little of the natural science. "And by knowledge are the chambers filled" (Prov. 24:4), "they empty themselves upon the earth" (Eccl. 11:3), with the science of geometry and the measures. And of this the rabbi, the author, wrote in the book *Ḥesheq Sh'lomo*, "There is no higher wisdom than that of the form of the world and its function, and likewise the measuring of the stars in relation and value."[3]

This passage, in enumerating the properties of gold, allows an interesting insight into the folklore of gold, which constituted an important part of the alchemical belief system in fifteenth-century Italy. Noteworthy, too, is the belief that alchemists can produce artificial gold which will be like true gold in every respect except one: artificial hot gold, if touched, will raise blisters, whereas true hot gold will not.

In addition to the two passages just quoted, there is in the *Shaʿar haḤesheq* a longer section in which alchemy is combined with the kabbalistic attribution of enormous secret power to the letters of the Hebrew alphabet. The basis of this combination seems to be the dual meaning of the Hebrew verb *l'ṣaref*, which means both "to refine" and "to combine." The passage in question is much too complex to present here, since it would require lengthy explanation of practically every phrase. We will only mention that it opens by stating that Bezalel, the biblical craftsman who is characterized in Exodus as skilful in working in gold and silver (Ex. 31:2ff.; 35:30ff.), and who in the Middle Ages became the prototype of alchemists, "knew how to combine (*l'ṣaref*) the letters with which heaven and earth were created. . . ." Then Alemanno goes on to explain that originally the Torah comprised an entirely different order of letters, words, and passages, in which there was such a mysterious power that had men known it they could have healed the sick and resuscitated the dead. Therefore God changed over the entire order of the Torah to its present text, which cannot be used for mysterious purposes. Only a very few of the greatest figures in Jewish history had access to that original sacred and awesome text, such as Abraham, of whom R. Abraham ben David wrote in his commentary to the *Sefer Y'ṣirah*, the earliest Hebrew mystical treatise, that "our father Abraham looked and saw and engraved and hewed and combined and created and thought."[4]

Alemanno explains (quoting older books of mystery) that the Hebrew alphabet contains four groups of letters, each of which is derived from or is representative of one of the four elements: fire, wind (i.e., air), water, and dust (i.e., earth). This being the case, the name of each person indicates his character, since the letters contained in his name are indicative of the elements that preponderate in him. The sage who was the greatest master of this science, Alemanno informs us, was Rabbi Meir, "who would weigh the number of the elements of the letters in the name, and according to the elements which outweighed the others it indicated [to him] righteousness, honesty, or wickedness." Finally, Alemanno refers to a passage in the *Zohar*, section *B'shallaḥ*, which tells about "how they saved a sick man in whom the elements of water and the element of dust prevailed. When these elements prevail over the elements of fire, the life of the person is endangered. Therefore he [Rabbi Meir] reversed the letters [in the name of the sick person and changed them into letters] which show the strengthening of fire over the dust and the water," and thus was able to save his life.[5]

The few passages quoted here should give us a glimpse of the mental world of this fifteenth-century Italian Jewish scholar who was thoroughly at home in astrology, alchemy, and all the sciences, as well as in the Kabbalah, the power of the letters of the Hebrew alphabet, and yet was a deeply religious person with an unshakable belief in God, and also a serious scholar who had at his fingertips the entire Jewish literature of all the past ages and of his own time. We do not know whether he was an active alchemist, but from his writings it is clear that he knew alchemy and believed in it, and that it served for him as a kind of intellectual philosophers' clay that luted together the disparate elements of his scholarly and mystical comprehension.

For our investigation into the history of Jewish alchemy it is instructive to have a look at the *haskamot* (approbations) printed in Alemanno's *Sha*ʿ*ar haḤesheq*. In Jewish book publishing it was the established custom over hundreds of years for authors or the publishers of their works to obtain approbations from the leading rabbis and scholars of the age. The typical haskamot contained praise of the author and his book, and expressed the signatories' agreement with the ideas put forward in it. The approbations were thus a guarantee for the reader that the ideas expressed in the book conformed to the generally prevalent view of the religious leadership, and were therefore orthodox. They came nearest in the world of the Jewish book to what the imprimatur and nihil obstat meant for the Catholic readership.

The haskamot of the leading Livornese rabbis of the eighteenth century, the time of publication of *Sha*ʿ*ar haḤesheq*, conform to this pattern. They term Alemanno "the universal sage, the famous philosopher," and heap praises upon him and his book. It is clear from these approbations that the religious establishment of eighteenth-century Livorno unhesitatingly identified itself with the alchemical ideas expressed by Alemanno. Moreover, it stands to reason that had the rabbis not been acquainted and in agreement with the alchemical worldview long before they read its presentation in *Sha*ʿ*ar haḤasheq*, they would not have given the book their approbation.

The signatories of the haskamot are R. David Mal'akh, S. Ṭ. (S'faradi Ṭahor, i.e. "pure Sephardi"), Israel Serusi, S. Ṭ., Raphael Benjamin Ḥayyim Moreno, S. Ṭ., Jacob ibn Naim, S. Ṭ., and Joseph Azubib, S. Ṭ., several of whom have books of their own to their credit. The approbations are followed by a lengthy introduction written by Jacob Barukh, who brought the book to press. In it Barukh extolls the importance of the subjects discussed by Alemanno, which include (as he transliterates them in Hebrew characters) *geometria, astrometria, mekhaniqa, esoropiqa* (?), *perspeqtiva*, and *algebra*. He refers by name to several of the great masters in these sciences—Ptolemy and his Almagest, Archimedes, Copernicus, Tigon (Tycho Brache?)—and asserts that "the purpose of the sciences is to comprehend the existence of God, to cleave to Him always, and not to separate oneself from Him in one's thoughts, and this is also the purpose of the Torah."

Joseph Albo

Joseph Albo was an early fifteenth-century Sephardi philosopher and religious polemicist, whose lasting fame is based on a single book, the *Sefer ha*ʿ*Iqqarim* or "Book of Principles," first published in 1485. It was subsequently republished in many editions, several of them with commentaries, and achieved great popularity in Jewish circles. Albo took part in the famous Disputation at Tortosa and San Mateo in 1413–1414 as representative of the Jewish community of Daroca (Province of Saragossa), and completed his *Sefer ha*ʿ*Iqqarim* in 1425 in Soria in Castile. He was a disciple of Ḥasdai Crescas, and was influenced by Crescas's *Or Adonai* (1410) and by Simon ben Ṣemaḥ Duran's formulation of the principles of the Jewish faith contained in the latter's commentary on Job, written in 1405. In addition to rabbinic literature and Jewish philosophy, Albo had a wide knowledge of Islamic philosophy and Latin Christian scholasticism, and was versed in mathematics and medicine.

In the *Sefer ha*ʿ*Iqqarim*, Albo, following Thomas Aquinas, distinguishes three kinds of law: natural law, conventional law (*dat nimusit*), and divine law. It is while arguing the superiority of divine law over conventional law that Albo betrays his familiarity with alchemical theory and practice; and, by using an alchemical simile in order to make his argument more easily understandable, he shows that alchemical procedures were well known to the Jewish audience for whom he wrote. He writes:

> Divine law, being derived from divine wisdom, determines for all times what is proper and what is improper. Hence the aversion to [that which is] improper which one acquires from it [the divine law] will admit of no change or diminution, because it is pure of all dross and refuse. And for this reason it can persist forever, like the silver that is pure of all dross, as is the saying of the poet, "The words of the Lord are pure words, like silver tried in a crucible on the earth, refined seven times" (Ps. 12:7). Explanation: the counterfeit silver which is made in the work of alchemy, some of it if smelted once will not reveal its falseness, but if it is smelted a second time it reveals its falseness, and there is such that will stand two smeltings, and such that stands three or four or five, but in the end it will reveal its falseness. And there is such that will not reveal its falseness if it is smelted in a melting pot, but if it is smelted in the bowels of the earth it reveals its falseness. And the silver which is refined in the bowels of the earth and is purified many times is pure of all falseness and dross and refuse, and it is impossible for it to change thereafter even if it is smelted many times. And this is why the Poet [i.e., the Psalmist] compares the words of God which are pure to the pure silver that is tried in the crucible of the earth, which is in a place discovered in the bowels of the earth, purified seven times, and there is no suspicion of any falsification in it. And likewise the aversion to the improper that one acquires, which occurs in the Torah, "is pure, enduring forever" (Ps. 19:10), since no change and diminution can occur in it as it occurs in the conventional law.[6]

Albo and his readers were evidently familiar with counterfeit silver produced by alchemists, and knew that, if smelted several consecutive times, the base metal it consists of will show up. It is clear that the passage quoted could have been written only in an environment and for an audience that was well acquainted with, and subscribed to, the alchemical theory of the gradual purification of metals in the bowels of the earth. If we consider people who knew of this theory and accepted it as a fact of nature to have been alchemists, then Albo lived in, and addressed his magnum opus to, an alchemist society.

Chapter Twenty-four

PSEUDO-MAIMONIDES

WHEN Maimonides (1135–1204) turned the searchlight of his genius on the religion of the people he called the Sabaeans, whom he considered the society in which Abraham grew up, he had nothing but scorn for their misguided, foolish, and superstitious beliefs. The Sabaeans believed, Maimonides writes in his *Guide of the Perplexed* (3:29)[1] that the universe was eternal (that is, not created, as the Bible teaches), and that the stars were deities—in fact, the only divine beings. They "manufactured ridiculous stories" about Adam, Seth, and Noah, and "attributed the metals and the climates to the influence of the planets." Abraham was the first to recognize "the absurdity of the tales in which he had been brought up," opposed the Sabaean theories, and proclaimed "the name of the Lord, the God of the Universe." Among the books from which one can gather an idea of the absurdities of the "Kasdim, Chaldeans, and Sabaeans" Maimonides mentions the book *On the Nabatean Agriculture*, a book entitled *Istimachis* (that is, *Stoecheiomatikos*, or *Astrologer*), falsely attributed to Aristotle (whom Maimonides greatly admired), and several other books, including one ascribed to Hermes. Since in Arabic literature numerous astrological, magical, and alchemical books were attributed to Hermes, we cannot be sure which of them Maimonides had in mind, but we know that the books of Hermes were considered by him especially execrable, for in a letter to his translator Samuel ibn Tibbon, Maimonides warned him not to waste his time by reading them. This being the case, there can be little doubt that Maimonides was a staunch opponent of alchemy.

Whether or not Maimonides' anti-alchemical stand was known to medieval Jewish alchemists in general, the fact is that some of them (their names and identities are unknown) wrote brief alchemical treatises and attributed them to Maimonides. These writings are preserved in several manuscripts four of which I was able to examine—those of Munich, Moscow, Jerusalem, and Manchester.

The Munich manuscript is in the Bavarian State Library in Munich.[2] It consists of nine pages (ffs. 29b–33b), and is among other Hebrew alchemical texts that are unattributed and written by a different hand. The pseudo-Maimonidean treatise is superscribed "Epistle of Secrets by the Rambam [Maimonides] of Blessed Memory," and is addressed to an unnamed disciple, probably in imitation of the *Guide*, which is addressed to Maimonides' "dear pupil," Joseph ibn Aknin. The treatise starts as follows:

> In the name of God the Helper, we shall begin the book of wisdom of the true divine philosopher Rabbi Moshe of blessed memory. Said the philosopher: God gave [me] wisdom and understanding to recognize the honesty of your nature and the goodness of your qualities and the strength of your mind yearning for wisdom [and] giving up for it all worldly affairs. And I saw that you need money sufficient for your essential needs, without which it is not possible for you to free yourself for wisdom, for the degree of richness is the ladder to all the degrees and benefits which God, blessed be He, bestows upon His creatures. Without it one cannot reach any of them, and especially the degree of wisdom, for how can one devote oneself to it if in his house there is no garb and no dress, and is lacking food? I have already informed you in the esteemed treatise *Guide of the Perplexed* that God does not change the constancy of the nature of existence, except at a certain time, and I gave the reason of this in the treatise on the *Resurrection of the Dead*, that man cannot live and devote himself to the service of God without food and drink. . . .
>
> Therefore, I thought it proper, O esteemed disciple, to let you know very wonderful things, how great is their benefit and how wonderful it is to gather richness and property and honor without undue toil, on condition that you do not abandon the secret [of] its power and do not divulge it to anybody . . . (f. 29b).

After this introduction, which evidently has as its purpose to establish the moral basis for engaging in alchemical operations, the author gets down to specific alchemical instructions:

> (f. 30a) Behold, I now begin the secrets. Know that the *mahriah* [A. *muhra*, shell, conch] stone, which is called in Laʿaz *perla* [pearl], is a very precious stone, whose precious virtues I have already revealed to you face to face. And when it is big in size, because of its rarity its value is greater than that of gold. And I shall reveal to you how to make out of a large number of small pearls one big stone as you wish, without losing its virtues and changing its appearance. Take the juice of *saqlade* [Moscow and Manchester MSS: *asqalide*], in Laʿaz *limone* [lemon], and pass it through the vessel called *anbiqi* [I. *alambicco*, alembic] in Laʿaz, and in Arabic *al-baḥār* [plural of A. *baḥra*, basin; Moscow and Manchester MSS: *al-badwār*], and preserve it, and then take of the stones [i.e., pearls], as many as you want to make of them a big one [of that] size, and grind them and pass whatever you want through a sieve, and put them into that water [i.e., juice], and let them soak there nine days. Then take that powder, and you will find it

tightly glued together. Then you can make of it whatever shape you wish, and round that thing until it will be of the shape you want. And then tear open a fish [marginal note: the fish named *r'ina* is the best for this], and put the stone into it so that it should not be squashed and lose its roundness, and put the fish into dough as is the custom of women when they prepare it for food, and put it on fire or into the oven until it becomes baked, and once it is baked open everything, and take the stone, and you will find it a little hard, but not according to the natural custom, nor [usual] in its appearance. Therefore, now in turn feed it to a cock, and instantly slaughter it, and you will find it hard as is its nature, and restored to its color (See Figure 24.1).

Figure 24.1. "These are the craftsmen who make pearls." MS Ebr. 395, Biblioteca Apostolica Vaticana, Rome.

Also I let you know, so that you succeed in your wisdom, a thing of high degree and wonderful of benefit. But its making is a little difficult. Take [some] of the best gold you can find and beat it to utter thinness, then take *ashinsa* [?], and dry ethrog [citron] peel, and *alyazmīn* [A. *yāsamīn*, jasmine] and *violas* [S., violets], and *alqaft* which is *qust* [A., costus, a maritime medicinal plant], and *zarnīkh* [A., arsenic], in equal amounts, and copper in the weight of all of them together, and grind them well to fine powder, and then mix with this weight twenty *sheqel*s of the mentioned stone, and then take flour called *riza* [A. *aruzz, ruzz*, rice], and pass it through a sieve, and mix of it one-half of one-tenth of the weight of the compound, then take *guma arabiqa* [gum arabic], and the sap of fig twigs which is like milk, and mix it with all this as the eyes of your mind see fit, until you can knead it, and after having kneaded it dry it in the sun forty days, not less, until it becomes well dried, (f. 30b) and then take lemon juice and alum juice and *maribulas* [?] juice, in equal amounts, and mix with them, that is with this water, a little *ṭuṣiah* [A. *ṭuṭia*, tutty, crude zinc oxide] as much as you wish, for whether you give more or less will neither help nor harm. Also of the gratings of the *qorale* [I., coral]—a little of it is very good—and put it in the juice of the lemon and the alum until it thickens a little, then put here what is dry, and soak it thirty days until it becomes thin, and let it thicken, and it will grow, and add to its quantity three times a like [amount of] what you put into it, and it will purify until it will become clear, even though not like the sapphire. Then put it into horse manure, well hidden, and let it stay there three days, and on the fourth day, if it has hardened like a stone take it, and if not leave it there another day but not more, for then it will undoubtedly harden. And then take it out from there, grind it well, and take two weights of copper and put with it one weight of this stone, and put everything into the melting pot, and take yourself the work of the secret.

Take ashes of vine-twigs and pass them through a sieve and then knead them in urine, and put into them a little ground salt, and be careful to put there only a little of the urine, so that you should be able to knead the ashes and make of them whatever you want, and make it in a melting pot, and put into it all the copper and the mentioned stone, and melt it in strong fire with a big flame. Out will come seven times purified and refined gold, which will stand a thousand meltings without losing its nature and color. I let you know these things which are great of benefit and small of trouble, so that you should succeed in wisdom.

Moreover I shall let you know a secret whose benefit is not as great as that of the previous things, but its trouble is less than theirs, and the benefit is not small for him who understands and succeeds. Take well-ground sulphur and put [some] of it on any metal you choose, upon all its surface, and then [put it] on fire, and let it burn until all the sulphur is consumed, and be careful that nothing of the sulphur should remain on the metal at the time when you remove it from there after the flame goes out. And you will be able to peel the whole metal off its surface where the sulphur has reached. However, according to the measure of the sulphur that you put on the metal will be the measure of the peelings which you peel from it: if you put much, it will be much, and if little, it will be little. And if that metal is copper, you will not need to purify it in order to melt it, but for silver and gold you will have to (f. 31a) put the peelings into lemon juice or into the juice of *atages* [Moscow MS *aranges*; Manchester MS *naranjas*, oranges], in case there are no lemons available, but if they are available, the virtue of their water is wonderful, for the strength of its juice is great, and its nature and virtue is to purify the silver and the gold. And it has not only this virtue alone.

But let us return to where we were, which is that after having soaked the peels in lemon juice one day or more, take them out and put them in the pot whose work I mentioned to you in connection with the work of gold. And let there be before you fire with a flame, and put there the pot with the peels in it. But after the peels begin to be melted, there should be half of their weight of lead prepared, and put it in the pot with the peels. But it is important that you be most careful not to put the lead in it until the silver or the gold begin to melt. The reason for this is that the lead is worked much more easily than they, and if you put it in the pot at the time you put the silver or the gold, it will melt a long time before them, and all will be lost and you toiled in vain. Therefore it is sufficient for you to put it there when they begin to melt, and you will see that the lead will cover the silver or the gold and will emit smoke until all the lead is consumed, and when it is consumed the smoke will cease, and then the silver or the gold will remain pure and refined.

But I want to add and remind you and warn you that you should be most careful to remove from them all the sulphur before you put them in the melting pot, for if any of it is left on them it will cause everything to be lost. And let this thing not be light in your eyes, for if you perform it with wisdom and modesty it will benefit you very much in little time and without much trouble. And this is so because the matter is very easy to perform, and its work is not great, while the operation of the others is great and their work is difficult.

HOWEVER, [another] matter which is known to some wise men in the work of alchemy is of great benefit, but one must be an expert in the Work and well versed. And I shall tell you now its Work, for this is the proper place to talk about it. And it is not easy, and also the things which I mentioned are not easy. And I leave this treatise for your benefit, O esteemed disciple, for I wish that you succeed in any case in all negotiations and in all buying and selling. And the reason for this is that we have seen that the selection you have made and the desire you have had and have embraced lack nothing (f. 31b) but completion in deed, and if this book will be with you as intended, you will complete the condition [knowing] what happened to me explicitly and what occurred to me justly, and you will rise and reach the high grade and rank of the sages. And truly, it was your good luck that you reached us. And I shall say that the sages of this Work take tutty and burn it in fire and quench it in water, and then pound it, and then take alum and put it alone in a vessel on the fire until it melts. Then they put on it the powder of the tutty and mix it together, and take it off the fire, and take human blood burnt in a vessel until it becomes black, and take scrapings of the fatty blood and of the alum and of the tutty mixed together, and salt, in equal amounts, and mix all of it, and take copper and silver in the same amount and melt it together, and put on it [some] of the mentioned powder, and it will be gilded silver.

This procedure is famous among the masters of that Work who divide the matter of its wisdom into two kinds. And if they are treated [here] under one heading, it is because there is no difference between them except for name. And the two kinds are silver and gold. And I will explain to you the famous difference between them, which is as follows. This work which I mentioned has been tried, and as for trouble, its value makes it easy. But I shall let you know what I myself tried and saw: that it is supreme and its benefit more vast, and it is of the gold kind. And you, take of tin any amount you wish, and melt it, and after the melting put it immediately into lemon juice or citronjuice. Then put it into melted fat, then into cold water, and then into onion juice, and then into garlic juice, and then into water in which *faisoles* [S. *frisoles*, beans] have been boiled. And then melt it once more with one weight of incense, and it will be very good gilded gold. This matter is more wonderful in its benefits than everything [else] I mentioned in this matter of this Work. And since I want you to benefit, and my soul wishes you to benefit, to bring you to human perfection, beside which there is no other perfection, nor is after it any benefit like it, therefore

I SHALL LET YOU KNOW what is in my heart, and shall inform you of the virtues of my secrets, and reveal to you another matter, whose degree and benefit are great, and it is of this Work, the work of alchemy. And I shall not expatiate in its praise for well known to me is the immensity of its virtue, and this is it.

TAKE *lauṭon* (I. or S. *laton*, brass) and melt it up to four times, and each time put into the melting pot pulverized glass with the brass an equal [Moscow MS half] part of its weight. And the same of tutty, and after the melting melt it in *lanṭisqole* [I. *lentisk*, mastic tree] oil in which burnt tutty has been quenched. After this out will come for you gold good and beautiful in every respect and appearance. And if it appears to the eye that it needs more purifying, take ox gall and *zāʿfrān* [saffron], and mix them together and put them upon it until they become warm, and put the mentioned into it, and it will be good gold. Behold this matter is wonderful in its benefits, and its work is light in relation to the greatness of the benefit, and it has been tried by me (f. 32a–b).

Moreover I shall let you know a matter with which God has enlightened the eyes of my heart. If you fill your barrels with clear, clean, and pure water, and put one *sheqel* of *muḥibb al-mulūkh* [lover, or beloved, of kings] which is called in Laʿaz *grāna* [I., grain] into a hundred of the water, and put the same proportion of one part of saffron and two parts of *mal ms balasān* [A., . . . balsam] which is *qarpo balsamo*, as well as two parts of cinnamon, and also one hundred parts of peeled oranges, and in the proportion mentioned above four *liṭras* [pounds] of *suqo reqoliṣia* [?], and the same proportion of garlic, and in the same proportion one and half parts of *alume* [alum] tree, and let all this soak there in the barrel thirty full days—you will find that water colored, become in appearance like wine, and also a little sharp in its taste, and like wine in its smell. And to complete the enormous work, put in the aforementioned proportion half of a sixth part of *galanga* [A. *juljulān*, coriander seed, sesame], and half of a half of an eighth part of *basbās* [A., fennel, rue, nutmeg], and two parts of pomegranate rinds, and the same amount of their pits, and four weights of the finest wine that you can find, which is strong in its smell and its taste, and has escaped all change in appearance and all accidents and remained unchanged, and put all this in the barrel in which there is the aforementioned water, and leave it there eight days, and you will find the wine boiling [effervescent], that is the wine has become real wine, it will boil, and on its surface will appear a great foam, and all the refuse of that which you have put there will remain on top as a refuse on top of the wine. And clean away that refuse by removing from there everything that is found there, lest it become moldy and be spoiled, and everything be lost. And then leave it for three days, and you will find valuable and good wine, the like of which is not found in good (f. 32b) taste and smell and spiciness. And this is the potion which I give to those who suffer epilepsy, and the *ḥolī haraʿash* [H., trembling disease], and to the paralytic, and to the melancholic, because of its effect on them, that is to say, this blackish potion, when they [the patients] are about to suffer bodily damage or to be seized by madness, for the virtue of this potion is very wonderful, without the properties of real wine being found [in it]. And the general rule is that this helps all illnesses, and strengthens the heart, and cleanses the passages of the [word illegible] and the liver, and reduces the unnatural fever, and increases the natural warmth, and waters the brains and the stomach and the head, and purifies the feelings, and sharpens the mind.

> And you, my brother, know that if this would become known to the mass of physicians, they would sell a weight of it at twice the price of gold, if it were to be found in their hands and if they knew its value and characteristics. And I have already tried it, and have found it to work fast. This potion is constantly with me, as commanded by the Honored One [the prince], may God lengthen his peace, to be ready to send it to him.
>
> And I also have another remedy which protects against deadly poisons. If one drinks it, and thereafter takes a deadly poison, it will not harm him at all. And this I tried out on myself when the physicians once gave me deadly poison to drink. And if somebody was given deadly poison to drink—and the sign of it is that when the food reaches the stomach he is seized with pain in the stomach, and his sight darkens—then it is necessary that one should quickly give him to drink some of this wine, which will induce diarrhea and cause all the deadly poison to be eliminated in the diarrhea without leaving any part of it in the stomach and in the limbs. And when I informed the Honored Prince, may God lengthen his peace, of this matter this was the reason for my finding favor in his eyes, to be able to shelter in the shadow of the wing of his grace, and to tell about the glory of his rule. And this potion is always in my possession, with the description of another wonderful medicament, [so that] the person who takes it [can] be saved from deadly and bitter poisons, and it is necessary for every king to have it, when there is somebody who wants to kill him. He should take two parts of *lawres* [L. *laurus*, laurel] seeds and two parts of *terra sigillata* [fine clay], let all of it be kneaded in olive oil, and the taking [i.e., dosage] of it should be like the size of an almond, with one-third of an ounce of honey water. Let him drink this, and even if he takes thereafter a deadly poison, it will remain in its place [that is, will save him]. And if he drinks thereafter (f. 33a) a deadly poison, the *qambasa* [?] will be renewed and the deadly poison will have to come out in vomit due to its cleansing power.

The remaining page and a half of the text deals with astrological-magical matters, with divination with the help of a homunculus created by melting certain metals at a certain astrologically determined hour, and with methods of obtaining honor, riches, happiness, and so forth. It closes with this personal note:

> Do not let this become known to anybody besides you, O esteemed disciple. May God bless you with the good and even path which I myself have taken when I came out of the cave in which I hid and was secluded, and this is the reason of my rising high and of the greatness of my wisdom, and of the respect people have for me. I advise you to make one [magic homunculus] for yourself, and carry it with you hidden and always, and you will succeed in all your affairs, with the help of God.

This conclusion, added to the rest of the contents of the *Iggeret ha-Sodot*, makes it clear that this treatise could not have been written by Maimonides. Who, then, was its author? He is anonymous, but we can make an educated guess as to where he lived. He uses Arabic terms and translates them into Laʿaz, that is Spanish or Italian—it is often difficult to distinguish between the two in the Hebrew transliteration. For example, he repeatedly uses the Arabic term for zinc oxide and other chemical substances, which in the original Arabic is *tutiyah*, but in most cases spells it *ṭuṣiah*, which reflects the Spanish form of the word, *tucia*. This, together with the other Laʿaz words he quotes, indicates that the author was a Sephardi Jew who was familiar with both Arabic and Spanish alchemical terminology. He probably lived in Christian Spain, or in one of the Arabic-speaking countries in which the Sephardi exiles found refuge after their 1492 expulsion from Spain.

The Moscow manuscript of the treatise[3] is not identified as attributed to Maimonides, probably because its beginning is missing, but the very first extant lines say (as does the Munich manuscript), "I have already informed you in the esteemed treatise *Guide of the Perplexed*," and so on. What follows is the translation or description of those parts in the Moscow manuscripts which are not contained in the Munich version.

> (F. 87b) Another thing. To make *aljawhar* [A., pearls], many in number, big in size. Take them and pound them to dust, cleanly, in a glass or metal mortar, and put it into the juice of lemons *almustaqtir* [A., destillateur] in a *qarʿah* [A., *qaʿran*, bowl] and alembic, and let them soak there nine days, and take of that dough and make a round shape as you wish, let it [sit or soak] *fī ṣadaf al-baḥr* [A., in a sea-shell] of the weight of three *pelras* [*perlas*, S., pearls], and the juice of two *limones* [S., lemons], and put it in a glass vessel into the sun, and then make it round and pierce it with the hair of a pig, and [put] in it the hair of a horse, and dry it well in the shade, and then take it and put it into the back of a fish called *dintul* or *diltabah* in Laʿaz (which you should tear open at its back, and then put it into the back) or into a piece of old beef meat, and cut it in two, and make holes in the middle of the cut part on both sides so that those stones should each fall into a hole, and tie it with a copper thread or another thread, very strongly, so that it should not open, and put it into dough and bake it and put it into the oven at eventide, and it should stand there all night, and in the morning take it out and let it cool, and after its baking and cooling you will find them [the pearls] hard like stone. Wrap them in a cloth with barley bran, and if you don't find them clear give them to a cock or to a pigeon to eat, and slaughter it right away, and you will find them clear *tārām* [?] stone. Then wrap them in a cloth with barley bran, and behold this procedure is very good. DO IT AND SUCCEED! And be very careful about their purity at the time of pounding and kneading and baking, lest dust or pow-

der or any other thing dull its shine. And in another version I found that one should keep it in its [the fowl's] belly two or three days, or a day and half a night. And if you don't find them in the feces, in any case slaughter it, and experience will show the truth.

(F. 88a) ANOTHER. Take the small pearls which are called *lūlū* [A., pearl], and put them in a small flask and hang them inside a barrel of strong vinegar, fifteen days, and let the flask be two fingers above the vinegar. And at the end of fifteen days you will find that all of them have become a kind of dough. Break that flask and take out the dough, and make of it round shapes as you wish, and glue them and pierce them with the hair of a pig, and put them in the shade, in cleanliness, for three days, until they dry thoroughly, and then put them into a fish in a dough of barley, and bake it in the oven as proper, and take it out and leave it until the bread dries, and then take them out: they will be strong and hard, but not clear. Give them to eat to a pigeon or a cock, let it hunger two days, and then slaughter it, and take them out and wash them in rice water, and wrap them in a cloth with barley bran, and then they will be pure, clean, and clear.

THE CUTTING OF CRYSTAL. Grind the crystal very thoroughly, and then soak it in the sour water of the *ethrog* [citron] and in a little *tinkār* [A., chrysocolla, silicate of copper], and then melt it, and it will become like yeast, and roll it in the intestines of a sea fish, and pierce it with the hair of a pig, and then put it into the belly of the fish, and put it in dough into the *forno* [I., oven], and then take them out, and behold it is finished.

(f. 89a) ANOTHER MATTER. Take of tin as much as you like, and melt it, and after the melting put it instantly into juice of lemons or juice of sour citron, then put it in melted fat, and then in cold water, then in the juice of onions, then in juice of garlic, and then in water in which *allabi* [?] fruit was cooked, then melt it another time with its own weight of moon [i.e., silver], and it will be very good yellow [i.e., gold].

The long section contained in Moscow manuscript, folios 89b–91a, is identical (except for minor variations) with the text of Abufalaḥ's alchemy, folios 8b–10a, which we presented above in Chapter 7. The inclusion of this section in a treatise attributed to Maimonides is an example of the nonchalance with which medieval alchemical writers manipulated source material, disregarding its original authorship and attributing it to more famous and hence more prestigious authors. Alchemical instructions written by the relatively unknown Abufalaḥ were of no great moment; the same instructions, if presented as originating from the great Maimonides, gained enormously in value and significance.

Then the unknown author continued:

(f. 91a) KNOW my brother that just as there exists and is known the virtue of the precious stone for the transmutation of all kinds of metals into a kind of gold, so there exists the virtue with which they can be transmuted into a kind of silver, if in its composition silver is put instead of gold, and you follow all the rules of the operation as mentioned, but each time put silver instead of gold. But do all the mentioned [word illegible] with quicksilver and *salamoniaq* [sal ammoniac] alone as mentioned in that operation, and you do not need to add anything else. And this is the operation which King Alexander used to perform for a long time, until the operations of the soul water and the hair water and the ashes of the viper and others were verified by him, and then he returned to the practice of the Work of this precious stone.

AND BEHOLD here are other descriptions, also in the operation of the congealing of quicksilver as stipulated, and it is an honored and important operation, and the abovementioned kind was used to perform it, and I extracted it from the book of Baraḥia the Indian. Take a loadstone and put it in a new pot, then put [a mixture] of quicklime stone and *zarnīkh* [arsenic] powder on top and below until it is well covered, and then seal its mouth well, and put it on gentle fire for six days, and remove it during the nights, and then when it cooled down open it and you will see some powder, and if it is not yet a powder return it to the fire until it becomes a powder when it cools, and then take [some] of the quicksilver and heat it in fire in a melting pot, and put on it one part of the powder for six of it, and shake it all around on the fire until it is mixed well, and it will become hard like a stone, and you can do with it all Work as with good silver.

(f. 91b) ANOTHER DESCRIPTION. This was the custom of our friend. Take of the quicksilver water and the sal ammoniac whose work in the operation of the precious stones is known, eighteen parts, and combine them with five parts of good and powdered silver, and put everything in a glass vessel on the fire in the pot with oil, and cook it well in the vessel with oil, and it will become congealed. If you put one part of this on fifty parts of quicksilver it will become good silver.

ANOTHER DESCRIPTION, also his. Take juice of the roots of *zarāwand* [P., A., aristolochium] and *sūsī* [sūsan, A., lily], and put into it [some] of the quicksilver, and there it will thicken a little, and then sublimate it in the known vessel according to the known method, and then put it in the live burning water whose work is already known among the expert physicians, and one should not expatiate on telling its Work, and there it will also harden, and then put it in the melting pot and melt it and throw it into the abovementioned water, and it will become very hard, and it will do for every Work.

ANOTHER, and this is from among the secrets of the esteemed desertic f[lower] *hāl ʿalbīn* [marginal note: another version: *hāl ʿalkan*], its round variety, for it has two, one long and one round. Take it and dry it and mix it with one-third of its weight of *ʿaqarqarha* [A. *ʿāqarqarḥā*ʾ, dracunculus, pyrethrum], and knead it with the juice of aristolochium and lily, and dry it, and make a powder. If you put a little on it on quicksilver in a melting pot, it will congeal it within an hour, and it will become hard like silver good for doing any work.

Here ends the Moscow manuscript of the pseudo-Maimonidean alchemical treatise. It is followed by four pages written by a different hand, containing brief alchemical and medical prescriptions (ff. 91b–93a), one of them attributed to "R. Moshe Zaqen," i.e., Rabbi Moses the Elder. The last piece is interesting: a conjuration in which the words of incantation to be recited are given first in German, then in Hebrew, and then in Laʿaz, that is, Italian.

CONTAINED in the Moscow manuscript is a prescription for the multiplication of saffron, which is an example of the efforts some Jewish alchemists made to increase the supply of certain plants that were valuable and hence sought after for alchemical operations, but not always readily available. The text is found on folio 210a of the Moscow MS 315. It is squeezed in between two unrelated passages, the first dealing with agricultural magic, the second with a philosophical discussion about the character and the attributes of God. It reads as follows:

Take sixty *onqia*s [ounces] of *karkom* [H., saffron], which is the most beautiful of flowers, and this number sixty corresponds to the number of queens King Solomon had, who was the choicest of those anointed. And [take] according to the value, that is to say, the weight, of the saffron oil and honey, that is thirty ounces of oil and thirty ounces of honey. And the oil should be very bright. . . . And take eleven ounces of the finest red wine, and seven ounces of *amiro* [?], and one ounce of *guma rabiqa* [gum arabic], and one ounce and two-thirds of *alume* [alum] *satiqo* [or *patiqo*, ?] which is the head of the bitters. Mix all these things together, and put them into the sixty ounces of saffron. Let them be dried, and spread out to the sun or to the wind, and they will become ninety ounces. And do thus always according to the amounts. Behold, you will gain thirty ounces.

However, the good advice is that you should take half of the weight of all these things we mentioned, and put them into the sixty ounces of saffron, and then you will gain fifteen ounces, and do this always according to the weight. And this is its description: Take five *litra*s [pounds], that is, sixty ounces of saffron, and take fifteen ounces of oil, and fifteen ounces of honey, eight ounces and a half of red wine, and three and a half ounces of the *amiro* [?], half an ounce of gum arabic, two thirds and a half of *roza* [?], one ounce of alume, which is close to three quarters. Pound what is suitable for pounding in a mortar, and then mix everything with the sixty ounces of saffron, and mix them well, and spread it out to the sun or to the southern wind so that it should dry. And then all of it will be transmuted generously, and you will gain fifteen ounces.

Saffron (*Crocus sativa*), cultivated in Mediterranean regions since ancient times, has been used as a coloring and aromatic agent for food and medicines, and was valued as an antispasmodic drug. The above recipe shows that it was an expensive substance, then, as now, which made it worthwhile for alchemists to bother with procedures to increase its weight by 50 percent, or even by only 25 percent. In addition, saffron also had considerable symbolic value; in fact, the yellow color of the saffron was considered the color of the sun, and as such had a close affinity to gold. Since much of alchemical gold-making concentrated on giving base metals a golden yellow, color, the innate vegetative yellowness of the saffron was considered in itself of great value. Yellowing (Greek *xanthosis*) was one of the four coloring processes—the other three were blackening (*melanosis*), whitening (*leukosis*), and reddening (*iosis*)—which were essential parts of the transmutation of base metals into gold.

THE third (Jerusalem) manuscript containing texts attributed to Maimonides[4] contains major parts of the material found in the Munich and Moscow manuscripts (with minor variations), identifies the author as "the Rambam of blessed memory," and states explicitly that Maimonides "sent this version to his important pupil." The main value of this manuscript lies in additional lexicographic material it contains. Thus the *ashinsa* of the Munich manuscript (here spelled *ansinas*), is identified as *lubān* (A., benzoin). The Hebrew term for *ethrog* peel is translated into Arabic as *qishr utrunj* (citron peel); the Italian or Spanish word *violas* is translated into Arabic as *banafsaj* (violet); the Hebrew "rice flour" is explained by the Arabic *ris* (that is *ruzz* or *aruzz*, rice); the Italian or Spanish *guma arabica* is translated into Arabic as *ṣamgh alʿarab* (gum arabic); alum is explained as *shabb* (Arabic for alum or vitriol); the *maribulas* of the Munich manuscript appears here as *mirabulanos qibulas*, and so on.

Two passages of the pseudo-Maimonidean alchemical treatise are found in yet another manuscript, one preserved in the John Rylands University Library of Manchester.[5] That entire manuscript is alchemical, and will be described in Chapter 31. Relevant here are two passages which deal with the pseudo-Maimonidean treatise.

The first is found on folio 15a, and begins as follows: "FOR SUN. The version of the Rambam [Maimonides] of blessed memory which he sent to his important disciple: I shall let you know and enlighten you, so that you should succeed in your wisdom, a thing of high degree. . . ." The rest of the passage is practically identical with the text which was presented above, from the Munich manuscript, except for a few explanatory additions.

The second passage is on folio 16a and starts with an introduction almost identical to that of the Munich manuscript: "SAID the divine philosopher, to whom God gave wisdom and understanding, our rabbi and master, son of Rabbi Maimon of blessed memory: Since I know the honesty of your nature and the goodness of your qualities and the strength of your mind yearning for wisdom. . . ."[11]

The passage ends on folio 16b with the words, "until here from Rabbi Moshe." Although we learn nothing new from this manuscript, it completes the picture in one respect: a manuscript of which four versions have survived must have been popular and often copied. In more general terms one can say that the existence of this treatise in this many versions, some complete and some partial, is another indication of the interest taken in alchemy by Jewish scholars in the late Middle Ages.

Chapter Twenty-five

THREE *KUZARI* COMMENTATORS

IN THE fifteenth and sixteenth centuries, several Jewish scholars wrote commentaries on Judah Halevi's *Kuzari* (on which, see Chapter 11), and when dealing with the passages in which Halevi speaks of the alchemists they not only explained them but also recorded their own knowledge and expressed their own opinion of alchemy.

SOLOMON VIVAS AND NETHANEL KASPI

One of the first of these commentators was Solomon ben Judah of Lunel (1411–?), also known as Solomon Vivas, a Provençal philosopher. Solomon was a child prodigy, who at the age of thirteen composed his *Kuzari* commentary entitled *Ḥesheq Sh'lomo* (Solomon's Desire), which is extant in a manuscript in the Bodleian Library.[1] Much of this work is based on the oral explanations of Solomon ben Menaḥem (Frat Maimon), of whom Solomon ben Judah was a disciple. Another *Kuzari* commentary is based on the same oral explanations, written by a second disciple of Frat Maimon, Nethanel ben Nehemia Kaspi, completed in 1424, and preserved in a Parma manuscript.[2] The passages dealing with Halevi's view on alchemy are appended to *Kuzari* 3:53, and are practically identical in the two commentaries. They read as follows (in my translation from the Hebrew):

> And from natural science is also separated the science of refining, which is called alchemy, and is known for the making of gold and silver out of that which is not gold and silver in actuality, and likewise other metals, and this is because it is understood that the existence of metals is not due to an accidental thing but that each thing develops out of a material that is related to it, and was prepared, as far as its effect and special impulse is concerned, to receive that form. And it is understood that the materials which are related to the metals are the minerals, and they are their origin. And the scholars of this Work—he [Halevi] intends to say the work of chemistry—are always searching for the things that are the materials related to each of the metals, and they want them to be salts, and [want] to induce them to produce the metals, whether by the combination of many things or by the making of certain known waters and powders and limes. And they complete those operations with fire which in the human Works stands in place of the

sun in the work of nature, and for this they need many different vessels of various appearance, such as ovens and furnaces and others of varying appearance and without number.

And they have in these matters books which divide the science and the Work into two parts, and indeed that science is the study of establishing the beginnings of this Work and its foundations, and establishing the causes and reasons of the transmutation of materials from one form into another, for the wondrous [thing] in these matters is that they can transmute any material they want into any other material they want, by divesting it of its form and causing it to assume another form which is near or far [i.e., similar or different]. And the proof of this is that they make silver and gold out of milk and blood and the brain of the skull, and the yolk of eggs, and urine, and the horn of animals, and the roots of many herbs, and the like. And about this they have spoken at length, and [adduced] proofs by analogy, and proofs derived from deduction by reason of having been verified by experiment many times.

And the second part is the description of the Works and the values of the mixtures and the making of strong waters which will dissolve everything, and the pots, and the waxes and the salt and the known manures which are renewed, and the *habaṭa* [? perhaps *hanaḥa*, placing] of the mixtures on the fire, and the measure of their staying on the fire, or all the other vessels which have been named by them, and the description of the vessels which are used in this Work, whether ovens and stoves, or alembics, and the description of the ovens which blow by themselves, and the other ovens and stoves which are different, and of what thing [or dust] they are made, and many other things like these.[3]

In another passage the same commentators discuss the relationship between alchemy and astrology:

Abū Naṣr wrote in his aforementioned book that behold there are natural devices that are common to the science of the stars, such as the work of the shapes [geometry] and the *ṣ'lamim* [images] and the *talasmaot* [A. *tilasm* (sing.), talisman], which is based on the special relationship of certain metals or certain minerals or certain stones or resins [or juices] or herbs to certain planets or certain constellations. And the scholars of this work mix [them] together by collecting their powers, and with it they observe that those stars should be in limited places—you could say by way of example, in their houses or in the house of their honor—where they will have a conjunction under such and such conditions, by observations and an understanding of the evil powers, and many things like these. And when there is a conjunction under those conditions it will produce such [and such] an effect upon the completion of the Work with burnings of incense and fumigations and sprinklings, and this and this will come to pass with the influ-

> ence of spirituality, in a certain known shape it will presage the future and in other shapes avert damage and heal certain illnesses. And [some] of these operations in agriculture will speed up the coming out of fruits, and the ways of grafting, and the manners of planting plants, with devices or strange acts at certain determined times, and they have in these things too many acts to be counted.[4]

These comments betray a thorough familiarity with both the theory and practice of alchemy and astrology, and despite their overt intention, which is to explain and elucidate Halevi's skepticism concerning alchemy, they are based on an overall acceptance of the premises that underlay the alchemical work of their day and age.

Judah Moscato

About a century after the aforementioned two authors, there lived Judah ben Joseph Moscato (c. 1530– c. 1593), one of the most outstanding rabbis, authors, and preachers of the Italian Renaissance. One of his favorite ideas, which Moscato expounds repeatedly in his major works, is that all the great philosophers were disciples of the ancient Hebrew kings and prophets, and that philosophy, as well as other arts and sciences such as music, were parts of Israel's ancient culture, lost during the long period of exile and preserved only in the works of non-Jewish disciples of Jewish masters. Moscato was thoroughly at home in the secular sciences of his age, and at the same time was a follower of the Kabbalah. He left behind two major works: a book of sermons entitled *N'fuṣot Y'huda* (The Dispersion of Judah)[5] and a commentary on Judah Halevi's *Kuzari*, titled *Qol Y'huda* (The Voice of Judah).[6] In the latter work, in discussing Halevi's statements on alchemy, Moscato shows himself familiar with, and at the same time critical of, alchemy:

> The masters of alchemy and spirituality did not know that what they envisaged were aspirations of falsehood and vanity. For behold the masters of alchemy thought that they could achieve the calculation of the heat of fire in a scale and a precise balance until a kind of metal would be transmuted for them into another kind, and in place of copper they would bring gold, just as natural heat could transmute food into blood and flesh. And what misled them was that they saw one species develop out of another, such as the coming into being of bees out of the flesh of cattle and gnats out of wine. And their heart enticed them to do the same with their charms, for they said, "Have we not seen with our own eyes the transmutation of one substance into another through measured natural heat? We too shall bring fire from the ordinary and shall measure it in such a manner that the process of transmutation of substances should be completed through it." And through this similarity they pointed to the feasibility of their work.[7]

To the second passage in which Judah Halevi discusses alchemy, Moscato appends these comments:

> The masters of alchemy . . . think that by means of measured heat they can bring into being what they want, and that measured fire will transmute for them the substance of copper into the substance of gold, or that the fire will bring them what they want, and that there is male fire and female fire. And they exert themselves to find such a fire, but their operations are in vain for they can never calculate it sufficiently for their intention. And they were misled by the experiments which they found, etc. This refers to those who are mentioned there in section 23 concerning the origin of bees out of the flesh of cattle and others that come into being out of putrefaction, which has no relevance, for only [precisely] measured heat causes them to come into being. And their heart enticed them to do likewise, and they did not understand that even though they knew of the existence of something, they did not know its cause, how to measure it in a manner that would lead from it to that innovation, nor could they thereafter derive a proof from it to bring about something like it with the work of their own hands. That is to say, they found [those results] by chance and not by calculation, and this is called an experiment by chance, when they don't know its measure and the manner of its regeneration through the degree of that calculated heat. And he [Judah Halevi] says that this is not similar to what we find concerning the origin of man through the placing of the semen into the womb, for in that matter the human being has no *pissul* [formative role?] at all except for the active one approaching the passive one, but the measure of their relationship and their value in the proper manner for the formation of the embryo upon the ready material—all this is hidden from the eyes of every living [being], and man can learn nothing from it applicable to his work in transmuting one substance to another. And only God can dispose of these proportions in devising their value, as its explanation is completed in the mentioned section.[8]

PART SEVEN

The Sixteenth Century

Introduction to Part Seven

THAT THE SIXTEENTH century was a time of special achievement for Jewish alchemy is due primarily to two major Hebrew alchemical treatises written in that period. One of unknown authorship, entitled *Esh M'ṣaref*, The Refiner's Fire, a quotation from Malachi 3:2, is the most complete extant example of the combination of alchemy, the alchemical interpretation of biblical passages, Kabbalah, gematria, and the utilization of magic squares for alchemical purposes. The treatise must have been more popular among the gentiles than among the Jews, for although its Hebrew original is lost, it has been preserved in Italian and Latin translations made in the seventeenth century, and in an English version produced in the early eighteenth.

The second sixteenth-century Hebrew alchemical treatise is important for two reasons. First, because it is the first book-length Hebrew alchemical compendium of known authorship, and second, because its author was none other than the famous Safed kabbalistic master Ḥayyim Vital, whose voluminous writings are practically the only source from which the kabbalistic doctrines of Isaac Luria have become known, and due to which Luria came to occupy undisputed leadership in the Kabbalah from the sixteenth century on. It has long been known in Jewish scholarly circles that Vital was interested in alchemy, but this fact has been disposed of in a brief footnote in the histories of Jewish mysticism. Vital's deep involvement with alchemy, his sustained work in that field, his systematic alchemical experimentation, his insistence that a procedure should be repeatable before it could be accepted as correct, and his detailed and precise description of alchemical processes—all this has been unknown until now, and is presented in Chapter 28 for the first time as fully as possible on the basis of Vital's own manuscript.

Less significant, but still worth mentioning, are the contributions to alchemy of five known Jewish scholars, as well as those of several anonymous ones, whose work survived in unidentified manuscripts. Taken together, these alchemical works make the sixteenth century one of the most original times in the history of Jewish alchemy.

Chapter Twenty-six

ESH M'ṢAREF: A KABBALISTIC-ALCHEMICAL TREATISE

THE METAPHYSICAL-theosophical-kabbalistic foundations of medieval Jewish alchemy are most fully presented in a treatise entitled *Esh M'ṣaref* (The Refiner's Fire), written originally in Hebrew or Aramaic, probably in the sixteenth century. The original is lost,[1] but an Italian translation of it was known to Christian Knorr von Rosenroth (1636–1689), who included major parts of it in his Latin work entitled *Kabbala denudata seu doctrina Hebraeorum transcendentalis et metaphysica atque theologica* (The Kabbala Uncovered, or the Transcendental and Metaphysical as well as Theological Doctrine of the Hebrews). The three volumes of this work were printed in Sulzbach by Abraham Lichtenthaler in 1677, 1678, and 1684, respectively. My translation is based on von Rosenroth's Latin text contained in volume 1 of *Kabbala denudata* (hereafter *Kab. den.*)[2]

The brief introductory passage alludes to several important alchemical traditions and concepts. The Prophet Elisha is presented as an "exemplar of natural wisdom," for which there is no basis either in the Bible or in the rich corpus of Jewish legend literature, but which was a commonly held tenet among the alchemists.[3] More significantly, the true alchemist, compared to Elisha the healer, is termed "the true healer of impure metals," in accordance with the general alchemical view that the impurity of metals was something like a disease of which the adept can heal them. The first to state this view was Maria the Jewess who, we have seen, is quoted by Zosimus to the effect that metals can be transmuted by the application of a remedy or medicine. The analogy between the alchemical process and the healing of the human body appears frequently in alchemical literature; what is new, and typically Jewish, in this introductory statement of the *Esh M'ṣaref* is the notion that "the true healer," that is, the expert alchemist, must be a person as contemptuous of riches as was the Prophet Elisha. In my translation, which now follows, I retained the names and words given in the original in Hebrew characters, but substituted the customary English transliteration for words given in Latin characters in the original.

CHAPTER 1 (AS QUOTED IN *KAB. DEN.* 1:116–18)

[*Elisha*] was a most notable prophet, an example of natural wisdom, and a despiser of worldly goods, as shown by the story of Naaman,[4] 2 Kings 5:6, and was therefore truly rich, in accordance with that which is said in *Pirqe Avot* ch. 4, "Who is rich? He who rejoices in his portion." For thus the true healer of impure metals has not a show of external riches, but is rather like the תהו [*tohu*] of primeval nature, empty and void. This word has the same numerical value as אלישע [*Elisha*], namely 411.[5] For it is a most true saying in Baba Qama 71b that "The thing which causes riches (such as natural wisdom) is instead of riches."[6]

Learn, therefore, to purify Naaman coming from the north, from Syria, and recognize the powers of the Jordan which is, as it were, יאר דין [*Y'or din*], the River of Judgment, flowing out of the north.

After a quotation from B. Baba Bathra 25b to the effect that the south is the place of wisdom, whereas the north is that of riches, the author offers a remarkable parallel between alchemy and the kabbalistic sefirot:

But know that the mysteries of this wisdom [i.e., alchemy] do not differ from the supernal mysteries of the Kabbalah. For just as there is a reflection of predicaments in sanctity, so there is also in impurity. And the sefirot which are in the Aṣilut [Emanation, the highest world of the Kabbalah] are also in ʿAsiya [Action, the lowest world of the Kabbalah], yea, even in that kingdom which is commonly called Minerals, although on the supernal plane their excellence is always greater. Therefore the place of Keter [Crown, the first and highest of the sefirot] is here [in the mineral kingdom] occupied by the Metallic Root, which has an occult nature, involved in great obscurity, and in which all metals have their origin. Even so, the nature of Keter is occult and from it emanate all the other sefirot.

Lead has the place of Ḥokhma [Wisdom, the second of the sefirot], and, just as Hokhma is next to Keter, so lead proceeds immediately from the metallic root, and is called in enigmatic similes "the father of the subsequent natures."

Tin holds the place of Bina [Intelligence, the third of the sefirot] showing age by its greyness, and adumbrating severity and judicial rigor by its crackling.

Silver is placed by all masters of the Kabbalah under the class of Ḥesed [Mercy, the fourth of the sefirot] because of its color and use.

Thus far the white natures. Now follow the red.

Gold, according to the most common opinion of the Kabbalists, is placed under G'vura [Power, the fifth of the sefirot]. Job 37:22 also refers gold to the north, not only because of its color but also because of its heat and sulphur.[7]

Iron is referred to Tif'eret [Beauty, the sixth sefira], for it is like a man of war, according to Exod. 15:2, and has the name Z'ir Anpin [Impatient One] from its swift anger,[8] according to Ps. 2, last verse.

Neṣaḥ [Lasting Endurance] and Hod [Majesty, the seventh and eighth sefirot], the two median places of the body,[9] and the seminal receptacles, are the places of the brass of androgynous nature. Likewise the two pillars in the Temple of Solomon, referring to these two modes, were made of brass, according to 1 Kings 7:15.

Y'sod [Foundation, the ninth sefira] is quicksilver, for it, characteristically, is given the name "living."[10] And this living water is the foundation of all nature and of the metallic art.

But to Malkhut [Kingdom, the tenth and lowest of the sefirot] is referred the true medicine of metals, for many reasons. Because it represents the rest of the natures under the metamorphosis of both gold and silver, right and left, judgment and mercy. Of all this more will be said elsewhere.

Thus I have delivered to you the key to unlock many closed gates, and have opened the door to the innermost secrets of nature. But if anyone has placed these [things] in a different order, I shall have no argument with him, since all tend to one truth.

For it may also be said that the three supernals [of the sefirot] are the three sources of metallic things. Thick water is Keter, salt Ḥokhma, sulphur Bina for known reasons. And, likewise, the seven inferiors [of the sefirot] represent seven metals, namely G'dula and G'vura silver and gold, Tif'eret iron, Neṣaḥ and Hod tin and copper, Y'sod lead, and Malkhut will be the metallic woman and the Luna of the wise, and the field into which ought to be cast the seeds of secret minerals, namely the water of gold, as this name occurs in Gen. 36:39.

But know, my son,[11] that such mysteries are hidden in these things as no human tongue can utter. Therefore I shall no more offend with my tongue, but will keep my mouth shut, from Ps. 39:2.

Chapter 1 (continued in *Kab. den.* 1:235–36)

גיחזי, Gehazi, the servant of Elisha, is of the type of the vulgar students of nature who set about contemplating the valleys and profundities of nature, but do not descend into its secrets, wherefore they labor in vain and remain servants forever. They give counsel about procuring the son of the wise, whose generation is impossible for nature, 2 Kings 4:14. But they can contribute nothing to this generation (for which a man like Elisha is required). For nature does not open her secrets to them, cf. verse 26, contemns them, verse 30, and the resuscitation of the dead to life is impossible for them, verse 31. They are covetous, 5:20, are liars and deceivers, verses 22, 25, and garrulous, narrators of others' deeds, 2 Kings 8:4, 5, and instead of riches they acquire leprosy, that is, disease, contempt, and poverty, 5:27. For the word גיחזי [*Gehazi*] and the word חול [*ḥol*], profane, common, both have the same numerical value.

Chapter 2 starts in *Kab. den.* 1:227–28, which contains a lengthy discussion of the various kinds of gold, and the analogy between them and the ten sefirot. The same subject is continued in *Kab. den.* 1:301–2. Then, on pages 303–5, it speaks of the office of the physician:

I, the insignificant one,[12] write these things according to the tenuousness of my knowledge, having diligently searched the occult for the healing of creatures. However, what moved me was that which is transmitted in *Zohar Haazinu*, fol. 145, chapter 580,[13] about the office of the physician, that I should not desist from the good and right way until I find the best medicine. The words there are as follows: "It is written in Deut. 32:10, 'He found him in a desert land, and in the waste, a howling wilderness, he led him to find the causes and made him understand, etc.' Rightly so, because he compelled all the husks to serve him. Thus far it was written in the Book of Kartaneus [Qartana] the physician. He then extracted from this text various observations necessary for the wise physician, about the healing of the patient who lies in the chamber of sickness, where the king's prisoners (Gen. 39:20) may worship the Master of the World. For when a prudent physician comes to him, he finds him in a desert land, and in the wilderness of howling solitude, which are the diseases by which he is afflicted, and he finds him in the captivity of the king.

"Here it may be objected that, since the Holy One, blessed be He, commanded that he be caught [by illness], man is not permitted to cure him. But this is not so. For David says, Ps. 41:2, 'Blessed is he who understands the weak.' And weak is he who lies in the house of sickness. And if the physician is wise, the Holy One, blessed be He, heaps blessings upon him in relation to him whom he cures. That physician finds him in the desert land, that is, in the place of death, where he lies. And in the waste, howling wilderness, which are the diseases afflicting him? What is to be done for him? etc.[14] R. El'azar said: 'Until now we have heard nothing of this physician, nor of his book. Except that once a certain merchant told me that he had heard from his father that in his time there was a certain physician who, having seen a sick man, instantly said, "This one will live, that one will die," and that it was reported to him that he was a just and true man who feared sin, and that if anyone was unable to get the things he needed, he himself would obtain them, and supply them from his own. And it was said that in the whole world there was no wise man like him, and that he achieved more with his prayers than with his hands. And when we supposed that this man was the very same physician, the merchant replied, "Certainly, his book is in my possession, having obtained it from the inheritance of my father. And all the sayings of that book are hidden in the mystery of the Law. And in it we find profound secrets and many remedies, which it is not permitted to apply save to those who fear sin, etc."[15]

"R. Elʿazar said: 'If that book is in your possession, lend it to me.' He answered: 'I shall, so as to show you the power of the sacred light.' And we have heard that R. Elʿazar had said: 'That book was in my hands for twelve months, and we found in it sublime and precious lights, etc.' And we have found in it many kinds of remedies, ordered according to the requisites of the Law, and profound secrets, etc., and we said, 'Blessed be the Merciful One who bestows wisdom on men from the supernal wisdom, etc.' Thus far there."[16]

This moved me to seek similar good and secret books, and with the good hand of God over me I found that which I now shall teach you. And the camea[17] of this metal is altogether wonderful for it consists of six times six partitions of reticulations, everywhere showing the admirable virtue of the letter *vav*,[18] related to Tif'eret [Beauty]. And all the columns and lines, as well as from the bottom to the top and from right to left and from one corner to another, give the same sum, and you can vary the same ad infinitum. And the various totals always observe the position that their lesser number[19] is always either 3 or 9 or 6, and again 3, 9, 6, and so on. Now I shall present an example whose sum represents the number 216 [which is the numerical value of] אריה [*arye*], our wonderful lion, 14 times, which is the numerical value of זהב [*zahav*], gold [see Figure 26.1].

11	63	5	67	69	1
13	21	53	55	15	59
37	27	31	29	45	47
35	33	43	41	33	25
49	57	19	17	51	23
71	9	65	7	3	61

Figure 26.1. Magic square for gold: "Compute and grow rich!"

CHAPTER 3 (IN *KAB. DEN.* 1:483–85)

כסף [Kesef], silver, is under G'dula on account of whiteness, which denotes mercy. And in *Raʿya Mehemna*[20] it is said that by fifty [pieces of] silver, Deut. 22:29 etc., is understood Bina, because it inclines to the side of G'dula [Silver] from fifty gates, *Pard. Rim.* trac. 23, ch. 11.[21]

About metallic things R. Mordecai[22] wrote: Let the red mineral of silver be taken, let it be ground most finely, then add to six ounces of it an ounce and a half of the calx [lime] of Luna [silver]. Let it be placed on a sand bath in a sealed vial. Let it be given weak fire for the first eight days lest its radical humidity be burnt up. In the second week, one degree stronger, and in the third, yet stronger; and in the fourth [even stronger] so that the sand should not be red hot, but that when water is dripped upon it it should hiss. Then, on top of the glass, you will have a white matter, which is the materia prima, the dyeing arsenic,[23] the living water of metals, which all philosophers call dry [water], and its vinegar. This is how it is purified: R_x [Take some] of this sublimated crystalline pure [matter]. Let it be ground on marble with calx of Luna in equal parts. Let it be put in a sealed vial, again in sand, in the first two hours with gentle fire, in the second with stronger, in the third with a yet more violent, and increased until the sand will hiss: and our arsenic will again be sublimated, with starry rays being sent forth. And since a large quantity is required of this, augment it thus: R_x of this six ounces, and of the purest filings of Luna one ounce and a half, and let it be an aaa. [amalgama], and let it be digested in a sealed vial in hot ashes, until all the Luna is dissolved, and converted into arsenical water. Take of this prepared spirit one ounce and a half, put it in a closed vial of hot ashes, and it will ascend and descend; which heat should be continued until it no longer sweats, but lies at the bottom, having the color of ashes. Thus the matter is dissolved and putrefied. Take of this ashy matter one part, and of the aforementioned water half a part, mix them and let them sweat in a glass as before, which will happen in about eight days. When, thereafter, the ashy earth begins to whiten, take it out, and let it be imbibed with five washings of its lunar water, and be digested as before. Let it be imbibed the third time with five ounces of the same water, and coagulated as before, for eight days. The fourth imbibition requires seven ounces of the lunar water, and once the sweating is ended this preparation is finished.

Now for the white work. Take of this white earth twenty-one drachmas. Of lunar water, fourteen drachmas. Of the calx of purest Luna, ten drachmas. Let them be mixed on marble, and committed to coagulation until they harden. Imbibe it with three parts of its own water, until it had drunk up this potion, and repeat this until it flows without smoke on a glowing copper plate. Then you will have a tincture for the white, which you can increase in the aforementioned manner. For [the tincture of] the red, calx of sol [sun, i.e., gold], a stronger fire must be applied. And this is a work of more or less four months. Thus [says] he.[24] This should be compared with the writings of the Arab philosopher,[25] in which he describes the arsenical material in more detail.

Chapter 3 is continued in *Kab. den.* 1:359, which contains further scriptural quotations to prove the correspondence of the sefirot and silver. It is then continued in *Kab. den.* 1:206–8, which begins with scriptural references to prove the correspondence between the sefirot and iron. Then it goes on:

> In the natural sciences this metal [iron] is the middle line reaching from one extreme to the other. This is that male and bridgegroom without whom the virgin is not impregnated. This is the Sun of the wise, without whom the Moon would be in perpetual darkness. He who knows its rays works in the day. The others grope in the night. פרזלא [*Parzᶜla*, Aramaic for iron], whose minor number is 12, has the same value as the name of that bloodthirsty animal דוב [*dov*], bear, whose number is also 12. And this is that mystical thing of which it is written in Dan. 7:5[26] "And behold another beast, a second like unto the bear, stood on one side, and [there were] three ribs in its mouth, between its teeth, and thus they said to him: Arise, devour much flesh!" The meaning is that in order to constitute the metallic kingdom, iron must be taken in the second place, in whose mouth or opening, which comes to pass in an earthen bowl, a threefold scoria will protrude from within its whitish nature. Let him eat בשר [*basar*], meat, whose minor number is 7, that is, פוך [*pukh*], stibium, whose minor number is the same, 7. And indeed much flesh, because its proportion is greater than that of the other, and indeed such a proportion as is that of פוך [*pukh*], that is, 106, to ברזל [*barzel*], i.e., 239, such shall be the iron to *pukh*.

Our text continues in this vein to explain alchemically Dan. 7:6, 7, 11. Then follows the conclusion of chapter 3.

Chapter 3 conclusion (in *Kab. den.* 1:683–84)

> In the history of metallic natures pertains the story of Phinehas, Num. 25:7, where by fornicators is understood the masculine [arsenical] sulphur and the dry water[27] improperly mixed together in the mineral. By the spear of Phinehas is meant the force of iron acting upon matter to expurgate it of dross. By which iron not only is that masculine [arsenical sulphur] completely killed, but also the woman herself is at length mortified. So that the miracle of Phinehas can be applied to this not unfittingly. See Targum, ad loc [Num. 25:7]. For the nature of iron is wonderful, which is also shown by its camea, which is as follows [see Figure 26.2], where the number ה [5] and its square כ״ה [25] denote the feminine nature which is corrected by this metal.

Chapter 4 (in *Kab. den.* 1:185–86)

> בדיל [*B'dil*] tin. In natural science this metal is not greatly used. For, since it is derived by separation, its matter remains separate from the universal medicine. Among the planets Ṣedeq [Jupiter] is attributed to it, a whitish wandering planet to which the gentiles applied an idolatrous name whose mention is forbidden, Exod. 23:13 [and for which] a major extirpation is promised, Hos. 2:15; Zech. 13:2. Among the beasts no allegory is better

11	24	7	20	3
4	12	25	8	16
17	5	13	21	9
10	18	1	14	22
23	6	19	2	15

Figure 26.2. Magic square for iron.

referred to than that, because of its crackling, it should be called חזיר מיער [*ḥazir miyaʿar*], a boar out of the wood, Ps. 80:14, whose [letters give the] number 545, which is not only produced by five times 109, but whose minor number shows a quinary, as does the name [*ṣedeq*], 194, which numbers, if added up, make 14, and they [if added up] make 5. Which, taken twice, is 10, the minor number of the word בדיל [*b'dil*], by adding together [the two digits of] 46. But five times ten shows the fifty gates of Bina, and the first letter of the sefira Neṣaḥ, which are the sefirotic classes to which this metal is referred.

In particular transmutation of its sulphurous nature does not come forth, but with other sulphurs, especially of the red metals, it reduces thick water duly terrified into gold, so also into silver if it is introduced into thin water of a subtle nature, by quicksilver, which among others is made well enough by tin. But its viscous and watery nature can be ameliorated into gold if it be pulverized with the calx of gold for ten days, through all degrees of fire, and if it is thrown upon liquid gold in the form of little globules, gradually, which, I am taught, is to be done also with water. But no man is wise unless experience is his master.

I add no more. He who is wise can correct natures and where they are deficient help by experiments.

Chapter 4 continued (in *Kab. den.* 1:676)

קסטרא [*Qastra*, or qassitera], tin. See בדיל [*b'dil*]. Its camea[28] is as follows [see Figure 26.3].

4	14	15	1
9	7	6	12
5	11	10	8
16	2	3	13

Figure 26.3. Magic square for tin.

The number resulting from every side is ד"ל [*dal*, 34], representing the tenuity and vileness of this metal[29] in metallic operations.

Chapter 5 (in *Kab. den.* 1:271–73)

הוד [Hod, Majesty] in the wisdom of nature is of the class of brass. For its color expresses the nature of G'vura [Power] which this sefira has. And the use of brass was not alien to instruments of praise and music, 1 Chron. 15:19. And in war brazen bows were used, 2 Sam. 17:5, 6, 38.

But just as Hod is girded by the serpent, so the name נחשת [*n'ḥoshet*], brass, refers in its root to נחש [*naḥash*], serpent.

The seventy talents of brass of the offering, Exod. 38:29, represent seventy princes. For around this place the power of the husks [evil spirits or entities] is the greatest. Hence Hod is a degree of prophetic representation, since from the root נחש [*nḥsh*] comes נחשים [*n'ḥashim*] enchantments, Num. 23:23; 24:1. But he who wants to be careful will find that Hod has its special decade, and likewise in the history of brass he can easily gather a decade from the Law. For can that offering of brass, in general form, from which subsequently vessels were made for the Tabernacle, Exod. 38:39, not be referred to Keter, since all other degrees originate from it? Does not the laver of brass, Exod. 30:18, refer to the nature of Ḥokhma [Wisdom] from which a flow is sent down to all the inferiors? But its basis, which was also brass, is Bina [Intelligence], for it is in it that Ḥokhma resides.

In the sequel our author continues in the same vein to discuss the significance of brass, its relationship to the sefirot, and its correspondence to the planet Venus. The conclusion of chapter 5 is found in *Kab. den.* 1:570.

Chapter 6 (in *Kab. den.* 1:345–46 and 625–26)

In metallic doctrine Ḥokhma is the grade of lead, or the primordial salt in which the lead of the wise lies hidden. But how can such a sublime place be attributed to lead, which is such an ignoble metal? And which Scripture so rarely mentions?

But here lies Wisdom! Both of its grades are kept very secret, hence very little mention is made of it. Yet there will be no absence of a number of particular sefirot. For may not that which in Zech. 5:7 is called "a lifted-up talent of lead" and brought up from the deep, represent the grade of Keter? And that which is called, Zech. 5:8, "stone of lead" sets before itself the letter Yod which is in Ḥokhma.[30] Then in Ezek. 27:12 lead is referred to the place of the congregation, the like of which is Bina. And in Amos 7:7 אנך [*anokh*], a leaden plummet, denotes the thread of Ḥesed. For אנך [*anokh*] with the whole word[31] gives 72, the number of ḥesed. But in Num. 31:22 lead is enumerated among those things which can abide fire, [it] will be G'vura. But in Job 19:24 an iron pen and lead are joined together, from whence you have Tif'eret, a writer.[32] Again in Ezek. 22:18, 20 there is the furnace of testing, or of grace, and the furnace of judgment, in which there is also lead. Hence Neṣaḥ and Hod, for thence ought to flow a river of silver.[33]

And Jer. 6:29 [refers to] the furnace of testing out of which, by means of lead, good silver is expected. Is not the just man, and he that justifies, the Y'sod [Foundation]?[34] But if you seek the bottom of the sea, contemplate the passage in Exod. 15:10, where occurs the notion of Malkhut. This is the Red Sea from which can be extracted the Salt of Wisdom, and across which the ships of Solomon fetched gold.

The continuation of chapter 6, containing further kabbalistic and alchemical explanations of the significance of lead, is found in *Kab. den.* 1:625–26, not translated here. This is followed, pages 151–52, by kabbalistic and alchemical explanations of the various Hebrew names for lion, likewise omitted here, except for our author's comments on *k'fir*:

Moreover, the words כפיר [*k'fir*], young lion, and ירק [*yereq*], greenness, have both the numerical value of 310. And it is known in the metallic mysteries that at the very outset there occurs the enigma of the Lion of the green growth, which we call the Green Lion,[35] which, I pray you, do not reckon that it is thus called for any other reason but its color. For unless your matter be green, not only in that immediate state before it is reduced to water, but also after the water of gold is made thereof, you must remember that you must thus amend your universal dry process.

Chapter 7 (in *Kab. den.* 1:455)

ירדן [*Yarden*, Jordan] denotes a mineral water, useful for cleansing metals and leprous minerals. This water flows from two sources, one of which is called יאר [*y'or*], that is, fluid, having the nature of the right and benign. The other is called דן [*dan*], that is, rigorous and of a rough nature.[36] But it flows through the Salt Sea, which ought to be noted, and finally it is thought to be mixed with the Red Sea,[37] which is a sulphurous matter, masculine, and known to all true artists.[38] . . . But know that the name זכו [*zakhu*],[39] purity, multiplied by 8, the [minor] number of Y'sod [Foundation: 33], produces the number of סדר [*seder*], order, 264. Which number is also contained in the word ירדן [*yarden*], so that you remember that at least eight orders of purification are required before true purity ensues.

Chapter 7 continued (in *Kab. den.* 1:441–43)

Y'sod in natural things contains under it quicksilver because this is the foundation of the whole art of transmutation. And as the name אל [El, God] indicates the nature of silver, because both belong to the class of

Ḥesed (but here the inferior Ḥesed, Y'sod), so the name אל חי [El Ḥay, the Living God] is, as it were, the same as כסף חי [*kesef ḥay*], living silver [i.e., quicksilver]. And so כוכב [*kokhav*, Mercury], star, the name of the planet under which is this material, is, together with the whole word, 49, which is the number of אל חי [El Ḥay].

But remember that not all quicksilvers are conducive to your work, because they differ even as flax and hemp or silk [differ], and you would in vain prepare flax so that it attain the fineness and splendor of byssus [fine linen cloth].

And there are also those who think that it is a sign of legitimate water if, mixed with gold, it presently effervesces. However, the solution of common quicksilver precipitated by lead evinces this; and what will it effect? Verily, I tell you that there is no other sign of a true quicksilver but this: that in proper heat it invests itself with a skin that is the purest of refined gold, and this in a very little time, yea, in one night. This is that which, not without mystery, is called כוכב [*kokhav*], star, from which, according to the natural Kabbalah, Num. 24:17, "Out of Jacob comes a star," or, plainly, arise the shapes of rods and branches, and from this star flows this influence of which we speak.

This quicksilver is called in the Gemara, tractate Gittin, chapter 7, folio 69b, אספירכא [*ispirkha*],[40] that is *aqua spherica* [spherical water], because it flows from the mundane sphere. And in Gen. 36:39 it is called מהיטבאל [Mehetabel], that is מֵי הַטְּבְלָא [*me hat'vula*], water of immersion, by a transposition of letters, because in them the king is immersed to be purified; or, as it were, מי אל הטוב [*me el hatov*], by a similar metathesis, "the water of the good God," or living silver, for life and good have equal power, as have death and evil. This is called "The daughter of מטרד [*Matred*]," that is, as the Targum teaches, the goldmaker laboring with assiduous weariness.[41]

For this water does not flow from the earth, nor is it due out of mines, but is produced and perfected through great labor and much diligence. This wife is called מי זהב [Me Zahav], water of gold, or such water as emits gold. If the artist be betrothed to her, he will beget a daughter who will be the water of the royal bath. Although others consider this bride to be waters which are made out of gold, however, the poor men leave her to be espoused by magnates.

The husband of Mehetabel is that Edomite king and [king] of redness[42] who is called הדר [Hadar], splendor, that is, the splendor of the metallic kingdom (Dan. 11:20), which is gold. Namely, such [gold] which can be referred to Tif'eret, for הדר [Hadar] represents 209, which number is obtained also from the Tetragrammaton multiplied by 8, which is the number of [the day of] circumcision, and of Y'sod if the whole word is added.

But so that you may know that what is understood is Tif'eret of the degree of G'vura, know that the same number added to the whole is also contained in יצחק [Yiṣḥaq], which, in like manner, is of the class of gold.

The city of that king is called פָּעוּ [Paʿu], from brightness, according to Deut. 33:2. Both this name and the name יוסף [Yosef], by which Y'sod is designated, have the number 156, so that you should know that quicksilver is required for the work, and that outside this splendid city royal glory does not reside.

Here belongs another epithet, אלהים חיים [*Elohim ḥayyim*, Living God], as if it were called "living gold," for Elohim and gold denote the same measure. But this water is so called because it is the mother and principle of the living gold. For all other kinds of gold are thought to be dead, only this one excepted.

Nor will you err if you attribute to it another epithet, for it may be called מקור מים חיים [*m'qor mayim ḥayyim*], source of living waters. For by this water the king is revived, so that he may give life to all metals and living things. The camea[43] of this water is evidently wonderful, and it exhibits in like manner the number חי [*ḥay*], living, [by yielding] eighteen times the same sum in a square of 64 numbers which is the sum of the name מי זהב [*Me Zahav*], water of gold, in infinite variability, in this manner [see Figure 26.4].[44]

8	58	59	5	4	62	63	1
49	15	14	52	53	11	10	56
41	23	22	44	45	19	18	48
32	34	35	29	28	38	39	25
40	26	27	37	36	30	31	33
17	47	46	20	21	43	42	24
9	55	54	12	13	51	50	16
64	2	3	61	60	6	7	57

Figure 26.4. Magic square for *mē-zahav*, water of gold.

Here you have the sum of 260 from bottom to top, from right to left, and diagonally. Of which the minor number is 8, the number of Y'sod. Also, the root of the whole square is 8. The symbol of the first sum is 260, which is סר [*sar*], [meaning] went back, because in going forward the sum always goes backward through the units. For example, if you begin with 2, the sum will be 268, which can be resolved in 7. Beginning with 3, it will be 276, which can be resolved in 6, and so forth, through the rest.[45] And likewise, when the number of purifications increases, the weight of your waters decreases.

Chapter 8 (in *Kab. den.* 1:430)

Among the enigmas of natural things [is the fact that] the name of a Dove is never applied to metals, but [only] to the ministering and preparing of nature. He who understands here the nature of the burnt offering will not take turtles but two young male doves, Lev. 1:14; 12:8; 14:22. But count the word בני [*b'ne*, sons of] 62, and a pair of doves, whence the word נוגה [*nogah*, splendor, or Venus], 64, which is the name of the fifth of the planets, and you shall go the true way. Else, "labor not to be rich, from thy own wisdom cease. Wilt thou cause thine eyes presently to discern it? That will not be. But [the disciple of the wise men] maketh for himself wings and like the eagle flieth [so as to obtain the minerals of the star] to heaven. Prov. 23:4–5.[46]

Chapter 8 continued in (*Kab. den.* 1:456)

ירח [*Yareaḥ*], moon. This is the Shekhina. . . .

In the history of natural things Luna is called the medicine for the white, because it has received its whitening splendor from the sun, which, through a similar shining illuminates and converts to its nature the whole earth, that is, the impure metals. And from this can be understood mystically the passage in Isa. 30:26, because, the work being finished, she [the moon] has acquired solar splendor, and in this state the passage in Cant. 6:9 pertains to her.

By the same name is called the material of the Work, and so indeed it is like the sickle-shaped moon in the first state of consistency, and like the full moon in the last state of fluidity and purity. For the word ירח [*yareaḥ*], moon, and רזיא [*razaya*], secrets, have in gematria the same numbers, also רבוי [*ribbuy*], multitude, because in this material are found the secrets of multiplication.

Chapter 8 continued (in *Kab. den.* 1:241–42)

גפרית [*Gofrit*], sulphur. In the science of minerals this principle is referred to Bina, to the left, because of its color: and to that side is gold also referred as a rule. And חרוץ [*ḥaruṣ*, lit. grooved] is a species of gold referred to Bina, having the minor number 7, which agrees with [that of] גופריתא [*gufrita*, Aramaic for sulphur]. Therefore the gold of natural wisdom ought to be *ḥaruṣ*, dug up, or the like, not melted out. And this is that sulphur which gives a fiery color is penetrating, and changes the impure earths. To wit, sulphur with salt, Deut. 29:22; sulphur with fire, raining down upon the wicked, that is, the impure metals, Ps. 11:6. This sulphur you must dig up. And it is to be dug up from water, so that you may have fire out of water, and if your way be right before the Lord, your iron will swim upon the water, 2 Kings 6:6. Go then thy way to the Jordan with Elisha, 2 Kings 6:4. But who shall declare the G'vurot of the Lord, Ps. 106:2. Many seek other sulphurs, and he who has entered the house of particular paths, Prov. 8:2, will understand. For the sulphurs of gold and iron, whose extraction is taught by many, is easy. Also of gold, iron, and brass; also of gold, iron, copper, antimony; which are gathered together after the fulmination by vinegar out of the lye (*lixivium*), are changed into red oil with moist *hydrargyrum* [artificially prepared quicksilver] and they tinge silver. But a desirable treasure and oil are found in the dwelling of the wise, Prov. 21:20.

On this moralistic note ends the *Esh M'ṣaref.* It is evident from its text that the author was well versed in the Hebrew and Aramaic languages, in the Bible, the Targum, and the Talmud, in the Kabbalah, and the methods of gematria, and in alchemical theory and practice. His treatise can be considered an attempt at unifying these separate disciplines. According to him both the Kabbalah and alchemy contain the same "mysteries of wisdom," and the transmutation of metals, hinted at by gematria correspondences, is analogous to the healing of the sick.

The value of the treatise lies primarily in typifying a specifically Jewish, kabbalistically oriented, trend in alchemy, which differed considerably from the alchemical methodology as practiced by most Muslim and Christian alchemists. We find in its presentation of alchemical theory and procedure an organic connection between alchemy on the one hand and biblical, talmudic, and kabbalistic tradition on the other. By interpreting biblical passages alchemically, our author has, in true alchemical fashion, transmuted the Bible into an alchemical source book. In his view, a true master of alchemy had to be conversant not only with run-of-the-mill alchemical techniques, mythologies, and theories about nature, but also with Jewish tradition; and, over and above all this, he had to be a moral, pious, God-fearing Jew.

One last point deserves mention. In reading this text one feels that its author was only tangentially, if at all, interested in making gold. One looks in vain in the *Esh M'ṣaref* for alchemical recipes such as the famous diplosis of gold attributed by Alexandrian alchemists to Moses. Instead, our author's attention is focused on deciphering the secrets of nature with the help of gematria, which reveals unsuspected connections between stars and metals, and among various metals, thus pointing to the greatest of all mysteries, the unity of God-created nature.

Chapter Twenty-seven

TAITAZAK AND PROVENÇALI

JOSEPH TAITAZAK was an important talmudist, Bible scholar, and Kabbalist who lived in Salonika in the fifteenth to sixteenth centuries. The exact dates of his birth and death have not been definitely established, but from 1520 on he was recognized as an outstanding scholar and halakhic authority in Salonika, and Joseph Caro in a letter to him called him "the light and the holy one of Israel, the crown of the Diaspora." Taitazak left behind several biblical commentaries and halakhic works, was the head of a kabbalistic circle in Salonika, and the first to develop and utilize the concept of the Maggid, a personalized divine voice, from whom several Kabbalists subsequently claimed to have received communications.

In one of his as yet unpublished manuscripts, Taitazak offers a kabbalistic-alchemical explanation of "the mystery of gold and silver." He states that the mystery of Jacob's ladder (Gen. 28:10ff.) will explain

> also great and fearsome things: how you can ascend in the mystery of the ladder, and this is a mystery. . . . And thus will be explained to them the mystery of the seven [metals] in the mystery of the ascent and descent. . . . And thus will be explained to them the mystery of the supernal gold and silver, and the mystery of the lower gold and silver: how you can make it, effectively, in nature, out of all kinds of the seven metals. And this is the real natural science, and all of it is embedded in the mystery of the ladder.

In the sequel Taitazak states that Jacob and Moses knew this mystery, and in a later context he returns to, and expands, the same idea:

> And instantly you will know and understand the whole mystery of the lower world and the mystery of the supernal and the lower silver and gold. If you know this great wisdom, you will instantly know how to make, in effect, in the lower world, and easily, each of the seven kinds of metal. And this is the science of alchemy, and it is the divine science, as you will understand further when you reach it. And he who does not first know the wisdom of the upper world will not be able to achieve it. [But he who knows] will be able to make each one of all the seven kinds of metal, and quicksilver, quickly.[1]

Scholem, in discussing this passage, expresses regrets that the part in which Taitazak promised to deal with the mysteries of alchemy has not been preserved, and explains that Taitazak hints that the "select gold of the real Kabbalah is the sefirah of Binah (Understanding), and the mystery of the purification of gold is anchored in the mystery of the godhead. The melting-pot of the alchemist, in which the metals are purified, is therefore but a natural model of the melting-pot in which one attains the mystery of the godhead in the purification of the holy names."[2]

A study of the alchemical references in the writings of Taitazak, who seems to be the only Jewish scholar to term alchemy "the divine science," is one of the desiderata of the history of Jewish alchemy.

Jacob ben David Provençali

A glimpse into the interest in alchemy among Italian Jews in the late fifteenth century is afforded by the correspondence between two Italian rabbis of that period. It was initiated by David ben Judah Messer Leon (1470/72–1526?), who served as rabbi in Florence, Salonika, and Valona, Albania, a man of vast erudition in Jewish subjects, as well as of interest in the natural sciences. In search of information on the latter subject, Messerleon (as he was generally referred to) requested information from R. Jacob Provençali on "the views of the talmudic sages about the study of the natural sciences, logic, philosophy, and medicine." Jacob ben David Provençali (dates of birth and death unknown) was a scholar who resided first in Marseille, where he engaged in maritime trade, and subsequently moved to Naples, where by 1480 he was one of the rabbis. His response to Messerleon was written from Naples in 1490, and in it he speaks about alchemy:

> Let the complete Torah of ours not be like the empty talk of theirs [the gentiles], for that should not be believed in, but only [what they say about] the nature of things, and natural experiments, such as experiments with poisons and herbs, and the powers and mixtures in which the hand of the philosophers is good and reliable, since they stole this from the books of Solomon, peace be upon him, who, as is known, wrote a great book called *Book of the Mystery of Natures*. And he wrote that book before the *Book of Medicaments*. . . . And our forebears . . . the sages of Babylonia were more versed in the natural sciences than all the other sages . . . and they praised this science very much, I mean the science of the mysteries of nature, which reaches the point where some of the sages give a new mixture to the quicksilver to become real silver, or they make good gold anew by an operation, as it is said in the Jerusalem [Talmud] at the end of chapter [?], on the verse "And wisdom keepeth its masters alive (Eccl. 7:12): R. Elʿazar said, Like the rich men of the House of Marqoʿaya who were experts in the nature of congealing gold, and in the pealing [i.e., removal] of silver from dross. Thus far his language. And this important saying is explained by R. Asher

> in his commentary to the Jerusalem Talmud: That family of Marqoᶜin were experts in the science of alchemy and caused the juices of certain herbs to congeal, and made gold out of them. And another science which was in their hands was that they were able easily to separate the dross from the silver, and that science is known and famous today. But they did not want to reveal the herbs which they congealed and which became gold. Thus far the language of the master. Hence the conclusion from all that has been said is that the natural science is not at all known today in its secrets. For what people today call natural science is but an invented [i.e., untrue] science, and empty talk, for these [people] know no real natural mystery, but [only] a linguistic expression, and ways of disputations, in which there is no substance for those who know, and it is not wanted by the enlightened. But the science which is hidden today was praised among our sages of blessed memory, for it gave sustenance to its masters in great honor, for by means of that science man achieves great riches in no time, and when man becomes rich he reaches the degree of wisdom.[3]

This passage is puzzling for more than one reason. First of all, the two books mentioned by Jacob Provençali as written by King Solomon are unknown, although other magical books, such as the *Book of the Key of Solomon*,[4] attributed to him, were well known and often referred to. Second, the Jerusalem Talmud does not contain the statement Provençali quotes in the name of R. Elᶜazar. Third, no commentary by Rabbenu Asher (Asher ben Yeḥiel, c. 1250–1327) on the Jerusalem Talmud is known, and therefore his explanation of the statement about the House of Marqoᶜaya (or Marqoᶜin) cannot be located.[5] Since Provençali included these references in a writing he addressed to a fellow scholar, it is almost impossible to imagine that he simply invented them: he would have exposed himself to instant critical censure by David Messerleon. Can it be, then, that Provençali had in his possession, or at least knew of, two books attributed to King Solomon, as well as a different text of the Jerusalem Talmud, and a lost commentary on it by Rabbenu Asher?

Leaving these questions aside, one thing is clear: Jacob Provençali had knowledge of a tradition about the existence of alchemical expertise in talmudic times possessed by certain families and by the sages in general.

Let me conclude this brief section by quoting what Immanuel Löw had to say on the subject in his *Die Flora der Juden*.[6] After referring to the passage quoted by Provençali from the Jerusalem Talmud as "invented," and the comment quoted by him from Rabbenu Asher as "alleged," Löw reports that he wrote to the noted historian of alchemy, Edmund O. von Lippmann, and asked him what he thought about the method of making gold by congealing the juice of a plant. Lippmann responded saying that he suspected that the passage referred to the "signature theory," which held that yellow plant juices become congealed into gold, white into silver, and so on. "Of course," Lippmann wrote, "this theory goes back to Dioscorides, but it came in vogue in the fifteenth century in a form developed especially by Paracelsus, and an author writing ca. 1490 could well have taken it from this type of writing."

Chapter Twenty-eight

ḤAYYIM VITAL, ALCHEMIST

AFTER MOSES DE LEON, the greatest figure in the history of Jewish mysticism was Isaac Luria (1534–1572). Whereas De Leon produced a great many books, Luria left behind practically no writings of his own, and his impact on the Kabbalah and the recognition of his stature as a highly original mystical thinker are due almost entirely to the presentation of his teachings in the voluminous writings of his chief disciple, Ḥayyim Vital, who effectively played Plato to Luria's Socrates.

Ḥayyim Vital (1542–1620) was born in Safed, Palestine, as son of the scribe Joseph Vital Calabrese, who, as his name shows, had come to Ereṣ Israel from Calabria in southern Italy. In his autobiographical notes Ḥayyim Vital reports that when he was twelve an expert in palmistry predicted that at the age of twenty-four he would spend two years neglecting his Torah studies, after which he would have to choose between the road to Paradise and the road to hell.[1] The prediction came true in the sense that after studying under various mystics in Safed, Vital devoted the two years 1566–1567 to studying and practicing alchemy. In 1570, when Luria arrived in Safed from Egypt, Vital became his chief disciple and remained closely associated with him for the two years that were granted to Luria before he died in 1572, at the age of thirty-eight. After Luria's death Vital jealously claimed to be the sole, or at least the most authentic and reliable, repository of Luria's teachings, and devoted a major part of the remaining forty-eight years of his life to putting in writing what he heard Luria utter during those two short years, elaborating the Lurianic ideas, telling what he knew about Luria's life, and building up in his voluminous writings an image of Luria that was to secure him pride of place not only among sixteenth-century Safed Kabbalists, whose circle included many other luminaries, but also in the history of Jewish mysticism in general. At one point during those two years Luria warned him off alchemy, but soon after his master's death Vital returned to it, and within a few short years thereafter wrote his large untitled book, which deals with alchemy and "practical Kabbalah," and which is the subject of the present chapter.

From 1577 to 1585 Vital was rabbi and head of a yeshivah in Jerusalem. From 1586 to 1592 he again lived in Safed. In 1593 he returned to Jerusalem a second time, and by 1598 we find him in Damascus, where for a time he served as rabbi of the Sicilian community, and stayed until his death. In all the places of his residence and while fulfilling various official rabbinical functions, however, his main preoccupation remained his scholarly writing, most of it devoted to Luria's Kabbalah. In these books it is not easy to distinguish between Luria's original teachings and their interpretation, presentation, and reinterpretation by Vital, so that ultimately it is difficult to decide whether Vital stood on Luria's shoulders or Luria on Vital's. But one thing is certain about Vital's place in the history of Jewish mysticism: he was unquestionably the most influential author in the Safed circle, and the teachings of "the Holy ARI" ("Lion," as Luria has been referred to by now for four hundred years, from the initials of his name, *Ashkenazi Rabbi Yiṣḥaq*), which have been in the center of Jewish mysticism ever since his death, made their impact in the form in which Vital presented them.

Vital's interest in magic and alchemy has been underplayed to such an extent by the historians of Jewish mysticism that one has the impression that they were embarrassed by the fact that this great Kabbalist devoted much of his attention to such subjects. Typical in this respect is Vital's long biography in the *Encyclopaedia Judaica* by Gershom Scholem, in which he discusses in detail each of the books and manuscripts of Vital. This, however, is all he found necessary to say about Vital's alchemy: "He . . . spent two years (1563–65) in the practice of alchemy which he later regretted." Scholem's statement that Vital "later regretted" that he had devoted time to alchemy is based on a passage in Vital's *Sefer haḤezyonot* (Book of Visions) in which he wrote: "[Luria] also told me that he saw written on my forehead the verse 'To devise skilful works, to work in gold and in silver' (Exod. 35:32), which hinted at the two and one-half years during which I desisted from Torah study and dealt with the science of alchemy."[2] However, Vital here quotes the view of his master Luria, and does not express his own attitude to alchemy, which was to remain one of positive interest and active involvement. He may have suspended his alchemical and other practical work during the two years while he was Luria's disciple, but after the death of the master he returned to alchemy, technology, and medicine, as shown by the manuscript discussed in this chapter.

Scholem's article was written in 1971. Fifteen years later Meir Benayahu of Tel Aviv University discussed the Vital manuscript in a paper titled "Medical Matters in an Unknown Manuscript of Ḥayyim Vital,"[3] in which he mentioned that the manuscript contains alchemical material as well. For some reason Benayahu came to the conclusion that the manuscript was written by Vital in his old age in Damascus. However, on top of folio 110a of the manuscript we find these words: "I, the youth, Ḥayyim Vital, disciple of our master the ARI of blessed memory . . .". This entry, written in the same hand as the text of the whole page, shows that the manuscript was probably written soon after the death of Luria, when Vital was in his early thirties. It also shows that soon after Luria's death Vital took time off from his kabbalistic studies to write this large book, which contains more than 1,500 medical, technical, alchemical, magical, and other prescriptions.

It is time now to have a close look at the manuscript itself, the original of which is in the Moussaieff Collection in Jerusalem.[4] The manuscript consists of 7 + 153 folios of about 7 by 10 inches in size. It begins with seven folios (numbered 2–5 and 7–9) that contain miscellaneous notes in a handwriting other than Vital's, and are evidently of later origin. They are difficult to decipher, but most of them are of alchemical content. The first reads: "*Alanbīqī* [alembic]. In Laʿaz: *aqua ardenṭe* [S., burning water, that is nitric acid], a vessel of burnt water . . . white alum . . . in Arabic *shāb* [vitriol]." This is followed by twenty similar notes giving the names of alchemical substances in Spanish, Arabic, and occasionally in Hebrew. Evidently this is an attempt to compile a vocabulary of the terms appearing in Vital's manuscript. These notes also comprise magical remedies and magical squares for incantations, so-called *qameʿot*, amulets, with angelic and divine names, and so on.

These first seven folios are followed by folios numbered in Hebrew alphabetic numbers, beginning with *beth.* The first few contain another vocabulary and magical recipes, squares, and figures, in two or three different hands. Two of these recipes give instructions for preparing ink for the writing of Torah scrolls and for writing on paper (f. 6a).

On folio 7a begins the clear and neat two-column text written by Vital's own hand. The six folios prior to this are missing, as one can gather from the index prepared by Vital's son Samuel, which is appended to the end of the volume. From that index we also learn that the missing superscription of this first part of the book was "Operations that are performed with holy names or with permutations, which are the external names, or with seals, or with incantations." The prescriptions contained in this part are either medical (remedies for curing various pains and ailments), or magical (interpretations of dreams, how to speak to the dead, the magical use of the herb *santa* [?], and so on).

On folio 10a begins the second part, superscribed "On operations which are performed through nature, and on medicaments and operations that are performed not with nature, which are the ones called *s'gullot* [H., charms]." This part contains a great variety of prescriptions, such as how to fry eggs or fish in a frying pan made of paper so that the paper should not be burned, how to expel smoke from the room, how to make ants flee the house, how to make honey out of grapes and raisins, how to make sour milk, and how to dye woollen cloth. It also contains a great number of instructions for the preparation of practical remedies, such as ointments, kohl for the eyes, and so on. Although in the actual entries Vital does not separate the "natural" from the "not natural," that is, magical, operations, the title of the section makes it clear that he was well aware of the differences between the two categories. Moreover, the details given in these instructions and descriptions show that Vital was not only a medical author and an avid collector of what other physicians before him had said and written, but also a practicing pharmacist and physician, who had many patients and treated them, if need be, for days and weeks. However, the following presentation will be limited to Vital's alchemy, which takes up about one-fourth of his manuscript.

A quite remarkable aspect of Vital's alchemy is its purely factual, technological nature. Vital, as is well known, was a great Kabbalist, a man who formulated mystical doctrines, dwelt at length on the great secrets of the relationship between the Above and the Below, was painfully conscious of the fierce ongoing struggle between the powers of Good and Evil in the world and in man—and yet of all this not a word is found in his alchemical writings. This is the more noteworthy since most Jewish kabbalistic alchemists in the Middle Ages and the Renaissance loved to give a mystical flavor to their alchemical notes by insisting repeatedly that this or that alchemical observation or insight was "a great secret," and it was precisely by doing so that they achieved a fusion, or at least a combination, of alchemy and Kabbalah. Nothing of all this can be found in Vital's long and painstakingly detailed alchemical prescriptions. One gets the definite impression that Vital was able to compartmentalize his thinking and writing: when he cogitated and wrote about the Kabbalah, he was a mystic. When he described magical remedies, *s'gullot, qameʿot*, incantations, adjurations, and magic squares, he was an undoubting believer in angels and demons. But when he worked, thought, and wrote about alchemy he was nothing but a natural scientist who observed keenly what went on in the course of his experiments, and described them with an eye to the smallest detail—at such times the world of the spirit simply did not exist for him.

Vital was also a man of considerable linguistic versatility. Although he wrote his book in Hebrew, in some minor parts of it he switched to Arabic (written in Hebrew characters), and he translated many medical, botanical, and alchemical terms into Arabic. His knowledge of Arabic extended to a familiarity with the differences between the urban and Bedouin dialects. In one recipe, for example, he writes, "For nose bleeding. Take powder of the herb called *ghalqa* [a bitter or poisonous shrub] in the language of the Arabs who dwell in the desert, and throw it into the nostril which bleeds . . ." (f. 24b). In a similar manner he translates words into Turkish, Persian, Latin, Italian, Spanish, Portuguese, and

German. In the continuation of the above recipe he writes: "And if it still bleeds a little, take the juice of *ḥarulim* [H., nettles. brambles], and in Laʿaz *urtigas* [S. *urticas*], and in the language of Ashkenaz [i.e., German] *urtias*, and put three drops of it into the nostril which bleeds, and let him lie back." On the same page we have this example of linguistic virtuosity: "To kill the lice which grow on the head of a woman. Take *mio bazaj* in Arabic, and it is called in Latin *estafiza agrias*, [S. *agriaz*, china berry] in the Ajami [Persian] language *vazjibāl jayāl*, and take Armenian *bola* which is called in Arabic *ṭīn Armīnī* [Armenian clay], and take sulphur and white *sirdisinqi* [?] and *minio* [minium] in Portuguese, and it is *azarqon* [*azarcón*] in Spanish. Of each of these five things take one *dirham* and pound them well."

As for the alchemical operations themselves, Vital carefully distinguishes among those of which he heard or read, those which he tried unsuccessfully, and those which he tried with occasional success—he groups the operations he describes under these three headings. Interestingly, he does not have a category of operations that he performed with consistent success.

Folio 34a carries this superscription: "THE THIRD PART of operations of the *qimiya* [alchemy] in matters of the seven metals, and I shall start with the making of the melting pot." The first of the numbered sections that follow describes in meticulous detail how to make a melting pot, and is a good example of Vital's interest and expertise in technology:

> 1. To make a melting pot for melting gold and silver, know that there is a special mineral dust of which the pot is made, but there are in it various kinds, for the earth in a certain country is stronger than that of another. . . . And we shall tell of it in several ways. Behold, if you have [some] of the earth of which the pots are made do this: take two parts of that earth, and one part of cotton-wool, and if it is old cotton it is better, and if it is chaff of flax it is better. And shred the cotton-wool into very small, fine, and separate pieces, and then put the earth on a smooth marble stone floor, and put it in a little cotton-wool spread and shredded in pieces as mentioned, and put on it two or three drops of water, and pound it with a sledgehammer, etc., so that all the cotton-wool should be absorbed, and also that it should be ground and powdered totally until it cannot be recognized and becomes, with the earth, a kind of waxy paste. And this is the essence of the whole work. And you should have ready a wooden mold of a pot, and press [this waxy paste] onto it and make the pot you want, or shape it between your hands and with your fingers. And so that it should not become [too] soft in your hands while you work it, strew on it ashes, little by little, while doing it, and thus it will not become soft in your hands while you work it. And make it thin little by little between your hands, until it is finished. And

> beware lest there be cracks and fissures in it. And then do not put it either into the sun or in the shade, but put it on ashes that are a little hot, which are called cinders, and the heat should be very gentle, or beneath the oven, under the place on which one puts the pot for cooking, and leave it there until it becomes very dry. And after it has dried completely put it on cinders and fire, and blow it with the bellows until the melting pot burns and becomes red like coals which are a little fiery, and then remove it and put it a second time on hot cinders. And all these things are done so that the melting pot should not crack when one melts in it.

In the sequel Vital describes alternative methods of making melting pots, how to repair them if need be, and how to preserve them. Then he goes on to describe the various methods of making *ṭiṭ haḥokhmah* [H., clay of wisdom], that is, philosophers' clay, and the preservation and use of glass flasks (f. 34a–b). The subsequent eleven folios (34b–45b) constitute a veritable handbook of alchemy, containing close to a hundred recipes, covering a great many aspects of treating metals, transmutations, separation of alloys, and much more. Among other things he discusses "how to clean a touchstone, called in Laᶜaz *toqe* [S. *piedra de toquel*, of the gold and silver that adhere to it" (f. 34b, no. 11). Interesting from the point of view of information on the material culture of Vital's world is his recipe for recovering by burning the silver and gold threads used in embroidering gala clothes (f. 34b, no. 15)—evidently the society in which he lived included rich people who could afford such very expensive clothes. Incidentally, these pages contain most of the standard alchemical vocabulary used by Vital, and, for that matter, by the other medieval and Renaissance alchemical authors, derived mainly from Spanish, Arabic, and Persian. Here is a sample (f. 37a, no. 43):

> This is the best operation, in which I succeeded more than in anything else I have tried until now. It is to improve the color of gold which is of fifteen *qīraṭ* [A. *qīrāṭ*, carat] and make it of twenty carats in its color and its tint in the view of the touchstone and in the view of the eye, and it is soft for the hammer and good and beautiful. Prepare three operations. One is putting together a combination of metals; and the second is kinds of powders, and this is how they are done: 1. The combination of metals is this: take sixteen carats of purified gold to the value of twenty-four carats as is known. And five carats of silver refined with lead, as is known. And three carats of copper. And first you must purify the copper in this manner: take red new copper or [copper] in which nothing of other metals had been mixed, not even the smell of heating tin, as is known. And melt it five times, and each time extinguish [quench] it in linseed oil. And if need be, heat the copper in fire until it becomes red like coals, and extinguish it in linseed oil twelve times, but if you melt it as mentioned, it will be much better. And melt the three

metals together in a new earthenware melting pot, and throw it in the iron *ḥarīṣ* [H., mold], and its weight will be found to be a full *mithqāl* [A., a weight equalling twenty-four carats], and preserve it. And then prepare the two kinds of powders. One of them is of prepared silver and *rasukhṭ* [A., orig. P., antimony], and the second powder is of prepared antimony alone. And this is their matter: the first powder is thus: take *salniṭri* [S. *sal de nitro*, saltpeter] and sulphur in equal parts and pound them well and put them in a new earthenware vessel which should not be glazed at all, and put it on gentle fire so that the sulphur should get inflamed, but only to the point of becoming fluid. And when it begins to be melted mix them well with a wooden stick, and not with iron. And when they melted and are well mixed, pour them out on a wooden tablet to cool. And then take of this mixture one part, and *jinjufr* [A. *zunjufr*, minium or cinnabar] one part, and *zunjār* [A. *zinjār*, verdigris] and in Laᶜaz *verdete* [S., verdigris], one part, and *vitriol Romano* which is white from the outside but in the inside it is like the purity of glass which inclines toward the color of sky blue and the color of the leek, and take of it one part, and one part of *bol Armeniqo* [S., Armenian bole, red clay] which, if you break it should be red inside and there should be no blackness at all in it, and *nishādir* [A., P., ammonia] one part, and it should be the cleanest and whitest that it can be, and one part of *alum yamini* [A.-H. Yemenite alum], and it is like the alum with which they dye the clothes and which is called *alum de roqa* [S. *alum de roca*, rock alum], and there are in it white pieces without any redness at all, and they are almost like the *qristal* [S. *cristal*, crystal], and this is called *alum yamini*. So that all in all there are eight drugs: of six of them there should be one part each, and of the first two, the sulphur and the saltpeter, there should be only half a part of each. And pound well all the mentioned to be very, very fine. This is the powder which is called the powder of eight ingredients. And then take two parts of this powder and eight parts of red clay, and two parts of *sforea de qana* [S. . . . *de caña*, . . . of reed] which is called in Arabic *samg ᶜarabī* [A. *samgh ᶜarabī*, gum arabic], that is to say gum of almonds. And pound well each of them alone, and then mix them again very, very well. And this powder is called the powder in which there is the *spodio* [?]. And take one part of the burnt powdered silver which we shall explain below, with the help of God in no. 45, which was burned with the sulphur and the red clay, and do not burn it in any other way but in that manner precisely. And take also one part of good and choice antimony, and pound the two of them together very well, and also mix them together, and take of this mixture only one part separately, and four parts separately from the powder in which is the *spodio*, and take the one part of the mixture of the burnt silver and the antimony, and tie it into a thin linen cloth, and make it like a round ball, and cut off that part of the cloth which remains outside the ball, cutting away of it as much as you can so that nothing should remain but the ball itself, very narrowly. And take the four parts of the powder, and divide it and put half of it into an earthenware pot, and make in its middle a kind of pit, and dip the ball into urine, that is water of feet, thoroughly until it becomes very wet. And when it is wet put it immediately into the pit, and put on it the half of the powder which was left, and push it well and squeeze it strongly with your fingers on the stone until it is very well crushed, and then put the melting pot on mild coal fire, and cover it on its sides with dark coals that have not yet been lighted, and it will transpire that the fire will be under the melting pot and not on its sides, until the fire will spread to them by itself, without your having blown it at all, and they will slowly catch fire. And when you see that smoke rises from the pot, remove the coals which are at the sides of the pot, and uncover the pot a little, and pour into it a little urine so that the powder should become well moistened, and then cover it again as at first. And half an hour later pour into it again a little urine as at first so that it should be well moistened, and do thus three times, every half hour. And be careful that the pot should not become red in the fire, for if it becomes red the pot will lose everything that is in it. And this is why I told you that it has to be moistened every hour with urine, as mentioned. And when the three times are up, as mentioned, then give it a somewhat stronger fire. And then take the pot out of the fire and let it cool, and you will find that the silver and the antimony have remained in the place in which you put them in the middle of the powder, and you will find that they have become a little hard like a small ball that is somewhat hard. And take it and clean it well of the powders that adhere to it, and then grind it very well, and then wash it in water three or four times until the water comes out clean and pure. And then put this powder in a new earthenware vessel or an iron vessel on the fire until it dries, and then take it off. And this powder is called the powder of the mixture of prepared silver and antimony. With this the matter of the first powder has been explained.

THE SECOND POWDER. Take one part of antimony, the best and the choicest that you can find, and take two parts of the abovementioned *spodio* powder, and put them into an earthenware pot after you have tied it into a ball, and extinguish it in urine three times, everything precisely as was done with the first ball of the mixture of the prepared silver and antimony. However it is not necessary that you should burn this antimony with sulphur, as you did with the silver. But all the other things remain the same in all their details. And behold this is called the powder of the prepared antimony. And know that if you leave this mixture on the fire twenty-four hours and every hour you extinguish it in urine as mentioned, then when you put the weight of one carat of it into one *mithqāl* of gold melted in fire, it will have the color and quality of three carats. And if you leave it three days and nights on the fire it will give the color and quality of six carats, that is to say, if you throw one carat of it upon one *mithqāl* of melted gold of eighteen carats it will improve it to become twenty-two carats. However it will not stand up to more than three or four meltings, that is to say, if you melt that gold three or four times it will lose this high quality which it received. But if you do this it will not add gold to every *mithqāl* but will only [give] an improvement of one carat alone and it will remain thus forever.

And now I shall explain the completion of their combinations. Behold, one which is the powder of the mixture of the prepared silver and the antimony. Take of them one carat and take very good and choice *ṭīnqār* [A. *tankār*, alcali, borax] which should not be moist, and it is called good *boraz* [borax], and is also called *bora*, and burn it on coals in a vessel until moisture is removed and its smoke ceases and it becomes very dry and its color becomes black, as is the usage of the refiners. And take of this black borax three carats and mix them with one carat of the abovementioned prepared powder of silver and rasukht and pound them well and mix them very well. And melt the three metals mentioned at the beginning of this operation, and after they are well melted throw the abovementioned mixture into them. And then take of the prepared antimony alone one carat and pound it and mix it well with one carat of the burned borax and throw it into the remaining three metals as mentioned. And then pour it into the known iron mold, and then taste it with the touchstone which is called *toqe* and you will find it gold of twenty carats, beautiful and good and soft. And it will be found that there are in it only sixteen carats of refined gold and now it has the weight of twenty-five or twenty-six carats gold, approximately twenty carats for the *mithqāl*. And as for the two aforementioned powders, which are the powder of the mixture of the prepared silver and antimony, and the powder of the prepared antimony by itself, these two powders, if you mix them with the burnt borax as mentioned, they will not survive long but will consume each other. And therefore if you wish them to survive a long time, take these powders after they are well washed, as mentioned, and the water comes out pure, and they are well dried. Take of them a hundred parts and take of the burnt borax five parts, and mix them well together, and put them aside to be preserved, and they will survive even for ten years. And if you wish to operate with them, then take these 105 parts and wash them very well, and dry the metals in fire, and then again mix new burnt borax into them as much as is suitable for its work, as above, and it will be good. But as for the powder of the eight substances, including the first powder of the mixture of the prepared silver and antimony, you can make it on one occasion and it will remain good for ten years.

And behold, by the aforementioned acts the color of the gold will tend a little to redness, like the color of the copper. And therefore, by [following] what I shall explain now, its color will be very superior, tending to the color of the greenness [i.e., yellowness] of gold and to the redness of copper, and even with a touchstone itself this change can be recognized. And this color will remain in it forever, even if you heat it in fire, unless you melt it.

TAKE an earthenware or iron vessel, and put into it the powder of the eight substances as mentioned, and heat the abovementioned gold after having made it into something like a long rod, or after having made it into a finished ornament. And once it gets hot and red in the fire, put it into the powders in the mentioned vessel and cover the gold well on all sides and above with these powders, and then put the earthenware vessel on gentle fire until the powders are almost consumed and melted. And then throw the gold immediately into urine to extinguish it. And this procedure will greatly improve its color and its interior and exterior hue, and will also add to it some weight.

AND THEN if you want to give it a better external hue, but not an internal one, as the one mentioned, do this: heat the gold well in fire, until it becomes red, and then put it immediately into crushed grain or bran of wheat flour, or into fine sawdust of the craftsmen, which falls down when new boards and logs are sawed, and cover it well with what has been mentioned, on all its sides, and leave it until it cools by itself. And repeat doing this once more, and then the color will come out very red. And then give it the color which is usually achieved by the refiners of salt and alum and ammonia and saltpeter, as is described above in no. 36. And do it twice, and its color will come out very superior. But this last branlike color will not remain forever, for when you put it into fire it disappears; but it is a very nice color, and is valued more than all the other exterior colors that I have seen, and also it remains as long as it is not put into fire. And this color is useful for all inferior gold, to make its color like that of good refined gold, and it remains as mentioned. But the color mentioned before is good for all gold in which is mixed copper and which, for that reason, tends to redness, and through it, it will have the color of really green [yellow] gold, even for the touchstone, and even if you heat it in fire, except if you melt it, as mentioned.

ALSO know that all gold, if you wish to heighten its color and weight by four carats in every *mithqāl*, you can do it in the above manner. For example, if you have one *mithqāl* of gold of twenty carats per *mithqāl*, and after it is melted you put into it one carat of the powder of the mixture of prepared silver and antimony as mentioned, after you have mixed it with three carats of borax as mentioned, then, behold, it will add one carat to the weight of the gold. And if you take one carat of the prepared antimony alone, as mentioned, after you have mixed it with one carat of burnt borax as mentioned, and you put it into melted gold, it will add one more carat to the weight of the gold. And also it will add to the quality of the gold, that is, it will improve its color, by one more carat above what it was. So that it will add two carats to its weight, and one carat to the improvement of the color of the gold, or a total of three carats. And if you prepare the color for it in an earthenware vessel with the powder of the eight ingredients, it will improve the color of the gold by one carat. That is, it will add two carats to the weight of the gold, and add two carats to the improvement of its color, improving it by four added carats in its total weight. And know that I saw it written concerning these four added carats that there is in it no blemish, nor any forgery at all, but it is a natural thing that even if the gold is melted many times, and even if you give it the known strong water [i.e., aquafortis], it will not lose that which has been added to it. And now:

44. I shall explain the manner of the above operations, and from them you can draw conclusions concerning all the other operations in the *kīmīya* [alchemy]. Know that every [product of] alchemy, which consists of a mixture of metals with one another, and especially if there is in it any admixture of antimony, is very hard and not soft for the hammer. And therefore the main thing is to be very careful that the gold should come out soft and good and beautiful by performing all your works in a new melting pot into which no refuse has ever entered. Also the drugs should all be choice, so that according to their high quality they should add to the quality of the work. Also, pound the drugs only on a marble stone, and not in a copper mortar, and if it is possible for the mortar to be of silver, it will be much better. For a copper mortar, and in particular if it is *al-mabrī* [A., cut, scratched], that is, one in which sand and other metals such as lead and tin and the like had been mixed, they cause two bad things: 1. they make the gold into which are put the drugs which are pounded in the mentioned mortar very hard under the hammer; and also [2.] such a mortar attracts and takes all the strength and power of the drug which is being pounded in it. And beware of this very much. Also know that when you mix gold melted in fire, or silver, don't mix it at all with an iron, but with a wooden stick, or with a long [piece] of coal taken with the tongs, and with it mix the melted gold in the pot (f. 38a).

On folio 38b, under no. 47, Vital writes:

All persons who engage in alchemical work must beware of the many kinds of strong drugs that are mixed into silver and gold when they are being melted in fire, and must stay away from their smoke. Also they should beware of the smell and smoke of the strong water [aquafortis] which separates silver from gold, as known. And above all one must beware of the smoke that issues from quicksilver when it is on the fire, for it is the quicksilver itself which becomes smoke and rises in the air, and it is a danger if it enters your nose, for the quicksilver is a mortal poison, for out of it is made *soliman* [S. or A. *sulayman*, mercury chloride, corrosive sublimate]. Therefore be extremely careful about the smell of all things that are of quicksilver when it is on the fire, such as mercury chloride, and cinnabar and the like, or when you put quicksilver itself on the fire with drugs.

The subsequent items deal with the following subjects:

48. How to refine gold from all the impurities in it.

49. How to separate gold alloyed with tin, lead, or *alatun* [S. *laton*, copper].

50. (f. 39a) How to soften hard gold.

51. How to liquify the mercury chloride.

52. What to do to enable gold alloyed with other metals to "endure the hammer." Also, "How to soften all hard metals or all hard *al-qīmīya*." Evidently Vital here uses the term "alchemy" to designate any alchemically produced substance. He describes five alternative methods.

53. (f. 39b) To purify silver or gold mixed with some copper. I did not find this written, but I myself succeeded in it after having tried it. To begin with, reach an estimate in your mind as to how much copper is mixed in it, and then melt the gold or silver, and when it is completely melted put into it a little saltpeter, as much as is the measure of the copper, and throw it into it little by little, and then pour it into the iron mold, and you will find that at the end of the stick there will be the purified silver alone, and at the other end there will be the burnt copper, something like antimony, and it will break up like dust, and then beat the metal with a hammer, and the rest of the silver will remain, and the copper will jump and break like dust. And you must be very accurate about the measure of the copper, so that you don't put more saltpeter than its weight, for then it will also consume [some] of the silver itself. And if it is less than the weight of the copper, the silver will not be completely purified.

54. How to soften brittle silver.

55. How to make gold and silver melt faster.

56. How to melt silver or gold which are in the form of thin threads.

57. The best way of refining silver and gold.

58. (f. 40a) How to make two pieces of gold stick together, "and in Laʿaz *soldar* [S., to solder]."

59. How to remove a skin from gold, silver, or copper.

60. How to burn copper so that it should become a kind of antimony.

61. How to burn tin or lead, "in Laʿaz *qalṣinar* [S. *calcinar*, to calcine]."

62–64. (f. 40b) Various methods of purifying and treating tin and lead.

65. (f. 41a) How to make edible salt out of nonedible.

66. How to purify and harden lead.

67. How to transmute gold, silver, tin, or lead into black dust.

68. How to purify copper.

69. The differences between tin and lead on the one hand and the other metals on the other, and the differences between tin and lead among themselves.

70. (f. 41b) On the various uses of *tutia hindia* [A., Indian zinc oxide], arsenic, sulphur, verdigris, vitriol, etc.

71. How to "kill" quicksilver.

72. How to increase the weight of a golden dinar by one or two grains.

73. How to shave gold coins so that it should not be noticeable.

74. How to make a new coin look old.

75. (f. 42a). Operations with *ṭarṭīr* (A., tartar).

76. How to counterfeit any seal, "even if it is on wax." How to counterfeit coins, or seals made of hard metal.

77. (f. 42b) How to engrave and write on iron, "even if it is strong *aziro tinfilado* [S. *acero* . . . , steel]," and how to make molds with which to stamp seals and coins. This is a very long item (over five tightly written columns with two illustrative sketches), which must be the result of extensive research.

78. (43b) The virtues of "the water called *soliman verdete* [S., sublimate of verdigris], with which, if mixed with lemon juice, one can whiten copper coins so that they should be like silver."

79. How to melt lead or tin so that no slag should remain.

80. How to separate gold from the tin, lead, or copper mixed into it.

81. "For all wounds, whether due to a fall or to being smitten with a sword, or a *postema* [S., abcess], and all kinds of growths and *geranqo* [?]. Two kinds of *inguintes* [S. *unguentos*, ointments]. . . ." These medical prescriptions are inserted here because the medicaments prescribed are of an alchemical (or rather chemical) nature: antimony, *mordisenqe*, etc.

82–83. (ff. 44a–b) Recipes for etching letters into iron, and for purifying gold.

Folios 45a–b contain one long unnumbered item which discusses the uses of "strong water," that is, aquafortis.

Part Three continues on folio 48, but under a new heading. It reads: "And these are the operations which I tried, and sometimes they succeeded, but they were not verified by me sufficiently many times." Most of the recipes in this part—numbered again beginning with 1—are medical. On folio 50b, beginning with item no. 43, Vital switches back to alchemy.

43. How to remove the *shibbur* (brittleness) from tin.
44. Recipe for making gold.
45. Recipe for making silver.
46. How to harden quicksilver.
47. How to write protruding letters on soft stone.
48. How to make a candle rise.
49. "To freeze [i.e., curdle] milk without a stomach."
50. (f. 51a) How to dye a sheet of paper green "and in Laʿaz *verde* [S.]."
51. How to remove an oil spot from a silk dress.
52. How to remove grape juice, lemon, or vinegar spots from a silk dress.
53. How to remove a wine spot from a linen dress.
54. How to remove an inkspot from a woollen or linen dress.
55. This item is crossed out.
56. How to clean glasses and glass lamps.
57. Recipe for yawning.
58. How to turn a red rose white.
59. How to protect the water of a cistern from worms, leeches, and bad smell: "throw into it powdered asphalt, or better still, tar."

After this item, quite incongruously, there are three religio-magical items:

60. "I have heard, and also saw proven to some extent, that he who prays the *Nʿīlah* prayer [the closing prayer] in a loud voice serving as a prayer leader on Yom Kippur, will be in danger, God forfend, in that year. Therefore he should be the prayer leader also in another prayer, such as the *mussaf* or the *minḥa* or *shaḥarit* of Yom Kippur."

61–62. (ff. 51a–b). Similar dangers connected with other religious functions.

63–64. Recipes for protection against flees and lice.

65. To know whether milk has been diluted with water.

66. "For him who has suddenly lost something, and it happens sometimes that the demons play with a person and take it." The intrusion of such "superstitious" items among Vital's alchemical, technological, and medical prescriptions occurs in several places in the book.

67–75. (ff. 51a–52a) Medical recipes.

76. "For cheese that it should not grow worms."

77. (f. 52b) For a hen that has been hurt or that does not lay eggs.

78. Very long instructions as to what to do at the time of an epidemic.

79. (f. 53b) General instruction for the preservations of one's health.

80. "For the illness of *azma* [S. *asma*, asthma]."

81–88 (ff. 53b–54a). Recipes for various illnesses.

89. (f. 54a). "For strange fire, which is called *ḥumra* [A., boil carbuncle, erysipelas, St. Anthony's fire]." This recipe is again exceptional,

because it prescribes treatment by an incantation in Spanish, whose text, in Hebrew characters, takes up ten lines in the manuscript.

90–92. More incantations for various ailments.

93–102. (ff. 54a–b). More recipes for various ailments.

103. Another incantation in Spanish for an ailment.

104. For protection against Lilith.

On folio 55a, still continuing Part Three, there is a new heading as follows: "And these are the operations which I have not tried myself, but heard them from tellers of truth. And I shall divide them into two parts: the first part what I have found written in books, which were tried by the authors of those books, and the second part what I heard and received from the mouth of tellers of truth." The material in the first part is medical and is taken from several Jewish and non-Jewish medical authors with whom we need not concern ourselves, beyond mentioning that quotations from Galen, Aristeas, Dioscorides, Tabari, and so on (ff. 55b–58a), are eloquent testimony to Vital's wide reading and familiarity with the Greek and Arabic medical literature available in his times.

On folio 58b begins "The second part on *s'gullot* [charms] and experiments which I got from the mouth of tellers of truth who tested them, and they became verified." This part contains again alchemical, medical, and magical prescriptions.

1. Rub the *qoral* which is called *almogim* [H., coral] with ground nuts, and it will yellow its redness.
2. How to restore the green color of *turqiza* [S. *turquesa*, turquoise].
3. How to "kill" quicksilver.
4. How to purify tin and harden it.
5. How to make a *perla* [S., pearl] which lost its color shiny again.
6. How to use "strong water."
7. How to make lead out of *mordisenqe* [?].
8. How to melt copper quickly.
9. Remedy for scorpion bite.
10. What to do if one swallows deadly poison.
11. "A deadly poison to kill a man."
12. To differentiate between a virgin and a married woman.
13. "Put the tongue of a frog on the clothes of a sleeping person, and he will tell you everything you ask."
14. How to remove an oil spot from clothing.

15–53. (ff. 59a–60b) Mostly medical and magical prescriptions. They include prescriptions for and against pregnancy, against miscarriage, for preventing a small dog from growing, cocks from fighting, wine from going sour, for protecting a person against the evil eye, increasing the milk of a suckling mother, knowing whether the prince is favorably inclined to you, escaping from a person who pursues you with a drawn sword, forcing the demon to leave the body of a person, and so on. After this excursion into the realm of magic, Vital returns to alchemy.

54–56. (ff. 60a–b) Methods of hardening quicksilver, the use of Indian *tutia* (zinc oxide), and other purely technical matters. It is fascinating to see that the moment Vital speaks of alchemy he becomes the critical scientist whose accuracy and acumen leaves no room for either good spiritual or evil demonic influences. The following can serve as an additional example:

> 57. (f. 60b) To make antimony. Take an oven and put into it burning coals, and put on the coals two stones or two bricks on the two sides of the oven as shown here [Figure 28.1], and again put other long coals which should lie on top of the two stones like beams, in so that there should remain a space between the two stones, and also between the lower and the upper coals. And take a red copper plate with tongues, and sprinkle on it sulphur powder so that the plate should be well covered from above, and with the tongues put this plate in the space between the coals, until the smoke of the sulphur is finished, and then remove it and extinguish it in strong vinegar, and repeat this three or four times, until it is finished, becoming antimony. And its sign is that if you hit this plate with a hammer it will break like glass. And know that if the fire is strong, put into it much sulphur so that it should be done quickly. And even if the copper plate is very thick, about a handbreadth, there [should be] no apprehension. But if the fire is mild, put only a little sulphur, just enough to cover the surface of the copper.

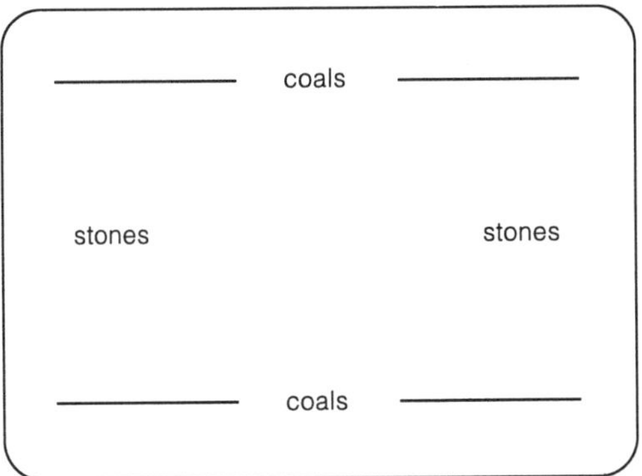

Figure 28.1. Plan for oven to make antimony.

58. (f. 60b) Detailed and complicated instructions for transmuting copper into a silver-like metal.

> Take white *rahj* [A., dust], and it is the *rejalgar* [A. *rahj al-ghār*, cave-dust, whence the Latin and English realgar, arsenic sulfide], and mash it like

beans or almonds. And take seven eggs, and twenty-five *dirhams* [drachmas] of olive oil, twenty-five drachmas of old butter, and mix the eggs and the oil and the butter well until they are like a paste. Then take twenty drachmas of tartar and mash them well, and then mix them very well with the mentioned paste, and it will become like hard dough. And divide it into two, and make of it two cakes. And take a new earthenware pan, coated with ashes, and put one of the cakes into it, and flatten over it the realgar, sprinkled on the cake. And let it enter into it a little, and it will stick to it. And then put on the realgar the second cake, and it has already been said above that these cakes should be like dough, a little hard. And it will be found that there will remain [a little] of the paste that did not mix with the two mentioned drugs, and therefore pour that which is left of the paste over this cake which you have made, and put the pan on mild fire, only under it, and put it on the roof because a strong smell of the realgar will issue from it, and people will feel that it is being prepared. And leave it until the upper cake dries a little, as is done by the women when they make egg cakes baked in oil upon the fire. And it should not burn, but only remain a little hard. And you will find the realgar between the two cakes like moist white cheese. And take it and throw away all the mold that cleaves to it. And take of good red copper eight drachmas, and shape it into thin leaves like paper, and burn them in coal fire, and put them into a mixture of *nishādir* [A., sal ammoniac] and powdered garlic and strong vinegar, up to seven times, and it will become purified as mentioned in section [word missing]. And then melt this copper, and put two drachmas of the mentioned realgar on it after it has melted thoroughly, and wait a little until it thickens and mixes with the copper. And then throw into it one drachma of tartar and one drachma of alum, well powdered, and put it to burn, and then when it is finished pour the copper into an iron mold, into olive oil, and it will come out white like half silver, and better.

59. (f. 60b) The preparation and use of *sal alqali* [S., alkali salt].
60. How to "kill" quicksilver.
61. (f. 61a) How to improve the quality of gold.
62. How to prepare mercury chloride.
63. How to melt copper easily.
64. How to recognize high-quality white sulphur.
65. How to recognize prepared cinnabar.
66. How to make quicksilver fire-resistant.
67. How to improve the color of inferior gold.
68. How to remove the *shibbur* [H., brittleness] from tin.
69. How to prepare gold and silver for alchemical operations.
69(bis). How to "kill" quicksilver and harden it.
70. The treatment of quicksilver with aquafortis.

71. More on quicksilver.

72. How to harden lead.

73. An operation with antimony, sulphur, and cinnabar.

74. (f. 61b) How to *sublimar* [S., sublimate] drugs.

75. The preparation of salt and its alchemical use.

76. How to make the gold heavier.

77. How to harden sulphur.

78. An operation with purified silver and antimony.

79. How to make gold with cinnabar, antimony, iron filings, copper filings, etc.

80. How to make saltpeter.

81. How to prepare *blanqete* [ceruse].

82. How "to give strong *ṭinfila* to the iron so that it should cut."

83. How to recognize the true value of an alloy of gold and other metals.

84. How to prepare a *solver* [?] in an animal's bladder.

85. How to prepare a bladder for the above operation.

86. How to extract salt from urine.

87. How to extract silver or gold from ore.

88. (f. 62b) The true procedure of refining gold.

89–159 (ff. 63a–66b). Incantations, magical procedures, some remedies. However, even here Vital could not deny that he was an alchemist, as can be seen, for example, from the following recipes, which show his use of alchemy for household purposes:

160. To make the roasting spit turn by itself. Put quicksilver between the skin and the meat of the chicken which is roasted on the fire, and sew up the place so that the quicksilver should not come out from there.

161. To make the fish jump and leap out of the frying-pan or of the fire, put quicksilver into its belly.

162. To make wine come out of the barrel, put the weight of two *zuz* [H., a silver coin] of quicksilver, and also a little sulphur, and the wine will come out [by itself].

163–164. Two more similar recipes.

165–170. Medical prescriptions.

171. To remember a dream.

172. How to rid a man of his addiction to gambling with dice.

173. How to make a coin you spend return to your pocket.

174. From the *Sefer haRimmon* [Book of the Pomegranate] by R. Saʿadia ben Saʿid:[5] "He who is bitten [*nashukh*] by a snake [*naḥash*], if he sees copper [*n'ḥoshet*] he will die instantly."

175. How to prevent ink from becoming unclean.

176–181. (f. 67a) More medical prescriptions.

182. An experiment with a *diamanṭ* [S. *diamante*, diamond].

183. An experiment with good mercury chloride.

184–187. More medical prescriptions.

188–192. More magical recipes.

193–196. Again medical prescriptions.

197. On the use of aquafortis, "from the mouth of a reliable expert."

198. (f. 68a) "From the same person," how to refine gold.

199. How to clean the melting pot of the slag remaining in it.

200. "I got this from the aforementioned person." How to improve the color of inferior gold.

201. "Also from the same person." How to recognize *afars'mon* [H., balsam] oil.

202. "I got this from the aforementioned person." The virtues of balsam oil.

203. (f. 68b) From the same person: How to whiten crystal stones which are black when coming from the mine, and sapphires which are sky-blue, and all other precious stones except the ruby.

204. Prescription for tooth ache.

205. How to clean a copper vessel of the tin adhering to it.

206. "Tried. Without any doubt." How to purify silver.

207–208. Medical prescriptions.

209. "A procedure without any doubt to kill quicksilver."

210–395 (ff. 68b–77b). Various medical, magical, and prognostic (divinatory) prescriptions, with occasional mention of the source, such as Rabbi Sh. Sidlit, Rabbi David ben Rosh, "from the *Book Kaf Q'toret*" (Ladle of Incense), a Bible commentary titled *Mar'ot haṢov'ot*, and so on. Dispersed among these are cosmetic prescriptions such as (324 on f. 74a) "for reddening the hair to make it gold," in which Vital's chemical and alchemical expertise is apparent. Later, on folio 79a, there is another recipe for a dye to tint a white beard black. Evidently, attractive appearance was an issue in Vital's circle.

396–397 (f. 77b). Again alchemical prescriptions for hardening quicksilver.

398–435 (ff. 77b–78b). Mostly medical and magical prescriptions, interspersed with occasional chemical or alchemical recipes. Thus 427 is a recipe for hardening iron. Of special interest in this group is 359 (f. 75b), which is a prescription for strengthening loose teeth magically: the "power-word" Vital employs is *tetragran-matan*, that is *tetragrammaton*, which shows that he was familiar, at least to some extent, with non-Jewish magic in which this word was frequently used.

Folio 79a carries the superscription of Part Four, Sub-part Three. It reads: "These One Hundred Tried *S'gullot* [Charms] Were Copied from the Book *Sod Y'sharim* [Secret of the Just]." The numeration of the items begins again with 1 and goes to 111. They constitute a miscellanea of practical magic, including items that are closer to the realm of prestidigitation than to that of magic. For example, no. 12 (f. 79a): "To make an egg fly in the air. In the morning, prior to sunrise, gather dew and fill with it an egg, and seal the hole well, and put it against the sun, and it will fly in the air." Or, no. 48 (f. 80a): "To show a snake running in the house. Fill the intestines of an animal or a bird with quicksilver, and tie it well on both ends, and put it into the bath or in a warm place, and it will run like a snake."

Folio number 81 appears by mistake on two folios, one after the other. Folio 81a bis contains two large magic circles, and the text next to them explains that their purpose is to prognosticate whether a sick person will live or die. On folio 81b bis there is a new superscription: "I copied this from a book that was brought from the city of Fez." The text begins as follows: "This is from the handwriting of our grandfather the outstanding rabbi, R. Moshe, son of the great rabbi, the saintly R. Levi, of blessed memory, and this is his language: This procedure is according to what my friend R. Abraham son of Levi Almadaʿ testified before me." The procedure itself is a magical prayer for success. (On f. 84a Vital quotes again "R. Abraham Halevi who wrote a book.") The items that follow are again numbered beginning with 1 and reaching 282 (ff. 81b–101a). Again the material is mostly magical and medical, with a few alchemical recipes interspersed. One of the latter, no. 80 (f. 86a, which happens to be missing), was titled according to Samuel Vital's index, "*Qīmīya* for making silver out of tin." Among the authorities quoted in this part are: "In the commentary to the prayers by R. Yosef Ṣīaḥ of blessed memory I found . . ."; "I heard from the mouth of the experimenter . . ."; "Rabbi M. haṢarfati wrote to me . . ." (all these on f. 88a); "A tradition from R. Yehuda haḤasid . . . "(f. 89a); "I received this name as it was told to my teacher and master, peace be upon him [Yiṣḥaq Luria] from the mouth of the G'vurah [divine power] . . . (f. 90b). In between the medical and magical recipes appear two alchemical prescriptions for the "freezing" of quicksilver (f. 92a, nos. 178–179). The second one, after three introductory lines, switches from Hebrew to Arabic, written, as was usual among the Jews, in Hebrew characters, and continues in that language for fifteen lines, describing a method of making gold, and, incidentally, supplying proof that Vital was at home in Arabic. In fact, in these Arabic recipes Vital uses relatively more alchemical terms than is his custom in writing about alchemy in Hebrew, so that one gets the impression that when writing on alchemy he was more fluent in Arabic than in Hebrew, in which he wrote all his kabbalistic works. An interesting detail in this connection is that when writing in Hebrew he never uses the words *shemesh* (sun), the favorite cover name of alchemists for gold, nor *l'vanah* (moon) for silver, but in this Arabic passage he calls gold *shams* (sun), and silver *qamar* (moon), as do Arab alchemists in general.

On folio 93b there is a recipe for making ink, and another, very long one, for making twenty-four carat gold, followed on folio 94a by instructions for the preparation of arsenic. Still on folio 94a follows no. 193, which demonstrates the extent to which Hebrew-writing alchemists were dependent on Spanish and Arabic. Vital writes:

> 193. The way of *taḥmīr al-ᶜabd* [A., reddening the "slave"], that is, the quicksilver. Take the *ᶜabd wayadhabuhu bil-bid* ["slave," and gild it with eggs] and then *yuṣaᶜᶜiduhu* [volatilize it]. Then take lime, one *roṭl*, and four *roṭl* water, and one *roṭl sal alqali* [salt of kali, i.e., potash], and four *roṭl* water, and let it soak two days, and the water will become clear, and take it when clear, and then put again one *roṭl* of the potash on it . . . .

The same observation can be made in connection with no. 194 (f. 94b), which deals with making gold:

> 194. Take cinnabar, and *zāj* [A., vitriol], and verdigris, and red arsenic, and sulphur, and antimony, and *zaᶜfrān ḥadīd* [A., iron saffron], and in Laᶜaz *qroqos feri* [S. *croco de fierro*, iron oxide], one part of each of these seven. Indian zinc oxide and *dam al-akhawayn* [A., dragon's blood, a red resinous substance, obtained from a plant], and sal ammoniac, of each of these three half a part, and pound all of them well. And take ten boiled eggs and take of their yolk one part, and bees' honey two parts, and knead the mentioned powders in them, and liquify them in the *alanbiqi* [A. *al-inbiq*, alembic] once, and take the remaining residue and pound it well and mix it with the water which flowed out of it, and put it in a glass flask luted with philosophers' clay, and put its mouth down and its bottom up, and seal its mouth with cotton or with cotton-wool, and put strong fire on top of the bottom [of the flask], and put the mouth of the flask down into a bowl which should receive the water that flows from the mouth of the flask, and leave it a day and a night. And again take the residue which is left in the flask and pound it and drench it with the water that flowed down, as mentioned. Do thus until all the water becomes red. And take one part of gold and put it in the melting pot on the fire for a short time, as do the goldsmiths when they melt the gold with which they gild silver. And put on it three parts of quicksilver until they mix like a *m'lugma* [A. *malgham*, softening ointment, whence amalgam], and take it and put it in an iron vessel on mild fire, and put with it [some] of the red water, and leave it to cook gently.

For some reason these two detailed alchemical recipes, as well as the subsequent one, which deals with the treatment of thin silver threads used for embroidering gala clothing, are omitted from Samuel Vital's index, which lists for folio 94b only the four-line religio-magical recommendation for quieting a stormy sea by reciting a psalm and the magical name *Adiriron*, which emerges from that psalm. That charm, incidentally, concludes with these words: "Tried and tested several times by the writer." It is difficult to believe that these lines were written by the same man who, on the very same page, prescribes the precise and detailed chemical procedures in which religious, spiritual, magical powers have no place at all.

This seafaring magic is followed on folio 95a, no. 195 by a quotation "From R. Netanel the astronomer" discussing methods of dealing with demons, which that astronomer attributed to a certain Asaf ben Berekhia, the author of the *Book of the King*. In Muslim folklore Asaf ibn Barakhya was the vizier of King Solomon. Nos. 196–200 (ff. 95a–b) also deal with controlling demons and angels. Nos. 201–238 (ff. 96a–97a) are a mélange of magical and medical recipes. These are followed by one of the very few statements made by Vital on general alchemical principles:

> 239. (ff. 97a–b) Great rule in the science of alchemy in making gold or silver. Know that there is body which are the metals, and there is soul which is quicksilver, and spirit which are all the drugs that are consumed in the fire and fly up and become spirit and are not preserved, and they are *rahj* [A., dust], which is called *rejalgar*, and sulphur, and the sal ammoniac, and the cinnabar and arsenic, and vitriol, and the like. And one must at first prepare [or improve] the spirit, which are the aforementioned drugs, until they are preserved in the fire and their impurities are removed from them, which cause them to be consumed by fire. And then one must prepare the soul, which is the quicksilver, by removing the impurity from it, so that it should be preserved in the fire, and then one must prepare the body, which are the metals, such as gold or silver or copper or tin or lead or iron, and the like. And after all three have been prepared one must melt them and mix them together, and this is called leaven and *īqsīr* [A., elixir]. And then, when you put a little of this leaven on some dough, such as gold or silver or copper, etc., it will change into what you wish.
>
> In fact, there are two kinds of preparations [or improvements]. One is for whiteness, and it is for making silver, and the other is for redness, and it is for making gold, and these two kinds of preparations are in [or: done with] all the three, the mentioned spirit and soul and body, and therefore the nature of [all] the spirits is not the same, for there is such that is of benefit for whiteness, and another for redness. The examples for this are vitriol and sulphur and cinnabar and red arsenic, and the like, which are for gold, and realgar and white arsenic and the like, which are for silver. There is yet a fourth aspect, which are the kinds of other drugs through which the mentioned soul and spirit and body are prepared [or improved], as you will find their operations described in books. And now I shall explain some works and preparations which are tried.

True to his promise, Vital devotes several of the ensuing items to alchemical operations, to wit:

240–241. (f. 97b) How to purify tin.

243. How to purify antimony.

244. The use of oil made of egg yolk.

245. "The preparation of *armoniaq* salt, which is called *nishādir* [sal ammoniac]."

246. How to prepare sal ammoniac oil.

247. "The preparation of sulphur and realgar and tartar, to whiten them and to make them resist fire."

248. "To purify sulphur of its oiliness and to extinuish its fire."

249. "To prepare sal ammoniac."

250. (f. 98a) The making of iron scrapings which are called in Arabic *zaʿfrān al-ḥadīd* [saffron of iron], and in Laʿaz *qroqos feri*."

251. How to calcine thin gold leaves.

252. How to transform quicksilver into a white liquid by soaking it in a decoction of *shinān* [A. *ushnān*, saltwort], which is a herb out of which they make *qalyi* [alkali, soda ash].

253. The preparation of cinnabar.

254–255. How to give gold color to silver and increase its weight.

256. How to whiten copper.

257–258. How to transmute copper into silver.

259. (f. 98b) In this item Vital describes how he himself experimented with an alloy:

> Take two drachmas of good silver, and melt it, and after it melted put on it two drachmas of purified tin, and make all of it like crumbling lime, and grind them well, and take fifteen drachmas of quicksilver. I tried it without grinding the mixed silver and tin, but instead I took fifteen drachmas of quicksilver and put it into a melting pot, and 2 fingers of olive oil over it, and heated it a little, and then I took the mixed silver and tin when they were well melted in another melting pot, and poured them into the melting pot with the oil and the quicksilver, and they instantly got all mixed together. And then I took of this *m'lugma* [amalgam] four drachmas, and eight drachmas of white realgar, and eight drachmas of saltpeter, and ground them well together, and kneaded them with egg white until sufficient, and made of them small round balls, and I melted thirty-six drachmas of purified copper, and after it melted I pelted them with these balls one by one until all were used up, and I poured it out, and then I mixed the copper with one-third of its weight of purified silver, and it came out white and good for all tests.

From this description, and some others like it, one can conclude not only that Vital maintained a well-equipped alchemical laboratory, but that he experimented with formerly untried procedures—that is, he was a true alchemist.

260–265. (ff. 98b–99a) Alchemical recipes for making silver.

266. How to harden quicksilver.

267. How to "whiten" an alloy which is half silver and half copper.

268. How to make new coins look old.

269. (f. 99b) Remedy for bloody diarrhea, and for piles.

270. "The stone called in Arabic *ḥajar al-ḥayy*, that is, snake stone," found in the heads of old snakes of the land and of the sea—protects against snake bite.

271 ff. (numbers illegible; ff. 99b–101b) Medical prescriptions.

Folio 102a is superscribed: "These are the things I heard from tellers of truth with complete experience." The numeration again begins with 1.

1–193. (ff. 102a–109). Medical and magical recipes.

Folio 110a has the superscription: "I, the youth, Ḥayyim Vital, disciple of our master the ARI [Yiṣḥaq Luria] of blessed memory." The rest of folio 110a is crossed out, and over it is written, "This *drush* [homily] does not belong here." This is followed by a folio again numbered 110, which is superscribed, "These are the operations of medicaments which I found written in books." They are numbered 194–247 (ff. 110a–111a), and contain medical and magical recipes. Folios 111b–113b contain more magical recipes, amulets, and texts of conjurations, with "names" and drawings. These items are not numbered, and these folios are passed over in silence in Samuel Vital's index.

Folio 114a carries this superscription: "These are the operations which I tried among those which I found written in books, and they were not verified in my hands, and I did not succeed in performing their operation." The items listed are numbered from 1 to 27 (ff. 114a–115b), and they are mostly alchemical. They are, in general, variations on material covered in earlier parts of the manuscript. Although in the title Vital states that he tried these operations unsuccessfully, nevertheless he presents them in the style of "take this and this . . . ," that is, in the form of instructions for effective operations. This stylistic peculiarity aside, these items are additional proof that Vital was a true experimental alchemist, as well as a "teller of truth," who reported his failures as frankly as his successes.

Number 10 on folio 114b is interesting because it quotes an alchemical recipe in the name of Maimonides:

> 10. TO MAKE gold out of tin, by the Rambam [Maimonides] of blessed memory to his disciple. And this is his language: I am letting you know what I tried and saw that it was the best, and its advantages are enormous,

> and it is a kind of gold. And you take of the tin and melt it, and after the melting put it immediately into *ethrog* [citron] juice or in *alsqolde*, which is lemon, then put it in melted tallow, then in cold water. Then in onion juice, then in garlic juice. Then in water in which *frijolas* [S. *frijoles*, beans], which are *ginaros el birgunes* [?], were cooked. Another version: *faisaules*. And then melt it once more with its own weight of *l'vonah* [H., incense], and it will be good yellow gold. Another version ends thus: And needed are sal ammoniac and *saljimana* [S. *sal de gema*, rock salt], one next to the other, mixed before the melting with the tin, and one must burn them together until nothing is left of them."

As we have seen, a similar alchemical recipe is found among the Pseudo-Maimonidean treatises.

Folio 115b (nos. 19–27) contains medical and magical prescriptions. Folio 116a is superscribed: "I tried also these practical traditions, and I did not succeed." Under this heading there are twenty-two items (ff. 116a–117b), all magical and medical prescriptions.

Folios 118a–123b contain again magical matters. Of special interest are nos. 9 and 10, because they contain words written in Arabic, including the name *Allah* three times. From this one can conclude that Vital was as eclectic in his approach to providing magical help as he was in collecting and presenting alchemical prescriptions.

Folios 124a–129b are missing in the manuscript. On folio 130a begins Samuel Vital's index to the book, which continues until folio 153b. The total number of items (prescriptions) contained in the manuscript is upward of 1,500, covering an astounding variety of alchemical, medical, and magical subjects. The variations in the handwriting show unmistakably that the book was written by Vital not in one stretch, but at different times, probably with considerable hiatuses in between. This, in turn, indicates that he maintained his interest in these subjects for a long time, probably for several years. The wording of many items also shows that he was a practicing alchemist, physician, and magician (meaning a provider of magical amulets and methods of healing and helping) for many years.

This is what we can learn from the Moussaieff manuscript about Ḥayyim Vital the alchemist. A portrait of Vital the physician, for which there is ample material in the same manuscript, awaits the attention of a medical historian fluent in Hebrew.

Chapter Twenty-nine

AN ALCHEMICAL MISCELLANY

The Vatican Manuscript

The Vatican Library has a Hebrew manuscript dating from the sixteenth century, and possibly written in Italy. Its folios 65–72 contain alchemical recipes for making gold, silver, and so on.[1] The manuscript is in poor condition, and is difficult to decipher. In the following I present a few illustrative excerpts.

(f. 1) To make ammoniac [I. *armeniaca*, ammoniac] salt *fisso* [I., fixed] for the Work. Take ammoniac salt, as you wish, and *solima* [I., sublimate] it, then pound it and mix it with the same amount of lime, and put everything in an earthenware pot, and give it fire and warm it for two or three hours, then put all of it in pure water, then *distila* [I. *distilla*, distill] it in a *filtro* [I. filter]. And then mix the sediments in clear water again and distill it in a filter, and thus do until the water becomes sweet. And put all this water in a glazed earthenware pot, and boil it up on pure and light fire until the water is almost gone, and you will find fixed ammoniac on the water. Put it in a glass vessel and let it dry, put it on a marble stone to dissolve, and in one night it will turn into water from the ammoniac salt, fixed for the mentioned Work. . . .

(f. 4) Moon [silver]. Take one part of purified silver and melt it and combine with it the same amount of lead, and mix them together, and throw them into a *gar'ine* [granules?]. Then take one part of good and fine *borase* [I. *borace*, borax] and one part of ammoniac salt and one part of live sulphur, and two parts of *sinabario* [I. *cinabro*, cinnabar] and one quarter [part] of copper *limatura* [I., filings], and one quarter of spider's webs which are found in the houses of millers, and make out of all of it a fine powder, and of these powders *simento* [I. *cimentare*, to cement] the *gar'ine* of the silver with the lead in a *farmakos* [vessel], and bury it in ashes in the *qapelo* [coppella] in the oven, and give it light fire at first and then give it middling fire for twelve hours, then leave it to cool and take it out and put it to be refined in the coppella, and do this three times, and it will become a dough and it will stand the test of strong water [aquafortis].

This water is good for coloring the aforementioned silver. Take *vitriole Romano* [Roman vitriol], salt, *nitro* [natron], *alum daroqo* [I. *allume di rocca*, rock alum, i.e., ordinary alum], of each one *liṭra* [pound], *ṣinabarion* one ounce, *verdoramo* [I. *verde rame*, verdigris] four ounces. Take four ounces of the aforementioned vitriol, and four ounces of the aforementioned alum, and put them pounded on burning coals in a vessel, and powder of which all its moisture has gone out, then [mix] all the things together, and put them to distill in a well-sealed vessel. Make strong water and then take half of the sediment out of the aforementioned water, and pound them, and take other, new powders, as you did at first, and put them into a *buṣa* [vessel], and put on them the aforementioned strong water, and seal the vessel and let it stand thus for a day, then put it to distill as the first time, then *purga* [purify] them as required, and combine the *peso* silver with its weight of refined silver which is not *peso*, and put it to a part, and sufficient [for him who understands]. . . .

(f. 6) *Water more precious than pure gold.* Take ammoniac salt, salt *niṭro* [saltpeter], salt *qomuno* [common], three pounds of each, cooked and whipped honey five ounces, [called] *siro* in La'az. Of milk, which should be sour and liquified five times, four ounces. Urine of boys of twelve years, fifteen ounces. Mix all of it together and put it to dissolve in a glass vessel in warm and moist dung eight days. Then put it to dissolve in warm dung for three days, and preserve that water, for it congeals the quicksilver without *solimaṣione* [I., sublimation] and without other mortification. Only put the quicksilver *'oreg* [?] in a melting pot on burning coals, and when it begins to raise smoke put three drops of this water into the melting pot and it will coagulate the quicksilver in *elissire* [I., elixir], that is, the taste of this *elosir* [elixir] will change the copper into silver without limitation. And likewise it changes all metals into silver, and it causes the spirits not to fly off, by the power of its strength, and it provides a way of entering and dissolving and refining all the salty [elements] in the metals, and they are good for silver and gold. . . .

The work of permanent moon [silver]. Take of green Roman vitriol four *liṭras.* You [can] turn it red in this manner: Take an earthenware vessel not *viṭriato* [glazed], and put into it one pound of the mentioned vitriol, and put the vessel on coals until you see (f. 7) that it almost turned to water. Add into the vessel half a pound of the mentioned vitriol which also turned to water, and do like this until you have put all of it into the vessel. Let it stand on burning coals until it becomes dry, and watch it that it should not raise bubbles nor make noise. Remove the vessel from the fire and let it cool. Then take out the vitriol from the vessel with iron and pound it fine, and put it into another vessel, and see that the vessel should not be full, only half, and put that vessel on burning coals until the vessel becomes red, for six hours, and occasionally stir inside the vessel with an iron so that what is in the bottom should come up, then remove it from the fire and leave it to cool, and preserve it for the time of need.

Perperaṣione [I. *preparazione*, preparation] of vinegar. Take of very strong white vinegar ten pounds, bring it to a boil in an earthenware vessel, then take two pounds of new quicklime, divide these two pounds into two parts, put one part into a glazed new pot, and the other part put into another vessel. And put half of the mentioned boiled vinegar into another vessel, and the other half into another vessel, and stir it with a stick, and let them stand thus for three hours, then distill it with a filter three times.

As can be seen from the above examples, the interest of the author of the Vatican manuscript extended beyond the manipulation of metals, and included such matters as the production of household vinegar.

The language of this work, like many other alchemical manuscripts of the Middle Ages and the Renaissance, is characterized by the frequent use of Italian terminology in Hebrew transliteration. Since the Hebrew *bet* can stand for both b and v in the Italian, the Hebrew *pe* for Italian p or f, the Hebrew *ṣade* for Italian soft c or z, the Hebrew *vav* for the Italian o or u, the Hebrew *yod* for the Italian e or i, and in the Hebrew unvocalized transliteration the Italian a is either not reproduced at all or indicated by an inserted *alef*, it is at times difficult to recognize the original Italian as reproduced in Hebrew. Also, more than occasionally the transliteration, even within these limits, is not accurate. Take, for example, a word that appears on the very first page of the manuscript: transliterating accurately its Hebrew letters into Latin, it reads *pyrpyraṣi'ony*, but evidently it stands for *preparazione*. Likewise the Hebrew *pwlyy'tw* stands for *foliato*; *qwmwny* for *commone*. At times the author (or the copyist) is inconsistent in his transliteration: the Italian *coppella* appears as *qwpylyw*, *qwpyl'*, or *qwpyl*; *elissire* appears once as *'ylisiri*, and in the next line as *'ylosir*; the Italian *cementa* appears once as *ṣymyt*, and on the same page a second time as *ṣymnth*, a third time as *ṣymynth*, a fourth as *ṣymntw*, a fifth as *ṣymyntw*; *alambic* is once *'lnbyqw*, once *'lbyqw*, and a third time *'byqw*; Italian *amalgama* becomes *mlgm'* and *mlgma*. Despite these difficulties, in most cases it was possible to identify the origin of the foreign terms appearing in Hebrew transliteration.

The Jewish Theological Seminary Manuscript

In the manuscript collection of the Jewish Theological Seminary of America in New York there is a small volume (no. 2,556) containing a miscellany of writings in Hebrew and in Arabic, several of which are of interest for us in the present context. It comprises forty-seven folios in small quarto, is in a neat old Sephardi hand, and seems to have been written in the sixteenth century.

It begins with a treatise entitled *Book of Minerals* written in Arabic in Hebrew characters. It was identified by a cataloguer of the manuscript as containing excerpts from Aḥmad ibn Yūsuf al-Tīfāshī's (d. 1253) well-known book *Flowers of Thoughts on the Precious Stones.*[2] Since the manuscript is written in Hebrew characters it was evidently aimed at a Jewish readership, and is thus an indication of interest among the Jews in mineralogy. It devotes a short chapter or a brief paragraph (ff. 2b–8b), to each of the minerals which, thanks to the studies of Alfred Siggel, can be identified without problem.[3]

Folio 9a carries the Hebrew title "The Gate of Understanding Various Kinds of Knowledge and Events."

Folio 10a is titled in Hebrew "The Gate of Great Science of Rains."

Folio 11a is titled in Arabic "The Treatise of the Science of the Herbs that are Useful in the Science of Wellbeing." This Arabic title is followed by a Hebrew subtitle which reads: "Comprises *S'gullot* [Charms] in Hebrew and Arabic with Conjurations and Spells and Amulets and Medicines and Dream Interpretations from the RAB"D [Rabbi Abraham ben David, c. 1125–1198] of blessed memory."

On folio 12a begins "The Gate of the Science of the Kinds of Metals" (in Hebrew with some Arabic notes).

Folios 14a–23b contain medical prescriptions.

Folio 24a offers a magical prescription for becoming invisible (in Hebrew), and an Arabic medical treatise.

Folios 25a–45b discuss interpretation of dreams, and magic and divination.

Folios 46a–47a deal with the seasons.

A few illustrative excerpts are presented in my translation from the Hebrew and Arabic of the manuscript.

> (f. 8a: A.) The twenty-fourth Gate on the Crystal. The origin of its formation is in its mine. Galenus said in the *Book of Causes and Effects* that the crystal is a shining white stone [word illegible] which is found in it [the mine], and its origin is the sapphire. Just as the glitter of silver is the formation and origin of the gold, likewise the crystal; there is in it moisture mixed with dryness.
>
> (f. 11b: A.) Description of the herb called wild cotton, which is similar to cotton except that its wool is yellow. When you find it, take its leaves and squeeze out their water, and then soak silver in it, and change it [the water] six times, and behold it will become pure gold. And seal this.
>
> (f. 11b: H.) Take sulphur and melt it and pour it into honey with its wax, and do thus up to one hundred times, and take purified silver and melt it, and put of this sulphur into the melting pot, and it will come out black. And take of this one part, and two parts of gold, and the *dibs* [A., honey] together, and it will come out very good. Finished.
>
> TO SOFTEN the silver, take *ḥiltit* [H., asafetida] and throw it into the purified silver and dry it, and it will be soft.

(f. 12a: H.) *The Gate of the Science of Kinds of Metals*

KNOW that if you take a piece of lead and put it in a closed vessel into quicksilver for twenty-four hours, that entire piece will be transmuted into quicksilver.

TAKE *allatūn* [S. *laton*, copper, brass] and melt it four times, and each time add to it ground glass in one-half of the weight of the *allatūn*, and the same way *tūtia* [A., tutty, zinc oxide], and after the melting quench it in *buṭm* [A., terebinth] oil or in linseed oil. Then it will become heavy and thick, and thereafter out will come sun [gold], good in every respect and shape. And if it seems to your consideration that it needs more purification, take ox-gall with *zaʿfrān* [A., saffron] and mix them together, and put them on the fire until they become hot, and put into it the aforementioned, and it will become pure sun.

TO ADD weight to gold, take *salmoniaqo* [sal ammoniac] and scrape it and put it upon the gold, and then put it to soak in strong vinegar for about half a day, and it will become heavier by nine parts. Also: Take the gold and heat it until it becomes like fire, and quench it in *balqa* [A. *baqla*, kohlrabi] juice, and it will increase its weight. Another: Heat it as mentioned, and quench it in the juice of *verdolāga* [S., purslane], which is called in Arabic *baqla al-ḥamqa*. This is how I have heard.

(A.) Gold. Calcify it in mouse droppings as it is calcified in lead. . . . And if the gold is mixed or impure, it will become of fine quality. And if *marqasiṭa* [marcasite] is smeared on it in melting it will become sulphur, which protects the body from harm. The *dahnaj* [malachite] softens the gold and removes its solidity, and makes it fluffy if it is melted in it. And if *tinkar* [chrysocolla] is mixed in it, it hastens its melting, and water of henna is squeezed out of it. If impure gold is heated and is quenched in it repeatedly, it becomes very soft. And salt increases the redness of gold very greatly. And the silver blackens in sulphur, and can be treated with salt. And *lāzward* [lapis lazuli], if it is mixed with gold, increases its beauty.

(A.) RULE. Take of white powder 2, tartar 2, borax 2, alum 2, sal ammoniac 1, white eggshell 2, antimony 12. Heat all of them together, and mix them in egg white, and put it in a small melting pot, and on top of all of it glass, and melt it, and mix it in henna, and add [word illegible] one-third moon, and if God exalted wants it.

(H.) If you take the roots of desert cabbage, and remove from them the water in an *al-anbiq* [A., alembic], it will congeal the quicksilver and whiten the face of women if they wash their face in it.

(H.) For pearls, that they should become white. Take *trementīna* [S., turpentine] and salt in equal parts, in *al-anbīqī* [A., alembic], in mild fire, and something like oil will come out of them. If you put the pearl into this oil for the time required to count a hundred for the most [?], it will become white.

(H.) To add weight to gold. Take dust of lead and put it into an alembic, and put the gold into the water that comes out of it, and let it stand about an hour. And also if human feces are put in the alembic in that water, and if he soaks the gold in that water, it will help as mentioned. Another matter: Take *nushādir* [A., sal ammoniac] and pound it well and put it on the gold, and then soak it with the sal ammoniac in strong vinegar, and let it stand in the vinegar about half a day. To increase the weight of gold: Smear it with the brain of a sheep's spinal cord, and throw it into the fire. It will add to its weight.

Folio 13a is again in Arabic and carries the superscription "Treatise on the Work of the Kinds of Colors of Ink." It contains eight prescriptions for making various kinds of inks, the seventh of which is attributed to "Ezra the Scribe." Although the recipe is, like all the others, in Arabic, these words in it are in Hebrew, which makes us suspect that we have here the work of a Jewish alchemist, and not merely the copy in Hebrew characters of an Arabic text written by a Muslim Arab. It reads:

THE DESCRIPTION of the ink of *'Ezra haSofer, 'alav hashalom* [Ezra the Scribe, peace be upon him]. And it is: Take myrtle leaves one part, and olive leaves one part, it should be green, and gallnuts half a part, and one part of pomegranate peel, and of the leaves of the skin of green walnut one part. Cook all of it in water, most thoroughly, and take it off the fire, and leave it a day and a night, and thereafter it will become purified, and put on it half a part of Cyprian walnuts, and write. And there has never been one like it.

The Oxford Manuscript

In the Bodleian Library is preserved an Arabic fragment from the Geniza folio 13 which contains three alchemical recipes for reddening and purifying gold. It is written in Hebrew characters, in Temanic cursive script.[4] A letter in a very similar script is found in the Cambridge University Library (T.–S.20.173), and is dated from 1133, which makes it possible that the Oxford manuscript also dates from about that period, but its contents and style point rather to the sixteenth century.

The Gate of reddening gold. Take *qalaqant* [colocynth] one part, and salt two parts, and *zinjar* [verdigris] one part, and one part of *zunjufr* [cinnabar], and half a part of red *za'frān* [saffron]. Pulverize everything, and [place it] in the fire for one hour. Then dry it and roast it in its *qarur* [?] in dung fire for a night, and lift it out. If you wish, use it, take of it what you wish and let it melt in fire, tint the gold with it, and place it in the fire until it becomes hot. Then put it aside until it cools off, then polish it. If you are pleased with its color [fine]; if not, tint it again until it achieves it. If you pulverize this medicine in the fire for [several] days, it will be improved, God willing.

The Gate of purifying gold. Take cinnabar, and saffron, and colocynth, and *martaq* [A. *martak*, litharge], and gall, and pulverize them together, and cast the gold into them, and place it in a narrow-mouthed crucible or a new *sirag* [A. *siraj*, lamp] and lute its mouth, and bury it in ashes throughout the night. When you remove it in the morning it will be purified.

The Gate of reddening the gold well. Take colocynth, and hemp, and verdigris, and *zig* [A. *zaj*, vitriol], and burnt copper, and salt, one part of each; Yemenite alum, one part and a half. Pulverize well and sift. Put it in a small *ajājah* [flask?] in the urine of young boys, and place it in the sun for three days, and leave it in the light. Three times dry it, pulverize it, and take it out.

Jewish Writings in the *Theatrum chemicum*

In addition to the treatises of Khālid ibn Yazīd, Artephius, Themo Iudaei, and the Hollanduses, the *Theatrum chemicum*,[5]—that greatest of all early alchemical collections—and Manget's *Bibliotheca chemica curiosa*[6] contain writings by several other alchemists whose Jewishness is indicated, or hinted at, in some ways.

One of them is attributed to Zadith filius Hamuel, also called Senior Zadith, or briefly Senior, and the title of his treatise is given as *Senioris antiquissimi philosophi libellus*, that is "The Booklet of Senior, the Most Ancient Philosopher." Its incipit is *Dixit Senior Zadith filius Hamuel.*[7] Nothing is known of an author by this name, but Berthelot, who discusses him in his work on medieval alchemy, states definitively that "this is a Jewish writing." He describes it as being full of parables and "commentaries on mystical figures," including the names of Maria the Jewess, Hermes, Khālid ibn Yazīd, Aros, the alchemist Plato, and Solomon. He also mentions Marcos, (whom Berthelot identifies with Marcus Gracus) conversing with King Theodore, Rosinus (that is, Zosimus), and, lastly, Averroes (Ibn Rushd) and Avicenna (Ibn Sīnā). However, no more recent authority is mentioned in it. Berthelot also finds in Senior Zadith's *Libellus* several phrases characteristic of the Greek-Hellenistic alchemical tradition, such as "Our copper is like man—it possesses a spirit, a soul, and a body"; "Three and three are one, and all results from the unity"; and so on.[8]

For lack of additional data, the Jewishness of this alchemist cannot be considered as established, even though his name, Zadith ben Hamuel, sounds like a Jewish name: Hamuel is a biblical name (Ḥammuel, 1 Chron. 4:26), and Zadith could be a distortion of Zabad (1 Chron. 2:36, etc.) or Zadok (Ṣadoq, 2 Sam.15:24, etc.).

Another treatise contained in the *Theatrum chemicum* (4:114ff., 5:101–90, and Paris MS 6514, f. 88–101) and considered "a Jewish work" by Berthelot is titled *Platonis libri quatuorum cum commento Hebuae habes Hamed. . . .* The word *habes* could be a misspelling of *aben*, that is, *ibn*, so that what we have here is the name Hebua ibn Hamed as that of the author of the comments. However, a variant reading of the name is Hebuhabes Hamed son of Gahar. It seems that Berthelot made his determination on the Jewishness of the author solely on the basis of the phrase *Aron noster* (our Aaron) which occurs in the treatise.[9] The passage in question is found in the dialogue between Hamed and Thebed. Thebed says: "I testify that there is one living God, because my zeal is not a zeal which ought to be censured." At a later point in their dialogue, Hamed says: "When Aaron says that the preparation of the body from beginning to end is rather easy, this is also more sustainable than another [proposition]. Our Aaron [said]: Because a thing is not free once from alterations, as we have previously mentioned. Since, however, the matter is thus, the body always has with it by natural force, and in radical composition, that which is in a member." And still later Hamed says: "You know that the science of the ancients, in whom sciences and virtues have been found, is that the substance from which substances exist is the invisible and immobile God, by whose will intelligence has been established, and by whose will the spirit of intelligence is simple. There is one God whose quality cannot be comprehended."[10]

Although the words of both Hamed and Thebed have a Jewish flavor, we must reserve judgment as to the Jewish authorship of this treatise. Berthelot was also of the opinion that the *Turba philosophorum* (*Bibliotheca chemica curiosa* 1:445–79) was originally written in Greek, then translated either into Arabic or into Hebrew, and from that language into Latin.[11] An investigation of the Jewish contents and references in such early classical alchemical collections as the *Theatrum chemicum* and the *Bibliotheca chemica curiosa* should be a prime task of any further work toward a history of Jewish alchemy.

Ben Zvi Institute Manuscript 2238

This Yemenite manuscript from the seventeenth century, written in beautiful Temanic Mashait script, is partly in Hebrew and partly in Judeo-Arabic.[12] Four pages of it (ff. 29a–70b) contain alchemical prescriptions in Judeo-Arabic, and in the following I present my translation of its first page which is entitled "The Way of the Sufi," and deals with "the philosophers' gold."

> THE WAY OF THE SUFI. Let there be taken the animal, vegetable, and mineral stone, and [let it] be washed with washing and then with warm clay, and let its water and oil be distilled, and half of the water put aside, and be distilled by itself, until there appear in it at least three distillations, and in seven of its middle (?) and where you want it, and as you increase it so you will have increased the benefit. And let the oil be mixed with the same amount of water, and these are the two leads. And [of] this pour the white upon the grey, and purify also both of them until they unite. And when they have united [and] mixed, they will become very clear. Then take the dye of the stone, and [do] this by soaking the clear pure water in its fourfold, and cook it in gentle fire until the water becomes red. Then distill the water from the dye and preserve it, and this is the philosophers' gold, and their fire, and their sun, and the red gum. And after this, behold the soil will turn it dead, black [and] soft. Continue [putting] on it the sweet water in gentle cooking and purification in stronger fire than at first, until all the blackness departs and it becomes white [and] soft, and it is the seed of the land of silver. Then return to the water and put in it one-sixth of its weight *nushadir* [sal ammoniac] of the stone, and put it in a covered still, and bury them in dung for three days, and it will become sharp [i.e., acid]. And take the white earth and incerate it with the sharp water, drench it and broil it until it melts with the inceration, and that time it becomes the earth foil, and that earth is the seed of gold. And the more you increase its drenching and broiling you will increase the inceration and the dye. And when you dilute and condense it it becomes silver elixir. And when you wish, take this silvery elixir, or of the earth foil, together with the same amount of the red gum, and it will become copper, and this is the body. And incerate it with the water preserved at first, which is the lead, and drench it and broil it until it totally dissolves in the inceration. Then drench it with the two leads, and heat them with three times their amount, and with seven drenchings and seven heatings.

BEFORE concluding this chapter let me mention in passing a number of additional Hebrew alchemical manuscripts, xerox copies of which were kindly put at my disposal by the Jerusalem Institute of Microfilmed Hebrew Manuscripts.

The Hebrew University has a Yemenite Judeo-Arabic manuscript (MS 47434) of sixty-six pages containing a rich alchemical miscellany. It quotes Harmas rayyis al-ḥukamā, that is, "Hermes, head of the wise men" (p. 20; cf. also p. 26), Aflaṭūn (Plato, p. 19), Arasṭaṭilis (Aristotle, pp. 18, 19), Farfīrus (Porphyrius? p. 19), al-Razi (p. 18), Jābir ibn

The Natures	Hot	Moist	Cold	Dry	The Kings	This is the table about the assembly of the numbers and the assembly of the minerals finished complete with the help of Allah exalted the argument
The minerals	The natures					
Zībaq (quicksilver)	1	7	7	1	Mercury	
Usrub (lead)	2	6	6	2	Saturn	
Dhahab (gold)	3	3	5	5	Sun	
Ḥadīd (iron)	4	1	4	7	Mars	
Fiḍḍa (silver)	5	2	3	6	Moon	
Nuḥās (copper)	6	4	2	4	Venus	
al-Qastīr (tin)	7	5	1	3	Jupiter	

Figure 29.1. Table showing the seven metals and their rulers.

	The Natures				
The Kings	Hot	Moist	Cold	Dry	The Minerals
Zuḥal (Saturn)	1	7	7	1	Lead: cold dry
Mushtarī (Jupiter)	2	6	6	2	Tin: . . . of the naturals
Mirrīkh (Mars)	3	3	5	5	Iron: cold dry
Shams (Sun)	4	1	4	7	Gold: hot dry
Zuhra (Venus)	5	2	3	6	Copper: the most temperate of the four
Uṭārid (Mercury)	6	4	2	4	Quicksilver: cold moist
Qamar (Moon)	7	5	1	3	Silver: cold moist

Figure 29.2. Table showing the ruling planets and their associated metals.

Ḥayyān (p. 36), Masīḥ ibn Ḥakīm (p. 2), Muḥammad ibn Yūnis of Bukhara (p. 18), ʿAlī al-Kandī (p. 18), Muḥammad ibn Līth al-Rasā'ilī (p. 18), ʿAlī al-Aṭlāqī (p. 19). In addition to the usual assortment of alchemical recipes, this manuscript contains (on p. 14) two tables listing the seven metals, their "kings," or "rulers," that is, their associated planets, and two different evaluations of the gradings of their qualities. In translating these tables (see Figures 29.1, 29.2) I substituted for the Hebrew numbers A, B, G, D, H, W, Z our usual numerals from 1 to 7, and added the English names of the planets to the Arabic ones appearing in the original.

MS Günzburg (Moscow) 315, which contains one of the known versions of the pseudo-Maimonidean alchemical treatise (see above, Chapter 24) also contains a miscellany of alchemical recipes, written by several hands. On folio 93a there is an incantation which is interesting from a linguistic point of view: it presents the words of the incantation first in *l'shon Ashkenaz*, that is "the language of Germany," then translates it into *l'shon haqodesh*, "the holy tongue," that is, Hebrew, and then also into *l'shon la'az*, "the foreign tongue," that is, Ladino. This is followed by a recipe for tinting any white substance gold. On folio 210a the manuscript contains a quotation from "The Book of the Fruit" by "Talmai [Ptolemy] the wise," and a recipe for increasing the weight or bulk of *karkom* (H., saffron), which we presented above in Chapter 24.

MS Or. 9861 in the British Library in London has on its folios 58b–59a Hebrew alchemical recipes for adding weight to gold, for preparing *lantisqole* [I., *Lentisk*, mastic tree] oil, and for separating gold from silver.

MS Ogp. 204 in the Bodleian Library of Oxford contains two pages of alchemical recipes, including one in Ladino for working with arsenic, and one in Hebrew for giving gold color to silver.

In the Countway Library of Medicine of Boston (MS Heb. 12), and in the Saltykov Public Library of St. Petersburg (MS Ebr.-Arab. II. 2349) there are Hebrew alchemical treatises.

Chapter Thirty

LABĪ, ḤAMAWĪ, AND PORTALEONE

THE MAJOR works to which these three men devoted their lives had little in common. The first was a Moroccan-Tripolitanian rabbi, Kabbalist, philologist, and poet, the second a Moroccan miracle worker and kabbalistic anthologist, the third an Italian court physician who wrote with equal facility in Latin and Hebrew. What they had in common was an interest in alchemy, either in its theoretical aspect (Labī), or in its technique of producing gold (Ḥamawī), or else in its promise to satisfy the age-old quest for the mysterious quintessence, the elixir of life (Portaleone).

The extant references of these three men to alchemy, meager though they are, tell us that Jewish scholars around the Mediterranean basin in the sixteenth century, with the most varied interests, were familiar with alchemical theory or practice or both. They did not doubt the reality of the alchemists' claims; they themselves dabbled, at least occasionally, in alchemy, and considered it important enough to include passages dealing with it in their writings, or even devote special treatises to it. Thus the three little vignettes of the present chapter round out the picture that emerges from our overview of Jewish alchemists in the thirteenth to the seventeenth centuries, revealing that half millennium as a period in which alchemy was an important preoccupation of the Jewish intellectual elite.

SIMEON LABĪ

Simeon Labī (d. 1580 or 1585) was a North African Kabbalist, philologist, and liturgical poet, who was familiar with, and believed in, alchemy. Of Spanish origin, Labī grew up in Fez, Morocco, and set out in 1549 to go to the land of Israel, but when he reached Tripoli on his way, he decided to stay there and become a teacher of the local Jewish community. His most important work is a detailed commentary on the book of *Zohar*, entitled *Ketem Paz* (Fine Gold), of which only the volume covering the book of Genesis was published. Of particular interest is his *Bi'ur Millot Zarot sheb'Sefer haZohar* (Explanation of Foreign Words in the Book of *Zohar*), which was published in Abraham Miranda's collection *Yad Ne'eman* (Faithful Hand) in Salonika in 1804. His most popular piece of writing is a mystical poem in honor of R. Shimʿon bar Yoḥai, the Palestinian second-century teacher who was believed to have been the author of the *Zohar*. This poem, entitled *Bar Yoḥai nimshaḥta ashrekha* (Bar Yoḥai, you have been anointed, happy are you), is sung to this day by Middle Eastern Jews on the Sabbath eve and at the tomb of Shimʿon bar Yoḥai in Meron, Galilee.

In the following passage Labī presents the well-known alchemical theory about the origin of metals in the earth, in combination with some kabbalistic mystical ideas:

> Know that the nature of the origin of silver and gold, their basis and their ore, is one. And pay no attention to those who say that they are two separate substances, for they see that there is a mineral [from which] originates silver, and there is a mineral [from which] originates gold, and they say that there is a difference between them. But that is not so, for there is no difference between them except for the color, for the essence of gold is silver at first. And there are [various] minerals present according to the places where silver comes into being. And from the power of the sun and its spark, which is strong, they become red in the course of many days, and it becomes gold, for the heat increases over it and its white color changes to red color, as you can see it happen in the fruits of trees, that the side which turns toward the sun is red, and the side which is not toward the sun remains white or green, for it is the nature of the sun to make everything red, according to the preparation of its material, or to make it black or white, and likewise in the minerals. . . .
>
> Therefore you will find that the wise men among the masters of alchemy do not deal with other metals, nor do any work with them, but only with silver, to make it red, for these two minerals exist in themselves, and they have one common origin, as we were told by men of truth who came from Ophir, that they had found a mineral of which half was gold and half silver, because it did not ripen sufficiently in the earth, in the heat of the sun, and they purify it and extract the gold separately, and the silver separately. And I wrote this in order to let you know their wisdom, for nothing remained hidden to them. . . . For also the masters of the Kabbalah called the gold sun and the silver moon. . . .
>
> Because of the strength of the sun upon that dust, that is to say, upon that mineral, it makes it red and turns it into gold, and from his words he lets the knowledgeable know that the lower sun and moon, those which are over our heads, are influenced by the power of the higher sun and moon which are souls for them. . . . The dust of silver, which is related to the moon, is the side of judgment.[1]

Abraham Ḥamawī

So little is known of the next sixteenth-century Kabbalist-alchemist to whom we turn that even the pronunciation of his name is in doubt. It is spelled in Hebrew ḤMWY, which is read by Gershom Scholem in his

Encyclopaedia Judaica articles one time "Ḥamoy," and another time "Ḥammawi (or Ḥamoj),"[2] and there is no entry under his name in that most modern and most complete Jewish encyclopedia. Since there were several Arab authors and personalities with the surname al-Ḥamawī, it seems to me that we can assume that this was also the name-form of our author.

His full name, then, was Abraham Shalom Ḥay Ḥamawī. He lived in Morocco, where he, like a number of other rabbis, had the reputation of being able to put an end to drought and make rain fall with his prayer.[3] Ḥamawī was a very prolific author: he wrote no fewer than forty-five books[4] most of which were anthologies of kabbalistic prayers. One of his books contains a number of kabbalistic treatises, including one on chiromancy. Of this entire literary output only two books have survived: *Nifla'im Maᶜasekha* and *Sefer Abīᶜa Ḥidōt* (The Book of "I Will Utter Dark Sayings").[5] It is in the latter (f.7a), that we find this alchemical recipe:

> There is also a herb called in the holy tongue *yarḥī* and in Arabic *al-hilālīlī* [correctly *al-hilālī*, both meaning "of the moon"]. And its height is about one cubit, and its stem is green like spinach. And the stem is quartered into eight parts, and it has only three leaves at its top. Gather it and dry it, not in the sun but in the shade, and make it a powder, and take lead and melt it, and put into it [some] of the aforementioned powder, and you will find that froth will rise upon the lead, and throw it away. And put also a little quicksilver [into it] until all the froth is gone, and it will turn . . . , and it will be real silver. And [this is] a tried thing. Thus did I find it in a manuscript book. And see in the holy book *Ger Hayītī* [I was a Stranger], in section 4.

In his *Nifla'īm Maᶜasekha* (ff. 24a–25a) Ḥamawī presents a prescription for making gold which contains elements familiar to us from Abufalaḥ's recipe of the miraculous "basilisk ashes":

> Gold. See, this is what I found in a manuscript. It is written as follows: A prescription (*s'gullah*) to make gold out of copper, and blessed is he who knows whether the words are true. And this is its description: Take nine eggs from hens, and put them into lime, and cover them well with lime, and put them under dung, covered, and let them remain there thirty days or more. Then take and open the eggs, and you will find a worm in each of them. Put everything into another pot, and cover the pot, and the worms will grow and eat the other things. And then they will eat one another, until only one big worm will remain. Then burn that worm in the pot, [but] you should stand afar, because of its bad smell which is like a deadly poison. And burnt powder will remain of it. And take that powder to pre-

serve it. And take pure copper and melt it, and put a little of that powder into it after it had melted, and it will become gold.

The subsequent passage contains a quote that repeats almost verbatim what Jacob Provençali said on the House of Marqoʿaya (see above, Chapter 27). The duplicated sentences are in italics:

> And behold, when I was a youth I set my heart to know the science of alchemy: upon what are its pillars founded? That is, how, by means of herbs, can tin and lead become gold? And that herb is called in Arabic *ḥashīshat al-dhahab* [herb of gold]. And I saw that herb [described] by our master and teacher Rabbi Ḥayyim Vital in the chapter on the Holy Spirit, and *in the Jerusalem Talmud, tractate* Shʿqalim, *at the end of the chapter, on the verse "And wisdom keepeth its masters alive" (Eccl. 7:12): R. Elʿazar said, Like the rich men of the House of Marqoʿaya, who were experts in the nature of congealing of gold, and in the pealing [removal] of silver from dross. Thus far his language. And this language was quoted by Rabbenu Asher in his commentary on the Jerusalem Talmud, and he wrote about it as follows: This family of Marqoʿin was versed in the science of alchemy, and they would cause certain juices of herbs to congeal, and make gold out of them. And [they knew] also another science: they knew how to separate easily the dross from silver. And that science is known and famous. But they did not want to reveal the herbs whose juice they would make to congeal so that it becomes gold. Thus far his language.* Hence it is established that that herb does exist in the world. And the real natural scientists have achieved [the ability] to make real silver out of quicksilver. And see in the holy book *Abiʿa Ḥidot*, section *ʿayin*, par. 4, at length.

The interesting thing about the above passage is that Ḥamawī disclaims belief in the prescription for goldmaking. This indicates a certain skepticism, quite rare among the literati of his age. Nevertheless, Ḥamawī identifies the herb allegedly used by the talmudic Marqoʿaya (or Marqoʿin) family with the herb known to him by both its Hebrew and Arabic names, and probably familiar to him from the Arab-Jewish folk belief of his North African environment.

Abraham Portaleone

The Portaleones, named after the Portaleone (Lion Gate) quarter of Rome where they originated, were a famous Italian Jewish family which, from the fourteenth century on, produced more than a dozen outstanding rabbis, physicians, authors, and poets. One of them was Abraham ben David Portaleone (1542–1612), a physician and encyclopedist, who in 1573 became body physician to the ducal house of Mantua, received in 1591 papal authorization to treat gentile patients despite the official restrictions, and wrote several important books in Latin and in Hebrew. Thoroughly versed in the secular sciences, Portaleone nevertheless remained a tradition-abiding Jew and, after suffering a stroke in 1605 that partly paralyzed him, he devoted his time to writing his magnum opus, *Shilṭē haGibborīm* (Shields of the Mighty, published in Mantua, 1612), which he composed for his children and in which he included everything he felt a Jew had to know in order to be able to live a full Jewish life.

At the request of the Duke of Mantua, Portaleone wrote several Latin works, of which two have survived: one is a book of medical guidance (*consilio medica*), the other entitled *De auro dialogi tres.*[6] This book is of interest to us in the present context because it contains, as the title indicates, not only a presentation of the medical use of gold, but also a number of other subjects that belong to the domain of alchemy. It is written in the form of a dialogue between Achryuasmus and Dynachrysus, and contains no direct reference to the author's Jewish beliefs, but is studded with frequent invocations of "the best and highest God," and "the immortal God." It also makes frequent reference to the *ars spagirica*, which was for centuries a term used to denote the art of alchemy.

Among the alchemical subjects discussed in the book are the aurum potabile (drinkable gold, 9, 42–43, 97), and the quinta essentia (quintessence, or elixir, 42–43). Portaleone also speaks about the golden calf and the gold in the Temple of Jerusalem (81–82), and about uniting gold and *hydrargyrus* (quicksilver, 121). A detailed index (179–204) facilitates the use of the book. It is thus evident that Portaleone belonged to that group of medieval and Renaissance physician-alchemists who were able to combine and harmonize the tenets, experiences, and practices of both disciplines.

Chapter Thirty-one

THE MANCHESTER (JOHN RYLANDS) MANUSCRIPT

AN ALCHEMICAL manuscript, numbered 1435, in the John Rylands University Library of Manchester was formerly owned by Moses Gaster, the renowned British Sephardi folklorist. The text is written in a clear Sephardi hand, probably in the sixteenth or seventeenth century. There are indications in it to show that it was copied from older manuscripts that were written in Spain and in Venice. It quotes several books and authorities, and their recipes, including (Pseudo-)Aristotle, (Pseudo-) Maimonides, R. Yaᶜqov Alqasṭila, Mestre Ventura, Michael, Sobola, *Sefer haMaor* (The Book of Light), *Sefer haLoᶜazim* (Book of Foreign Expressions), the *uman* (artist), Almoli, "a woman expert," and "an old book."

Most of the recipes contained in the manuscript are very brief, some pages containing as many as seventeen prescriptions. Its forty-eight pages contain a total of 374 individual prescriptions. The Hebrew language of the manuscript is grammatically more correct than in many other alchemical writings, but it shares with them the use of a great number of foreign technical terms taken from Spanish, Italian, Arabic, Turkish, and even German. Quite frequently the meaning of these terms is explained by translating them into another language.

The 374 prescriptions cover the entire field of alchemy, and give a rare picture of the many interests, endeavors, and purposes of alchemical work not often matched by other Hebrew (or even non-Hebrew) alchemical manuscripts and a full listing and description of its contents will be given here. Most of the recipes I identify merely by their incipits, or by stating their contents in my own words. Several of the more interesting ones I give fully, including, wherever I was able to ascertain it, the translation of technical terms.

Folios 2a: 1. To tint iron in the color of gold. 2. To write letters of gold upon iron. 3–4. To gild iron. 5. To gild iron or copper. 6. To tint moon [silver]. 7. *Bertolo* [?] color.

Folio 2b: 8. To improve silver. 9. Sweetness of metals [fragment only].

Folio 3a: 10. To make *presto* [?] of moon. 11. To color *Saturno* [Saturn, i.e., lead]. 12–13. To tint moon. 14. To tint *bertolo*.

Folio 3b: 15. To give green color to silver. 16–17. To make silver weigh as much as gold. 18. To transmute lead into gold. 19. To lighten the weight of a dinar and to return it to its original weight, so that of each fifty ducats one ounce should be left over. 20. To collect gold. 21. To tint silver.

Folio 4a: 22. To tint lead or silver to the color of gold. 23. To increase gold by half. "Take *salnitri* [sodium nitrate] and *armoniaq* salt [sal ammoniac], and Roman *vidriol* [vitriol], of each one *unsa* [ounce], *verde ramo* [verdigris] six *oqias* [ounces], and pound all of it well. And take the gold and pound it, and put it into a *maṣaʿ* [H., middle-sized] melting pot, as mentioned, and lute it with philosophers' clay, and give it the proper fire, and it will come out." 24. To make philosophers' clay. 25. *Lega presta* [I., quick alloy]. 26. To purify and improve gold. 27. *Liga* [alloy] for gold.

Folio 4b: 28–30. To extract the gold from a gilded silver vessel without ruining all of it. 31–32. To increase the weight of gold. 33. To separate the gold from a gilded vessel. 34–37. To increase the weight of gold.

Folio 5a: 38–44. To increase the weight of gold. 45. To make ducats heavier. 46. To separate gold from lead, "from the mouth of R. Yaʿaqov Alqastila." 47. To separate iron from tin. 48. To purify a gold thread. 49. To purify a gold chain. 50–51. To add weight to any metal. 52–53. To add weight to gold.

Folio 5b: 54–55. To add weight to gold. [The second recipe ends:] "From the mouth of Sobola, and remember what Michael[2] said, that it is necessary at first to purify the gold well." 56. To add weight to gold. 57–58. To add weight to silver. 59. For gold which does not come under the hammer [i.e., to soften gold]. 60. For gold in which there is an admixture of *alaṭon* [brass] [how to separate them]. 61–63. For gold mixed with copper and silver or tin [how to separate them]. 64. To remove the copper. 65. To separate the gold from gilded vessels.

Folio 6a: 66. To remove gold from silver. 67. For gilded work in which quicksilver is mixed. 68. To separate the gold from a gilded vessel. 69. To extract gold from silver and copper. 70. To extract the gold from a silver vessel. 71–72. To extract the gold from another vessel. 73–74. To remove the gold from a gilded vessel. 75. To remove the gold from an iron vessel.

Folio 6b:

76. Sun [gold] and moon [silver]. Take the herb which is called *ilarino* [?], which makes its leaves grow neither very long nor very wide, and they are like grass, and its stalk becomes of the size of a span, and in a few places a little longer, according to the soil in which it grows. And from the stalk grow kinds of knobs, and in each knob it raises a flower whose color is

green and *mulada* [?], and it is made like a *lirio* [?], except in its color, and there is of it a male and a female. The male produces one head, and the female three heads or four like *zaʿfrān* [saffron]. And it is found in the mountains of Jaqa and on the way to Marseille, and in Monaco, and in the forests of Segovia close to Rastafariah. Take of that which produces soft heads, and they are good for moon [silver]. And the others are good for sun [gold]. And cover them and pound them very fine, and keep their powder. And take prepared and purified *merqurio* [mercury] and put it into a glass cup or into one plated with glass, and put it in hot ashes. And when it gets warm and wants to fly away, put on it as much of the powders as you wish, and stir it with a stick, and then cover it for the duration of one hour, then throw into it a little white vinegar. And when the vinegar is completely swallowed up take it out and you will find it completed and good. And some say that it has to dry in bread in the oven. 77. Gold. The herb called *borisa* which is similar to *mangorana* [?], its leaves are of the color of the sun [gold], and this herb grows without leaves, and on the first day of the month it raises one leaf, and likewise every day, until it becomes full of leaves, and then its leaves fall off, one every day, and it again becomes naked as it was in the beginning, and it can be found on the seashore, and the banks of rivers, and in the mountains. Its leaves are round like a dinar, and its color is red, and its flower is black. Its fragrance is like that of the musk, its milk is *sitrina* [lemonlike]. Take the juice of this herb and throw it on the mercury, and boil it on fire, and it will become like a red stone. And of it put one weight upon a hundred, and it will become gold. And if you put the aforementioned juice on moon [silver] it will become gold. Put of this sun [gold] on lead, and it will become gold. And this herb is also called *benedita* [blessed].

78–79. To make gold or silver. 80. To make *sal preparado* [prepared salt].

[Folio 7 missing]

Folio 8a [mistakenly paginated 9a]: 81. To make silver. 82. Silver. "In Guadalcanal and in other places there grows a herb called *flamosa* or *sintilia* [I. *scintilla*, spark]." . . . Description of the use of this herb for making pure silver. 83. To make silver. 84. Sweetness—to boil powdered gold in *tartaro* oil [cream of tartar, potassium bitartrate?]. 85. Strong water [aquafortis] for the aforementioned work.

Folio 8b: 86. *Blanqimento* [whitening]. [The recipe concludes with:] "Some say that one must throw into it burned sulphur, and others say that it is not necessary, and you should test the way of both." 87. To make silver. 88. Glue for the above operation. 89. To make silver.

Folio 9a: 90. To harden quicksilver, "from the mouth of Mestre Ventura." 91. To increase gold. 92. To purify gold. 93–94. To whiten Venus [copper]. 95–96. To whiten anything that you cover with it.

97. To whiten anything you want. 98. To improve, purify and whiten copper.

Folio 9b: 99. To silver any copper vessel. 100. To silver copper. 101. To silver brass or copper. 102. To whiten brass or copper, and for counterfeit and bad silver, so that it should not look as if plated with lead. 103. To tint copper like silver. 104. To gild. 105. To gild a silver platter. 106–7. To make goldlike writing.

Folio 10a: 108. To write in gold color. 109. To gild. 110. Colored letters. "Take stone of corals, which is a green stone with which they sharpen razors, and grind it until it will be all *niato* [?], and mix this powder with rosewater in which there should be *guma* [gum], and write with it, and the letters will be green, and when the letters dry rub them with a pure gold or silver or copper ring." 111. To make letters have the color of gold or silver or any metal. 112. To write writing like gold or silver. 113. To make ink of gold. 114. To make silver writing. 115. To make gold ink.

Folio 10b: 116–18. For gilded letters. 119. To write like tin or lead. 120–21. To write like gold. 122. To give color to gold. 123–24. To gild. 125. To write and the writing should become the color of any metal you want. 126. To melt the gold *waraq* [leaf]. 127. To write or draw upon leather, and the drawing should remain gilded. 128. "Know that all metals are not pure to get color until they are purified by burning and quenched in living water. From the *Sefer haMaor* [Book of Light]."[3] 129. To whiten. 130. To gild with gold leaf.

Folio 11a: 131. "Now we ask what is the difference in gilding with leaf? It is that instead of going for one it goes for three." 132. To recognize whether a silver object is gilded with gold leaf or with gold. 133. To repair a broken copper vessel.

> 134. Take three parts of *oropimento* [orpiment] and one part of mercury, and grind it with *guma arabiqa* [gum arabic], and write with it, and you will make it beautiful like ivory. 135. A good glue, that is *soldadora* [S., solder]. Take filings of Iovis [Jupiter, i.e., tin], and ground *sulfar* [sulphur], which is *razina* [?], and *harṣ*, that is tar, and mix them together, and besmear the *shafut* [H., potted] metals with fat, and sprinkle the powder on top and heat from below the potted [metals] with a candle until the powder on top becomes melted, and then it will be glued together with the potted [metals]. This is for Venus [copper], but for tin and lead do not put sulphur and don't heat with a candle but with coals, and hurry to remove it from the fire.

136. To improve the quicksilver. 137. An operation for burning quicksilver. 138. The philosophers' clay [two methods of its preparation]. 139. Explanation of a few names: *armoniaqo anosanire*; *alqali*

salitri qe is *suza*; *antron* is the waste of glass; *atinkar boras* [borax],[4] *obin ablutos* [I., washed] is oil washed many times and turned white; *azarniqos* is *asirniqo* [arsenic] and *oro pimento* [orpiment]; *alume yaminos* is *alume de paloma*; *agrimino verde* [I., green *agrimonia*, agrimony], *azingar* cup of *soliman*; *vitrioles azij* or powder of *skolia*; *alfano de sirizuelo azair* powder of *skolia*; *al saralige alfur ser pirizuelo*; *afas blanqo* [I. *blanco*, white] *alume botiso*. 140. To improve inferior gold, which is called *astraimento de oro* [atrament of gold] . . . From the mouth of Mestre Ventura."

Folio 11b: 141. Good tint for inferior gold. 142. To gild or to silver any metal. 143. To make water of *nishādīr* [sal ammoniac]. 144. To make ammoniac oil. 145. To make *ṭarṭaro* oil [cream of tartar?] which is called *razuras* [I. *rasura*, scraping, shaving], and that oil is like water. 146. *Ṭarṭaro* oil in another way.

Folio 12a: 147. To make *ṭarṭaro* oil which preserves all spirits, and all the bodies which are lime will become water. 148. To make *azij* [?] water of *atramento* [?] or ashes of *savilia* [?], all of which is one. 149. To make strong water [aquafortis]. 150. To make scorpio oil which is sulphur. "From the mouth of the *uman* [H., artist]." 151. To make oil to give *ingres* [I. *ingresso*, entry] to all medicaments.

> 152. To make sulphur oil. Turn an *orinal* [flask] with its mouth down, and under it put a bowl in which you should collect the oil, and put burning coals in a bowl, and put the sulphur upon the coals so that the flask should get its smoke and the oil should drip into the bowl under it. From the mouth of Almoli. And it is better if you put a wide glass flask with its mouth turned down. 153. To make sulphur oil. Pulverize well live sulphur and put it in a glass flask, and lute with it another flask mouth-to-mouth [see Figure 31.1] . . . and this way put them into warm horse manure and let it stand thus fifteen days, and the sulphur oil will come out into the empty flask.

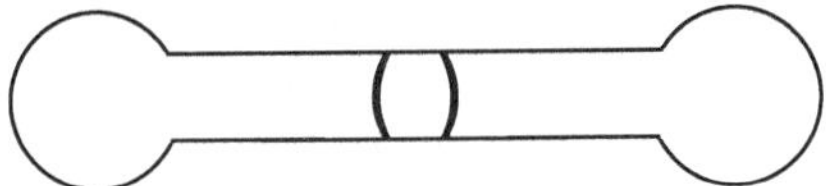

Figure 31.1. Sketch of two flasks, luted.

154. To make scorpio oil which is sulphur.

Folio 112b: 155–156. To whiten the scorpio [sulphur]. 157. To make water out of the *qafar* [or *qafrah* ?]. 158. To make strong water [aquafortis]. 159. Water to preserve all spirits. 160. To make water out of mercury and *luna* [moon, i.e., silver] together. 161. To *fisar* [fixate] the sulphur. 162. To make sulphur white.

Folio 13a:

163. Glue out of gold. Take two ounces of ammoniac salt, half an ounce of *pirite de Espania* [I., pyrite, fool's gold, of Spain], half an ounce of *vitriol Romano rubifiqato* [reddened Roman vitriol], that is, put the vitriol in a small covered pot on the fire until it gets red and then take it out. This is called reddened vitriol. Another, exact version: the vitriol will not become reddened. Pound all this well, and put them in a glass flask, and lute it up to its half [mark] or less with philosophers' clay, and put the flask, as you know it, on an oven with fire to *asuplimar* [sublimate], and give it fire for ten hours, and then let it cool, and put the glass flask upon the fire and let it cool, and then take one quarter of an ounce of this medicine on two ounces of refined silver, *qopelia* [I. *coppella*, cupel, test] in Laʿaz, and melt the silver at first, and when it is melted throw the aforementioned medicine into it, thus three times, and then throw it as mentioned, and then take a part of this alloy, and one part of good gold, and you will find it good. From the mouth of Mestre Ventura.

164. Oil of *atutia* [*ṭuṭia*, tutty, zinc oxide]. 165. Another oil of tutty called oil of *tusia*. 166. *Saʿdun*. "Take two flasks mouth-to-mouth and covered. And put sulphur into one and lute it, and put it on *lutada* [I., luted] fire. And the smoke of one should go into the other. And this is the spirit of *zinjifra* [A. *zunjufr*, cinnabar], the spirit of *ṭuṭia zinjar* [A. tutty of verdigris]." 167–68. To make spirit of sulphur. 169. A color of twenty carats, one for thirty moon [silver].

Folio 13b: 170. Color for silver of twenty-two carats. 171. Color to *qalsina* [calcine] the tutty. 172. Color made of thin gold leaves. 173. To purify lead and to color it gold.

174. Gold. Take tin of Ferrara, one *uns* [ounce] of sulphur and one ounce of orpiment, half of *alqali* [alkali] salt, pounded, and mix them, and put them to boil in a little goat's milk for half an hour, gently, and take it out and let the aforementioned powders dry in the sun, and then take cupeled silver, and make of it a *maṣaʿ* [H., foundation] four times six hours in ashes, and then *aqopilalo* [refine it] and put it in strong water [aquafortis], and it will be strong and will remain gold.

175. To increase the weight of gold. 176. "The work of *zilata*[?]. Put *merqurio qonzilato*[?] one *liṭra* [pound] with three ounces of leaf of copper. . . ." 177. Another one.

Folio 14a: 178. Sun [gold]. To establish half gold so that it should become twenty-two carat. 179. To make *fizar* [fixing] for moon [silver]. 180. To fixate moon. 181. Moon. 182. To purify copper. 183. *Purifiqar* [to purify] verdigris. 184. *Qalsinar* [to calcine]. 185. *Suplimar* [to sublimate]. 186. *Banio Maria* [*bain Marie*, water-bath].

Folio 14b: 187. Moon. 188. Sun. 189. "Take one part of silver and one part of gold [these words are in Arabic], and melt them together. . . ." 190. To freeze [solidify] mercury. 191. *Fizasion* [fixation]. 192. To make gold-lime. 193. For gold. 194. To freeze [solidify]. 195. Sun and moon. 196. To make *zirnikh* [arsenic] permanent.

Folio 15a: 197. "Good *alizīr* [elixir]. Take sublimated arsenic which does not make silver black, and put it layer upon layer with the silver, and roast it with it, and put on it another layer of arsenic and roast it as at the first time. Do this many times until it is consumed and is melted like wax. . . . And put it with quicksilver, and this is a good elixir." 198. For moon [silver]. 199. For sun [gold]. "The version of the Rambam [Maimonides]. . . ."[5]

Folio 15b: 200. [Continuation of the above with the following personal note added:] "And if it seems to the eye of your brains that it needs to be more purified, I did not find more, I the writer." 201. "Color for silver, from the mouth of Mestre Ventura. Take *tarab* [A. *turab*, dust, earth] color, which is called in the Venetian language *habatasan samrias* [?] of Veneṣia [Venice]. . . ." 202. Color [word illegible].

Folio 16a: 203–4. To separate gold from silver. 205. "Said the divine philosopher. . . ."[6]

Folio 16b: 206. "In the Book of Sadidi.[7] *Qāl Arisṭuṭalis* . . . " [a quotation in Judeo-Arabic from Aristotle]. 207. To make *perlas* [pearls]. 208. To make big pearls out of small ones.

Folio 17a: 209–12. To make big pearls out of small ones.

Folio 17b: 213–17. To make one out of several pearls.

Folio 18a: 218–22. To whiten pearls. 223–24. To purify pearls. 225. To whiten pearls. 226. To give good color to pearls. 227. To whiten pearls.

Folio 18b: 228. To clean and purify pearls. 229. To whiten pearls.

> 230. And this is the work of the real crystal. Take of it the amount you want, and put it into the middle wall of the oven until it becomes calcined white like snow, and this will happen within one hour or less. Then take it out and preserve it and put [some] of it into an *albūt* [A. *būṭa*, melting pot] made of philosophers' clay, and put on it one-fourth or one-fifth of *ḥūṣa* [A. *ḥaṣan*, pebbles]. And it will instantly dissolve and will be like real glass in every respect. And here I show you the shape of the oven so that you don't err in making it [Figure 31.2]. And it too you should make of philosophers' clay so that it should be strong, and give it fire of thick logs. And there are many kinds. The kind of crystal that breaks easily is called in Laʿaz *franjibile* [I. *frangibile*, breakable]. And for this you will need to mix with the pebbles a little *ladasqos* [?], so that it should melt and run immediately.

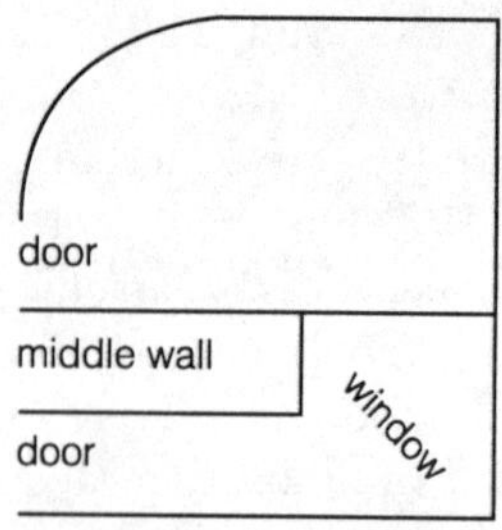

Figure 31.2. Cross section of an oven.

231. To separate alum water from crystal water. 232. To soften crystal. 233. To tint crystal and to make of it precious stones. 234. To soften a horn. 235. To soften stone like wax.

Folio 19a: 236. To soften crystal. 237–39. To melt crystal. 240. To make *esmeralda* [emerald], "from the mouth of Mestre Ventura." 241. To melt crystal. 242. To tint crystal sky-blue color.

243. To tint crystal the color of *margada* [G. *maragdos*, emerald]. Take *alum de pluma* [?] one part, white and pure ground crystal one part, mix everything seven days, and on the seventh day take one-third of a part of arsenic, and cook everything in an iron vessel, and that soup with *zaʿra*, that is, *ayara* [?], which is *verdete* [green] in Laʿaz, clean and pure, and melt it and put it in any form you wish. The herb *darganah* [?] melts the crystal.

244. To soften crystal.

Folio 19b: 245. To melt crystal. 246. "To tint crystal the color of *qrizolitos* [I. *crisolito*, chrysolite]. Take crystal and put it into alum water twelve days, and cook it in *arseniq* [arsenic] or orpiment, and it will become greenish like chrysolite. And if you cook it in *sfangasron* [?] it will be like *smaraq* [emerald]. *Sfansagron* [*sic*], that is *qolitia* or *verderis*, that is *verdet*, which is *qalame jinjir* or *azmar* [A. *asmar*, brown]." 247. To soften crystal. 248. "To tint crystal or another hard stone, or to engrave on it. Take the juice of *milfolio* [I. *millefoglio*, milfoil, *Achillea millefolium*], and put it wherever you want to engrave, and then put it in the sun, and you can engrave what you want." 249. To make artificial crystal. 250. To soften crystal. 251. To tint crystal the color of *rubin* [ruby]. 253. To tint crystal like *granata* [I., garnet]. 254. To make emeralds. 255. To tint glass any color you want. 256. Color. To make glass panes, glasses, and flasks any color you want.

Folio 20a: 257. To tint the aforementioned the color of gold.

258. To soften precious stones or glass like dough. Take dragon's blood [a resinous substance obtained from tropical plants], and blood of *irizo*,

which is an animal with spines [porcupine?], and blood of desertic [i.e., wild] or domestic geese, and wine sediment, and strong vinegar, in equal parts. They should all be cooked together on gentle fire, and after their cooking put into them the stones, and they will soften like wax, so that you can impress into them any seal you want. From an old book.

259. To soften glass so that it should be soft like wax. 260. To purify *qorales* [corals]. 261. To make the coral shiny after it has dried. 262. To make corals and other things *moldasas* [?]. 263. To soften corals. 264. To join together brittle corals. 265. To soften small stones.

Folio 20b: 266. To soften bones. 267. To melt bones and ivory. 268. To pour a horn into a mold. 269. To soften any horn. 270. To tint bones or wood red. 271. To tint green. 272. To tint a bone green. 273. To tint a bone *rozāṭo* [pink]. 274. To tint a bone green. 275. To make combs black, if they are made of horn. 276. To make *almārjīn* [A. *marjan*, small pearls]. 277. To soften the bones of an elephant. 278. To tint bones green or pink. 279. To tint *mārfīl* [I. *marfilo*, elephant's tusk] or another bone pink color. 280. To tint writing or any other thing.

Folio 21a: 281. To tint any object black. 282. To tint the *sapir* [sapphire] white. 283. To give a stone the color of sapphire. 284. "*Rubis.* Take red coral and dragon's blood [a kind of resin], and pure *laqa* [I. *lacca*, lacquer] in equal parts, and grind all of it very well, and knead them in egg white, and make your stones, and put them for nine days in strong sun, so that it should dry." 285. *Matista* [?] . . . to make glass beads. 286. "To make *maistobanio*, and it is like white sapphire, but it is a little greenish. If you want to make it like a diamond. . . ." 287. Black color. 288–89. To whiten sapphire. 290. To make good and pure *azūl* [lapis lazuli].

Folio 21b: 291–93. To make *lāzuward* [A., lapis lazuli]. 294. To tint *turqiza* [turquoise]. 295. To bring out the color of turquoise. 296–98. To tint the turquoise, "from the mouth of the artist." 299. To make *aṭuṭia qalamina* [I. *tuzia calamina*, calamine, a zinc ore]. "Thus did I find it, I the writer."

Folio 22a: 300. To make *ṭuṭia Alisandrina* [Alexandrian tutty, zinc oxide], "from the mouth of Mestre Ventura." 301. To make spirit of tutty.

Folio 22b: 302. "To remove the skin. Take *sālmoniaq* [sal ammoniac], *reagal* [I., realgar], *maṣṭiq* [I. *mastica*, mastic] in equal parts, and *boras* [I. *borace*, borax] water, and put it together in a melting pot until they melt, and let it dry, and it will become a powder. And put that powder upon skin, and put it in fire until the powder melts, and the skin will separate." 303. To remove the skin from moon [silver]. 304. For skin. 305. To remove the skin from silver and gold. 306. To remove the skin from silver. 307. "To skin any coin of silver and also gold. First soak it in water and then put on it quicklime and old cheese in equal parts, and heat it on gentle fire or wax fire until the powder that is on the coin is consumed, and the skin will separate. And if you want, whiten it thereafter because it will get black due to the fire." 308. To remove the skin from silver. 309. To give weight to gold. 310. To remove the skin from gold. 311–12. To remove the skin from gold flower. 313. "To peel off the skin from a vessel, from any metal you wish, from its whole surface. The version of the divine philosopher the Rambam [Maimonides] of blessed memory. . . ."[8]

Folio 23a: 313. Continued. 314. "To purify the aforementioned peelings. . . . All this from the mouth of Mestre Ventura." 315. Treatment of silver peelings. 316. If you want to melt the peelings. 317. "I heard from a woman expert."

Folio 23b: [317 continued:] "in the Work that you should melt the peelings as they are in a melting pot, and always stir it in it with an iron spit [H. *shipuda*], and it does not need an iron pot, nor pieces of *aziro* [?], nor anything else." 318. To peel a silver coin or silver. 319–20. To purify the aforementioned peelings. 321. For gold: to make it better than it is. 322. To give color to a vessel of which part is gilded. 323. If you wish to gild part of a silver vesel. 324. To gild rings of iron or lead.

> 325. To elevate gold in assaying. Melt the gold and pour it into a tube, and there should be prepared a melting pot. When you put into it sal ammoniac. Grind two parts and one part of *niṭro* salt [saltpeter], all ground well. And take the gold which you have poured into the tube while it is still hot and put it into this melting pot with the aforementioned powders, and cover the mouth of the pot with a piece of wooden plank or another thing, and do nothing else but shake the pot with everything that is in it, and put it into assaying. And you will see a marvel. All this from the mouth of Mestre Ventura.

326. To tint an iron ring.

Folio 24a: 327. To *asmaltar* [I. *smaltar*, to smelt, enamel] *de Jovis* [Jupiter, i.e. tin] 328. To smelt. 329. To make color. 330. To make *nieil* [I. *niello*, a black glaze]. 331. "To remove the *istrido* [I. *strido*, shriek, crackling] and the softness from Jupiter [tin], and to make it pure. Take two parts of sulphur and one of *laton Morisqo* [Moorish brass], and melt at first the brass, and throw it into *andimonia* [antimony] water." 332. "To improve tin. Take Iovis, that is, tin, and melt it in vinegar in which there is mercury, and it will be beautiful and hard, and it will give off a voice." 333–35. To make borax which is *atinkar* [A. *tinkar*, a calcareous salt].

Folio 24b: 336–38. Three more recipes for making borax. 339. To make *vermilian* [I. *vermiglio*, vermilion], which is cinnabar. 340. To make it in another way. 341. To make cinnabar which is vermilion. 342. *Figasion* [fixation] of *sinabra*, that is, cinnabar.

Folio 25a: 343–45. To make alkali salt. 346. To make *azarqon* [A. *zarqūn*, cinnabar] which is *soligin* in the Togar [Turkish] language. 347–49. To make *algalia* [= *alqali*?]. 350. Take *ardij* [?] in the Togar language, ten drachmas; *qitran* [A., tar, pitch], five drachmas; and make a potion of honey with rosewater, and put it to boil on fire, and remove the scum, and take of this ten drachmas, and one drachma of pure *algalia*, and mix it together, and it will be good *algalia*. 351. To make *musq* [A. *misk*, musk].

Folio 25b: 252–54. Three more recipes for making musk. 355. For *musqo* [musk] which lost its fragrance. 356. To try out the musk. 357–59. To recognize *balsamo* [balsam], whether it is good and pure. 360. To concoct *balsamo rubarbaro* [I. *balsamo reubarbaro*, rhubarb balsam].

> 361. In the *Sefer haMaor* [H., The Book of Light][9] par. 30: To make *ambar* [A. *ʿanbar*, amber]. Take egg white and melt it in gum arabic and a little good saffron, and dry it in the sun. It will become like glass, and it will be amber." 362. In the *Sefer haMaor*, par. SNT [or SKT?]: To make saffron cook the flesh of an ox and dry it in the sun, or dried fishes which are called *stoq fish* [G. *Stockfisch*, stock-fish, dried cod] and grind them fine, and take good saffron and melt it in rosewater. Wet the fish with this water until it becomes red. Look in the *Sefer haLoʿazim*, page 39."

363. To purify saffron. 364. To add weight to saffron. 365. To increase saffron.

Folio 26a: 366–67. Two more recipes for increasing the weight of saffron. 368–69. To increase wax. 370. To make *qwintas* [fifths?] of amber into one *libra* [pound]. 371. To make amber.

Folio 26b: 372. Brittle *quintas* that they should become smearable. 373. "The secret of fragrant water superior in its purpose, and its advantages are many, and it was tried by me."

> 374. To make *būkhūr* [A. *bakhūr*, incense] *swai* [?]. Rosewater one ounce, *kinjia*, that is *ḥaṣīl* [H., eggplant] *kinṭ* [?] three drachmas, *asturq* twenty-five drachmas, white *sandalos* [A. *sandal*, sandalwood] one drachma, *lingalia* [?] one drachma. Pound all of it and cook it in a vessel called *paila* [I. *palla*, flask; or *pala*, bucket] in Laʿaz, and cover it well with dough so that its vapor and smell should not get out, and let it cook until you see that it smells good. That is a sign that it is cooked. Remove the *paila* from the fire and let it cool one day, and then open it, and throw the water into small flasks. The sediment which remains in the bottom of the vessel, take it out and put it in a *ṭāfsar* [?] on gentle fire, and take a little and make [pieces] like bricks called askaros, and if it is very dry put a little rosewater

into them, or spring water. 375. To make *mandragola* [I. *mandragola*, mandrake]. Take two *lirio* [?] and draw the shape of a whole man, and bury it in the field until it grows thick leaves. And take a razor and prepare [word illegible], and pass it along all of it except its eyelashes and the hair of its head. And in every place where a man has hair, leave it. And after you let it grow, bury it for one day until the *raidores* [?] become smooth, that is, what is pulled off them. 376. To make a *blanqet* [ceruse] prepared for the work, take the ceruse . . .

Here the manuscript breaks off. Attached to it are four pages (unnumbered), written by a different hand, in Judeo-Arabic, except for two brief paragraphs that are in Hebrew.

PART EIGHT

The Seventeenth Century

Introduction to Part Eight

WHEREAS in the sixteenth century most of the Jewish authors who wrote on alchemy lived in Arabic-speaking lands, not a single Jewish alchemical author who lived in that part of the world is known to us from the seventeenth century. Although these seventeenth-century authors were still Sephardi Jews, all of them lived in the West, in a Christian environment—in Italy, the Netherlands, or else in north-central or northeastern Europe.

This geographical shift reflects two movements that took place toward the end of the sixteenth century. One was an internal Jewish one: the intellectual leadership that in the sixteenth century still belonged to those branches of Sephardi Jewry which lived in Muslim countries passed to the western Sephardim who lived in Italy, Holland, and adjacent areas, and to the Ashkenazi Jews who lived in central and eastern Europe. The other movement was one that took place outside the Jewish orbit but could not fail to influence the Jewish intellectual orientation. During the Renaissance, the center of alchemical work shifted from the Muslim world to Christian western Europe. By the seventeenth century this shift was complete, and was paralleled by a corresponding shift in Jewish alchemical work, experimentation, and writing.

This activity, carried out by Sephardi Jews in Christian Europe, was but one manifestation of the openness of the Sephardim to gentile culture, not matched even remotely by their Ashkenazi brethren. Although the dominant positions in Halakha and rabbinical scholarship had been taken by Ahkenazim, they manifested, with a very few exceptions, a negative attitude toward the sciences, arts, and other cultural activities of the Christian environment. One of those activities was alchemy. It was not until the eighteenth century that this situation began to change.

A clear indication of the openness of Sephardi Jewish intellectuals in western Europe to the preoccupations of gentile culture, including alchemy, may be found in the life of Baruch (Benedict) de Spinoza (1632–1677), one of the greatest philosophers of all times. Little attention has been paid to the fact that Spinoza was keenly interested in chemical and physical matters in general, and alchemy in particular. In letters he wrote to Heinrich Oldenburg, a German scholar from Bremen who lived in London, where he became a member and subsequently secretary of the Royal Society, and editor of its *Transactions*, Spinoza repeatedly discusses salts and saltpeter.[1] On March 25, 1667, Spinoza wrote a letter to

Jarrigh (or Jarrich) Jelles, a Mennonite merchant in Amsterdam, who was a friend of his and whose writings Spinoza translated into Dutch after Jelles's death.[2] The first part of that letter deals with alchemy, and from the introductory sentence it becomes clear that Spinoza and Jelles had already discussed Helvetius's experiments mentioned in it:

> Concerning the matter of Helvetius, I have consulted Vossius, who (in order not to relate the whole contents of our conversation) laughed uncontrollably and was astonished that I asked about such babble (*nugis*). However, unconcerned about it, I betook myself to that goldsmith (*aurificem*) himself, who had assayed the gold, his name is Berchtolt (Berchtelt). But he said something quite different than Mr. Vossius. He maintained that the weight of the gold increased between the melting and the separation (*liquescendum et separandum*), and that it became heavier by the weight of the silver which he threw (*iniecerat*) into the melting pot (*crucibulo*) for the purpose of separation; so that he believed firmly that this gold, which transmuted his silver into gold, contained in itself something special. Not only he, but also various other gentlemen who were present, have confirmed that this indeed was the case. Thereupon I went to Helvetius himself, who showed me both the gold and the melting pot, whose inner walls were still gilded over, and he related that he had thrown barely a quarter of a barley-corn or mustard seed into the molten lead. He added that he would soon publish the entire course of the thing, and further informed me that a man (whom he considered to be the same as the one who had been with him) had carried out this same operation in Amsterdam, about which you have undoubtedly heard. This is what I could find out about this thing.[3]

Helvetius, mentioned in this letter as an experimenter in goldmaking, was an important alchemist in The Hague in the second half of the seventeenth century. His original name was Johan Frederick Schweitzer (1629–1709), but he became known, by the Latin translation of his last name, as Helvetius. He wrote several books on alchemy, and in the year in whcih he told Spinoza about his successful transmutation of lead into gold, he published the book he mentioned to Spinoza. In it he discusses several alchemical subjects, but evidently he considered that particular transmutation the most important of all, and therefore described it in the title of the book. It reads (in my translation from the Latin): "The Golden Calf which the whole world adores and prays to, in which is discussed the rarest miracle of nature in transmuting metals, namely how the total substance of lead within a moment with a minutest particle of the true philosophers' stone was changed into pure gold in Hagae Comitis, Amsterdam, 1667."

Helvetius's book contains the explanation of why Spinoza does not mention in his letter what substance it was that Helvetius threw into the motlen lead: Helvetius did not divulge its secret to him. This becomes clear from the fact that even in his book Helvetius passes over this point in silence. What he tells in Part Three of his book is that he was visited by a strange and peculiarly dressed man, who identified himself as "Elias Arista." We recognize under this name that of the prophet Elijah, whom the alchemists considered the great master of their art—this is why they call him "Elias Arista"—and who, they expected, would upon his second coming reveal to them the secret of the philosophers' stone. Helvetius goes on to say that Elias Arista showed him the philosophers' stone, which he had in his satchel, and gave him of it "as much as a coriander seed" (almost the very words of Spinoza's letter), but he refrains from even hinting at what that mysterious stone consisted of. Hence we can assume that he said nothing about it to Spinoza, either.

What Helvetius does instead is to quote the sacred words Elias Artista wrote down for him. They were: "Holy, holy, holy is the Lord our God, and all things are full of His honor," which is a free rendering of the Jewish *q'dusha* prayer quoted from Isaiah 6:3. Next Elias Artista wrote: "Of Yehova of the wonderful wonderworking wisdom in the general book of nature, I am made [?] on August 26, 1666"—evidently the date of his visit with Helvetius. And then he wrote: "Wonderful is God, nature, and the Spagirian Art. Do nothing gratuitously. Mostly holy spirit, Hallelujah, Hallelujah. Phew to the Devil! Without light don't speak of God. Amen." "Spagirian Art" is a frequently used designation for the art of alchemy. Chapter 4 of the treatise is a dialogue between Elias Artista and a "Medicus," who is presented as a physician seeking alchemical knowledge. These sections are preceeded in Part One by quotations from various alchemical authors, and descriptions of experiments in goldmaking.

Isaac Vossius (1618–1689), to whom Spinoza referred, was a historian, philosopher, and naturalist, who moved from The Hague to Windsor, where he became *canonicus* in 1673.[4] He wrote several books on natural sciences, and, as can be gathered from Spinoza's reference, was more than skeptical about the possibility of transmuting base metals into gold.

The second alchemist mentioned by Spinoza, the goldsmith Berchtolt (or Berchtelt), did not claim to be in possession of the philosophers' stone, and had a different method for producing gold. He threw silver into the crucible, ostensibly in order to effect a separation of the melted gold from another, unnamed, substance, with the result that the original weight of the gold increased by the weight of the silver, that is, that the silver was transmuted into gold. This operation, Spinoza writes to Jelles, was witnessed, and its results confirmed, by several men.

In his letter Spinoza embraces no position either for or against alchemy. Nevertheless, he spent a good bit of time in trying to find out whether there was any basis in reality to the alchemists' claim that they could transmute silver and lead into gold. This in itself shows that despite his considerable knowledge of the sciences and his great critical acumen, Spinoza, a man of his time, considered transmutation at least a possibility.

Chapter Thirty-two

LEONE MODENA, DELMEDIGO, AND ZERAḤ

LEONE Modena (also known as Leon da Modena, 1571–1648) was possibly the most colorful character in Italian Jewish history. Born in Venice, brought up in Ferrara, he was an infant prodigy, studied Hebrew, Italian, and Latin, and became rabbi in Venice, where his sermons (in Italian) attracted large Jewish and gentile audiences. He wrote with equal facility in Hebrew and Italian, was an acute polemicist, and attacked with equal sharpness Uriel da Costa, the *Zohar*, Yiṣḥaq Luria, and Christianity. He possessed an extensive talmudic and rabbinical knowledge, wrote numerous responsa of a liberal character, and also produced Italian, and occasionally Latin, prose and poetry. He suffered from an addiction to gambling from which, despite repeated vows, he could not tear himself away, and consequently he was almost constantly in deep financial trouble. He tried to earn money with a great variety of occupations; on occasion he worked as a broker, translator, letter-writer, writer of poems and sermons for others, playwright (he wrote at least one Italian comedy), amateur actor, marriage broker, writer of amulets and teacher of the art of amulet writing, and he was even *maestro di cappella* of a musical academy established in the Venetian ghetto in 1632, when he was sixty-one.

An interest in alchemy ran in the Modena family. This we know from Leone's own account of his life, which is the first "frank" autobiography to be written in Hebrew.[1] In it Leone tells of his uncle Shemaᶜya, who was killed because of his alchemy, of his own attempts at making gold, and of his son Mordecai's death as a result of his protracted work in alchemy. At the same time it becomes clear from Leone's account that in his days it was not unusual in Italy for either Jewish physicians and rabbis or Christian priests to engage in alchemical experimentation.

Of his uncle Shemaᶜya, Leone writes as follows:

> Shemaᶜya lived in Modena and was in charge of the management of a loan-shop there, and his heart inclined to dealing in alchemy, and a gentile cheated him, for he showed him fake increment, and persuaded him to take all the silver and gold that was in the store to a courtyard, by telling him that he would melt it and increase it many times. And there he thrust a sword into his belly and killed him, and took all the silver and gold, and ran

away. And this happened on the eve of the removal of the leavened bread [the eve of Passover]. And next day they noticed the matter and found him and buried him. And three days later the murderer was caught with all the silver and gold, nothing was missing, and they cut him in four quarters.[2]

Of his own involvement with alchemy Leone reports briefly: "In the winter of 5363 [1603; he was thirty-two years old at the time] I was without pupils, and I went after the foolishness, the work of alchemy, for I was enticed by the physician, the sage R. Abraham di Cammeo of the city of Rome, who was at that time a young man, and was here with his father, and also on this I spent a great deal of money" (30). Abraham di Cammeo is known to have become rabbi of Rome fifteen years later, on April 22, 1618.[3]

Mordecai Modena's death as a result of his unceasing and protracted work in alchemy was a terrible blow to his father, who reports it in detail:

It happened on the tenth of Tishri 5375 [the fall of 1614] that my son Mordecai of blessed memory traveled abroad because an ungodly evil man oppressed us, and he [Mordecai] abandoned at that time his studies with the students of the society. And he returned in the month of Kislev [December 1614], and began to occupy himself with the work of alchemy with the priest Joseph Grillo, a great sage, and he exerted himself greatly, and became well versed in it to the point where all the masters of that science, who had become old and aged in it, marveled at what a youth like him knew of it. Finally, in the month of Iyar [spring 1615], he set up for himself a house in the *Ghetto Vecchio* [in Venice], and made all the preparations necessary for the work, and he repeatedly performed there an experiment that he had learned and tried in the house of the priest, which consisted of making ten ounces of refined silver out of nine ounces of lead and one ounce of silver. And I saw this and tested it twice as it was done by him, and I myself sold the silver, six pounds and half an ounce, which stood up in the coppella [assay], and I knew that it was true, even though it was a matter of great effort and exertion, and it required two and a half months each time. The end of the matter was that [we were able] to earn about a thousand ducats in a year. Nor was this all, for I too spent my life in trying to understand such things, and I would not have misled myself had sin not caused it. During the Feast of Sukkot 5376 [fall 1615], suddenly much blood flowed down from his [Mordecai's] head to his mouth, and from then on he ceased performing that work, for they said perhaps the vapors and the smokes of the arsenics and the salts that enter into it injured his head. And he stayed thus for two years until his death, doing some easy things (34).

A few paragraphs later Leone describes the symptoms of his son's illness, and the medicaments administered to him. His end came due to high fever on the ninth of Ḥeshvan 5378 (October 1617), at the age of twenty-six. At that point Leone mentions that he is writing these lines three years later, that is, in 1620.

Although some details in the account are not clear, the picture Leone paints of the involvement in alchemy by his uncle Shemaya, the physician-rabbi Abraham Cammeo, the priest Joseph Grillo, and his son Mordecai, as well as his own alchemical work, is unmistakably that of a society in which alchemy was practiced, in which people, including Leone himself, believed in the reality of alchemical transmutation of base metals into precious ones, and in which Christian masters of alchemy taught alchemy to Jewish youths. An interesting feature in this picture is the acceptance by laymen, that is, non-alchemists, of the so-called silver produced by the alchemists as real, on the basis of unreliable assay, which enabled the alchemist to acquire a considerable fortune within a short time.

As for Mordecai Modena's tragic death as a result of the "vapors and smokes" produced by his experiments, such occurrences seem not to have been extraordinary in medieval alchemy. This, at least, is what we can conclude from the description of the alchemist's life given five centuries earlier by Baḥya ibn Paquda, which includes the warning that "it can happen that the smell and the smoke will kill [the alchemist] due to the constant work and the length of the effort he devotes to them night and day."[4] The fact that Mordecai Modena died in precisely such circumstances shows that in this respect the hazards of alchemy had not improved since the days of Baḥya.

Delmedigo and His Disciple Zeraḥ

One of the most outstanding Jewish scholars of the seventeenth century was the polyhistor and encyclopedic author Joseph Solomon Delmedigo (1591–1655). As the son of Elijah Delmedigo of Candia (Crete), whose disciple and patron was the famous Renaissance figure Pico della Mirandola, Joseph received a thorough Jewish and classical education, and at the age of fifteen was admitted to the University of Padua, where he studied astronomy and mathematics under Galileo. Simultaneously, he also studied medicine, and was influenced by Leone Modena, rabbi of neighboring Venice, of whose interest in alchemy we have just heard.

In 1613, aged twenty-two, Delmedigo returned to Crete and started practicing medicine, but before long he set out on an extensive journey, visited Egypt and Turkey, and then settled in Vilna, where he became personal physician to Prince Radziwill. His services were much sought after by both Jewish and gentile patients, but his busy life as a physician did not prevent him from producing an impressive number of important works in arithmetic, astronomy, geometry, geography, chemistry, mechanics, medicine, logic, ethics, metaphysics, philosophy, and Kabbalah. Of this colossal output only two books have survived, the *Sefer Elim* (Book of Elim) and the *Taᶜalumot Ḥokhma* (Secrets of Wisdom), both of which are of interest to us in the present context. Toward the end of his life Delmedigo moved to Frankfurt, and finally to Prague, where he died at the age of sixty-four.

The antecedents of the *Sefer Elim* throw light on the international contacts Delmedigo maintained throughout his life. While sojourning in Egypt and in Constantinople, he became friendly with Karaite leaders, and in 1620 his disciple Moshe Metz made the acquaintance of the Karaite scholar Zeraḥ ben Nathan (b. 1578) of Troki, Lithuania. Encouraged by Metz's glowing reports about Delmedigo's scholarship, Zeraḥ began to write, in the same year, scholarly Hebrew letters to Delmedigo, grouping his inquiries under the headings of twelve "springs" and seventy "palm trees," which, according to the biblical account (Exod. 15:27; Num. 33:9), the Children of Israel found at Elim, a station of their wanderings in the desert. Zeraḥ's letters deal with mathematics, astronomy, Kabbalah and the occult, astrology, alchemy, medicine, metaphysics, and theology. He evidently was a learned man of wide interest, who sought further enlightenment in all the sciences of the day from Delmedigo, whom he recognized as a master in all of them.

In 1623 Delmedigo responded in considerable detail, and a few years later he included the full text of Zeraḥ's letters in his *Sefer Elim*, which was published in Amsterdam in 1629 by Manasseh ben Israel.[5] Under the title "The Eighth Spring," Zeraḥ writes about alchemy as follows:

> The Eighth Spring in the Works of Hermes, and his medicaments, and on the rules of the natural secrets. Several books have been printed recently in the languages of the *goyim* [gentiles], and in them are precious things about all the Works, such as how to write scrolls of secrets and how to heal strange diseases, and on agriculture, and on useful compounds, and on the operation of alchemy, and on the transmutation of metals. And my heart desires to know whether there is any use in it in relation to its great expense and the troubles and the loss of time in carrying out a thing wanted. And behold, there fell into my hands a booklet full of wisdom, a wreath of beauty, attributed to the Rambam [Maimonides] of blessed memory, who spoke wonders in it, as is his wont in all the sciences. Also the ancient ones, Greeks and Arabs, extolled it, such as Hermes and Geber, and Ben Sina and Alberto, and Tomaz and Baqon, and thousands with them. And in it are all

the affairs of the lands of China and Japan, and there is no nation or kingdom that its fame has not reached, and not the whole world "cuts reeds in the meadow."[6] For it is certainly an exalted science, and my ears have perceived only a morsel of it from the mouths of the masters. They tell of your honor [this is Zeraḥ writing, addressing Delmedigo], and the makers and merchants of spices tell of the works of your hands, for you have many secrets, all tried and tested, to you are revealed all the mysteries, and with you kings confer and princes take counsel.

And behold, this my desire has only recently been awakened, for never before did I have any dealings with these sciences, and especially not with alchemy. I had only heard rumors about it, and I put it as a seal upon my heart, and now we have heard the tidings from your disciple [Moshe Metz] that you reign over all the expanses of this science, and rule over all its properties, its nobs and nests. He also showed us some of your signs, several kinds of colored glass-stones which you have produced, and strong iron which you had made out of weak, and choice silver [you made] of strips of *ṣinfario* [cinnabar], and coin of half silver and half gold, and quicksilver which you produced from several metals, and *talqo* [talc or mica] oil for making faces bright until ripe old age, and a ring in which there is a stone which, if you soak it in wine or beer and give it to a man to drink, it will make him eliminate, and it will suffice to make him eliminate [urinate] as long as he lives, without pain, and other operations, and priceless works. He filled our belly with your delicacies, you greatly enriched us with your wisdom, he showed us marvels, for indeed your thoughts are exalted over the thoughts of others like the height of heaven, and "deep calleth unto deep at the voice of Thy cataracts" (Ps. 42:8), "the waters stand above the mountains" (Ps. 104:6).[7]

Although the letter is written in an effusive and exaggerated style, the factual basis underlying it must have been that Delmedigo's fame as a successful practicing alchemist had reached Zeraḥ, and that Moshe Metz not only told him about Delmedigo's experiments but actually showed him artificial gemstones and other objects Delmedigo produced with his alchemy. However, this letter reveals more about Zeraḥ and his familiarity with alchemical literature than about Delmedigo's expertise in alchemy.

Zeraḥ begins by referring to alchemy as "the Works of Hermes," which is in conformity with the generally prevalent Hellenistic and medieval alchemical traditional about a mythical Hermes as the originator of the Great Art of alchemy. The first alchemical treatise Zeraḥ mentions is a "booklet" attributed to the Rambam, that is, Maimonides; this could refer to the Pseudo-Maimonidean treatise discussed above in Chapter 24. Next Zeraḥ mentions "Geber," who, of course, is none other than Jābir ibn Ḥayyān, with whom we are by now quite familiar. "Ben Sina" is Ibn Sīnā (980–1037), known in the West as Avicenna, one of the greatest scholars and scientists of the Arab Middle Ages, considered a leading light by the alchemists. "Alberto" is Albertus Magnus (c. 1206–1280), the German Scholastic philosopher and theologian, another great alchemical luminary. "Tomaz" is Thomas Aquinas (1225–1274), yet another Catholic philosopher and theologian, who became a great authority for the alchemists. "Baqon" is Roger Bacon (1214?-1292), the English philosopher and scientist, who was also adopted by the alchemists as a great master of the art. By throwing out these illustrious names Zeraḥ invokes the most prestigious figures of alchemy, and demonstrates that he was indeed well acquainted with the standard literature on the subject. Moreover, by quoting a talmudic saying, which refers to ignoramuses as those who "cut reeds in the meadow," Zeraḥ shows himself to be at home in rabbinic literature as well, not a common accomplishment among Karaites. Interesting is the account Zeraḥ gives of the antecedents that led him to the study of alchemy: at first doubtful, when he read the treatise of Maimonides he became convinced that alchemy was a great science, whereupon he embarked on studying it to the point of becoming quite an expert in it.

In a later part of his *Sefer Elim* Delmedigo included a piece of writing by his disciple Moshe Metz that seems to be a response to the above epistle of Zeraḥ:

> You have also asked me to let you know some valuable things about the natural secrets and the operations of alchemy, which I learned from my master. And you asked me about the production of quicksilver out of Shabtai [Saturn, lead] and moon [silver], and about the transmutation of iron into *stal* [Ger. *Stahl*, steel] and into copper, and *ṣinfario* [cinnabar] into choice silver, and how to add color to gold, and weight to moon, and the freezing of KTB [?; probably *kesef ḥay*, quicksilver], and how to separate the metals that are mixed together, and how we can draw one of them to the periphery while the other should remain in the center, and how we can bring the precious metals, such as gold and silver, in vessels, when we first melt them to [the consistency of] oil and water, and how we can take them a long distance so that those who look should not notice them, and how to soften glass like wax in fire, and other things about the important medicaments which help severe diseases, such as to heal the cramp and the looseness and the epilepsy and the illnesses of the stone and the like, on which the members of the sect of Hermes pride themselves, and you dwelt at length on telling their praises according to what you tried, etc. My learned sir, the mastery of the secret is a wonderful thing and is useful, but it is not known in public, as if you would say: change saltwater into sweet, and keep

> gunpowder which, even if fire touched it, would not burn, and preserve wine so that it should not become sour, and lemon juice so that it should not become moldy, and make a very fragrant *borit* [soapwort or borax] which will shave the hair like a razor when one washes with it in water, and remove spots from all kinds of clothes, and other endless things which are unknown to the whole world, except to a few, and they are very effective, and if they were known to the masses they would be considered nothing, and he who would teach how to do them would be like him who teaches the cooking of meat with onions, of which Ben Roshd [Ibn Rushd, Averroes] wrote in his compendium. . . . I shall let you know this time of a secret writing kept hidden with me, from the Book of Bosmath, which deals with the strange disciplines . . . [Signed] Moshe Metz.[8]

The Book of Bosmath Bath Shlomo mentioned above is an unpublished encyclopedic work by Delmedigo.[9] The whole tenor of this letter shows that Moshe Metz, too, was thoroughly at home in the world of alchemy.

Simultaneously with the *Sefer Elim* was published part of Delmedigo's *Taʿalumot Ḥokhma* under the title *Maṣref la Ḥokhma* (Crucible of Wisdom).[10] In its chapter 7 he extols experimental science, especially alchemy, and deprecates abstract theoretical discussion. He writes (48–49):

> Hear, O wise artificers, this is not the straight path which you are following in the ways of research. The [true] natural science is to know how to create a creation or a formation, not to waste time in logical and philosophical discussions, and in building a thousand questions about the wings of ants as they wander about in movement. Your thoughts are totally empty, you err about the beginnings of materia and form, and [rehash] incidental chatter collected by idle priests whose books are heaps upon heaps of vain mockeries. Being engaged in them all day long with their disciples they appear to be able to answer every question, even if it be "terrible as an army with banners" [Cant. 6:4]. . . . But I do praise the inventors of definite works for the benefit of many, and the occupations of those who transmute metals, the sages among the philosophers of alchemy, who show manifestly the truth of their philosophizing, and likewise those [who work] in seafaring and in agriculture and in the devices of bringing water, and the like, who help the many in times of peace and times of war, for truly they are the accomplished sages who have invented marvels, and not the philosophers who write empty words. . . . For "let him who glorieth glory in this" [Jer. 9:23]—that he knows how to perform a superior thing of great qualities. Such a man alone can stand up before kings, and not he who asks great questions and scrutinizes words.

In the sequel Delmedigo recounts several fantastic stories known to him from talmudic and medieval Jewish sources about sages who allegedly "created" animals and human beings. He does this in order to show that, by the grace of God, and with serious application, man can indeed achieve marvelous things. The presentation of these stories by Delmedigo right after he gives a realistic appraisal of the value of technical inventions in agriculture, water supply, and the like affords a striking insight into the mind of this late-Renaissance figure: he is fully aware of the value of technology for the improvement of the human condition, but when it comes to stories transmitted by and about prestigious Jewish religious authorities (he quotes the Talmud, the *Sefer Y'ṣirah*, Saadia Gaon, Abraham ben David, Ibn Ezra, and so on) his attitude is one of unhesitating suspension of disbelief, even though these stories run counter to everything he knew as a student of medicine and the natural sciences. We have here the same phenomenon we encountered in looking at the personality of Ḥayyim Vital, who lived a generation before Delmedigo: a combination in one and the same mind of precision, realism, critical observation, and experimentation on the one hand, and unquestioning belief in magic, in spirits and demons, in mysterious powers and influences, on the other.

An additional remarkable feature in the case of Delmedigo is his derisive attitude toward what he calls the "chatter" of "idle priests," whom he leaves cautiously unidentified but whom he characterizes as wasting their time with discussions of "a thousand questions about the wings of ants." We would express the same idea by saying that they were discussing how many angels could dance on the head of a pin. As against this scornful view, Delmedigo praises "the occupations of those who transmute metals," in which he sees a particular manifestation of the truth of the alchemists' philosophy, of which, regrettably, he says nothing further. In any case, it appears from the quoted passage that although Delmedigo disdained purely theoretical discussions of minutiae, he did believe in the feasibility of transmutation. Clearly, he was a man of broad knowledge, a polyhistor and scientist, but at the same time a son of his age.

FOUR SEVENTEENTH-CENTURY MANUSCRIPTS

Berlin MS Orient. Oct. 514

One of the most valuable Hebrew alchemical manuscripts preserved in the Berlin Staatsbibliothek, was discussed in part in Chapter 8.[1] It consists of ninety folios, about 4 by 6 inches in size, written in a clear Sephardi hand, probably in the seventeenth century. From references contained in the text it is evident that the manuscript is a copy of an older one, in fact one so old that parts of it were no longer legible when it was copied. Thus on folio 62b, under the superscription, "This is another way of cleaning the pearl of *lazule* [I. or S., lapis lazuli]," the copyist begins his text as follows: "I did not find the thing explained, for the paper was erased, and I wrote what I was able to." And on the next page (f. 63a) he again writes: "What I shall write here, a little of it was erased in the copy of the paper due to the length of time, and I wrote what I found." In fact, on several pages (e.g., ff. 88a–90b) the copyist left empty spaces in the middle of lines, or even left several lines blank, evidently because he was unable to decipher the writing in the original. In addition, the beginning of the manuscript is missing, and the extant copy begins with folio 45a (numbered in Hebrew), which a later user has renumbered from 1 in Arabic numbers. The following discussion uses the more recent numeration.

The manuscript itself is an alchemical anthology, similar in intent and method to the larger contemporary Gaster manuscript found in the British Library (see below). At one point during the history of the manuscript one of the copyists (not necessarily the last one) added many supplementary notes of his own, explaining what he understood the intention of the author to have been, or supplying alternatives to the author's prescriptions, or else correcting him. Thus the manuscript as it stands is the product of at least two Hebrew-writing alchemists: the original author, and the copyist-editor. The additions are always introduced with the Hebrew abbreviation *n"l*, standing for the words *nir'eh li*, that is, "it seems to me . . ."; and they are either written into the text or placed on the margin.

The author quotes a great many authorities, some known, some unknown, some in a single sentence, others at great length. A listing of these references conveys an idea of the author's familiarity with the history of alchemy, and of the great variety of alchemical subjects he covers in his book.

On the first extant page (f. 1a) he writes: "And I have heard from MNSH [Menaseh?] that one needs the light of a candle. . . ." The manuscript contains no clue as to the identity of this MNSH. Also on folio 1a he writes: "In the Book of Seventy it says, the *borașe* [borax] with the iron is a secret." The *Book of Seventy* is one of the famous alchemical treatises attributed to Jābir ibn Ḥayyān. Still on the same page our author writes, "In the Book of Poisons it says that burnt iron and also burnt copper are deadly poisons." A *Book of Poisons* by Jābir is known and has been published in a German translation.[2]

On folio 1b the first item reads: "MAMYSQRT. Glass and frozen sulphur and *zarnikh* [arsenic] and *kokhav* [H., the planet Mercury, mercury]. . . ." It would be too hazardous to guess the identity of the alchemist referred to.

Folio 2b: "BYRRDO [Berardo?] told me: be careful about the salt, to prepare it so that it should melt like wax, for you will not succeed without it."

Folio 3b: "The philosophers said. . . ."

Folio 11a: "In the *Book of the Amendments of Yeber* [Jābir] it says: Pound well the whitened sulphur with the same amount of *nishdera* [A. *nushādir*, sal ammoniac].

Folio 11b: "A real act which GSPNP tried. . . ."[3]

Folio 13a: "Remember, and let not depart from your eyes that which is said in the *Book* QUPYRYTTE [?] and in the *Book of K"Ḥ* of the dissolution of the spirits. . . ." The letters *K"Ḥ* can stand for the number 28 or for *Kesef Ḥay*, quicksilver. Later in 13a is written: "Miriam [Maria the Jewess] said: 'Make copper white, and burn the books.' It seems to me because thereafter it will become yellow. . . ." No such saying of Maria the Jewess is known to me, but the style is definitely hers. The "It seems to me" note is the copyist's addition.

Folio 13b: "Said Yeber [Jābir] in this book, the *Book of the Moon*, which is Book thirty-eight of the seventy. . . . Said RYSKR [?]. . . . "The act of MAWRYLO [Aurelio?] who burned copper. . . ."

Folio 14a: "In the *Book of Succor* which is twenty-seven out of the seventy, it says. . . ."

Folio 16a: "In the book *The Treatise of Copper*, which is sixty-eight of the seventy, it says. . . ."

Folio 16b: "In Book thirty-eight of the seventy, which is similar to the Gate of Moses [?]. . . ."

Folio 17a: "On the compound salt which is called *sapon* [H., soap?]

of the sages, see in the *Book of Arqilus*. . . ." On the margin the words "King Solomon" are added.

Folios 19b–36a contain a Hebrew version of the famous *Book of Alums and Salts*, which we discussed in Chapter 8.

Folio 36a has a new title in the middle: "Flowers of Explanations of the Wise Men, which I sealed [in the sense of copied?] from those books with the help of God." On the same folio there is a quotation, "Said Hermos," that is, Hermes.

Folio 36b quotes "other people. . . ."

Folio 42a again quotes Yeber ben Ḥayyan, that is, Jābir ibn Ḥayyān.

Folio 46b carries a title "from a Latin book," and quotes Aristotle.

Folio 47a: "From the mouth of MSH [Messer?] Rinaldo of Villa Nova: To make sun [gold] and its water, and in the language of the *goyim* [gentiles] *ana* [read *aqua*] *solis* [L., water of the sun]." Arnaldus de Villanova (1245–1313) was one of the most famous medieval alchemists.

Folios 48a–b contain quotations from a *Book of Elim*.[4]

Folio 52a is identified on the margin as being "From the Hindī [Indian language] of Rabbi Y'udah," and it contains the description of an operation performed by "the Hindī" and instructions given by the same "Hindī," both pertaining to the making of what is called "Venetian gold."

Folios 52b–54a: "From Ḥajjī Aḥmed. . . . From Shaykh Nūr al-Dīn. . . . From Sultan BAZYT [Bayazit?]. . . . From an Arab Shaykh. . . ."

Folio 85b prescribes the use of *ḥammam Miryam* [A. *ḥammām M.*] that is, the bath of Maria, the well-known water-bath whose invention, as we have seen in Chapter 5, was attributed to Maria the Jewess.

The Hebrew of the manuscript is typical of the language used by most medieval and Renaissance Hebrew-writing alchemists. Many of them were guilty of lapses in observing the rules of Hebrew grammar, which require that adjectives, pronouns, and verbs conform in number and gender to the noun to which they refer. Instead, they (and our manuscript among them) often use a masculine verb, pronoun, or adjective with a feminine noun, or a singular verb, pronoun, or adjective with a plural noun. For instance, in the paragraph I quote below, the Hebrew text has *n'ḥoshet adom* (red copper), where grammar would require *n'ḥoshet adumah*, and *haz'khukhit yehafekh* (the glass will become), where correctly it should be *haz'khukhit tehafekh*. And, as we have often seen before, the limitations in the Hebrew technical vocabulary lead these writers simply to transliterate in Hebrew characters the foreign terms familiar to them. In the following example, taken from folio 85b of our manuscript, the italicized words are all Arabic.

Usrub aḥmar [red lead]. Put in the bottom of the melting-pot five *dirhams* [drachmas] of *mashūq* [ground] glass, and upon it five *dirhams* of *rasukht mashūq* [ground antimony], and on it one *ṣaḥīfa* [leaf] of lead—4 *dirhams*, and on it five *dirhams* of *rasukht*, and on it five *dirhams* of glass, and lute the mouth of the pot, and dry it, and put in into fire with bellows, and the *zuhal* [Saturn, lead] should melt like red copper. This is *usrub aḥmar*, and the glass will become like *marjān* [pearl].

Evidently, such an alchemical recipe was useful only for a Jewish alchemist who knew both Hebrew and Arabic. In an interesting passage (f. 39b) our author explains how he proceeded in translating Arabic and Italian alchemical terms into Hebrew:

It seems to me [necessary] to include this rule for you: In every book which I translated, in every place where you find the expression *taasᶜūd* [A. *taṣᶜūd*, or *taṣᶜīd*, distillation], then it is with dry *solimare* [I., to sublimate]. And thus *haᶜala'ah* [H., sublimation] is also *solimare.* But if you find *tasᶜud* or *haᶜala'ah* in the wet, then he wants to say *destilare* [I., to distill] in fire, without the means of ashes and water. And where [you find] the expression *dilluf* [H., dripping], it is *destilare*, that is, as they make rosewater.

The Hebrew style is not very smooth, but the meaning is clear.

In this connection it should be stated that roughly until the middle of the manuscript the author used mostly European (Italian or Spanish) sources, and that accordingly most of the foreign words he uses are Italian or Spanish; often it is difficult to establish which of the two was the original language reproduced. From the middle of the manuscript on, the author relied primarily on Arabic sources, and consequently almost all the foreign words he uses are Arabic.

Now for a few examples from the manuscript. First a very simple and brief prescription:

(f. 4a) Philosophers' clay. Very important. Take ashes and sift them through a cloth. And take salt, and dissolve it in water, and knead it with the ashes, and dry it in the sun. Do this three times. Then grind it in a vessel, and when you want to remove it, soak a cloth and moisten the clay in the vessel, and cleanse it, and when you need it for luting, knead it with the water of the salt.

The next one is interesting because of the limitation it imposes on its dissemination; it has a marginal note: "I found this in a book."

(f.12b) THIS operation is called the Messiah of the Righteous, and it is forbidden to give it to the ignorant. Take smooth green sulphur and quicksilver, and mix them together, and grind them well, and cook them together with rosewater at night in a glass vessel, and the fire should be gentle, and the vessel should be sealed on top, and in the morning take it out and grind it and mix it with strong vinegar, and then return it to the vessel as it was. Do thus six times until the quicksilver dies. Then take these powders and grind them and distill them in a distillation, and of twelve ounces three ounces will remain. Then take one part of *sal armoniaqe* [sal ammoniac] and one part of saffron of iron and *ʿubr* [A., eagle, sal ammoniac], and one part of linseed oil, and grind it all and mix it with what you obtained from the distillation, and grind and mix it well, and put these powders into a new glass flask, and put it into a pit full of dung, and cover it well for seven days, and at the end of the seven days you will find in the flask something like a piece of metal, and make a powder and take the metal, whatever it will be, and heat it and put [some] of this powder on top and [word illegible] it, and then take of lead one part, and cut it up and throw its powder upon two parts of quicksilver, and when you see the smoke from the quicksilver rising, throw on it [some] of this powder, and take of this mixed quicksilver one part, and one part of gold, and mix them together, and it will color it to gold which will be good for all tests, and try it. And he who understands from this will be right, and will live to the end of days.

The only question in connection with this is a run-of-the-mill alchemical prescription is why it should be given such an extravagant name as "Messiah of the Righteous."

(f. 13b) SAID RYSKR: Combine the spirit with the soul and dissolve the strong body—it seems to me: *qroqo di ferro* [I. *croco di ferro*, iron oxide] or any one of the bodies—and mix it with them, and it will restrain it and conquer it. Or put the soul into the body and then put the spirit. Or dissolve both of them and mix them and freeze them.

OIL of sulphur, purified, transmutes burnt copper into gold.

IT HAPPENED to Maurilo [or: Aurilo] that he burned *nogah* [H., Venus, copper] in the same amount of yellow live sulphur—it seems to me arsenic is better—and he washed it in water and salt and *alume* [alum], and it became white. I heard that if you mix with it *sal niṭri* [sodium nitrate], that is to say with the *nogah*, it will make it white.

(f. 15a) IN THE NAME OF GOD IT WILL BE. AMEN

THANKS TO Him who graces with knowledge, Who is the first and the last, etc. The performance of the *kīmīyah* [alchemy] of which the philosophers have said: He who observes my commandments will attain that which he desires. And if he does otherwise, he will err. And let him begin when the sun is in Aries at its height, without fault. And likewise he says: If you do it, it is necessary that the moon should be in Taurus. Take the herb called *moltobona rizinate*[?] without any other thing. And thin it in *viminie*[?], and wash it well, and put it in a pot without water. And put this *ququrbita*

[I. *cucurbita*, currurbit, gourd-shaped flask] in another pot in which there should be water with ashes, and mix this with gentle fire, and do it until the oil that comes out is red. Then make a strong fire under it. And the water which you will find in the pot, which has come out of the stone, put it aside in a glass vessel. And do thus with the oil, and preserve it in another place in *al-roṭībah* [A. *ruṭubah*, moisture]. And on this throw fire. And when all the water and the oil comes out, and the sediment remains in the pot dry and black, preserve them separately. Then take the water and filter it up to three times. And put that pot into a pot in which there should be ashes without water. Then turn it around and grind it well with its water in a glass *ṭablah* [A., bucket]. And preserve it in a covered glass vessel. And put on it enough of that water so that it should cover it [by] two fingers. And seal the cover well. And bury it in soft and warm dung. And the cover should stand above it, and leave it there fourteen days. And every four days change the manure, and on the fifteenth day take it out and filter the water and preserve it. And put the stone into an *anpulah* [I., ampulla] of glass, in the sun. And seal its mouth and dry it. And then grind it with water. And put it in a glazed vessel covered with clay on all sides. But its mouth should be open. And make a gentle fire under it for six hours. Again grind it well and drench it with the abovementioned water until it becomes soft. Then put it in a glass vessel and bake it on the fire for twelve days, and thus it will become white. And then take the oil and add to it three parts of urine from a twelve-year-old boy, and mix it well together, and let it stand in the pot, and leave it, and it will become very red. And keep the red and throw away the rest. Then put it into that pot, and put it once more into very warm dung, and it will be white. And that which is in the pot will be red. And preserve it wisely in a glass vessel well covered. And this is the root upon which the philosophers relied and in which they trusted. The red is a medicine for the sun [gold], and the white for the moon [silver]. Put one part of it on a thousand and nine hundred of Mercury. And if you wish to make it more pure, put it on a thousand and three hundred. And if you don't have Mercury put it on Mars [iron], one ounce on nine hundred (f. 16a), and I believe that this is the same for Sun and Moon. And the artist Yeber ben Ḥayyan said that he took of the mentioned thing the weight of one *garah* [carat?] and put it on ground *qristalo* [crystal] of four dinars, and melted it, and out came wonderful *yaqut* [ruby or sapphire].

(f. 49a) [On the margin: From Ḥajji Muṣṭafa.] Take ten *dra* [drachmas] *ṭuṭia* [A., tutty, zinc oxide], ten *drachmas zībak* [A., mercury], and put the tutty to melt, and put in it *ʿabd* [A., slave, quicksilver], and make a *malgama* [A., amalgam], and put into it five *drachmas* of sublimated *zīrnīkh* [A., *zarnīkh*, arsenic, realgar, auripigment], and five *drachmas* of white purified *sījān* [?] and thirty *drachmas* of purified good *burada ḥadīd*

[A., filings of iron], and thirty *drachmas* of copper leaves like *fārah* [?] and knead them with egg white, and put them into two copper bowls, and lute them well, and put them into dung, and make over it a fire like that for maintaining *zīnjīfra* [cinnabar], and remove it from the *dims* [container], and put it into a melting pot and melt them in sesame oil. If it comes out *taqlīs* [A. *taklīs*, calcination], put into it the same amount of copper, and mix it with whatever you want.

(f. 50b) THIS IS HOW one extracts oil from egg yolks. Take the yolks after they have been cooked, and put them into a flask, all well luted, and seal its mouth with [word missing], and put it in an earthenware bowl in the bottom of which there is a hole for the neck of the flask to go through, and place (f. 51a) the bowl upon an *istrivade* [?] and put the receiver under it, and put the flask with its mouth downward so that it should go through the hole of the bowl, and lute the hole of the bowl around the neck of the flask, and when it has dried put into the bowl ashes up to four fingers, and on the ashes make fire around the flask at a distance of one or two fingers, little by little, and from the heat of the fire the oil will descend from what it is into the receiver, and this is its sketch [see Figure 33.1, top]. And this is called *istanzal* [A., receiver]. And there is a thing that needs stronger fire, and they make [for it] the *istanzal* in a bowl and in a flask even more luted, and they put another bowl as a lid on top of the bowl, and the flask sits wholly in the ashes, and they make the fire on top of the bowl which is the lid, and from its heat whatever has to descend will descend into the receiver. And this is its sketch [Figure 33.1, bottom].

(f. 51b) OIL of scorpio [sulphur]. Take seven small flasks that can stand the fire, and fill them with ground scorpio, and lute them well, and let the clay dry, and put on it more clay, and let it dry, and put on it more clay, so that it should be luted three times, so that it should be thick, and dry it well, and make a long pit in which there should be room for the seven flasks, and the flasks should be at a distance of about a span from one another, and take sand and cover them lightly, and put under them sand four fingers [deep], and upon that sand put the flasks at the distance stated, and fill the whole hole with the aforementioned sand, until full, and it should extend above the flasks four fingers, and the pit should be well filled, and make on it a fire with cattle dung until it becomes ashes, and when it cools press the ashes well with your two hands, and then make a great wood fire on the ashes for about four hours, and when it cools open the sand. If you find one flask whole, it should be enough for you.

(f. 52a) [On the margin: From the Hindī of R. Y'udah.] OIL of sulphur. Take four drachmas of ʿ*uqāb* [A., eagle, sal ammoniac] and grind it and put it in a flask by itself, and sublimate it, and take of what was sublimated three drachmas and grind, and grind four drachmas of green sulphur, and

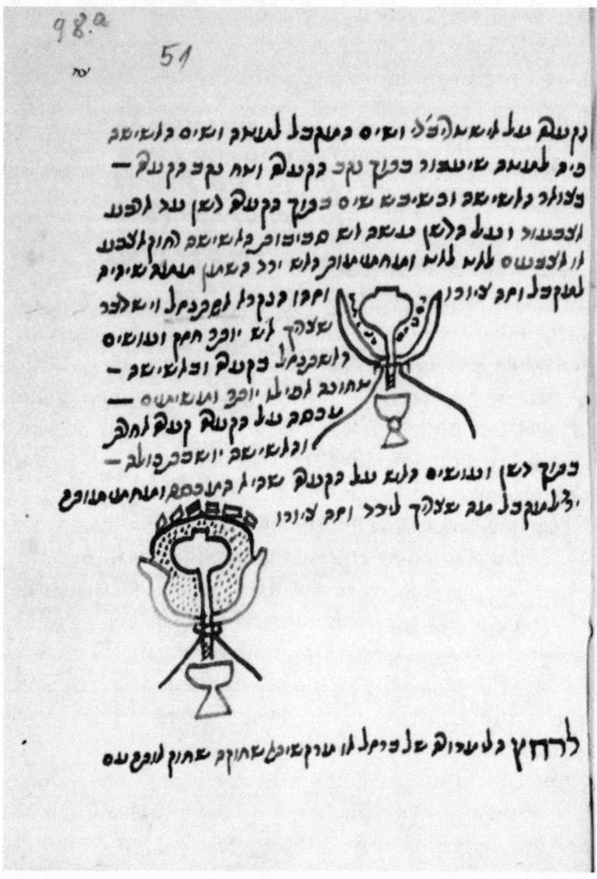

Figure 33.1. Two sketches of *istanzals* (receivers), that is, stills.

grind one drachma and *saf* [A. *sāf*, pebbles], and grind one drachma of *nishisti* [?], and grind twenty-five drachmas of live lime, and mix all the ground substances and put them in a *storta* [I., retort], which is a crooked flask, and put the retort into sifted ashes in an earthenware pot which is well luted, into the oven, and put under it middling coal fire, and let it sit until white smoke rises from its mouth and you see that red comes from its mouth into the receiver, and then oil-like drops, and green smoke. When there is in the receiver about twenty or fifteen drachmas, remove it from the fire and preserve the oil. And then the Hindu took about twenty drachmas of *nogah* [H., Venus, copper], and made of it a thin leaf, and melted it and made of it a thin leaf, and melted it and made of it a thin leaf, up to three times, and he melted it and threw upon it, while it was in the melting pot, three drops of the oil, and threw it in a *verga* [?], and put the *verga* next to the fire, and it became whole sun [gold]. And the Hindu also said that this sun is not whole, for it lasts [only] up to twenty years and then it returns to its root. And then he took a golden quart [a coin], and made it thin as the goldsmiths do, and put it in the melting pot, and when it was close to melting he threw into it three drops of the mentioned oil, and it all became (f. 52b) like ashes, and he preserved it. Then he took twenty drachmas of *zuharah* [A., Venus, copper], and melted it once by itself, and took of the mentioned ashes and threw into it what the head of the *ilal* [?] could stand, and threw it into a *verga*, and out came Venetian gold, and he gilded with it a ring of *ariento* [?].

(f. 63a) TAKE three red beans of the kind that is called the white bean, on those which there are with all kinds of eyes, and big and bright, and put them into a flask, and fill the flask with donkey's blood, and seal the mouth of the flask well, and let it sit, and it will produce kinds of worms, and one will eat the other, and at the end only one big one will remain, and when it grows put it into another flask, and beware lest it bite you for it is a kind of viper, and give it donkey's blood to eat, and when you see that it has become big let it starve two days, do not give it blood, so that its strength should diminish, and take sharp scissors and cut off its head, and take its blood and dry and preserve it, and put one drop with any metal you wish and it will become sun [gold].

(f. 69b) PHILOSOPHERS' CLAY. [Take] glass, if you can, the known iron, in equal amounts, grind them well and knead them with the blood of a sheep, and it will become good clay. There is nothing better than this.

(f. 70a) When you want to operate with spirits and souls, such as *zarnīkh* [arsenic] or scorpio [sulphur], you must thin it in this manner: cook it on gentle fire with sesame oil, but at first one must pound it with *qalia* [kali] salt, and at the cooking when the oil becomes black remove it and wash that which is cooked with *qalia* water, and cook it with new oil. Do this until it becomes white.

Know that if you cook the spirits or the souls with oil to purify them, if you must purify them of the oil there is no other way except that you cook it with lemon water, and with nothing else.

This last example from the manuscript shows that the author was well aware of the dangerous nature of some of the experiments he describes:

(f. 79b) To make *mā zarīn*. Grind *bārūd* [A., saltpeter]—two, *ʿuqāb* sal ammoniac—one, and put them in a bowl, and make a pit at the bottom of the oven, and in that pit make coal fire, and fasten the *īnbīq* [A., alembic], and have the receiver not luted, and when you see that the likeness of a white cloud rises, quickly put an iron cover over the pit, and put on the *anbīq* [alembic] the edge of a leaf, and you should stand afar, and you will see that the receiver becomes full of white cloud like cotton-wool. And when no whiteness is left in the alembic, strengthen the luting of the alembic, and seal the alembic with the receiver, and then remove the iron cover which is over the fire, and from time to time strengthen the fire until it becomes flames, and you will see that the cloud which is in the receiver will shrink into the bottom of the receiver and will go down like oil into the receiver. And when it ceases, remove it and keep it. And if you put sun [gold] into it it will become water and will go over into the receiver. And when you have distilled it three times the gold at the bottom will remain dust.

Berlin MS Orient. Qu. 543

The three pages of another Hebrew manuscript in the Berlin Staatsbibliothek[5] written by an anonymous alchemist present a summary of the alchemists' philosophy, the Jewish alchemists' claim to be the only true heirs of the ancient and secret alchemical knowledge, the alchemical worldview of the nature and properties of the four elements, and the most sublime goal of all alchemical endeavor: the production of the elixir of life. It is written in beautiful Yevanic Mashait script, probably in the seventeenth century, and its author had a fine command of Hebrew.

Listen to me my sons and lend me your ears. I shall reveal to you the secrets of the science hidden by the philosophers, and I shall reveal secrets, transgressing the commands of my teacher, for I considered it wrong to withhold what is good from those who should possess it, so that this science should not become lost but should belong to him whose heart moves him to approach it, to the man who raises the candle of science over his head and protects it and surrounds it. He will find it, and take it into his heart, and will be able to translate these hidden things from theory into practice, will draw water from a deep well, and after having reached the heights of science he will find what he desires, and will be proud of it, and will show the fools and the ignorant who have seen no light the hidden things which one must reveal only to a single adept, [otherwise] it would be better had he been an abortion and never seen the light of day, for this secret is so great that the ancient ones ceased to search for it and could never attain it, for the first ones hid it deeply and wrote their words in hints, and after them no man possessed enough spirit to reach it, because of its depth. And this science is a gift of God, and no man can achieve it except with an elevated spirit and a pure heart which God, blessed be he, has filled with wisdom and understanding to know all works.

And this science no man can deny, because it is true, for the false scholars did not study it well enough and did not learn its true meaning, so that their words are worthless, for they did not understand the words of the great scholar Aristotle. But we, the young ones of the flock, have followed the footsteps of the great wise men, and we exerted ourselves until we grasped the meaning of the great philosopher, and until no doubt was left with us. And in this science we found things whose wonders of wonders the eye will not be satisfied seeing and the ear hearing. Blessed is he who knows the thing whose value no man has known, and happy is the woman-born who attained it.

And now my son I shall open to you the gates of wisdom, I shall reveal a little and conceal twice as much, and you will understand its depth in a blessed hour, and will draw water in joy, and will extract the elements as you know how, and put each element separately, and guard it from the air.

Thus far the words of our author present no difficulties. What follows is more problematic, because while ostensibly he speaks of the four elements, what he actually discusses are four quasi-miraculous medicaments he terms water, oil (which he equates with air), fire, and dust. Moreover, after arousing the reader's curiosity by asserting that he is the heir of great and secret ancient wisdom which he will divulge to the son whom he addresses, he fails to fulfil the promise, and all he does is to state that there exist these miraculous elixirs, and to describe in considerable detail their medical use, but he says almost nothing about the manner of their preparation, except for the last one, that made of earth ("dust").

THE WATER is useful for all illnesses, both the cold ones and the hot ones, because it is hidden in its nature, and is very helpful for him who has stabbing pain in the chest, and it removes poison from the heart, and moistens the nerves and strengthens them, and revives them. All illnesses that affect the lungs, such as thick wetness [phlegm] which sticks to them, and weakness, and damage, it cleanses it and heals it. It also cleanses worn-out blood and its rancid wetness, and after the natural purification it guards it so that it should not come to a weakening of the breathing vessels. And a person who has suffered his illness for a long time and his nature has given out, if he can manage to drink of it three or four times, you will see its effect, and there is hope.

THE OIL is the air, and it helps the sucklings and establishes them in health and beauty, and keeps them from illnesses all the days of their lives, and delays old age. And he who takes of it should take a small amount in soup. And the reason is that it preserves the blood in its health, and also the white humor so that it should not become dominant over the blood, and it subdues the black humor so that it should not dominate the nature [of the body]. And it preserves the red humor so that it should not burn and should not produce sediments. And it increases the blood and the semen, and because of this those who are accustomed to take the water and the oil must undergo blood-letting at certain times, and cleanse the body, according to the advice of the experts of medicine. And this oil opens the obstructions of the sinews and nerves, and if a limb has denegerated it heals it and returns it to its nature. And this is tried. If a person, while he is growing up, until the age of twenty, has lost the sight of one eye or of two eyes, let him put one drop of this oil into the eye every day, and let him refrain from all work, and let him rest up to one month. Moreover, if a limb seems to become weakened due to excess of exertion, this will heal it by the power of its effect.

THE FIRE is wonderful in producing great effects, for it helps all kinds of . . . diseases, like the oil, and more so. Its effect is to make the old young because it cleanses his nature, and makes him rejoice, and returns him to the days of his youth. But do not imagine that it can resuscitate the dead, for that key has not been delivered into the hands of any man, only the Creator of All alone has the dominion. But he who lies on a bed of suffering and is near death, give him one drop to drink: it will enter the chambers of the heart, will make him rejoice, and return him to health, and it expels the poison from the heart quickly, and it dispels and removes all the bad humors, and it revives the nature and returns it to its proper state. And if old men get used to taking this oil at the proper time, and drink of the abovementioned water one sip, it removes all the illnesses of old age, such as belching, and yawning, and weakness of digestion, and the flowing of urine, and the shattering of [word illegible], at times they are constipated, and at times suffer looseness of the bowels, and eczema, and halitosis. . . . And this is why it is called *elixir vitae*, for just as leaven is good for dough so this elixir is good for the body, for it makes it healthy and establishes nature on a healthy basis.

AND THE DUST too has wonderful qualities, if you prepare it and make it into lime, and dissolve it in burnt water, and distill it in a *pito* [?] and then congeal it, it will become like salt, and this is how you should do it: sublimate it in the alembic, and what remains in the bottom of the alembic is the salt. And this salt can congeal the quicksilver, so that it becomes another body and no longer becomes sublimated in fire. And the water that you have sublimated through the alembic will congeal all the other spirits, and make them resist fire. And if you take fire [probably: the salt] and dissolve it in burnt water the water will become red, and put the quicksilver which is *fiqs* [I., fixed] in the water upon small fire, then the quicksilver will instantly dissolve in the water, and when it is dissolved mix into it one-third of the water of the *su'l* [?], on weak fire, and everything will instantly become one body. And then put into it a little alum, then it will become hard and become a red stone. And this stone, if you wish to prepare it, treat it with *mercurios* [mercury] oil, and it will become elixir for the quicksilver, and one part of it on a thousand of quicksilver.

Having finished discussing the four elements (or, rather, the elixirs he calls by their names), our author switches to a new theme, and without any introduction or explanation begins to talk about a herb as if the reader would be familiar with it from a previous discussion. Nor does he say anything that would enable the reader to identify the herb, or to know how to go about finding it. Yet that herb is the supreme elixir of life, and it appears that everything he said earlier was merely an introduction to his presentation of this essential medico-alchemical substance.[6]

> BEND your ear and understand that this is the manner in which you can find this herb any time. And let your clothes be white, for the ancient ones did not want to reveal this work, except for the remnants whom God calls the Faithful of the Spirit. And this herb gives love and brotherliness to him who knows it, and its ashes are beloved and dear . . . and it makes the heart rejoice, and encourages it to be victorious over everybody who opposes him, and he will not retreat from anybody. And there are those among the adepts who do not know how to separate the four elements, and they put this herb together with its flower into burnt water which was sprinkled twelve times in its known vessels, and that water extracts the nature of the herb, and the water becomes red. Collect of that water about as much as a whole hazel, and give it to him to drink every morning with wine. And all the philosophers have agreed that this water helps all illnesses, and if you take a *magneta* [I. *magnete*, magnet] stone, and wrap it in this herb with this flower, and put it in a clean white cloth, and carry it with you, you will be liked and favored by kings and great men, and all those who rise up against you will not succeed and will flee from you, all spirits, and demons and harmful beings. And nobody was able to find a wisdom such as this anywhere in the earth or the seas, for it is the beginning of the medicine of the philosophers and the chief crown of all wisdom, for the person who knows it is transformed by it into another person, adorned with rows of gold adornments, and all those who see him will recognize him, and it gives him dominion, dignity, and respect, and raises him above all things. And it assures the healthy body of its health, lest any bad thing happen to it, and he will dwell in the dwelling of peace. And if the illness is renewed, it will heal him in one day, and if it has persisted for a year it will heal him in twelve days, and if it is an old illness it will heal him in one month. And therefore this medicine has to be sought above all others, for its effect is greater than that of all other medicaments produced by the wise researchers.

In the concluding part of the treatise, the author introduces yet another magic elixir, that of "gold water." The search for the aurum potabile, drinkable gold, has been a favorite preoccupation of alchemists throughout the ages, but our author speaks of it as if it were a known medicine, of which he had a supply in his possession, and on whose preparation he does not have to waste a single word.

> And now I shall reveal to you the secrets of gold water. And one has to know that he who takes of it is cured of all the illnesses that are in the body, even absolute leprosy. And it gives the barren woman pregnancy, and strengthens the nature of him who is impotent, and raises his rod, and it protects all bodies from all internal and external diseases, and it cleans all the spots and maculae from all faces. And it helps the darkening of the eyesight, and strengthens the nature, and protects the health, and he who takes it regularly will rejoice and be happy forever, and the skin of his face will not change, and his juice will not dry up, but he will remain in his beauty all his days, and it helps jaundice, and removes all the bad humors from the heart, and it protects the body against poison. And since water is purer and lighter and more convenient to enter into all the limbs of the body than powder, we made this compound. And happy is he who understands and knows it, and happy is she who gave birth to him. After all, God is merciful.
>
> The spirit of wisdom and understanding
> Finished and completed

The last six lines of the page contain a prescription given in the name of "Maester Arnalo Devila Nova" (Arnaldo de Villanova) recommending a medicament composed of a mixture of herbs, goat's milk, and rose water, with the addition of "sixty or seventy gold leaves." Since Villanova—one of the most famous names in the annals of alchemy—lived from 1245 to 1313, the manuscript discussed above could not have been written earlier than in the beginning of the fourteenth century. But its style and the terminology employed (including the absence of Arabic terms), in addition to the script, point to a seventeenth-century origin, possibly in Italy.

The Gaster Manuscript

A major seventeenth-century Hebrew alchemical manuscript was acquired by Moses Gaster (1856–1939), rabbi of the English Sephardi community, Zionist leader, and pioneer in Jewish folklore studies. In his article on "Alchemy" in the *Jewish Encyclopaedia*, Gaster called it "an important manuscript" and "as complete a *bibliotheca alchemica Judaica* as one could desire."[7]

The manuscript, evidently a copy of an older one, was written in 1690. It contains 173 folios and consists of two parts: the first deals mostly with the early Greek-Arab period, the second with the Latin world. It begins with a note about the "moon" (silver), and recipes for making gold and transmuting copper into silver (f. 2a–b). This is followed by a recipe for transmuting tin into "moon and sun" (silver and gold). Throughout, arsenic, alkali, *zag* (A. *zāj*, vitriol), mercury, tin, lead and *metal* (S., brass) figure prominently (ff. 2b–9b).

Next comes the full text of the treatise of "Ibn Aflaḥ" (= Abufalaḥ) of Syracuse (ff. 3a–21a), presented above in Chapter 7 from an older manuscript. Several subsequent excerpts are stated to be "without a name"(ff. 21b, 23b, 24b). In between are recipes for making gold and silver out of base metals (ff. 14a–15a), and for "adding to the weight of the sun," that is, multiplying gold (f. 15b). Folio 23a contains an excerpt "from the Book of Yoḥanan Asprmantt," which name, despite Gaster's guess, cannot be satisfactorily identified. On folio 25a begins the *Book of Astutah* (or *Astuto*), which name, as Gaster suspects, is probably a corruption of Ostanes, the famous ancient alchemist.[8] On folio 45a is found a drawing of an alembic.

Book Two (ff. 45a–52b) is ascribed to Aliberto Manyo, that is Albertus Magnus (c. 1206–1280), the German Scholastic philosopher and theologian, sainted by the Church, who wrote extensively on a great variety of subjects, and to whom alchemical writings were attributed.[9] Folio 2a contains instructions for the preparation of *luna* (moon, silver) out of arsenic, *sid luna* (H.-L. "lime of silver"), etc., ground and mixed with water of sal ammoniac.

Book Three (ff. 53b–58b) is stated to be "The Book of Spiros," whom I am not able to identify. He is quoted as having "performed great works," including the preparation of the elixir. In this book (Pseudo-)Democritus and "Arquitinus" are quoted, and several recipes are given for making gold and silver.

Book Four (ff. 58b–64a) is "The Book of the Shining Star," which again starts with recipes for the transmutation of "metals into sun and moon."

Book Five (ff. 64a–70a) is "The Book of Aristotle." It discusses the use of vitriol, tutty, alum, Saturn (lead), the urine of boys under twelve years of age, red water, white water, and "white philosophers' oil."

Book Six (ff. 70a–76a) is "The Book of Yeber," that is, Jābir ibn Ḥayyān. This book discusses orpiment, atramento (black dye), elixir, and the alchemical use of salts. It includes a "Book of the Great Stone" as well as a discussion of the *supostorio* (*suppositorio*?), arsenic, and so on.

Book Seven (ff. 76a–78b) is "The Book of Arcturus."

Book Eight (ff. 78b–82a) is "The Book of Arkhilus [Archelaos]," who seems to have been a Byzantine alchemist. Ruska identifies him with Archelaos of Miletus, the pupil of Anaxagoras,[10] who is referred to several times in alchemical treatises. This book also mentions the process of *qagular* (*coagulare*, to coagulate).

Book Nine (ff. 82b–90a) is "The Book of Light," a name resembling those borne by many alchemical books, including the *Liber lucis* of John de Rupescissa, the well-known fourteenth-century alchemist.[11] Among the items discussed in it are antimony, tutty, DRGNT (*dargent*, silver?), salt, gold, silver, lead, sulphur, asphalt, cinnabar, copper, balsam, other substances, and a method for solidifying mercury.

Book Ten (ff. 90b–94a) is entitled "The Book of Maestro Irimans of Qostantina" who, perhaps, is none other than Morienus (variants: Marianus, Morienes), the Byzantine (Qostantina = Constantinople = Byzantium) monk, the legendary teacher in alchemy of the Umayyad prince Khālid ibn Yazīd (see Chapter 9.) To Marianus is attributed the treatise *Sermo de transmutatione metallorum.*[12]

Book Eleven (ff. 94a–97a) is entitled "The Book of the Thirty Paths," which could refer to a part or parts of Jābir ibn Ḥayyān's well-known "Book of Seventy." Following a brief presentation of the thirty paths, we again learn of orpiment, and then of sulphur.

Book Twelve (ff. 97a–103a) is "The Book of Avi Sina," that is, Ibn Sīnā, known in the West as Avicenna (980–1037). Although Ibn Sīnā was in fact rather critical of alchemists—he argued that the transmutation of base metals into gold was merely a matter of appearances, while the substance of the base metals remained unchanged—he was nevertheless adopted into the alchemical canon, and a fourteenth-century Latin practical alchemical treatise bears his name.[13] This book also discusses the use of borax, alums, and stones.

Book Thirteen (ff. 103b–115a) is "The Book of Razes." Razes (or Rhazes, Muḥammad ibn Zakariyya al-Rāzī (c. 854–c. 925), was a great Persian physician who practiced in Baghdad, and whose writings were for centuries required reading for medical students in both the Muslim world and Europe. No less influential in alchemy was his *Kitāb al-Asrār* (Book of Secrets).[14] This book in the Gaster manuscript contains instructions concerning sal ammoniac, orpiment, how to calcinate; it mentions ḤRMS (probably Hermes), cadmium, marcasite, and gold making.

Book Fourteen (ff. 115b–118a) is "The Book of Plato." Alchemical works written by, or attributed to, Hermes, Plato, Jābir ibn Ḥayyān, Ibn Sīnā, and Rāzī are standards in the literature of alchemy.

This part of the manuscript concludes with a valuable glossary of Arabic and Greek words, which awaits study by a linguist at home in those two languages.

On folio 118a begins the second part, called "Kolel Sheni," or Second Collection, which contains excerpts in Hebrew from the writings of Christian European alchemists. In this part, Italian terms in Hebrew transliteration appear frequently. It includes (f. 119b) excerpts from Mestre Arnaldus, that is Maestro Arnaldus de Villanova (c. 1300), the famous alchemist, many of whose works have been translated into Hebrew.[15]

This is followed by a quote from Ioane Ashkenazi (ff. 121b–122b), which name, Gaster suspects, could be a Hebrew translation of "Teutonicus," originally "Theodonicus" or "Theotonicus," mentioned by Berthelot.[16] Then we learn of purgation (f. 121b), following which comes a reference to "the well-known man" (f. 123a), and several mentions of fixation (ff. 123a, 123b, 125a). Next comes "the work according to Messer Piero Dabano" (ff. 125a–b), who is Petrus Bonus or Pietro Antonio Boni, the author of *Margarita pretiosa*.[17] This is followed by short recipe-extracts from several alchemical authors: Niccolo di Ingliterra (ff. 125b–126b), Mestero Ermano de Normandia (f. 126b), Messer Andrea di Napoli (ff. 127a–130a), Jacopo da Venesia (f. 127b), Bartolomeo d'Altenpio (f. 129a), and Giaspare (Gaspare) di Bologna (f. 130b).

These excerpts are interrupted by a long recipe entitled "Operation According to the Abifior della Luna" (ff. 130b–131a). "Abifior" (in correct Hebrew spelling *apifiyor*) means "pope," and "Pope della Luna" could perhaps refer to the anti-pope Benedict XII (pontificated 1334–1342), born Pedro de Luna, of a noble family of Aragon.[18]

On folios 131b–133a there is a long discussion (all superscribed "Abifior,") based on the sayings of "ancient philosophers" about the correspondence between mercury in metals and the soul in the human body, which is translated below. These quotations are several times stated to be taken from the *Turba philosophorum* (Philosophers' Assembly), one of the most famous medieval collections of alchemical discussions. The Gaster manuscript quotes many philosophers by name (transcribed in Hebrew as Pramenidas, Mugais, Furnias, Filipelino, Magrines, Mariares, Morienus, Astamus, Artabanus), of whom only a few can be identified with the names actually appearing in the *Turba*.[19]

Now follow references to more alchemists: "Cristoforo of Abolonia who operated in our house" (f. 133b), Messer Joane Botrio (ff. 133b–134a), Frati Elia (ff. 134b–135a), Messer Simone (f. 135b), "Nico who made a white suit of clothes" (ff. 135b–136a), Gulielmo da Monte Polaseno (f. 136a), and an instruction "according to the Romito who speaks of *particulare*" (ff. 136b–137a).

This part of the manuscript concludes on folio 137b with the following colophon (in Hebrew): "Finished and completed are the books of alchemy, today, the 25th of Ṭeveth, in the year "*matay* (when) will the Redeemer come." The letters of the word *matay*, which stands for the year, have the numerical value of 40, 400, 10, or a total of 450, which corresponds to the civil year 1690. The copyist added: "As I merited to copy all of it, so may I merit to reach the light [i.e., the Messiah] which we await every day."

The conclusion of the text (ff. 138a–140b) is followed by drawings of alchemical vessels (alembics, retorts, furnaces, etc.) with Hebrew explanations (see Figures 33.2–33.7).

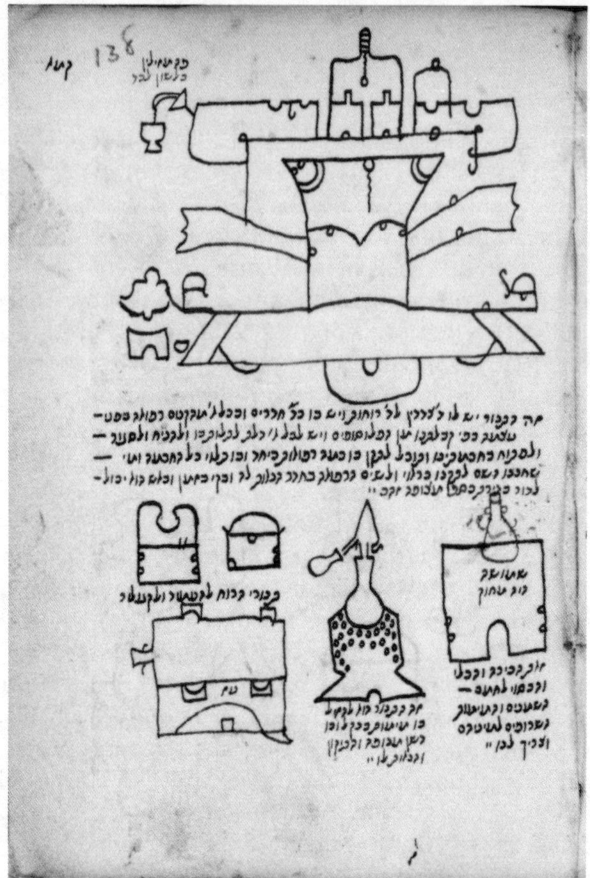

Figure 33.2. Alchemical apparatus in the Gaster Manuscript, folio 138a. Top left: "Here they flow through a tongue into a jar." Middle: This furnace has four sides toward the four winds, and there are in it twenty-four chambers, and in each of the tubes there is a separate medicine as we received them from the philosophers, and each one has a door to hang on it and to put, and to shut and to open, in our wisdom. You can set up in it several medicines together, and on it depends the entire science, and he whom God has graced by blessing him properly and [letting him] put each medicine in the chamber which is suitable for it, and he who is an expert in timing and firing, can dwell in a dwelling of silver overlaid with gold." Bottom right, inside figure: "Its use has been erased." Under it: "This is the furnace and the vessel and the lid to heat the burnt oils and the waters according to their kinds, and we need it." Bottom middle: "This is the furnace to liquify in it the waters easily, and in it are weakened ashes, and the preparation, and what is suitable for it." Bottom left: "The furnaces of spirit to make it stand and to coagulate."

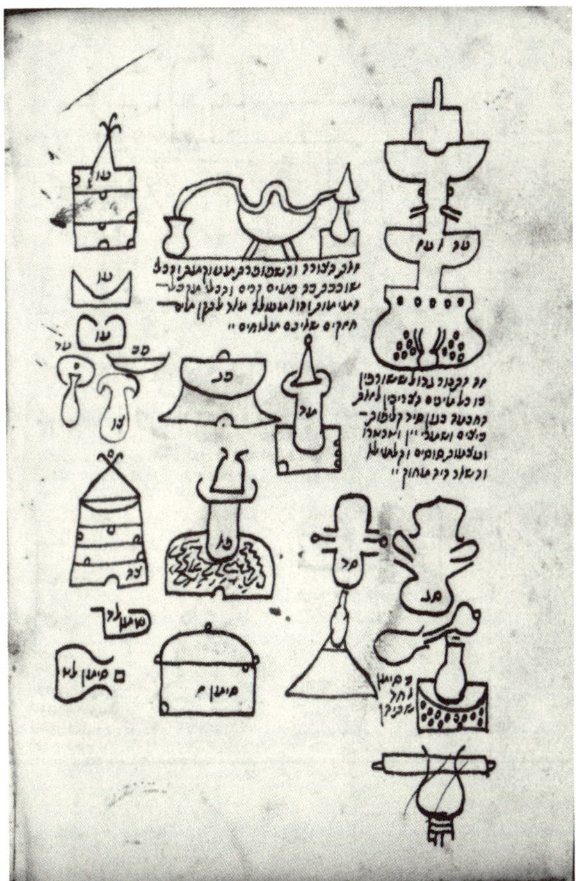

Figure 33.3. Folio 138b of the Gaster Manuscript. Top right, in figure: illegible; under the figure: "This is the big furnace in which are burned all kinds which are needed for this science, such as the lime of eggshells and sediment of wine, and tartar, and bones of horses and calomel, and the rest was erased." Top middle: "This is the shape and the crooked tube, and the vessel lies in it in cold water, and the vessel receives the water, and it is very superior for the preparation of strong water which is not salty." Lower right: "There is one sign for both." In each figure there is a number called "sign."

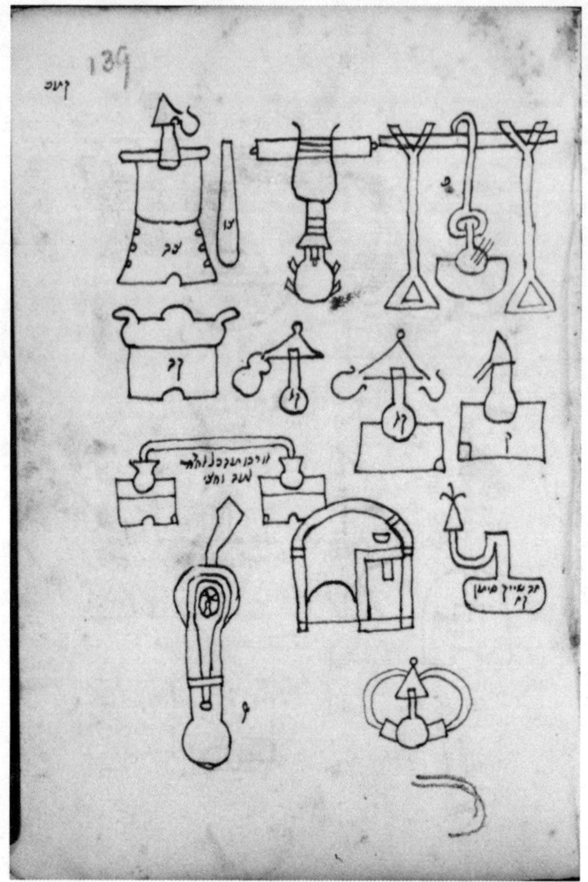

Figure 33.4. Folio 139a of the Gaster Manuscript. Middle right: "This belongs of sign 107." Middle left: "Its total length is one cubit and a half."

The six pages of figures are followed by detailed indexes of names and subjects (ff. 143a–169a). Finally (ff. 170a–173b), there are four leaves in Arabic, with many words written in unconnected letters. In the same disconnected manner is penned the Muslim invocation of God, *Bismi-llahi l-raḥmāni l-raḥimi* (f. 172b), "In the name of Allah the compassionate, the merciful." The very last page of the manuscript (f. 173b) is written again in Hebrew and deals with mercury.

A few excerpts from this manuscript follow.

(f. 55a) FOR SOL. DEMOCRITUS said: Take white *ṭuṭia* [arsenic] and *merqurio* [mercury] and red alum and *ṭarṭarus* [tartar], and throw it on tin and on lead which are prepared together.

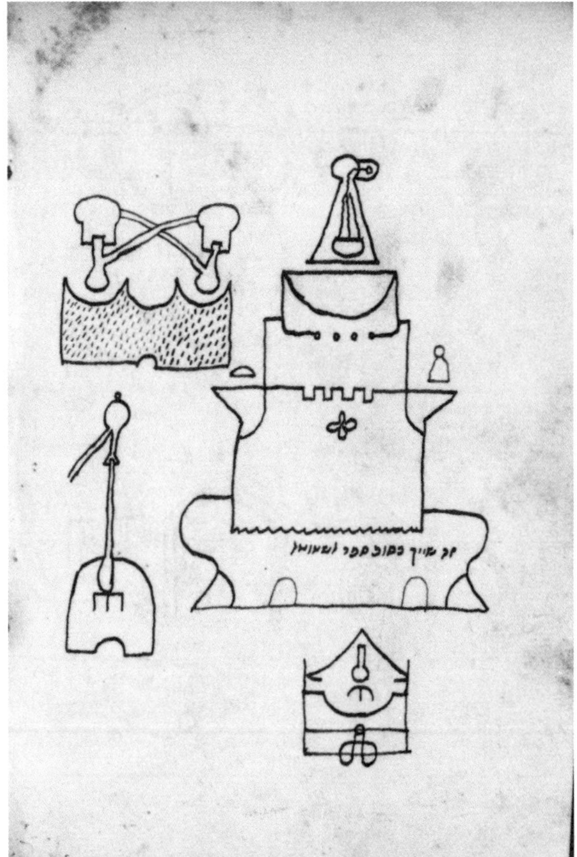

Figure 33.5. Folio 139b of the Gaster Manuscript. Middle: "This belongs to the end of the Book of Astuta."

FOR SOL. Take mercury and red alum and *ṭuṭia* [tutty, zinc oxide], and grind them together in red oil of blood which had become red from *sal armoniq* [sal ammoniac], and with other red things, and throw it on *luna* [silver] or on Venus [copper] four times, and it will be *sol* [gold].

(f. 128b) TO REMOVE hair so that it should not return. Take green frogs called *raqno*, [I. or S. *rana*], three of them, and put them into a bowl in which there should be good wine, and let it stand in the sun two months, that is Yulio [July] Agusṭo [August], and then wash your face or the roots of the hair, and it will be removed not to return again.

TO MAKE hair black. Take fig leaves and burn them and make of them a *lisia* [solution], and with this solution wash the hair, and it will be black.

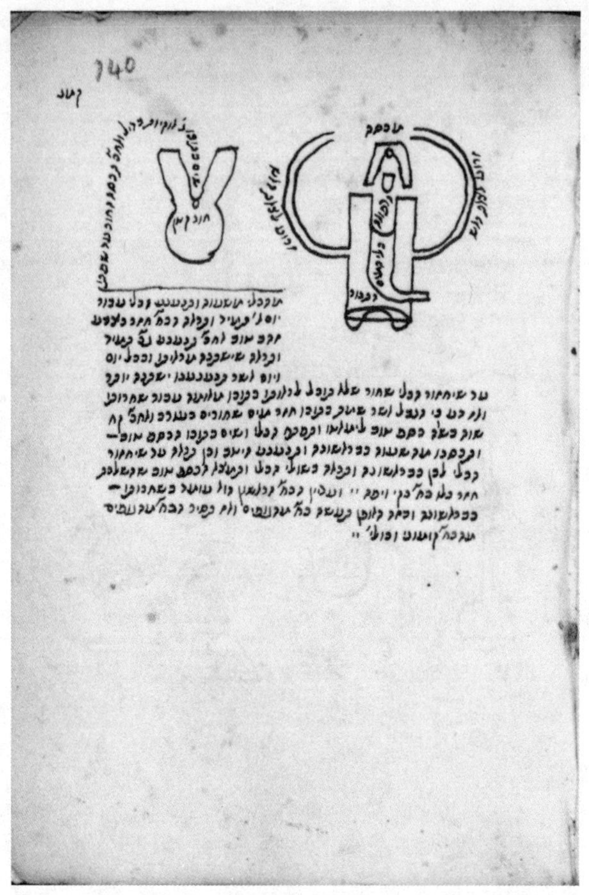

Figure 33.6. Folio 140a of the Gaster Manuscript. Top right (written around the figure), right arm: "arm for the exit of the fire"; top: "lid"; left arm: "arm for the exit of the fire"; inside the vessel: "the medicine; the water vessel; the furnace." Top left figure, inside: "a small hole"; descending from top of vessel: "Put a piece of three ounces of tin, and then plug up the hole up to the lip of the vessel with wax, and shake the vessel for one day always, and you will see the quicksilver become the color of good gold. Then shake it again constantly, and you will see that its appearance has changed, and every day that you shake it, it will change more, until the vessel becomes black so that you can see nothing inside it because of its blackness, and then know that the *nevel* [?] which you put into it became water black like the raven. And then take equal amounts of good filed silver, and open the vessel and put into it the good silver and cover it with wax as at first, and look at the bottom of the vessel and you will find that the good silver that you have thrown in has all become pure and beautiful quicksilver. And the first quicksilver will still remain in its blackness as at first, and in this manner you will make quicksilver out of the bodies, and then remove the quicksilver from the bodies from the common quicksilver, etc."

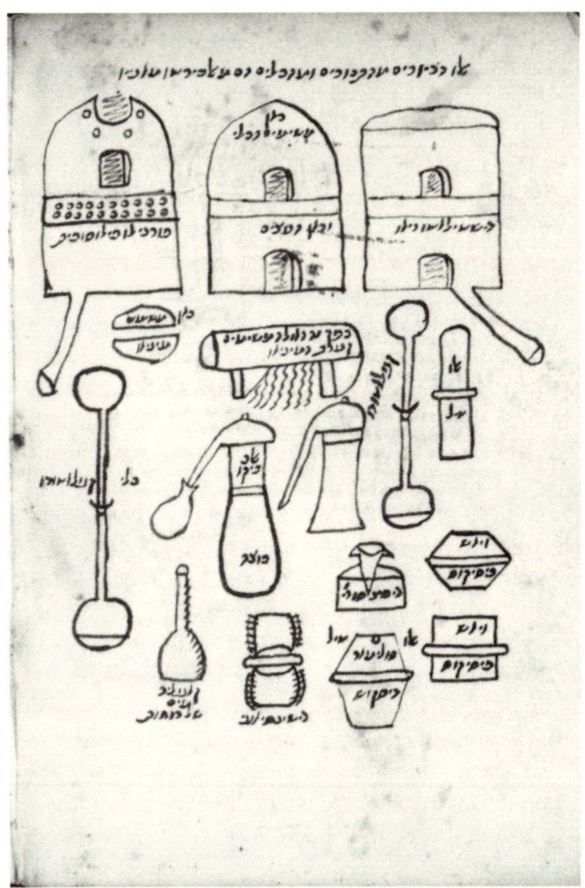

Figure 33.7. Folio 140b of the Gaster Manuscript. Top: "These figures of the furnaces and of the vessels are from Alberto Manyo [Magno]." Inside top right figure: "Disṭilaṭorio [distilling apparatus]." Inside top middle figure: "Here one puts the vessel and here the wood." Inside top left figure: "*fornillo filosofit* [philosophical small furnace]." Under top middle figure: "Into this loop one puts the bowl of minium." On its right, next to long-necked figure: "*ganelatūdo* [cane-like]." On its left: "Here they put the minium." Middle left: "cane-like vessel." Middle, inside vessel, top: "alembic"; bottom: "flask." Lower right, inside both vessels: "*vias fisiqos* [physical . . .]." To their left, inside top vessel: "*disinsorio* [?]"; inside and around bottom vessel: "aludel, to sublimate discs." Bottom center: *resensione* [receiver?]. Bottom left: "*qagulir* [coagulate] water of spirits."

For red color. Take *qrisṭalo* [crystal] and make a fine powder, and mix it with vinegar ten times, and dry it. Then mix it with vinegar of the juice of *grānāṭe* apples [pomegranates] ten times. Then *rofifiqa* [*rarifica*? rarify] *viṭriolo* [vitriol], and put it into the urine of a boy until it becomes water, and in this water put sal ammoniac, and grind it in it, and then soak the crystal ten times. Then put it in a moist place, and it will become water. Dry this water, and it will become stone crystal. Throw one part of this on four parts of tin, and it will turn into the color of gold.

(f. 130b) The operation according to the Abifior della Luna on the stone. Take one *liṭra* [pound] of *limaṭo* [filed] copper, and let it be in pure *limaṭura* [filings], and mix it with four pounds of quicksilver, and put it into a *ṭorṭiro* [S. *tortera*, baking pan] with a little salt and vinegar until they become *amalgamaṭe* [amalgamated] (f. 131a) together, and when they are well mixed and glued together, put on them a great quantity of quicksilver, and put all this in the *orinale* [flask], in a flask which should be in the ashes upon very weak fire, which should be like the heat of the sun, for one full day. Then remove it from the fire and let it cool, and when it cooled put it into strong and tough linen cloth, and squeeze the quicksilver forcefully through that cloth, and what will come out of the quicksilver and of the filings should be *desilaṭa* [*distillata*, distilled] like the quicksilver. Put it aside in a flask. Also take other quicksilver and mix it with the aforementioned filings left in the linen cloth and return to the weak fire for a full day as you did at first, and then let it cool and pass through the linen cloth all that has melted of the filings in the quicksilver as you did at first, and continue to do thus until all the limaṭura filings melt and become quicksilver and all of it goes through the linen cloth. If you take all this quicksilver with the filings limaṭura which have become quicksilver, and put it in a *viṭriaṭo* [glazed] vessel as it is proper to do, and put it on a gentle fire and bake it until you see on its surface some blackness, and remove that blackness as you can with one [word missing], and continue to do so and to remove the blackness until it no longer produces blackness, and do this on a weak fire, and after the quicksilver remains pure and clean then you will have the element of earth and water prepared. And after the quicksilver becomes pure then take all this *maṭeria* and put it in a flask, and put on it the quicksilver that floats on it, and bake it on a weak fire four full days. And again put on them quicksilver and bake it and do thus until the earth becomes white and clear, and this is what the Philosopher said. Take this earth with the aforementioned water that should be *montrafiqata* [?] which, if it will be pure in this manner, all our work will be done. Then take all this combination and put it in a flask, and put on it a *lamiqo* [?] and distill it as much as you can in strong fire so that the choice [part] should ascend and the earth should remain in the bottom of the vessel *qalṣinaṭo* [calcinated].

THEN take yeast of whatever you want, one-third of a part, that is, if the impure body is one pound take half a pound of the wheat [soul] of the sun [gold] or of the moon [silver], and don't take any other wheat but of sun and moon, and make of this wheat a *malgama* [amalgam] of the sun or the moon prepared in the manner mentioned above, and bake it together three full days. Then put on them quicksilver, and bake it as you did at first, and do thus until these two bodies become combined, and the sign is that they are combined when the color returns to them. Then put on them other quicksilver, little by little gently until they drink of them as much as can be drunk, and always put on them new quicksilver to drink.

(f. 131b) AND KNOW that in this combination they make the bodies so that the spirit mixes with them and becomes one thing with the bodies, and they are transformed into one nature. And thus *luṣirme* [?] that is to say, the substance that will be born out of these substances will become pure with the bodies, which could not happen before the bodies were pure of their [word illegible] and of their muddiness, and thus they grow and multiply in number of *Vertigero* [?].

In the sequel to this section our author quotes the views of various "philosophers" from the Book Turba on the four basic elements of water, earth, air, and fire, identifies water with quicksilver, and gives instructions concerning the re-creation of the elements in the alchemical work. He subsumes these topics under three "sayings," the first of which concerns the transmutation of the impure bodies into quicksilver, the second the making of earth, and the third the purification of the produced earth. Then, in the "fourth saying," he gets down to a discussion of the analogy between the relationship of body and soul in the human being and in the elements. In doing so, he uses the term "wheat" [H. *ḥiṭṭah*] to designate the soul that informs both the human body and the body of the elements:

THE FOURTH SAYING is that the water can *ababorare e solimaṣione e asènṣione* [I. *evaporare e solimazione e ascensione*, evaporate and sublimation and ascension] and that earth will become air, for at first it was thick, that is, *sfisa* [I., fixed] with the earth and the water. And behold, I showed you the earth and the water and the air, and behold it is what the philosopher Felipelino said in the Book Turba: "You should always whiten it with dry fire until out of it comes the powder which you will find in it." And it is what is called [word illegible] by the philosopher ARMS [Hermes?]. And the philosopher NGRIDES [?] also said that calcinated earth will remain in the bottom of the vessel which is of the nature of fire. And in this manner we shall have four elements in the mentioned work, and of the mentioned dust of which the philosophers and the philosopher Mariaris [Morienus] said, "Don't beat and don't disdain the ashes which are found in the bottom of the vessel, for in them is the crown of the heart, for they are the *firminato* [I., solidified] ashes." And thereafter put the mentioned wheat into the mentioned dust [which is] the soul of the philosophers, for just as the human body without its soul is nothing and is like dregs, so the impure body [of an element] without its wheat, which is called soul, is nothing. And just as the soul when combined with the human body is its substantial life, so the wheat is prepared and ready for the body [of the elements], which is not yet pure until you combine the one with the other, and the wheat supplies it with its substantial life, and takes it out of its nature and transmutes it to its [own] nature.

And know that there is no other wheat but the wheat of the sun [gold] or of the moon [silver], for just as the sun and the moon rule over the other stars, so these two metals rule over the others, and they are better and more honored than the others, and therefore are called wheat.

Then it is necessary that the wheat, that is, the soul, should be put into the body so that the body should be capable of becoming pure and should receive vitality, and this is what the philosopher Moranais [Morienus] said: "If you don't purify the impure body to make it white, you will not be able to put into it the soul in such a manner that the color should become white, and nothing of your work will become purified."

Then it is necessary that you combine the wheat, that is, the soul, with the pure body, and then the vital spirit will become combined with it, and will rejoice with them [i.e., the soul and the body], because they are pure and clean of their impure nature, and are now bright and fine. And this is what the philosopher Astamus [Ostanes?] said in the Book Turba: "The spirit will not combine with the body until the body becomes pure of its turbid material, and is purified thoroughly and is divested of its dustiness."

And know that at the time of their combination the greatest marvels are seen that can occur in the world. And then the body which is impure receives the color of the complete and permanent color, and this is on behalf of the wheat which is called soul. And the soul, that is, the quicksilver, on behalf of the power of the soul, will combine with the body, and unite with it, and the color from the wheat transmutes and becomes one combined thing. Then, with the mentioned saying, every wise man can see and know that the philosophers, in clear speech and with fine discernment, spoke the truth and uttered deep sayings.

Next our author goes on to discuss other aspects of the relationship between body and soul as they bear on alchemical operations:

(f. 132a) THE PHILOSOPHERS SAID that our stone is of four elements, and they likened it to them. And behold I have shown you that there are in this stone four elements, that is, earth and water and air and fire. And so they said that our stone is composed of body and soul and of spirit, and they spoke the truth about this, for it is spirit. They likened the impure body to ashes and water, while the quicksilver they likened to the spirit of the wheat. They said that it is the soul, because it gives life to the impure body which is the copper, which previously did not have vitality, and it also transmutes it into a good shape. And other philosophers said that if you don't transform the corporeal thing into a non-corporeal, and the incorporeal into a corporeal, you have not yet found the way.[20] And about this they spoke the truth, for the impure body, that is, the copper, will at first turn into water, that is, into quicksilver, and then it will become incorporeal, and then, at the time of the combination with the spirit, that is, with the quicksilver, it will turn into body. There are other philosophers who said something exactly like this in other peculiar words: Artabanes [said:] one to the other, you will find what you are seeking. And they spoke the truth, for our work is to make out of the thick thing a thin [thing], that is, out of the body we make water which is quicksilver, and then (f. 132b), we make it dry, that is, out of the water which is quicksilver we make earth. And also of the quicksilver which is the moist [element] we make dry, that is earth, and in this manner we make and transmute the corporeal thing into a spiritual, and the spiritual into corporeal, as we said. And we make also something which is supernal into something which is lower, and vice versa, that is, that the spirit will become body and body will become spirit, and this will be in the beginning, through the *solimaṣion* [I., sublimation] of the impure bodies [when] they become quicksilver. Thus it will be seen that our stone is of four elements, [and] of body and soul and spirit, and this stone is made of one thing. They spoke the truth about this, for we perform our whole work out of quicksilver, which is called in general by all the philosophers "living blessed water," which has such power and virtue that it dissolves every metal and transmutes it into itself.

And don't believe that it dissolves the bodies *de solṣione* [I. *de soluzione*, by dissolution] just a little, as the peoples of the land [the ignorant] believe, but it is a real and natural *disolṣione* [I., dissolution] and *qalṣinare* [I., to calcinate], and it transforms the *qalṣinas* [I., calcinated things] into ashes and whitens it and purifies it as the philosopher Bonays [?] said that everyone must bake the quicksilver in fire with the copper which will remove the blackness and the darkness from the copper, and then combine the two pure bodies together in the aforementioned manner, and they will so combine in strength and mixture that no power of the fire will be able to separate them, nor can any *azminaṣione* [I. *azzimazione*, embellishment] and *ṣtinṭaṣione* [I., coloring] separate them from each other, but let him protect them from burning and the scorching of fire, and let him put the power of the virtue from the one into the other in a manner so that it will no longer be possible to call them two bodies, but [they will be] like one body in shape and quality. And also *solima* [I., sublimate] the bodies not in the sublimation which most people say; we are not speaking here of the superiority of the vessel, that is to say to take the quicksilver with *arseniqo* [I., arsenic] and to make them sublimated with strong and rapid fire. And they said that in this manner the bodies are pure and sublimated. And the truth is that they are in a great error in this, for the bodies will then be more impure than at first, [and] then our work is not in the highest place, that is, *solimare* [I., to sublimate], but it is sublimation which the philosophers call "lower *solimare.*" And it means to change the thing which is muddy and make of it a thing which is supernal and pure and clean and sapphire-like [spiritual].[21] The people say "This man is *solimaṭo,*" that is, that he ascended to the highest degree from the first, or that he had *dinaiṭare* [cf. I. *renato*, reborn]. And thus we say in our Work, when the bodies are *solimaṭe*, that is, when they are *asoṭiliaṭe* [I. *assottigliata*, thinned], and are combined with the highest nature, and from the muddy thing they become not muddy, that is to say not *qoroṭe* [I. *corrotte*, corrupt]. And likewise this will make the living water a sacred water, that is, quicksilver. And then many colors will become visible before they become white, and in the end there will remain the white color. But the combination of the water with the body will be clean, and the wheat is called many colors, but without purpose, one cannot count them. (f. 133a) In this manner it will appear to you that our Work is of one thing and is made of one independent thing, that is, the sacred water, the living water, and it is the quicksilver, and it is of four things, water, earth, air, fire, as we have said above, and it is of three things, namely body, spirit, soul, as I have shown to you above in the explanation.

The Budapest Manuscript

In the Kaufmann Collection of Hebrew manuscripts in the Hungarian Academy of Sciences there is a one-page Hebrew alchemical manuscript (Kaufman, 454), of apparently Italian provenance, written in what probably is a sixteenth- or seventeenth-century Sephardic hand.[22] It contains three recipes: one for making gold out of silver, one for solidifying quicksilver, and the third describes a method of "revivification" by means of verdigris. Linguistically the manuscript belongs to that category of Hebrew alchemical writings which use a great number of foreign terms for the alchemical materials, instruments, and operations for which no Hebrew terms were available, or at least were unknown to the writer. In the following translation, all the foreign terms are Italian.

To make out of half gold and half silver, out of *qōpūla* [linking together] so that together they should be good gold of twenty-two *qarāṭe* [carats] gold suitable for every test

First make *qalṣikalisone* [*calcinazione*, calcination] of the *luna* [silver] in this manner: take silver and pass it through a *lima* [file] so that all of it be *limaṭo* [filed] finely, and take three times as much quicksilver as is the weight of the good silver, and smelt the two together, and take as much sulphur as is the weight of the aforementioned two silvers [together], and get *qomuno* [common] *kalṣinaṭo* [calcinated] salt twice the weight of all the aforementioned things, and put it in a well-covered earthenware pot, and put it on the fire, and when you put it [off] it will no longer be liquid. Let him take the aforementioned salt and sulphur and quicksilver and good silver, and put it all into *al morṭaro* [the mortar], and pound everything until it becomes fine, and put everything in a melting pot which must be well *luṭāṭo* [luted] with clay, and put it on great fire which does not have to be blown, and leave it on the fire until you see that it no longer makes flame, and then remove it from the fire and throw it into a vessel in which there is hot water, and there they will separate, and the silver will remain a powder in the bottom of the aforementioned vessel. And remove the water from the aforementioned vessel slowly, and you will find everything at its bottom. And then put everything in a vessel on high fire, and when everything is dry take sulphur twice the weight of all the aforementioned things, and also the same amount of common salt, and repeat twice what you did before, without any quicksilver. Thereafter let whatever rises from all of it sink to the bottom, as is written before us about this.

To make quicksilver stand [i.e., coagulate], take an equal amount of gold and quicksilver and *verde rāmo revifiqāṭo* [revivified verdigris], and one part of calcinated silver, and the same amount of *salmoniaqo* [sal ammoniac] as the weight of the silver and the verdigris and the gold, and grind all this well on a marble stone so that all of it should be well mixed together, and put all this into a glass *buṣa* [vessel] with a long neck, and which is so large as to be able to receive three times all the aforementioned things. And put the aforementioned vessel on weak fire, and give it fire all the time two days running, and at the end of the two days make under it a great and mighty fire, burning for two hours, and then remove the vessel from the fire and break it, and take the powder which is on its bottom from the aforementioned things, and then take the same amount of silver and of gold as the weight of the aforementioned powder, and put it into a melting pot with the *boraso* [borax, saltpeter], and when it is melted make of it a *verga* [rod, bar], and pound it with a mallet on an *inqorina* [?] so that it should be fine like the *qarlino* [*carlino*, a coin], then take *viṭriolo romano* [Roman vitriol, ferrous sulphate] and verdigris in equal amounts, and sal ammoniac weighing as much as the two together, and *qroqonfero* [*croco di ferro*, iron oxide], and put the iron in *limaṭura* [filings] as the weight of all this, and knead all of it together in the urine of a virgin boy, and dry it all on weak fire, and do this four times. Then take the aforementioned *baṭuṭo* [*battuto*, beaten] silver, and cut it into small pieces, and fill a melting pot with the pieces of the silver, and then with the aforementioned *misṭura* [mixture] until the melting pot is full, and then cover the pot with the *luṭa* [clay], and leave a little hole in its roof, and give it weak fire for one hour until the aforementioned clay becomes dry. Then give it great fire for the duration of two hours so that it should melt, and remove the pot from the fire and make of it a rod, and this will be twenty-two *qaraṭo* [carat] gold by any test.

METHOD OF *REVIFIQAṢIONE* [REVIVIFICATION] WITH *VERDIGRIS*

Take verdigris and put it in a melting pot covered with a brick, and give it great fire for one hour, and it should be made to make iron oxide. Take filings of iron and sulphur, and put them in a melting pot and give it fire until smoke rises, and when the mentioned smoke rests remove it from the fire and put it in another melting pot, and do thus three times. Then take all that is in it and put it in a vessel of glass, and put in the mentioned vessel as much strong vinegar as will cover all the mentioned things by two fingers, and put it on strong and powerful fire for two hours until you see that everything is red like the appearance of blood. Then remove everything from the fire and it will be done.

Chapter Thirty-four

BENJAMIN MUSSAFIA

BENJAMIN ben Immanuel Mussafia (1606–1675), a descendant of Spanish Marranos, was probably born in Spain, but lived in Hamburg, where he gained fame as a physician and a man of wide learning in Hebrew, Arabic, Latin, and Greek. He became personal physician of King Christian IV of Denmark, and dedicated to him one of his books, entitled *Mē haYam* (Water of the Sea), dealing with tidal flow. It was published in Amsterdam in 1642.

Upon the king's death in 1648, Mussafia moved to Amsterdam, where he became one of the intellectual and administrative leaders of the Jewish community. Like many other Jews in Amsterdam, Mussafia was an adherent of Shabbatai Zevi, the false Messiah, and consequently was attacked by Jacob Sasportas, a zealous fighter against the Shabbateans.

Mussafia's most important work is the *Musaf he'Arukh* (Supplement to the *'Arukh*). The *'Arukh*, written by Nathan ben Yeḥiel of Rome (1035–c. 1110), is a lexicon of the Talmud and the Midrashim, with comments on all the words found in that literature in need of explanation. Mussafia's supplement, printed in 1655 in Amsterdam, corrected the Greek and Latin words explained in the *'Arukh*, based largely on Johannes Buxtorf's 1640 *Lexicon Chaldaicum Talmudicum*. This book, published in no fewer than twenty editions, secured Mussafia a worldwide reputation.

Among the works of Mussafia that are of special interest in the present context is a short treatise in Latin under the title *Mezahab epistola* (The Epistle Mē-Zahav), which was first published in Hamburg in 1638. Addressed to a learned friend of the author, who remains unnamed, the young Mussafia (he was about thirty) presents an overview of how gold figures in the Bible, and a compendium of the explanations rabbinical scholars, including medieval commentators, appended to those biblical passages in which gold is mentioned. The main value for us of Mussafia's treatise lies in the fact that it gives a detailed and reliable picture of Jewish views in his day on the role gold played in the life of ancient Israel, and on biblical references to alchemy.

The name of the treatise, *Mezahab*, correctly *Mē-Zahav*, is taken from Genesis 36:39 (= 1 Chron. 1:50), where, in the listing of the ancient kings of Edom, who "reigned before there reigned any king over the Children of Israel," we find this statement: "And Baal-Hanan the son of

Achbor died, and Hadar reigned in his stead; and the name of the city was Pau; and his wife's name was Mehetabel, the daughter of Matred, the daughter of Mē-Zahav." Modern biblical scholarship has very little to say about Mē-Zahav, even whether it is the name of a man or a woman. The literal translation of the name is "water of gold," or "goldwater" (see Chapter 2 above).

The alchemists had, of course, much more to say about Mē-Zahav. Blithely disregarding that it appears in the Bible as the name of a person, they took it to mean "gold-water" and, combining it with the story in Exodus in which Moses gave to the Children of Israel water to drink into which he had mixed the powder of the golden calf (Exod. 32:20), they built upon it the assumption that Moses was a great alchemist who knew the secret of the aurum potabile, one of the never-attained goals of alchemy. This was the subject that Mussafia tackled in writing his *Mezahab epistola*.

Following its publication in 1638, Mussafia's treatise was included in several standard collections of alchemical writings, with detailed comments by the compilers of those anthologies. The Latin text was copied faithfully from one edition into the next, and the Hebrew names and expressions contained in it were also copied consistently, with exactly the same corruptions repeated again and again.

The most detailed and most learned comments on Mussafia's *Mezahab epistola* are contained in Johann Jakob Schudt's monumental *Jüdische Merkwürdigkeiten.*[1] Schudt was no great friend of the Jews, but he was an indefatigable collector of information which he presented objectively and accurately. The following includes most of the material on pages 327–39 of volume 3 of the work. It consists of three parts: Schudt's introductory remarks in German; the Latin text of the *Mezahab epistola*;[2] and further explanations by Schudt in German. The many faultily transliterated Hebrew names and words have been retained as they appear in Schudt's text, followed in square brackets by their correct transliteration and where applicable, their translation.

A Jewish Epistle Called Mesahab Concerning Alchemy and the Art of Making Gold

Since . . . we promised to present a detailed account of how also the Jews meddled in alchemy and the art of making gold, therefore we enter here the totality of the epistle *Mesahab*, which is not unknown to scholars, the more so since there occur in the same also a few other curious and noteworthy things, which rightly belong to the Jewish curiosities.

§1. When we dealt above . . . with some money- and gold-hungry skinflints, and on that occasion mentioned that also the Jews meddled in gold making by means of alchemy, and at the same time we promised—since in the mentioned place we did not want to make use of the opportunity for inserting such a lengthy discourse and printing an entire epistle as an authentic curious document of this matter—to discuss it in Part III, therefore we now wish to keep that promise rendered. And we will not enter in an extensive disputation with the gentlemen alchemists about whether gold making is a real transmutation (by means of the *lapis philosophorum* [philosophers' stone] or gold tincture) of one substance into another, namely lead and copper into gold, and tin into silver, in which case the *theologi* will hardly admit that such a thing is possible, because to transmute one entity into another is reserved to the divine omnipotence alone, as Christ did it when he transmuted water essentially into wine at the wedding in Cana in the Galilee, John 2:7seq. Therefore, neither will it be conceded to the devil that he can truly change men into wolves or cats, but it takes place by deluding the eyes so that they see themselves and others as if they were wolves or cats; or else it [gold making] is only a *perfection* and a completion of the baser metals, in which, with the help of fire and other things, one advances in a short time the incomplete metals of lead, copper, tin to the highest perfection of gold, which the sun, together with the subterranean fire-heat, would have attained in quite a lot of years. The best advice was given by the devil to several alchemists who asked him for his advice how they should proceed with the process they had begun when he said: *travaillez, travaillez*, work, work, for this is God's order: to nourish oneself by work, and to obtain God's blessing, as well as gold and money. But they understood it erroneously that they should zealously continue their alchemistical work, and that is what they did, and became beggars by it, and got *pro thesauro carbones*, coals for gold. Nevertheless the gentlemen alchemists are so dogged (*verbast*) about it that even the good Mr. Christian Eisenmenger[3] sacrificed his life to it, and became a veritable alchemical martyr, as we have mentioned above. . . . Others, who sacrificed to it only their fortune, got away more mercifully, but worst off are the deceitful gold makers who have to make and stand the last test on the gallows-assay (*Galgen-Capell*).

§2. Until the present time those scholars have possessed an old Jewish epistle in the Latin tongue entitled *Mesahab* about gold, which in Hebrew is called זהב *Sahaf* or *Sahab* [*zahav*], in which the *auctor* [author] (whose name and lifetime or place are just as little known as are those of the person to whom he wrote), a good alchemist, writes to an intimate friend about the art of making gold. This epistle was brought to light in the Latin language by Mr. Joh. Ludov. Hanneman, Medic, Doct. and Professor at the Hollstein Academie, Kiel, *An.* 1694, in 8 at Frankfurt-am-Main, with many curious *Annotationibus*, under the title OVUM *Hermetico-Paracelsico-Trismegistum, i.e., Commentarius Philosophico-Chemico-Medicus in quandam Epistolam* MEZAHAB *dictam de* AURO.

Despite Schudt's assertion, the identity of the author of the *Epistola* is well known.

The Latin text of the *Mezahab epistola* is contained on pp. 329–34 of Schudt's *Jüdische Merkwürdigkeiten*. It begins with a descriptive title that reads:

MEZAHAB EPISTOLA

On the Potable Gold Extracted from the Repository of the Sacred Literature and the Rabbis' Doctrines, for His Most Learned Friend, Already Well Known in all Europe, Carefully Written by a Certain Erudite Who at Present Chooses to Remain Unknown.

The text begins, as was the custom widely followed in the Middle Ages, by effusively complimenting the author's unnamed friend for his great learning and studiousness. Then, as Schudt summarizes in his comments following the Latin text, the author adduces examples to show that the ancient Hebrews were masters of all the arts and sciences which his contemporaries claim had been recently invented. This is followed by a discussion of the central subject of the treatise, namely, the various kinds of gold known to the ancient Hebrews, and the operations they were able to perform with them. Since this part is not covered in Schudt's summary, I present here its literal translation:

The Holy Scripture mentions not only potable gold but six other varieties of gold, of which two have remained unknown until now to the hunters of secrets, nor have their names been explored, while the other four are termed by the Hermetics, the first purified gold, the second gold calx, the third essence of gold, and the fourth vegetative gold—names that are in fact not suitable to them, and to which I shall now set about to refer one by one.

First: potable gold, *mezahab*, obviously called water of gold, Gen. 36:39.

Second: termed purified gold, *zahahme zucac* [*zahav m'zuqqaq*], purified gold, 1 Chron. 28:18.

Third: clearly calx of gold, *zahab saruff*, burnt gold, Exod. 32:20.

Fourth: that is to say the essence of gold, *zahab tahor*, clean gold, 2 Chron. 9: 16, 18.

Fifth: that is to say vegetative gold, *zahab parvaim* [*zahav parvayim*], 2 Chron. 3:6, 8, and in the rabbinical language *zahaf mothi peroth* [*zahav moṣi perot*], gold that produces fruits. Sometimes also [called] *zahab sehru haseh peroth* [*zahav shehu ʿose perot*], gold that makes fruit, brings fruit.

Sixth: a gold unknown to the Hermetics, *zahab muphaz*, strong gold, 1 Kings 10:18. According to the rabbis *dome legofrit mutsehet baes* [*domeh l'gofrit muṣetet ha'esh*], similar to sulphur set on fire. Sometimes, however, it is actually taken to mean *dome lapaz*, similar to the precious stone *spaz* [*paz*].

Seventh: also unknown to the Hermetics, *zahab sachut* [*zahav shaḥuṭ*], stretched gold, 1 Kings 10:16, said by the rabbis to be *zahab senitva cahut* [*zahav shenitvah kaḥuṭ*], gold which is spun like a thread. Sometimes, however, called *seminsach que sa hava* [*shenimshakh k'shaʿavah*], which can be stretched like wax.

In the sequel Mussafia presents an erudite assortment of sources, explanations, opinions, and so on, on each of the seven kinds of gold, gathered from the Bible, the talmudic and midrashic literature, and the writings of the medieval exegetes Abraham ibn Ezra, Moses Gerondi, and David Kimhi. He also refers to Suidas, that is, the *Suidae lexicon*, the great historical and literary encyclopedia compiled in the tenth century.

He concludes his *Epistola* (334) with a reference, unusual in Jewish sources, to the alchemical expertise of the Jews in Hellenistic Egypt:

> The rabbis, in *Sh'mot Rabbah*, assert that this [stretchable] gold was very rare some time after the destruction of the [Jerusalem] Temple. For they say that now, indeed, it is found nowhere in the world. Adrianus [Hadrian] possessed a portion of the aforesaid gold the size of an egg; Diocletian, indeed, possessed the weight of a *denarius*. But the race of the Romans have no such thing in their presence. From this assertion I conclude, not undeservedly, that the books of *chymia* where were collected and burned by Diocletian, as Suidas mentions, belonged not, as he says, to the Egyptians, but to the Hebrews. For rather many things are attributed in histories to the Egyptians, above all when there is a discussion about the sciences, which, on stronger grounds, are connected with the Hebrews; because, I think, the Hebrew race was envied or held in contempt, or, what I deem more kind, because the wisest Hebrews dwelling at that time in Alexandria were called Egyptians—this is what I consider most likely.
>
> Whatever I had of gold I offered willingly to you, not ordinary gold but one fetched from the Sacred Treasury, which no other gold has the power to equal. Job 28:17. Farewell![4]

As we can see from the above summation and excerpts, Mussafia's erudition that enabled him to write his *Musaf heʿArukh* is evident in his *Epistola* as well. Most interesting for the history of Jewish alchemy is his assertion that the Hellenistic Alexandrian alchemists were not Egyptians but Jews, whose books were falsely attributed to Egyptian authors. As we have seen above in Chapter 4, this view had its origin among the Hellenistic alchemists themselves, who ascribed the origin of their art to Jewish adepts.

Immediately after his presentation of the Latin text of the *Epistle*, Schudt proceeds to comment upon it in German, without any intervening subtitle. Since he presented the entire *Epistle* as part of his paragraph 2, he numbers the beginning of his commentary as paragraph 3:

§3. This is material that belongs either exclusively or at least largely to scholars, who will surely grasp the meaning of the author from the Latin language, and the matter, obscure in any case, would become even more obscure and more unclear if one were to translate this epistle word by word into German. Therefore, in order to make the matter clearer to the gracious reader, we wish to present the contents of the letter in sequence.

§4. At the outset of the letter the author praises the skill, excellence, and zeal of his friend to whom he writes, and promises to answer the question which was put to him: whether the Jewish teachers knew also of the auro potabili, or liquid and potable gold, to dissolve it so that he [they] should have joy and pleasure from it. Then he begins and says that all the arts and sciences which nowadays pass as newly invented were long known and familiar to the ancient Jews. As a proof of this he adduces two pieces: first, the art of printing, for which purpose he refers to the two stone tablets upon which was *impressus*, imprinted, the *Decalogue* or the Sacred Ten Commandments, as well as to the frontal plate and little breast-shield of the high priest of the Old Testament, upon which various letters and names were engraved. But since the letters were written upon the stone tablets and upon the frontal plate and the little shield of office by the finger of God, I am surprised that Mr. Hannemann in those *Annotations*, p. 13, gives the Jewish *scribenten* [scribes] his assent in his matter, saying: *proinde ego huic Rabbino pollicem premo, quod & Judaeis isto tempore, ut & Salomoni, quaedam ars libros aeque celeriter imprimendi fuerit cognita*, that is, "Therefore I give approval to the rabbi that the art of thus rapidly printing books was known to the Jews of those times as well as to Solomon." That the Chinese already had before us Europeans some art of printing books is not denied, but nobody has so far dreamt this about the ancient Jews. The proofs adduced by Mr. Hannemann are: 1. Since at the building of the Tabernacle of Moses and the Temple of Solomon all sciences and arts came together through the inspiration by God into the hearts of the master craftsmen, therefore nothing remained hidden to them, and especially not to the wisest Solomon, of all that which human diligence can invent. But I answer: God taught them those sciences and arts which were necessary for the building of the Tabernacle and the Temple, but not others. One can, after all, build the most beautiful royal palace without the science of the noble art of printing. 2. He says that the Chinese got their printer's art *per traditionem* [by tradition] from the Jews, but he gives no proof for this; not to mention that the Chinese were already a famous people in the times of Moses and Solomon, and had printing.

§5. In the second place, the Jewish rabbi in his gold-epistle further adduces gunpowder as proof of his statement that all the newly invented arts were already known formerly to the ancient Jews; this invention is otherwise ascribed to a German monk, Barthold Schwartz, who was a good *chymicus*, An. 1378. The rabbi, quite inappropriately, refers to the words of Moses where God threatens the disobedient people of Israel that He would burn their whole land with brimstone and salt so that it could not be sown, nor would any grass grow therein, etc. *Deut.* 29:23 [in the Hebrew Bible Deut. 29:22], in which Mr. Hannemann, p. 15, likewise considers him correct, since, after all, the nature of brimstone and saltpeter was not unknown to Solomon and to other ancient sages of the world, even though they did not utilize it for such a ruination of people as we are doing nowadays with gunpowder. However, even though its nature may not have been unknown to them, they still did not therefore understand all the effects of the same.

§6. Now he continues and comes nearer to his aim: Adam, although he did not practice *chymie* himself, taught it nevertheless, and from him Tubal-Cain acquired metallurgy, and Moses, David, and Solomon practiced it.

§7. He not only describes at length six different kinds of gold from the Holy Scripture, but also wants to show us in it the aurum potabile, or liquid gold, referring to Gen. 36:39, where the name Mesahab (from which he takes the title of his epistle) occurs. Now in Hebrew, where it is written in two separate words, this name reads מֵי זָהָב, *aquae auri*, gold water. Now since the Hebrew names of the Holy Scripture were not given at random but purposely with reference to some remarkable event, therefore the ancient Jews wanted to make of Mezahab a gold-smelter and alchemist who could prepare the aurum potabile. Therefore our rabbi refers to the Chaldean translation of Onkelos, who renders it מְצָרֵף דַּהֲבָא, *conflator auri*, a gold smelter. He refers to the Chaldean *Targum Hierosolymitanum* [the Jerusalem Targum], which translated it in the same manner, and added that because he could transform gold *in liquorem* [into fluid] and other metals into gold, he valued silver and gold lightly, and asked, מָה הוּא דַהֲבָא מָה הוּא כַסְפָּא, "What is gold? What is silver?" as we are wont to sing: Gold is only red earth, the earth is not worth much. Also R. Solomon Jarchi [Yarḥi, i.e., Rashi] says that the word Mesahab means מה הוא זהב ? היה עשיר ואין זהב חשוב בעיניו לכלום. What is gold? He was rich, and gold counted in his eyes for nothing. The R. Aben Esra [Ibn Ezra] writes about the word מי זהב the most judiciously thus: כן שמו והגאון אמר צורף זהב ואחרים אמרו רמז לעושים זהב מנחשת ואלה דברי רוח, that is, "Thus was his name (Mesahab), and the *R. Saadia Gaon* says that he was a goldsmith; others say that he discovered how one could make gold out of copper; but these are empty words." It can be that this name Mesahab did not arise accidentally, but must it therefore signify the *aurum potabile*? How if he found gold in a river or in water, and discovered a river carrying such gold, and therefore was given the epithet Mesahab, gold stream, gold water? But to assert that also the Jews were goldmakers ever since primeval times makes one wonder that they did not hit upon [the idea] that Solomon in the Song of Songs described the art of making gold in allegorical words. Otherwise too Mr. D. Hannemann wants to maintain that most of the ancient rabbis were *adeptos*, or such as could make gold, and he opines that they presented that art in dark words and in fables, when he writes page 12:[5] "What pertains to the writings of the rabbis, they transmit these and many remarkable things in all kinds of disciplines, and many of them are such that they seem old-womanish fables: under them, however, lies hidden great wisdom which nobody can obtain unless he is acquainted with the secrets of mystical philosophy. Many therefore read the writings of the rabbis either because of the philology, or because of curiosity; when they encounter some fable they do not further inquire into what is hidden under that fable. But for us it is firmly established that under those fables the rabbis wanted to hide other things whose knowledge they did not want to transmit to others. And most of the ancient rabbis were known to have been adepts of philosophy."

The *chymici* used to present their alleged gold art in such veiled words, as he adduces on page 32 the words of Theophrastus Paracelsus:[6] "He commands to cast the red Jew into the Caspian Sea until he dissolves in it, then to burn it to ashes which first will become white, then red." In which riddle he describes the whole art, etc. For the wise men this and similar locutions are all *oracula* [oracles] and veils of mysteries.

§8. He moreover wants to present two examples from the Holy Scripture of transmutation of metals which actually did occur. First, that silver was transmuted into gold, and then also copper into gold: *praedicti liquoris forsan appositione*, perhaps by adding the aforementioned *liquor* [fluid] of the aurum potabile or liquid gold. That David transmuted silver into gold should therefore be obvious, for otherwise the text of the Holy Scripture could not be reconciled. For in 1 Chron. 30:4 [actually 1 Chron. 29:4] one reads that David gave 7,000 talents of refined silver wherewith to overlay the walls of the Temple, but from 2 Chron. 3:6, 7, 8 one learns that Solomon overlaid the walls of the House with gold. Therefore, the silver allocated for it by David must have been transmuted into gold according to the statement of the rabbis. That also brass was transmuted into gold, of this he opines to have found a good basis in the words of Ezra 8:27: And twenty bowls of gold of a thousand darics, and two vessels of fine bright brass precious as gold. Then he opines that since these two brass vessels are counted among so many silver and gold vessels, they surely must have been something quite special, especially since the text testifies that they were in no way less valuable than gold. Therefore one must assume that they were of brass which was transmuted into gold. This he proves first by a rather weak *argumentum grammaticale* [grammatical argument]: because the word נחשת, brass, is *generis foemin.* [of feminine gender], but the *epithetum* [adjective] מֻצְהָב, *fulgens* [shining] is construed *genere masculino* [in masculine gender], which reflects his secret allusion to the word זהב, gold, which is *generis mascul.* [of masculine gender]. This, however, can easily be countered by saying that it is *enallage generis mascul. pro foemin.* [a change of the masculine gender for the feminine], which is quite usual in Hebrew in *verbis nominibus* [words of names] and *participiis* [participles], as both R. Solomon Jarchi [Yarḥi, Rashi] and R. Aben-Ezra [Ibn Ezra] remark here. The other is also an *argumentum grammaticum*: if one replaces the צ with a ז, the word מְזֻהָב results, which means golden; it then would mean golden brass, that is, such gold as was formerly brass. This exchange of letters is based on the well-known Hebrew rule *literae unius ejusdemque organi facile inter se permutantur*, letters of the same sound are easily exchanged for one another. Although this rule in itself is quite good, and is sufficiently confirmed by examples from the Holy Scripture, such as צעק and זעק, to cry, still the question remains whether this exchange of letters has taken place in this word as well, because of this there is no example at all in the Holy Scripture, and without a precedent we are not allowed to change even a single letter.

§9. Furthermore, he deals with gold dust or powder, how one can make gold into dust or powder, and attributes such art to Moses, because in Exod. 32:20 it is said of Moses, "And he took the calf which they had made, and burnt it with fire, and ground it to powder, and strewed it upon the water, and made the Children of Israel drink of it." Many have written that Moses had to be a good *chymicus*, of which Mr. D. Hannemann quotes much in *Annotat.* p. 42. We ourselves, in *Historia Jud.* L. 1, Cap. IX, p. 86 *seq.*, after describing the manyfold wisdom and science of Moses, have also commented[7] that "it appears that he knew also *chymia* in that he made the golden calf into powder so that one could drink it."

Borrichius de Ortu & Progressu Chemiae p. 47 writes:[8] "Certainly none but an excellent *chymicus* can accomplish that which the Holy Scripture tells about Moses [and what] he accomplished, namely, to burn the golden calf in fire, to grind it to powder, to strew it into water, and give it to the Children of Israel to drink." But those patrons of the *chymia* go much too far who alleged that Moses wrote a book of *chymia*, as Mr. D. Hoh. Andreas Schmidius, provost at Helmstadt, states in *Pseudo-Veteri Testamento*, p. 49.

§10. When the author describes all kinds of gold, it is somewhat difficult to believe that there exists also an *aurum vegetativum* [vegetative gold], which has its *semen*, seed, within it, and therefore grows. He quotes the opinion of the rabbis that Solomon made in the Temple trees of such gold, which trees brought forth golden fruit at certain times. Mr. Hannemann in *Annotat.* p. 63 agrees with him, but we attribute this to Jewish fiction.

§11. The *autor* [author] concludes by saying that the *chymical* books about the preparation of gold and silver, which the Emperor Diocletianus, according to the testimony of Suidas, collected and burned, were not of the

Egyptians, as Suidas opines, but of the Jews who, because so many of them resided in Alexandria in Egypt, were often called Egyptians, of which Mr. D. Hannemann discourses at length in his *Annotat.*, p. 116 *seq.*

§12. If the ancient Hebrews knew the art of making gold and silver, it is most astonishing that their descendants, the money- and gold-hungry Jews, disregarded this art of their ancestors and let it be lost. In conclusion we want to point to the best goldmaking art which consists of true repentance, conversion, and fear of God, which process the primeval Oriental *Philosophus* Eliphas of Theman described very beautifully and quite clearly in Job 22:21 seq.: "Acquaint now thyself with Him (the Lord God), and be at peace, thereby shall thine increase be good. Receive, pray, instruction from His mouth, and lay up His words in thy heart. If thou return to the Almighty thou shalt be built up, if thou put away unrighteousness far from thy tents. And the Almighty shall be thy gold [in the original: treasure], and silver will accrue to you."

Chapter Thirty-five

BENJAMIN JESSE

As we have seen, some Jewish alchemists, even though they have left behind writings, remain anonymous; others are known by name because they are referred to by non-Jewish alchemical authors who discuss their works, but we know nothing of their lives, nor have any of their works survived; still others are mentioned only in passing in the available sources, and we know nothing of either their works or their lives outside that single tantalizingly brief reference. The man Benjamin Jesse belongs to none of these categories. None of his works has survived, he is mentioned only in one source, which happens to be of Christian provenance, but that single source is an eyewitness account, which contains more information about him than we have about many a Jewish alchemist who left behind voluminous treatises. The single existing source is a letter written in 1730, some time after Jesse's death, by his Christian disciple and heir (whose name and identity are unknown), and published in excerpts a hundred years later by Schmieder in his history of alchemy.[1]

Schmieder introduces the letter by stating that in the early eighteenth century there were many alchemists in Germany of whom nothing was known during their lifetime, and whose very names became known only after their death. He adds, "It almost seems that the vow of unconditional concealment was easier for the Jews than for the Christians; for we have the first example in Flamel's Abraham, the second in the two Hollanduses, who are considered Jews by some, and the one of whom we shall speak now was also a Jew, by the name of Benjamin Jesse, who lived for a long time in Hamburg without attracting the slightest notice. One would have learned nothing about him even after his death, had he not had a Christian heir, whose letter follows here in excerpts." Schmieder does not say to whom the letter is addressed, how long after Benjamin Jesse's death it was written, nor how it fell into his hands.

Honored Friend!

You wished to have news of the life and death of my late master Benjamin Jesse. By birth he was a Jew, but in his heart a Christian; for he honored our Savior. He was a gentle person, helped many in secret, and healed the sick whom nobody else could heal. When I was ten years old he took me in out of a foundlings' home, and employed me as a helper in his laboratory. He had me instructed in Latin, French, and Italian, and taught me also Hebrew. I served him to the best of my ability for twenty years.

One morning he summoned me and said that, being in his eighty-eighth year, his life's balsam was drying out and his end near. In his will, he said, he remembered two cousins and me. It was on the table in his little prayer room. He led me to its door. He covered the lock and the hinges (*fugen*) of the door with a transparent glass pulp which he kneaded in his hands like wax, and pressed his golden seal on the pulp which very quickly became hard. He placed the keys to the door in a little box, sealed it in the same manner, and gave it to me with the instruction to give it only to his cousins Abraham and Solomon, both of whom lived in Switzerland at that time. Thereupon he dropped his seal into a glass flask full of clear water, where it melted like ice, while a white powder gathered at its bottom, and the water became red like a rose. He sealed the flask with his glass pulp, and entrusted me with handing it to his cousin Abraham.

After he had done this, he prayed on his knees, reciting Hebrew Psalms, then seated himself in his armchair, drank a little malmsey, fell asleep placidly, and an hour later expired in my arms. I informed the cousins of his death, and much sooner than I could have expected both of them arrived. When I expressed my astonishment about it, I noticed a gentle smile on the face of Abraham; but the other had a very serious mien.

Next day Abraham Jesse took the flask with the water and broke it over a china bowl to catch the water. With this water he moistened the crystal seals which became quite soft and could be removed easily. Thus he opened the little prayer room. In its middle stood a table of ebony with a gold tray. On it were lying and standing many different singular books and instruments, and among them a box full of an important scarlet powder. Of this Abraham smilingly took charge, for all these things were bequeathed to him in advance in the will.

We found four big crates full of gold bars. These were to be inherited by the cousins in equal parts, and to me six thousand ducats were to be paid out of it; but they gave me twice as much. Abraham renounced his half, for he knew the same art which my patron had possessed, and knew well that he had received in advance more than all this. He designated it for dowries of poor girls. Since up to that time I had to remain single, they persuaded me to marry a poor girl, who then would bring me a part of Abraham's gift. Solomon returned with his gold to Switzerland; but Abraham went with his share of the inheritance to East India.

Schmieder adds that this story is especially interesting because it gives a clear idea of the famous Hermetic seal, which is often mentioned by alchemists. When the alchemists teach us that the *sigillum Hermetis* is in fact glass, this seems to indicate that the mouth of a glass flask becomes closed by being melted, but that does not at all seem suitable for operations in whose course a repeated opening is prescribed. The contradiction, however, is well explained by this description of the letter-writer. It is characterized by a guileless ingenuousness, and therefore deserves credence.

Schmieder goes on to explain that Jesse had undoubtedly written to his cousins as soon as he felt that his end was near, and asked them to come to Hamburg. The surprise of the helper at their unexpected early arrival indicated to them the simplicity of the well-intentioned man, and it amused them to make the instruments they found appear as magical wonderworks. From this remark it appears that the letter contained a description of some surprising acts, performed by Abraham Jesse, who seems to have been an adept, which seemed to the helper to be works of magic, but which Schmieder found unnecessary to print.

At the end of his account Schmieder remarks that nothing is known of the heir of Jesse's art, his cousin Abraham, who left Europe with his treasure, except that he remained single, and that after some time he adopted the eldest son of Jesse's helper. That is, the art did not die out with him, "and one should therefore not consider it surprising that later South Asia made a contribution to the history of alchemy."

A brief comment in conclusion. The story as told in the unnamed helper's letter is certainly fascinating, and seems to be true, despite, or rather because, of the minor contradictions it contains. The letter tells that the Jew Benjamin Jesse was a Christian believer at heart, but also that he maintained a Jewish prayer room in his house, and that when he felt his death near he recited Hebrew Psalms—which shows that he remained an observant Jew. His cousin Abraham is said to have given up half of the gold, but then we hear that he took along "his share in the inheritance" to East India. But perhaps the latter statement refers to the red powder, which must have been most valuable, and it was that which Abraham took along. If Abraham adopted the eldest son of the helper, born to him after he married the poor girl made rich by her share in the gold, Abraham and the helper must have remained in touch for several years after the former left for East India. Was reference to this also made in the letter, in those parts which Schmieder did not print?

In any case, here we have a unique report of a Jewish alchemist, who was born in 1642 at the latest, who lived in Hamburg for many years in total anonymity, who healed sick people unable to find succor elsewhere, who knew how to soften and harden and again soften a glass-like material, who knew how to melt gold in a water-like liquid, who produced an "important scarlet powder" (used in transmuting base metals into gold?), and who maintained a well-equipped alchemical laboratory. We also learn that the Hermetic Art of which this man was a master was transmitted by him to his cousin who then carried it to faraway East India.

PART NINE

The Eighteenth Century

Introduction to Part Nine

ABOUT THE END of the seventeenth century a remarkable change took place in the identity of the people who engaged in alchemical operations. After Maria Hebraea, until about 1700, almost all the alchemists were men. One of the few exceptions known to us was an anonymous Jewish woman "expert in the Work," who is quoted in the Manchester manuscript discussed above in Chapter 31. However, from about 1700 on women took their place next to men in alchemical laboratories, as indicated, among other things, by the illustrations printed in books from that time on. Thus in the *Mutus liber*, included in Johannes Jacobus Manget's *Bibliotheca chemica curiosa* (Geneva, 1702) many illustrations show a man and a woman working jointly on alchemical operations. In fact, alchemy became something of a fashionable pastime for women of the upper layers of society. Thus Rousseau's friend and mentor Madame de Warens "inherited her father's taste for empirical medicine and alchemy," and in 1728–1731 engaged in the preparation of "elixirs, tinctures, balsams, and magisteries" with the help of all members of her household, and made drugs and medicaments from plants; her house "was never free from quacks, manufacturers, alchemists, and promoters of all kinds." Some years later (1747–1749) Rousseau himself became interested in chemistry, which at that time was scarcely distinguishable from alchemy, and, together with his friends filled "quires of paper with our scribblings upon this science."[1] The social vogue of alchemy could not fail to spread into Jewish circles.

The eighteenth century was a period of great transformation in the social, religious, and cultural life of the Jewish people. The Ashkenazim became firmly established as the dominant sector in Jewry, while the Sephardi-Oriental element receded into relative insignificance both numerically and culturally. In eastern Europe a new Jewish religious development, that of Hasidism, became a vital factor, and almost simultaneously in central Europe the rejuvenating winds of the Haskalah, the Jewish Enlightenment, began to rise. And western Europe witnessed the first stirrings of what in the following century was to become the emancipation of the Jews.

These developments inevitably left their mark on Jewish alchemical activity. Up to the eighteenth century, the Sephardim had a virtual monopoly in alchemy among the Jews, but the exhaustion of the élan that characterized their communities in general was accompanied by a diminution of productivity in this field as well. This did not mean that interest in alchemy and the practice of alchemy did not continue among them, even into the nineteenth and twentieth centuries. Evidence shows that they engaged in alchemical practice and also produced copies of earlier Hebrew alchemical works, added annotations to them, compiled alchemical vocabularies, and the like. But all this was merely a faint afterglow of the creativity in alchemy that had secured them for centuries a position of preeminence in the alchemy of the Western world. In my search for information on what alchemy meant to eighteenth-century Sephardi rabbis I came across only one author who makes fleeting references to it: Ḥayyim Yosef Azulai (1724–1806), the Jerusalem-born polygraph, who in one of his minor works, entitled *Midbar Q'demot* (Primeval Desert), mentions in passing that Ḥayyim Vital was a master of alchemy.

On the other hand, for the first time in the millennial history of Jewish alchemy, Ashkenazi Jews appear in its annals. This development undoubtedly came about under the influence of gentile alchemy, which first became accessible to them when some Jews in central and western Europe began to take an interest in the culture of their non-Jewish environment in the eighteenth century. The two eighteenth-century Ashkenazi alchemists who will be discussed in this part represent a new type of Jewish adept: that of the magician-conjurer-alchemist-adventurer, whose work was directed toward the top echelons of the gentile world, who gained the favor of princes and rulers by impressing them with their mystical power, for whom alchemy was but one arrow in their quiver, and whose main ammunition was their ability to project a captivating, overwhelming personality.

One of them, Ḥayyim Sh'muel Falck, flaunted his Judaism in German princely courts, lecturing to, and actually berating, his noble audience in German (the mere fact that he knew German proves that he was an assimilated Jew), and claiming supernatural powers. The other, the Comte de Saint-Germain, on the contrary, never openly acknowledged his Jewish origin, claimed royal parentage as well as a millennial lifespan, and became *persona grata* in many European royal and princely courts, admired for his charm, wit, knowledge, and, to a considerable extent, his alchemical expertise.

In addition to these two remarkable characters, we shall discuss in this part the interest in alchemy displayed by a Sephardi-influenced Ashkenazi rabbi and an alchemical manuscript written in the eighteenth century, mostly in Hebrew and partly in Ladino, by a Sephardi Jew who probably lived in Italy, and whose epigonic character is manifested, among other things, by his admission that he copied some of the things he found in older manuscripts without understanding them.

Chapter Thirty-six

ḤAYYIM SH'MUEL FALCK

In or about 1736 a Jewish magician, who later was to become famous in London as an alchemist, was a house guest in the castle of Alexandre Leopold Antoine, reigning count of Rantzow and free count of the Holy Roman Empire. His name, as spelled in contemporary sources, was Chaim Schmul Falck, and he was in his twenty-eighth year at the time. The reigning count's son, Count George Louis Albert de Rantzow, left behind a detailed account in his *Mémoires* of his impression of Falck, and of Falck's doings in the castle.[1]

> This extraordinary personage is, at the time of my writing, twenty-seven years and eight months old. Of medium stature, he is well proportioned to make him an agreeable man. Without being stout, he is not thin. He has a brownish visage, beautiful and big black eyes, long rather than round and full of fire, an aquiline nose, a mouth of medium size. In his appearance, which is very noble and grand, pleasantness predominates and prevails over pride. His ordinary garb is a robe [*talard*] of purple color, unless he has a reason to dress differently. He has all the appearances of virtue, of probity, yet with all this, beware of his devilry![2]

As one can gather from these words, Falck was a man of prepossessing appearance and personality. The words of caution with which young Rantzow (he was twenty-one years old at the time) closes his brief pen-portrait reflect his ambivalent reaction to the remarkable feats he saw Falck perform. He witnessed those acts in the company of his family and friends, and was totally baffled by them, but at the same time, being a good Christian, he simply could not accept as a fact that a Jewish "priest" should be able to summon angelic and divine powers and make them do his bidding. His description is valuable because he describes in precise detail the magic of Falck, who, it would seem, was at that early stage of his career primarily a magician and conjurer—arts that appear to have served him as a good preparation for his alchemical mastery which later brought him fame as "the Baʿal Shem of London." Despite young Rantzow's reluctance to believe his own eyes, he must have been greatly impressed by Falck's magic since he devoted to their description no fewer than twenty-seven pages in his *Mémoires*.

Young Rantzow tells us nothing about the origin of Falck or his life prior to his sojourn in the castle of the reigning count. However, since

Figure 36.1. Ḥayyim Sh'muel Falck, by Copley.
Reproduced with permission of Mrs. Cecil Roth.

Rantzow penned his observations between 1736 and 1739, and he states that at the time Falck was twenty-seven years and eight months old, we can conclude that Falck was born between 1708 and 1711. From other sources it appears that the place of Falck's birth was either Furth in Bavaria or Podhajce in Podolia. Since Rantzow says that Falck had "a brownish visage," it is possible that his ancestors were Jews from the Mediterranean area.

Rantzow begins by telling that upon his return from a voyage he found that his father secretly sheltered "the famous Prince and Grand Priest of the Jews, Chaim Schmul Falck," who claimed descent from King David. Rantzow learned that before being taken in by his father, Falck had sojourned for a long time at Geilberg as a guest of the Baron de Donop, court-councillor of the empire, a person of spirit and merit, and a man unlikely to let himself be dazzled by deceptive appearances. Prior to that, says Rantzow, "this Jew" was banished from several German states, because he "performed things that were above the prodigies that one can relate." He adds that "one must see him with one's own eyes" in order to be better convinced of the reality of Falck's powers than is possible by a mere recital, and goes on to list the noblemen and statesmen for whom Falck performed "a thousand marvelous spectacles": "Is it necessary to recount that which he did with the Comte de Westerloh, the Marquis Damis, and the Duc de Richelieu, at the time ambassador to the Court of Vienna?" Next he reports an unfortunate incident:

> These gentlemen, all present when the unfortunate valet of the Comte de Westerloh had a fatal accident, could not deny that he [Falck] possessed kabbalistic devilry. The twisted neck of that poor young man, who, had he lived after the accident that took his life, could have seen only backward, proved only too well that the Devil was after the Grand Priest and all those who let him approach them. My father, who was among those listening, and who wanted to test me, approached me at that moment and took me to this pretended Prince of the Jews. As much in deference to the orders of my father as from curiosity by which one is easily overcome at the idea of an extraordinary thing, I let myself be led to the apartment of this famous Kabbalist.
>
> Having arrived there, this new pontiff began by telling me that he was not unaware of what I had in mind. "You, sir," he said to me, "are of an unbelieving sentiment concerning our ancient Jews of whom Jesus Christ said, 'This race will never believe in me unless it sees miracles and figures; I promise to show such to anyone struck by incredulity." "You speak," I answered him, "of the New Testament as if you were a Christian." He responded, "Quite possibly I have read it as much as you." I answered, "That can be, but in that case I am surprised that you still remain in your error."
>
> "I am so little in error," the Jew answered, "and love it so little, that I work at freeing all my brothers from it. They are waiting for somebody to liberate them from the oppression and the slavery in which they are. The time is approaching, but I cannot say more about it. Your law assumes," the Jew continued, "that we are rejected by the people elected by God. But one would have to prove to me that God, who is immutable, could change His decrees. It is quite apparent that He has not changed them with regard to our people, that we are actually under His hand which beats us on our heads like the hands of a father who punishes his children. The Christians bask in the glory of the world. The Jews are in ignominy, so that in a true sense they are the only Christians. The death of Jesus Christ has come about in order to announce to us a humiliating state, after which we must fill the earth, to the very ends of the universe, with the cry of the magnificence of God and the glory of the Jewish nation. This nation has withstood the injuries of all times, it preserved its name, its unity, despite all the efforts of the powers of the earth. Unsuited to perform impostures, and very indifferent to the politics of the century, we do not count except in the thunder of heaven that will be detonated by the ministers of His vengeance. One should not say that we are blind. We always see the finger of God

over our heads. Would you, Monsieur, cease to recognize your father as your father because he punishes you? Is it not that chastisement is the most beautiful sign which the true tenderness of a father can give? When all the Jews will be humble of heart, in sackcloth and ashes, He shall respond with their deliverance."

Assuming that young Rantzow reproduced Falck's words faithfully—and there is no reason to doubt it—this is quite a self-assured, almost provocative, statement coming from the mouth of a Jew in the house of a Christian nobleman. At that moment the arrival of the Baron de Donop was announced. Young Rantzow left "the pretended liberator of the Jews with a shrug," and hastened to meet the baron to ask for more information about Falck. Baron de Donop's response shows that he did not doubt Falck's powers:

"I knew him, having seen him first in Cassel, where his reputation was above suspicion. He cured at that time the daughter of the Court Jew who had suffered almost daily attacks of the falling sickness. He cured her of this illness with kabbalistic talismans, without making her take any medicament. Nor is this all. At one time the Court Jew had to leave the city on some business, and inadvertently took along the key to his cellar. The pretended Grand Priest was taken aback: he thought that this was a trick played on him by his friend. When he sat down at the table and saw that no wine was served, he raised one corner of his napkin, wrote a few characters on it, and said very loudly, 'My host will be quite surprised when he returns.' When the Court Jew returned and went down to his cellar, he saw that all the wine barrels were standing on their bottom. He went back up, and saw that the would-be Grand Priest was laughing very loudly. Then he gave his host a few characters to attach to the barrels. The Jew went back to the cellar, did as he was told, and saw that the barrels instantly returned to their original position."

The recital of these incidents did not impress young Rantzow, who reports that "the more the Baron de Donop seemed intent on affirming this, the more I laughed."

"Right you are," answered the Baron, "go on, laugh. I too laughed and was incredulous to the point of wanting to prove to my own eyes that this was not a case of imposture. I therefore took along to my home in Geilberg this Jew, who was no longer safe in Cassel due to the great fuss occasioned by his prodigies."

Rantzow then reports the many marvels the Baron de Donop told him had been performed by Falck in Geilberg, all the time protesting his own disbelief that they were anything but imposture. He continued:

The greater my repugnance to approach this man, so famous, the more I was pressured to have some confidence in him. I acquiesced, giving in to the importune pressure to which I was subjected. I went to see the Grand Priest in very good company. He started by telling me that I should go and purchase a sheet of paper, mark it with my seal, so as to remove all my suspicions concerning that which he was about to make me see.

In this case I had confidence only in myself. I left the castle, went to town to buy the paper, being distrustful of everything that he had there in the house. I returned; I gave my sheet of paper to the Grand Priest, after having put my seal on its four corners. He did not set his eyes on it except for the time he needed to write the Hebrew word *Jehova* on it. Then he returned it into my hands, telling me to attach it with pins to the tapestry, and to keep my eyes on it all the time. Then he made a circle with his *magne*,[3] and began to chant in Hebrew. After about an hour one could hear three knocks which were louder than canon shots.

The castle shook to its foundations. One could see neither fire nor smoke; one felt no odor, no similarity at all between this noise and the noise of a canon. A moment later my sheet of paper on which I had my eyes fixed, appeared to me to be full of writing: I called the attention of the Grand Priest to it; he fell on his knees, and prostrated himself. A moment later, with eyes bathed in tears, he raised his head, and told me to detach the paper in order to see what was written on it. I saw under the [word] *Jehova* a person sitting in a fauteil, and two cherubim covering him with their wings from above. Under this figure, which seemed to me to be an inimitable painting, I read in green letters everything remarkable that had happened to me ever since my birth. I also read a prediction that I was to see come true to the letter.

The Grand Priest asked me whether I had seen everything, and said to me that this was not all. Thereafter the Baron de Donop and my father asked me what I thought of the Grand Priest, and what ideas I had about the facts that they had related to me. "Excuse my incivility," I answered them, "if I am one who does not easily accept the marvelous. At present I do condemn my incredulity, but this does not keep me from doubting that all this was done by permitted means."

"In other words," said the Baron de Donop [turning to my father], "the day before yesterday he told us that he did not believe his eyes; today he believes, but on condition of apparently crediting it to the Devil."

After witnessing another vivid demonstration of Falck's powers, this time involving control over angelic spirits, Rantzow was now forced to acknowledge that this Jew was helped by divine approval. This made Jewish religion appear in his eyes as legitimate, something that, as a good Christian, he simply could not accept. He felt that it was a sin to witness that demonstration of Jewish mystical power, that what he had seen jeopardized his Christianity, his very salvation. He retired to his room, and poured into an emotional improvised prayer not so much what he believed as what he wanted to, or felt he should, believe. Having thus calmed his qualms of conscience, and duly recorded the words of his prayer, he continued his account of Falck's baffling performances:

> There is nothing in the world to be feared as much as the spirit of fanaticism. Let him who so wishes embark upon it. As for me, whatever prodigies this famous personage can perform, I shall let him do them without moving me, because I firmly decided not to let myself be found again at his kabbalistic shows. I have attended one, that much is true, in very good company. Present at that spectacle were the Baron de Donop and his younger son who is an officer in the service of the King of Sweden, the Baronesses de Koening, Mr. Rincius, counselor of the Regency, Madame de Malhous and one of her sons, my whole family, and several other persons of standing.
>
> While it lasted, it was done with such mysterious gravity that one lost the inclination to laugh at the two demoiselles and the one lady of high rank. Curious, as women ordinarily are, they were seized with a violent passion to see the Grand Priest operate. They arrived a little late at the house, almost at the moment when the kabbalistic work was about to begin. My mother spoke to them, apparently to warn them that one could approach the mysterious place only in a state of purity. The mother and the two daughters did not dare to present themselves. At any other time I would have given free play to hilarity; but I contented myself by telling them with a very serious mien: "I am sorry, my ladies, that you are not in accordance with the orders of the pontiff."
>
> To compensate them for not being able to satisfy their curiosity, when these surprising mysteries were over, the Baron de Donop and my father showed them the pieces of silver that were found. These were very many, from the times of the triumvirs and Otto the First.
>
> After this I asked the Grand Priest, how he could dare to claim that he worked with God after the valet of the Comte de Westerloh had his neck broken, when he performed his famous sacrifice of the black calf in the garden of the Comte, in the presence of the Duc de Richelieu.
>
> He answered me that that misfortune happened to the unfortunate young man because he dared to appear at that sacrifice in a state of impurity, of which he should have been free, as he was warned. . . .
>
> I know from a very good source that this Jew requested a great prince to give him refuge and give him the freedom to work at his Kabbalah in the Prince's states for forty days.
>
> Even though the Jew suggested to the Prince to have his work examined by such theologians as the Prince deemed reliable to ensure that he did

> nothing except with the help of God, the Prince refused to entertain his propositions. The Jew offered the Prince, as the price of his head, four million écus upon the end of the forty days. How beautiful is the response of that generous Prince: "That Jew," he said, "should rather multiply bread for the poor, if he performed miracles with the help of heaven, and not address himself to rich people offering to augment their treasuries."

Although the entire story tells only of Falck's activities as a religiously inspired magician and conjurer, this paragraph seems to indicate that even at that early stage of his life he was also an alchemist. His offer to enrich the prince's treasury by four million écus—a huge sum by any calculation—and to do so at the end of forty days of "Work," is precisely in line with the modus operandi of many alchemists in his time and in the preceding centuries. In several earlier chapters we have heard of Jewish alchemists working for kings and princes in this manner: they entered into agreements under which the rulers financed and authorized their alchemical work in exchange for the alchemists' undertaking to deliver the precious metal they were to produce into the rulers' hands. This is, it would seem, what Falck offered the unnamed prince, although it is not clear whether he promised to produce the millions of écus by alchemical or by magical, "kabbalistic," work. However, given the fact that subsequently, in London, Falck became famous not as a "kabbalistic" conjurer but as an alchemist, one is inclined to assume that when seeking entry into the states of the German prince he held out to him the promises of the alchemical way of producing gold.

Rantzow's account of that early phase of Falck's life ends with a reference to Falck's emigration to England:

> The Jew was ordered to leave the house of my parents. His Highness the Reigning Duke of Brunswic and Lunebourg wrote in strong terms to my family who resolved to abandon the famous Chaim-Schahul-Falck [*sic*], sovereign pontiff of the Jews, descendant of King David, if one wants to believe it on the faith of a passport of the *Grand Seigneur*.
>
> He departed for England, where the Portuguese Jews of the highest reputation rendered him honors as their prince and sovereign pontiff.
>
> One of my friends informed me from England that Parliament had him arrested in London, and that afterwards he was released on condition that he would no longer kabbalize.

The value of this detailed eyewitness account of the acts and words of the young Falck is enhanced by the fact that its author was not only predisposed by his religious convictions to disbelieve whatever he saw Falck perform, but in addition had no sympathy whatsoever for the man whom he calls, with evident sarcasm, "the Grand Priest," "sovereign pontiff of the Jews," and, most frequently, simply "the Jew." This being the case, one cannot doubt that the skeptical young count actually believed that he had seen the prodigies performed by Falck, and that he found Falck to be truly a grand master of magic.

Some four decades later a Swedish historian and traveler, Johann Wilhelm von Archenholz (1743–1812), visited London, and while there he learned some particulars about Falck. In his book *England und Italien*[4] Archenholz briefly describes the two Jewish communities he found in London, the Portuguese and the German. He goes on to speak of Falck:

> For the last thirty years there has lived among his people a peculiar man who is very famous in the annals of the kabbalists. His name is Chaim Schmul Falk but he is called here by everybody Doctor Falkon. A certain Count of Ranzow, who recently died as Marechal de Camp in French service, gives in his printed memoirs an account of so-called kabbalistic and magical operation, which he allegedly saw performed by this Falk in Braunschweig [i.e., Brunswic] county, on an estate of his father, in the presence of many respected persons, all of whom he names in his book, and whom he calls upon to contradict him if he does not speak the truth. Whether Falk made use of the cupper's arts, I don't know; however, this man lives in London without ever having played here publicly the role of a kabbalist. He occupies a splendidly decorated big house, in which, apart from him, nobody lives, except for a few domestics. He carries on no trade, lives very modestly, and gives many alms to the poor. Very rarely does he go out, and if that happens, he wears a long robe which suits him very well with his long white beard and noble facial features. He is now about seventy years old. I do not want to enumerate here the wonderful things that are told about him. It seems most probable to me that this Doctor Falkon is an able chymist, and that he possesses in that science a very personal knowledge which, however, he definitely does not want to reveal to anybody. A royal prince, who is seaking the philosophers' stone with great zeal, wanted to see him a few years ago; he drove up to Falkon's house, but had the annoyance of being denied admittance.[5]

The forty-year gap between Rantzow's portrait of the young Falck in Brunswick, and that of the old Doctor Falkon in London given by Archenholz is filled only to a very unsatisfactory extent by writings left behind by Falck himself and by his faithful famulus Zevi Hirsch of Kalisch. Falck kept a diary, a kind of kabbalistic notebook, in which he recorded his dreams, his charitable gifts, and a medley of other items, including cooking recipes. This manuscript, preserved in the library of the Beth Hamidrash of the United Synagogue of London, although interesting for a study of the personality of Falck, contains little or no information about his alchemical activities.

Chapter Thirty-seven

THE COMTE DE SAINT-GERMAIN

THE COUNT of Saint-Germain was one of the most fascinating characters to figure in the annals of alchemy, and certainly the best known all over Europe. Voltaire, whose contemporary he was, referred to him with his typical irony—in a letter he wrote on April 15, 1760, to King Frederick of Prussia—as the only man to whom the Duke of Choiseul, Prince Kaunitz, and William Pitt confided their secrets, "who had souped in the past in the city of Trent with the Fathers of the Council [in the sixteenth century], and who probably will have the honor of seeing Your Majesty in some fifty years. He is a man who does not die and who knows everything." Two weeks later Frederick, who evidently had known of Saint-Germain's reputation before he received Voltaire's letter, responded by commenting caustically, "the Comte de Saint-Germain conte pour rire" (loosely, "counts as a joke").[1]

In the event, Voltaire's prediction came partially true, not in fifty but in a mere seventeen years: in 1777 Saint-Germain submitted to Frederick a memorandum offering him all kinds of quasi-miraculous technological services. It is remarkable that a few years thereafter Frederick completely changed his mind about Saint-Germain, and said to the French ambassador Comte de Saint-Maurice that all the marvels circulating about Saint-Germain "don't prevent me from having for this psychologist of human nature a residual weakness that I would not admit to him but that moves me to admire him."[2]

Much of the second half of Saint-Germain's life took place in the public eye, and hence a good deal is known about it. He was, from 1745 to his death in 1784, a celebrated alchemist, diplomatist, adventurer, the confidant of kings and princes, a personage generally regarded with awe and even adulation, a man believed to possess mysterious knowledge and powers. He was, in addition, a polyhistor, a painter, a composer, and an industrial innovator. The first half of his life, however, has remained totally unknown, despite the prodigious efforts by several nineteenth- and twentieth-century authors who wrote book-length biographies of Saint-Germain, trying to throw light on his origins, childhood, and youth.[3] The fact remains that Saint-Germain was so successful in keeping everything pertaining to his early life completely hidden that even his original name is still unknown.

In contrast to the absence of facts, once Saint-Germain became famous, rumors about his parentage abounded. Some of them are anonymous in origin; others were said to be based on statements made by princely personages who knew him; and at least one or two claimed to be based on the words of Saint-Germain himself. The most fantastic was the one to which Voltaire alluded: that Saint-Germain was a man who knew not death, that he was in possession of the fabulous elixir of life—the ultimate quest of all alchemists—and that he was hundreds, even thousands, of years old. It was fabled about him that he had known personally St. Anne, the grandmother of Jesus, and that several centuries later he was instrumental in having the council of Nicea (325 C.E.) approve her canonization. He knew Jesus, too, and intervened with Pilate in his favor. It was reported of him that he astonished his interlocutors by speaking of Jesus with the greatest familiarity. "I knew him intimately," he supposedly said, "he was the best person in the world, but was romantic and inconsiderate. I often predicted to him that he would come to a bad end."[4]

Saint-Germain himself—this much is clear from contemporary records—was quite pleased with these beliefs, and contributed to them. Baron de Gleichen, who knew him well, reports that one day Saint-Germain said to him, "These stupid Parisians believe that I am five hundred years old; I confirm them in this idea since I see that it gives them much pleasure. However, this does not mean that I am not infinitely older than I look."[5]

Shortly after Saint-Germain's death, his patron, friend, and disciple, the Landgrave Charles of Hesse (1744–1836) recorded in his memoirs that Saint-Germain had told him that

> he was the son of Prince Ragozky [a misspelling of Rákóczi] of Transylvania[6] and his first wife, a Tékély [Thököly]. He was under the protection of the last Medicis, who made him sleep as a child in his own bedroom. When he learned that his two brothers, sons of the Princess d'Hesse-Rheinfels or Rothenburg, if I am not mistaken, surrendered to the Emperor Charles VI and received the name of St. Charles and St. Elisabeth, after those of the Emperor and Emperatrice, he said to himself, "Well, then I shall call myself Sanctus Germanus, or holy brother!" I cannot, in truth, guarantee his birth; but that he was prodigiously protected by the last Medicis that I have also learned from another side. That house possessed, as is known, the highest sciences, and it is not surprising that he derived from it his first knowledge.[7]

We must join the landgrave in his doubts; it is almost impossible to accept Saint-Germain's claim that he was born a Rákóczi. Among other things, although Saint-Germain was reputed to have known many languages, Hungarian does not figure among them. On the other hand, he was reputed to have spoken Spanish and Portuguese "to perfection,"

Italian "admirably," German and English "very well," and French "with a slight Piemontese accent."[8]

Count Kobenzl, the powerful plenipotentiary of Maria Theresa in the Austrian provinces of the Netherlands, who was a friend and admirer of Saint-Germain, once said to the leading Austrian statesman, Prince Kaunitz: "Even though the history of his [Saint-Germain's] life and his origins are veiled in a mysterious obscurity, I found in him outstanding talents for all the sciences and all the arts. He is a poet, musician, writer, physician, chemist, a mechanic if need be, and an experienced connoisseur of painting. In brief, he is a man of universal culture, as is but rarely found in one person; he speaks all the languages, Hindustani as Italian, Yiddish as French. He has traveled in the whole world, and since he is very generous with his knowledge, I have spent very agreeable hours of leisure in his company. I can reproach him only for frequently boasting of his talents and his origins. When I asked him about his parents, he answered me emphatically, "Only the House of Bourbon is equal to mine in birth!"[9]

In the eighteenth century only a Jew would know Yiddish, that exclusively Ashkenazi-Jewish language. Although Hebrew was by that time studied by some gentile scholars because of their interest in the Bible, a knowledge of Yiddish seems to be prima facie evidence of a Jewish background. Since Saint-Germain was determined to keep his origins under veil, one must assume that he divulged his knowledge of Yiddish to Count Kobenzl in a moment of inadvertence.

The great pains Saint-Germain took to let nothing at all become known of his true origins can be indicative of only one thing: he was afraid lest a leakage of his actual parentage cause him irreparable harm. In eighteenth-century Europe, prior to the emancipation of the Jews, nothing would have been more damaging to a man whose entire existence depended on the personal admiration he was able to elicit in the circles of the high nobility than to be unmasked as having Jewish parents. Yet despite all his efforts to hide the circumstances of his birth, it was precisely Jewish origin that rumor most persistently attributed to him.

Those who claimed to be privy to details about Saint-Germain's background said he was the son of a Jewish physician of Strasbourg named Daniel Wolf; his real name was Samuel Samer; he was born in Frankfurt on October 12 or 13, 1715, as the illegitimate son of a poor Jew and a grande dame. The Troyes writer Pierre-Jean Grosley reported that "a Dutchman told me that it was public knowledge in Holland that the Comte de Saint-Germain was the son of a refugee princess in Bayonne and a Jew from Bordeaux."[10] Other rumors had it that he was of German-Spanish-Jewish extraction; that he was the son of a Jew and a princess known to Louis XV; that he was the natural son of the widow of Charles II of Spain, the charming and frivolous Marie-Anne of Spals-Neubourg—father unknown.

Some of his recent biographers have considered the possibility that Saint-Germain was of Jewish descent, and rejected it on rather peculiar grounds.[11] But, as we shall see, in addition to the persistent rumors, there are other indications pointing to Saint-Germain's Jewish origins. It is time to recapitulate briefly what is known about Saint-Germain's life. The first concrete data come from London in 1745, when several songs composed by him were published under the name of Comte de Saint-Germain.[12] On December 9 of that year, Horace Walpole, the Earl of Orford, wrote to Sir Horace Mann:

> the other day they seized an odd man, who goes by the name of Count St. Germain. He has been here for two years, and does not tell who he is, or whence, but professes that he does not go by his right name. He sings, plays on the violin wonderfully, composes, is mad, and not very sensible. He is called an Italian, a Spaniard, a Pole; a somebody that married a great fortune in Mexico, and ran away with the jewels to Constantinople; a priest, a fiddler, a vast nobleman. The Prince of Wales has had unsatiated curiosity about him, but in vain. However, nothing has been made out against him; he is released; and what convinces me that he is not a gentleman, stays here, and talks of his being taken for a spy.[13]

Early in 1746 Saint-Germain went to Germany, and in February 1758 he arrived in Paris.[14] The Marechal de Belle-Isle, who had known him in Germany, introduced him to Mme de Pompadour, who, in turn, presented him to Louis XV. The king found him so entertaining that he invited him to his "small suppers"—a great and rare privilege—and gave him an apartment in Chambord. For a time Saint-Germain was the toast of Paris, and given unquestioning credence for even the most fantastic claims.

How could Saint-Germain get away, even in the credulous time of the mid-eighteenth century, with such preposterous claims as having lived for two thousand or more years, and possessing quasi-miraculous powers? The *Nouvelle biographie générale*, published in the late nineteenth century, raises the question, and offers two factors that may have contributed to that credulity. One was that the *philosophes*, "by casting Paris into skepticism, did not extinguish the belief in the marvelous that seems to be one of the essential conditions of human life; and, replacing the belief in the miracles of religion, there arose a belief in other miracles and another supernatural. Thereupon men arose, coming from who knows whence, who promised prodigies . . . were listened to and generously remunerated, and saw the best of people gather around their magic mirrors. No one became more fashionable than the Comte de Saint-Germain, and soon there was no talk except about him."

The second factor was the extraordinary personality of Saint-Germain himself. On this point the *Nouvelle biographie* quotes Friedrich Melchior Grimm, the famous historian of French literature, who was Saint-Germain's contemporary, to the effect that "Saint-Germain appeared to all those who knew him as a man of much *esprit.* He had the natural eloquence that is best suited to seduce; he knew much chemistry, and history as few people had acquired it. He had the talent to evoke in conversation the most important events of ancient history, and to tell them as one tells anecdotes of the day, with the same detail, the same degree of interest and vivacity." To this the *Nouvelle biographie* adds it was not possible to deny "the domination Saint-Germain exercised all about, an extrordinary domination, especially if one does not seek an occult basis for it. For in that case one can attribute it only to his power of personality, that is to say, to the superiority of his intelligence or the energy of his will."[15]

On the basis of such eyewitness accounts, supplemented by the studies of his modern biographers, one can state with confidence that Saint-Germain must have been a man not only of extraordinarily wide knowledge and phenomenal memory, but also of great charm and grand manners, a spellbinding conversationalist, a person who inspired everybody who met him with liking and admiration (Figure 37.1). Highly educated people, princes, powerful statesmen, refined noblemen, all fell under his spell, and believed that he had miraculous powers. What Heine says about the troubadour Bertrand de Born must have been true to a multiple degree of Saint-Germain: he had the ability of making the world believe whatever he wanted.

He was also thoroughly at home in the natural sciences, was an eminent chemist, and was able to support with actual experiments his claim of knowing how to make gold and of having discovered the panacea, the universal remedy. On the other hand, his acts and words indicate that he believed in the eternity and unity of substance, which throughout the centuries was a basic tenet of alchemy. He himself was surrounded by myths, and was a legend in his lifetime.[16]

His lifestyle was a curious combination of asceticism and grand luxury. He never ate at the houses to which he was invited, and never invited anybody to a meal in his house. He always prepared his own meals, ate with the greatest frugality, mostly nothing but some vegetable gruel, and never took a drink with his meals. On the other hand, he dressed most luxuriously, loved jewelry, and traveled in a seignorial manner. His way of life involved considerable outlays, and although nothing is known for certain about the sources of his income, some suspected him

Figure 37.1. The only known portrait of the Comte de Saint-Germain. Engraving by N. Thomas, made in 1783, after a painting by an unknown artist-friend of the Comte, which he presented to Mme d'Urfé.

of having received lavish payments for espionage activities, for which he had ample opportunity in his travels all over Europe. He himself claimed, or was rumored to have claimed, that his riches were literally self-made, in the sense of being produced—manufactured alchemically—by himself: it was his mastery of the Great Art that enabled him to make as much gold and as many precious stones as he wanted.[17]

It is a rather puzzling fact that although his biographers and the memoirists who wrote about him never fail to mention his seductive charm, they give no information whatsoever about his relations with women. It is known that women of the high aristocracy, for instance Mme de Pompadour and Mme de Hausset in Paris, were greatly impressed by him, but no gossip has survived about any amorous affair he might have had. It is not even known whether he was ever married. The sexual aspect of his life is as much a mystery as are his true name and origins.

More is known about Saint-Germain's diplomatic activities. It is a documented fact that in February 1760 he was given full powers by Louis XV and an authorization by Marechal Belle-Isle, the minister of war, to go to Holland and obtain there a loan of thirty million florins (an enormous amount at the time) for France. Upon his arrival in Amsterdam, Saint-Germain presented himself to the Jewish bankers Thomas and Adrien Hope. It would seem that the leading bankers both in Amsterdam and The Hague knew, or believed, that Saint-Germain was of Jewish origin (the son of "Wolf"?), and it was possibly due to this that he had ready access to them. However, Saint-Germain's mission aroused the displeasure of the Duc de Choiseul, and he sent instructions to his representative in Amsterdam to have the "the pretended Comte de Saint-Germain," as he referred to him, arrested and sent back to France. Luckily for Saint-Germain, he learned of the order in time, and managed to obtain a personal loan of 2,000 florins from the Jewish money-lender Boas against the surety of three opals, evade capture, and flee to England (in June, 1760).[18] In London Saint-Germain was given to understand that he was unwelcome there, too, whereupon he proceeded to The Hague and thence to Nimègues, near the German border, where he bought a large estate, and engaged in the research of dyes.

In April 1762 Saint-Germain received, and accepted, an invitation from the Count Pierre Rotari to come to Russia.[19] There he became an intimate friend of Count Orlov, and was believed to have played a part in the coup d'état carried out by the three Orlov brothers against Peter III. Thereafter nothing is known about Saint-Germain until 1770, when he appeared in Livorno in the uniform of a Russian general.

The last chapter in Saint-Germain's life was played out in Germany. He participated in the Masonic movement. For a while he achieved complete domination over Margrave Charles-Alexander of Anspach, who took him along wherever he went. Finally, in 1779, he became a close friend of Landgrave Charles of Hesse, whom we have already met. The landgrave was keenly interested in alchemy, and provided Saint-Germain with a laboratory and a home to the end of his life. Saint-Germain became not only a friend of the landgrave, but also his mentor in alchemy and things spiritual. The story of the relationship between Saint-Germain and the landgrave is best told in the latter's own words:

Upon my return to Altona I saw the famous Comte de St. Germain, who seemed to take a liking to me, especially when he learned that I was not a hunter, neither had other passions contrary to the study of the high things of nature. He told me then: "I shall come to see you at Schleswig, and you will see the great things that we shall do together."

I made him understand that I had good reason for not accepting, for the moment, the favor he wanted to do me. He answered, "I know that I must come to you, and must talk to you." I knew no other way of avoiding all explanations except to tell him that Colonel Koeppern, who was staying behind sick, would follow me in a couple of days, and that he could talk to him about it. Then I wrote a letter to Koeppern to tell him to prevent, and if possible dissuade, the Comte de St. Germain from coming here. Koeppern arrived in Altona and spoke to him. But the comte answered him, "You can say what you want, I must go to Schleswig, and I shall not change my mind. The rest will come about by itself. You should take care of providing me with prepared lodgings, etc." Koeppern told me of this result of their conversation, of which I could not approve.

I have gathered much information about this extraordinary man from the Russian army where I had spoken about him in particular with my friend Colonel Frankenberg. He told me, "You can be sure that he is not a *trompeur* [charlatan], and that he possesses great knowledge. He was at Dresden; I was there with my wife. He showed goodwill toward both of us. My wife wanted to sell a pair of earrings. A jeweler offered a small sum for it. She spoke about it in front of the comte, who told her, "Do you want to show them to me?"—which she did. Then he said, "Can you confide them to me for a couple of days?" He gave them back to her after having enhanced them. The jeweler, to whom my wife showed them thereafter, told her, "These are beautiful stones, they are totally different from the previous ones that you showed me!" and paid her more than double.

St. Germain arrived soon thereafter at Schleswig. He talked to me about great things he wanted to do for the good of humanity, etc. I had no desire for them, but then I had scruples about rejecting knowledge, very important in all respects, because of a false idea of wisdom or avariciousness, and I made myself his disciple. He spoke a lot about the improvement of colors which cost almost nothing, of the amelioration of metals, adding that one should absolutely not make gold, even if one knew how, and remained absolutely faithful to this principle. Precious stones cost much to buy, but if one knows how to ameliorate them, they increase infinitely in value. There is almost nothing in nature that he did not know how to improve and utilize. He confided in me almost all the knowledge of nature, but only its beginning, making me thereafter search myself, by experiments, for the means to succeed, and was extremely pleased with my progress. This concerns metals and stones, but as for colors, he gave them to me effectively, and also some more important knowledge. One will perhaps be curious to know his story, and I shall trace it with the greatest veracity according to his own words, adding the necessary explanations.

He told me that he was eighty-eight years old when he came here; he was ninety-two or ninety-three when he died. . . . He pretended to have acquired the knowledge of nature by his own application and his researches. He knew the herbs and plants completely, and had invented the medicaments that he used continuously, and that prolonged his life and health. I still have all his prescriptions, but the physicians turned against his science after his death. There was a Dr. Lossau, who had been an apothecary and to whom I gave 1,200 écus each year to work on the medicaments that the Comte de St. Germain dictated to him, among others, and principally, his tea that rich people purchased and that the poor received for nothing—as they did also the care of this doctor who cured many people—of which tea, to my knowledge, nobody died. But after the death of this physician, disgusted by the remarks I was hearing from every side, I withdrew all the prescriptions, and did not replace Lossau.

St. Germain wanted to establish a factory of dyes in this country. The one of the late Otte at Eckernfoerde was vacant and abandoned. Thus I had the opportunity to purchase those buildings next to the town at a good price, and I set up the Comte de St. Germain there. I bought silks, wools, etc. It was necessary to have a lot of utensils for such a factory. I saw there fifteen pounds of silk being dyed in a big cauldron according to the method that I had learned and carried out myself in a cup. This succeeded perfectly. One therefore cannot say that this was not done on a large scale.

Unfortunately, the Comte de St. Germain, when arriving at Eckernfoerde, stayed in a humid room where he contracted very bad rheumatism, from which, despite all his remedies, he never recovered completely. I often went to see him at Eckernfoerde, and never went away without new, very interesting instructions, often making notes of the questions I wanted to ask him. Toward the end of his life I found him very sick one day, and he believed that he was about to die. He was visibly losing weight. After having dined in his bedroom, he made me sit down alone next to his bed, and spoke to me then more clearly about a lot of things, foretelling much. He told me to come back as soon as possible, which I did. Upon my return I found him somewhat better, but he was very silent. When I went in 1783 to Cassel, he told me that if he died during my absence I would find a sealed note by his hand which should be sufficient for me. But this note was not found, having perhaps been entrusted to unfaithful hands. Often I pressed him to give me during his life that which he wanted to leave in that note. This distressed him, and he said, "Ah, how unhappy I would be, my dear Prince, if I dared to speak!"

He was perhaps one of the greatest philosophers who had ever lived. Friend of humanity, wanting money only to give it to the poor, friend also

> of animals, his heart was occupied only with the happiness of others. He thought he could make the world happy by providing it with new pleasures, more beautiful fabrics, more beautiful colors, at better prices. For his superb colors cost almost nothing. I have never seen a man who had a clearer mind than his, and with it an erudition, especially in ancient history, the like of which I have rarely found. . . .
>
> He traveled to all the countries of Europe, and I know almost none in which he did not sojourn a long time. He knew them all thoroughly. He has often been to Constantinople and Turkey. Nevertheless, France seemed to be the country he loved most. . . .
>
> His philosophical principles in religion were pure materialism, but he knew how to present them with such refinement that it was very difficult to counter him successfully with reasoning. Still, I often succeeded in confounding his views. He was the opposite of an adorer of Jesus Christ, and permitted himself to say things about him that were rather disagreeable to me. I said to him, "My dear Comte, it depends on you what you want to believe about Jesus Christ, but I admit frankly that you cause me much pain in making remarks against him, to whom I am so completely devoted." He remained pensive for a time, then answered, "Jesus Christ is nothing, but to cause you pain is something. So I promise you never again to speak about him." On his deathbed, during my absence, one day he asked Lossau to tell me when I returned to Cassel that God granted him the grace to make him again change his views before his death, and added that he knew how much this would please me, and that I shall still do much for his happiness in another world.[20]

This document is most important as an authentic eyewitness account of the last five years of Saint-Germain's life. It shows that while he still engaged in mystifying people whom he encountered (as in the incident with the jewels of Colonel Frankenberg's wife), he concentrated on practical methods of improving technological production, the production of medicaments, the fabrication and dyeing of materials, and the like. Most remarkable is that he dared to risk offending the landgrave's religious sensibilities by making "rather disagreeable remarks" about Jesus, and by giving unrestrained expression to his disbelief in him. Could it be that these views were survivals of attitudes he had absorbed many decades earlier in his Jewish parental home, views which now, in his extreme old age, he no longer felt constrained to hide?

The landgrave's account is supplemented by that of another eyewitness. The Hamburg physician, Dr. Kelemann, was present at a conversation between the landgrave and Saint-Germain. He heard Saint-Germain say: "I carry the burden of centuries. I shall die like all others, at least as far as appearances go, but my spirit will be reabsorbed into the bosom of the Great All (*Grand Tout*) who inspires me." Next Saint-Germain expressed the belief that he would be reincarnated in the body of a newborn child, and then said to the landgrave:

> You doubt the existence of Satan. Yet he does exist and is powerful. But he is the spirit of evil, and will ultimately succumb. It is due to Satan's maleficent influence that man must exist as he does. Two currents, one good, one bad, did inevitably go into the making of your ancestor. The All did not desire man. It was the rebellion of Satan that brought about the creation of Adam. Do not proclaim this, for many people cannot conceive this truth. This secret, should it be divulged, could not be admitted by human pride.

The landgrave objected to this view of the origin of man, but Saint-Germain answered, "So it is, life springs from the union of the sexes. One is of a diabolic order, the other of a divine order." At that point the landgrave asked him why he did not believe in Jesus, but before Saint-Germain could answer, Dr. Kelemann had to leave the room and thus could not record his response.[21]

Saint-Germain's view of the mixed divine-diabolic origin of man bears too close a resemblance to the well-known midrash about Cain having been fathered on Eve not by Adam but by Satan to be mere coincidence. It would appear that, as his final hour approached, Saint-Germain remembered that midrash which he may have studied, or heard, in his Jewish youth.

Saint-Germain died on February 27, 1784, at Eckenfoerde, in the Duchy of Schleswig. Upon his death Landgrave Charles inherited all his papers, burned them all, and thereafter refused to give any information about the mysterious man.

Saint-Germain's death, far from putting an end to his legend, added new chapters to it. Rumors began circulating that he had not died, and more and more people claimed to have met him personally: he was seen in Paris in 1835, and even as late as 1926. For the Society of Theosophy Saint-Germain became one of the "immortal initiates"; he was sighted again in Paris in 1934; it was believed that he would be reincarnated in December 1939, and that he would appear in a district of the Midi in 1945 and resume his occult activities.[22]

More relevant to our present interest is the alchemical knowledge Saint-Germain claimed to possess. The most authentic document in this respect is the memorandum he submitted—signing himself as "L.P.T.C. de Welldone", a name he used at one time—to M. d'Alvensleben, Frederick II's ambassador to Dresden. In this document, comprising twenty-nine points, Saint-Germain offered to set up industrial, chemical, and technical operations that would greatly benefit the economy of the Prussian state. They included, under points 19 to 29, the following:

19. Diverse processes for precious metals, that is to say, without gold or silver, being of great utility and of great economy, which will surely astonish every good chemist, and which will also reduce the enormous prices of perishable articles of luxury.
20. The preparation of a totally new metal whose qualities are amazing.
21. Diverse processes for precious objects which seem perfectly impossible.
22. The preparation of paper, feathers, ivory, bone, and wood tinted in very fine splendid colors.
23. Good chemical processes for various wines.
24. The preparation of Rossoli liqueur out of fruit-stones, etc. of superior quality and at advantageous prices.
25. The preparation of other useful things about which I keep silent.
26. Preventive measures against illnesses and all kinds of nuisances.
27. True purgatives that remove from the body only harmful elements.
28. True, sure, and beneficial cosmetics.
29. Superfine olive oil produced in Germany within twelve hours. That which concerns agronomy is reserved for later.

L.P.T.C. de Welldone

On another point one cannot say anything here for various reasons. It is reserved, etc.

The execution of this new industrial plan can serve the political economy to the highest degree, and introduce an indissoluble union among certain great nations.

De Welldone

On June 25, 1777, this memorandum was forwarded to Frederick II by D'Alvensleben who added: "The secret procedures about which he does not want to give information concern the transmutation of fine stones into precious stones."[23] Considering the risk to which an individual exposed himself if he disappointed the expectations of an autocrat such as the king of Prussia, the least one can conclude from this document is that Saint-Germain had supreme confidence in his ability to fulfill the alchemical and technological promises he made in it.

In addition to the above memorandum, unquestionably written by Saint-Germain, two manuscripts are attributed to him. One is titled *La magie sainte revelée a Moyse*, which is basically a handbook of magic ceremonial ritual including descriptions of rites for the purpose of discovering various hidden things, such as "mines of diamonds, of gold and silver, in the bosom of the earth," of prolonging life for more than a century in full health and strength, and so on.[24] It contains this statement: "Moses found it [the manuscript] in an Egyptian monument and conserved it piously in Asia under the device of a winged dragon." One remarkable feature of this manuscript was that it was triangular in shape.[25] As we shall see, the triangle (and the number three) had special fascination for Saint-Germain.

The second manuscript, preserved in the Municipal Library of Troyes, France, is entitled *La trés sainte trinosophie*, and is essentially a description of a fantastic voyage undertaken by the author in search of alchemical-kabbalistic secrets. As to its authorship, there is no unanimity among the scholars who studied it, several of whom doubt that it was actually written by Saint-Germain.[26] The body of the book contains a fantastic and repetitious travelogue. Written in first person singular, this travelogue has a depressing, nightmarish quality: the author crosses terrifying landscapes, moves in and out of vaguely described imaginary and bizarre palaces designated often by repulsive names, encounters strange human beings who are stated to be hoary with the wisdom of the ages, and yet whatever they are quoted as saying amounts to very little. In the course of his fantastic journey the author is accosted by dangerous fires and waters, wades through sandy and salty deserts and lakes of putrefaction, sees phantoms, hydras, and lamias, and an assortment of fearsome birds. But in all this there is no mention of either alchemy or mysticism. On the other hand, we do get a large number of Hebrew-Aramaic, and somewhat fewer Arabic, words and expressions, penned partly in the original characters. The text of the book begins as follows:

> It was night, the moon hidden by dark clouds cast only an uncertain glimmer over the blocs of lava that surround the solfatara [sulphur springs]. My head covered with a linen veil, holding in my hand the golden bough, I advanced without fear toward the place where I had been ordered to spend the night. Walking on scorching sand, every instant I felt it give way under my steps. The clouds piled up over my head, lightning streaked through the night and gave a blood-red coloring to the flames of the volcano. . . . Finally I arrive, find an altar of iron, I place on it the mysterious bough. . . . I pronounce the terrible words. . . . Instantly the earth trembles under my feet, there is a clap of thunder. . . . The roarings of Vesuvius respond to its redoubled blows, its fires join the fires of the lightning. The choirs of spirits rise up into the air, and reach the praises of the Creator. . . . The consecrated bough that I have placed on the triangular altar bursts into flame; suddenly a thick smoke surrounds me, I can see no more. Plunged into darkness I feel that I am descending into an abyss. I do not know how long I remained in this situation, but when I opened my eyes I searched diligently for the objects that had surrounded me some time earlier. The altar, Vesuvius, the open country of Naples had vanished from my sight, I was in a vast subterranean realm, alone, removed from the whole world. . . . Next to me was a long white robe; its loose fabric seemed to me to be composed of linen yarn; on a granite block rested a copper lamp; on

top, a black tablet inscribed with Greek letters indicated the route I was to follow.

In the sequel the author describes his trials and tribulations while traversing a terribly frightening landscape. After an "immense march" he arrives at a square place. He enters through the northern portal, then proceeds across more fantastic lands. He sees a boat, and says to the boatman, *Bonum est sperare in domino quam confidere in principibus*, which is the Latin translation of Psalm 118:9, "it is better to take refuge in the Lord than to trust in princes." Then he comes to a lake of fire, and crossing it finds a hall upheld by columns of fire. He sees all kinds of phantoms. This section closes with an emblem inscribed in unskilled Hebrew script with the words *esha ḥolit*, that is, "sandy fire" in Aramaic letters.

The book is literally studded with Hebrew and Aramaic words, names, and expressions that a non-Jewish author would be most unlikely to know, and that would be familiar only among Jews who had a good talmudic education. Only part of these Hebrew and Aramaic words can be identified; many of them are reproduced by the person who prepared the Troyes copy of the manuscript so badly that it is impossible to recognize what words they intend to stand for. The same holds good for those Hebrew words which are given in French transliteration.

Among the illustrations contained in the Troyes manuscript there is one that shows a bird, an altar, and a lamp stand supporting a candle (See Figure 37.2). Above the picture there is a Hebrew inscription: *kohen, rofe, ashaf*, "priest, physician, wizard (or: magician)." Since of these three nouns the first is biblical, and the second and third are talmudic, their use again indicates the author's familiarity with both biblical and post-biblical Hebrew.

In contrast to the gloomy mood that pervades the whole book, it ends on an upbeat, almost triumphant note: "I took the sword, and striking the sun reduced it to dust. Then I touched it, and each molecule became a sun of gold similar to the one I had shattered. 'The work is accomplished,' a strong and melodious voice cried out instantly" (237). Since "sun" is the ubiquitous alchemical name for gold, these words could indicate that the traumatic voyage related in the book was meant to be a symbolic and mystical description of the Work of the alchemist, that of making gold, which, in the end, he succeeded in accomplishing.

The last page of the *Trinosophie* is inscribed with four lines of mystical signs at the bottom, and over them is a triple circular diagram containing Hebrew words (see Figure 37.3).[27]

Figure 37.2. Illustration from *La très sainte trinosophie*, attributed to the Comte de Saint-Germain. Hebrew at top: "priest, physician, wizard."

The author of the *Trinosophie* evidently had more than a working knowledge of biblical and post-biblical Hebrew and of talmudic Aramaic. The latter is evidenced, for example, in his ability to find no fewer than four synonyms for "decomposition": *ṣaḥan, raqav, bash,* and *ne'elaḥ*. This points to an author who had received in his youth a thorough talmudic education. In addition, he also had at least some familiarity with Arabic, including some Arabic alchemical terms, which he may have acquired at a later age. He must have acquired Yiddish, too, in his adulthood, while he lived in places (such as Strasbourg) inhabited by Yiddish-speaking Ashkenazi Jews.

Figure 37.3. Last page of *La très sainte trinosophie*. The Hebrew words, from the top, clockwise: Outer circle: "*Adonay* [Lord]. And the spirit of God. Supernal world. Infinity." Middle circle: "Supernal. Middle. World of the angels. Infernal." Inner circle: "*Ispirkha* [white lead]. Flower. Sulphur." The French words in the center read: "Réunion des principes. Unité. Création. Conservat[rice]. Génératrice [Union of principles. Unity. Creation. Keeper. Generative]." I am unable to deciper the four lines at the bottom.

WHAT can be said in conclusion of the life and work of the famous, fabulous, and mysterious Comte de Saint-Germain? I think that the data contain sufficient evidence of his Sephardi (Spanish-Portuguese) background, of a childhood spent in Piemonte (he spoke French with a Piemontese accent), and of talmudic education. Being gifted with a prodigious memory, the knowledge he acquired even in the earliest stages of his life remained with him as long as he lived. After striking out on his own and embarking on a career of international adventurism, he found it essential to conceal his Jewish origin. He assumed many guises and names, always pretending to be a nobleman, usually a count, and hailing from a country other than the one in which he happened to be. Exploiting the credulity of the times, he claimed—or at least encouraged the rumors to the effect—that he was hundreds or even thousands of years old, that he was in possession of the elixir of life, and that he knew how to make gold and precious stones, in a word that he was a master of the Great Art of alchemy. Most importantly for his success in being admitted into, and admired by, the highest circles of nobility in one country after the other, he had such a winning personality that he was able to cast his spell over all people whom he met, including princes and even crowned heads. Another side of his talents was his aptitude in diplomacy, business, and industry, of which Louis XV, the Landgrave Charles, and leading French and possibly Russian statesmen made use. Although to the very end of his life he never revealed his Jewish origin, in his old age he made no secret of his disbelief in Jesus, nor of his knowledge (among the many tongues he knew) of the Jewish languages of Hebrew, Aramaic, and Yiddish.

As for his alchemy and chemistry, although no documentation has survived as to whether he made any original contribution to them, he certainly played a significant role in keeping alive the belief and interest in the former, and possibly contributed to laying the foundations for the industrial use of the latter.

Chapter Thirty-eight

JACOB EMDEN; THE BAR ILAN MANUSCRIPT

THE TWO eighteenth-century Jewish alchemists discussed so far were primarily professional magicians and mystifiers whose orientation was very remote from the traditional pre-Haskala Jewish mentality. The third man, to whom we now turn briefly, was in contrast, a rabbi, a halakhic authority, and Kabbalist, one of the most outstanding Jewish scholars of his generation. He devoted much of his life to combating those of his co-religionists who still adhered to what he considered the dangerous Shabbatean heresy, and those who initiated during his lifetime the equally heretical Frankist movement. He was the son of Zevi Hirsch Ashkenazi, known as Ḥakham Zevi, and like his father was a man of a stormy, independent, and uncompromising character.

His name was Jacob Emden (1697–1776), and the little that is known of his life indicates that he was in many respects an exceptional character in the north European Jewish environment of his age. For one thing, despite his great knowledge and voluminous scholarly literary output, he occupied a rabbinical position, in the community of Emden, for only a short period in his long life. For another, he established a printing press in Altona, providing himself with a certain economic and intellectual independence that enabled him to disseminate his views, often strongly critical of the traditions and social mores of the Jewish community in which he lived. He became embroiled in numerous controversies, of which the most envenomed was that with Rabbi Jonathan Eybeschuetz, who became rabbi of the "Three Communities" of Altona, Hamburg, and Wandsbeck in 1751, and was suspected (by Emden as well as by others) of being an adherent of Shabbatai Zevi, the false Messiah. The fight between the two rabbinical giants reached such a point that Emden was forced to escape to Amsterdam, from where, however, he continued his attacks on Eybeschuetz. From fighting the Shabbateans, Emden went on to a criticism of the *Zohar*, the holy book of the Kabbalah, and even dared to question its antiquity (it was considered by the Kabbalists to be the work of the second-century Palestinian sage Rabbi Shimʿon ben Yoḥai), and ultimately its sanctity as well. This, of course, aroused strong opposition, and contributed to the controversy that surrounded Emden.

In addition to his halakhic works, his commentaries on Scripture and the prayer book, and his polemical writings, Emden wrote an autobiography, which is unique in the rabbinical world. Apart from all this, he was interested in the natural sciences, knowledgeable of Hebrew grammar, and familiar with the Latin, German, and Dutch languages. As for alchemy, although there is no evidence in his voluminous works that he engaged in alchemical experimentation or that he believed in alchemical tenets and teachings, one of his responsa shows that he took the claims of alchemy very seriously and, more than that, that he was eager to obtain information about alchemical doctrines and achievements. In Emden's great responsa collection, entitled *Sh'elat Ya*ᶜ*vetz* (printed in Altona, 1738–1759), there is one long letter which he wrote in answer to a question addressed to him by a certain Wolf Ginzburg, who wanted to know whether it was permissible to learn sciences, and especially medical science, from the gentiles. In his responsum (no. 41, ff. 65a–74a), Emden inserts a question of his own in which he asks Ginzburg for information on alchemy in general, and on Hebrew (or Jewish) alchemical writings in particular. What follows is my translation of the relevant passage (ff. 73b–74a) from Emden's Hebrew. Emden was not familiar with Hebrew alchemical terms, but managed to convey what he wanted to say by using Hebrew words whose basic meanings were near enough to the terms he lacked (these words are in parentheses).

> Inform me, please, whether there is there somebody who is skilled in the analysis (*nituaḥ*) of elements (*y'sodot*), and their extraction from compounds (*murkavim*), and the separation of the three pillars of alchemy, and the science of their combination and mixing in all the low existing things down to plants and herbs, and metals and minerals. I would like to know whether that science still exists, and whether those things, such as the transmutation (*hishtanut*) of the substances of metals (*ᶜatzme hamatakhot*), have been verified with a full certainty. And [whether] the greatness of the medicaments, about which the masters of that sect (*kat*) sang exaggerated praises and told great marvels, is actually as rumored. And whether there is anything about it in any book of ours. And recently I saw a book printed in the foreign language (*La*ᶜ*az*), in the name of an ancient one of the sons of our people, which is considered among them [the gentiles] of very great value, and they say that they have several Jewish authors who were great in that science. And this makes me wonder greatly: if the thing is really true, how did their memory totally disappear from among us, nobody knows how far, even though the author of the *Duties of the Hearts* [by Baḥya ibn Paquda] mentions the virtues of alchemy at the beginning of his chapter on Trusting, making it clear that he verified its existence? Also Rabbi Abraham ibn Ezra seems to assume its reality. But the *Kuzari* talks

> about them in two places, and mentions them disparagingly and mocks them. However, I have neither seen as yet nor heard that our early sages mentioned anywhere that they knew of any book written in the holy tongue on that science. Therefore my soul yearns also to know whether perchance somebody among us still possesses such a book. In the great houses of books [libraries] and in the collections of the honored houses of study [universities] there are [such books]. My soul would greatly enjoy to know what their wise men think about this matter. And from our old ones, may their memory be for a blessing, we know that one should not, heaven forfend, leave the precious, holy study for the sake of this. But, happy is he who can hold on to the one without leaving the other, to do as they do. But to go a long way to their houses of study is, to my mind, not a proper thing to do. Even though it does not have to be condemned as has learning from a magus. In any case, don't go near the door of its house, and don't dwell with them in their ornamented rooms and courtyards and palaces, to learn their customs and manners.

Several interesting points are supplied by this passage. One is that Emden had some general knowledge about the basic tenets of alchemy, including its claim to be able to transmute metals, but was not sure whether that "science" was still in existence in his day. Second, he was familiar with the views of the medieval Jewish philosophers on alchemy and understood clearly that some of them believed in alchemy, while others rejected it. Third, he had read at least one alchemical book in a foreign language (*Laᶜaz*) written by a Jew and greatly valued by the gentile alchemists. Fourth, he knew that the gentile alchemists possessed, and valued, several books written by Jewish alchemists, which were unknown to him. Fifth, he was puzzled as to how it was possible that those old Jewish alchemical books were unknown to Jewish scholars, and regretted that this was the case. Sixth, he was keenly interested in finding out whether such alchemical books of Jewish authorship could still be found anywhere. Seventh, while he cautions his interrogator not to abandon Torah study for the sake of alchemy, he offers the opinion that "happy is he" who can pursue both studies simultaneously.

Jacob Emden was an exceptional figure among the Ashkenazi Jews of the eighteenth century. Whereas the Sephardi Jews could by that time look back upon several centuries of achievement in all fields of sciences (in addition to halakha, philosophy, poetry, and mysticism), so that interest in alchemy was for them, so to speak, a natural given, Ashkenazi Jewry (with a very few exceptions) concentrated exclusively on halakha and Talmud study, and opened up to new trends, such as Hasidism and the Enlightenment, only in the latter half of the eighteenth century. For a halakhically anchored Ashkenazi Jew of those days to take an interest in sciences, and especially in alchemy, was in fact so unusual that one is prompted to look for special factors in trying to account for it.

In the case of Jacob Emden such special factors can easily be found. His father, Zevi Hirsch Ashkenazi (1660–1718), although he was of Ashkenazi stock and lived in Moravia in his childhood, was sent at the age of fifteen to Salonika, to study there in the yeshiva of R. Elijah Covo. Zevi Hirsch stayed in Salonika for some twelve years, then spent another year in Belgrade. During this time he adopted Sephardi customs, manners, and outlook, and even assumed the Sephardi title *ḥakham* rather than its Ashkenazi equivalent, rabbi. As for the surname "Ashkenazi," it was adopted by, or given to, some Jews of Ashkenazi descent who lived in a Sephardi environment. (The most famous of them was Yiṣḥaq Luria Ashkenazi, or Ashkenazi Rabbi Yiṣḥaq, whence his acronym "the Holy ARI.") Subsequently Ḥakham Zevi was appointed *ḥakham* of the Sephardi community of Sarajevo. He was close to thirty when he returned to the Ashkenazi world, accepting the position of *av bet din* (which can be translated as "suffragan rabbi") of the "Three Communities" of Altona, Hamburg, and Wandsbeck. In 1710 he was invited to serve as rabbi of the Ashkenazi community in Amsterdam, where he maintained close relations with the Sephardim, and had the highest regard for them and their traditions. His son, Jacob Emden, was greatly influenced by him, and was imbued by him with Sephardi views and attitudes, and the Sephardi positive approach to the secular sciences. This is the background that explains Emden's interest in the sciences, in medicine, and in alchemy.

The responsum quoted above affords us a fleeting glimpse into the status of alchemy among the Ashkenazi rabbinical scholars of the eighteenth century. The interest of the run-of-the-mill Ashkenazi scholar was in that period still largely confined to "the four cubits of the halakha." Their general silence concerning alchemy indicates that they were, in all probability, unaware of its meaning, scope, tenets, and possibly of its very existence. Even Jacob Emden, despite his much broader Sephardi-influenced approach to the world of intellectual endeavor, had only a vague idea of what alchemy meant and what it tried to achieve, and although he knew about the existence of Jewish alchemical treatises, he was unable to identify their authors. No wonder that, as we proceed from the eighteenth to the nineteenth century, we find the last Jewish alchemists not among the Ashkenazi but among the Sephardi Jews. There remains but one manuscript from the eighteenth century to discuss, and it too is evidence of some continuing interest in alchemy among the Sephardi community.

Bar Ilan Manuscript 625

This manuscript, found in the Margaliot Collection of Bar Ilan University, Ramat Gan, Israel, consists of ten folios, paginated 4–6, and 8–14. It is in poor shape, with several pages partly illegible. It seems to date from the eighteenth century, although it undoubtedly is but a copy of an older manuscript. Nineteen of its twenty pages are in Hebrew; folio 6a and part of folio 7b are in Ladino. Most of the foreign technical terms appearing in it are in Italian. Hence it stands to reason to assume that its author was a Sephardi Jew who lived in Italy.

The most interesting part of this manuscript is a long recipe for the preparation of a liquid "philosophers' stone," which can transmute silver into gold:

> (f.8a). THE MAKING of a precious stone which is called the philosophers' stone. Take one *liṭra* [pound] of purified and white *armoniaqo* [ammoniac] salt in which there should be no blackness at all. Pound it very fine, and pass it through a very dense sieve. Then take fifteen wet [fresh] eggs, one day old, and boil them in water until they become very hard, and take the egg whites and cut them into small pieces, and take a marble stone and put on it layer (*ʿaliyah*) upon layer, one layer of the aforementioned ammoniac salt, and one layer of the aforementioned egg whites, until the aforementioned salt and egg whites are used up. And then put it into a receptor [until] all the salt becomes water. Take that water and put it aside to keep. Then take two pounds of *sublimaṭo* [sublimated] quicksilver which should be of the best, and pound it to a very very thin powder which the wind can blow away, and put the powder with the aforementioned water into an *orinal* [flask], and put it [in] very gradually, and all the time mix it well with a [word missing] of wood, and when it is well mixed cover the flask immediately, and lute well the joints so that is should not be able to blow through, and then take four or ten hard-boiled egg whites as mentioned, and cut them into small pieces, and put them into the water which is mixed with the aforementioned powder, and mix well. And cover the flask well, and put it into a *bagno tineiro* [bath], until all of it is saturated with water, and it should be [there] for four days. And when all has become *resolvido* [dissolved], pour the aforementioned water through a *filṭro* [filter] cloth in cleanliness.
>
> In the name of God. Take two pounds of good *anṭimonio* [antimony], which should not be counterfeit but should have *samforot arutat* [?], and he will see written some *samforot zufiyot* [?], and grind the aforementioned two pounds on a marble stone, very very fine, then take a glass flask whose neck should be long, and lute it with the philosophers' clay, and let it dry,

and put into it the aforementioned ground antimony, and on it put the aforementioned water, and instantly seal its mouth with wax made with *asṭize* [?] which should close well, so that the spirits should not get lost, and put the aforementioned flask in your oven upon two iron sticks so that it should not move at all, and then put into it the receptor as customary, and the aforementioned receptor must be as big as possible, and lute well the joint with a glue made of quicklime and egg white and fine flour, and make it so that it should not be able to breathe, and let it stand like this until the glue hardens, and then make a fire in the oven with two coals [several illegible words], until the oven and the flask get hot, and then increase the fire little by little three hours [words illegible] water white like milk, which when it falls [words illegible] it appears that it has frozen, and after four hours have passed [put?] it on the fire with eight or nine coals which should not be big, but like small apples, and you will see the shape of color, either *stanire* [?] or *verde* [*amordo* green]. And you will see in the receptor that a black cloud has developed with other colors, and continue the aforementioned fire for another four hours, and when the said cloud disappears you will see another color, and know that a drop red like blood will drop down, and then give it more fire for another four hours. Then you will see another color like gold drop down. Give always fire for another four hours, and after those colors have become mixed you will see that another black color like burnt blood comes, then for eight hours give very strong fire of wood which makes a clear and strong flame like that of the *reverbero* [?], and after those eight hours put coals above the flask so that the ascent of the fire should be strong, and leave it until it becomes extinguished by itself. And when you see that the fire is weak, take the aforementioned receptor cleverly and cover it with cotton-wool and wax or something similar, so that it should not breathe, and cover that wax with glue made of flour and egg white, and cover it very well, for it is the key of keys and the secret of secrets. And then remove the mud which is on the flask, until it remains pure and you can see in it a tree like a tree with fruits and flowers, and this is one of the signs that the operation is going well—and when everything is nice and pure take what is in it and pound it well until it becomes very fine powder, and put it in an unglazed pot and cover it with another pot like it, mouth to mouth, and tie [?] them with an iron thread, and cover it with mud so that it should not breathe, and so that the mud should be one finger [thick] over them. And when you have dried them, put them into an oven to [word illegible], and make light fire for one hour. Then cover that pot with burning coals [word illegible] for about four hours so that the fruits should be well covered, and after that time take them and let them cool, and when they are cool open it and see: if that powder is colored red, that is *melone* [?] in Laʿaz, good; and if not, repeat and cover it in the pot upon fire as at first, for twelve hours or until it becomes very red, and then take that powder and pound it fine, then put on it strong *desṭillaṭo* [distilled] vinegar, and take care that when you liquify it you should put into every pound of vinegar half an *onqia* [ounce] of *armoniaqo preparaṭo* [prepared ammoniac] salt. Then put that vinegar [upon] that powder so that it should cover it by two fingers, and cover everything well so that it should not breathe. Then put it into horse manure or a bath for about four hours. Then take it and you will find that vinegar red. Empty it gently into the other vessel and put on that powder new vinegar, liquified as the aforementioned, and put it into manure or a bath for about four hours, and do this each time until the aforementioned powder dissolves completely in the vinegar, by putting each time enough vinegar to cover the powder and two fingers [above it]. And when you see that the vinegar no longer brings color, take all the aforementioned colored vinegar and combine it, and liquify it like that oil of the aforementioned antimony, and lute well the joints. And know that at first will come pure water like rain water, and when you see that it begins to change color, that it comes tinted like gold, then take the receptor and give it strong fire at last, when you see that it stopped flowing give it very strong fire, and when all of it is collected take it and mix it with the oil of the aforementioned antimony, the oil of the colors for the powder, [and] put aside the aforementioned and preserve it well, and you should keep in great secret, for this is the precious oil of antimony of the philosophers with which they tint the silver to good gold.

Although the above recipe is contained in an eighteenth-century Hebrew manuscript, it obviously goes back to a much older original, from which it was copied in that century. It is in the traditional genre of instructions of how to prepare the invaluable "philosophers' stone" (which in this case is not a stone at all but a liquid), which can be used for "tinting silver to good gold," that is, either to transmute silver into gold, or, at least, to give silver the appearance of "good gold."

Despite some illegible words in the manuscript, and a few technical terms that could not be identified, this recipe is one of the most complete and detailed in Hebrew alchemical literature for the preparation of the secret substance termed here "the precious oil of antimony of the philosophers," and in many other tracts "the elixir of life." Particularly interesting in this recipe are the instructions which require the adept to spend an inordinate number of hours tending the fire, supervising the procedures, repeating them again and again. One gets the impression that the author's intention was to make the operation so difficult as to make it almost impossible for the average alchemist to undertake it.

Also, the complexity of the operation is such that it makes the committing of errors almost inevitable. One wonders how many alchemists, reading this recipe, were actually prepared to embark upon this operation, and how many of those who did so were able to carry it through correctly. In any case, "the precious oil of antimony" must have been among the rarest of substances ever produced by alchemists.

PART TEN

The Nineteenth Century

Introduction to Part Ten

By the nineteenth century, active engagement in alchemy was largely a thing of the past in the Western world. Chemistry, the triumphant heir and successor of alchemy, left no room for either the theories believed in or the operations performed by alchemists ever since the Hellenistic age, although the debt of chemistry to alchemy is a fascinating and as yet insufficiently explored subject. In the rare instances where isolated alchemical work still did continue in nineteenth-century Europe, it had become a quaint and queer fringe phenomenon.

The same situation did not obtain in the Muslim Middle East, where many venerable traditions were able to survive the century almost intact, among them the interest in, and practice of, alchemy. Islamic alchemy has been relatively well studied, but only in its classical period. Practically no research of later Islamic alchemy has been undertaken. Under the entry *al-Kīmīya* in the authoritative *Encyclopedia of Islam* (5:110–15), published in 1979, one finds not a word about what work Muslims did in alchemy, or what Muslim authors thought about it, after Ibn Khaldūn, who lived in the fourteenth century. The *Encyclopedia of Religion*, published in 1987, also stops with that century in its article "Islamic Alchemy" (1:196–99). This being true, the material I present here on Jewish alchemical activity in North Africa in the nineteenth century opens a window to the extension of Muslim alchemy by five centuries. Jewish alchemy could not have survived in that part of the world, even in the diminished form in which it did survive, unless alchemy was still a constituent part of the cultural atmosphere breathed by Jews and Muslims alike.

Chapter Thirty-nine

AN ALCHEMICAL MANUSCRIPT FROM JERBA

THE TUNISIAN island of Jerba (Djerba), despite its isolation from the North African mainland, was the home of a centuries-old Jewish community, which survived persecutions under the Almohads in the twelfth century, under the Spaniards in 1519, and under the Nazis in 1943. In the twelfth century Maimonides, in a letter to his son Abraham, expressed a very low opinion of the Jerban Jews, calling them "dull and of a crude nature."[1] However, by the nineteenth century, the period with which we are concerned in the present context, the yeshivot of Jerba produced many rabbis and writers, and provided religious leaders for the communities of North Africa. The Jewish community numbered 4,900 in 1946, before most emigrated to Israel. The manuscript which we are discussing in this chapter shows that, in addition, some of them were also engaged in alchemical study and practice.[2]

The manuscript, written in 1865 in Sephardi cursive, measures approximately 6 by 4 inches, and contains 145 folios. The title page, which carries the date-line "In the Island of Jerba, in the year 625," which corresponds to 1865, is surrounded by a primitive decorative frame, and it reads as follows:

> This is the gate of the Lord the righteous shall enter into it [Ps. 118:20]
>
> THE BOOK
> OF THE SCIENCE OF BKRṬNṬB[3]
>
> Behold here are before you wonderful and precious sciences, pleasant and honored, they are very very straight, and are revealed only to the honest sages whose hearts are pure and choice in the fear of God, and who do not reveal anything, for this science should not be explained to everybody, lest they spoil its secret and pleasantness and shine and splendor. Therefore it comes in a very hidden way, and very very obscurely, and what God has granted a person in knowledge and wisdom is properly kept hidden. And let him give thanks to God for the benefits He granted him, and for having raised up his horn [i.e., honor] and luck, and let him turn all his days to His service and His Torah, and let him hold on to the hand of [i.e., support] the wise and

the poor and the destitute, in order to learn the Torah of God and to serve Him, and to augment and exalt the Torah which is more precious than pearls, and to write books and print them and also those of others. And let him make the Torah a constant preoccupation for the old and the youth, the small and the young. And of the Lord, the God of heaven and earth, I beg that He save me from all evil and trouble, and let me attain this science, and guide me in His pure and flawless Torah. And what I arranged above I vowed and shall fulfill, with His help who gives knowledge and wisdom. And then I shall offer Him a song and praise, and shall bless Him, "in the congregations will I bless the Lord" [Ps. 26:12].

Written
on the Island of Jerba, may our city be rebuilt,
in the year
625 [1865]

As one can see from this literal translation, the author is not a great stylist, but he makes up for that deficiency by intense piety, and considers "this science" (the term he uses is *ḥokhmah*, which can also mean "wisdom") closely related to the Torah.

The text of the book begins on the reverse of the title page. The many non-Hebrew technical terms, mostly Italian and Arabic, include words in the local North-African Arabic dialect that are not found in the Arabic dictionaries:

> The science of alchemy. In all parts of the melting of metals and the nature of minerals it is necessary to understand the meaning of the building of the Sanctuary and the Tabernacle, which is for silver and which for gold and which for copper and iron, and the meaning of the precious stones and their virtues, and likewise the secrets of nature, *simpaṭiyah* and *anṭipiaiṭiya* [I. *simpatia* and *antipatia*], and it is necessary to know for each thing what is the limit and the virtue of its nature, and that there is in it nothing of the ways of the Emorite [i.e., idolatrous matters], and whatever does not belong to the roots of this science is of the ways of the Emorite.

The next two lines refer the reader to a later part of the book, dealing with *purgaṣione* (purgation), then follows another introductory statement which is of considerable interest due to its kabbalistic connotations. It begins by identifying the author (or the copyist) as "the youth Barukh Abraham HaKohen, S"Ṭ." The family name HaKohen is the same as that of the author of the book, but that is not an indication of relationship, since the majority of the Jews of Jerba were of Kohanite, that is, priestly, descent. S"Ṭ stands for *S'faradi ṭahor*, meaning "pure Sephardi," the proud self-identification of men who boasted pure

Sephardi descent even centuries after the expulsion of the Sephardi Jews from Spain in 1492.

> SAYS THE AUTHOR, the youth Barukh Abraham HaKohen, S"Ṭ: In my humble opinion, before you start reading in this honored and precious science you should recite this prayer that I composed. In my humble opinion it will be considered in the eyes of my Creator, blessed be His name, amen, and except for what you find written in it, do as God favors you with knowledge and wisdom, for the Lord our God is compassionate, and then also its study in which you will engage, and the neglect [of Torah study] it involves, will count for you as if you had studied His holy Torah, for the Holy One, blessed be He, adds the good thought to the deed. And this is the text of the prayer, with the help of heaven:
>
> For the unification of the Holy One, blessed be He [with His Shekhina], in fear and in trembling, to unite the name *YaH* with *WeH* [i.e., Yahweh] in a complete unity, in the name of all Israel, behold I come to study the science of TKDYMMT,[4] so that if the Lord our God will grant me to understand it and to succeed in working in it, I shall print the books of our brothers, the righteous and pious Children of Israel, and to study the Torah of the Lord day and night, to learn and to teach and to do and to raise up the horn [i.e., glory] and the banner of the Torah, and to strengthen the hands of those who devote themselves to it, and to work the holy work without trouble, with a full heart, and without turning anywhere else.

The first few lines of this prayer consist of a somewhat shortened version of the well-known *yiḥud* formula, whose full text contains the words "with His Shekhina," in brackets above. This brief dedication prayer was instituted by Yiṣḥaq Luria, the leading sixteenth-century Safed kabbalistic master, who is quoted as having said categorically, "One must always be careful to say before everything, 'For the unification of the Name of the Holy One, blessed be He, in fear and love and awe, in the name of all Israel,' for one must always unite the male and the female." Luria's influence was so powerful that ever since his time the unification formula has been faithfully recited by traditional kabbalistic and Hasidic Jews many times a day, at the start of each of the daily prayers, and before performing any religious or otherwise significant act. Underlying it is the mystical conviction that the destruction of the Temple of Jerusalem and the exile of the People of Israel brought about a separation between God the King and His mate the Shekhina (the feminine Presence of God), that as a result of this cleavage in the godhead God Himself was not complete, and that therefore it was the duty of the pious to dedicate everything they did to the overarching great purpose of bringing about the unification of God and the Shekhina.[5] The recommendation of the author of our book to recite the *yiḥud* before embarking on alchemical work brings that work most definitely within the compass of licit, and more than that, approved and valuable, religious activity. Among the hundreds of manuscript and printed alchemical texts I have perused, this manuscript is the only one in which I found a reference to the *yiḥud*.

After some more religious admonitions and recommendations of prayers, the author (f. 1a) identifies, first of all, the provenance of his treatise:

> This esteemed book I found in a manuscript . . . of our master and teacher R. Moshe HaKohen, son of the great rabbi R. Shaul HaKohen of blessed memory.
>
> Know that every passage over which you find a half-moon is by the aforementioned R. Moshe Kohen, and where you [do not] find a half-moon, it is by me, I the young Abraham Kohen, S"Ṭ.

Nowhere in the book is a half-moon (or any other identification mark) to be found. However, scattered in the text of the manuscript are additional indications concerning the provenance and authorship of the book. On folio 54b, introducing the third part of the book, we find some more details about the manner in which the copyist, Barukh Abraham HaKohen, obtained the material he included in the book:

> SAYS THE COPYIST: after having presented to you the first and second parts of the aforementioned book which I found in a manuscript . . . of his honor Rabbi Moshe Kohen . . . son of the great terebinth, the master of the land, . . . Rabbi Shaul HaKohen of blessed memory . . . author of the book *Leḥem haBikkurim* [Bread of the Firstfruits] and other books, I now come to put before you some pearls which I found in a manuscript of my master and father, may his light shine, and which are not contained in the aforementioned book; and my master and father told me that he had copied them from writings of the aforementioned RM"K [Rabbi Moshe Kohen].

Dealing with a manuscript of such composite origin it is difficult to determine whether certain specific statements, made in the first person singular, represent the words of the author or of the copyist. Thus, for example, on folio 58a we find a recipe for making "silver-water with which you can write as with ink," which is introduced with these words: "I found it written in a manuscript, and this is its language." We are at a loss in trying to determine whether the author or the copyist speaks here. If the latter, then he made use of sources in addition to Rabbi Moshe HaKohen's manuscript.

Another reference to an extraneous source, if it can be taken at face value, seems to indicate that the author, Moshe ben Shaul HaKohen, lived in the sixteenth century in Bologna, Italy. On folio 40b we find this statement:

> Know that I received from a wise man, and his name is Paṭīsṭa, here, Bologna, the 9th of Marṣo [March], year 5308 [1548], *s'gullot* [H., remedies] of two herbs: the herb *ṭorah* [?] and the herb *anṭorah* [?]. And they are found only in the mountains of France. One of them is good for hardening iron, and the other for softening it. Also the herb *sfera qaṣwalo* [?] is good for breaking and crushing all iron vessels and all copper, and it is found only in Napoli [Naples].

This is a very intriguing entry. I have not been able to identify a sixteenth-century Bolognese alchemist named Paṭīsṭa (probably Batista), nor could I find traces of a Moshe ben Shaul HaKohen, or his book *Leḥem haBikkurim*. However, in about 1500 one of the Jews expelled from Spain, Abraham ben Moshe HaKohen, was appointed rabbi of Bologna, and it is possible that our Moshe ben Shaul HaKohen was of the same family. In 1568 the Jews were banished from Bologna, and it could have been at that time that Moshe ben Shaul moved to Jerba. Since most of the alchemical terms used in the manuscript are Italian, it is more than likely that its author was an Italian Jew.

The actual alchemical text of the manuscript begins on the same folio 1a:

And This is My Desire with the Help of the Lord my Rock and Savior

> The kinds of salt are many but all of them are of three kinds: natural, heavenly, and artificial.
>
> The natural comes from the mountains and some of it is dark and some of it is pure like the onyx, and is called *sal gemma*, that is salt whose glitter sparkles like a precious stone. And there is of it a kind of mineral which is called *sal indi*, that is, it comes from India. And there is another mineral one which is called *sal natiqo* [?]. And there is yet another mineral one called *sal niṭro* [saltpeter] which comes from Egypt and its borders. And there is another mineral, scented and good smelling, which comes from *al-Yaman* [Yemen]. And there is another one whose color is black. And there is another one, white like glass, with whose pieces one can see the face of man, and therefore it is called *speculare* [I., mirror] salt. And there is a kind which is red of an essential redness, similar to *qarma* [garnet]. And there is a kind of it whose redness is clear like that of the rose. And there is [a kind] of it which is yellow like saffron.
>
> The heavenly is the salt of Sodom which came down from heaven, and it is bitter and very salty. It burns easily, and its grains do not burst in fire, as do the other salts.

THE ARTIFICIAL: some of it comes from the soil and is called *sal misiṭro* [I. *sal mastro*, brackish salt], and it is the one out of which they make the *polvere* [I., powder] for guns. AND THERE IS THE ONE which is made out of the water of the sea, as in Sicily and Italy. AND THERE IS ONE which is made out of the blood of domestic and wild animals. AND THERE IS ONE which is made out of gold. AND THERE IS ONE which is made out of silver. AND THE ONE made out of honey. AND THE ONE made out of the sediment of wine called *ṭarṭaro* [tartar]. AND THE ONE made out of burnt olives. AND THE ONE made out of the *lipio santo* [?]. AND THE ONE made out of the *ienpiro* [I. *giunipero* or ginepro, juniper] tree. AND THE ONE made out of wormwood roots. AND THE ONE made out of the *absinsio* [I. *absintina*, absinthe, wormwood] tree. And thus it can be made out of all the fruits and plants, and the salt of each thing is good for particular diseases according to the nature of the fruit or the plant of which it is made. AND THERE IS ONE made out of urine. AND out of the *saraṭānes* [A. *saraṭan*, lobster]. And see in the book ShLH"G[6] at length.

The last two lines of folio 1a are only partly legible, but they deal with "a dust taken out from under the sand . . . big stones, and it is called *salarmoniaqo* [sal ammoniac], that is, salt that is found under the sand."

Folio 1b contains a table of contents listing the forty-one chapters of the book, each with its page number. The foreign terms are Italian in the first part (numbers 7 to 16), then follow several Hebrew terms (numbers 17 to 25), and finally (numbers 26 to 39) terms in Arabic. I have put all the Italian and Arabic terms in italics, and added my translations and explanation in square brackets.

INDEXES OF THE BOOK IN GENERAL TERMS,
WITH THE HELP OF GOD AWESOME IN PRAISES

1. Kinds of salt, 1a
2. Explanation of some things, 2a, 8a
3. Introduction to the book, 4a
4. Operations of abridgments, 5b
5. The waters, 9a
6. The oils, 11b
7. *Solimaṣione* [I., sublimations], 13a
8. *Asolimāre* [I., to sublimate], 13b
9. The *fisaṣione* [I., fixations], 13b
10. *Afisāre* [I., to fixate], 15a
11. *Purgaṣione* [I., purgations], 15b
12. *Apurgāre* [I., to purgate], 16a
13. The *preparaṣione* [I., preparations], 16b
14. *Aprepārāre* [I., to prepare], 16b

15. The *qalṣinasione* [I., calcination], 17b
16. The *qalṣināre* [I., to calcinate], 18a
17. *Hasʿarah* [H., sublimation], 18b
18. The preparation [or improvement] of some things, 19a
19. The purification of metals, 20b
20. Freezing [i.e., congelation], 21a
21. Whitening, 25a
22. Reddening and tinting, 28b
23. The long operations, 31b
24. Separate operations, 41b, 55b
25. The work of the pearls, 45a, 55b
26. The *taṭhīr* [A., purification], 49a, 55a
27. The *taḥmīr* [A., reddening], 50a
28. The *tabyīḍ* [A., whitening], 50a, 55a
29. The *tathbīt* [A., fixation] 51a, 54b
30. *Thabāt* [A., fixation] for the *ʿabd* [A., slave, i.e., mercury], 51b
31. The *tarṣīṣ* [A., coating with lead or zinc], 52a
32. The *taḥṣīn* [A., cementing or solidification], 52b
33. Particular expression, 52b, 55a
34. The *taqṭīr* [A., distilling or filtering], 53a
35. The *taklīs* [A., calcifying], 53a
36. The *tarzīn* [A., explained as *libbun* [H.], whitening], 53a
37. The *tarṭīb* [A., wetting], 53b
38. For *ḥal* [A., dissolving], 53b
39. *Hajrān wal ʿaqd* [A., expanding and tying, i.e., fixing of the spirits], 54a
40. The work of writing, 55b
41. Separate operations, 55b

This listing comprises most of the standard alchemical operations, indicating that the author was thoroughly at home in all aspects of alchemy. The next four pages (ff. 2a–3b) contain explanations of alchemical terms, the great majority Italian words that are translated into Hebrew with supporting elucidations. The material contained in this brief vocabulary has been included in the general vocabulary of the Jerba manuscript in the Appendix.

Following that brief vocabulary our manuscript presents (f. 3b) some technical information on weight measures taken from the book *Oṣar haḤayyim* (Treasury of Life), an encyclopedic work written by Jacob ben Isaac Ṣahalon (1630–1693), which was published in 1683 in Venice. Ṣahalon intended to write a general encyclopedia of all the sciences, but only this (the third) part, which deals with medicine, was published. Since Ṣahalon lived more than a century after Moshe ben Shaul, it is evident that this entry was added by the copyist. It reads:

The order of the proportions copied from the book *Oṣar haḤayyim*, page 43b and 44a: One *liṭra* [pound] is twelve *onqias* [ounces]. The ounce is divided into eight *drāme* [drams] and one *ottava* [I., eighth]. The dram is divided into three *scrupalo* [I. *scrupolo*, the twenty-fourth part of an ounce]. The *scrupalo* is twenty-four wheat [seeds]. Thus far, and see there.

Then the copyist goes on to add material of his own:

And I found in a manuscript the names of the weights as follows: *drakhma, dirhām, grāno, qimḥa, scrupalo*, twenty-four wheat [seeds]. One *riṭla*—twelve ounces; one ounce—eight *dirhām*; one *dirhām*—three *scrupalo*. Thus far. The rule of how you should behave with all the frozen [congealed] matters. See its description in part one, in the Freezing [Congealing], par. 10. Remember it and don't forget it.

Ṣīnērāṣio. ᶜAMSh''L [H. acronym: "see what I wrote above"]. And to QᶜAD''N [H. acronym: "the shortness of the poverty of my mind it seems"] that *S''D* [H. acronym: "the end of the matter is"] that it is not closed, for the *ramāṣ* [A., read *ramaḍ*, hot cinders] of the oven are themselves *taṣfīya'* [A., purification] if you make it into a kind of *aljūja* [?], and many persons, in places where they have no *zakhs* [?] to make of it a combination, make a place to feed the oven, but they say that the hot cinders of the oven swallow much of the silver, however, the *zakhs* stone is better . . .

OUR ORDER of measures in the Island of Jerba, YᶜI''A [H. abbreviation of "May our city be rebuilt, Amen"]: the *qintār* [A. *kantar*] is one hundred *raṭl*, and the *raṭl* is fifteen *onqiot* [ounces], and the ounce is eight *tas*, and the *tas* is twenty carob seeds, and the carob seed is two wheat [seeds]. The *mithqāl* is twenty-four carob seeds. The *dirhām* is fifteen carob seeds. We say that the *grāno* is half a wheat [seed], it is the weight of a *pruṭah* [H., farthing] of RZ''L [our masters of blessed memory].

Now the copyist is finally ready to begin with the actual alchemical text of his book. Italian and Arabic words are transliterated at first appearance, translated where possible thereafter.

BᶜE''H [WITH THE HELP OF GOD]. PREFACE WHICH CONTAINS THE RULES OF THIS PRECIOUS SCIENCE

1. IN THE BEGINNING all those who enter this work must know the four spirits, that is the *prēpārāṣione*, and the preparation out of the seven bodies, that is to say the seven known metals.

2. AND THE FOUR spirits are *sālarmoniāqo* [sal ammoniac], *k''ḥ* [H. abbreviation for quicksilver], sulphur, *arsēnīqo* [arsenic], and they are called spirits because they do not tolerate fire, but fly off into the air like a vapor and a wind, unless they are mixed wisely and carefully, for one must sublimate them in special vessels of glass and clay, which are called *solimaṭore*, for if you do not sublimate them you cannot cleanse them of their moisture.

3. AND THE SEVEN metals, if they were not made into lime, that is *qālṣināre* [to calcinate], and if you did not extract from them their moisture and then drench them on a marble in sharp water, and then retransform them into water, your operation is worth nothing, for in the beginning one must make lime out of them, and then transform them into water, and then they will rise like the aforementioned spirits, and then one must mix the water from those metals together with the waters of the aforementioned spirits, and then one must transform them into one body, and then into water, and in this way your operations will be complete and good, and this is the great secret in this work, and there is nothing higher than it, and the philosophers hid it, and the proof is that you cannot mix together two things well even if you grind them. Moreover, if you mix together two waters, or if they become more colored . . . when this medicine is added to them, for their first nature has already departed from them and they acquired a different nature, and they have a wonderful effect on the metal if you put the prepared medicine upon it in the aforementioned manner. And do not be astonished at the way the metal is transmuted into another nature, for, see, even glass was originally a herb and then transformed into glass, and apart from this also many other things change but it would take too long to describe them. And the best of the spirits and the bodies should be prepared, that is *prēpāraṣione*, and then they should be connected and made into one body. And so that you should know the sublimation and the preparation out of the four spirits and the seven metals easily, behold I wrote them down for you B"H [with the help of God], and they are described above, each one in its place in the manner of sublimation and preparation.

4. AND THE PREPARATION of the seven metals can be done in four ways. One is to calcinate, that is their transformation into lime; the second, *inṣeraṣione*, that is to drench them and to mix them on marble so that they should unite well; the third, *risolaṣione* [I. *risoluzione*, dissolution], that is to transform them into water; the fourth [*qonyelaṣione*], to freeze [congeal] that water and to turn it into stone. And he who does not know this will not be able to operate with any completeness in this science.

5. AND THE DRENCHINGS and the manner of doing them, which is called *inkikirāmenṭo*. The manner of doing them: take any one you want of the spirits or of the metals, and drench it upon a marble stone, steadily grind and drench it with the best sharp water such as vinegar and *wenirame* [?] urine, sal ammoniac, and you must know that this will be a superior operation, and it will work better.

6. AND KNOW that the philosophers have a nice saying, very *singolāre* [I., singular, i.e., excellent]. They said: all the bodies of metal can *arorifiqare* [I. *rarefare*, to rarify] with *ziya* water, that is *witriolo* [vitriol], but you should add something finer and more honored.

7. THE SULPHUR *minerale* is a fat from the earth, and the mineral sulphur of the philosophers is (f. 4b) *eksṭeraso* [extracted] of all its *sorișe* [?] and of all things that are *qorumpionaṭe* [cf. I. *corrompere*, to corrupt, spoil].

8. AND THE K"Ḥ [quicksilver] *minerale* is for the philosophers *wiskosa* [I. *viscosa*, viscous] water, which is in the bellies of the earth, and the philosophical quicksilver is extracted from the impure things and of all things corrupted.

9. AND KNOW that if you make lime out of silver and then transform it into a body, it will no longer be damaged, and then the sulphur if you put it. . . .

10. LEAD is composed of quicksilver and *inṭuoso* [?] sulphur, and the quicksilver is dark and not pure, and it is weak from being cooked, and it also weakens in combination, and therefore one must extract from it the blackness and impurity, and it will become *reisaṭo* [?] in this manner. MELT the quicksilver and then remove it from the fire, and throw upon it [marginal note: one quarter of it] *purgaṭo* [purified] quicksilver, and then grind it on a marble stone, and grind with it its own weight of crushed *qomano* [I. *comuno*, common] salt until it does not crackle upon the fire, and grind it together until the salt becomes black, and then remove the salt with warm water, and do thus as many as six times, and then put upon it its own weight of salt and grind it well and boil it with strong vinegar, and boil it a full day, and the blackness will come out, and it will become purified of its blackness and its sulphur, and then remove the salt with water, and it will be a powder of lead and quicksilver, which will be *repuraṭo* [I. *ripurgato*, purified] in a *miraoqare* [I. *miracoloso*, miraculous] manner and white. Return to doing the grinding and the boiling as at first until that lead will be found to be white and pure, and whatever you want to do so, it will be so well purified and good.

11. TIN is a body composed of quicksilver that has been purified in a miraculous manner, and impure, white and weak from cooking sulphur, as well as other *wwari* [I. *vario*, varied] metals, and dry and less *poroso* [I., porous]. Therefore melt it with one quarter of its weight of purified quicksilver which will reduce its *stridore* [I., noise, crackling] *tiri'i* [?], and it is because it is purified like *muḥraq* [A., burnt] for *qontrișione* [I. *contrazione*, contraction] with burnt common salt, that is to say *riqoṭo* [I. *ricotto*, burnt], due to boiling with the salt and the vinegar. Then let it stand a long time with the *reṭifiqaṭo* [I. *rettificato*, rectified] oil, until it becomes very *omitato* [?]. When there is no [more] crackling upon it, either drench it with pork fat, that is *asukia*, and extinguish it in it until it receives the moisture that is in it . . . so as to diminish its dryness and to open its *porosiṭaṭe* [I., porosity] which was reduced due to it, until it becomes *pransibile* [I. *prendibile*, takable, catchable], which is *misustosia porisma* [?] which breaks all the metals by its dryness and reduces their viscosity. Therefore

understand and work, for if it is not *separato* [I., separated] well it breaks all the other metals except lead, for it [lead] is *fisimo* [?] and *inifiṭo* [?], which is called in the science of alchemy *leproso* [I. *lebbroso*, leprous], and if it is purified well it will accept the medicine and will be very good.

12. INQALLARE [I. *incollare*, to paste, glue] the *yuntore* [?] from the vessels. Take eggs of *greqa* [?], and pound them and put them in a *qasa* [A. *kuza*, flask] to melt on fire, and put in it a little *maṭone* [I. *mattone*, brick] finely ground, until it becomes like a *liqwida* [liquid] dough, and grind with it the *yuntore* from the vessels when it is warm, and it is good.

13. TO MELT the four spirits and the seven metals, which is called *resolimēnṭo*. Take sal ammoniac water and drench with it whatever water you want, that is of the four spirits and the seven metals, and drench it (f. 5a) three times, and dry it three times in the sun or by gentle fire, and the last time when you drench it put it as it is, wet, into a flask and seal its opening and put it in dung forty days or more if necessary, and at the end see: if all of it turned into water, fine; and if not, renew it in the dung another seven days and another seven days, and leave it there until all of it becomes *resolaṭo* [I., dissolved]. In this manner you can transform all the lime into water, and this is a great secret in this Work. AND IF YOU WANT to operate in this Work take the two waters, that is, the water of the spirit and the water of the lime that was made out of the metal, and mix them and put them into a flask, and seal its mouth with philosophers' clay, and put the flask into a kettle in which there are already ashes, and put it on the oven on gentle fire until the water in the flask becomes frozen [congealed] and becomes a stone, then your work is good and superior. And if you persist to make water out of that stone, and then congeal it to make it again a stone, in the aforementioned manner, it will be better and it will function as suitable: any metal which you put there will become powdery, and strew [some] of that powder upon hot plates and it will become moon [silver]. And if you put [some] of this powder upon any metal when it is melted, you will see wonderful colors that the metal will get. AND KNOW that lime of gold is made in the aforementioned manner, and then it is turned into water with the spirit, and then turned into stone and ground. If you put some of it on any one of the seven metals it will color it very much and turn it into its own quality and color. And thus you can do with lime of silver as you did with lime of gold with one of the spirits.

14. IF you take one ounce of *alume* [I. *allume*, alum] and an ounce of sal ammoniac, and you extract from them the water in the *alambiqo* [I. *alambicco*, alembic, still], and put into that water *solimaṭo* [sublimated] silver, it will melt it and turn it into water. And if you freeze [congeal] the water and turn it into the shape of a stone, and grind it and put one ounce of the aforementioned powder on tin or on quicksilver, it will work wonders. . . .

15. TO MELT common salt, so that it should melt like wax and should be *fisibile* [I. *fissibile*, fixable] and good to soften anything takable, and should congeal quicksilver, take common salt and *ṣementa* [cement] with quicklime and put it into the oven twelve hours, and then remove it and put on it water and *disṭila* [distill] the water and dry it, and then return it with other new lime and return it into the oven a second time and a third, and everything as at the first time, until you see that if you put it on a *lamina* [thin plate] it melts like wax, and if you put it on quicksilver in a melting pot or *alutilo* [I., aludel], it will congeal it, and if you throw it upon a takable thing it will sweeten it definitely. This is the end of the preface B'E"H [with the help of God] "who hangeth the earth over nothing" [Job 26:7].

This is followed, on the bottom of folio 5a, by an evidently later addition which is a kind of index, with several page numbers after each entry. Folio 5b is superscribed by a new title:

B'E"H OPERATIONS OF ABRIDGMENTS

1. TAKE sublimated silver and prepared salt, in equal parts and sublimate together, and do thus five times and each time put new salt, and take this sublimation with the same amount of sal ammoniac, sublimate with *pomiṣe* [I. *pomice*, pumice] (another version: *pumize*), and let the sublimation be white. Then take both of them and grind them together well, and sublimate that which rose up with the *pise* [or *fise* ?] (which is *larṣie* [?]) mentioned among the Waters, par. 17. . . . and also in the Oils), and grind and sublimate until the quicksilver becomes *fisso* [I., fixed] (hence we learn that the silver mentioned in the beginning is quicksilver and not silver, and see its description in the *Solimaṣione*, par. 4, and in *Solimare*). Then take *disṭilāṭo* [distilled] vinegar and put it on the fixed thin quicksilver, and it will melt in the vinegar. Then congeal it in weak fire, and when it is congealed let it cool, and then grind it well and put it in a moist place for thirty days, and when it has turned into water take of that water one *riṭla* [12 ounces], and four ounces of *foliaṭo* [foliated] silver, and put it in warm dung one [?] day, and then congeal in weak fire, and then grind and put it to melt and congeal, thus do ten times, and you will have more riches than can be imagined, for one part of this upon thirty parts of *purga* [purified] quicksilver put into the melting pot to be heated will harden it so much that it will stand up in the *qupela* [cupel].

2. ANOTHER matter of superior congelation. Take bricks, the oldest ones you can find, and make them red hot in fire, and leave them to cool, and then granulate them to the size of beans, and put them in a pot which should not be *wiṭriaṭa* [glazed], and put it on three [word illegible], and

give fire until they become hot but not red, and shake it well as do the perfumers to the *ʿaṭarye'a* [literary A. *ʿiṭriyāt*, perfumes]. And when they are hot throw them into a glazed *lanila* [or: *lawila* ?], in which there should be as much old oil as you can find, and let it cool, and put it *adisṭilāre* [to distill] (there it is written *asṭilāre*, and it seems to me that it is a *ṭ"s* [ṭʿut sofer, H., scribe's error]) in an *orināle* [flask] with weak fire at first for four hours (and then strengthen the fire) and what flows out at first is not good, and take the last one which is select oil. And there are those who make out of this oil that flowed out two ounces with one ounce of *ṭarṭaro* [tartar] oil, because it is more *arisṭino* [?]. Then [take] purified quicksilver and put it in a *kuza luṭa* [luted flask] up to its half, and put enough oil on the quicksilver to cover it [to a depth of] two fingers, and put it into the oven with a burning candle which you should put in the bottom of the flask, for eight days, and make sure that the candle never goes out, and let it cool, and you will find your desire congealed and full. . . . (And one must repeat and write it as it is witten there and not as it is written here.)

3. TAKE very thin *lamine* [leaves] of copper and make them red [hot], and cover them in a *morṭaro* [mortar] in which there is tartar salt and urine and strong vinegar, and do this ten times and then take these leaves and smear them with olive oil, and wrap them in *iropimenṭo* [?] dust, then cement these leaves in a pot with common salt, and seal the mouth of the pot with a lid, and put it into a *rewerbero* [?] oven for four hours, then take this calcinated copper and lute it well and wash it with warm water as many times as [needed] until the lime remains pure, and then dry it in the sun or in fire in a ladle, then take one *riṭla* of this copper and one ounce of saltpeter, and one ounce of lime of eggshells, and one ounce of calcinated tartar and mix everything together with egg white until it becomes like dough, and put it to melt through a *foṭos* [or: *poṭos*] [another version: *foṭos barbuṭos*] . . . *barbāṭos* [?], and it will come out a nice *lege* [or: *lego*, I., alloy].

4. TAKE the whites of hard-boiled eggs, and grind them well, then put them in a wet place to become moist, and then put them into an earthenware vessel for fifteen days in a wet place, then mix them with lime of eggshells [marginal note: (there it is written : to make a *fisso* oil take etc.)] (f. 6a) and put in a flask sealed with warm dung fifteen days and then *disṭila fiso* [distill fixed?] water, and thus you can do out of the yolks to tint red [i.e. yellow] and then take general *fusibile* [I. *fissibile*, fixable] salt, and put it in this water in a flask whose neck is long, and put into it the quicksilver to boil until the water is finished, and dry it, and you will find it very good silver.

5. TAKE sublimation and smear it on a marble stone with tartar oil like *salṣa qlara* [I. *salsa clara*, clear sauce], and put it into a flask whose neck is

long, and put it into dung into the oven and distill in very weak fire, and when the flask is hot increase the fire a little and dry your medicine with the flask open, and let it cool, and break the flask and you will find a hard stone. Then take it and grind it with *ṭarṭaro* oil as the first time, on marble, and put it into a flask and dry it as at first, and do thus seven times, and in the last flask take it and put it into warm dung for twenty-five days, and it will become water. Then put the flask to congeal in very gentle fire and it will become fixed spirit, and make it into powder, and of this powder put one part [blank space] and one part of it on sixty parts of *rāe qālṣinato* [I. *rame calcinato*, calcinated copper] will transmute it into silver for all tests.

6. TAKE water of *sālarmoniaq fisso* [fixed sal ammoniac] three ounces, and one ounce sublimated silver, and grind it on marble five times, and drench it with the aforementioned water as much as you can, and place it on *marmaro* [marble], and it will become water, and you should have quicksilver water (hence one understands that the sublimated silver is quicksilver and not *mukallas* [A., calcincated; or *mukhlas*, A., unadulterated] silver, and this is meant above par. 1), and the sal ammoniac water together, and make it so that all the sal ammoniac water should take three ounces of sublimated silver, to drench together and become water. And then take for each ounce of sublimated silver two *dirhām*s of good silver, and the silver will be very *limaṭura* [I., filing], and put it into the flask with the aforementioned water, and put it into warm dung for eight days, and you will have three waters: the quicksilver water, and the sal ammoniac water, and the good silver water, and then congeal these waters and dissolve and congeal many times, and then one part on three (another version: fifty) parts of quicksilver [will transmute it into real silver].

7. TAKE prepared salt, and grind it and put it in an earthenware *fisiqa* vessel suspended in strong vinegar, and it will dissolve into water, and congeal it and dissolve it and congeal it many times until it will run on the iron, and put [some] of this on the quicksilver, and it will make it good moon [silver] for all tests.

8. TAKE *olibāno serafino sarqāqula* [?], common prepared salt, and grind it well, and knead it well in tartar water, as well as in *alume suqarino* [I. *allume zuccherino*, sugared alum] (another version: *saquṭrino* [?]), and make of them a lid and a melting pot, and fill it with *luton* [brass] quicksilver, and it seems to me that he wanted to say washed and killed with *rogririo* [?] and *sināpe* [I., mustard] and vinegar, and cover it well, and put it on hot ashes six hours, and it will congeal again, and on the quicksilver make *riqone* [?] of quicklime and of lime of eggs, and the melting pot should be luted with philosophers' clay all over, and the clay should be made of ashes and salt and water, and dry it well, and it should be put with the quicksilver into the melting pot. And see below par. 34 something close to this.

9. TAKE (in its beginning it is written, I shall tell you secrets of wisdom, etc.) quicksilver sublimated three times, and make of it ounces of *arseniqo solima* [sublimated arsenic] water, three times ounces, and if it is steady it is better. And make of it also *sālqali prepāra* [prepared sal alcali] water two ounces, and make of it sublimated sal ammoniac water three times, and make of it water two ounces, *solimato qalsinato* [sublimated calcinated] silver one ounce, and mix together all the waters, and with them knead and grind the good silver on marble, and if you know how to make water out of it too then it is better, and then mix all the waters together and it should suffice for you. Then put all these waters into dung three or four days, and then distill them in a *banio Maria* [I. *bagno Maria*, water-bath], and then distill them in fire, dry as is customary, and take what is found in the bottom of the vessel and leave it, and return the (f. 6b) water that came out and distill a second time, and then take what is left in the bottom of the flask and put it into strong water made of vitriol and nitrous salt and *alume di roṣa* [or *rocea*, rock alum] in equal parts, in the amount that all the medicine should dissolve well from the strength of the water, and distill thereafter as is customary, with gentle fire, and then increase it, and return the water that comes out a second time upon the medicine, and if you grind it it will be better, and when it is distilled twice take the medicine which is found in the bottom and grind it and drench it with the I. tartar oil, and then dry it three times and then drench it with the egg white water three times, and then dry it, and then you will have a wonderful medicine whose effect cannot be imagined, and if you throw one part of it on thirty parts of pure *rāme* [I., copper] as is proper, when it is melted, and if you put the medicine into copper put it in tied into new wax, and out will come a thing that will make your heart rejoice. And if you put [some] of this medicine upon quicksilver when it is hot on the fire, it seems to me that it will congeal it in a good manner, and the experiment will prove it.

10. TAKE sublimated arsenic, sublimated sal ammoniac, one part of each, and grind them separately, and then mix them together, and then sublimate all of it with a full amount of copper shavings twice, and then cook it one day in water made of liquid egg white in the alembic, on a gentle fire, like the warmth of the sun, then cook it one day in *pasṭela* [I. *pastella*, batter] vinegar on a gentle fire, then mix it with its own weight of silver shavings, and combine all of it together on marble with tartar oil, and then put it *arisensoria* [?], and it will come out for you a small and good philosophical stone. One ounce of it on forty ounces of *rāme purga* [I., purified copper] will become moon [silver] good for all tests. From the *gallaḥ* [H., priest or monk].

11. TO MAKE the *d* [abbreviation of *dahab:* A. *dhahab*, gold] of fourteen carats, take of live permanent sulphur three ounces, *rubifiqa* [I., reddened] quicksilver (see its abbreviation in the Redness, par. 3) four ounces, *verde*

rāme [I., verdigris] sublimated with lime one ounce, permanent sal ammoniac three ounces, *tutia Alessandrina purga* (I., purified Alexandrian tutty), two ounces, *qroqo ferro* [I. *croco di ferro*, iron oxide] three ounces, gold dissolved in water three ounces, and sublimate all these things together, and always grind them with their sediments, three times. And then take twice the amount of Roman vitriol water, and drench these things until all that water becomes dry in them, and then take this medicine and sublimate it once more, and then put it *apoṭrifaṣione* [?], and then dissolve it on a marble stone, and congeal it, and dissolve four times, and one part of this medicine on twelve parts of Shabtai [H., Saturn, lead] will work wonders, and give thanks to God, and don't teach them to any creature, except to your sons. From the *gallaḥ* of Prato [or: Frato].

12. TAKE common strong water [aquaforte] [marginal note: (this is the explanation of common strong water, see in the Color, 8, and read carefully)] two ounces, and one ounce quicksilver, and dissolve it in the aforementioned juice, and after it is soaked make it *ewaporare* [I. *evaporare*, to evaporate] (it seems to me that he intends to say to boil it as mentioned in the Whitening, par. 15) on hot ashes until the water is gone, and then take a melting pot and put the quicksilver into it, and give it temperate fire until it becomes red, and then it is done. And preserve it for the Work which you know (it seems to me that he should throw it upon moon [silver], one on six parts, as below), and know that thereafter I found a man who said to me that his *qomosāre* [?] gave him this *pratiqa* [I. *pratica*, practice], and he swore to me that it is true and good, but it goes on six parts, that is, once one part on six, the second time one on twelve, the third time one on twenty-four, and thus you can multiply until a hundred. And then I want to reveal to you a great secret: that if you take one leaf of silver, and make it red hot in fire, and quench it in this compound (it seems to me that it should be dissolved before it congeals), it will color it [into gold] of twenty-four *qiraṭe* [carats], and he did this several times, and did not want to reveal it to anybody.

13. TAKE half a *riṭla* of live sulphur, and half a *riṭla* of red arsenic, and grind them on a marble stone with strong vinegar, and then take half of one eighth of sal ammoniac, and half of one eighth of common salt, and mix everything and dry them, and make of them a powder, and put them into the alembic, and make water like the water made to separate gold from silver, and preserve this water like a treasure, and when you want to operate, put well-washed quicksilver into this water, and the water must cover the quicksilver by two fingers, and cook it in gentle fire until the water dries, and the quicksilver will be congealed and hard, and this is true and clear, with the help of God.

14. TO MAKE out of Z"K [?] one pure one, and this is an honored work, take one ounce of quicksilver, and wash it several times (there it is written

once and a second time, and thus in the second star mentioned after it), and each time pass it through a *qomoṣa* [sieve?], and then take one ounce of pure and purified silver, which should be filed very fine, and mix it with the quicksilver and make a *malgama* [amalgam], and again wash them twice (there it is written once and a second time, etc. as mentioned) with pure water and then take one ounce of sal ammoniac, and one ounce of saltpeter, and one ounce of glass, and grind everything very fine, and mix them with the abovementioned amalgam very thoroughly so that everything should become one body. And then put everything in a flask on the oven which is prepared as you know how, and light under it gentle fire, that is, light a candle under the flask, and let that candle burn thirty days, and at the end of the thirty days take out the flask and scrape off what is in it and preserve it. And when you want to perform an operation take one *riṭla* of washed and pure quicksilver, and put it into the melting pot, and put one quarter of an ounce of the medicine which you have preserved, with a little paper, and put on it a little melted wax, and then cover the melting pot with philosophers' clay, and put it on a fire to melt, and start with gentle fire, and then increase the fire a little, and then give it fire to melt, and throw it in the *qānāl* [I. *canale*, tube], and out will come for you purified moon [silver] of *carlina* [I., a coin].

15. TAKE wax and make of it a round ball, and cover it with philosophers' clay, and let it dry, and make for it an additional cover, and do this with four covers of clay, and then make a small hole in it and put it next to the fire, so that the wax should melt and run out, and the clay should remain hollow, and then put into it through the hole linseed oil with *totomilo* [I. *titimaglia*, spurge, euphorbia] juice, and put into it quicksilver, and seal the hole well with philosophers' clay, and then put it on burning coals until you see that it is thoroughly burnt, and then it will be like a hard stone.

16. TAKE one *roṭl* of sal ammoniac, and two *roṭls* of quicklime, and mix them together in pure water, and boil it upon the fire until it is reduced to one-third, and let it dry, and put that pure water in a *kāṣīn* [?], and put other pure water on the sediment, and bring it to a boil as the first time, and let it dry, and put it into the *kāṣīn*, and do thus until all the saltiness comes out of the sediments, and the sediments become sweet. And then take all these waters and put into them two *roṭla* of quicklime, and do as at the first time (thus repeat four times, that is, until you put for each *roṭl*) sal ammoniac eight *roṭls* of quicklime, and then take all these waters and distill through a *filṭro* [I., filter], and then congeal it, and it will become like a stone, and it will be fixed like oil, and then take one *dirhām* of good gold, and four *dirhāms* of quicksilver, and make an amalgam in the pot on a gentle fire, and always stir it with an iron rod, and calcinate the gold as is customary, and then take this lime of gold and grind it on marble with the abovementioned oil, and put it in a flask, and put of the oil as much as

needed to cover the lime, and cover it and *luṭ* [I. *luto*, seal, cement] it well, and put it in warm dung ten days, then take it out and you will find that the lime has been transmuted into quicksilver. (f. 7b) Then take of this quicksilver of the gold [?] one *dirhām*, and of other purified quicksilver three *dirhām*, and amalgamate them together, and put it in an *orinale* [flask], into hot ashes in light fire, for seven days, and in the end strengthen the fire for six hours, and it will be congealed, then instantly restore it to become a body with the melting pot, and sal ammoniac and *salpeṭro* [saltpeter] in equal parts, pulverized and dissolved in white wine, and let the salts be two parts and the body one part, and put it on marble and drench all of it together, and cause it to return to a body in a melting pot, and it will become wonderful sun [gold], and it is an honored amalgam.

17. TAKE *sālarmoniāq* [marg. note: (another version: *armoniāqo* salt, and it is the same)] sublimated three times seven times (it seems to me that he did it on purpose and wrote it thus: three times seven times, in order to satisfy the reader, and it surely needs seven times, or he wanted to say between them twenty-one times), with the same amount of common salt, and then grind it and put it on marble until water issues from it, and take of that water four ounces and put into it a quarter of an an ounce *ia probio* [?; marg. note: (another version: *oprobia*)], and put it into the *banio Maria adisṭila* [water-bath still; marg. note: (*adisṭilāre*)], and take the abovementioned water and preserve it, and take quicksilver and heat it in the melting pot, and while it is hot throw it seven times into the abovementioned water, and it will congeal. And then throw it seven times into oil, whose description is this: take three ounces of linseed oil, and half an ounce of *oprobio* of leaves (*ṭasin*)[?], and pass it through the alembic in the water-bath, and preserve the abovementioned oil and into it throw seven times the congealed quicksilver while it is hot from the melting pot, and it will congeal and become hard, and then place it into the abovementioned oil a third time, and it will become good for every thing, for the hammer, and for melting only for cupel, and I received it [on condition] not to tell it to anybody.

18. TAKE one ounce of good silver, and three ounces of quicksilver, and make an amalgam, and then put it in one *riṭla* of olive oil and three ounces of *oprobio*, and boil them up together until the oil dries and it will become congealed.

19. TAKE gumma arabica [gum arabic], *gumma derengānṭe, [?] orpimenṭo* [orpiment], in equal parts, and make them into water, and put in it the quicksilver for three full days, and then take *nitro* [niter] salt, common salt, *salyemma* [I. *salgemma*, rock salt], lime, *werde rāme* [I. *verderame*, verdigris] in equal parts, and make of them a powder, and put it on the abovementioned thing, and it will become very hard. And know that the juice of the *werbena* [I., verbena] congeals the quicksilver, by experiment.

20. TAKE sublimated quicksilver seven times three ounces, and grind it with three ounces of sal ammoniac, and sublimate three times, then dissolve it in moss, and in this *resolāṣione* [solution] put one ounce of calcinated moon [silver] and one ounce of *arseniqo solimāṭo* [sublimated arsenic], and half an ounce of *alume yāmāni preparāṭo* [I., prepared Yemenite alum], and grind all of it, and put it *arisolvere* [to dissolve] in strong water [aquafortis] made of nitric salt and *alume diroṣa* [I. *allume di rocca*, rock alum]. Then congeal, and then again dissolve and congeal. Thus do three times, and then one part on one hundred hot quicksilver in the melting pot will congeal it, and if [you put] one part of it on ten *rāme purga* [I., purified copper] it will be silver better than Venetian.

Here follows a second short vocabulary of Arabic and Italian terms which have been included in the general vocabulary in the Appendix.

On folio 9a begins the detailed discussion of each topic in the order as listed in the index on folio 1b, starting with chapter 5, The Waters. Each chapter is subdivided into numbered sections. These sections contain mostly recipes, that is, instructions for alchemical procedures involving the substances or the procedures figuring in the title of the section. Thus, for instance, the chapter on "The Waters" contains thirty-six sections, most of which describe methods of "turning into water," that is, liquifying, such substances as arsenic, mercury, silver, sal ammoniac, vitriol, lead, virgin milk, talc, "anything," any salt, and so on. What is missing in these recipes (and in all the recipes contained in the manuscript) is a statement of the purpose subserved by these liquifications and other alchemical procedures. Take as an example recipe no. 25 on folio 11a:

Water of the *qosmim* [H., wizards], that is to say water of *revenāṣione* [I., ?] Take egg whites cooked in water so that the water should cover the egg whites, one part, [and] quicklime two parts, and mix them together, and put it in a *kuza* [A., flask] well sealed and its mouth luted, and put it in warm dung until it becomes like moldy mud, and then let it drip in an alembic, and take the water that drips, and then remove the sediment from the bottom of the vessel, and take new quicklime and mix it with the abovementioned water, and let them drip in an alembic, and then put in the water a little lime of eggshell, and put it in a sealed flask and put it in warm dung or in the *banyo Maria* [water-bath] nine days, then let them drip in the alembic as mentioned, and do thus three times, and then the wizard's water is completed, and the philosophers call it *rosa ṣeleste* [I., heavenly rose], and he who reveals the secret of this water is called a thief.

The section on "Congelations" (ff. 21a–25a) contains no fewer than seventy-six prescriptions, some of them titled *reseṭṭah ṭovah* [I.-H., good recipe], or *reseṭṭah nikhb'dah* [I.-H., honored recipe].

Although most of the manuscript is in Hebrew, there are major parts in it written in Arabic, more precisely in the Judeo-Arabic of northwest Africa, the cultural and linguistic area to which the island of Jerba belongs. Folios 49a–55a are written in this language, and so are parts of the subsequent folios. On folio 72a, for example, there is a recipe in Arabic for the transmutation of copper into gold with the admixture of quicksilver. These pages deal mostly with such alchemical procedures as the purification of metals, processes of coloring red, white, and so on, and the treatment of quicksilver, lead, calcination, and so on.

A few samples of the Arabic passages contained on folio 51a of the manuscript demonstrate that Hebrew expressions are frequently mixed into the Arabic text:

> The fixation of the *ʿuqāb* [A., eagle, sal ammoniac]. Take of it a *roṭl*, and like it [the same amount] of saltpeter salt, and pound them, and burn them well in a sufficient fire, and take them out and fill them, and what *ʿuqāb* is reduced add to it, and do thus until the weight of the *ʿuqāb* is fixed.
>
> *ʿAyin alef* [H. abbreviation of *ʿOd aḥeret*, "another one"]. Its fixation and making it yellow. Take two [amounts] of *ʿuqāb* and one of *asad* [H., lion, could stand for *al-asad al-barri*, "the wild lion," sal ammoniac, or for *al-asad al-akhḍar*, "the green lion," copper], and one quarter of reddened *zāj* [A., vitriol], and purify them well, and put them in a baking pan, and seal it, and put it on the fire. And before you seal it you will be wise to work it well until it becomes consumed in the fire until you know its time. And AH"K [H. abbreviation of *w'aḥar kakh*, and then] throw it down, and diminish it, and return it to the fire. Do thus seven times [these words are in Hebrew], until the work rises up yellowed, and in it is red color. [Then] know that it is fixed.
>
> *ʿAyin alef* [H., another one]. Take cooking salt and let it stand [overnight], and after the stars, and in the morning take what remained in the *hasefel* [H., cup], and dry it, and spread it out, and soak of it in the *ʿuqāb*, and let it stand. . . . And repeat this *kaniz' d"p* [H., as mentioned, four times]. It will be fixed.

Several of these sections are superscribed by technical terms (in Arabic) which do not appear in the vocabularies.

Since the Jerba manuscript, as mentioned earlier, is the composite work of two authors, we cannot be sure whether any characteristic revealed by it pertains to the first or to the second. However, it appears that both authors were deeply religious—a trait shared with the Jews of Jerba in general, whose exceeding piety was observed and commented upon by Maimonides in the twelfth century. Both authors considered studying alchemy and working in it as ways of serving God, and of exalting the Torah. In addition, the junior author was also a Kabbalist, a follower of the Lurianic Kabbalah.

Another trait is shared by the two authors. The copyist proudly identifies both himself and the senior author as "pure Sephardi," that is, men of pure Spanish-Jewish descent. There can be little doubt that the senior author, like the other Kohens of sixteenth-century Bologna, either was himself born in Spain or was the son of an immigrant from Spain, which means that he surely must have spoken Spanish. Likewise the junior author, a "pure Sephardi" living in Jerba in the nineteenth century, could be expected to use Spanish (Ladino) as his colloquial. And yet in the entire manuscript (written in Hebrew), which is full of Italian and Arabic technical terms, there are only a very few and doubtful traces of Spanish (such as the Spanish *s* ending for the plural). Evidently both authors had acquired their alchemical expertise from Italian and Arabic alchemical literature, and not from Spanish works. This becomes especially clear from the vocabularies contained in the manuscript (see Appendix). That they had not only a reading knowledge of Italian but also spoke it can be concluded from the manner in which they transliterate the Italian words into Hebrew characters: their transliteration invariably reflects the pronunciation, and not the spelling, of the Italian terms. For example, they spell in Hebrew *banyo* for the Italian spelling *bagno, conyelaṣi'one* for *congelazione*, and so on.

The frequent and expert use of Arabic in the manuscript makes us suspect that the share of the junior author in it was greater than he claims. The senior author, even if he settled in Jerba immediately after the expulsion of the Jews from Bologna (1568), by which time he was an elderly man, is unlikely to have acquired Arabic quickly and thoroughly enough to be able to translate into, and to explain in, that language the hundreds of Italian alchemical terms appearing in the book. One is therefore inclined to assume that the Arabic translation and explanation of these terms is rather the work of the junior author, who was a native of Jerba and whose mother tongue was the Judeo-Arabic spoken by his community. This assumption is strengthened by the passages in the book (e.g. on folios 51a, 71a–72b) in Arabic, which indicate an equal facility in both languages. Also, quite a number of times the author does not translate the Arabic technical terms he lists into another language, but instead adduces Arabic synonyms for them, or uses only the Arabic term without any translation or explanation at all. The latter is the case especially with terms denoting alchemical procedures; terms such as *taṭhīr* (purification), *taḥmīr* (reddening), *tabyīḍ* (whitening), etc., are given only in Arabic, despite the fact that these procedures were widely designated by Latin-derived alchemical terminology.

Apart from these three languages (Hebrew, Arabic, and Italian) the authors (or one of them) knew, or claims to have known, "Latin and the languages of the ancients," as stated in the superscription of one of the vocabularies.

In addition to being alchemists, Kabbalists, and linguists, our authors were also naturalists, thoroughly at home in the fields of mineralogy and botany. This becomes evident when they speak of three groups of salt (natural, heavenly, and artificial), and enumerate and define ten kinds of salt belonging to the first group, and more than twelve belonging to the third, or when they refer to various kinds of rare plants.

Finally, our authors were also historians of alchemy and medicine, and were acquainted with the literature in Hebrew and Arabic covering both subjects. Their reference to sources can not always be identified. For instance, the older author mentions Batista of Bologna and the priest Prato, whom I was not able to trace. But he also refers to works by some of the well-known figures in alchemical history, such as Ibn Sīnā, Joseph Kimḥi, Ḥayyim Yisr'eli, Simeon ben Ṣemaḥ Duran, and Jacob Anatoli. The younger author mentions treatises by Abraham Portaleone and Jacob Ṣahalon. Since in the sixteenth century, or even in the nineteenth, books or manuscripts by authors such as these were not easy to come by anywhere, and especially not in a relatively isolated place such as the island of Jerba, one must conclude that our authors had contacts with sources around the Mediterranean which were able to supply them with copies, and had the money to pay for them.

All in all, we can conclude by saying that this book is a worthy last fruit of the almost two millennia of Jewish alchemical work and writing.

Chapter Forty

MORDECAI ABI SEROUR

THERE EXISTS evidence that the copyist of the *Book of Wisdom* discussed in the previous chapter was not the last North African Jew to take an active interest in alchemy. It is supplied by Charles de Foucauld (1858–1916), the French officer, explorer, and later missionary, much of whose work was concentrated on Morocco. At an early age Foucauld became an officer of the Hussards, and was sent to Morocco to gather information on local conditions. Such intelligence was considered important by France, engaged at the time in strengthening its influence in Morocco in competition with other European powers. Since it would have been extremely dangerous for Foucauld to appear in Morocco as a French officer, that is, a Christian, it was decided that he would adopt the disguise of a Jewish rabbi. The Jews, although a *declassé* community in Morocco, were able to move about relatively freely. Foucauld employed a Jewish guide, and thus was able to visit many places in the country. This first trip of Foucauld took place in 1883, when he was twenty-five years old, and the information he gathered about the almost completely unknown country proved very useful for its penetration by the French. Subsequently Foucauld became a missionary, and settled in Tamanrasset in the central Sahara, where he was ultimately assassinated by the Touareg of the Hoggar.

Foucauld's guide on that first Moroccan trip was Mordecai Abi Serour, a Moroccan Jew born about 1830 in the oasis of Aqqa in Southern Morocco, and living in Algeria, where he was an alchemist, albeit not a very successful one. He probably agreed to enter the service of Foucauld and go with him into the depths of the Moroccan countryside because he needed the money Foucauld was willing to pay him. The relationship between the two men was tense, as can easily be understood if one considers that the fifty-four-year-old Jew, who was the guide and life insurance for the twenty-five-year-old Frenchman, could easily have felt unhappy being subordinated to a youngster almost thirty years his junior. After a final quarrel they parted, and Mordecai returned to Algeria to his family.

Once back home, Mordecai took up the alchemical experiments interrupted by his Moroccan trip. With the money he received from Foucauld he purchased mercury, an essential ingredient in his operations to transmute base metals into gold. What happened thereafter was a repetition of the pattern known to us from the lives of several alchemists. As René Bazin, Foucauld's biographer, put it, "since he [Mordecai], remained all day long bent over his crucibles, the mercurial vapors, without much delay, poisoned this last of the alchemists."[1]

I doubt that Mordecai Abi Serour was indeed the last of the alchemists. Morocco in particular has remained a country of widespread folk rituals and folk beliefs; no wonder Edward Westermarck chose it for the subject of his classic *Ritual and Belief in Morocco.* Because of self-imposed limitations, Westermarck does not speak about alchemy in that exceptionally thorough study, but it nevertheless contains indications of interest and belief in the possibility of producing gold. Thus he mentions that in Fez he was told that "if the *jnūn* [jinns] cause the water supply in the house to cease at night, there is a splendid opportunity for anybody who notices it to enrich himself: he gets up and puts into the basin . . . an object of silver or gold, with the result that the water there is transformed into the same metal. Many persons have made a fortune in this way through the kindness of the *jnūn.*"[2] The procedure described by Westermarck is but a variant of the widespread alchemical operation of multiplying gold or silver by placing some of it into another substance.

As late as the 1940s, in the course of my own studies of Moroccan Jewish folk custom, I was told by an old Moroccan Jewish woman in Jerusalem that on rare occasions one could find an object or growth called *wars* in the gall of a cow that had eaten a grass called *qamia*, and that *wars* could be used for making gold. Since *wars* is an Arabic term for saffron, and *qamia* seems to be a distortion of the Arabic term *kameh*, meaning "cameo" or precious stone, it appears that my informant inadvertently switched the two terms, and what she meant to say was that if a cow eats a plant called *wars*, one could find in its gall a precious stone.[3] In any case, the belief, which she recalled from her young days in Fez, shows that the interest in making gold, and the idea that it was possible to do so, were still alive in Morocco in the 1920s.

With the penetration of modern European culture into the Jewish communities in central and western Europe, the decline of alchemical belief and practice that took place about the end of the eighteenth century was parallelled by a similar practice developed among the Jews. However, only the faintest echoes of the European Enlightenment had reached the Muslim countries by the nineteenth century, and their Jewish communities remained practically untouched by the Haskalah, and continued in their age-old religious beliefs and practices. Among the Jews of Morocco, perhaps more than among their co-religionists in other Muslim countries, the belief in the efficacy of amulets was widespread, for example, and many a rabbi was engaged in writing *qameʿot* (amulets) which were worn by practically everybody. The amulets were usually small pieces of paper or parchment, or else small platelets of metals, always inscribed with magic names and formulas. After the mass immigration of Middle Eastern Jews to Israel, as the younger people among them began to assimilate to the prevalent Israeli non-religious (or even anti-religious) mood, they sold these amulets by the thousands to antique dealers in the Tel Aviv and Jaffa flea markets, and it was possible to buy them for relatively little money.

We know from our historical review of the work of Jewish alchemists that in many cases they also engaged in providing amulets that were supposed to serve all kinds of apotropaeic needs, such as protection against dangers and illnesses, and, on the positive side, to give success in all possible types of quests—the same assortment of purposes that were served by the amulets that passed through the hands of the dealers in the Tel Aviv flea markets. The best example to illustrate this combination of alchemy with amulets is the manuscript of the great sixteenth-century Kabbalist Ḥayyim Vital. This being the case, it stands to reason that at least some of the rabbis who produced the great profusion of amulets from Middle Eastern Jewish communities that came to light in Israel must also have been engaged in alchemy, but this activity did not leave behind such tangible traces as represented by the amulets.

Adding this argument to the case history of Mordechai Abi Serour, and to the testimony of the book-sized alchemical manuscript discussed in the preceding chapter, I believe we are safe in assuming that as long as the Middle Eastern Jewish communities continued to live in their traditional home environments, the persistence among them of the belief in and use of amulets points to the survival of alchemical practices among some of them.[4]

A PROFILE OF JEWISH ALCHEMY

HAVING REACHED the end of our trek through eighteen centuries, we are faced with the task that confronts all conscientious travelers upon the conclusion of their voyage: they must try to answer the question of what they have learned in the course of their explorations. What have the records taught us about the many Jewish men and one or two Jewish women who pursued the alchemical quest? Did they truly believe in the feasibility of transmuting base metals into gold? Were such transmutations the major, or at least a major, goal of their alchemical work? What were the theoretical foundations of their work in the Great Art, which was both a philosophy and a technology, both a quasi-religious world-view and a skill requiring manual precision and dexterity? Was the search for the philosophers' stone (also known as the elixir of life) another of their main concerns? Were they among the ranks of the many alchemists who, ever since antiquity, persisted in pursuing the elusive Faustian goals of restoring youth, regaining health, achieving long life, and finding happiness? Did they merely follow the alchemical theories and practices established by the gentile adepts, or were they pathfinders and inventors in one or both of those fields? If the latter was the case, did they significantly advance the theoretical foundations of alchemy and the techniques utilized in its operations? And, apart from the question of innovation and originality, were there any essential differences between the alchemy as practiced by the gentiles on the one hand and by the Jews on the other; in other words, was there such a thing as a *Jewish* alchemy?

Let us begin with the last question first. By asking whether there was such a thing as a Jewish alchemy what we mean is, can we speak of Jewish alchemy in the sense in which one can distinguish between Jewish philosophy and the philosophy of the Muslims and Christians, because the former, being suffused through and through with Jewish religious ideas, had an unmistakably Jewish character? Or was the alchemy practiced by the Jews rather comparable to medicine, to which Jewish doctors made important contributions as both practitioners and theoreticians, but which, in the hands of the Jews, was an art devoid of any particular Jewish component?

It seems to me that in this respect alchemy occupied a middle position between philosophy and medicine. It was like medicine in the sense that the basic alchemical views of the composition and evolution of substances, the apparatus used, the operations performed, and the goals pursued were shared by Jews and gentiles. In all this, religio-national affiliation or commitment, whether gentile or Jewish, did not come into play. On the other hand, alchemy was like philosophy in that a complex network of conceptual connections ran between it and the religio-ideational structures that until the Enlightenment were the most important components of every cultural environment, whether Muslim, Christian, or Jewish. The Jewish alchemists who, like practically all the Jews until the nineteenth century, were religiously observant, saw in alchemy a God-given gift, and therefore considered engaging in alchemical work a God-pleasing religious activity. As a corollary of this attitude, some Jewish alchemists felt that their achievements in the Great Art should not go beyond the confines of the Jewish people—an early representative of this view, as we have seen, was Maria the Jewess. Others, while not going quite that far, were convinced that the Jews, being heirs to an age-old religio-cultural tradition, of which alchemy was a part, and which included familiarity with the Hebrew language, the Bible and its exegesis, Jewish ritual and moral precepts, and, from the later Middle Ages on, also the Kabbalah, were much better equipped to become master alchemists than the gentiles who lacked that essential background. As we have seen in several chapters of this book, this view was shared by many gentile alchemists, who were therefore prompted to learn Hebrew, to study the Bible, and to delve into the mysteries of the Kabbalah and gematria, and to seek out Jewish mentors from whom to acquire the true and full measure of alchemical mastery.

Related to this feature is another characteristic of all the Jewish alchemists: they considered their art a specialization closely interwoven with religious observance. We know of no Jew who was a full-time alchemist; all the Jewish alchemists were also engaged in other work, and in most cases in work that was either directly religious or was sanctioned by religious tradition. Thus many Jewish alchemists were rabbis, or teachers or students of religion, or else were physicians (probably the majority), or communal heads, or money-lenders.

Focussing on their alchemical work, we know from the sources that some Jewish alchemists were independent entrepreneurs who engaged in alchemy to satisfy their personal drive for knowledge and achievement, or in search of fame, recognition, and riches; others were employed by kings, princes, and potentates, and served them as unofficial court or house alchemists. Our book contains several examples of both kinds of Jewish alchemists, some of whom enjoyed positions of considerable influence in royal and lordly courts, or basked in the protection of princes of the Church. Of particular interest are the records or reports telling of contractual arrangements entered into by royalty with Jewish alchemists, under which the rulers extended all kinds of privileges to the latter, and undertook to finance their operations, in exchange for which the alchemists were supposed to make gold to replenish the royal treasury. The most interesting case in point is that of Raymund, who stipulated in his agreement with Edward III that the king would use the gold he was to produce for financing a military expedition against the Turks.

One curious byproduct of the prestige Jewish alchemy and Jewish alchemists enjoyed is the attribution of Jewish authorship to alchemical treatises that were actually written by non-Jewish adepts. Such attributions were variants of the more frequently encountered claim in ancient, medieval, and Renaissance writings whose true authors hid under the pseudepigraphic names of famous authorities. When an anonymous gentile alchemical author gave out that his treatise was written by, say, Raymond Lull, or when an anonymous Jewish alchemical author attributed his treatise to Maimonides, this was clearly done in order to ensure favorable reception of the work by having it accepted as that of an author of great renown. Likewise, when a known non-Jewish alchemical author was, long after his death, pronounced Jewish, this was done because by transmuting him into a Jew, his status in the alchemical community was enhanced, and thus his treatises could claim greater prestige, greater authenticity, greater veracity. At the same time, the very occurrence of such pseudepigraphic transmutations from gentile into Jew are eloquent testimonies to the standing of Jewish alchemy at the top of the alchemical value system. No cases of reverse transmutations of Jewish alchemical authors into gentiles have come to my attention.

Do the sources permit us to draw any definite conclusion as to whether or not the Jewish alchemists believed in the authenticity of the Art? In the course of studying the sources I repeatedly asked myself this question, and the conclusion I reached was that they did sincerely believe that the recipes they presented in their treatises as "tried and true" were actually accurate descriptions of procedures that led to the results they promised. This conclusion is based on the Hebrew alchemical texts themselves, which, on the one hand, occasionally include frankly stated reservations as to the reliability of the prescriptions, while, on the other, present the most complex recipes for transmuting base metals into gold in the same matter-of-fact style in which they offer simple chemical instructions for making, for instance, various kinds of inks or cosmetic preparations.

A consideration of the life, work, and character of the few Hebrew alchemical authors of whom we have information leads to the same conclusion. To mention only one example—the most outstanding one—it is quite impossible to imagine that a man of the stature and probity of Ḥayyim Vital, a leading light of the Safed kabbalistic school, should describe alchemical operations in meticulous detail, state that he himself performed them and that the results were in some cases satisfactory, in others not, and do all this with the fraudulent intent of misleading his readers. In addition, there is another important general factor that practically vouches for the honesty of Jewish alchemical tracts: for a religious Jew to write something that he knew to be untrue would have been a grave transgression that, he firmly believed, would bring about severe punishment in afterlife.

In this connection we must touch, at lest fleetingly, upon a question that has often been asked in connection with alchemy as a whole but never satisfactorily answered: leaving aside the issue of whether the alchemists themselves believed in the feasibility of transmuting base metals into gold, how was it possible that the thousands who were their clients, among them intelligent and cultured people of power and means, continued to believe that gold could be manufactured in retorts, alembics, and crucibles, when the simple (and for us easily ascertainable) fact is that such a thing is not within the realm of the possible?

Among the explanations, most of which sound like excuses for human credulity, are: for many centuries many alchemists, and most of their clients, were unable to distinguish between gold and other metals that had the color of gold, that is, looked like gold; because of loose terminology any metal that looked like gold was called gold; there were hundreds of ready excuses for lack of success in gold-making operations, which enabled the adept to hold out the hope that next time he would be successful; lack of success in one particular type of experiment did not necessarily translate into distrust in the alchemists' ability to perform other types of operations; those other types of operations, and especially the search for the philosophers' stone (that mysterious compound substance which was believed to be the elixir of life), were at least as important goals within the general realm of the Great Art as gold making.

But let us set aside the hopeless issue of alchemical verification, and return to the profile of Jewish alchemy, taking up the matter of the philosophers' stone. The overall impression one gains from a comparison of Jewish with gentile alchemical texts is that in the former the quest for the philosophers' stone was more closely associated than in the latter with the humanitarian purpose of healing the sick. Hebrew alchemical texts, generally speaking, devote more attention and hence more space to the medical use of alchemically produced substances than to the methods and procedures of producing those healing liquids, unguents, or powders. The examples presented in this book show quite clearly that the Jewish adept was in many cases as much a physician as an alchemist, and that his major purpose in committing his prescriptions to writing was to enable his disciples to make use of his accumulated knowledge in their efforts to heal the sick. The most eloquent example of this procedure can again be found in the treatise of Ḥayyim Vital.

In this connection yet another characteristic feature of the Hebrew alchemical writings must be mentioned. The Jewish adept, as a rule, did not distinguish between procedures aimed at the transmutation of substances and others based on what we know are valid, experimentally correct, chemical or physical effects. In other words, no distinction was made by them between alchemy proper and what today we would subsume under chemistry. On the same page of a typical Hebrew alchemical manuscript we find prescriptions belonging to the first category alternating with recipes belonging to the second, and, in addition, with a third type consisting of charms, magic, incantations, conjurations, and divinations. This being the case, the scope of the Jewish alchemist's activity is found to comprise practically the entire range of human needs, whether physical, economic, political, social, cultural, psychological, or religious. In view of this global interest the Jewish adept evinces in all aspects of the welfare of his fellow man, and the many disparate methods he employs and proposes to avoid dangers, alleviate suffering and anxiety, and provide relief for painful states of body and mind, one could say in general terms that for the Jewish adept alchemy was but one of several paths he followed in his all-embracing concern for his fellow man, and in his dedication to translating into action in every possible manner and fashion that most basic of all biblical commandments, "Thou shalt love thy neighbor as thyself."

As for the relationship between theory and practice in the work of the Jewish alchemists, the extant sources seem to indicate that its balance tilted toward the latter. Jewish alchemists were, of course, interested in and knowledgeable about alchemical theory. From their extant writings alone one could easily reconstruct a full picture of alchemical theory, alchemical worldview, and the alchemical understanding of the nature of nature and of the divinely ordained natural processes that resulted in the present configuration of the mineral, vegetable, and animal kingdoms. But, reading what they had to say about these subjects, one has the impression that they were not intrinsically interested in these issues. They spoke of them only because they felt that some theory was required in order to provide the underpinning for the technical instructions in the hundreds of recipes with which they filled their treatises.

This being the case, one would not expect the Jewish alchemists to have made any significant contribution to alchemical theory. In fact, and practically everything they have to say about theory is taken from ancient Greek and medieval Arabic sources. I say "practically," because there is one area in which the Jewish alchemists did make a significant contribution, and that was in the field of what can be called "mysticization." This process, and the influence of the kabbalistic gematria on gentile alchemists, have been dealt with in Chapter 12, to which I want to add here only one point: under the impact of the Kabbalah and its *gematria* the medieval alchemical tradition underwent a noticeable change, and became during the Renaissance a more mystically and religiously oriented discipline.

As for the technical instructions contained in Hebrew alchemical treatises, they are, in general, of a high quality, in the sense that they are precise and detailed. This, of course, does not mean that they are easy to follow. First of all, in many cases we cannot be sure of the exact meaning of the technical terms used in Hebrew alchemical texts to designate substances, apparatuses, processes, and procedures. Many of these are given in foreign languages (especially Arabic, Spanish, and Italian) in Hebrew transliteration, which does not help, because the precise meaning of terms is uncertain in those languages as well. Precision in terminology was not a strong point of ancient, medieval, and Renaissance alchemy in general. Even frequently recurring terms, whose derivatives are still in use in the modern European languages, do not necessarily mean the same in the alchemical texts as they mean today. Second, many substances are called not by their proper names, but by a confusing variety of cover-names: gold is called "sun," silver "moon," mercury "slave," sulphur "scorpio," and so on. Similar difficulties arise in connection with terms used for apparatuses, measures, and alchemical processes. That is, an old Hebrew alchemical text, even in the few cases in which it is not too difficult to decipher, cannot simply be read; it has to be carefully and often painstakingly interpreted. Once one has done the work, what emerges is a prescription containing precise and detailed instructions.

It is also characteristic of the Hebrew alchemists' treatises that they often state that they themselves invented a procedure, or that they carried out a certain recipe not exactly as prescribed, but with certain modifications, and they don't hesitate to mention whether, in performing an operation, they were successful or not. In fact, some even state that they succeeded with an operation only occasionally. Such details indicate the beginnings of an attitude characteristic of the modern experimental scientist who knows that the foremost criterion of the validity of a discovery is procedural repeatability.

THIS book has, I think, lifted out of obscurity a field of Jewish cultural activity which, although not entirely unknown, had been grossly neglected. Its significance has consistently been denied, or at least belittled, by those few Jewish historians who deigned to refer to it in their works. In view of this situation one cannot blame the authors of general histories of alchemy for not paying attention to Jewish alchemy, and presenting the history of alchemy as comprising only Chinese, Indian, Greek, Hellenistic, Arab, and Christian-European branches. The present book shows, however,—as far as this was possible on the basis of the insufficiently explored source material—that alchemy was throughout the ages an important Jewish occupational specialization, comparable to Jewish work in medicine. Jewish alchemists were engaged in experimentation, introduced new apparatus, techniques, and procedures, were employed as court alchemists, and enjoyed a high reputation in those societies of the Muslim and the Christian worlds in which alchemy was practiced.

This book also shows that alchemy was a unique field of activity in which Jews were able to have contact with gentiles on an equal footing, and, occasionally at least, they occupied a higher position than their gentile colleagues, serving as teachers and masters of aspiring gentile adepts. In this connection it would be of considerable interest to look into the question of whether the position of the Jews in general was better in those countries in which alchemy was a recognized Jewish specialization than in those in which this was not the case. My guess would be that such a positive correlation would indeed be found.

Finally, in the modern world Jews have occupied an important position in chemistry in which, as the *Encyclopaedia Judaica* puts it, "the percentage of Jews achieving eminence has been high compared to their number in the general population." The *Encyclopaedia Judaica* contains no general article on the role of Jews in chemistry, only a listing of Jewish chemists with a few lines of biographical notes (s. v. Chemistry), and thus it provides no basis for any consideration of the roots of this intensive Jewish interest in the field. Since, as has been generally recognized, alchemy was the father of chemistry, it stands to reason that the attention Jews paid to alchemy throughout the ages became the cultural heritage that led relatively more Jews than gentiles into specializing in the successor science of what for many centuries was considered and termed the Great Art.

Appendix

AN ALCHEMICAL VOCABULARY FROM JERBA

THE MOST VALUABLE part of the Jerba manuscript discussed in Chapter 39 is the alchemical vocabulary found in it. In fact the manuscript contains no fewer than three vocabularies: a short one on folios 2a–3b; a second short one on folios 8a–b; and a long one on folios 136a–144a, which contains most, but not all, of the items listed in the first two.

The purpose of the vocabularies is stated in almost identical terms in the heading of each of the three. The first heading (f. 2a) reads: BIN"U ᶜAM"I ᶜAS"U: Specific Explanations of Some Things that Belong to the Work. The first three words are acrostics of the Hebrew *b'shem adonay naᶜaseh w'naṣliaḥ—ᶜezri meᶜim adonay—ᶜose shamayim wa'areṣ*, that is: "In the name of God we shall do and succeed, my help is from God the maker of heaven and earth." The second vocabulary is headed as follows: "Explanation of some names in Latin and in the languages of the ancients." The third: "BIN"U ᶜAM"I AS"U: Explanation of Some [Words] Hard to Understand."

Most of the words explained in the vocabularies are either in Italian or Arabic. A few, to judge from the appended -s plural, are in Spanish. A very few are in Hebrew. Despite the superscription of the second vocabulary, none of the words listed in it can clearly be identified as Latin. All the words, whatever their language, are given in Hebrew transliteration. The Arabic words are occasionally transliterated in accordance with their Judeo-Arabic Maghrebite (Western) pronunciation: *sams* (sun, gold), instead of the literary Arabic *shams*; *qāṣiḥ* (thick), for *qāshiḥ*; the article *al-* is abridged into *l-*; and so on.

The language into which the "difficult words" are translated is in almost every case Arabic. Occasionally, one Arabic term is translated (or rather explained) simply by a synonym. In a few cases the explanation-translation is given in both Arabic and Italian; for example; "*anṭūn*: *nuḥās* [A.], that is *rāme* [I.]," both of which mean copper. On a few occasions the explanation is given in Hebrew, or in what appears to be Latin or Greek. Sometimes, however, an Arabic word is translated into Italian (e.g., *bīlār* [in literary A., *bilawr*]: *qrisṭalo* [I. *cristallo*]). Occasionally, when translating an Arabic word into Italian, the author states that it is in Laᶜaz, using the traditional Hebrew term for "foreign tongue."

The explanations or translations are occasionally bilingual: the author uses expressions compounded of Arabic and Hebrew. For example, he explains the Italian *alūmē diroqa* (I. *allume di rocca*) as *shabb maḥṣavī* (A.-H., mineral vitriol). Or, he uses an Arabic or an Italian word with the Hebrew article *ha-*: *ha-nār* (the fire), or *ha-numero* (the number).

On a few occasions the author is not satisfied with simply giving the equivalent of the word to be explained in Arabic (or in another language), but instead appends a sentence explaining in detail what the word means. These sentences are either in Hebrew or in Arabic, or in a mixture of the two languages. For example, "*Barbīna* [L. verbena officialis]: *ʿesev qanyī ya'sir yusayyib hadam* [a reedy herb which stops the flow of blood]," where the first two Hebrew words are followed by two Arabic words, and then the last word is again Hebrew.

The Hebrew transliteration of the Arabic, Italian, and other words is in general adequate, although by no means consistent. For example, the Arabic word *zuwaq* (quicksilver) is transliterated *zwq, zāwāq, zāwwāq*; the Italian *salgemma* (rocksalt) as *salgemah, saljemah, salyemah*; and so on. This difficulty in transliterating the Italian soft *g* is parallelled by the problem the author had in transliterating the Italian *z*: he vacillates between the Hebrew *zayin, samekh*, and *ṣade*.

An interesting feature in the vocabularies is the listing of Hebrew *Decknamen* (cover names). The use of *Decknamen* for the alchemical designation of substances is very common in Arabic, and our author uses quite a few of them, e.g., *shams* (sun) for gold, *qamar* (moon) for silver, and *zuhrā* (Venus) for copper, and so on. The use of the Hebrew equivalents of these names is not unusual in Hebrew alchemical literature, in which one finds *shemesh* (sun), *l'vanah* (moon), and *nogah* (Venus) for these three metals. Unusual and original, however, is our author's occasional use of Hebrew *Decknamen* that do not seem to appear in other Hebrew alchemical texts. Thus for *zuwaq* (quicksilver) he uses the phrase *ʿof haporeaḥ ba'awīr* (bird that flies in the air); for sal ammoniac the expression *ʿof haqam b'vehalah* (bird that rises in fright); for tin, Arabic *qazdīr*, he uses both the Hebrew *Deckname m'ṣoraʿ*, leper, and the Arabic *Deckname mustarī*, lion (the planet Jupiter). He also lists the Arabic *zabad al-baḥr* (foam of the sea) and explains it only as *isquma maris* (that is, *scuma maris*) meaning the same, without any further translation.

An additional interesting feature in the vocabularies is that the author frequently describes the substances listed as being "hot and dry in the third degree," or "cold and wet in the second degree," and so on, using (in the second half of the nineteenth century) the classification of substances according to the degrees of heat and dryness, or cold and wetness, established by the famous second-century Greek physician Galen. On the other hand, our author was up to date as far as the division of the world into a Christian and a Muslim realm was concerned, as can be gathered from the comment he makes in explaining the word *'onqi'ah* as a measure of weight which "in the cities of Edom" (that is, in the Christian world) is divided into eight drachmas, while "in the cities of Ishmael" (that is, in the Muslim world) into ten. The one authority whom our author quotes frequently is Ibn Sīnā (980–1037), to whom he refers either by name or as "the Physician," and whose *Kānūn* he seems to have known well.

The entries in the vocabulary that follows are arranged in this manner: the entry words are listed in English alphabetical order, and in careful transliteration of the Hebrew letters in which they appear in the manuscript. If I was able to identify the original language of a word, it is followed in square brackets by an abbreviation indicating that language; then, wherever necessary, I added in *italics* the original spelling of the word or my transliteration of it; then comes my translation of the word into English. This is followed by a dash, after which comes in *italics* the translation of the word as given in the manuscript. Then, in square brackets, my identification of the language of the translation, and my translation of that word (or words) into English. If the manuscript contains, in addition to the translation of the word, an explanation (which is always in Hebrew), I give that explanation in my English translation. That is, all the material contained in the manuscript of the vocabularies is given outside the brackets; whatever is inside the brackets is my translation or explanation. In many cases I had to leave words unidentified and unexplained. I am aware that this vocabulary is but a first attempt at the presentation of this rather complex multilingual material whose full treatment has to await the attention of future researchers.

a'awrum [L. *aurum*, gold]—*dahab* [A. *dhahab*, gold]

ʿabd [A. slave, *Deckname* for quicksilver]—*zawaq* [A. *zuwaq*, quicksilver]

abrū'ol—*antimonio* [I., antimony], *kuḥl* [A., antimony]

adraṣogane—*ʿunṣul* [A., wild onion, leek]

affināṭo [I.]—that is, refined

afroniṭum [I. *afronitro*, foam of nitre, *spuma nitri*, saltpeter]—*burāqas* or *nītrī*

al'abar, al'ahbar [A. *al-ābār*, lead]—*raṣāṣ* [A., lead]

ʿalam—*zarnīkh* [A., arsenic]

alambiqo [I. *alambicco*, alembic]—kettle in which burnt water is extracted.

al'anaq [A. *al'anuk, al'anaq*, tin]—*qazdīr* [A., tin]

al'anūq albar'ī [A. . . . *al-burā'ī*, tin shavings]—*b'dil wʿoferet* [H., tin and lead]

al'asirāngē—*limatura plombo* [I., filings of lead]

alaṭqad, al'aṭqī—*antimonio* [I., antimony], *kuḥl* [A., antimony]

albūno—*sheten* [H., urine]

alīga [I. *aliga, alga*, seaweed]—that is, pearl shell. Refine as mentioned in the *libbun* [H., whitening]

alīqālī—*vitriolo* [I.], *zāj* [A., vitriol]

alīzmārīr—*shenāder* [A., see *nushādir*]

almārqashīṭā [A., marcasite]—*litarigiri'o* [I. *litargirio*, litharge]

almiṣādīr [I. *almizadir, almicadir, almisadir*]—*shenāder* [see *nushādir*]; *salarmoni'aqo* [I., sal ammoniac], and likewise *alīzmārīr* [see above].

alqālṣinārē [I. *calcinare*, to calcine, with the A. article *al-*]—that is, that it should be like lime

alqāsīdēs [A. *al-qasid*, broken]—*ʿoferet* [H., lead] *qrispus* [L., crisped, curled], *raṣāṣ* [A., lead].

alqībrīṭ [A. *al-kibrīt*; or I. *alcubrith*, sulphur]—white sulphur.

alqūsūr [A. *al-qaswar*, the old one, lion, *Deckname*?]—*antimonio* [I., antimony]

alrā'ī—*nitrozisqo*

alrāsīs—*shenāder* [see *nushādir*]; *salarmoniaqo* [I., sal ammoniac]

alṣērārē [I. *cerare*, with A. article, to cerate, to wax]—this is to melt the solid thing which is not capable of being melted and when it becomes *liqwido* [I., liquid] then it is called *igtarāto* or *inṣērāto*

alṭālīq [A., the separated or the mild]—*sal* [I. salt], and it seems that it is *talq* [A., talc]

alūmē [I. *allume*, alum]—*shabb* [A., vitriol]

alūmē difiūma [I. *allume di fiume*, river alum?]—*shabb yamanī* [A., Yemenite vitriol]

alūmē diplūma [another spelling of the above]

alūmē diroqa [I. *allume di rocca*, ordinary alum]—*shabb* [A., vitriol] *maḥṣavī* [H., mineral]

alūmīn [I. *allumina*, alumina]—*zarnīkh* [A., arsenic]; *orpimento* [I., orpiment]

al'unon—*qazdīr* [A., tin]

alwānās, salarmoniqo, shenāder [see *nushādir*]

alyas [A., lion, a *Deckname*?]—*melaḥ* [H., salt]

amīr lmilḥ [A. *amīr a-milḥ*]—*melaḥ* [H., salt], *milḥ nuʿās* [A., sleepy (?) salt]

amrūn [A. *al-amrān*, the two most bitter things, aloe and mustard]—*ashrah baqarā'* [A. *shara, asharr*, worst, colocynth, bitter apple], hot and dry in the third [degree]

andadān [see *angira'*]

anfiyum [A. *afyūn*, opium]—*tusmirat*

angira'—*urtiga* [L. *urtica*, nettle], it and its seeds are dry

angīrā [A. *anjudān*, asafetida]—*waraq alḥiltīt* [A., leaf of asafetida], hot and dry in the third [degree]

anī'odīn—*waraq alḥiltīt* [A., leaf of asafetida]

anṭīmonī—it seems to me that it is what is called *antimonio*, it is *atmad* [A. *ithmad*], which is *kuḥl* [A., antimony]

anṭīmonīo [I.]—that is, a kind of metal called in Arabic *magnīṭiā*, and in Lat[in] *dīmībūzan* [marginal note:] *dimirkuzan*. And in the *Kānūn* he [Ibn Sīnā] wrote that it is similar to *marqashīṭa* [A., marcasite]

anṭron—it is *shuman zkhukhit* [H., glass-oil, glass-fat]

anṭūn—*nuḥās* [A., copper], that is *rāme* [I., copper]

anverga—*shabīkah* [A., net]

aposārē—that is, *rīposārē* [I., to repose], that is, *yirtāḥ* [A. *yirtakh*, tarry]

apoṭrīpāṣione—that is, a vessel *yakhmur wayaʿban* [A., sealed and big]

aqālṣīnārē [I. *calcinare*, to calcine]—that is, that it should be like lime

ʿaqrab [A., Scorpio, *Deckname* for sulphur]—*bukhārah* [A., smoke, fog, steam]

arēsolvārē [I., to dissolve]—that is, *ḥulhum* [A., error for *maḥlūl*, dissolved]

argenṭos vivos [I.-S.]—*zībaq* [A., quicksilver]

arinṭano vivos [I. *argentovivo*, quicksilver]—*zauwāq* [A. *zuwaq*, quicksilver]

armanos—*niṭros*

armīkh—*qarfa* [A. *qirf*, skin, peel, rind]

armoniaqo [I. *ammoniaco*, ammonia]—*ūṣaq* [A. *ushshaq*, ammoniac]

aroni'āqos [S.]—*shenādir* [see *nushādir*]

aropniqārē—that is, *taḥrīk* [A., encouragement, moving]; or *taḥrīq*, [A., burning]

arsēnīqo(s) [I. *arsenico*]—*zarnīkh* [A., arsenic]

arṭīfīqārē [I. *artificiare*, to work with artifice]—that is, *ṣafiyy* [A., pure]

'arubīsqārē [I. *arrubinare*, to make red]—that is *taḥrīk* [A., read *taḥrīq*, burning]

āsa fāṭīda [I. *assafatida*]—*ḥiltīt* [H. and A., asafetida]

asad [A., lion, a *Deckname*]—*rahj* [A., dust]

aṣē'ēy [thus vocalized, I. *azey*]—*vitriol shāṭār* [I.-A. *v. shaṭr*, half vitriol]

asenṣio [I. *ascensione*, ascent]—*sujrat Maryam* [A., basin of Maria, i.e., bain-Marie]

aṣēto [I. *aceto*, vinegar]—*khall* [A., vinegar], *zāj waḍīf* [A., quick vitriol]

aseṭum [I. *acetum*, vinegar]—*khall* [A., vinegar]

asfīnārē—*bāhuq* or *bāhnaq*

asfōdē, asfōdium [I. *asfodelo*, asphodel]—*ṭabāshīr* [A., the pebbly substance in bamboo, chalk]

aspōne [I. *asabon*, *sapone*, soap]—*ṣābūn* [A., soap]

ass—*ḥiltīt* [A. and H., asafetida]

aṣṭuraq—*qālāmīṭa* [I. *calamita*, a fossil plant], hot and dry in the third [degree]

ʿaṭ [A.]—it seems it is *zāwāq* [A. *zuwaq*, quicksilver]

aṭaq—*ūṣaq* [or *usaq*; A. *wushshaq*, ammoniac], hot at the end of the third [degree]
ᶜaṭārd—*zāwāk* [A. *zuwaq*, quicksilver]
atmad [A. *ithmad*, antimony]—*kuḥl* [A., antimony], *anṭimonio* [I., antimony]
aṭrāmēnṭūm [or *aṭrāmēntōs*; L. or I.]—*zāj* [A., vitriol], that is, *vitriolo* in Laᶜaz
aṭrāmēnṭūm soṭorium [I. *a. sotorio*, sulfate of copper or of iron]
awwis—*qazdīr* [A., tin]
ayres [I. *aeris*, copper]—*n'ḥoshet sarūf* [H., burnt copper]
azāfāran—*zaᶜfarān* [A., saffron]
azarīqon—*zārqūn* [A., cinnabar]
azīg, or *azīq* [I. *azec*, vitriol]—*zāj* [A., vitriol]
azimar [I., minium, vermilion, copper]—some say that it is *zinjār* [A., verdigris] which is *sqāliya* [I., scalings] of copper, others think it is *sqāliya* of iron [I., *scaglie di ferro*]
azīq [see *azīg*]
azōg [see *zāg*]
azwar [read *azwaq*; A. *zuwaq*, quicksilver]—*kesef ḥay* [H., quicksilver]

bālbaḥ anqarde—hot and dry in the fourth [degree]
banyo arēna [I. *bagno arena*, sand bath]—that is, *yaḥūṭ ha-raml fī burma wayaḥūṭ liklī fawq ha-raml wayaᶜṭi ha-nār taḥt l-burma* [Judeo-A.: throw the sand in a kettle and throw it in a vessel over the sand and give it fire under the kettle]
banyo Maria [I. *bagno Maria*]—as is known . . .
barbīna [I. *verbena*]—a reedy herb which stops the *yusayyib* [A., flow] of blood
baṣal haᶜakhbar [H., mouse onion]—*ᶜunṣul* [A., wild onion, leek]
basbā'īg [A. *basbā'īj, e. polypodium (Filice)*] *solifāre*—hot in the third [degree] and wonderful in its dryness
basīrāg, basīrāj—*shemen shumsh'min* [H., sesame oil]
baure—*ṣurqi* or *ṣudqi*
bi'aqa [I. read *bianca*, white]—*bārūq* [A., white lead, ceruse]
bīlār [A. *bilawr*, crystal]—*qrisṭalo* [I. *cristallo*]
blānqēṭ [I. *bianchetto*, ceruse, stannic oxide pigment]—*bārūq* [A., white lead, ceruse]
bōl armīnī [A., Armenian clay]

dam tanīn [H., dragon's blood]—*damm lakhwa* [A. *d. al-akhawayn*, dragon's blood, the juice of the *dracaena draco*]
damm alkhawīn [A., variant of the preceding]
dī'ai mīdīli—*b'dil o qali'ah* [H., tin or kali]

disōlūṣione [I. *dissoluzione*, dissolution]—this is to turn into water anything that has become lime [was calcinated]
dīstīla in rēsqonṭaro [I. *distilla in . . .*]—that is, between the *lambiq* [A. *al-anbīq*, alembic] and the *qābilah* [A., receptor], as known
disṭilaṣione [I. *distillazione*] or *haṭafah* [H., distillation]—making the vapors rise from the things that are in the vessel, to collect them in another vessel

esh meha-grado ha-bet [H.-I., fire of the second grade]—that is, *taḥūṭ* [A., put] the vessel *qurbī* [A., near] *ha-nār* [H.-A., the fire], *watashūf* [A., and you will see] *ha-numero* [H.-I., the number]
ewaporare [I. *evaporare*, to evaporate]—that is, you should let it boil gently until all the moisture goes out and the thing remains dry

ferrum [L., iron]—*ḥadid* [A., iron]
filṭro [I., filter]—this is a piece of woolen cloth; that is, the *anbīq* [A., alembic], and they hollow out in it a *pūma sīqa* [Aramaic, correctly *sika*, "mouth of a pin," i.e., pinhole]
fisaṣione [I. *fissazione*, fixation]—this is to gather the thing that flees from the fire and does not stand heat, and they keep it *per artifiṣio* [I., for an artifice], also for that which flees from strong water
fiṣṣe [I. *fisso*, fixed]—*hashmarim* [H., sediments]; they are the sediments in Laʿaz
fi'umah [see *pli'umah*]
flor da'irim [from the L. *flos aeris*, copper oxide, verdigris]—*nuḥās* [A., copper]
fornello [I., furnace]—*maṣref* [H., melting pot], and it means *kur* [H., melting pot], that is melting pot for gold
friṭṭa [I. *frits*, the partly fused mixture of sand and fluxes of which glass is made]; in Laʿaz it means glass-fat
friṭṭo di Aspania [I. *frits* of Spain]

gale, galos [I. *galla*, gallnut]—ʿafṣ [A., gallnut]
gandaba dasṭar [A. *jundbadastar*, castoreum]—*qāsṭūr* [L. *castoreum*], hot at the end of the fourth and dry in the third [degree]
ganti'anah [L. *gentiana*, gentian]—*nasi'anah.* Hot in the third and dry in the second [degree]
garīr, ṭartaro, ṭarṭār [A. *ṭarṭīr*, tartar]
gāshīr [A. *jashar*, spring herbs]—*apoponago*, hot and dry in the third [degree]
gawzbō [A. *jawz bawwa*, muscat nut]—*nusse musqade* [I. *noce moscado*, nutmeg tree], hot and dry in the third [degree]
gīrārāsīro—*gofrit ḥay* [H., live sulphur], *qībrītē* [A. *kibrīt*, sulphur]

gisos [I. *gisisun*, a kind of gum]—*jāsū*
gofrit [H., sulphur] is of five kinds: green, red, black, white, *zinjārī barṭi*
goma [I. *gomma*]—*ṣemeg* [H., rubber], that is, *s'raf* [H., resin]
goma arabiqa [I. *gomma arabica*]—*ṣemeg ʿaravi* [H., gum arabic]
goma rossa [I. *gomma rossa*, red gum]—*lūkh* or *lūk*

ḥadīdah lkalwiya [A., explanation illegible]
hawīrmaṣe or **huwirnīse**—is made of linseed oil and quicklime melted together
ḥōm [H., heat] *ṭemperāṭo* [I., tempered, temperate]

i'adrosero, idrosero—*kesef ferro* [H.-I., iron silver], *iqtra'iros, fuzrah* [A. *fiḍḍah*, silver]
idrogorias [I. *idrargirio*, quicksilver]—*zawaq* [A. *zuwaq*, quicksilver]
il'asṭīrob [cf. P. and A. *usrub*, lead]—*ʿoferet sale* [H. *ʿoferet*, lead, I. *sale*, of salt]
imunqabiʿal—*zanzafūr* [A. *zunjufr*, cinnabar], *zinafario* [I. *cinnabrio*, cinnabar]
in esso [I. in himself or itself]—and it seems to me *fīhī* [A., in it]
infaṭānṭa—that is, *banyo di Maria* [I. *bagno di Maria, bain Marie*]
ingresso [I.?]—that is, *shaḥrut* [H., blackness]
īnoq—*zāwāq* [A. *zuwaq*, quicksilver]
īnos [G. *oenos*, wine]—*sharāb* [A., a drink]
inpola [I. *ampolla*, ampulla]—*kūza* [A., flask with a narrow neck], that is a vessel like a *ṭāṣa* [A. *ṭassa*, or I. *tazza*, cup, mug]
inqolare [I. *incollare*, to paste, to glue]—that is, *taṣʿīd* [A., sublimation or distillation]
insenṣio, inṣīnaṣio [I. *incensario*, fleabane, a kind of gentian]—*lūbān* [A. *labūn, lubān*, juniper, benzoin]
inṣērāṣione [I. *incerazione*, ceration, waxing]—that is, to drench and to mix on marble until they combine
inṣēre sālis [I. *essere salis*?]—*salyema* [I. *salgemma*, rock salt]
insūlīṭos [S.]—*ṭarṭaro* [I., tartar, or A. *tartir*, tartar]
i'owuṣīsṭon—*damm lkhawā'* [A. *damm al-akhawayn*, dragon's blood], *dam tanin* [H., dragon's blood]
iqtrā'iros [S.]—*fuzrah* [A., read *fiḍḍah*, silver; see *i'adrosero*]
is [L. *aes*, metal, copper]—*nuḥās* [A., copper]
ʿīsah [H., dough]—*liqwida* [I. *liquido*, liquid], that is, soft, that is, *jāriwah* [A., correctly *jārīyah*, liquid, in feminine]
isfīdāg [A. *isfīdāj*, white lead, ceruse]—*bārūq* [A., white lead, ceruse]
isīrī salis [I. *essere salis*?]—*saleyma* [i.e. *salyema*, I. *salgemma*, rock salt]
iṣīṣīṣī—*zāj* [A., vitriol]

isqīl, isqoalla [A. *isqīl*, sea-onion, *scilla maritima*]—*ʿunṣul* [A., wild onion, leek]

isṭīs [cf. L. *aes ustum*, burnt copper]—*zāj* [A., vitriol]

kāṣīn—a vessel

kesef foliaṭo [H. *kesef*, silver, I. *foliato*, foliated]—that is, *waraqī* [A., leaflike]

kesef fitto [H. *kesef*, silver, I. *fitto*, counterfeit]—it is permanent silver, that is *marzan*

kesef ḥay [H., quicksilver]—which has been passed through leather, and a linen cloth is good instead of leather

kesef ḥay sōlīma [H. *kesef ḥay*, quicksilver, I. *solima*, sublimated]—that is, which has been made to rise [i.e., sublimated]

kesef qupēlah [H. *kesef*, silver, I. *coppella*, cupelled]—that is, pure, purified

kesef qupēllāṭo [H. *kesef*, silver, I., cupelled]—that is, *waraqah* [A., leaf]

kesef sōlīma [H. *kesef*, silver, I. *solima*, sublimated]—that is, dead, and possibly he intended dead quicksilver

kesef sōlīmāṭo [H. *kesef*, silver, sublimated]—it is the *kesef sōlīma*

kuḥl [A., antimony]

kurqomah [I. *curcuma*, curcuma]—*nuḥās* [A., copper]

kūza [P. and A. *kūz*, pitcher, jug]—I saw a few times that he calls it *batlis igfula*

labgīn—*fuzrah* [A., read *fiḍḍah*, silver]

lamine [I. *lamina*, thin layer]—*ṣafā'iḥ* [A., leaves]

lane or **li'ane, li'one** [I. *lana*, wool, and *leone*, lion]—*shemen pishtan* [H., linseed oil]

lapis [L., stone]—*ḥajar* [A., stone]

lapis al'āgi'us [L.-A.]—*ḥajar lʿāj* [A. *ḥajar al-ʿāj*, ivory stone]

lapis ametitis [L. *l. amethystus*, amethyst stone]—*ḥajrat almas* [A., diamond stone]

lapis antimoni [L.-I., antimony stone]—*kuḥl* [A., antimony]

lapis apodogi'on—[L.-G.] *ḥajar alqadūḥī* [A. *ḥajar al-qaddāḥī*, firestone]

lapis aqwa'iṭor [L.-I. *l. acquatura*, watering stone]—*ḥajar almisann* [A., whetstone]

lapis arminos [L.-I. *l. armeno*, Armenian stone]—*ḥajar aromīnī* [A., Armenian stone]

lapis guda'iqan [L.-I. *l. giudaicon*, Jewish stone, i.e., calcium carbonate]

lapis lūne [L.-I. moonstone]—*ḥajar lqamar* [A. *ḥajar al-qamar*, moonstone]

lapis molades [L. *l. molaris*? millstone]—*ḥajar haraḥah* [A. *ḥajar*, stone, H., smelling]

lapis nigrorum [L., Negroes' stone]—*ḥajar lḥabas* [A. *h. al-ḥabash*, Abyssinian stone]

lapis serpentos [L. or L.-S., snake stone]—*ḥajar (a)lḥayyah* [A., snake stone]

lapis y'hūdīt [L., stone, H. Jewish]—*ḥajar alyahūd wahuwa ḥab haranḍ* [A., Jewstone, and it is a grain of rice]

lasērābā [A. *al- usrub*, lead]—*ʿoferet* [H., lead], *raṣāṣ* [A., lead, tin], *martero* [I., pounded]

lima, limaṭo [I., filed, polished]—*madwūk* [A., ground, triturated], for turning into water

liminios [I. *limone*, lemon]—*limon* [H., lemon]

liqwide [I. *liquido*, liquid]—*ʿisl* [A., honey, juice]

lunah [I. *luna*, moon]—*fuzrah* [A., read *fiḍḍah*, silver; a *Deckname*], *l'vanah* [H., moon, *Deckname* for silver]

luṭa [I., sealed]—*sadda* [A., seal], that is, *satum* [H., sealed]

luṭāṭah [I. *lutata*, sealed]—that is, *muṭaynah* [A., luted, coated with clay]

lutēmētālium, limasinas, orpimento—*zarnīkh* [A., arsenic]

luṭōn [I., copper]—*nuḥās* [A., copper]

luṭum absoluṭe

luṭum arminum [L. *lutum armenicum*, Armenian clay]

luṭum sigillaṭum [L. *terra sigillata*, sealed earth, i.e., fine clay]

mā' ʿabd [A., mercury water]—*mā'ḥalyu* [A. *mā'ḥulla*, melted water]

ma'adīm [H., planet Mars, iron]—*ḥadīd* [A. iron]

mābūr [A., pierced, punctured]—*fazra* [A. *fiḍḍah*, silver], *kesef* [H., silver]

mah shahayta [A., what you desire]—that is, *mah shetirṣeh* [H., what you wish]

malfa, mu'allafa [A., composite, a *Deckname* of lead]—*khābīza*

maliar—*zanzār* [A. *zinjār*, verdigris]

maroqurio [I. *mercurio*]—*zawaq* [A. *zuwaq*, quicksilver]

marrīkh [A., planet Mars, iron]—*ḥadīd* [A., iron]

masālaṭu—*abra*

māshīt [see *mah shahayta*]

māsqīṭ nos [I. *moscato noce*, muscat nut]—*maṣṭari* [A. *mustarī*, planet Jupiter, tin]

masṭīṣe [I. *mastice*, a vegetable resin]—*maskatah*

mayim ḥazaqim [H., strong water, i.e., *aquafortis*]—*mafartire* [?]

mayyit ḥay [A. *mā' al-ḥayāt*, living water, or *mā al-ḥayya*, serpent water, *Deckname* for quicksilver]—*mā' yaṭirsī min hanār walākin bāqī ḥay yutaharraq* [Explanation: What is taken off the fire, and therefore remains living (and) burning]

melaḥ klali [H., common salt]—it seems to me that it is the *milḥ ṭaʿām* [A., kitchen salt]

melaḥ petra [H. *melaḥ*, salt, L. *petra*, rock: rocksalt]—it is the *milḥ yema* [A.-I. *m. gemma*, rock salt]
melaḥ prēparāṭo [H.-I. prepared salt]—see *bārukhes* [?]
mīlbūraq [A. *mā' al-būraq*, borax water]—*sālīma* [I., solution] *milḥ qardam* [A., cardamum salt]
milḥ alqālīy [A., alcali salt]
milqa lqālīy [A. *milḥ al-qālīy*, alcali salt]- *sāl qālīy* [I., alcali salt]
minio [I., minium]—*zārqūn* [A. *zarqūn*, cinnabar]
mīra [A. *murr*, bitter]—*mar* [H., bitter]
mōlībārōn—it is burnt
mōlifiqārē [I. *mollificare*, to soften]—that is, *rākhaf* [A. *rakhif*, thin and watery]
morṭario, morṭaro [I., mortar]—*māhrāz* [A. *mihrās*, mortar]
morṭaro b'porfiro morṭaro—that is *mihrās* [A., mortar] and *porfiro* [I. *porfire*, marble], that is, the thinnest of the thin. And in Laᶜaz *morṭaro*
mqoroqorio [I. *mercurio*]—*zawwaq* [A. *zuwaq*, quicksilver]
m'ṣoraᶜ [H., leper]—*qazdīr* [A., tin., a *Deckname*]
muṣīnṣībar—see *nusha'idira* [*nushādir*]
mustarī [A., lion, *Deckname* for planet Jupiter, tin]—*qazdīr* [A., tin]

naqar—*fuzrah* [A. *fiḍḍah*, silver]
nās [A., contraction of *nuḥās*]—[A., copper]
nashdār [A., colloquial for *nushādir*, which see]
nāṭrōn [I. *natron*; A. *natrūn*, niter]—*būraq* [A., borax, saltpeter]
niṭro—*niṭrum* [I., soda, natron]
nobile [I., noble]—*nikhbad* [H., honored person]
nogah [H., planet Venus, *Deckname* for copper]—*nuḥās* [A., copper]
nūnsōmāṭo
nūra [A. *nūrā'*, depilatory]—*jayr* [A., quicklime]
nushādir [A., sal ammoniac, often spelled *shenāder*]
nushī'ādīra—*shenāder* [A. *nushādir*, sal ammoniac]
nuṣīnṣībar, nushdār, *salarmoniaq* [synonyms for *nushādir*, sal ammoniac]

ōda fāsa or **ōra fāsa**—*zabīb* [A., raisins]
ᶜof haporeaḥ ba'awir [H., bird that flies in the air]—*zāwāq* [A. *zuwaq*, quicksilver]
ᶜof haqam b'vehalah [H., bird that rises in fright]—*shenāder* [see *nushādir*]
oli'oṭodos—is silver and gold mixed
onqi'ah—a measure of weight of the cities of Edom [i. e., Rome, the Christian world], divided into eight *drame* [drachmas], and in the cities of Ishmael [the Arab world] ten *drahes* [drachmas]
origano [I. *origan*, marjoram]—*ṣaᶜtar* [A., thyme]

orinale [I.]—that is, a glass vessel like a *ṭāṣā* [A. *ṭassa*, cup], or *qandīl tawīl* [A., long lamp]
orpimento [I., orpiment]—*zarnīkh* [A., arsenic]
osṭrāqum [G. *'ostrakion*, L. *ostracium*, mussel]—*ṣedef* [H., seashell]

pelosā'irim—*nuḥās* [A., copper]
peripiṭah, perpeṭa—that is *naḍif* [A., unclean], or *waḍif* [A., quick]
pīla [I. *pila*, basin, font; cf. *pīwa*]
pīlūle [L. *pilula*, globule]—*ḥubūb* [A., corn, a plague-boil], that is, *ḥarābes*
pīrīṭo dī aspania [I., pyrite of Spain]—according to the Physician [Ibn Sīnā] *khuyūṭ nuḥās* [A., threads of copper]
pīṣe [I. *pece*]—*zefet* [H., tar, pitch]
pīwa [I. read *pila*, basin, font]—that is, *maʿūn* [A., pot]. *Qāl* [A., he said] that this should read *pīla*, that is, a vessel
pīwa luṭāṭah [I. *pila lutata*, luted vessel]—that is, *maʿūn muṭayyan* [A., luted pot], and according to his [Ibn Sīnā's] words it is a *ṭass* [A., saucer, tray], and it has to be read *pīla*
pli'umah—it should say *fi'umah* [cf. I. *fumo*, smoke], it means *dūkhān* [A., smoke, steam] or *dunaṣ* [A. *danaṣ*, impurity]
polmone [I., lung]
porfiro [I., porphyry]—that is, the thinnest possible
prānṣībīle [I. *prendibile*, takable]—*qāṣiḥ* [A. *qāshiḥ*, thick], that is, hard
prēṣiaso [I. *prezioso*, precious, costly]
p'tīlah [H., wick]
purga [I., purified]—that is, *ṣarūf* [H., refined]
purgaṣi'one [I. *purgazione*]—that is, *naḍif* [A. read *naẓif*, clean], that is, to clean and thus to refine
purgāṭo [I., purified]—that is, *naḍif* [A. *naẓif*, clean], that is, purified
puro [I., pure]—that is, *naḍif* [A. as above]

qālami'onah, qālamīṭa [I. *calamita*, magnet]—*ḥajarat alamas* [A. *ḥajarat al-mass*, touchstone]
qāldīr—I do not know whether it is a repetition of *sālqalīy*
qalʿi [A. *qalʿiyy*, Indian tin]—*qazdīr* [A., tin]
qalīmasṭīqā—*lītarīgiros* [I. *lithargiro*] also *qrīsīsos*
qālqadīs, qalqanṭum, isīsīsī, ru'anīj, īstīq—*zāj*, vitriol [evidently synonyms]
qalqanṭum, qālkānte, qālkāntos—*zāj* [vitriol; alternate spellings]
qālsināṣi'one, qalṣinaṣi'one [I. *calcinazione*, calcination]—this is *siyyud* [H., plastering, calcifying], and it seems to me to transmute into lime, and it is to pulverize the thing and remove the moisture from it and from the thing you want to calcify
qālsīṭrān—*salqaliy* [see *saleqaliy*]

qālṭīqrī'on—a glass vessel . . . [illegible]
qamar, qamarah [A., moon, silver]—*fuzrah* [A. *fiḍḍah*, silver]
qāmfōrah [I. *camfore*]—*kāfūr* [A., camphor]
qānābar [G., *kinnabari*, cinnabar]—*minio* [I., minium], *zarqūn* [A., cinnabar]
qapīṭīlan, qapīṭīlo [I. *capitello*, or *capitellum*, watery solution of soap, lye]—this is *līsa'ah* [I. *lisi*, lysis] made of quicklime and ashes of *ṭarṭaro*, wine sediment
qāreṭūre—*dahab* [A. *dhahab*, gold]
qārīnā', *qīrīnā'* [read *qārūre*, I. *carure*, glass bottle, urinal]—*orinale* [I., flask]
qāṭīmī'a—*ṭuṣī'ah* [I. *tutia*, tutty, white arsenic]
qawqo—*zawak* [A. *zuwaq*, quicksilver], *kesef ḥay* [H., quicksilver]
qīlīqīmī'āre—*purgāmenṭo* [I. ?, cleansing agent]
qonyelaṣione [I. *congelatione*, congealing]—this is to make it moist after it has become lime
qonyelāṭo [I. *congelato*, congealed]—that is, *yābis* [A., dry], and possibly it should be *consēlāṭo*
qopēla [I. *copella*, cupel]—*maṣref* [H., melting pot], and it means *jūja* [A.]
qorālo [I. *corallo*, coral]—*marzān* or *marwān* [A.]
qori'o [I. *corio*, corium for tanning]—*zāᶜfarān* [A., saffron], *karkom* [H., saffron]
qrīso jāled [G. *chrysos*, gold, A. *jalīd*, frozen]—*zahav o 'iril* [H., gold or . . .]
qrīsos [G. *chrysos*, gold]—*dahab* [A. *dhahab*, gold]
qrispus [L. *crispus*, curled, crisped]—*raṣāṣ* [A., lead]
qroqos [I. *croco*]—*zāᶜfarān* [A., saffron]
qwilasione [I. *acquilazione*, turning into water]—after it has been calcified to bring it to its humidity

rāme [I., copper]—*nuḥās* [A., copper]
rāme purgāṭo [I., purified copper]—that is, pure
raroṭaq—*vērnīz* [I. *vernice*, varnish, glaze]
rāṣ hasabōn [A.-H., . . . of the soap]—this is the *liyān* [A., softness]
rāsah dī fīn or **rāsah mifīn**—this is *qalafonia*
rasās [A., lead]—*raṣāṣ* [A., lead]
rēmōlaṭo [I. *remollato*, resoaked]—that is, *maḥlūl* [A., dissolved]
remolwe—that is, sand
rē'oqīq—*ḥadīd* [A., iron]
rē'oqiq stomā'oqos—*b'dil* [H., tin]
rēsēnsorio [over-the-line correction: *reskonṭario*]—that is, *yaḥuṭ burmah maqlūbah min qāᶜaha wayaḥūṭ ᶜalayha burmah thāniyah manqūbah g'k* [H. abbr. *gam ken*] *min qāᶜaha w'aḥ"k* [H. abbr. *w'aḥar kakh*, and then]

yaḥūṭ ʿalayha burmah g' [H. 3] *min gīd naqūb wayashad liwaṣl bayna kulhum wayuṣʿad* [A., let him put a vessel upside down from its bottom, and let him put on it another vessel with holes in it also at its bottom, and then put on it a third vessel with a long perforated neck, and let him tie it as a connection between them, and let it sublimate]

rēṣipi'ente [I. *recipiente*]—that is, a vessel in which there is a receptacle

rēṣipērazione—that is, *ṭarian* in fire, *yamshī filanir* [read *fi'lnār*, put it into the fire], that is, enliven the fire, it should go on the fire

rēsolaṭo—that is, *maḥlūl māh* [read *mā'*, A., dissolved in water]

rēsolusione [I. *resoluzione*]—this means all things that were made into lime to make them again water [i.e., to liquify the calcinated substances]

rēsolwamenṭo—this is *ḥalhūm* [A. read *maḥlūl*, dissolved]

rēsolwe [I. *resolve*]—that is *ḥalhūm* [A. read *maḥlūl*, dissolved]

rēwērbēro [I. *riverbero*], *rēwērbērāsione* [I. *reverberazione*]—that is, close to the *nār muqābilathā mahushi taḥt* . . . [illegible] [fire opposite it . . .]

rīqoṭo [I. *ricotto*, burnt]—that is, *sarūf* [H., burnt]

rīse taqazqilo

ro'anig—*zāj* [A., vitriol]

ro'ārē palombah—*ʿoferet ub'dil* [H., lead and tin]

rubīfīqa [I. *rubifica*]—that is, in fire [illegible], set it near fire

rukhifqa—that is, in fire, *yawli nūr* [A. *yawli nār*, set near fire]

rumor [I. *rumore*, noise, clamor]—*gaṭros rufi'os*

sādārāqah [I. *sandracca*, realgar]—*sandarūs* [A., sandarac, red arsenic]

sāfārāno [I. *zafferano*]—*zaʿfarān* [A., saffron]

sal [I. *sale*, salt]—*melaḥ* [H., salt]

sālāmoniāqo [I. *sale ammoniaco*, sal ammoniac]—this is salt that comes from beneath the sand, big pebbles, *shenāder* [see *nushādir*]

saleqaliy [I.-A. *sale kalīy*, alkali salt]

salgemah or **salyemah** [I. *salgemma*, rock salt]—it is the real *qomane* [I. *comune*, common], *lākin ṣāfī mlīḥ* [A., therefore it is very pure] . . . [Another definition:] salt that shines like a precious stone

saljema niṭrissima [I. *salgemma nitrissima*, most nitric rock salt]—*qāl* [A., he said] that this is *ṣāfī* [A., pure]

salkomune or **salqomune** [I. *sal comune*]—*milḥ ṭaʿām* [A., kitchen salt]. [Another definition:] the one found among us, and it comes from water or from the sea

salmesṭro [I. *salmastro*, salt, brackish]—*milḥ bārūd* [A., powdered salt]

salmesṭro raffināṭo [I., refined *salmastro*]—*milḥ bārūd* [A., powdered salt]

salniṭro [I. *salnitro*, saltpeter]—*būraq* [A., borax, saltpeter]; [another definition:] it is of the *pulvere* [I., powder]

samāq—*samgh ʿarabī* [A., gum arabic]

ṣamās—the same as the preceding

sams [A. *shams*, the sun, gold]—*dahab* [A. *dhahab*, gold]

sanbuqo [illegible]

sāndaria, sāndariār, sāndariāre—burnt orpiment or burnt arsenic

sangi'os draqonis [L. read *sanguis draconis*, dragon's blood]—*dam lkhiwwa* [A. read *damm al-akhawayn*, dragon's blood, a resinous substance]

sango'is [I. *sangue*, blood]—*dam* [A. or H., blood]

sangwe darqon [I. *sangue di drago*, dragon's blood]—this is a kind of resin which drips from a tree that is born in *Andi'ah* [India?], which is called *draqona*, and it is cold and dry. This is what the *Oṣar Ḥayyim* wrote, and it seems that it is *dam al-khiwwa*, and this is the language of Ibn Sīnā: *damm al-khawin*, in Latin *sanguis draqonis*, called *si'ān* (or *shay'ān*), it is kind of red, it is known

ṣangwides [no definition. Possibly variant spelling of sango'is.]

saqīla—*ʿunṣul* [A., wild onion]

sarusah [I. *cerussa*, white lead]—*bādūq* [A., white lead]

saṭīṣtīrī'ah—*shab* [A., vitriol] *mal'akhuti* [H., artificial]

sāwī'ah—*zawak* [A. *zuwaq*, quicksilver]

sawi'ah unuq za'ikht, tresaron, 'idrogori'as

sawres—*arseniqo sarūf* [I. *arsenico*, arsenic, H. *sarūf*, burnt]

sawṣīr—*b'dil* [H., tin], *qazdīr* [A., tin]

ṣedeq [H. planet Jupiter, tin]—*qazdīr* [A., tin]

ṣemenṭa [I. *cementa*]—that is, *faras* [A., to break, grind, crush]

sība marīna [L. *caepa marina*, I. *cipolla marina*, great sea squill]—*ʿunṣul* [A., wild onion, leek]

sībaseros, sibasiores [S.]—*tusī'ās* [S. or I., *tutias*, tutties, white arsenics]

sīdrārāqī—*zawak* [A., *zuwaq*, quicksilver]

sīhra [Aramaic, moon]—*fuzrah* [A. *fiḍḍah*, silver]

ṣīnābrio [I. *cinabrio, cinabro*]—*zanzafur* [A. *zunjufr*, cinnabar]

sīnapeo—*khardal* [A., mustard]

ṣīnērāṣio [I. *cinerazio*, burning]—*ramāṣ* [A. *ramaḍ*, burning]. According to the *Kānūn* of Ibn Sīnā. However, it seems that it is *aljūma*, or a kind of *taṣfiya* [A., purification]

sīra—*fuzrah* [A. *fiḍḍah*, silver]

sīrā', 'idrosiro, 'iqṭara'iros—*kesef* [H., silver]

sīrī'āre—*zawaq* [A. *zuwaq*, quicksilver]

sīrī'āre sīdrāwāre—*kesef ḥay* [H., quicksilver]

soliēnē, antimonio—*kuḥl* [A., antimony]

sōlīmāṣione [I. *sublimazione*, sublimation]—this is *haʿala'ah* [H., sublimation] of the hard substances that adhere to the bottom of the melting pot due to the heat of the fire, and the fire makes several kinds join together, as is known to the masters of the *sōlīmāṣione*. And according to the Physician [Ibn Sīnā] it is *taṣʿīd* [A., sublimation]

spodium [L., dross of metals, scoria; I., ivory black, spodium]—*ṭābsīr* [A.]

sqālia [I. *scaglia*, scale]—that is, *qashūr* [H., tied], for thus *qasqeset* [H., fish-scale] is *sqalia* in Laʿaz, and according to the Physician [Ibn Sīnā] pieces of *ṣijād* [A.]

sqālia di ferro [I. *scaglia di ferro*, scalings of iron]—that is, "tied," for likewise *qasqeset* [H., fish-scale] is *sqalia* in Laʿaz

sqālia di ramo [I. *scaglia di r.*, scalings of copper]

sqrupalo [I. *scrupalo*]—one of the measures of weight, and there are in it 24 grains

sṭanio [I. *stagno*, tin]—*qazdīr* [A., tin]

sṭerqos [I. *sterco*, excrement]—*zevel* [H., dung]

sṭēsosīrī'o—*ʿoferet* [H., lead] *figutos*

sṭomawqos [I. *stomaco*, stomach]—*ḥadīd* [A., iron]

sūbāres—*kuḥl* [A., antimony]

sūkar alfar [A. *sukkar al-fa'r*, mouse sugar]—*rāqiz* [A., jumping?]

sūlfo [I. *zolfo*, sulphur]—*sublimaṣio fī hasfīsīriya wahuwa ʿawdi mayin* [I.-A. sublimation of the . . . , and it is turning to water]

sūlfūr [I.]—*gofrit* [H., sulphur]

surmīṭāse—*kuḥl* [A., antimony]

ṭalq [A.]—*milḥ taʿām* [A., kitchen salt]

ṭarminṭanah [I. *trementina*, turpentine]—*tamartinah* [I., turpentine]

ṭaron—*ṭarmah* [A. *tarm* (?), butter, honey]

ṭarq—*salyema* [I. *salgemma*, rock salt], hot and dry in the second [degree]

ṭāso barbāso [I. *tasso barbato*, bearded yew tree, possibly mullein with downy leaves]—it is a herb . . . it is one kind of the *totomalio* [I. *titimaglia*, spurge, euphorbia], and it is found in the words of the Physician [Ibn Sīnā]

ṭāso werbāso [I. *verbasco*, mullein]—according to the Physician [Ib Sīnā] it is the great *totomalio* whose leaves are broad; but the leaves of the small one are long, as is known. However, from the *purgāṣione*, par. 2, which he wrote, it appears that white *ṭāso* is not a herb

ṭemperāṭo [I., tempered]—see *ḥōm ṭemperāṭo*

tiqqun [H., reparation]—wherever it says to repair a thing it means to purify it, that is, in *rēpāraṣio* [I. *reparazione*, reparation]

ṭīnṭūra bilṭīn [I. *tintura*, tincture, A. *bi'ltin*, with clay; or *biLatin*, in Latin]—that is, *ṣabāgh* [A., dyeing], and according to the Physician [Ibn Sīnā] it is a medicine

ṭoṭomalio [I. *titimaglia*, spurge, euphorbia]—see *ṭāso barbāso* and *ṭāso werbāso*

ṭrīsāron—*zawaq* [A. *zuwaq*, quicksilver]
ṭora [I. *torà, tora, bubalis tora*]—it is *laʿanah* [H., wormwood], as Ibn Sīnā has written in the vegetable poisons, section 2, chapter 8
ṭuṣī'ah alessandrina [A.-I. Alexandrian *tutiyah*, tutty]—*tutiyah zarqah* [A., blue tutty]
ṭuṭiyah [A.]—tutty, white arsenic

ubar fāso—*zabib* [A., raisins]
unsilāṭos—*ʿarʿār* [A. *ʿarʿar*, juniper; or *ʿarʿarah*, stopper, cork]
uqab [A., sal ammoniac]—*shenāder* [A. *nushādir*, sal ammoniac]
uranginṭos wiwos [I.-L.? . . . *vivos*]—*zawaq* [A. *zuwaq*, quicksilver]
uraniaqos—*shenāder* [A. *nushādir*, sal ammoniac]
urīna [I. *urina*, urine]—*sheten* [H., urine]
urṭīnas—*ʿafṣ* [A., gallnut]
urṭīqa [I. *urtica*, nettle]—*ḥārīq* [A., burning, glowing]
ushaq—*waṣq* [P. and A. *ushshaq*, ammoniac]
usrub [A., lead]—*raṣāṣ* [A., lead]
ustu—*raṣāṣ* [A., lead]
uzīfur—*zanzafur* [A. *zunjufr*, cinnabar]

werde [I. *verde*, green]—name of the green color
werderāme [I. *verderame*, verdigris]—*zinzār* [A. *zinjār*, verdigris]
werga or *wirga* [I. *verga, virga*, rod, cane]—it seems it is the *rāt* [A., straw]
wermilion or **wermilon** [I. *vermiglio*, vermilion]—*zanzafur* [A. *zunjufr*, cinnabar], *sināfaro* [I. *cinabro*, cinnabar, vermilion]
wiṭrī'āṭa, wiṭrīāṭo [I. *vitreo*, vitreous]—*metaliya* [I. *metalia*, metallic?], *metali*
wiṭri'olo [I. *vitriolo*]—*zāj* [A., vitriol]
wiṭri'olo romāno [I., Roman vitriol]—*zāj naṣīf* [A. read *naẓīf*, purified vitriol], that is pure, and I also heard that it means that it comes from Rome

yanās [probably Venus, i.e., copper]—*nuḥās* [A., copper]
yasāsīṭiri'on—*kularminio* [A. *khall armīnī*, Armenian vinegar]
yowis [Iovis, Jupiter, i.e., tin]—*yazdīr* [A., tin]
yenāli'ār—*zanzafur* [A. *zunjufr*, cinnabar], *sinabārio* [I. *cinabro*, cinnabar]

zabad lbaḥr [A. *zabad al-baḥr*, foam of the sea], *isqoma maris scuma* [Ger. *schaum*, foam] *maris* [L., of the sea: *Deckname* for quicksilver], hot and dry in the third [degree]
zāfārāno [I. *zafferano*, saffron, crocus]—*zāʿfarān* [A., saffron]

zāg [A. *zāj*, vitriol], *wiṭriolo* [I., vitriol], and likewise *azīq* and *azōg*
zāhāfāran [I. *zafferano*, saffron, crocus]—*zāʿfarān* [A., saffron]
zahara [A. *zuhrah*, the planet Venus, copper]—*nuḥās* [A., copper]
zarawand [A., *aristolochia*, birthwort]—*aristoligia* [L.-I. *aristolochia*, birthwort], hot in the third and dry in the second [degree]
zarī—*pinpinella* [I. *pimpinella*, a plant of the primrose family], hot and dry in the third [degree]
zarī'ūn—*zārqūn* [A. *zarqūn*, cinnabar], *minio* [I., minium]
zarnīkh [A., arsenic]—*orpimento* [I., orpiment], hot and dry in the third [degree]
zarnīkh sarūf [A.-H., burnt arsenic]—*orpimento sarūf* [I.-H., burnt orpiment]
zarqūn [A. cinnabar; see *zarī'ūn*]
zawaq [A. *zuwaq*, quicksilver]
zayqaṭ—*zawaq* [A. *zuwaq*, quicksilver]
zāzag [A. *zajāj*, glass]—*zkhukhit* [H., glass]
zībaq [A., quicksilver]—*zawaq* [A. *zuwaq*, quicksilver], cold and wet in the third [degree]
zili'ar—*zanzār* [A. *zinjār*, verdigris]
zīnyār—*zinzār* [A. *zinjār*, verdigris]
zīya—is *vitriolo* [I.], zāj [A., vitriol]
zuwaq [A.]—quicksilver

NOTES

Chapter One
Introduction

1. C. G. Jung, *Psychology and Alchemy*, Bollingen Series XX (Princeton, 1968), 25.

2. Henry and Renée Kahane, "Alchemy: Hellenistic and Medieval Alchemy," *Encyclopedia of Religion* (New York, 1987), 1:195.

3. See Chapter 5 below.

4. Modern Jewish scholarship is still scandalized by this attitude of Graetz; for example, the entry devoted to him in the 1972 *Encyclopaedia Judaica* faults him for having shown "no understanding for mystical forces and movement such as the Kabbalah and Hasidism, which he despised and considered malignant growths in the body of Judaism."

5. On this subject see my *The Jewish Mind* (New York, 1977), chapters 6 and 8.

6. Moritz Steinschneider, "Typen," in Joseph Kobak's *Jeschurun* 9 (1873): 84; cited by Joshua Trachtenberg, *Jewish Magic and Superstition* (New York, 1939), 304 n.1.

7. *EI*[2], 4:929.

8. In *Monatschrift für Geschichte und Wissenschaft des Judentums* 38 (1894): 39ff.

9. Berthelot, *Grecs*, 3:232–37.

10. Marcellin P. E. Berthelot, "Alchimie," in *La grande encyclopédie* (Paris, no date), 2:13.

11. Cornelius de Pauw, *Recherches philosophiques sur les Egyptiens et les Chinois*, vol. 1 (Berlin, 1773), 288ff.

12. August Schmölders, *Essai sur les écoles philosophiques chez les Arabes* (Paris, 1842), 105.

13. G. Monod-Herzen, *L'Alchimie et son code symbolique* (Paris, 1978), 24, 62.

Chapter Two
Biblical Figures as Alchemists

1. See Berthelot *Grecs*, 3:95, 223. There is more on Zosimus in Chapters 4 and 6 below.

2. See Bernard Gorceix, *Alchimie: Traites alemandes du XVIe siècle . . .* (Paris, 1980), 190. Cf. also pp. 21, 68–69, 189.

3. See *EJ* (B), 2:140, s.v. Alchemie.

4. *Theatrum chemicum*, vol. 1 (Argentorati [Strasbourg], 1659), 331–61.

5. Alfred Edward Waite, *The Secret Tradition in Alchemie* (London and New York, 1926), 261–62. On the parallel between the world and man the microcosm, see R. Patai, *Adam va'Adamah* (Jerusalem, 1942–1943), 1:165–76.

6. Maurice P. Crosland, *Historical Studies in the Language of Chemistry* (Cambridge, Mass., 1962), 10.

7. Grillot de Givry, *Witchcraft, Magic, and Alchemy* (London, 1931), 350; Crosland, *Historical Studies*, 19.

8. Hermann Kopp, *Beiträge zur Geschichte der Chemie* (Braunschweig, 1869), 319, 398, quoting Vincent de Beauvais (d. 1264), *Speculum maius*, part 1, *Speculum naturale* (Venice, 1591), f. 82a.

9. Hermann F. Jellinghaus, ed., *Das Buch Sidrach*, Bibliothek des Litterarischen Vereins in Stuttgart, vol. 235 (Tübingen, 1904), 96–98. On its sources, see Moritz Steinschneider, *Il Buonarotti*, vol. 6 (Rome, 1872), 241.

10. Waite, *Secret Tradition*, 182–83.

11. Ben Jonson, *The Alchemist* (London, 1612), act 2, scene 1, line 80.

12. Hermann Kopp, *Die Alchemie in älterer und neuerer Zeit* (Heidelberg, 1886), 2:370.

13. John Read, *Prelude to Chemistry* (New York, 1937), 112; Alfred Edward Waite, ed., *The Hermetic Museum Restored and Enlarged* (London, 1893), 1:236. In his *Secret Tradition*, 349 n. 1, Waite overlooked the biblical source of this tradition.

14. Waite, *Hermetic Museum*, 1:236; Read, *Prelude*, 24.

15. Elias Ashmole, *Qui est Mercuriophilus Anglicus?* (London, 1652), 1:449, as quoted by Read, *Prelude*, 124.

16. Ashmole, *Mercuriophilus*, 312, as quoted by Read, *Prelude*, 128.

17. Shams al-Dīn Abū ʿAbd-Allāh Muḥammad b. Abi Ṭālib al-Anṣārī al-Ṣūfī al-Dimashqī, known as Ibn Shaykh Ḥittīn, d. 1327. Cf. *EI*², s.v. Dimashqī.

18. Edmund O. von Lippmann, *Entstehung und Ausbreitung der Alchemie* (Berlin, 1919), 1:258, citing al-Dimashqī and Chwolson.

19. Johann Ludwig Hannemann (1640–1724) wrote a thesis about him entitled *Tubalkain stans ad fornacem* (Tubal-Cain Standing at the Furnace). Kopp, *Die Alchemie*, 2:314–17.

20. 1 Enoch 7:1; 8:1, 3. Cf. also Clemens Romanus, *Hom.* viii.11, 14; Clemens of Alexandria, *Strom*, v.1.10; Tertullian, *Cult. fem.* 1.2; cf. 11.10. Cf. also Marcellin P. E. Berthelot, *La chimie au moyen age* (Paris, 1893), 2:xxvi, xxx, 238.

21. Marcellin P. E. Berthelot, *Les origines de l'alchimie* (Paris, 1885), 9, citing Syncellus, *Chronographia*, ed. Goar (Venice, 1652), 12, 14.

22. Berthelot, *Moyen age*, 2:xx, xxx, 214 n.1, 238, translating a Syriac manuscript (MS 6.29) in the Cambridge University Library. See also Chapters 4 and 6 below.

23. Lippmann, *Entstehung*, 1:308. Cf. also Hoffmann, in Ladenburg, *Handwörterbuch der Chemie*, 2:516ff. as cited in Pauly-Wissowa, *Realenzyklopedie der klassischen Altertumswissenschaft* (Stuttgart, 1894), 1339, s.v. Alchemie; Berthelot, *Grecs*, 3:181 quotes a passage from Zosimus in which he speaks of "the prophet Chymes."

24. Nicolas Lenglet Du Fresnoy, *Histoire de la philosophie hermetique* (Paris, 1742), 1:4, 5, 7–8.

25. Ibid.

26. Daniel Georg Morhof, *Polyhistor*, 3rd ed. (Lubeck, 1732), 89–91.

27. Kopp, *Die Alchemie*, 1:209.

28. Johannes Albertus Fabricius, *Bibliotheca Graeca*, edited by Gottlieb Christophorus Harles (Hamburg, 1790), 1:76. My translation is from the Latin. According to John Ferguson, *Bibliotheca chemica* (Glasgow, 1906), 1:393, the *Tabula smaragdina* was first printed, together with other tracts, in *De alchemia* (Nuremberg, 1541), after it had been known for at least three hundred years.

29. Johannes Jacobus Manget, ed., *Bibliotheca chemica curiosa*, 2 vols. (Geneva, 1702), as quoted by Read, *Prelude*, 156. Read also refers to Ashmole's mention of Jacob's ladder, p. 92. Cf. also *Mutus liber*, or the Book of Silence of Hermes (Rupella [La Rochelle], 1677).

30. Waite, *Secret Tradition*, 400–401.

31. Kopp, *Die Alchemie*, 1:209.

32. B. Suler in *EJ* (B), 2:140, s.v. Alchemie.

33. Kopp, *Die Alchemie*, 1:302–9.

34. Suler in *EJ* (B) 2:142. Cf. figure there in col. 143. A treatise entitled *Keren ha-Pukh* will be discussed in Chapter 10 below.

35. Cf. sources in *JE*, 7:556, and *EJ* (J), 10:1192–93, s.v. Korah.

36. Cf. sources in *EI*[2],4:673, s.v. Karun, and *EJ* (J), 10:1143, s.v. Korah.

37. Included in the *Theatrum chemicum*, vol. 5 (Argentorati [Strasbourg], 1622), 16, 240. Cf. Ferguson, *Bibliotheca chemica*, 2:87.

38. Wisdom of Solomon, in R. H. Charles, *The Apocrypha and Pseudepigraphia of the Old Testament* (Oxford, 1913), 1:545.

39. Kopp, *Die Alchemie*, 1:209; 2:370.

40. Berthelot, *Moyen age*, 1:242, 243; Lippmann, *Entstehung*, 92. See also below, Chapter 5.

41. Berthelot, *Grecs*, 2:389, 390; 3:373; Lippmann, *Entstehung*, 111.

42. Read, *Prelude*, 275.

43. See Julius Ruska, *Steinbuch des Aristoteles* (Heidelberg, 1912), 161, as quoted by Lippmann, *Entstehung*, 383.

44. Lippmann, *Entstehung*, 625. On Ibn Rusta see *EI*[2],s.v.

45. *Arabian Nights*, as cited by Lippmann, *Entstehung*, 423.

46. Bonaventure de Periers, *Cymbalum mundi* (1537), and *Nouvelles recréations* (Lyon, 1558), as cited by Lippmann, *Entstehung*, 503.

47. Kopp, *Die Alchemie*, 2:370.

48. Johann Joachim Becher (1655–1682), *Physica subterranea*, edited by Stahl (Leipzig, 1703), 696, as cited by Lippmann, *Entstehung*, 510.

49. London, 1652, p. 350, cited by Read, *Prelude*, 110.

50. See below, Chapters 7 and 23.

51. *Sefer Shaʿar haḤesheg*, edited with an introduction by Moshe Ḥayyim Barukh (Leghorn, 1790), 8+57 folios; see esp. ff. 2a, 3a.

52. See ff. 36a–37b.

53. See Berthelot, *Moyen age*, 2:265–66; Lippmann, *Entstehung*, 91.

54. Kopp, *Die Alchemie*, 2:246. On the origin and history of the Magen David as a Jewish symbol and talisman, see Gershom Scholem, "The Star of David: History of a Symbol," in his *The Messianic Idea in Judaism and Other*

Essays (New York, 1971), 256–81. In a brief paragraph on p. 271 Scholem refers to the alchemical interpretation of the Magen David.

55. Genesis Rabba, edited by J. Theodor (Berlin, 1912), 1:31, in the name of the third-century sage, Rav. See parallel passages, ibid.

56. *Physica naturalis rotunda visionis chemicae cabalisticae*, in *Theatrum chemicum*, vol. 6 (Argentorati [Strasbourg], 1661), 377.

57. Read, *Prelude*, 167–68.

58. The above four books are listed and described in Ferguson, *Bibliotheca chemica*, 1:338–41; 2:3, 320–21.

59. Suler, *EJ* (B), 2:142. See also Introduction to Part Eight below on Elias Artista's appearance to Johannes Fredericus Schweitzer.

60. Kopp, *Die Alchemie*, 1:209; Suler, *EJ* (B), 2:142.

61. Leyden Papyrus no. 75, edited by Reuvens, cited in Berthelot, *Les origines*, 54, and appendix, 158.

62. Berthelot, *Grecs*, 3:261.

63. See note 60 above.

64. MS. 6.29, ff. 116–20; Berthelot, *Moyen age* 2:xxii, xxxvi, 296.

65. Kopp, *Die Alchemie*, 1:207; Lippmann, *Entstehung*, 1:86; Ferguson, *Bibliotheca chemica*, 2:113. See also John G. Gager, *Moses in Greco-Roman Paganism* (Nashville and New York, 1972), which discusses the image of Moses in Greco-Roman literature, including his reputation as magician. Gager says very little (pp. 152–55) about the alchemical writings attributed to Moses.

66. Berthelot, *Grecs*, 3:209, 338.

67. Ibid., 2:304; 3:292.

68. Ibid., 2:300, 315; 3:287, 302. The Leyden Papyrus no. 75, written in demotic script and in Greek, contains several Hebrew names such as Jao Sabaoth, Adonai, Abraham, and parallel Hebrew, Egyptian, and Greek invocations. Ibid., 1:8–9; Berthelot, *Les origines*, 171, and sources there. Cf. also Kopp, *Beiträge*, 262, 354.

69. Berthelot, *Grecs*, 2:182, 183; 3:180, 181, 209, 338. In his Introduction (1:257), Berthelot quotes *Lexicon alchemiae rulandi*: "Kymus id est massa. Kuria vel kymia, id est massa, alchimia."

70. Lippmann, *Entstehung*, 1:69–70, and Chapter 5 below.

71. Lippmann, *Entstehung*, 1:69, and sources there in the footnotes.

72. Ibid., 1:69–70, and sources there in the footnotes.

73. Ibid., 1:68.

74. Thus the Greek philosopher Pappos (7th or 8th century), cf. Berthelot, *Grecs*, 3:30; Lippmann, *Entstehung*, 1:107.

75. These are listed in Kopp, *Beiträge*, 262, 273, 302, 397–98; and in Berthelot, *Les origines*, 61, 175, 188.

76. Cf. Berthelot, *Grecs*, 3:9, 40, 431; Lippmann, *Entstehung*, 1:69 suggests Kalais in the Sinai or in Persia. On Qalai or Callais, cf. Berthelot, *Moyen age*, 1:367–69.

77. Berthelot, *Grecs*, 2:38–39; 3:40; idem, *Les origines*, 54. In square brackets I added the variant translations by F. Sherwood Taylor, *The Alchemists: Founders of Modern Chemistry* (New York, 1949), 35. Since the prescription is called "diplosis," doubling, it seems that the text calling for one part of copper

and three parts of gold is corrupt: it should read one part of copper and one part of gold. Cf. also the comments of Taylor, *The Alchemists*, 35–36.

78. Philo, *Vita Mosis*, 1:5–7, and following him Clemens of Alexandria, *Stromata*, 1:23. Cf. additional sources in Louis Ginzberg, *The Legends of the Jews*, 7 vols. (Philadelphia, 1909–1938), 6:402.

79. Artapanus, *Peri Ioudaiōn* (About the Jews), 432ff., in Eusebius, *Praeparatio evangelica*, as cited by Ginzberg, *Legends*, 5:401 n. 59, and 402–3 n. 67.

80. Pseudo-Philo, *Philonis Alexandrini libri antiquitatum* (Basel, 1527), 19.10–13; *Mekhilta*, Amalek 2, 55b–56a; *Assumption of Moses*, 12, as quoted by Ginzberg, *Legends*, 6:151, 158.

81. Lippmann, *Entstehung*, 68–69; Kopp, *Beiträge*, 396ff.

82. Leyden Papyrus no. 76, as quoted by Berthelot, *Les origines*, 54. According to the doctrines of the Carpocratians, Monas was the ignored Great God; cf. Berthelot, *Grecs*, 1:17.

83. Berthelot, *Grecs*, 1:110–11, 271; Kopp, *Beiträge*, 354; Papyrus Kenyon (3rd century C.E.?), as cited by Lippmann, *Entstehung*, 74.

84. Berthelot, *Grecs*, 2:353; 3:338.

85. Pliny, *Historia naturalis*, 30:2 (Loeb Classical Library, 8:284–85).

86. Midrash Esther 68–69; Abba Gorion 29–32, as quoted in Ginzberg, *Legends*, 4:411.

87. Kopp, *Beiträge*, 367; Lippmann, *Entstehung*, 56, and references there; Fabricius, *Bibliotheca Graeca*, 1:46–94; Ferguson, *Bibliotheca chemica*, 2:113.

88. "Explicatio duorum primorum capitum Geneseos juxta Physicam," in *Theatrum chemicum*, 1:331–32.

89. See *EI*[2],s.v. Djābir b. Ḥayyān.

90. See sources in Paul Kraus, *Jābir ibn Ḥayyān: Contribution à l'histoire des idées scientifiques dans l'Islam* (Cairo, 1942–1943), 1:90; 2:32, 44.

91. *EI*,[2]s.v. Ibn al-Nadīm; Berthelot, *Moyen age*, 3:27.

92. Ginzberg, *Legends*, 2:125; 3:11, 286. See sources there, 6:99 n. 560.

93. Suler, *EJ* (B), 2:140. Kunckel's works are listed in Ferguson, *Bibliotheca chemica*, 1:483–85.

94. Berthelot, *Moyen age*, 1:254, 267.

95. Julius Ruska, *Turba philosophorum: Ein Beitrag zur Geschichte der Alchemie* (Berlin, 1931), 231.

96. Ruska remarks at this point that this is a jocular statement. The author, of course, knew that the egg symbolized the four elements.

97. My translation from the German of Ruska, *Turba*, 248–49. Cf. the English translation in Arthur Edward Waite, *The Turba Philosophorum or Assembly of the Sages* (London, 1896), 138–39, 181–84.

98. Petrus Bonus, *Margarita pretiosa*, first printed in Aldina, Venice, 1561, then included in Manget's *Bibliotheca chemica curiosa*. Cited by Ruska, *Turba*, 341.

99. See above at n. 10.

100. Waite, *Secret Tradition*, 182–83.

101. Ruska, *Turba*, 331. In this book the well-known dialogue between Maria the Jewess and Aros has become a dialogue between Maria and Aaron.

102. Hermann Conring, *De Hermetica Aegyptorum vetere et Paracelsicorum*

nova medicina (Helmstedt, 1648), 393; idem, *De Hermetica medicina* (Helmstedt, 1669), 431; both cited by Kopp, *Beiträge*, 399.

103. Johann Georg Schmid, *Der von Mose und denen Propheten übel urtheilende Alchymist* (Chemnitz, 1706). Cf. Ferguson, *Bibliotheca chemica*, 2:336.

104. Olaus Borrichius, *De ortu et progressu chemiae* (Copenhagen, 1668), 46–47; idem, *Hermetis Aegyptorum et chemicorum sapientia* (Copenhagen, 1674), 226; as cited by Kopp, *Beiträge*, 399.

105. Georg Wolfgang Wedel, *Excitationum medico-philologicarum* (Jena, 1699), 1ff. as quoted by Kopp, *Beiträge*, 399–400.

106. Published in London by John Starkey, 1670. Cf. Lenglet Du Fresnoy, *Histoire*, 3:62, 185. "Obrizon" is the English translation of the Latin *Obryzum*, pure gold.

107. Georg Ernst Stahl, "Observat. chymico-physico-medic. ann. MDCXCVIII, mensis Aprilis, quo vitulus aureus igne combustus, arcanum simplex, sed arcanum demonstratur," in his *Opusculo chymico-physico-medico* (Halle in Saxony, 1715), 585ff., as quoted by Kopp, *Beiträge*, 400.

108. Lenglet Du Fresnoy, *Histoire*, 1:18–19.

109. Ibid., 1:459.

110. See note 79 above.

111. Fabricius, *Bibliotheca Graeca*, 1:46, 49. Jacques Christian Basnage (1653–1725) was a French Protestant divine, one of whose works was the multivolume *Histoire des Juifs depuis Jesus Christ jusqu'à present* (The Hague, 1706–1711). The reference to Mercurius and Moses is in book 3, chapter 18, par. 18, p. 458.

112. W. Herapath, in *Philosophical Magazine and Journal of Science*, series 4, vol. 3 (London, 1852), 528, as quoted by Kopp, *Beiträge*, 401–2.

113. J. Denham Smith, in *Philosophical Magazine* 4:142. Some additional references to Moses the alchemist, made by Huetius, Fabricius, and Libavius, can be found in Ferguson, *Bibliotheca chemica*, 2:113.

Chapter Three
Alchemy in Bible and Talmud

1. More information can be found in the Hebrew *Enṣiqlopediya Miqrait*, s.v. Matekhet, and in the English *EJ* (J), s.v. Metals and Mining.

2. The *EJ* (J) covers the subject, and the material in Samuel Krauss's *Talmudische Archaeologie* (Leipzig, 1910–1912) is still valuable, after eighty years.

3. Cf. B. Sukka 51b.

4. Jerusalem Talmud Yoma 41d; Babylonian Talmud Yoma 44b–45a; Exodus Rabba 35:1; Canticles Rabba 3:9.

5. B. Yoma 44b–45a.

6. Numbers Rabba 12:4; Canticles Rabba 3:9.

7. Leviticus Rabba 16:2, quoting Psalms 34:13–14.

8. *Midrash Tanḥuma*, edited by S. Buber (New York, 1946), vol. 2, *M'ṣoraʿ*, pp. 45–46 and additional sources in note there.

9. Cf. B. Shabbat 88b; B. Yoma 72b; B. Qid. 30b.

Chapter Four
Jews in Hellenistic Alchemy

1. Berthelot published and translated the version of this treatise preserved in the Paris Bibliothèque Nationale MS. 2419 (dating from 1460): Berthelot, *Grecs*, 3:24.

2. Litharge: Greek alchemists used this term in the sense of "silver-producing stone" *claudianos*: a copper-lead alloy; *asem* or *asemon*: a lustrous alloy of varied composition, in which silver, copper, tin, lead, and mercury are frequent ingredients; *Diargyros* or *argyrite*: perhaps native silver sulphite, or argentiferous galena. T. Sherwood Taylor, "A Survey of Greek Alchemy," *Journal of Hellenic Studies* 50 (1930): 109–39.

3. Berthelot, *Grecs*, 2:24–25; 3:25–26.

4. Ibid., 3:37.

5. Ibid., 2:90; 3:98. Marcellin P. E. Berthelot, *Introduction à l'étude de la chimie* (Paris, 1889), 294.

6. Berthelot, *Grecs*, 3:120–21.

7. "Divine water" is sulphurous water, whose preparation is dealt with in long sections of the writings of Greek alchemists, and especially in those of the school of Maria the Jewess, but its use and nature remain obscure. Taylor, "Survey," 130–31. For Theosebeia, see Marrellin P. E. Berthelot, *Les origines de l'alchimie* (Paris, 1885), 9, 64.

8. "The bird" refers to the bird of Hermes, which was considered the spirit of the fire of nature, enclosed in the humidity of the Hermetic mercury, or the natural heat united with the radical humidity. Berthelot, *Grecs*, 3:140–41.

9. The tribikos was a widely used alchemical apparatus. See Figure 5.3.

10. Yellow arsenic sulphide, orpiment. Taylor, "Survey," 123.

11. Ceruse: white lead, but also perhaps other white substances such as arsenic trioxide. Berthelot, *Grecs*, 3:140; Taylor, "Survey," 124.

12. *Mine* is an abbreviated form of the Greek *ʿēmina*, the name of an old Greek measure.

13. Berthelot, *Grecs*, 3:140–41.

14. It seems likely that when Zosimus says "bloody earth" he means "blood-red earth." If so, his explanation may hark back to the Hebrew assonance of *Adam* and *adom* (red), even though Greek legend too tells of man having been formed by Prometheus out of red clay (cf. Pausanias, *Description of Greece*, X:4:4; James G. Frazer, *Folk Lore in the Old Testament*, 3 vols. London, 1919, [1:6]). Zosimus's notion that the name Adam signifies "virgin earth" is found in the writings of Josephus Flavius in the first century C.E. He says that the man whom God created "was called Adam . . . which signifies one who is red, because he was formed out of red earth . . . of that which is virgin soil and real earth," Josephus, *Antiquities of the Jews*, I:1:2. As for the meaning of the individual letters contained in the name Adam, what Zosimus says is a variant of the explanations found in several ancient Jewish and Greek sources. In Hebrew the name consists of the three letters, ADM, and accordingly, R. Yoḥanan (2nd century C.E.) explains that the name is the acrostic of the words *Efer, Dam, Marah*,

i.e., dust, blood, gall (B. Soṭah 5a: cf. Pirqe R. Eliezer 12). In the Sybilline Books (3:24–26) and elsewhere in Christian literature the name, consisting of four letter in the Greek transliteration (ADAM), is explained as being an acrostic composed of the initials of *anatolē* (east), *dúsis* (west), *arktos* (north), and *mesēmbria* (south), which goes back to 2 Enoch 30:13. The first Jewish source to state that the body consists of the four elements of earth, water, air, and fire was Philo of Alexandria (1st century C.E.). Cf. Louis Ginzberg, *Legends of the Jews* (Philadelphia, 1909–1938) 5:72; and R. Patai, *Adam va'Adamah* (Jerusalem, 1942), 1:159–61.

15. Hesiod, *Theogony*, pars. 521, 618.

16. Berthelot, *Grecs*, 3:223–25.

17. Ibid., 3:232.

18. Ibid., 3:233–34.

19. Ibid., 3:235–36.

20. Ibid., 3:337.

21. The book in question is preserved in a manuscript in Cambridge, which has been analyzed by Julius Ruska, *Tabula Smaragdina: Ein Beitrag zur Geschichte der hermetischen Literatur* (Heidelberg, 1926; reprint 1948), 41–42. See also above, Chapter 2, notes 20 and 21. Cf. Ginzberg, *Legends*, 1:151; 5:172.

22. Ruska, *Tabula smaragdina*, 41–42.

23. Abu-l-Qāsim al-ʿĪrāqī, *Kitāb al-ʿilm al-muktasab fī zirāʿat al-dhahab*, edited by E. J. Holmyard (Paris, 1923), Arabic text, 229.

24. In saying this I follow Edmund O. von Lippmann, *Entstehung und Ausbreitung der Alchemie* (Berlin, 1931), 2:229. See also Moshe Idel, "The Origin of Alchemy According to Zosimus . . ." *Revue des Études Juives* 144 (1986): 117–24.

25. Berthelot, *Introduction*, 16–18.

26. Berthelot, *Grecs*, 2:90, 99.

27. The catalogue of the Greek manuscripts in the Bibliothèque Nationale identifies this treatise as "Albumazaris excerpta." *Inventaire sommaire des manuscripts grecs*, part 2, *Ancien fonds grec* (Paris, 1888), 257.

28. *EI*², 1:139–40.

29. Berthelot, *Grecs*, 1:79.

30. Ibid., Greek text, 24, translation, 25. Most of the terms listed above are explained by Berthelot in his *Introduction*.

31. See for example ff. 39b–56b.

Chapter Five
Maria the Jewess

1. Marcellin P. E. Berthelot and Charles Emile Ruelle, *Collection des anciens alchimistes grecs*, 3 vols. (Paris, 1888). The introductory volume of this work is cited here as Berthelot, *Grecs* 1, the Greek texts as Berthelot, *Grecs* 2, and the French translation as Berthelot, *Grecs* 3. A critical edition of the Greek text of one of Zosimus's treatises, that on the letter Omega, with an English translation and annotations was prepared by Howard M. Jackson, *Zosimus of Panopolis on*

the Letter Omega (Missoula, Montana, 1978). On Zosimus's life, see Jackson, *Zosimus*, 4–5.

2. Berthelot, *Grecs* 3:172–73, 236.

3. Ibid., 180.

4. Jackson, *Zosimus*, 19, 42 n. 10.

5. Jack Lindsay, *The Origins of Alchemy in Graeco-Roman Egypt* (London, 1970), 243, says that Maria "probably existed not very long after Bolos," who, he says (on pp. 22, 66–67), seems to have lived c. 200 B.C.E.

6. Berthelot, *Grecs*, 2:224ff., 237; 3:216ff., 228; 2:201; 3:197.

7. Edmund O. von Lippmann, "Zur Geschichte des Wasserbades," in his *Abhandlungen und Vorträge zur Geschichte der Naturwissenschaften*. idem, 2 vols. (Leipzig. 1906–1913), *Entstehung und Ausbreitung der Alchemie* (Berlin, 1919), 1:50. The English usage is exceptional in that the name of the water-bath is not associated with that of Maria. The *balneum Mariae* was so popular in medieval and later alchemy that no fewer than eight symbols were used to denote it:

MB, MB, BM, ℞, To, ▽Mℓ, [symbol], Jrℓ

Wolfgang Schneider, *Lexikon Alchemistisch-Pharmazeutischer Symbole* (Wenheim/Bergstr, 1962), 32.

8. See the detailed description of the still, based on Zosimus, in Lippmann, *Entstehung*, 48–49, and the brief summary with figures in F. Sherwood Taylor, *The Alchemists: Founders of Modern Chemistry* (New York, 1949), 46–49. Cf. also Berthelot, *Grecs*, 1:142ff., 148.

9. Pliny, *Historia naturalis*, 35:31 (Loeb Classical Library 9:297–99).

10. Berthelot, *Grecs*, 1:146–49; Taylor, *The Alchemists*, 46–49.

11. Taylor, *The Alchemists*, 39. Cf. Berthelot, *Grecs*, 2:225–26, 236; 3:217–18, 228–29, and fig. 15 in *Grecs*, 1:139.

12. "Discourse of the Most Sage Maria about the Philosophers' Stone," as quoted by Ferdinand Hoefer, *Histoire de la chimie* (Paris, 1886), 1:283–84.

13. Berthelot, *Grecs*, 2:146; 3:148.

14. Cf. Lippmann's summary, *Entstehung*, 1:48, based on Berthelot.

15. Berthelot, *Grecs*, 2:146, 169, 273; 3:148, 168–69, 262.

16. Ibid., 2:93, 94, 273; 3:101–2, 262.

17. Ibid., 2:96; 3:104; cf. 3:92. Other names applied to this "four in one" are lead, magnesia, *molybdochalkon* (lead-copper), and *māza*, that is, dough or bread; Berthelot *Grecs*, 2:96, 192, 197; 3:104, 188.

18. Olympiodorus, in Berthelot, *Grecs*, 2:92; 3:101; cf. also 2:93, 93; 3:171–72.

19. Ibid., 2:146, 170; 3:148, 169.

20. Zosimus, in Berthelot, *Grecs*, 2:148, 149; 3:151–52; cf. 2:172; 3:171–72.

21. Lippmann, *Entstehung*, 1:47; Berthelot, *La chimie au moyen age* (Paris, 1893), vol. 2, *L'Alchimie syriaque* 281.

22. Berthelot, *Grecs*, 2:171, 199; 3:170, 194.

23. Ibid., 1:271; Lippmann, *Entstehung*, 1:50.

24. Berthelot, *Grecs*, 3:168.

25. Ibid., 3:188.

26. Ibid., 3:168.

27. Ibid., 1:389; 2:404.

28. Berthelot, *Moyen age*, 1:260, quoting the *Theatrum chemicum*, vol. 1 (Argentaati [Strasbourg], 1659), 461.

29. C. G. Jung, *Psychology and Alchemy*, vol. 12 of *Collected Works*, Bollingen Series XX (2nd ed., Princeton, 1968), 23.

30. Berthelot, *Grecs*, 3:389 n. 2.

31. A detailed comparison of the human body and parts of the world is found in *Avot diRabbi Nathan*, ed. Solomon Schechter (New York, 1945), version A, 91ff. Cf. R. Patai, *Adam va'Adama* (Jerusalem, 1942), 1:166–67. The *Avot* dates from the second century C.E. The passage on nourishment is given in the next chapter.

32. Philo of Alexandria (Philo Judaeus), *On the Creation of the World*, 51 (Loeb Classical Library, 1:115, 117). Cf. also Philo's *De decalogo*, 8 (Loeb, 7:21). In his *De somniis* [On Dreams], Philo says that man was created of earth and water, which is also a midrashic view, cf. Targum Yerushalmi ad Genesis 2:7. Cf. Patai, *Adam va'Adama*, 1:159–60; Berthelot, *Grecs*, 3:170.

33. Berthelot, *Grecs*, 3:196; cf. 3:124 n. 1, 147.

34. Ibid., 153.

35. Ibid., 153 n. 2, and 159 n. 2.

36. Ibid., 196.

37. Ibid., 153.

38. Ibid., 192.

39. Ibid., 2:93; 3:101. In a Syriac manuscript of Zosimus a somewhat different version is given of Maria's doctrine of volatilization: "The first mercury among the fugacious bodies determines only a partial volatilization. Instead of disappearing, it fixes the fugacious bodies, which are the sulphurs. Thus is verified the word of Maria who says that the sulphurs tint and are fugacious. They are fixed by mercury." Berthelot, *Moyen age*, 2:243.

40. Cf. Berthelot, *Grecs*, 3:101 n. 2, and 124 n. 1.

41. Berthelot, *Moyen age*, vol. 3, *L'Alchimie arabe*, 47. My translation from the Arabic. See also p. 88, and Berthelot, *Grecs*, translation of Synesius, 3:64 n.1.

42. Berthelot, *Moyen age*, 3:86; cf. 3:83.

43. Ibid., 3:90.

44. Ibid. My translation from the Arabic. I read the Arabic *ḥrsfly* as *ḥarr sufly* (deep heat), instead of *harrsefla*, which remains untranslated and unexplained by Berthelot, *Moyen age*, 94.

45. Ibid., 104.

46. H. E. Stapleton, G. I. Lewis, and F. Sherwood Taylor, "The Sayings of Hermes Quoted in the Ma al-Waraqi of Ibn Umail," *Ambix* 3 (1949): 72–73.

47. M. Turāb Ali, H. E. Stapleton, and M. Hidāyat Ḥusain, *Three Arabic Treatises by Muḥammad bin Umail (10 Century A.D.)*, Memoirs of the Asiatic Society of Bengal, 12:1 (Calcutta, 1933), 130, 134.

48. St. Mark MS, f. 178; MS 2,327, f. 214; MS 2,250, f. 163, as quoted in Marcellin P. E. Berthelot, *Les Origines de l'alchimie* (Paris, 1885), 56, 172.

49. Berthelot, *Grecs*, 3:112 n. 4.

50. E.g. Zosimus, see Berthelot, *Grecs*, 3:235; Olympiodorus, *ibid.*, 90–91.

51. Latin translation by Robertus Castrensis, in Johannes Jacobus Manget, *Bibliotheca chemica curiosa*, 2 vols. (Geneva, 1702), 1:515 col. 1; cited by Berthelot, *Moyen age*, 1:243.

52. Berthelot, *Moyen age*, 3:81–82.

53. Des Periers, *Cymbalum mundi* (Bell of the World) (1537), 43, 45, 314ff., and *Nouvelles recreations* (1558; repr. Paris: Jacobs, 1858), as quoted in Lippmann, *Entstehung*, 1:503.

54. *Artis auriferae quam chemiam vocant*, 2 vols. (Basel, 1610) 1:205–7. First published in Basel, 1593. For the publishing history, see John Ferguson, *Bibliotheca chemica* (Glasgow, 1906), 1:51–52, 2:106–7.

55. The words "scoyare Ade & Zethet" seem to mean "to study [two works called] Ade and Zethet." The root "scoya" appears twice more in our text: "in libris suis scoyas," which seems to mean, "in his study books," and "in societate scoyari," which could mean "in the students' society." The latter expression was taken by Jung to refer to a secret society, whose name, he says, "recalls the mysterious Scayolus in the writings of Paracelsus (*De vita longa*), where it means the adept. Scayolae are the higher spiritual forces or principles." Cf. Jung, *Psychology and Alchemy*, 314 n. 50.

56. Lippmann, *Entstehung*, 46.

57. Cf. J.-P. Migne, *Patrologiae cursus completus, Series graeca* (Paris, 1858), vol. 41 col. 173, and vol. 42 col. 832.

58. Ibid., 41:324–43. The words in square brackets are added from the Latin translation. The quotations are from John 3:12 and 6:62. I am indebted to Louis H. Feldman of Yeshiva University for the translation of the above excerpt from the Greek original.

59. Jung, *Psychology and Alchemy*, 160.

60. P. de Jong and M. J. de Goeje, *Catalogus codicum orientalium bibliothecae academiae Lugduno-Batavae* (Leiden, 1865), 3:196 and elsewhere; Hermann Kopp, *Beiträge zur Geschichte der Chemie* (Braunschweig, 1869), 406; idem, *Die Alchemie in älterer und neuerer Zeit* (Heidelberg, 1886), 2:208.

61. Berthelot, *Les origines*, 172; Paul Kraus, *Jābir ibn Ḥayyān* (Cairo, 1943), 43 n. 1, quoting *Kitāb al-Ḥajar*, ed. Holmyard, 15, 18.

62. Cf. Pliny, as cited by Kopp, *Beiträge*, 407.

63. Lippmann, *Entstehung*, 1:46, 66–67, 333–35; cf. Berthelot, *Les origines*, 163ff.; Kopp, *Beiträge*, 506–7.

64. Georgii Syncelli, *Chronographia*, edited by J. Goar (Venice, 1729), 198, as cited by Kopp, *Beiträge*, 506–7.

65. Berthelot, *Moyen age*, 3:90 (Arabic text). My translation.

66. See the poem at the end of this chapter.

67. Kopp, *Beiträge*, 405–6; idem, *Die Alchemie*, 207; Berthelot, *Les origines*, 172.

68. Michael Maier, *Symbola aureae mensae duodecim nationum* (Frankfurt-am-Main, 1617), 2:56. I am indebted to Louis H. Feldman and David Berger for their help in translating the above passage. Pyrgopolynices, the central figure in Plautus's *Braggart Soldier*, appears here as the "adversary of Chymistry and Chymists," whereas Maria is the courageous defender of the Hermetic Art; cf. John Read, *Prelude to Chemistry: An Outline of Alchemy*, 2nd ed. (Cambridge, Mass., 1966), 223, 225.

69. Maier, *Symbola*, 57–64.

70. John Read, *Prelude to Chemistry* (New York, 1937), 257–58.

71. Arnaldus de Villanova, "Carmen," as reprinted in *Theatrum chemicum*, vol. 4 (Argentorati [Strasbourg], 1613), 614–15, and *Artis auriferae*, 1:208.

Chapter Six
Zosimus on Maria the Jewess

1. The excerpts assembled here are my translations from the texts published in Berthelot, *Grecs*. Page numbers are given in parentheses after each passage.

2. The kerotakis is a complex still. See Figure 5.2.

3. The word "gum" (G. *kommi*) designates the material that provides the yellow coloring. Its nature is not explained. See Berthelot, *Grecs*, 3:148 n. 3.

4. Sulphur (G. *theion*) means not only the element sulphur but also similar substances such as arsenic sulphide.

5. This seems to signify that in the transmutation the copper and the silver do not retain their proper qualities or colors, nor their bodies, which become changed into that of another metal. As for plants, if one understands them in the sense of vegetable tinctures, they are in effect destroyed by the fire. In this sense, the metallic flowers and certain corresponding colorings are equally evaporated or destroyed by the fire. Berthelot, *Grecs*, 3:153.

6. "Magnesia" is not the modern magnesia, but usually an alloy of four base metals: copper, iron, lead, and tin; the term is used in a very wide sense. Antimony (G. *stimmi*) means antimony sulphide. Litharge (G. *lithargyros*) is used in the sense of "silver-producing stone": it is doubtful whether lead oxide was ever intended. See F. Sherwood Taylor, "A Survey of Greek Alchemy," *Journal of Hellenic Studies* 50 (1930): 123–24.

7. Molybdochalkon is a copper-lead alloy, or perhaps a metallic sulphide. Ibid., 123.

8. The four bodies are the four base metals listed in note 6.

9. "Divine water" is sulphur, the pale yellow, nonmetallic element. It can also mean sulphurous water.

10. Cf. Marcellin P. E. Berthelot, *Introduction à l'étude de la chimie* (Paris, 1889), 56, 60, 64.

11. *Ios* has the meaning of "rust," or "calx," and also that of the Latin *virus*. The use of the word is difficult to follow. See Taylor, "Survey," 124, and note 17 below.

12. Chrysocolla is apparently malachite, but is also used in other senses in the texts. See Berthelot, *Introduction*, 232; Taylor, "Survey," 124.

13. Alum (G. *stypteria*) is not always identical with modern alum, and is possibly used as a term for arsenic; Taylor, "Survey," 123.

14. Cinnabar (G. *kinnabaris*) is native mercury sulphide, but the term is also used of realgar, and perhaps of red lead, which are similar in color, and were imperfectly distinguished from one another; ibid., 124.

15. That is to say, use sulphur of arsenic instead of cinnabar or mercury; Berthelot, *Grecs*, 3:173 n. 1.

16. The reference seems to be to realgar (G. *sandarache*), arsenic sulphide, an orange-red mineral; Berthelot, *Introduction*, 238, 244.

17. *Iosis* has several meanings: 1. the operation by which metals are oxidized; 2. the purification or refining of the metals, such as gold; 3. the virulence or possession of a specific active quality, communicated, for example, with the help of oxidation; 4. the coloring to yellow or violet of metallic compounds, often produced by certain oxidations. Berthelot, *Introduction*, 255.

18. Natron (G. *nitron*) is native soda.

19. The term *māza* was used by the Greek alchemists to denote chemistry or alchemy. The term is discussed repeatedly by Berthelot in his *Introduction*, 209, 210, 257, 270.

20. Laurel wood is a symbolic name of a mineral substance; Berthelot, *Grecs*, 3:159 n. 2, and 178 n. 1.

21. Ocher (G. *ōchra*) perhaps has the additional meaning of realgar and cinnabar.

22. *Motaria* is the residue remaining in the linen wrapping used in operations with minerals, especially yellow sandarac; Berthelot, *Grecs*, 3:112, 157–58, 188. Sandarac is the resin of the sandarac tree, or a realgar.

23. Pyrites (G.), probably included iron and copper pyrites, galena, and mispickel; Taylor, "Survey," 124.

24. That is: if you do not transform the metals by taking away their metallic state, and if you do not regenerate them in that state with the new properties, by uniting several metals into one. Cf. Berthelot, *Grecs*, 3:101 n. 2.

25. Brine (G. *almyria, almē*): the term is perhaps also used figuratively for other liquids; Taylor, "Survey," 124.

26. *Misy* (G.), is basic iron sulphate; ibid.

27. One or more words missing in the original.

28. On the tribikos see above, Chapter 5 at note 11.

Introduction to Part Three

1. See the detailed bibliography in A.-M. Goichon's article "Ibn Sīnā" in *EI*², 3:945–47.

2. MS. 6514, f. 149r. It was printed in Basel, 1572, as pp. 1–471 of the *Artis chemiae principes.*

3. Cf. Marcellin P. E. Berthelot, *La chimie au moyen age* (Paris, 1893), 1:301–2. Berthelot himself comments on the"tolerance and community of sentiments established among the adepts of the alchemical science whatever their religious beliefs," which is evinced by Ibn Sīnā's quoted reference.

4. B. Shabbat 31a.

5. Cf. B. Yoma 86a, etc.

Chapter Seven
Abufalaḥ's Alchemy

1. British Library Hebrew MS 3659 consists of ten leaves, written in clear Sephardi cursive, and it is undoubtedly several centuries later than the eleventh century, when Abufalaḥ was supposed to have lived. Its incipit is *Amar Abulfalaḥ haSaraquṣṭi*, and it ends in medias res on folio 10v with the words "*y'ḥabber min hanushādir ḥaṣī mishqal min*" I wish to thank the British Library

for having put a photocopy of the manuscript at my disposal, and permitted me to publish my English translation on it.

2. The *Sefer haTamar* was published by Gershom Scholem in the Hebrew original and a German translation in Jerusalem, 1926, and Hannover, 1927.

3. Cf. F. S. Bodenheimer, *Gershon ben Solomon of Arles . . . Gate of Heaven* (Jerusalem, 1953), and especially pp. 19–34, which list "The Sources and Authors quoted or Used in the Shaʿar Ha-Shamayim." Abufalaḥ should be added to that list. A few of the many scholars who discussed this book are: Shneur Zacks, in *Kerem Ḥemed* (Berlin) 8 (1854): 152–58; Steinschneider, *Hebräische Übersetzungen*, 9–16; Lothar Kopf in *Tarbiz* 24 (1955): 150–66, 274–89, 410–25 (this excellent article lists the foreign words used by Gershon); and Kopf's article on Gershon in the *EJ* (J), 7:515–16.

4. Cf. Moritz Steinschneider, *Die hebräischen Übersetzungen des Mittelalters und die Juden als Dolmetscher* (Berlin, 1893; reprint Graz, 1956), 381–82, 850, s.v. *Sefer haHaqnatah*.

5. Cf. Yitzḥaq Sh'muel Reggio, in the Viennese *Kerem Ḥemed*, 2 (1836): 48–50.

6. Cf. Gen. 41:43.

7. Cf. 2 Kings 13:14.

8. Cf. 1 Kings 10.

9. The reference is to Ibn Rushd (1126–1198), the famous Arab philosopher.

10. In the excerpt from Abufalaḥ's manuscript contained in Gershon ben Shlomo's *Book of the Gate of Heaven* (Venice, 1547), which includes the above passage, the word *bdil*, tin, is substituted for the *barzel*, iron, of our text.

11. Marginal note: "explanation: that which falls off from the iron when the smiths beat it."

12. Marginal note: "I found in a copy that possibly it is dust of which clay vessels are made."

13. Marginal note: "one end of it in the water and the other end in the empty vessel."

14. Marginal note in Hebrew characters: *"soluzione, disṭilazione, solimazione, coniulazione, qalzinazione"*.

Chapter Eight
A Hebrew Version of the *Book of Alums and Salts*

1. Julius Ruska, *Das Buch der Alaune und Salze: Ein Grundwerk spätlateinischer Alchemie* (Berlin, 1935).

2. Ibid., 16, 23 n. 1, 38.

3. Moritz Steinschneider, *Verzeichniss der hebräischen Handschriften* (Berlin, 1878), 120.

4. The MS was received by the Staatsbibliothek in 1893, and some time later the cataloger renumbered the folios, designating the extant folio 45 as 1, folio 46 as 2, and so on, so that the original last folio, f. 136, became f. 89 (the discrepancy is due to some errors in the pagination). In the following we shall use this new pagination in referring to the folios.

5. I give the quotations from the Hebrew text in my translation. The many non-Hebrew words contained in the MS are given in transliteration in italics, followed by my translation in square brackets.

6. Folio 34a, which corresponds to Ruska's Latin text section, pp. 74–75, G. 58, and is missing in the Arabic.

7. Cf. Steinschneider, *Verzeichniss*, 120.

8. Cf. J. Ruska and E. Wiedemann, "Beiträge zur Geschichte der Naturwissenschaften LXVII: Alchemische Decknamen," in Physikalisch-medizinische Sozietät (Erlangen), *Sitzungsberichte* 56 (1924): 24–26, 28, 32; Alfred Siggel, *Decknamen in der arabischen alchemistischen Literatur* (Berlin, 1951), 12.

9. Cf. Martin Levey, *Early Arabic Pharmacology* (Leiden, 1977), 143.

10. Giovanni Battista Nazari, *Della Tramutazione Metallica* (Brescia, 1564), 135. Cf. Ferguson, *Bibliotheca chemica* 1:281–82, quoting Lenglet Du Fresnoy.

Chapter Nine
Pseudo-Khālid ibn Yazīd

1. Cf. *EI*[2], s.v. Marianus.

2. Johannes Jacobus Manget, *Bibliotheca chemica curiosa*, 2 vols. (Geneva, 1702).

3. *Azoth* (variant: *azoch*), also called *viriditas*, presumably verdigris, was considered by alchemical authors as the substance out of which gold could be made. See, e.g., *Artis auriferae quam chemiam vocant* . . . (Basel, 1593), 2:220. Cf. C. G. Jung, *Psychology and Alchemy*, vol. 12 of *Collected Works*, Bollingen Series XX (2nd ed., Princeton, 1968), 159, 286, 458.

4. Historians of Arabic literature are of the opinion that the books of alchemical and magical nature attributed to Maslama were actually written by a contemporary compatriot of Maslama named Abū Maslama Muḥammad al-Majrīṭī and the latter's pupil Ibn Bishrūn al-Majrīṭī, but this question of authorship is of no particular interest for us in the present context. Fuat Sezgin, *Geschichte des arabischen Schrifttums* (Leiden, 1971), 4:294–98.

5. Cf. Raphael Patai, *Adam va'Adamah* (Jerusalem, 1942), 1:216–26.

6. Josephus Flavius, *Wars of the Jews*, 7:6:3. Shakespeare, *Romeo and Juliet*, act IV, scene III; *Henry VI*, second part, act III, scene II. See also James G. Frazer, *Folk Lore in the Old Testament* (London: 1919), 2:384–85.

7. Cf. Genesis 30; Frazer, *Folk Lore*, 2:372ff.

8. Cf. J. Sontheimer's German translation (Stuttgart, 1840–1842), 2:14ff., 594.

9. Louis Ginzberg, *The Legends of the Jews*, 7 vols. (Philadelphia, 1909–1938), 5:297–98.

10. Cf. Jung, *Psychology and Alchemy*, Index, s.v. *lapis*.

11. Bauzan is perhaps identical with Bacsen or Bassen mentioned in the *Turba*. See Manget, *Bibliotheca chemica curiosa*, 1:454, 455, 482.

Introduction to Part Four

1. Cf. B. Suler, "Alchemy," in *Encyclopaedia Judaica* (Jerusalem, 1972), 2:547.

Chapter Ten
Artephius

1. Karl Christoph Schmieder, *Geschichte der Alchemie* (Halle, 1832), 125–27.
2. Ibid., 127.
3. *Fegfeufer der Chymisten* . . . (Amsterdam, 1702). There is a copy in the Bibliothèque Nationale, Paris.
4. Suler's article in the *EJ* (B), 2:152, states that the *Keren Happuch* mentions another Jewish alchemist, Tenellus by name, whom the "pious author" characterizes as "a despicable soul, a Jew." The fact is that under the category "Chief Lies," the author of Keren Happuch only says "No. 23. Tenelli MSt. eine liederliche Seele," with no indication that Tenellus was a Jew.
5. Johann Christoph Wolf, *Bibliotheca Hebraea*, 4 vols. (Hamburg, 1715–1733), 4:790.
6. *Theatrum chemicum*, published by Lazarus Zetzner (Argentorati [Strasbourg], 1613), 4:220. Just a year earlier P. Arnauld translated Artephius's *Liber secretus* into French and published it, together with alchemical treatises by Flamel and Synesius, under the title *Trois traitez de la philosophie naturelle* . . . (Paris, 1612). I wish to thank Louis H. Feldman for the translation.
7. Johann Friedrich Gmelin, *Geschichte der Chemie* (Göttingen, 1797), 1:22–23.
8. M. Chevreul, "Examen critique au point de vue de l'histoire de la chimie, d'un écrit alchimique intitulé *Artefii clavis majoris sapientiae*," in *Mémoires de l'Académie des Sciences de l'Institut Impérial de France*, 36 (1870): 27.
9. Thus according to Ibn Khallikān. Cf. Gildemeister, *Zeitschrift der Morgenländischen Gesellschaft* 30 (1876): 538, as quoted by John Ferguson, *Bibliotheca chemica*, 51.
10. Schmieder, *Geschichte*, 125–26.

Chapter Eleven
The Great Jewish Philosophers

1. See Raphael Patai, *The Jewish Mind* (New York: 1977), 126.
2. Baḥya ibn Paquda, *Kitāb al-Hidāya ilā Farā'id al-Qulūb*, edited by A. Yahuda (Leiden, 1912).
3. Cf. *Judah Hallevi's Kitāb al Khazarī*, translated from the Arabic by Hartwig Hirschfeld, new rev. ed. (London, 1931), 144 (3:23), 159 (3:53).
4. More on Mē-Zahav will be found in Chapter 34.
5. MS *Midrash haḤokhmah*, quoted by Moritz Steinschneider in his article "Typen," in Joseph Kobak's *Jeschurun* 9 (1873): 84–85.

Chapter Twelve
Kabbalah and Alchemy: A Reconsideration

1. *Zohar* 2:23b–24b.
2. Cf. *Zohar* 2:249b–250a.
3. See Chapter 27 on Taitazak and Provençali.

4. Cf. MSS 527, 596–98, 3663, 3667, Angelica MS 3, in the Bibliothèque Nationale, Paris.

5. Hermann Sprengel, "Alchemy," in Johann S. Ersch and J. G. Gruber, eds., *Allgemeine Encyklopädie* (Leipzig, 1850–1851), 2:416.

6. Cf. Henricus Cornelius Agrippa von Nettesheym, *De incertitudine et vanitate omnium scientiarum et artium* (On the Incertitude and Vanity of All Sciences and Arts) (The Hague, 1656); English translation, *The Vanity of Arts and Sciences* (London, 1676), vol. 2, ch. 15.

7. Printed in Hanau, 1602, and again in 1609.

8. Arthur Edward Waite, *The Secret Tradition of Alchemy* (London and New York, 1926), 255.

9. Jacques Van Lennep, Nicolas Séd, and Sylvain Matton, *Simeon ben Cantara: Cabala Mineralis* (Paris, 1986).

10. Gerhard Dorn, *Physica Trismegisti*, in *Theatrum chemicum*, (Strasbourg [Argentorati], 1659), 371; cf. also 359.

11. Cf. Raphael Patai, *The Hebrew Goddess* (Detroit, 1990), 78.

12. "Zur Terminologie der jüdischen Alchemie," In *Monatschrift für Geschichte und Wissenschaft des Judentums* (Breslau, 1925), 69:364–71.

13. Albert W. Greenup, ed., *Sefer Sheqel haQodesh* (London, 1911), 46–47. My translation from the Hebrew.

14. Ibid., 77.

15. Ibid., 120–22.

Introduction to Part Five

1. Emmanuel Le Roy Ladurie, *L'État royal: De Louis XI à Henri IV (1460–1610)* (Paris, 1987), 51–52.

Chapter Thirteen
Raymund de Tarrega: Marrano, Heretic, Alchemist

1. Italian translation by M. Pietro Lauro (Venice, 1557; English translation: Oxford MS, Ashmole 1507, Cat. Col. 1409. A somewhat abridged version of this chapter was published in *Ambix* 35 (March 1988): 14–30.

2. Enrico Cardile, *Il Trattato della Quinta Essenza ovvero d' Secreti di Natura di Raimundo Lullo a cura di Enrico Cardile* (Todi, 1924). This is more of a summary than a translation.

3. Lucas Waddingus (Wadding), *Annales minorum*, 25 vols. (Rome, 1731–1886); 3rd ed. (Florence, 1931), 4:477–78.

4. Ibid., 6:233; *Dictionnaire de theologie catholique* (Paris, 1926), 9:1086; *EJ* (J), 8:14; 13:1542.

5. Lucas Waddingus, *Scriptores ordinis minorum* (Rome, 1906), 192–202; A. Perroquet, *Apologia de la vie et des oeuvres du bienheureux Raymond Lulle* (Vendome, 1662).

6. Nicolas Antonio Hispalensis (1617–1684), *Bibliotheca hispana vetus* (Madrid, 1788), 2:126–41.

7. See the volumes of the *Boletin de la Sociedad Arqueologica Luliana*, Majorca.

8. Cf. Hispalensis, *Bibliotheca*, 2:126–41, and Joannes Baptista Sollerius (Sollier), *Acta B. Raymundi Lulli* (Antwerp 1708), 59ff. Arthur Edward Waite, in *Three Famous Alchemists*, (Philadelphia, n.d. [c. 1903], 50, counted 77 alchemical works attributed to Lull in the *Opera omnia catalogus librorum beati Raymundi Lullii*. See also Miguel Massuti y Alzamora, "Ramón Lull y la alquimia," *Boletin de la Sociedad Arqueologica Luliana* 28 (July 1942–Dec. 1943): nos. 695–703 on p. 526.

9. *Musaeum Hermeticum* (Frankfurt, 1625), 101.

10. Ibid., 271.

11. My translation from the Latin. Cf. *Codicillus seu vade mecum* (Cologne, 1563), and other editions; *Testamentum* (Rouen, 1663), part 1, "Theoria & Practica."

12. Waddingus, *Annales minorum*, 6:166, quotes passages from four books by Lull. See also Hispalensis, *Bibliotheca*, 2:136–37; Jaime Custurer (1657–1715), *Disertaciones historicas del culto immemorial del B. Raymundo Lulli . . .* (Majorca, 1700), 625; Erhad Wolfram Platzeck, ed., *Raimund Lull, Opuscula*, 3 vols. (Hildesheim, 1971–1973) l:xviii; 2:xlvii; *Acta sanctorum*, June, no. 5 (Antwerp, 1709), 657–61, 706. A number of anti-alchemical statements made by Lull are presented in Waite, *Three Famous Alchemists*, 49–50.

13. The Basel, 1600, edition of the *Testamentum novissimum*, which I consulted in the rare book division of the New York Public Library, has on p. 139 a slightly different version of this statement. St. Catharine's Hospital was located near the Tower of London, and in 1351 Queen Philippa, wife of Edward III, founded a chantry in it; cf. Robert Seymour, *A Survey of the Cities of London and Westminster* (London, 1733), 1:197.

14. Waddingus, *Annales minorum*, 6:266–67.

15. Ibid.

16. Massuti y Alzamora, "Ramón Lull," 526.

17. Montpellier was indeed a "celebrated place of study," famous for its medical school. See Alexandre Charles Germain, *L'École de medicine à Montpellier* (Montpellier, 1880).

18. The conclusion that the dates contained in the colophons of these manuscripts render Lullian authorship impossible has been emphasized by D. José Ramon de Luanco in his *Ramon Lull (Raimundo Lulio) cosiderado como alquimista* (Barcelona, 1870), 38ff., and after him by Massuti y Alzamora, "Ramon Lull," 515–17. By coincidence, Lull was in Montpellier in 1309 and in Paris in 1310; Joan Avinyo, *Les obres autentiques del Beat Ramon Llull, Repertori Bibliografic* (Barcelona, 1935), 207, 232; Leon Teissier, "La cité de Montpellier au temps de Raymond Lulle," *Revue des Pays d'Oc* 2 (Paris, 1933): 384–90.

19. Daniel Georg Morhof, *Polyhistor*, 3rd ed. (Lübeck, 1732), 1:81.

20. Lynn Thorndike, *A History of Magic and Experimental Science*, 8 vols. (New York, 1923–1958), 4:13–14.

21. Quoted by Waite, *Three Famous Alchemists*, 52. My translation from the Latin.

22. Michael Maier, *Tripus aureus hoc est tres tractatus chymici selectissimi* (The Golden Tripod which Is Three Most Selected Chemical Tractates), (Frankfurt-am-Main, 1618). A different version of *The Testament of Cremer* was reissued in 1983 by the Alchemical Press, Edmonds, Washington.

23. Waite, *Three Famous Alchemists*, 56; cf. 52.

24. See below, Chapter 15.

25. See below, Chapter 16.

26. Elias Ashmole, *Theatrum chemicum Britannicum* (London, 1652), 467. The poem "Hermes Bird" is on pp. 213–26.

27. My translations from the Spanish of Ramón de Luanco, *Ramon Lull*, 43–44, quoting the *Bibliothèque des philosophes chimiques* (Paris, 1741).

28. Robertus Constantinus, *Nomeclator insignium scriptorum* (Paris, 1555), as cited by Waite, *Three Famous Alchemists*, 60.

29. See the Oxford manuscripts listed by J. M. Batista y Roca, "Catalech de les obres Lulianes d'Oxford," in *Boletin de la Real Academia de Buenas Letras de Barcelona* 15:60 (Oct.–Dec. 1915): 220–22, 225–26. See also Johannes Jacobus Manget, *Bibliotheca chemica curiosa*, 2 vols. (Geneva, 1702), 1:780–90, 853–62, 863–72.

30. *Testamenti novissimi Raymundi Lullii Majoricani*, Regi Carolo dicati, liber primus, in Manget, *Bibliotheca*, 1:790.

31. Cf. Manget, *Bibliotheca*, 1:780.

32. See the Spanish *Enciclopedia Universal Illustrada*, 58 (1928), 762.

33. R. P. Alexander Natalis (Alexandre Noël, 1639–1724), *Historia ecclesiastica*, first published in 8 volumes in Paris, 1714; (Bingen, 1789), 15:212–13. See also the *Enciclopedia Universal*, 58:764, which says that "some call him Ramón Lull de Tárrega, neophyte, Jew, and rabbi. At the age of twelve he embraced the Catholic religion, and later entered the order of Santo Domingo." The author of the article seems to have overlooked the difficulty of how a boy who at the age of twelve converted to Christianity could have been a rabbi.

34. Cf. Francisco Peña's comment in Nicolas Eymeric, *Directorium inquisitorum*, first printed with copious notes by Peña in 1503, and reprinted five times between 1576 and 1607. I consulted the Rome, 1587, and Venice, 1607, editions in the rare book division of the Columbia University Library, in both of which the above statement is on p. 315.

35. Ibid., 316 This book was still of sufficient interest in 1973 to be translated into French in a greatly abridged version, with an introduction and notes by Louis Sala-Molino, *Le manual des inquisiteurs* (Paris, 1973). See pp. 11–12, 15.

36. Eymeric, *Directorium*, 262–64, and Peña's comment, p. 264, to the effect that the (unnamed) books in which Eymeric found the twenty-four heresies were written by Raymundus Neophytus, as also Eymeric himself states in question 27.

37. Eymeric in his *Directorium*, 264, has "hostile Mahomet."

38. Natalis, *Historia ecclesiastica* 15:212–13. My translation from the Latin. After enumerating Raymund de Tarrega's heresies, Natalis adds: "Let one read the same Eymericus, Question 27, and Franciscus Peña, Commentarium 52. From this should be corrected the error of Prateolus, Bernardus Lutzemburgus,

and Bzovius, who, misled by the similarity of the name, falsely attributed the errors and pernicious books of Raymundus Neophytus to the better known Raymundus Lullus."

39. Peña ad Eymeric, *Directorium*, part 1, question 27, as quoted in Custurer, *Disertationes*, 200–1.

40. As quoted by Jaime Custurer, *Disertationes historicas*, (Majorca, 1700), 200–1. In the sequel Custurer enumerates the observations of Odericus Raynaldus, Waddingus, Gubernantis, Luis Moreri, D. Nicolas Antonio, Athanasius Kirker (Kircher), Pedro Sanchez Arroyo, Francisco Porter, etc.

41. Custurer, *Disertationes*, 202, 213.

42. As quoted ibid., 404.

43. Giulio Bartolocci, *Bibliotheca magna rabbinica*, vol. 4 (Rome, 1693), 362. My translation from the Hebrew. In the sequel, written in Latin (p. 363), Bartolocci tells the story of the two papal letters, and again cautions against confusing the two Raymunds.

44. Johann Christoph Wolf, *Bibliotheca Hebreae*, vol. 3 (Hamburg, 1727), 289. Cf. also 1:1016.

45. Johann Jacob Hofmann, *Lexicon universale*, 4 vols. (Leiden, 1698), 4:vii.

46. Johannes Albertus Fabricius, *Bibliotheca Latina mediae et infimae aetatis*, 6 vols. (Hamburg, 1734–1736), 6:119.

47. Ibid. and 4:867. In the Florence, 1858, edition the passages about de Tarrega are in 3:575 and 5:346.

48. See Raymund de Tarrega's brief biography in Felix Torres Amat, *Memorias para ayudar a formar un diccionario crítico de los escritores catalanes* (Barcelona, 1836). The date 1368 for the incarceration of Raymund seems more probable than 1360, given in the *Enciclopedia Universal*, 58:764.

49. Cf. Greg. XI Decret. de Curia Anno I, Reg. Vat. 263, f. 225. I wish to thank the Director of the Archivio Segreto Vaticano for supplying me with photocopies of this document and of the one referred to in note 54, and permitting me to publish them. I also wish to thank Dr. Joseph Salemi for helping me to decipher the difficult handwriting of these two documents and translating them into English.

50. Eymeric, *Directorium*, 314.

51. The *De alchimia* is considered by all scholars who dealt with the problem as having been written by Raymund de Tarrega. Cf. Waddingus, *Annales minorum*, 6: 265; Natalis, *Historia ecclesiastica*, 15:212; Fabricius, *Bibliotheca Latina* (Florence, 1858), 3:575, 5:346; John Ferguson, *Bibliotheca chemica* (Glasgow, 1906), 2:54.

52. Torres Amat, *Memorias*, 615–16. My translation from Spanish.

53. Greg. XI Decret. de Curia Anno II, Reg. Vat. 263, f. 1919. See note 49 above.

54. See the text of the letter in Franciscus Peyna (Peña), *Litterae apostolicae diversorum Romanorum pontificum* (Rome, 1587), 67–68.

55. Cf. W. T. A. Barber, "Lullists," in *Encyclopaedia of Religion and Ethics*, edited by James Hastings (London, c. 1900); E. Grahit, *El inquisidor Fray Nicolás Eymerich* (Gerona, 1878). A list of documentary material concerning

Eymeric's work as an inquisitor is given by J. Avinyó, "Catalech de Documents Lulians," in *Boletin de la Real Academia de Buenas Letras de Barcelona* 12:47 (July–Sept. 1912): 395ff.

56. The Venice 1542 edition, of which I studied one copy at the Bibliothèque Nationale, Paris, and another at the National Library of Medicine in Bethesda, Maryland, is a small volume about 4" x 6" in size. It contains in its first 107 pages the Latin text of *De Secr.*, followed by the text, also in Latin, of *De mineralibus et rebus metallicis libri quinque* (Five Books on Minerals and Metallic Things) by Albertus Magnus.

57. I wish to thank Joseph Salemi for the translation of this page.

58. Actually the parable of the talents is in Matthew 25:14–30.

59. Exodus 4:12.

60. "Mumia" was a substance reputedly derived from the bodies of Egyptian mummies. For its use in folk medicine, see Raphael Patai, "Indulco and Mumia," *Journal of American Folklore* 77 (Jan.–March, 1964): 3–11.

61. A plant, *Centaurea centaurium L.*

62. Epithymus, flower of thyme.

63. A plant much used by the ancients as a remedy for mental diseases, epilepsy, etc. Lewis and Short, *A Latin Dictionary*, s.v. Elleborus.

64. Hypericon, chamaepitys, corion, groundpine. Ibid., s.v.

65. See sources in Louis Ginzberg, *The Legends of the Jews*, vol. 6 (Philadelphia, 1928), 289, 291, 292, 296.

Chapter Fourteen
The Quinta Essentia in Hebrew

1. *De secretis naturae sive quinta essentia.* No fewer than seven of these editions (Venice, 1514; Augsburg, 1518; Venice, 1521; Lyons, 1535, Venice, 1542, Nuremberg, 1546; Venice, 1557) are in the National Library of Medicine, Bethesda, Maryland. A copy of the Strasbourg, 1541, edition is in the Engineering Library, New York.

2. Printed in Basel, 1600, pp. 330–74.

3. E.g., *Raymundi Lullii tractatus brevis et eruditus de conservatione vitae: item Liber secretorum, sive quintae essentiae* (Strasbourg, 1616). Although my own perusal of contemporary papal and other documents leads me to accept Ramon de Tarrega as the author of *De secr.* for the sake of brevity I shall hereinafter refer to both *De secr.*, and *De med.* as "Lullian" works.

4. The *Allgemeines Gelehrten-Lexicon*, vol. 3 (Leipzig, 1752), 2,315–16, states that Rupescissa's *De consideratione* (Basel, 1597) "was almost entirely copied from Raymund Lull."

5. Fonds hébr. 1207, ff. 155v–158v.

6. Moritz Steinschneider, *Die hebräischen Übersetzungen des Mittelalters und die Juden als Dolmetscher* (Berlin, 1893; reprint Graz, 1956), 824–25.

7. It was this prefatory statement that misled Steinschneider, who evidently did not examine the whole MS, to state that it was a reworking of *De secr.*

8. Rupescissa, *De consideratione*, 18. My translation from the Latin. On the same page Rupescissa refers to *quinta essentia id est coelum humanum.*

9. Folio 155v.

10. Folio 156r.

11. Sussman Muntner, *Moshe ben Maimon (Maimonides), Poisons and Their Antidotes* (Jerusalem, 1942), 98ff.

12. "Their language" refers to Spanish. In his Hebrew transliteration, *qinta esensia*, the author uses the Spanish form of this term.

13. *ʿIppush* (H.): moldiness, decay, putrefaction, a term often used by medieval Hebrew medical authors.

14. The Hebrew *ṭivʿiyyim* can mean naturalists or physicists, i.e., scholars who devoted themselves to the study of nature.

15. Rupescissa, *De consideratione*, 16, says that the quinta essentia is *sicut coelum incorruptibile* (like heaven incorruptible).

16. "Human artifice" is again a phrase reminiscent of Rupescissa, who says (p. 17) that the quinta essentia was created by God and can be extracted from the body of nature *cum artificio humano* (with human artifice).

17. *HaSamim haLeviyyim* (H.): drugs pertaining to the heart.

18. Quotation, in a modified form, from 1 Sam. 26:10, which reads, "the Lord shall smite him, or his day shall come to die."

19. *Salidonia* (L. *chelidonia*): celandine, swallow-wort or pilewort, a weedy plant of the poppy family.

20. *Frasas* (S. *fresas*): strawberries. I am unable to identify *fraulas* or *praulas*, but cf. *fralles* in C. E. Dubler, *La "Materia media" de Dioscorides: Transmision medieval y renacentista*, 6 vols. (Barcelona, 1953–1959), 6:101. Laʿaz in medieval Hebrew authors usually refers to the local colloquial, which in this case would be Spanish. But since our author calls Spanish "their tongue," his Laʿaz seems to refer to Latin. The Latin *fragulae* could have easily been mistransliterated as *fraula*. *Jilek* is the Turkish *çilek*, strawberry.

21. *Mora sarsa: mora* is Spanish for raspberry or blackberry. *Sarsa* is the Spanish *zarza*, common bramble, or the European blackberry, *rubus fruticosus*. In modern Spanish usage the name of the blackberry is *zarzamora*; see Maria Molinar, *Diccionario de Uso del Español* (Madrid, 1967), s.v.

22. *Tartaro* (S.): explained in our text as *rasuras*, which in Spanish means argol, tartar in its natural form as deposited in wine casks.

23. *Perlesia* (S.): muscle weakness accompanied by trembling, paralysis.

24. *HaL'vana* (H.), lit. "the white one." Medieval Hebrew medical authors use this word for phlegm, one of the four humors which, since Hippocrates and Galen, were believed to be responsible for one's health and disposition. The preponderance or impairment of any one of these humors was believed to cause certain types of diseases.

25. Persian *farfayūn* or *farfiyūn*, is the euphorbium or gum euphorbium, an African plant. The yellow or brownish, very acrid, gum resin derived from the *Euphorbia resinifera* of Morocco and other African species was used medicinally as an emetic or cathartic. Also called *furbiyūn* or afarbiyūn in Arabic. Cf. Max Meyerhof, *Šarḥ Asmā al-ʿUqqār* (Explication of the Names of the Drugs, by Maimonides), in *Mémoires . . . Institute de l'Egypt*, vol. 41 (Cairo, 1940). *Turbid* (A., *turbidh* in Avicenna) is a purgative, cf. Sussmann Muntner, *Moshe ben Maimon Maimonides): The Book on Asthma* (Jerusalem, 1940), 142 and index.

26. *Shawqu* (probably A. *shawk* or *shawka*): thorn, thistle.

27. *Bazr qatūna* (A.; alternative form: *qutna*): cotton seed, *Plantago psyllium L.* See Alfred Siggel, *Arabisch-Deutsches Wörterbuch der Stoffe aus den drei Naturreichen* (Berlin, 1950), 20; Raphael Patai, *On Jewish Folklore* (Detroit, 1983), 347, 372.

28. *Tisiqa* (S. *tisica*): from the Latin *phthisica*, atrophy, asthma, pulmonary consumption.

29. *Melakhonia*: melancholy, the state of mind caused by the *melan-chole*, black bile, which our author terms *haSh'ḥora*, the black one.

30. *HaSh'ḥora haMuḥadit* (H.), the sharpened black, or acute melancholy.

31. *Fuagia*: I am unable to identify this term. Perhaps *phlegium*, cf. Dubler, *Materia media*, 3:III: 287; or a term derived from the Spanish *fuego*, fire.

32. *Peonia* (S.), peony. See Oskar von Hovorka and Adolf Kronfeld, *Vergleichende Volksmedizin*, 2 vols. (Stuttgart, 1908–1909), 1:186, 349.

33. *Toronjil* (S.): from the Arabic *taranjabil*, genet d'Espagne, waythorn, furze broom, genista, balm gentle, Melissa.

34. *Badrang buya* (P., *bardangbuya*): *Melissa officinalis*, mountain balm. Muntner, *Poisons*, 118. Also called *turunjān*; Meyerhof, *Šarḥ*, 22 n. 40, and note 33 above.

35. *Perforata*: perfoliate, St. John's wort, *Hypericum perforatum L.* Hovorka and Kronfeld, *Volksmedizin*, 1:228–30. The Spanish *perfoliata* means hare's ear, thoroughwort-wax, *Bupleurum rotundifolium*.

36. *Qorasonsolio* (S. *corazoncillo*): perforated St. John's wort, *Hypericum perforatum*.

37. *Adadores* (S. *aradores*): parasitic mites affecting animals and humans, and causing a skin disease characterized by scabby eruptions.

38. Word illegible. Perhaps *meha*ʿ*alim*, of the leaves.

39. *Muzaj*: probably Arabic *mazaj* or *mizj*, honey, bitter almond.

40. *M'nagdim* (H.): lit., opposed to.

41. *HaQadaḥat had'* (H.): quartan fever. Cf. Hovorka-Kronfeld, *Volksmedizin* 2:323–24.

42. *HaSh'ḥora* (H.): the black one, i.e., the black humor. See note 29 above.

43. *M'zagim* (H.): constitutions; lit., "mixtures."

44. *haQadaḥat haTmidit* (H.): perpetual fever. *De secr.*, ff. 51a–b list *tertiana febris, quotidiana febris, continuae febris* (this is our author's perpetual fever), and *febres pestilentiales* among the diseases which can be cured with the quinta essentia. To them are added in *De med.*, 369, the following types of fevers: *quartanae* (see n. 41 above), *acutae, pestiferae, sanguinaea, cholericae, phlegmaticae, melancholiae, venales, aestivales, autumnales,* and *hyemales.*

45. *Marqurial* (S. *mercurial*): all-good (a plant), mercury, *Mercurialis L.* Hovorka and Kronfeld, *Volksmedizin*, 1:69–70.

46. *Aduma w*ʿ*appusha* (H.): red and putrefied (fever). Perhaps redwater fever. No such fever is mentioned in the Lullian treatises. See note 13 above.

47. *HaMīṣ haNirpa'* (H.): the cured (?) juice or liquid.

48. *HaL'vana haM*ʿ*uppeshet* (H.): the white putrefied (fever), i.e., fever caused by the putrefied white humor or phelgm.

49. Cf. note 25 above.

50. Cf. note 26 above.

51. *Sirsam* (A. *sirsām*), which, according to Jār-Allah Zamakhsahri's *Lexicon Arabico Persicum* (Leipzig, 1850), means fever with headache and inflammation of the palate.

52. *Violas, boraja, lijunas* (S.): *viola* is violet; Muntner, *Poisons*, 97; Hovorka and Kronfeld, *Volksmedizin*, 1:403, 431–32. *Boraja* is the Spanish *borraja, borago L.*; *lijuna* is possibly the logania.

53. The next paragraph is inserted as a box in the top right corner of folio 157b of the manuscript. It is in Arabic, written in a different hand, in large Hebrew characters. It has been translated freely, since its syntax is extremely problematic.

54. *Darur* could be our author's transliteration of the Arabic *darūr*, meaning overflow or abundance, or of *dharūr*, powder, or an unusual form (plural?) of *dhurra*, a variety of sorghum. Or else it could stand for *darū*, mastic; Dubler, *Materia medica*, 3:55.

55. *M'shiḥat popilion* (H.-S.): popilion ointment. In modern Spanish *populeon* is a popular ointment prepared with pigs' butter, poppy leaves, belladonna, and other things, and used as a sedative. Its principal base consists of the first shoots of black poplar trees. Molinar, *Diccionario*, s.v. On the *papilonaceae* in folk medicine, see Hovorka and Kronfeld, *Volksmedizin* 1:350.

56. *Roda ganit* (S.-H.): garden rue, *ruta domestica. De secr.* ff. 19a, 38a; Hovorka and Kronfeld, *Volksmedizin*, 1:171, 356–58; Patai, *Jewish Folklore*, 347, 372.

57. *Mahut haDam* (H.): essence of the blood. See *De med.*, 341–42, which describes in detail how to produce essence out of human blood.

58. *L'shon haShor* (H.): ox tongue. In other medieval Hebrew medical works the term appears also in Aramaic as *l'shon tora* or *lishna tora*; in Arabic, *lisān al-thawr*. All these terms are translations of the Greek *buglosson*, cf. Latin *lingua bovis*. It is the *Picris echoides L.*, borage. See Immanuel Löw, *Die flora der Juden*, 4 vols. (Vienna, 1923–1924), 1:295, 299; 4:133, 170, 481; Siggel, *Wörterbuch*, 65; Patai, *Jewish Folklore*, 346.

59. The sentence in italics is in Spanish in Hebrew characters, and translates as "*agritas*, and if it is diluted with currant or with the syrup of it, it is much better." *Agritas* is the Spanish *agrito, Berberis vulgaris L.*; Molinar, *Diccionario*, s.v. *Ribas* is the Spanish *ribes*, currant, from the Arabic *rībās*, a kind of sorrel. *Jarope* is Spanish for syrup; Meyerhof, *Šarḥ*, 175, no. 350.

60. *Ṣabr suqutri* (A.), Socotrine aloe, *aloe socotrina* or *succotrina*, the resinous juice of the aloe from the island of Socotra, still sold under this name in the Cairo bazaar as a drastic and emmenagogue; Meyerhof, *Šarḥ* 158 no. 318.

61. See note 25 above.

62. *Gira pigra* (S. *gerapliega, hierapicra*): a cathartic powder made of aloes and canella bark. Muntner, *Asthma*, 139; idem, *Poisons*, 143.

63. *Lilio* (L. *lilium*): lily.

64. *Qapili veneris* (L.): Venus hair, *Adiantum capillus Veneris L.*

65. *Qevat ha'Egel* (H.): calf's stomach. I am unable to identify this disease.

66. *Ḥoli haQeveṣ* (H.): the disease of spasms; *De secr.* f. 53a: *vera cura spasmi.*

67. "Experimenters" seems to refer to alchemists who engage in medical experiments.

68. *Flamula*, see *De secr.*, ff. 37b, 53a.

69. *Agramonia* (L. *argemonia-agremonia*): agrimony, cocklebur; Hovorka and Kronfeld, *Volksmedizin*, 1:120, 328.

70. *Eshskhe haShuʿal* (H.): fox testicles. In other medieval Hebrew medical sources also called "fox eggs." According to Löw, *Flora*, 1:27, 652; 2:296, it is the *Kynos orchis*, a member of the *orchidaceae* family; according to Ben Yehuda, *Thesaurus*. s.v. *eshekh*, it is the *Satyrum album*.

71. *Asukar* (S. *azucar*): sugar.

72. *Shiqquy* (H.): dropsy.

73. *HaEsh haParsi* (H.): translation of Spanish *fuego Persico*, Persian fire, and alternative name for *herpes zona*, a cutaneous eruption. Molinar, *Diccionario*, s.v.

74. See note 60 above.

75. *Pinpinela* (S. *pimpinela*): burnet, a roseaceous plant. Hovorka and Kronfeld, *Volksmedizin*, 1:32, 66; 2:312.

76. *Perisil*, elsewhere spelled *pirosil* (S. *peresil*): parsley. Ibid., 1:33, 170, 349; Patai, *Jewish Folklore* 372.

77. *Maṣṭaki*, (A. *maṣṭaka*): mastic; the reference probably is to the mastic thistle, *Carlina gummifera*. Siggel, *Wörterbuch*, 68; Meyerhof, *Šarḥ*, 115, no. 232.

78. *Resentor*: an alchemical vessel; cf. Gino Testi, *Dizionario di alchimia* (Rome, 1950), 153: *restentorio*, a vessel for collecting the product of distillation.

79. *Neteq* (H.): scab, scabies, perhaps *tinea tonsurans*, or *herpes tonsurans*.

80. See note 23 above, and *De secr.* f. 46a on the cure of paralysis.

81. *Golondrinos* (S.): swallows.

82. *Qastorio* (S. *castoreo*, from L. *castoreum*, G. *kastorion*): A strong-smelling oily substance obtained from the sexual glands of the beaver, used as a stimulant in medicine, and in making perfumes. *De secr.*, f. 19a.

83. *Qashni* (A.): *galbanum*, a bitter, bad-smelling Asiatic gum resin used in medicine. Our author is in error in identifying *castoreum* with *galbanum*.

84. Word illegible.

85. *Avhal* (A. *abhal* or *abhul*): savin, *Juniperus sabina*, a Eurasian evergreen, with small berries. Its bitter, acrid tops were used in medicine for gout and amenorrhoea, and as an abortifacient. Siggel, *Wörterbuch*, 11; Meyerhof, *Šarḥ*, 14, no. 22.

86. *Akheronto* (perhaps S. *agerato*): sweet milfoil or maudlin, *Achilles ageratum*.

87. *Falij* (A. *fālij*): half paralysis, hemiplegia. Munter, *Asthma*, 137.

88. See note 19 above.

89. See note 60 above.

90. *Niqras* (H.): gout. Ben Yehuda, *Thesaurus*, s.v., lists several medicines for gout from medieval Hebrew medical authors. According to Muntner, *Asthma*, 114, *niqras* is podagra.

91. *Nolimitanjero*, i.e., *noli me tangere*, touch me not. This was the name of several skin diseases characterized by ulcers. In the Spanish usage it means a malignant ulcer on the face or the nose.

92. See note 79 above.

93. See note 76 above.

94. *Qanila* (S. *canela*): The inner bark of certain tropical trees, still used as a spice and a tonic. Patai, *Jewish Folklore*, 348.

95. *Artemisa* (S.): mugwort or wormwood. Hovorka and Kronfeld, *Volksmedizin*, 1:104–5.

96. *Polio* (L. *polium* or *polion*): perhaps the poley-germander. *De secr.*, ff. 18a, 36a, 37b.

97. See note 76 above.

98. *Papaver* (S.): poppy. Hovorka and Kronfeld, *Volksmedizin*, 1:209–11, 235.

99. See note 82 above.

100. See note 87 above.

101. *Salvia* (S.): sage, a plant of the mint family. Hovorka and Kronfeld, *Volksmedizin*, 1:171, 370–71; Patai, *Jewish Folklore*, 344, 346.

102. See note 96 above.

103. Approximate quotation from Prov. 17:22, which reads, "A merry heart improves the tonic."

104. *Al-buṭm* (A.): terebinth. "Water of the terebinth" is turpentine. See note 109 below. Also called *maṣṭaka*, mastic, see note 77 above. Meyerhof, *Šarḥ*, 36, no. 66.

105. *Ḥub al-qadhra* (A. *ḥubbat al-khadhrā*): fruit of the terebinth.

106. See note 82 above.

107. *Qanavos* (a mishnaic term): hemp. From the Greek *kannabos* or *kannabis.*

108. *Perselia*, probably a misspelling for *perlesia*, see note 23 above.

109. *Tarmintina* (S. *trementina*): turpentine. Hovorka and Kronfeld, *Volksmedizin*, 1:172; 2:29, 75.

110. *Aqwa vita* (L. *aqua vitae*): In alchemy it usually means alcohol.

111. *ʿAnd hindi*: Indian *ʿand*. I am unable to identify *ʿand.*

112. *Ṣandal* (A.): sandalwood. Spanish *sandalo.*

113. *Ṣemeg* (A. *ṣamgh*): gum. "Arab *ṣamgh*" is gum arabic; *ṣamgh al-buṭm* is the resin of the terebinth. Meyerhof, *Sarh.*, 159, no. 320.

114. *Juz bawwa* (A.): nutmeg.

115. *Kolanjan* (A. *khalanjān):*, *Alpinia galanga*, or *Maranta galanga. De secr.*, f. 19a.

116. *Kababa* (A. *kubāba* or *kabbāba*): cubeb, *Piper cubeba Tr. De secr.*, ff. 34a, 36a. Cf. Siggel, *Wörterbuch*, 62; Meyerhof, *Šarḥ*, 159, no. 320.

117. See note 77 above.

118. *Qaranfal* (A. *qaranful*): cloves. Patai, *Jewish Folklore*, 348.

119. *Sanbal* (A. *sunbul*): nard. Löw, *Flora*, 3:62, 395; Muntner, *Poisons*, 108; Meyerhof, *Šarḥ*, 129, no. 265.

120. *Barosnat*, cf. modern S. *barroso*: pimpled, full of pimples, *barros.*

121. *Nujmi tanjir: nujm* in A. is star; "Tangier star" evidently refers to a carbuncle-like boil on the face.

122. The words "mentioned above" indicate that our author considered *nujmi tanjir* an alternative designation for *barosnat*, cf. note 120 above.

123. Word illegible.

124. See note 45 above.

125. *Sukar qandero*: from the A. *sukkar qandī*, candy sugar, with the Spanish suffix *-ero*. Meyerhof, *Šarḥ*, 141, no. 289.

126. See note 82 above.

127. *Raubarbaro* (medieval L. *rheubarbarum*, modern S. *ruibarbo*): rhubarb. Muntner, *Asthma*, 98 (32), lines 8–9.

128. *Rubia* (S.): rhubarb, madder, a root used in medicines and dyes.

129. See note 76 above.

130. *Parro*, perhaps from Spanish *parron* or *parra*, wild wine.

131. See note 90 above.

132. See note 75 above.

133. *Qataras* (S. *catarata*): cataract.

134. *Romero* (S.): rosemary, *Rosemarius officinalis*, an evergreen shrub of the mint family, with a warm, pungent, bitterish taste, used in cookery, perfumes, etc.

135. *Ṭiṭ haḥokhma* (H.): clay of wisdom, the Hebrew name of philosophers' clay.

136. *Ṭirpola* (Skt. *triphala*): having three fruits, namely, the three myrobalans, *Terminalia chebula, T. bellerica*, and *Phyllantus emblica*. Monier Monier-Williams, *A Sanskrit-English Dictionary* (1899; reprint Delhi, 1974) 459; Alex Wayman, "Notes on Three Myrobalans," *Phi Theta Annual* 5 (Berkeley, 1954–1955): 63–77; Bhagwan Dash, "The Drug *Terminalia Chebula* in Ayurveda and Tibetan Medical Literature," *Kailash: A Journal of Himalayan Studies* 4 (1976): 5–20. Our author evidently mixed up the meaning of the two terms *tirpola (triphala)* and *ṭirqoṭa* (see n. 138 below), and attached the explanation of the first to the second, and vice versa.

137. *Zangavil* (A. *zanjabil*): ginger, or juniper berry.

138. *Ṭirqoṭa* (Skt. *trīkaṭu*): the three spices (black pepper, long pepper, and dry ginger). Monier-Williams, *Dictionary*, 458. The three kinds of pepper, *Piper longum, P. album, P. nigrum*, were part of the classical theriac Muntner, *Asthma*, 137.

139. *Mirabulanes* (S. *mirabolano*): myrobalan, a dried, astringent, prunelike fruit of India. Raymond Lull, *Secreta secretorum* (Cologne, 1592), 26, lists *mirabolani conditi* among the medicines. Cf. Muntner, *Asthma*, 132, and note 117 above.

140. *Amlaj* (A.): brownish. Our author refers to the *Myrobalan amilegum*. Cf. Muntner, *Asthma*, 132.

141. *Tangargayad* (Skt. *ṭankaṇa*), borax.

142. *Atinkar* (S. *atincar*): borax. Martin Ruland, *Lexicon alchimiae sive dictionarium alchemisticum* (Frankfurt-am-Main, 1612), 132: *Atincar, atinkar, id est borax de petra, baurach, boras, Burress von Felsen.*

143. *Ras* (Skt. *rāsa*): quicksilver. Monier-Williams, *Dictionary*, 869.

144. *Zibaq* or *zaibaq* (P. and A. *zi'baq*): quicksilver. Cf. Meyerhof, *Šarḥ*, 68, no. 139.

145. *Bis*, perhaps Skt. *bisa*, lotus plant, *Napellus moysis*. Cf. Adolf Wahrmund, *Handwörterbuch der arabischen und deutschen Sprache*, 2 vols. (Giessen, 1877), s.v.

146. *Gndek* (thus vocalized in the manuscript), (Skt. *gandhaka*): sulphur. Monier-Williams, *Dictionary*, 345.

147. *Arhertal* (Skt. *haritāla*): yellow orpiment or sulphuret of arsenic. Monier-Williams, *Dictionary*, 1291. Hindi *hartal*, arsenic: cf. C. Bulcke, *An English-Hindi Dictionary* (Ranchi, Bihar, 1968), 40.

148. *Zarnikh* (A.): arsenic. Siggel, *Wörterbuch*, 81.

149. *Apsantin* (G. *apsinthion*): wormwood. *De secr.* f. 36a; Muntner, *Asthma*, 131.

150. *Dār* (A.): house; here meaning pod.

151. *Darsini* (A. *dār ṣīnī*): cinnamon bark, canella of China, *Cinnamonum ceylanicum* or *aromatum*. Maimonides translates the Hebrew *qinnamon* as *dār ṣīnī*. Cf. Muntner, *Poisons*, 109 (with additional references to other medieval Hebrew sources on cinnamon—*dār ṣīnī*). Cf. Siggel, *Wörterbuch*, 34; Meyerhof, *Šarḥ*, 50, no. 95; Löw, *Flora*, 2:106.

152. See note 114 above.

153. See note 137 above.

154. *Zafran* (A. *zaʿfarān*): saffron. Meyerhof, *Šarḥ*, 66, no. 135; Patai, *Jewish Folklore*, 347, 372.

155. *Mesekh* (A. *misk*): musk. Siggel, *Wörterbuch*, 68; Patai, *Jewish Folkore*, 347.

156. *Jarīs* (A.): groat.

157. *Ḥukaro* (reading uncertain). *Jucaro* is the Spanish term for *Terminalia hilariana*, and *T. bucera*, a tree whose fruit resembles the olive. Molinar, *Diccionario*, s.v.

158. *Farazjat* (P. *farzaja*): suppository, clyster.

159. "Let the woman suffer": the *pónos*, suffering, of the patient was part of the Hippocratic therapy.

160. *Teriaq faruq* (A. *tiryāq fārūq*): special (?) theriac. On the various kinds of theriac, see Muntner, *Poisons*, Index, s.v. teriaqim. See also Hovorka and Kronfeld, *Volksmedizin*, 1:413; 2:312.

CHAPTER FIFTEEN
FLAMEL'S JEWISH MASTERS

1. Robert Halleux, "Le myth de Nicolas Flamel ou les mécanismes de la pseudepigraphie alchimique," in *Archives internationales d'histoire des sciences* (Rome) 33 (1983): 234–45. In the first group Halleux lists thirteen, in the second nine, books or studies. Another two dozen or so books on Flamel are quoted by Jacques Van Lennep, *Alchimie: Contribution à l'histoire de l'art alchimique* (Brussels, 1984), 256–62. English-language studies about Flamel, including Arthur Edward Waite's important analysis of Flamel in his *The Secret Tradition in Alchemy* (London and New York, 1926), 137ff., are overlooked by the aforementioned two scholars.

2. This book was subsequently reprinted many times from the seventeenth to the twentieth centuries, and translated into English and German. See Van Lennep, *Alchimie*, 256–57 n. 88.

3. Preface by Elie-Charles Flamand to Nicolas Flamel, *Oeuvres* (Paris, 1973), 45–58.

4. The carelessness that characterizes many authors writing about alchemy can be illustrated by this passage. The French original has *une verge et des ser-*

pents s'engloutissants, which I translated here literally. Waite, *The Secret Tradition*, 139, translates: "a virgin who was being swallowed up by serpents." F. Sherwood Taylor, *The Alchemists: Founders of Modern Chemistry* (New York, 1949), 164, following "a translation made in 1624" (that of Eirenaeus Orandus, London) writes, "a Virgin, and serpents swallowing her up."

5. Other manuscripts are: Bibliothèque Nationale, Paris, MS Français 22157 (Nouvelle Acquisition), ff. 256r–271r; Bibliothèque de l'Arsenal, Paris, MS 3012 (157 S.A.F.) dated from 1756; Bibliothèque Mazarine, Paris, MS 3680, no. 7, dating from the 17th century; etc.

6. *Voyage du sieur Paul Lucas au Levant*, 2 vols. (Paris, 1704); *Voyage du sieur Paul Lucas fait par ordre du Roy, dans la Grece, l'Asie Mineure, la Macedonie at l'Afrique* (Paris, 1712); *Troisième voyage de sieur Paul Lucas fait en MDCCXIV, etc. par ordre de Louis XIV dans la Turquie, l'Asie, la Sourie, la Palestine, la Haute et la Basse Egypt, etc.*, 3 vols. (Rouen, 1719).

7. This claim was often made by dervishes or on their behalf. For example, when Arminius Vámbéry (1832–1913), the famous Hungarian Jewish traveler and Orientalist, stayed in a Persian village disguised as a dervish, the villagers believed that his mystical powers enabled him to speak all the languages of the world. My relative Bernát Munkácsi (1860–1937), who was a student of Vámbéry, told me this in the master's name.

8. Note in the original: *Un ocque pese 3. livres* (one *ocque* weighs three pounds). The *ocque* or *oque* was a unit of weight used in Turkey, Greece, and elsewhere in the Orient. It corresponded to about 1 kilogram, but varied from place to place.

9. Paul Lucas, *Voyages* (1712), 1:98–112.

Chapter Sixteen
Two Spanish-Jewish Court Alchemists

1. Text printed in *Bolletin de la Societat Arqueologica Luliana*, Palma (de Majorca), January 1914, 6. David Romano in his article "*Trumata shel Yahadut Sfarad laMadaʿim*, in Hayyim Beinart, ed., *Moreshet Sfarad* (Jerusalem, 1992), 204, misunderstood the text of the indictment, which charges Menahem with being "a great experimenter and necromancer," and interprets these words as being Menahem's "title" (*to'ar*).

2. Fritz Baer, *Die Juden im Christlichen Spanien*, 1 (Berlin, 1929), 310–11.

3. Geronymo Çurita (Zurita) Chronista, *Los Cinco Libros Postreros de la Primera Parte de los anales de la Corona de Aragon*, 2 (Saragossa, 1610), 389a. See also *Indice de las cosas mas notables . . .* (Aragon, 1621), 532, which states that "Menahẽ Iudio fue Maestro del Rey don Pedro Quarto en la Astrologia," and also see p. 615. José Amador de los Rios, in his *Historia Social, Politica y Religiosa de los Judios de España y Portugal*, 2 (Madrid, 1876), 299, basing himself on Zurita, enlarges somewhat on the subject and says that King Pedro "showed deference to his Jewish physicians, and especially to Don Rabbi Menahem, whose disciple he declared himself to be," and that the king found in his physician Don Menahem a master in astrology and alchemy.

4. Pierre Vidal, "Les Juifs des anciens comté de Roussillon et de Cerdagne," *Revue des Études Juives* 15 (1887): 53.

5. Baer, *De Juden*, 1:452.

6. Antoni Rubio y Lluch, *Documents per l'Historia de la Cultura Catalana Mig-eval*, 1 (Barcelona, 1908), 319.

7. Ibid., 2 (1921), 346–47. I thank Joseph Salemi for translating this document.

Chapter Seventeen
Abraham Eleazar

1. In Hebrew letters.

2. The letters I. N. J. CXI stand for "in nomine Jesu Christi." They were undoubtedly added by Gervasius.

3. Johan Friedrich Gmelin, *Geschichte der Chemie*, 3 vols. (Göttingen, 1797–1799), 1:64.

4. See Julius F. Ruska, *Tabula smaragdina: Ein Beitrag zur Geschichte der hermetischen Literatur* (Heidelberg, 1926).

5. Hermann Kopp, *Die Alchemie in älterer und neuerer Zeit* (Heidelberg, 1886) 2:314–17.

6. Moritz Steinschneider, "Pseudo-Juden und zweifelhafte Autoren," *Monatschrift für Geschichte und Wissenschaft des Judentums* 38 (1894): 41.

7. John Ferguson, *Bibliotheca chemica* (Glasgow, 1906), 1:3.

8. C. G. Jung, *Mysterium conjunctionis*, Collected Works, vol. 14, Bollingen Series XX (2nd ed., Princeton, 1960), pars. 591, 597 note. An interesting addition to the bibliographic history of Abraham Eleazar's book is supplied by Dennis I. Duveen, who had a copy of it which was supplemented by a 12 ½ page manuscript vocabulary (in German) with this title: "German Key of those foreign words which are found in these books but are partly not explained in their registers, but which are contained in the Book of Zoroastro the Jew and Rabbi." Dennis I. Duveen, *Bibliotheca alchemica et chemica* (London, 1949), 2.

9. Actually Matthew 27:25.

10. Actually *Ant.* 1:2:2: "invented the art of making brass."

11. I am at a loss to explain this quotation. However, it could be a very corrupt transliteration of the Hebrew phrase found in Isaiah 60:16, which reads in the original: *kī anī Adonai moshī*ʿ*ēkh v'go'alēkh*—"that I am the Lord, thy Savior and thy Redeemer." These words are followed in v. 17 by the promise of "bringing gold for brass, silver for iron," etc., which was given alchemical interpretation by medieval and later alchemists.

12. See above, Chapter 15.

13. I. N. U. [J.] C. XI, again "In nomine Jesu Christ," added by Gervasius.

14. AZOTH is explained in the vocabulary appended to the second book of the *Werck* as "a running fire, *Mercurius animatus*" (animated mercury) or "*M. philosophorum*" (mercury of the philosophers). HYLĒ (written here in Greek letters) is explained as "a confused mixture." The Hebrew word, SHAMAYIM, heaven, is written in Hebrew characters but vocalized incorrectly.

15. The explanations I put in square brackets after the technical terms appearing in the text are taken from the vocabularies appended to Books I and II of the *Werck*.

16. Alchemical symbols like this one appear frequently in the *Werck*, as well as in many medieval and later alchemical treatises. They could have been added by the translator or by Gervasius. I added their meanings in square brackets.

17. Cf. Berthelot, *Grecs*, 1:11, 17, on "the eye of Python," and "the serpent Python."

18. On the libel of well-poisoning, the torture of Jews to extract admission of guilt, etc., see *EJ* (J), 2, s.v. "Black Death."

19. Preface by Elie-Charles Flamand to Nicholas Flamel, *Oeuvres* (Paris, 1973) 45–46. See above, Chapter 15. The idea that sacred texts were originally inscribed on metal tablets recurs in the Mormon belief that the *Book of Mormon* came down inscribed on gold tablets. Important documents were in fact inscribed on metal tablets and preserved in stone or marble boxes in Mesopotamia, Egypt, etc. H. Curtis Wright, "Ancient Burials of Metal Documents in Stone Boxes," in John M. Lundquist and Stephen D. Ricks, eds., *By Study and Also by Faith* (Salt Lake City, 1990), 2:273 ff. I am indebted to Dr. Lundquist, head of the Oriental Division of the New York Public Library, for this reference.

20. I wish to thank Louis H. Feldman of Yeshiva University for providing the translation of this and the subsequent four Latin passages.

21. Italicized passages are in Latin.

22. This Hebrew sentence contains two printer's errors which I put in parentheses and corrected in square brackets. Its precise translation is: "All medicine, without God's help, is of no use, and causes death." This seems to have been the Aramaic passage that Gustave Weil found to be erroneous.

23. See above, Chapter 15 at n. 3.

Chapter Eighteen
Themo Judaei

1. Pierre Duhem, *Études sur Léonard de Vinci.* 1st ser. (Paris, 1906), 164.

2. Ibid., 164–65, and sources there.

3. Ibid., 163–70.

4. Henri Huggonard-Roche, *L'Oeuvre astronomique de Themon Juif, maitre parisien du XIVe siècle* (Geneva and Paris, 1973) 13, 18, 22.

5. Johann Christoph Wolf, *Bibliotheca Hebraica*, 4 vols. (Hamburg, 1715–1733), 1:1257, No. 2,223.

6. Duhem, *Études*, 171ff.

7. Huggonard-Roche, *L'Oeuvre astronomique*, 13, 18, 22.

8. Folios 155b–213b in the 1516 edition, and folios 155b–214b in that of 1518. The book also contains treatises by Albertus of Saxonia and Johannes Buridanus.

9. Ibid., 203b (1516) or 202b (1518). The phrase about the potters, referring to professional jealousy, is found in Aristotle, *Politics*, 1312b 5, and in Hesiod, *Works and Days* 25. I am indebted to James W. Halporn of Indiana University for these references and for transcribing the difficult Latin print of the original text, and to Edward Grant of Indiana University for translating the above passage.

Introduction to Part Six
The Fifteenth Century

1. Cf. Fritz Baer, *Die Juden im christlichen Spanien* (Berlin, 1936), 515, quoting Archivo Historico Nacional, Inq. To., leg. 164, no. 530. Rendered in a free English translation in Yitzhak Baer, *A History of the Jews in Christian Spain* (Philadelphia, 1971), 351–52. I wish to thank Mrs. Joseph Adler for translating this passage from the Spanish.

Chapter Nineteen
Simeon ben Ṣemaḥ Duran

1. The text has *m'vaṭel* (annuls), which seems to be a printer's error for *m'vashel* (ripens).
2. C. Simeon ben Ṣemaḥ Duran, *Magen Avot* (Leghorn, 1785), 10a.
3. I discussed this stone in my book *Adam va'Adamah* (Jerusalem, 1943), 2:28–32.
4. Julius Ruska, *Das Steinbuch des Aristoteles* (Heidelberg, 1912).

Chapter Twenty
Solomon Trismosin and His Jewish Master

1. Paris, 1613. The book was actually on the market before the end of 1612: the copy in the Bibliothèque Nationale, Paris, is inscribed with a dedication dated Paris, 25 November 1612. A German manuscript of this book, entitled *Splendor solis* (Splendor of the Sun) and dated 1582, is found in the British Library (Harley MS 3469). Its text is largely identical with that of the Rorschach 1598–1599 edition. See John Reed, *Prelude to Chemistry: An Outline of Alchemy, Its Literature and Relationship* (Cambridge, Mass., 1966), 67ff.
2. *Aureum vellus* (Rorschach am Bodensee, 1598–1599), 4.
3. *Allgemeine Deutsche Biographie* (Leipzig, 1894); reprint Berlin, 1971), 38:625
4. Ibid., quoting Hermann Kopp, *Geschichte der Chemie*, 4 vols. (Braunschweig, 1843–1848), 2:179, 228; idem, *Die Alchemie in älterer und neuerer Zeit* (Heidelberg, 1886), 1:98, 242; 2:229; idem, *Beiträge zur Geschichte der Chemie* (Braunschweig, 1869), 1:12.

Chapter Twenty-one
Abraham ben Simeon's *Cabala Mystica*

1. Paul Lacroix, *Sciences et lettres au moyen age et à l'époque de la Renaissance*, (Paris, 1877).
2. I am indebted for this comment to Professor Gerald Strauss.
3. The above summary is based primarily on the untitled Hebrew manuscript in Oxford. I wish to thank the Bodleian Library for its permission to publish excerpts in my English translation.

4. I wish to thank the Bibliothèque Nationale for its permission to publish excerpts from the manuscript in my English translation.

5. Johann Christoph Wolf, *Bibliotheca Hebraica*, vol. 4 (Hamburg, 1733), 757–59. Adolf Neubauer, *Catalogi cod. MSS. Bibliothecae Bodleianae*, pars XII (Oxford, 1886–1906), no. 2051.

6. Moritz Steinschneider, *Die hebräischen Übersetzungen des Mittelalters und die Juden als Dolmetscher* (Berlin, 1893; reprint Graz, 1956), 381–82, 850.

7. Gershom Scholem, *Kabbala: Quellen und Forschungen zur Geschichte der jüdischen Mystik* (Leipzig, 1927), 2:2 n. 8.

8. Gershom Scholem, "Abraham ben Simeon of Worms," in *EJ* (J), 2:156.

9. Gershom Scholem, "Farben und ihre Symbolik in der jüdischen Überlieferung und Mystik," in *Eranos Jahrbuch*, 41 (Leiden, 1974), 1–49.

10. The Hebrew manuscript has not yet been published. The French was published by Robert Ambelain under the title *La magie sacrée d'Abramelin le mage* (no place, no date) under the auspices of the Kabbalistic Order of the Rosicrucians. The text as printed is somewhat different from that of the manuscript in phrases, expressions etc., and the spelling has been modernized. As for the German manuscript, a few pages of it (part of book one, chapter eight) have been published by Wolf in his *Bibliotheca Hebraica*, see note 5 above. A version rather different from the German manuscript was published in Cologne by Peter Hammer in 1725. That edition seems to be unavailable, but it was reprinted about 1900, without stating that it is a reprint, and a microfilm of this edition, entitled *Die egyptischen grossen offenbarungen* . . . was kindly put at my disposal by the Munich Bayerische Staatsbibliothek. Another German edition was published by Johann Richard Beecken, entitled *Die heilige Magie des Abramelin: Die Überlieferung des Abraham von Worms* (Berlin, 1957). An English translation was published by S. L. MacGregor-Mathers under the title *The Book of the Sacred Magic of Abra-Melin the Mage, as delivered by Abraham the Jew unto his son Lamech, A. D. 1458* (London, 1898). In none of these printed versions, except for the fragment published by Wolf in 1733, did I find anything useful for my search for the original version of Abraham's book.

11. Hermann Gollancz, *Sepher Mafteaḥ Shelomo* (Oxford, 1914).

12. See above, note 10.

13. The above overview of Abraham's references to popes and princes is based on Gerald Strauss's analysis of the text. Private communication February 23, 1991.

Chapter Twenty-two
Isaac Hollandus and His Son John Isaac

1. Cf. *Fegfeuer der Chymisten* . . . (Amsterdam, 1702), no. 31.

2. Karl Christoph Schmieder, *Geschichte der Alchemie* (Halle, 1832), 210.

3. E. O. von Lippmann, *Entstehung und Ausbreitung der Alchemie*, vol. 2 (Berlin, 1931).

4. Schmieder, *Geschichte*, 211, quoting Torbern Olof Bergman, *Historia chemiae medii aevi* (History of Medieval Chemistry) (Uppsala, 1782), 112.

5. Schmieder, *Geschichte* 211.
6. Nurnburg, 1676.
7. Published in Latin in Middelburg, the Netherlands, in 1600.
8. In addition to those mentioned above, the following works are attributed to the Hollanduses: To Isaac Hollandus: *Opera vegetabilia* (Vegetable Operations), in Latin (Amsterdam, 1659), elucidations of *Opera mineralia*; *De salibus et oleis metallorum* (On the Salts and Oils of the Metals), in Latin (no place, 1604); *Secreta revelatio operationis manualis pro universali opere et lapide sapientium, sicut filio suo Joanni Isaaco Hollando e Flandria paterno animo fidelissimo manu traduit* (The Secret Revelation of the Manual Operation for the Whole Work and the Philosophers' Stone, as He Transmitted it to His Son John Isaac Hollandus of Flanders with the Strongest Feelings of Paternal Fidelity), listed in the *Bibliotheca chemica* of Giovanni Aefonso Borelli (1608–1679).

To John Isaac Hollandus: *De urina* (On the Urine), included in the *Theatrum chemicum*, vol. 6 (Argentorati [Strasbourg], 1661), no. 204, pp. 566–68; *De lapide seu elixir philosophico* (On the Philosophical Stone or Elixir), in German (Frankfurt, 1669); *Manus philosophorum cum signaturis* (The Handwriting of the Philosophers with Their Signs), published in German together with the *Opus Saturni* (Frankfurt, 1667); *Rariores operationes chymiae* (The More Remarkable Chemical Operations), published in German in *Cureusen und raren chymischen operationen* (Leipzig and Gardeleben, 1714); *Fragmenta chemica de opere philosophico* (Chemical Fragments of the Philosophical Work), in Latin, *Theatrum chemicum* (Ursel, 1602), vol. 2, no. 33.

Chapter Twenty-Three
Johanan Alemanno and Joseph Albo

1. Paris MS 849. See *Kiryat Sefer* 5 (1929): 273–77.
2. *Sefer Sha*ʿ*ar haḤesheq* (Livorno, 1790), 29a.
3. Ibid., 55b–56a.
4. Ibid., 36a.
5. Ibid., 36a–37a.
6. Joseph Albo, *Sefer ha*ʿ*Iqqarim* (Book of Principles) (Rimino, Italy, 1522), unpaginated. The passage translated above is found in the first treatise, chapter eight. My translation from the Hebrew.

Chapter Twenty-Four
Pseudo-Maimonides

1. The *Guide of the Perplexed* has been published in the Arabic original, in three Hebrew translations, and in all the major European languages.
2. MS 14; the Bavarian State Library kindly put a photocopy of the manuscript at my disposal.
3. I was able to examine the Moscow manuscript, folios 87a–91b of MS Guenzburg 315 in the Moscow Lenin State Library, thanks to the courtesy of Benjamin Richler of the Jerusalem Institute of Microfilmed Hebrew Manuscripts, who kindly put a photocopy of it at my disposal. As soon as I started

deciphering it, it became evident that it was only another version of Munich MS 14 discussed above. Some parts contained in the latter are missing in it, but it is richer than the Munich manuscript by several pages of text.

4. I was also able to consult this manuscript thanks to the courtesy of Benjamin Richler.

5. MS Gaster 1435.

Chapter Twenty-Five
Three Kuzari Commentators

1. Bodleian Library, Opp. Add. 114; Moritz Steinschneider, *Hebräische Bibliographie*, vol. 16 (1876; reprint New York, 1972), 127.

2. Moritz Steinschneider, *Die hebräischen Übersetzungen des Mittelalters und die Juden als Dolmetscher* (Berlin, 1893; reprint Graz, 1956), 404, 427.

3. Steinschneider also refers to Encykl. Cod. Ascher 11 = Cod. Munich Bl. 63b. Cf. his "Alfarabi (Alpharabius) des arabischen Philosophen Leben und Schriften," in *Memoires de l'Academie Imperiale de St.-Petersbourg*, 7th Series, Vol. 13, No. 4 (1869), 244–45.

4. Ibid., 245.

5. Printed in Venice, 1589.

6. Printed in Venice, 1594.

7. Judah Halevi, *Sefer haKuzari*, with the commentary of Judah Moscato (Venice, 1594), 160a.

8. Ibid., f. 184a.

Chapter Twenty-Six
Esh M'ṣaref: A Kabbalistic-Alchemical Treatise

1. Cf. Gershom Scholem, in *EJ* (J), s.v. Knorr von Rosenroth. According to him the lost original of *Esh M'ṣaref* was written in Hebrew.

2. In my translation, I substituted the customary English forms of biblical names for the German given in *Kabbala denudata*. In 1714 a somewhat flawed English translation of its sections quoting *Esh M'ṣaref* was printed by a "Lover of Philalethes," which, in turn, was reprinted in 1894 by the Theosophical Publishing Society of London, with a preface, notes, and explanation by "Sapere Aude." Another, rather inaccurate, translation was edited by W. W. Westcott, and reprinted in 1991 by Sure Fire Press in Edmonds, Wa.

3. Cf. Louis Ginzberg, *The Legends of the Jews*, 7 vols. (Philadelphia, 1909–1938), 7, Index, s.v. Elisha. See Chapter 2, above.

4. In his chapter 6 the author explains that Naaman stands for "the matter of metallic medicine which must be purified seven times."

5. For an explanation of the exegetical method called gematria, see above, Chapter 12.

6. This saying is not found in B. Bab. Qam. 71b.

7. Cf. B. Bab. Bath. 25b: "R. Yiṣḥaq said: 'He who wants to be wise should turn to the south (Rashi adds, "while praying"); he who wants to be rich should turn to the north.' "

8. Here the author of *Esh M'ṣaref* anticipates G. Scholem by some four centuries in explaining the term *zᶜir anpin* as "Impatient One." Scholem seems to have been unaware of this: see his *Major Trends in Jewish Mysticism* (New York, 1961), 270.

9. The ten sefirot are often represented in the shape of a human body.

10. *Argentum vivum* in Latin, *kesef ḥay* in Hebrew.

11. To address one's treatise to one's son was a widespread literary convention.

12. Translation of the Hebrew *ani haqaṭan.*

13. The passage quoted is found in the *Zohar*, 3:299a in the standard editions.

14. Here our text omits some 17 lines of the zoharic passage.

15. Here again five lines of the *Zohar* are omitted.

16. End of quote from the *Zohar.*

17. Camea (H. *q'meᶜa*, amulet). Here and in the following the word is used in the sense of a magic square of numbers. Our author assigns a camea to each of the metals.

18. The letter *vav*, the sixth letter of the alphabet, stands for the number six.

19. By lesser or minor number is meant the sum of the digits comprised in a number. Thus the lesser number of 216 (2+1+6) is 9.

20. *Raᶜya Mehemna* (Aramaic, The Faithful Shepherd) is a part of the *Zohar.*

21. Our author frequently quotes Moses Cordovero (1522–1570), a leading Safed Kabbalist, whose major work is *Pardes Rimmonim* (H., The Pomegranate Orchard). Hence the *Esh M'ṣaref* could not have been written prior to the second half of the sixteenth century.

22. It is possible that this Mordecai was identical with the son of Leon de Modena of the same name, who attempted to transmute lead into silver, and died as a result of his experiments; see Chapter 32 below. If so, the *Esh M'ṣaref* could not have been written before the early seventeenth century.

23. The term can also mean orpiment, auripigment, or corrosive sublimate.

24. The aforementioned R. Mordecai.

25. The reference is probably to the most famous Arab alchemist, Jābir ibn Ḥayyān.

26. There follows a detailed alchemical explanation of Daniel's vision of the beast.

27. Water, *aqua*, has the feminine gender in Latin.

28. Sapere Aude in his English translation remarks here that "This is the true magic square of Jupiter."

29. Actually the Hebrew word *dal* means poor.

30. The reference is to the letter *yod* in the tetragrammaton YHWH, which the Kabbalists interpreted as representing Ḥokhma, Wisdom. See Raphael Patai, *The Hebrew Goddess* (Detroit, 1990), 116.

31. One way of calculating the numerical value of a word is to count the word itself as one, and add to it the sum total of the value of its letters. Thus the word ANKh (*anokh*) obtains the value of 72: the word (1)+aleph (1)+*nun* (50)+*kaph* (20)=72.

32. I am at a loss as to the meaning of this sentence.

33. Again, meaning unclear.

34. Reference to Prov. 10:25, "The righteous is an everlasting foundation."

35. On the Green Lion in alchemy, see Betty Jo Dobbs, *The Hunting of the Green Lion* (Cambridge, 1975).

36. There is perhaps a faint echo here of Philo's distinction of two natures in the deity, one gentle and beneficent, the other sovereign and chastising, and of the rabbis' concept of the two thrones of God, one of mercy and one of judgment. Cf. Patai, *The Hebrew Goddess*, 76, 78.

37. The notion that the river Jordan flows out of the Dead Sea and into the Red Sea is talmudic.

38. I.e., alchemists, who held themselves to be masters of the Great Art.

39. This is one of the Aramaic forms of the word *z'khuta*.

40. Correctly *isfdikha*, white lead; cf. Arabic *isfidāj*.

41. The Targum translates the words "the daughter of Me-Zahav" as "the daughter of a (or the) refiner of gold," using the word *m'ṣaref* which appears in the title of our treatise.

42. *Edom* is interpreted as *adom*, red.

43. Here the word is spelled *kamea*.

44. Sapere Aude remarks: "This is the usual form of the magic square of 8 related to Mercury."

45. That is, if in the first column on the right, instead of 1, 56, 48, etc., you write 2, 57, 49, etc.

46. That is, he volatilizes the metals, the earthly representatives of the stars. The translation above of the passage from Proverbs follows the author's Latin.

Chapter Twenty-Seven
Taitazak and Provençali

1. My translation from the Hebrew published by G. Scholem in his article "The Maggid of R. Joseph Taitazaq," *Sefunot* 11 (1971–1978): 86, 107a.

2. Ibid., 87.

3. Cf. *Divre Ḥakhamim*, ed. by Eliezer Ashkenazi of Tunis (Metz, 1849), 63–75.

4. Hermann Gollancz, ed., *Sepher Mafteaḥ Shelomo* (Oxford, 1914).

5. On Rabbenu Asher's lost commentary see Nissan Meir Feivel Zacks, *Massekhet Sh'qalim ʿim Perush haROSh* (Jerusalem, 1943), 10. I wish to thank Tuvia Preschel for having called my attention to Zacks's book.

6. Immanuel Löw, *Die Flora der Juden*, 4 vols. (Vienna, 1923–1924), 4:402.

Chapter Twenty-Eight
Ḥayyim Vital, Alchemist

1. Meir Benayahu, "Medical Matters in an Unknown Manuscript by R. Ḥayyim Vital" (in Hebrew), *Koroth: A Bulletin Devoted to the History of Medicine and Science* (Jerusalem) 34:3–4 (Spring 1984): 3–17; idem, "Collectanea from the Book of Medicines and S'gullot of R. Ḥayyim Vital," ibid. 35:5–6 (Spring 1987): 91–112.

2. *Shivḥe R. Ḥayyim Vital* (Ostrog, 1826); Ḥayyim Vital, *Sefer haḤezyonot* (Jerusalem, 1866).

3. See note 1 above.

4. A microfilm copy of it is found in the Institute of Microfilmed Hebrew Manuscripts of the Hebrew University of Jerusalem, which kindly put at my disposal a photocopy enlarged to the size of the original. On this occasion I want to thank my brother Saul Patai of the Hebrew University, who located the microfilm, and to Benjamin Richler of the Institute, who had the copy prepared for me, and to the Moussaieff Collection for its permission to describe it and to quote from it in my own English translation.

5. This seems to be an unpublished manuscript.

Chapter Twenty-Nine
An Alchemical Miscellany

1. MS ebr. 375. A copy was put at my disposal by the Institute of Hebrew Manuscripts of the Hebrew University of Jerusalem, and the Vatican Library permitted me to present it.

2. Aḥmad ibn Yūsuf al-Tīfāshī, *Kitāb Azhār al-Afkār fī Jawāhir al-Asjār*, translated by Reineri Biscia, 2nd ed. (Bologna, 1906), 53–54. I wish to thank the Library of the Jewish Theological Seminary, New York, for permission to publish excerpts from this manuscript.

3. Alfred Siggel, *Arabisch-Deutsches Wörterbuch der Stoffe aus den drei Naturreichen*. . . (Berlin, 1950).

4. MS Ox. Hebr. c. 55, cat 2659.5. I wish to thank the Bodleian Library for its permission to publish a translation of the manuscript, to the Jerusalem Institute of Microfilmed Hebrew Manuscripts for sending me a photocopy of it, and to Moshe Sokolow of Yeshiva University for deciphering and translating it.

5. *Theatrum chemicum* (Argentorati [Strasbourg], several editions in the 17th century).

6. Joannes Jacobus Manget, ed., *Bibliotheca chemica curiosa* (Geneva, 1702).

7. *Theatrum chemicum*, 5:215.

8. Marcellin P.E. Berthelot, *La chimie au moyen age* (Paris, 1893), 1:248–49.

9. Ibid. I might add that the names Hebua, Hamed, and Thebed could be corruptions of biblical Hebrew names. Hebua could stand for Ḥubba (1 Chron. 7:34) or Ḥavaya (Ezra 2:61); Hamed for Hamdata (Esth. 3:1) or Ḥemdan (Gen. 36:26); and Thebed for Ṭafat (1 Kings 4:11).

10. *Theatrum chemicum*, 5 (1622 ed.), 114, 120, 145. I wish to thank Leon Feldmann for the translation of these passages.

11. Cf. Berthelot, *Moyen age*, 1:250.

12. I wish to thank the Ben Zvi Institute fro permission to publish a translation of this excerpt.

Chapter Thirty
Labī Ḥamawī and Portaleone

1. Shimʿon Labī, *Ketem Paz* (Leghorn, 1795), 2:445a–b.

2. *EJ* (J), 5:479 and 10:641.

3. Abraham Ḥamawī, *Niflaim Maʿasekha* (Wonderful Are Thy Works) (Leghorn, 1881), 4b. The title is taken from Psalm 139:14.

4. Ibid., approbation.

5. *Abiᶜa Ḥidot* (Leghorn, 1879). The title is taken from Psalm 78:2. Also see note 3 above.

6. Its subtitle is: *in quibus non solum de auri in re medica facultate, verum etiam de specifica eius, & caeterarum rerum forma, ac duplici potestate, qua mixtis in omnibus illa operatur, copiose disputatur* (Venice, 1584). The author is identified as Abrahamo e Porta Leonis Mantuano Medico Hebraeo Auctore, and the book, published *cum licentia sanctae inquisitionis & illustrissimi senatus Veneti*, is dedicated to Guilelmo Gonzaga, Duke of Mantua.

Chapter Thirty-One
The Manchester (John Rylands) Manuscript

1. The manuscript consists of 48 pages, paginated in Hebrew numbers beginning with folio *beth/a*, that is 2, to folio *waw/a*, that is 6, and then continuing with *ḥet/b*, that is, 8, to *kaf-waw/b*, that is, 26. A later pagination running from 1 through 24 was added in Arabic numbers. In the following I have used the original pagination.

2. There were two famous alchemists with the first name Michael whose books were printed in the early seventeenth century: Michael Maier and Michael Sendivogius. Our manuscript's reference could be to either of them, or to yet another alchemist by that name.

3. *Sefer haMaor*: at least six books of this title are known in Hebrew literature, the oldest being that of the Spanish Halakhist Zeraḥiah ben Yiṣḥaq haLevi (ca. 1125–1186). However, none of them has alchemical contents, so that we must assume that our manuscript refers to a *Sefer haMaor* that is lost.

4. The Arabic alchemical term *tinkar* has many meanings: a stone of the class of salts, cf. Juluis Ruska, *Das Steinbuch des Aristoteles* (Heidelberg, 1912), (1895–1896) 11; alkali or borax, cf. Ernst Darmstaedter, *Die Alchemie des Geber* (Berlin, 1922), index; a calcareous salt from which glass is made, cf. Martin Levey, *Early Arabic Pharmacology* (Leiden, 1973), 112. The multiple meanings of terms such as this constitute one of the most difficult problems in trying to interpret alchemical recipes.

5. This long recipe, as well as the one that follows it (no. 200), are practically identical with the prescriptions translated above in Chapter 24.

6. This is another version of the pseudo-Maimonidean alchemical instructions, including operations with pearls, presented above, Chapter 24.

7. I am unable to identify the *Book of Sadidi.*

8. These pseudo-Maimonidean instructions are again largely identical with those contained in the Munich MS 14, presented above in Chapter 24.

9. See note 3 above.

10. I am unable to identify *Sefer haLoᶜazim* (Book of Foreign Expressions).

Introduction to Part Eight

1. Cf. Hugo Ginsberg, *Der Briefwechsel des Spinoza* (Leipzig, 1876), letters VI and IX, the Latin original; and J. Stern, *Spinozas Briefwechsel* (Leipzig, 1904), German translation.

2. They were published in 1677. Jelles wrote the introduction to Spinoza's *Ethics*, published likewise in 1677. Biographies of Jelles are contained in *Nieuw Nederlansch Biografisch Woordenboek*, 9 (Leiden, 1933), 459; and de Bie en Loosjes, *Biogr. Woordenboek d. Protest. Godgel in Nederland*, 4:535.

3. See Latin text in Ginsberg, *Briefwechsel*, letter XLV, 127ff.

4. For a biography of Isaac Vossius, see *Nieuw Nederlandsch Biografisch Woordenboek*, vol. 1 (Leiden, 1911), 1519–26.

Chapter Thirty-Two
Leone Modena, Delmedigo, and Zeraḥ

1. Leon of Modena, *Sefer Ḥayye Y'huda*, edited by Abraham Kahana (Kiev, 1911).

2. Ibid., 12.

3. Abraham Berliner, *Geschichte der Juden in Rom* (Frankfurt-am-Main, 1893; reprint Hildesheim, Zurich, New York, 1987), 2:54.

4. See above, Chapter 11.

5. Delmedigo's response, entitled *Iggeret Aḥuz*, was published by Abraham Geiger in *Melo Chofnajim* [*M'lo Ḥofnayim*], with a German translation and notes (Berlin, 1840). There was a new edition of *Sefer Elim* in Odessa (1864); I quote from this edition. On pp. xxvii–lvi, Geiger gives a biography of Delmedigo. Incidentally, in his response Delmedigo does not speak at all of alchemy.

6. This is a talmudic phrase, meaning ignorant, or illiterate. Cf. B. Shabbat 95a; B. Sanhedrin 33a.

7. *Sefer Elim*, 24–25.

8. Ibid., 73–74.

9. See Isaac Barzilay, *Yoseph Shlomo Delmedigo* (Leiden, 1974), 49. This book is valuable for its portraiture of Delmedigo.

10. *Maṣref laḤokhma* (Basel, 1629; new ed. Warsaw, 1890); I used the new edition.

Chapter Thirty-Three
Four Seventeenth-Century Manuscripts

1. A photocopy was put at my disposal by the library and the curator of its Oriental Department, Hartmut-Ortwin Feistel. Moritz Steinschneider in his *Verzeichniss der Hebraeischen Handschriften (Die Handschriften-Verzeichnisse der Königlichen Bibliothek zu Berlin)* (Berlin, 1897), 2:119–21, gave a brief description of this manuscript, though his reading of the Hebrew text was occasionally faulty.

2. Cf. Alfred Siggel, *Das Buch der Gifte des Ǧābir ibn Ḥayyān* (Wiesbaden, 1958).

3. Steinschneider misread the word as GSPWS, and guessed that it stood for Josephus (?).

4. Steinschneider, *Verzeichniss*, 121, says that he cannot explain this title; evidently he was not aware of Delmedigo's *Sefer Elim* (see Chapter 32 above).

5. A photocopy was put at my disposal by the Jerusalem Institute of Microfilmed Hebrew Manuscripts, with the kind permission of the Berlin Staatsbibliothek.

6. For "white herb from the mountain," see above, Chapter 5.

7. *JE* 1:330. The manuscript is in the British Library in London (MS Or. 10289), and copies of it are available in the Institute of Microfilmed Hebrew Manuscripts of the Hebrew University of Jerusalem, and in the library of the Jewish Theological Seminary of America in New York. The following analysis is based on the latter copy.

8. Cf. Marcellin P. E. Berthelot, *La chimie au moyen age* (Paris, 1893), 3:13, 116.

9. Ibid., 1:290ff.

10. Julius F. Ruska, *Turba philosophorum: Ein Beitrag zur Geschichte der Alchemie* 1 (Berlin, 1931), 23.

11. Cf. Johannes Jacobus Manget, *Bibliotheca chemica curiosa*, 2 vols. (Geneva, 1702), 2:84–85; *Theatrum chemicum* 3 (Argentorati [Strasbourg], 1659), 284–92.

12. Reprinted in *Artis auriferae quam chemiam vocant* (Basel, 1593), 2:7–54.

13. Berthelot, *Moyen age*, 1:213.

14. This work of al-Rāzī was so popular among the Jews that in a Yemenite Judeo-Arabic manuscript parts of it were copied in Hebrew characters under the title *Kitāb Sirr al-Asrār* (The Book of the Secret of Secrets), with the incipit "*Qāla* [said] Abū Bakr Muḥammad ibn Zakariyya al-Rāzī. . . ." Jerusalem Institute of Microfilmed Hebrew Manuscripts, film no. 47434, page 18ff.

15. Cf. Moritz Steinschneider, *Die hebräischen Übersetzungen des Mittelalters und die Juden als Dolmetscher* (Berlin, 1893; reprint Graz, 1956), 778ff., index, s.v. Arnaldus.

16. Berthelot, *Moyen age*, 1:213.

17. Cf. Manget, *Bibliotheca chemica*, 2:1–80.

18. On the anti-pope Benedict XII, see *Cambridge Medieval History*, vol. 7 (Cambridge: Cambridge University Press, 1968), index s.v.

19. Cf. Manget, *Bibliotheca chemica*, 1:444–509; Ruska, *Turba*, 341–42, 345.

20. This is the well-known and oft-quoted axiom of Maria the Jewess.

21. This sentence seems to be corrupt in the original. The above is the best I could make of it.

22. I wish to express my thanks to the Hungarian Academy of Sciences for its permission to present the translation of this manuscript.

Chapter Thirty-Four
Benjamin Mussafia

1. Published in 4 volumes in Frankfurt and Leipzig, 1714–1718.

2. I wish to thank Joseph Salemi for translating the Latin text.

3. The alchemist Christian Eisenmenger is not to be confused with Johann Andreas Eisenmenger (1654–1704), the anti-Semitic author of the notorious *Entdecktes Judentum* (Judaism Unmasked), published in Koenigsberg in 1711.

4. I wish to thank Louis H. Feldman for his help in translating this excerpt.
5. The Latin has been omitted.
6. The Latin has been omitted.
7. The Latin has been omitted.
8. The Latin has been omitted.

Chapter Thirty-Five
Benjamin Jesse

1. Karl Cristoph Schmieder, *Geschichte der Alchemie* (Halle, 1832), 523–26.

Introduction to Part Nine

1. Jean Jacques Rousseau, *Confessions*, Everyman's Library ed. (London, 1931) 1:43, 98, 161, 164, 314.

Chapter Thirty-Six
Ḥayyim Sh'muel Falck

1. George Louis Albert de Rantzow, *Mémoires du Comte de Rantzow, ou les heures de récréation a l'usage de la noblesse de l'Europe*, 2 vols. (Amsterdam, 1741), 1:197ff. I consulted the copy of this rare book in the Bibliothèque Nationale, Paris.
2. In inthe original: *Sauve qui peut la Diablerie!* Ibid., 1:223.
3. The word *magne* evidently refers to the rolled-up scroll Falck used as a wand. I am unable to find in any dictionary of the French language any mention of this word in the sense that would suit Rantzow's use of it.
4. Johann Wilhelm von Archenholz, *England und Italien* (Leipzig, 1785; new ed., Carlsruhe, 1791). This latter is the edition I used in the British Library, London. An English translation was published under the title *A Picture of England* (London, 1797).
5. The story of Falck's refusal to see the unnamed British prince is repeated by Cecil Roth in his paper "The King and the Kabbalist," published in his *Essays and Portraits in Anglo-Jewish History* (Philadelphia, 1962), 139–64. Roth also wrote a brief biography of Falck (Falk, Samuel Jacob Ḥayyim), for the *EJ* (J), 2:1159–60, where he says that Falk "about 1742 made his way to England." Since Rantzow's *Mémoires*, published in 1741, tell about Falck's move to London, his reception there by the Portuguese Jewish community, his arrest, and his subsequent release, it is clear that Falck must have arrived in London quite some time prior to 1742, probably as early as the late 1730s. On Falck's life in London, see Herman Adler in *JE*, 5:331.

Chapter Thirty-Seven
The Comte de Saint-Germain

1. Cf. *Oeuvres complètes de Voltaire*, new ed., *Correspondance* (Paris, 1880), 8:353, 376; *Nouvelle biographie générale* (Paris, 1864), 43:27. The *Biographie universelle (Michaud) ancienne et moderne* (Paris, Leipzig, c. 1860), 37:324–25,

mistakenly gives the date of April 15, 1758, for Voltaire's letter, and attributes, likewise mistakenly, to Voltaire Frederick II's bon mot about Saint-Germain.

2. Pierre Lhermier, *Le mystérieux Comte de Saint-Germain: Rose-croix et dilomate* (Paris, 1943), 243, quoting the memoires of the Comte de Saint-Maurice.

3. See entry "Comte de Saint-Germain," in *La grande encyclopedie* (Paris, 1895–1902), 29:168–69, and earlier literature in the bibliography there; Paul Chacornac, *Le Comte de Saint-Germain* (Paris, 1947; new ed. Paris, 1989); Maurice Heim, *Le vrai visage du Comte de Saint-Germain* (Paris, 1957); René Alleau, ed., *Comte de Saint-Germain, la très sainte trinosophie* (Paris, 1971). Cf. also George B. Kauffman, "The Comte de Saint-Germain," in *The Hexagon* (Iowa City, Iowa), Autumn 1979, pp. 20–22, and the bibliography therein.

4. *Biographie universelle*, 37:324.

5. Ibid.

6. The Rákóczi whose son Saint-Germain claimed to be was Ferenc Rákóczi (1676–1735), who led an uprising against Hapsburg rule over Hungary in 1703, was defeated by Austria, and after the Peace of Satmar (1711) found refuge in Turkey.

7. Charles, Prince of Hesse, *Mémoires de mon temps* (Copenhagen, 1861) 133–34.

8. Frederic Bulau, *Personnages énigmatiques: Histoires mysterieuses* translated by W. Duckett (Paris, 1861), 1:340 ff.

9. Lhermier, *Le mystérieux Comte*, 217–18.

10. As quoted by Chacornac, *Le Comte de Saint-Germain*, 269.

11. Ibid., 28, 86; Heim, *Le vrai visage*, 49. Jean Robin in a recent book presents several additional unfounded assumptions about the origin of Saint-Germain from Spanish noblemen of remote Marrano descent: *La véritable mission du Comte de Saint-Germain* (Paris, 1986), 14–15, relying primarily on Jean Lombard, *La face cachée de l'histoire moderne*, vol. 1 (Madrid, 1984).

12. Chacornac, *Le Comte de Saint-Germain*, 39, 44, 46; Heim, *Le vrai visage*, 63.

13. *Letters of Horace Walpole Earl of Orford to Sir Horace Mann*, edited by Lord Dover (New York, 1833) 1:383. Letter 145, dated Arlington Street, December 9, 1745.

14. Chacornac, *Le Comte de Saint-Germain*, 49.

15. *Nouvelle biographie générale*, 43:28–29. See also the testimony in Frederic Nicolai, *Description d'un voyage à travers l'Allemagne et la Suisse en 1781* (Berlin and Stettin, 1786) 7:109, addenda, as quoted by Chacornac, *Le Comte de Saint-Germain*, 190. And see the poem printed in the January 1785 issue of the *Berlinische Monatschrift*, under the caption "Le Comte de St. Germain célèbre alchimiste."

16. Heim, *Le vrai visage*, 37–40.

17. Ibid., 75–76; Lhermier, *Le mystérieux Comte*, 71.

18. Ibid., 18, 124; Pierre Andremont, *Les trois visages du Comte de Saint-Germain* (Geneva, 1979), 89–90, 99–102, quoting official Dutch documents.

19. Andremont, *Les trois visages*, 104–7.

20. *Mémoires de mon temps*, 132–36.

21. Lhermier, *Le mystérieux Comte*, 248–51, quoting Dr. Kelemann.

22. Heim, *Le vrai visage*, 226ff., 237–38, 277. Cf. also Andremont and Jean Robin, both of whom give details about the posthumous "sightings" of Saint-Germain.

23. Alleau, *Comte de Saint-Germain*, 287.

24. Chacornac, *Le Comte de Saint-Germain*, 207–8.

25. Lhermier, *Le mystérieux Comte*, 254.

26. Heim, *Le vrai visage*, 159; Alleau, *Comte de Saint-Germain*, 290. I had no opportunity to examine the Troyes manuscript, but Mme A. Plassard, curator of the Troyes Municipal Library, kindly sent me photocopies of several pages of it, including one that carries this colophon: "This manuscript is the only existing copy of the famous Trinosophie of the Comte de St. Germain, which he himself destroyed on one of his voyages. [Signed] J. B. C. Philotaume." The manuscript was published several times in the French original: in the *Annales maçoniques* (Paris, 1908); in *Le voile d'Isis* (April 1932), 269–88; and by Alleau in *Le Comte de Saint-Germain*; also in an annotated edition in English by Manly Hall, 3rd ed. (Los Angeles, 1949). In all of them the Hebrew words contained in the text are frequently misread and mistranslated.

27. I am indebted to Mme A. Plassard for deciphering the French in this inscription.

Chapter Thirty-Nine
An Alchemical Manuscript from Jerba

1. Raphael Patai, *The Jewish Mind* (New York, 1977) 464.

2. I received from my friend Benjamin Richler of the Jerusalem Institute of Microfilmed Hebrew Manuscripts a photocopy of this miraculously preserved book-sized Hebrew alchemical manuscript (MS Jerusalem, M. Feldman 15).

3. BKRṬNṬB is our author's cryptogram for the word ALQIMIA, as he spells alchemy in Hebrew. He arrived at the cryptogram by substituting for the Hebrew letters of the word ALQIMIA alternately the letters following them and preceding them in the Hebrew alphabet, which resulted in BKRṬNṬB.

4. TKDYMMT is another cryptogram which stands for ALQIMIA in the so-called ATB"SH code, in which *tav* is substituted for *aleph, shin* for *bet, resh* for *gimel*, etc. I am indebted to Benjamin Richler for this explanation.

5. See details in Raphael Patai, *The Hebrew Goddess* (3rd ed., Detroit, 1990), 161–201.

6. The abbreviation ShLH"G stands for the book *Shilṭe haGibborim* (Shields of the Heroes) by Abraham Portaleone, printed in Mantua in 1612. We have dealt with Portaleone's works in Chapter 30. The reference to this book shows that our junior author was in possession of rare books, and perused and excerpted them.

Chapter Forty
Mordecai Abi Serour

1. See René Bazin, *Charles de Foucauld* (Paris, 1921), 30–43.

2. Edward Westermarck, *Ritual and Belief in Morocco*, 2 vols. (London, 1926), 1:363.

3. Raphael Patai, *On Jewish Folklore* (Detroit, 1983), 375 and notes on 427.

4. This assumption is borne out by a research study on the Algerian-Moroccan alchemist Rabbi Makhluf Amsallam (1837–1927), who was for a while employed by the Sultan of Morocco, Mulay Al-Hasan (r. 1873–1894). See Joseph Yinon (Fenton), "Rabbi Makhluf Amsallam," in *Peʿamim: Studies in Oriental Jewry* (a quarterly): Jerusalem, Spring 1993.

INDEX

The forms of the non-Hebrew words that appear in the Hebrew alchemical texts and are reproduced here often differ from the forms of those words in the original languages. Those languages are identified by abbreviations (see p. xv) following the entry-words. Arabic names and words beginning with the article *al-* are listed under the letter following it. See also the entries listed in the vocabulary contained in the appendix, which are not included here so as to avoid duplication.